CW01150673

Destination Branding and Bias in Ecotourism

Muhammad Abrar
Lyallpur Business School, Government College University, Faisalabad, Pakistan

Muhammad Asim Nawaz
Lyallpur Business School, Government College University, Faisalabad, Pakistan

Faiqa Kiran
Lyallpur Business School, Government College University, Faisalabad, Pakistan

IGI Global
Scientific Publishing
Publishing Tomorrow's Research Today

Published in the United States of America by
IGI Global
701 E. Chocolate Avenue
Hershey PA, USA 17033
Tel: 717-533-8845
Fax: 717-533-8661
E-mail: cust@igi-global.com
Web site: https://www.igi-global.com

Library of Congress Cataloging-in-Publication Data

CIP DATA PENDING

ISBN13: 9798369367001
EISBN13: 9798369367018

Vice President of Editorial: Melissa Wagner
Managing Editor of Acquisitions: Mikaela Felty
Managing Editor of Book Development: Jocelynn Hessler
Production Manager: Mike Brehm
Cover Design: Phillip Shickler

British Cataloguing in Publication Data
A Cataloguing in Publication record for this book is available from the British Library.

Table of Contents

Preface xv

Acknowledgement xxiv

Chapter 1
Understanding Destination Brand Experience 1
Muhammad Abrar, Government College University, Faisalabad, Pakistan
Ahmad Sohail Khan, Government College University, Faisalabad, Pakistan
Rizwan Shabbir, Government College University, Faisalabad, Pakistan

Chapter 2
Social Media Influencers Shaping Ecotourism Destination Branding 23
Saqib Rehman, Lahore College for Women University, Pakistan
Nabeela Arshad, Lahore College for Women University, Pakistan
Aman Ullah, University of Melbourne, Australia
Nadia Noor, Lahore College for Women University, Pakistan

Chapter 3
Leveraging Social Media for Destination Branding 51
Muhammad Hamid Murtza, Islamia University of Bahawalpur, Pakistan
Muhammad Imran Rasheed, Surrey International Institute, Dongbei University of Finance and Economics, China & University of Surrey, UK

Chapter 4
Building Brand Authenticity and Strategies for Genuine Destination Experiences 75
Khalid Jamil, Beijing University of Technology, China
Aliya Anwar, North China Electric Power University, China
Sajjad Ahmad Baig, National Textile University, Faisalabad, Pakistan

Chapter 5
Destination Branding and Luxury Experiences in the Digital Age 105
Mario Sierra Martin, Universidad de Málaga, Spain
Marisol de Brito Correia, University of Algarve, Portugal
Nelson da Silva deMatos, University of Algarve, Portugal
Álvaro Díaz Caquero, Universidad de Málaga, Spain
Pilar Alarcón Urbistondo, Universidad de Málaga, Spain

Chapter 6
Artificial Intelligence and Destination Branding 141
Maha Khamis Al Balushi, Sultan Qaboos University, Oman
Mohammad Soliman, Sultan Qaboos University, Oman
Mohammed S. Al Hosni, Sultan Qaboos University, Oman
Amal Al Mamari, Sultan Qaboos University, Oman

Chapter 7
Analyzing Destination Branding Themes Using Co-Word Analysis 165
Hamid Derviş, Kastamonu University, Turkey

Chapter 8
Eco-tourism Branding Balancing Conservation and Community 187
Uma Pandey, Jagran Lakecity University, India
Hafizullah Dar, Lovely Professional University, India

Chapter 9
Balancing Bias and Sustainability in Heritage Tourism 217
Aditi Nag, Manipal University Jaipur, India
Anurag Singh Rathore, Indira Gandhi National Open University, India

Chapter 10
Developing Destination Brand Identity Through Stakeholder Collaboration ... 267
Serkan Gün, Siirt Universty, Turkey

Chapter 11
Leveraging Market Research to Enhance Destination Branding in Chiang Mai 287
Olukemi Adedokun Fagbolu, National Open University of Nigeria, Nigeria

Chapter 12
Wine and Cultural Tourism as Niche Opportunities in Slovakia, Czechia, and Canada 309
Marica Mazurek, University of Zilina, Slovakia

Chapter 13
Ecotourism and Sustainable Development in Chania 325
Panoraia Poulaki, University of the Aegean, Greece
Theodoros Rachiotis, National and Kapodistrian University of Athens, Greece
Nikolaos Vasilakis, Ionian University, Greece

Chapter 14
Fostering Ecotourism Brands Through Local Engagement in Peru and the Maldives 357
Gulen Hashmi, Glasgow Caledonian University, UK
Julie Roberts, Glasgow Caledonian University, UK

Chapter 15
Awareness of Ecotourism and the Creation of Ecotouristic Destination Brands in Türkiye 385
Nil Sonuç, İzmir Katip Çelebi University, Turkey

Chapter 16
Village Tourism Balances Brand Identity and Sustainability in Montegridolfo 411
Manuela Presutti, University of Bologna, Italy
Francesco Maria Barbini, University of Bologna, Italy
Valeria lo Presti, University of Bologna, Italy

Compilation of References 449

About the Contributors 529

Index 539

Detailed Table of Contents

Preface xv

Acknowledgement xxiv

Chapter 1
Understanding Destination Brand Experience 1
Muhammad Abrar, Government College University, Faisalabad, Pakistan
Ahmad Sohail Khan, Government College University, Faisalabad, Pakistan
Rizwan Shabbir, Government College University, Faisalabad, Pakistan

Ecotourism is one of the most vital catalysts of conservation and sustainable development in tourism. Ecotourism favours the production of economic and administrative support for protected areas, heightens the understanding of environmental and historical values, and improves the visitor's experience. The chapter explains the conceptual understanding and aspects of destination band experience and looks into the theoretical foundation of destination brand experience in the ecotourism industry. Furthermore, it explores the factors influencing destination brand experience, strategies, challenges and future trends in managing ecotourism. Destination marketers could design their marketing communication programs to better integrate with the expectations of intended tourists to augment their destination experience. Policymakers might also use this information to develop sustainable tourism plans and regulate how tourism influences the environment and the local community, ultimately leading to a refined destination brand experience.

Chapter 2
Social Media Influencers Shaping Ecotourism Destination Branding 23
Saqib Rehman, Lahore College for Women University, Pakistan
Nabeela Arshad, Lahore College for Women University, Pakistan
Aman Ullah, University of Melbourne, Australia
Nadia Noor, Lahore College for Women University, Pakistan

Influencers can use large online followings to create awareness about the destination, answer the tourists' queries, and structure the destination image, environment, and sustainable accommodations while staying in a particular landscape. Moreover, influencers may promote the ecotourists' destination, grab the trust of their followers, and be a carrier of promoting eco-friendly activities at destinations. The theory of planned behaviour sets the direction for this study. It offers a thorough framework for clarifying the factors that may affect or limit persons' intentions to perform certain behaviours. TPB can assist tourists in understanding the motivations behind their choice of destination by analyzing the elements influencing ecotourism. Influencers who engage with ecotourists can shape their perceptions of a region by emphasizing its unique attributes, like captivating natural scenery and sustainable tourism practices.

Chapter 3
Leveraging Social Media for Destination Branding 51
Muhammad Hamid Murtza, Islamia University of Bahawalpur, Pakistan
Muhammad Imran Rasheed, Surrey International Institute, Dongbei University of Finance and Economics, China & University of Surrey, UK

This chapter examines and understands social media's significance in destination branding. Social media has become instrumental in shaping perceptions, effectively interacting with and forming destination brands. This section will highlight the critical role of social media in inventing and promoting destination brands, provide a complete analysis of its upshots, and describe theoretical application and support from the literature. With the advent of social media, the methods for advertising destinations have significantly affected customer perceptions. Social media outlets have wide-ranging outreach with interactional features, portraying destinations in previously impossible ways. These outlets can easily express distinctive value propositions to travellers, establishing influential, enduring brands. This chapter will also cover the fundamental concepts and theories related to social media, such as social identity theory and the theory of planned behaviour and its uses and gratifications.

Chapter 4
Building Brand Authenticity and Strategies for Genuine Destination Experiences 75
Khalid Jamil, Beijing University of Technology, China
Aliya Anwar, North China Electric Power University, China
Sajjad Ahmad Baig, National Textile University, Faisalabad, Pakistan

This chapter is devoted to understanding the concept of constructing the destination brand authenticity, focusing on the delicate interplay between tourism and culture. This chapter discusses over-tourism, cultural commodification, environmental degradation, and economic dependency issues based on Bali, Venice, and Kyoto case studies. Every case presented in the paper describes specific actions taken to ensure that genuine values are preserved, including the involvement of the local population, the promotion of ecotourism, the use of the legal framework, cultural conservation, and the diversification of the economy. The measures taken by Bali regarding sustainable tourism, measures taken by Venice in terms of regulatory and artistic support, and measures taken by Kyoto in terms of cultural preservation and implementation of sustainable practices help preserve the true identity of places popular among tourists. The chapter ends by stressing that the approaches discussed should be integrated and dynamic, including community involvement and sustainability.

Chapter 5
Destination Branding and Luxury Experiences in the Digital Age 105
Mario Sierra Martin, Universidad de Málaga, Spain
Marisol de Brito Correia, University of Algarve, Portugal
Nelson da Silva deMatos, University of Algarve, Portugal
Álvaro Díaz Caquero, Universidad de Málaga, Spain
Pilar Alarcón Urbistondo, Universidad de Málaga, Spain

In an era where the digital image of a destination can be as influential as actual experiences, this chapter will evaluate how Spain and Portugal use digital platforms to cultivate and promote their identities as luxury destinations. Through a methodology that combines quantitative and qualitative analysis, the effectiveness of the digital marketing techniques employed will be examined, including content management on social media, user interaction, and the adaptation of marketing strategies to changes in consumer preferences and behaviours. Additionally, our research leverages user-generated content, specifically comments extracted from TripAdvisor, to gauge perceptions of luxury hotels in both countries. By analyzing these comments, we gain insights into customer satisfaction, expectations, and the overall reputation of the hotels. This comprehensive approach allows us to assess the strategies deployed by these destinations and their real-world impact on the luxury tourism market.

Chapter 6
Artificial Intelligence and Destination Branding 141
Maha Khamis Al Balushi, Sultan Qaboos University, Oman
Mohammad Soliman, Sultan Qaboos University, Oman
Mohammed S. Al Hosni, Sultan Qaboos University, Oman
Amal Al Mamari, Sultan Qaboos University, Oman

Artificial intelligence (AI) has become a significant focus of research and practical applications within the tourism industry. Tourism researchers and practitioners have recently changed their methods by incorporating AI tools, resulting in new approaches to generate and use insights. These AI-driven developments hold great potential for enhancing destination branding. The current chapter aims to showcase the main benefits of using AI in destination branding, examine how AI helps create and implement effective branding strategies, identify the key challenges and complexities of integrating AI tools for this purpose, and highlight the crucial ethical considerations that need to be addressed when using AI in destination branding. This chapter presents several theoretical implications and helpful practical recommendations for using AI in destination branding.

Chapter 7
Analyzing Destination Branding Themes Using Co-Word Analysis 165
Hamid Derviş, Kastamonu University, Turkey

The chapter provides practical strategies for leveraging Social Network Analysis (SNA) in destination branding, offering insights on using interconnected keywords to create a cohesive brand identity extracted from Clarivate Analytics Web of Science (WOS). Using Istanbul, Konya, and Kastamonu showcased as destination brands, the chapter demonstrates how SNA can be applied in real-world contexts, providing insights into the benefits of a strategic branding approach through SNA. The author emphasizes the significance of a connected keyword network and offers practical strategies for leveraging these connections to establish a sustainable destination brand identity. The findings serve as a guide for tourism and hospitality practitioners, assisting them in creating compelling, sustainable destination brands. Similarly, this methodology can be applied to investigate the complex relationships among stakeholders, including local communities, businesses, government agencies, and tourists.

Chapter 8
Eco-tourism Branding Balancing Conservation and Community 187
Uma Pandey, Jagran Lakecity University, India
Hafizullah Dar, Lovely Professional University, India

Balancing conservation and community development is a significant challenge, especially where natural resources are protected and serve as livelihoods for locals. This study focuses on Kanha National Park in central India, which conserves diverse flora and fauna, including tigers and swamp deer. Conservation efforts often conflict with the livelihoods of locals living in buffer zones, leading to socioeconomic issues. Eco-tourism offers an alternative income source, leveraging the park's natural beauty and biodiversity. This chapter analyzes Kanha's eco-tourism branding, highlighting sustainable tourism practices and their ecological importance. Sustainable measures, like eco-friendly lodging and income reinvestment in community projects, align local interests with conservation goals. Despite challenges, the chapter suggests Kanha's model as an example of effective eco-tourism branding, promoting conservation and regional development through inclusive management.

Chapter 9
Balancing Bias and Sustainability in Heritage Tourism 217
Aditi Nag, Manipal University Jaipur, India
Anurag Singh Rathore, Indira Gandhi National Open University, India

This paper examines the complex dynamics of biases in ecotourism and destination branding within the context of heritage site management. It explores how these biases influence perceptions, visitor experiences, and sustainable practices at iconic destinations such as the Taj Mahal, Machu Picchu and Serengeti National Park. The study identifies critical challenges and opportunities in promoting inclusive, authentic, and sustainable tourism by integrating insights from predictive analytics, cultural sensitivity, and ethical considerations. Drawing on case studies and theoretical frameworks, the paper offers practical implications for mitigating biases, enhancing visitor engagement, and safeguarding cultural and natural heritage. It concludes by advocating for integrated strategies that balance effective branding with responsible stewardship to ensure the long-term preservation and equitable enjoyment of heritage sites worldwide.

Chapter 10
Developing Destination Brand Identity Through Stakeholder Collaboration ... 267
Serkan Gün, Siirt Universty, Turkey

The brand helps make a significant difference in distinguishing goods and services and acts as an edge over the closest rivals (Aaker, 1991). Govers et al. (2007) claim that the consumption experience of travel "determines aspects of consumer behavior related to multiple emotional, sensory, and fantasy aspects of consumer behavior" (Hirschman and Holbrook, 1982). Morgan et al. (2004) state that location branding is a potent tool for marketing that can aid travellers in developing positive affective attachments and impressions. As they explain, the summation of perceived experiences that a tourist will encounter at a destination is the so-called "most important repertoire of beliefs that support the branding of a destination." (Barnes et al., 2014).

Chapter 11
Leveraging Market Research to Enhance Destination Branding in Chiang Mai 287
Olukemi Adedokun Fagbolu, National Open University of Nigeria, Nigeria

This chapter explores how a specific tourism destination can employ market research to develop a logo and slogan to gain a competitive advantage in the international and domestic tourism market through product differentiation, market segmentation, target marketing and branding strategies. It highlights possible strategies for destination brands to develop their marketing strategies and competitiveness. The study gathers historical data from existing literature about the selected destination for the study. Additionally, it observes the destination features and employs developed questions to interview the selected destination using a cluster sampling method to gather customer data. The study also makes recommendations for the destination for possible destination brand sustainability.

Chapter 12
Wine and Cultural Tourism as Niche Opportunities in Slovakia, Czechia, and Canada 309
Marica Mazurek, University of Zilina, Slovakia

This chapter will discuss recent advancements in the tourism industry, particularly in light of the COVID-19 time. Tourism destinations can profit from the sound effects of sustainable and niche tourism during economic downturns and unrest by enhancing their reputation, image, and level of service and utilizing their local cultural resources and legacy. The only travel locations that will be more successful and competitive are those that can investigate new product offerings and deal with the realities of the current environment. In tourist destinations, ecology and sustainability have begun to take centre stage. Niche tourism is a prime illustration of this kind of growth and provision. The study aims to explain the importance of wine tourism as a form of niche tourism and to add the importance of culinary and cultural tourism as additional niche tourism products. The Brand Niagara Region in Canada, Slovakia, and the Czech Republic will be the study's main subjects.

Chapter 13
Ecotourism and Sustainable Development in Chania 325
Panoraia Poulaki, University of the Aegean, Greece
Theodoros Rachiotis, National and Kapodistrian University of Athens, Greece
Nikolaos Vasilakis, Ionian University, Greece

This study investigates the potential of ecotourism in fostering sustainable development in Chania, Crete, focusing on environmental conservation, cultural preservation, and economic growth. A mixed-methods approach combines secondary research to establish a global and local theoretical framework with qualitative interviews with key stakeholders in Chania. The study assesses the current state of ecotourism, its impact on natural and cultural heritage, and barriers to sustainable tourism. Findings highlight ecotourism's role in raising environmental awareness and supporting local economies. However, challenges such as infrastructure, stakeholder cooperation, and ecological management persist. The study concludes that strategic planning and stakeholder collaboration are essential for ecotourism's success, balancing growth with resource preservation. Theoretical implications suggest ecotourism as a sustainable tourism model, while practical recommendations call for targeted policies, employee training, and marketing strategies to position Chania as a top ecotourism destination.

Chapter 14
Fostering Ecotourism Brands Through Local Engagement in Peru and the Maldives 357
Gulen Hashmi, Glasgow Caledonian University, UK
Julie Roberts, Glasgow Caledonian University, UK

As a subset of sustainable tourism, ecotourism has increased in protected tourism sites and biodiversity hotspots as increasingly more tourists look for meaningful natural experiences. This necessitates understanding how to leverage tourist-local community engagement in ecotourism branding. The chapter focuses on two case studies from two contexts, which harness tourist-local community engagement in their ecotourism branding. While the first case study relates to the conservation of nature and cultural heritage within an Amazonian rainforest in Peru, the latter refers to preserving the ecosystems of the ocean in the Maldives. Although both cases leverage tourist-local community engagement to a certain extent, they heavily focus on uplifting local communities, guest education and scientific research in their ecotourism branding. The study lacks empirical evidence, yet it has managerial and policy implications. It advises managers and policymakers to foster a sustainable ecotourism brand with the tourist-local community interaction in mind.

Chapter 15
Awareness of Ecotourism and the Creation of Ecotouristic Destination Brands in Türkiye 385
Nil Sonuç, İzmir Katip Çelebi University, Turkey

This chapter aims to define and understand the current perception of ecotourism by analyzing the academic literature and identifying the perspectives of international and related national organizations. Following a global view of ecotourism, the Türkiye case is dealt with by examining the potential of ecotourism and the evolving phases of the ecotourism development path of Türkiye on the way to the creation of ecotouristic destination brands in this country. Compared to the classical mass tourism of sun-sea-sand, ecotourism has adopted an alternative tourism path, which is carried out to be more considerate of the protection of biodiversity and much more attentive in terms of human-environment interaction. Therefore, as international organizations emphasize, the sustainable management of ecotourism is advised, and ecotouristic destination branding is suggested to be developed for Türkiye.

Chapter 16
Village Tourism Balances Brand Identity and Sustainability in Montegridolfo 411
Manuela Presutti, University of Bologna, Italy
Francesco Maria Barbini, University of Bologna, Italy
Valeria lo Presti, University of Bologna, Italy

This paper explores the role of village tourism in promoting sustainable practices and enhancing destination branding, using the case study of Montegridolfo and Palazzo Viviani, a luxury hotel in Italy's Riviera Romagnola. Through ethnographic research, we investigate the motivations behind establishing a high-end hotel in a small,rich village far from mainstream tourist routes. The study examines how luxury tourism can foster sustainable development, support unique destination branding, and balance tourism growth with the preservation of cultural heritage and local identity. The case of Palazzo Viviani demonstrates the integration of eco-sustainable strategies within the luxury sector, highlighting the interplay between environmental responsibility, economic growth, and cultural revitalization. Our findings suggest that luxury tourism when properly managed, can provide ethical and economically sound development opportunities for rural destinations. The paper concludes by offering strategic insights for developing sustainable luxury tourism models in similar small village settings

Compilation of References 449

About the Contributors 529

Index 539

Preface

As editors of this comprehensive reference book on "Destination Branding and Bias in Ecotourism," we are pleased to present a collaborative effort that delves into the multifaceted realm of Ecotourism and branding. Professor Muhammad Abrar, Muhammad Asim Nawaz, and Faiqa Kiran bring their collective expertise from Lyallpur Business School, Government College University, Pakistan, to unravel the intricate connections between ecotourism and destination branding.

The world of tourism is undergoing a significant transformation. No longer is travel simply about visiting new places; today, it is about embracing experiences that align with a traveller's social, moral, and environmental values. Environmental consciousness has evolved from a trend to an imperative, and this shift is driving the emergence of ecotourism as a robust and growing sector within the global travel industry. The book *Destination Branding and Bias in Ecotourism* explores how branding plays a crucial role in shaping ecotourism destinations and influencing perceptions, behaviours, and sustainable practices worldwide.

Destination branding is relatively new, yet it has garnered significant attention in recent years. As destinations strive to stand out in a crowded tourism market, branding, particularly with a focus on environmental sustainability and ethical tourism, has become a crucial factor in their success. Branding an eco-destination requires a careful blend of storytelling, marketing, and community engagement to highlight the natural beauty of a place and its commitment to sustainability. This process requires the involvement of local communities, stakeholders, and tourists to ensure that a destination's brand truly represents its values and fosters a sense of inclusivity and environmental stewardship.

This book serves as a comprehensive guide for destination branders, including managers, marketers, and ecological activists, offering the latest insights, strategies, and tools adopted by destinations worldwide. From the Northern regions of Pakistan to the coastlines of Hawaii, the case studies and theoretical frameworks included in this book are designed to inform and inspire those involved in developing eco-destination brands. It delves into how collaboration between local, national, and international entities, storytelling, and ethical considerations can help build stronger, more sustainable brands that resonate with residents and visitors alike.

The chapters in this book cover a wide range of topics related to destination branding, including the importance of brand image, the role of social media and AI in branding efforts, and how events, celebrity endorsements, and influencers can help promote eco-tourism destinations. Notably, the book also addresses the challenges and complexities of destination branding, such as destination brand attachment, authenticity, and different case studies. By understanding these branding facets, destinations can attract tourists and contribute meaningfully to environmental preservation and social well-being.

At the heart of this book is the belief that ecotourism offers a path toward a more sustainable future—where travel can be a force for good, preserving the natural beauty of our planet while supporting local communities. Through the combined efforts of researchers, authors, and practitioners, *Destination Branding and Bias in Ecotourism* offers an essential resource for those seeking to build meaningful, ethical, and sustainable travel experiences that leave a lasting impact on both people and the planet.

As editors, we sincerely thank the contributors who have brought their expertise to this book. Their research and insights will undoubtedly help shape the future of destination branding in Ecotourism, empowering both present and future generations to foster a world where tourism and sustainability go hand in hand. We invite you to engage with the ideas presented in this volume and to participate in the ongoing conversation about how we can all work together to build a better, more sustainable future for travel.

ORGANIZATION OF THE BOOK

Chapter 1: Understanding Destination Brand Experience

Ecotourism is one of the most vital catalysts of conservation and sustainable development in tourism. Ecotourism favours the production of economic and administrative support for protected areas, heightens the understanding of environmental and historical values, and improves the visitor's experience. The chapter explains the conceptual understanding and aspects of destination band experience and looks into the theoretical foundation of destination brand experience in the ecotourism industry. Furthermore, it explores the factors influencing destination brand experience, strategies, challenges and future trends in managing Ecotourism. Destination marketers could design their marketing communication programs to better integrate with the expectations of intended tourists to augment their destination experience.

Policymakers might also use this information to develop sustainable tourism plans and regulate how tourism influences the environment and the local community, ultimately leading to a refined destination brand experience.

Chapter 2: Social Media Influencers Shaping Ecotourism Destination Branding

Influencers can use large online followings to create awareness about the destination, answer the tourists' queries, and structure the destination image, environment, and sustainable accommodations while staying in a particular landscape. Moreover, influencers may promote the ecotourists' destination, grab the trust of their followers, and be a carrier of promoting eco-friendly activities at destinations. The theory of planned behaviour sets the direction for this study. It offers a thorough framework for clarifying the factors that may affect or limit persons' intentions to perform certain behaviours. TPB can assist tourists in understanding the motivations behind their choice of destination by analyzing the elements influencing Ecotourism. Influencers who engage with ecotourists can shape their perceptions of a region by emphasizing its unique attributes, like captivating natural scenery and sustainable tourism practices.

Chapter 3: Leveraging Social Media for Destination Branding

This chapter examines and understands social media's significance in destination branding. Social media has become instrumental in shaping perceptions, effectively interacting with and forming destination brands. This section will highlight the critical role of social media in inventing and promoting destination brands, provide a complete analysis of its upshots, and describe theoretical application and support from the literature. With the advent of social media, the methods for advertising destinations have significantly affected customer perceptions. Social media outlets have wide-ranging outreach with interactional features, portraying destinations in previously impossible ways. These outlets can easily express distinctive value propositions to travellers, establishing influential, enduring brands. This chapter will also cover the fundamental concepts and theories related to social media, such as social identity theory and the theory of planned behaviour and its uses and gratifications.

Chapter 4: Building Brand Authenticity and Strategies for Genuine Destination Experiences

This chapter examines and understands social media's significance in destination branding. Social media has become instrumental in shaping perceptions, effectively interacting with and forming destination brands. This section will highlight the critical role of social media in inventing and promoting destination brands, provide a complete analysis of its upshots, and describe theoretical application and support from the literature. The advent of social media, the methods for advertising destinations have significantly affected customer perceptions. Social media outlets have wide-ranging outreach with interactional features, portraying destinations in previously impossible ways. These outlets can easily express distinctive value propositions to travellers, establishing influential, enduring brands. This chapter will also cover the fundamental concepts and theories related to social media, such as social identity theory and the theory of planned behaviour and its uses and gratifications.

Chapter 5: Destination Branding and Luxury Experiences in the Digital Age

In an era where the digital image of a destination can be as influential as actual experiences, this chapter will evaluate how Spain and Portugal use digital platforms to cultivate and promote their identities as luxury destinations. Through a methodology that combines quantitative and qualitative analysis, the effectiveness of the digital marketing techniques employed will be examined, including content management on social media, user interaction, and the adaptation of marketing strategies to changes in consumer preferences and behaviours. Additionally, our research leverages user-generated content, specifically comments extracted from TripAdvisor, to gauge perceptions of luxury hotels in both countries. By analyzing these comments, we gain insights into customer satisfaction, expectations, and the overall reputation of the hotels. This comprehensive approach allows us to assess the strategies deployed by these destinations and their real-world impact on the luxury tourism market.

Chapter 6: Artificial Intelligence and Destination Branding

Artificial intelligence (AI) has become a significant focus of research and practical applications within the tourism industry. Tourism researchers and practitioners have recently changed their methods by incorporating AI tools, resulting in new approaches to generate and use insights. These AI-driven developments hold great potential for enhancing destination branding. The current chapter aims to showcase the main benefits of using AI in destination branding, examine how AI helps create and implement effective branding strategies, identify the key challenges and complexities of integrating AI tools for this purpose, and highlight the crucial ethical considerations that need to be addressed when using AI in destination branding. This chapter presents several theoretical implications and helpful practical recommendations for using AI in destination branding.

Chapter 7: Analyzing Destination Branding Themes Using Co-Word Analysis

The chapter provides practical strategies for leveraging Social Network Analysis (SNA) in destination branding, offering insights on using interconnected keywords to create a cohesive brand identity extracted from Clarivate Analytics Web of Science (WOS). Using Istanbul, Konya, and Kastamonu showcased as destination brands, the chapter demonstrates how SNA can be applied in real-world contexts, providing insights into the benefits of a strategic branding approach through SNA. The author emphasizes the significance of a connected keyword network and offers practical strategies for leveraging these connections to establish a sustainable destination brand identity. The findings serve as a guide for tourism and hospitality practitioners, assisting them in creating compelling, sustainable destination brands. Similarly, this methodology can be applied to investigate the complex relationships among stakeholders, including local communities, businesses, government agencies, and tourists.

Chapter 8: Ecotourism Branding Balancing Conservation and Community

Balancing conservation and community development is a significant challenge, especially where natural resources are protected and serve as livelihoods for locals. This study focuses on Kanha National Park in central India, which conserves diverse flora and fauna, including tigers and swamp deer. Conservation efforts often conflict with the livelihoods of locals living in buffer zones, leading to socioeconomic issues. Eco-tourism offers an alternative income source, leveraging the park's natural beauty and biodiversity. This chapter analyzes Kanha's eco-tourism branding, highlighting sustainable tourism practices and their ecological importance. Sustainable measures, like eco-friendly lodging and income reinvestment in community projects, align local interests with conservation goals. Despite challenges, the chapter suggests Kanha's model as an example of effective eco-tourism branding, promoting conservation and regional development through inclusive management.

Chapter 9: Balancing Bias and Sustainability in Heritage Tourism

This paper examines the complex dynamics of biases in ecotourism and destination branding within the context of heritage site management. It explores how these biases influence perceptions, visitor experiences, and sustainable practices at iconic destinations such as the Taj Mahal and Machu Picchu. The study identifies critical challenges and opportunities in promoting inclusive, authentic, and sustainable tourism by integrating insights from predictive analytics, cultural sensitivity, and ethical considerations. Drawing on case studies and theoretical frameworks, the paper offers practical implications for mitigating biases, enhancing visitor engagement, and safeguarding cultural and natural heritage. It concludes by advocating for integrated strategies that balance effective branding with responsible stewardship to ensure the long-term preservation and equitable enjoyment of heritage sites worldwide.

Chapter 10: Developing Destination Brand Identity through Stakeholder Collaboration

Stakeholder collaboration is essential in creating a strong and resilient destination brand. This chapter explores how collaboration between local communities, government agencies, and private enterprises can help develop a cohesive brand identity that resonates with tourists. Drawing on the works of Aaker, Govers, and others, the chapter discusses how emotional, sensory, and experiential aspects of tourism shape consumer behaviour and brand perceptions, offering strategies for building affective attachments to destinations.

Chapter 11: Leveraging Market Research for Destination Branding in Chiang Mai's Tourism Market

This chapter explores how a specific tourism destination can employ market research to develop a logo and slogan to gain a competitive advantage in the international and domestic tourism market through product differentiation, market segmentation, target marketing and branding strategies. It highlights possible strategies for destination brands to develop their marketing strategies and competitiveness. The study gathers historical data from existing literature about the selected destination for the study. Additionally, it observes the destination features and employs developed questions to interview the selected destination using a cluster sampling method to gather customer data. The study also makes recommendations for the destination for possible destination brand sustainability.

Chapter 12: Wine and Cultural Tourism as Niche Opportunities in Slovakia, Czechia, and Canada

This chapter will discuss recent advancements in the tourism industry, particularly in light of the COVID-19 time. Tourism destinations can profit from the sound effects of sustainable and niche tourism during economic downturns and unrest by enhancing their reputation, image, and level of service and utilizing their local cultural resources and legacy. The only travel locations that will be more successful and competitive are those that can investigate new product offerings and deal with the realities of the current environment. In tourist destinations, ecology and sustainability have begun to take centre stage. Niche tourism is a prime illustration of this kind of growth and provision. The study aims to explain the importance of wine tourism as a form of niche tourism and to add the importance of culinary and cultural tourism as additional niche tourism products. The Brand Niagara Region in Canada, Slovakia, and the Czech Republic will be the study's main subjects.

Chapter 13: Ecotourism and Sustainable Development in Chania

This study investigates the potential of Ecotourism in fostering sustainable development in Chania, Crete, focusing on environmental conservation, cultural preservation, and economic growth. A mixed-methods approach combines secondary research to establish a global and local theoretical framework with qualitative interviews with key stakeholders in Chania. The study assesses the current state of Ecotourism, its impact on natural and cultural heritage, and barriers to sustainable tourism. Findings highlight Ecotourism's role in raising environmental awareness and supporting local economies. However, challenges such as infrastructure, stakeholder cooperation, and ecological management persist. The study concludes that strategic planning and stakeholder collaboration are essential for Ecotourism's success, balancing growth with resource preservation. Theoretical implications suggest Ecotourism as a sustainable tourism model, while practical recommendations call for targeted policies, employee training, and marketing strategies to position Chania as a top ecotourism destination.

Chapter 14: Fostering Ecotourism Brands through Local Engagement in Peru and the Maldives

As a subset of sustainable tourism, ecotourism has increased in protected tourism sites and biodiversity hotspots as more tourists seek meaningful natural experiences. This necessitates understanding how to leverage tourist-local community engagement in ecotourism branding. The chapter focuses on two case studies from two contexts, which harness tourist-local community engagement in their ecotourism branding. While the first case study relates to the conservation of nature and cultural heritage within an Amazonian rainforest in Peru, the latter refers to preserving the Maldives' ocean ecosystems. Although both cases leverage tourist-local community engagement to a certain extent, they heavily focus on uplifting local communities, guest education and scientific research in their ecotourism branding. The study lacks empirical evidence, yet it has managerial and policy implications. It advises managers and policymakers to foster a sustainable ecotourism brand with the tourist-local community interaction in mind.

Chapter 15: Awareness of Ecotourism and the Creation of Ecotouristic Destination Brands in Türkiye

This chapter aims to define and understand the current perception of Ecotourism by analyzing the academic literature and identifying the perspectives of international and related national organizations. Following a global view of Ecotourism, the Türkiye case is dealt with by examining the potential of Ecotourism and the evolving phases of the ecotourism development path of Türkiye on the way to the creation of ecotouristic destination brands in this country. Compared to the classical mass tourism of sun-sea-sand, Ecotourism has adopted an alternative tourism path, which is carried out to be more considerate of the protection of biodiversity and much more attentive in terms of human-environment interaction. Therefore, as international organizations emphasize, the sustainable management of Ecotourism is advised, and ecotouristic destination branding is suggested to be developed for Türkiye.

Chapter 16: Village Tourism Balances Brand Identity and Sustainability in Montegridolfo

This paper explores village tourism through a case study of a luxury hotel in a small town on the hills of Riviera Romagnola in Italy. Montegridolfo is the name of this delightful village set in the countryside and characterized by rolling hills and olive groves; it has historical roots dating back to the Middle Ages. The walls of a castle enclose the ancient village that has recently been transformed into a 4-star hotel: the historic residence of Palazzo Viviani. What is the rationale of an entrepreneurial investment in a luxury hotel in a small village far away from the traditional tourist routes? Can it foster sustainable development and support peculiar destination branding processes? How can the choice to redevelop a town into a luxury destination maintain the sustainability of its tourism while ensuring ethically and economically sound destination development? Using ethnographic research, we discuss these research questions by illustrating how Palazzo Viviani exemplifies a brand destination creation, following an eco-sustainability approach.

In Conclusion

As the editors of this comprehensive volume on *Destination Branding and Bias in Ecotourism*, we have witnessed the unfolding of diverse perspectives and case studies that reveal the intricate interplay between culture, destination branding, and tourism. The chapters included here illustrate that the global tourism landscape is evolving rapidly, with sustainability and innovation at the core of this transformation. From village tourism fostering destination branding and ecological preservation to niche markets like wine and cultural tourism expanding in unexpected regions, the contributions offer fresh insights into how technology can drive preservation and progress.

The rise of ecotourism is emblematic of this balance, seeking to conserve natural and cultural heritage while engaging local communities in sustainable practices. Several case studies have emphasized the importance of local engagement, ethical entrepreneurship, and responsible tourism branding, urging stakeholders to consider both their strategies' environmental and socioeconomic impacts. Furthermore, the global scope of the research, spanning regions from Italy to Canada and from the Maldives to Türkiye, demonstrates the universal relevance of cultural and Ecotourism in shaping the industry's future.

By synthesizing these contributions, we hope to inspire tourism practitioners, researchers, policymakers, and students to reimagine the potential of cultural tourism. Integrating advanced technology, digital tools, intelligent systems, or sustainable innovation, opens up new possibilities for enhancing the tourist experience while safeguarding the assets that make destinations unique.

This volume is a testament to the potential of global collaboration, interdisciplinary research, and a forward-looking approach to tourism management. The insights presented here will guide future cultural and sustainable tourism developments, fostering a balance between conservation, technological innovation, and community well-being.

Muhammad Abrar
Muhammad Asim Nawaz
Faiqa Kiran

Acknowledgement

I am delighted to acknowledge the vital contributions of numerous individuals who made this pioneering book on Destination Branding and Bias in Ecotourism a reality. Firstly, I extend my heartfelt gratitude to my co-editors, **Muhammad Asim Nawaz** and **Faiqa Kiran**, whose tireless dedication, expertise, and collaborative spirit were instrumental in shaping this book.

The steadfast support and guidance from the staff of IGI Global are also greatly appreciated. Their professionalism and commitment to excellence ensured the seamless publication process.

I am deeply appreciative to the revered authors from diverse institutions and countries who contributed their valuable insights, expertise, and research to this book. Their collective efforts have enriched the content and enhanced the book's global relevance.

I would also like to express my sincere gratitude to the leadership of my institution, particularly former Deans Prof. Dr. Hazoor Muhammad Sabir and Prof. Dr. Sofia Anwar of the Faculty of Economics and Management Sciences, and worthy Vice-Chancellor Prof.Dr.Rauf-i-Azam. Their reinforcement, motivation, and support enabled me to balance this project with other academic responsibilities.

On a personal note, I am thankful for the moral support and inspiration received from Mohsin Bashir, Umair Arshad, Khalid Mahmood Zia, Sharjeel Saleem, Rizwan Shabbir, Ahsan Zubair, Muhammad Ishtiaq, Bashir Ahmad and Ayesha Sharif. Their presence and encouragement played a significant role in overcoming challenges during this project.

Lastly, I am grateful for the opportunity to work on this book, which has been a rewarding experience. I hope that this publication will contribute meaningfully to the field of ecotourism and destination branding.

Sincerely,

Muhammad Abrar

Chapter 1
Understanding Destination Brand Experience

Muhammad Abrar
https://orcid.org/0000-0002-1128-5350
Government College University, Faisalabad, Pakistan

Ahmad Sohail Khan
Government College University, Faisalabad, Pakistan

Rizwan Shabbir
https://orcid.org/0000-0003-0859-7465
Government College University, Faisalabad, Pakistan

ABSTRACT

Ecotourism is one of the most vital catalysts of conservation and sustainable development in tourism. Ecotourism favours the production of economic and administrative support for protected areas, heightens the understanding of environmental and historical values, and improves the visitor's experience. The chapter explains the conceptual understanding and aspects of destination band experience and looks into the theoretical foundation of destination brand experience in the ecotourism industry. Furthermore, it explores the factors influencing destination brand experience, strategies, challenges and future trends in managing ecotourism. Destination marketers could design their marketing communication programs to better integrate with the expectations of intended tourists to augment their destination experience. Policymakers might also use this information to develop sustainable tourism plans and regulate how tourism influences the environment and the local community, ultimately leading to a refined destination brand experience.

DOI: 10.4018/979-8-3693-6700-1.ch001

INTRODUCTION

The United Nations World Tourism Organization (UNWTO) states that tourism is one of the most significant sectors in the global economy; it brings progress, creates new avenues to synchronize different cultures, and facilitates sustainable development (UNWTO, 2024). Ecotourism is a form of tourism that serves as a window for tropical destinations to tap into their resources. Destination conservation goes hand in hand with ecological interferences and cultural values (Björk, 2000; Paul & Brad, 1997). This specialized type of tourism has gained considerable attention and transformed the orientation of the tourism industry. The core of this concept is the destination brand experience, which helps to form the ecotourists' perceptions and expectations.

Ecotourism is described as tourism that occurs in natural environments to preserve the environment and benefit the local community. Ecotourism is showcasing an opportunity to enhance the flow of visitors' knowledge and understanding of natural surroundings, people, and their culture (Junus et al., 2020). That is why this type of tourism focuses on preserving the environment, the development of the economy, and involving communities (Nematollahi et al., 2022).

The scope of the ecotourism destination brand experience memoirs the totality of a visitor's experience when interacting with a specific destination, including the physical environment, interaction with locals, and learning aspects (Stamboulis & Skayannis, 2003). The recent development in the marketing literature showed that positive destination image and experience are crucial to be the main components endorsing positive emotions and satisfaction for tourists (Quynh et al., 2021). It leads to a higher propensity to spread favorable word of mouth and revisit intention of a particular eco-destination (Quynh et al., 2021). This is essential in developing the impressions of ecotourists and their level of satisfaction and dependency on the destination. It is suggested that destination image appears to be one of the critical dimensions in the ecotourism experience because it contributes to the creation of feelings towards the tourist destination and, therefore, impacts the tourist's satisfaction level.

Empirical studies are available in the literature about the role of the tourist experience for a particular destination brand in developing a destination's image. Although preceding studies tested the relationships between experience, satisfaction, image and behavior, these need to be thoroughly understood in the context of ecotourism (Li et al., 2021). The tourism industry is witnessing the significance of experiential value in developing a positive visitor experience and enhancing customer satisfaction (Elayouty et al., 2023). Thus, understanding visitors' experience of a destination brand in ecotourism becomes highly important. In the context of ecotourism, defined by its focus on conservation, sustainability, and the natural environment, experiential value becomes even more critical to ensure positive visitor experiences and satisfaction. Thus, the literature finds a gap in holistically reviewing the destination brand experience.

Marketing management of the ecotourism destination brand experience holds benefits for the destination and the local community. Due to the intensity of the use of the ecotourism business, it is wise for destinations that offer the service to ensure that what they offer is different and genuine to appeal to the conscience of tourists and those who cherish the environment. This chapter discusses the conceptual foundations of destination brand experience and narrates different aspects of eco-destination brand experience, along with the application of experience-related constructs in ecotourism. Moreover, it discusses research approaches for measuring destination brand experience and strategies to improve that experience.

1.1 Aspects of Ecotourism

As a specialized tourism sub-industry, ecotourism captures a narrowly stipulated niche of the tourist market by offering clients qualitatively different propositions and experiences. Historically, ecotourism brands have different aims from traditional tourist products, emphasizing environmental conservation, social sensitivity, and the impact of improving communities' economies (Paul & Brad, 1997). The newer and more precise concept of ecotourism, according to The International Ecotourism Society (TIES), *"is ethical travel to natural areas that helps the well-being of local people and conserves the environment"* (Ouboter et al., 2021).

Ecotourism business activities aim to reduce their negative impacts on the ecosystem by adopting some of the principles like using environment-friendly energy sources, minimizing energy wastage and protecting local ecosystems. Another component of the brand experience is the efficiency in managing resources used in ecotourism activities. This would not only help the sustainability of the destinations for future generations but also appeal to consumers with a conscience who want to minimize their carbon footprint when traveling (Junus et al., 2020; Nematollahi et al., 2022; Paul & Brad, 1997; Roseta et al., 2020).

That is why, besides environmental issues, ecotourism brands pay special attention to indigenous people and their financial stability. Ecotourism supporters and entrepreneurs actively incorporate the economic advantages of ecotourism to disseminate the improvement of host communities and the provision for engagement in the preparation and delivery of services to the local people (Nematollahi et al., 2022).

2. ECOTOURISM AND DESTINATION BRAND EXPERIENCE

Destination branding has become significant in the tourism business because place marketing seeks to develop a unique and easily remembered brand image (Cai, 2002). The destination brand experience (DBE) concept offers a more comprehensive and complicated perspective of the destination brand.

2.1 Destination Brand Experience

Destination Brand Experience (DBE) is defined by the following components that originate from the branding and brand management literature. Destination brand experience refers to the sensory, emotional, cognitive and communicating customer reactions when interacting with the destination brand. This multiple-layered view is also consistent with the general marketing discussions of the brand experience concept, where the tasks are given to develop valuable and purposeful contacts between the brand and the consumer.

In tourism literature, brand experience has been defined as an essential factor that influences visitors' satisfaction, repeat visitation and recommendation intentions. Therefore, DBE could play a pivotal role in influencing the visitors' perceptions, feelings, and behavioral intentions about the decision to revisit the destination, as well as to recommend it to others. Brand experience is crucial to the success of businesses that are well-studied in the marketing field. However, its impact on the benefits of competitive differentiation and brand positioning, particularly in tourism, needs more research (Torres-Moraga & Barra, 2023).

2.2 Place Identity and Place Attachment

Based on environmental psychology, place identity is defined as an understanding or perception of the meanings and values that people or specific populations assign to a given place. In the concept of destination branding, it becomes very important that the visitor understands the destination's strengths and identity. When tourists travel to multiple destinations repeatedly, they interact directly with various spatial elements, which may influence their emotional connection with the destination, leading them to place attachment. According to a recent study, the impact of the destination's nature dimension positively affected place identity and dependence. The concept of place attachment includes people and their affective relationship with certain places. Place attachment could be cultured in tourists by providing positive experiences that make the tourists recommend the destination to others. It has also merged into the theoretical framework of destination brand experience.

2.3 Brand Identification

Brand Identification is the extent to which people perceive the destination brand as true to their self-identity and ideals. Destination brand commitment is significant because when people have a strong brand connection, they tend to exhibit positive behavioral intention towards the brand through destination loyalty and positive word of mouth. Destination management in ecotourism has emphasized the place identity constructed by public authorities and focused on place promotion, branding and promotion with a match between place identity and place image perceived by visitors and impact on their satisfaction (Nogueira & Carvalho, 2024).

2.4 Brand Love

Numerous brands can satisfy consumers' needs and desires. However, a few can create an emotional and exclusive connection with delighted consumers, known as brand love (Leroi-Werelds et al., 2014). It is conceivable that people love places, as can be understood in one of the most popular marketing campaigns of all time: "I Love New York." multiple studies have presented that love is an emotion that people feel for places, including cities (Aro et al., 2018). Brand love also serves as the theoretical foundation of destination brand experience. Tourism destination love is an extreme emotional relationship with a particular destination (Sharma & Nayak, 2020). Brand affection is a strong emotional bond that consumers create with a brand. Specifically, in tourism, brand love may enhance the degree of users' identification with the brand, thus increasing their satisfaction level, the likelihood of return visits, positive word-of-mouth and empowering the local communities (Barnes et al., 2014; Dekimpe et al., 1997; Hosany & Gilbert, 2010; Phon et al., 2024).

Due to the competitiveness in tourism destinations, destination managers have deemed it necessary to develop adequate branding strategies to help establish and attract tourism travelers (Cai, 2002). Thus, understanding the brand experience theories can help improve the experience of the tourism destination brand. The recent advancement in consumer behavior suggested that experience research is no longer limited to ecotourism sites and resources. This turns into a multi-stakeholder approach. Thus, the experience has been divided into three stages: pre-visit, on-site and post-visit. All of these stages have their relative significance in the formulation of positive experiences of the visitor regarding a destination brand (Sana et al., 2023).

2.5 Destination Image

Destination image and destination personality are two of the most interrelated concepts in the framework of which branding theories can be explained (Hosany et al., 2006). Destination image is the stored information in the consumer's memory regarding the attributes of a destination. At the same time, Destination personality entails the affective response to the destination regarding feelings and attitudes towards it. It is just established that the attitude of the tourist plays an integral part in contributing to the determinant of the destination personality, which in turn emphasizes the positive images that the tourists have towards a particular tourism destination, which ultimately leads to tourist satisfaction (Qu et al., 2011; Quynh et al., 2021).

2.6 Brand Equity

Another type of brand equity explored within the tourism literature includes brand awareness, brand image, perceived quality and brand loyalty. In a related study on destination image, social self-image and perceived value, a strong correlation exists in developing the loyalty bond with the visitor's destination. In addition, the 'unique image,' alongside the cognitive evaluations of a place, is highly influential as it defines the general destination image, not to mention the behaviors of the tourists (Qu et al., 2011). A recent study conducted in Malaysia examined the consequent relationship between sustainable tourism marketing and brand equity in the context of rural community-based home-stays. It concluded a highly significant relationship (Krishnapillai & Rehman, 2023).

2.7 Service-Dominant Logic (S-D Logic)

Value is co-created; it is a mutual exchange between providers and consumers (Vargo et al., 2020). This concept fairly works in destination branding. It implies involving the tourist, the host community, and others in the creation and sustenance of the brand image that is perceived by tourists, hence promoting a more meaningful experience for the tourist. Therefore, to enact the theories associated with brand experience, including the brand image, brand personality and brand equity, the destination managers engaged in enhancing the brand experience of travelers and consequently developed a closer rapport with them.

3. MEASURING DESTINATION BRAND EXPERIENCE

Destination branding has emerged as a significant facet of tourism marketing because for destinations to stand out, they must relay an image that visitors would remember to consider (Konecnik & Gartner, 2007). Both qualitative and quantitative research methods are used to measure the destination brand experience.

3.1 Qualitative Approach

Qualitative research is quite helpful in understanding the richness and complexity of the destination brand experience (Kladou et al., 2015). A recent study conducted in Indonesia has exercised focus group discussion to explore leading antecedents of ecotourism brand experience (Tarigan et al., 2023). The more objective methods of interviews, focus groups, and observational studies have given critical qualitative data that captures the subjective and emotional nature of the visitors' experience. Such methods have assisted in identifying the aspects that constitute destination brand equity, which includes aspects like awareness, image, perceived quality, and loyalty (Kladou et al., 2015). Previous scholars have employed a qualitative research method to determine the role of various touch points and touch events in the process of brand building of a destination (Barnes et al., 2014).

3.2 Quantitative Approach

Nevertheless, quantitative methodologies have also facilitated the establishment of a more standardized, systematic and generalizable examination of the construct, namely destination brand experience. Self-administered questionnaires have been employed since they offer a reliable and less costly way of creating and establishing scales, encompassing the destination brand experience (Konecnik & Gartner, 2007). One of the contemporary studies executed in Malaysia where the quantitative approach was applied, in which a structured questionnaire was used to collect 280 tourist responses through purposive sampling, resulted in destination brand experience positively impacting destination loyalty (Azinuddin et al., 2022).

It is noteworthy that past research has analyzed interactions between the destination brand experience components and crucial indicators like revisit intention and word-of-mouth communication intentions (Barnes et al., 2014). For instance, amongst the factors of destination brand experience, the sensory element has the highest significance in influencing the visitors' behavior.

3.3 Mix-Method Research

This chapter has demonstrated that the combination of qualitative and quantitative research, known as mixed-method research, will better study the brand experience of a particular destination. Qualitative data can be used to design quantitative variables, and quantitative data can help refine the identified theoretical constructs. In sum, theoretical and practical procedures for capturing destination brand experience as a strategic marketing and management tool aimed at improving the image of a destination brand are recommended. Therefore, it can be understood that the essence of the concept of destination brand experience can be quantified and evaluated based on both qualitatively and quantitatively driven tools. Qualitative methods are helpful when one wants more detail and a description of the sample, while quantitative methods allow for examining a sample as a whole.

4. FACTORS INFLUENCING ECOTOURISM BRAND EXPERIENCE

Ecotourism has become one of the possible substitutes for conventional mass tourism, providing tourists with an opportunity to explore nature. Hence, the most critical factor for ecotourism's success is the capacity to meet visitors' brand expectations, which satisfactorily matches visitors' motivation for the concept of ecotourism. The chapter establishes the critical determinants of the ecotourism brand experience concerning visitor motivation, expectations, and experiences. Ecotourists have been described as more conscious and responsible in their travels than mass tourists. However, some researchers have criticized this distinction, stressing that it is hard to distinguish between the motives, values, and consumption patterns of ecotourists and those of mass tourists. This raises several issues regarding the categorization of an "ecotourist" and the appropriateness of the current ecotourism marketing strategy in satisfying the needs of this distinct niche tourism market. Ecotourism is one of the fastest-growing sectors in which tourists can gain unique experiences while simultaneously respecting the environment and the local culture.

4.1 Authenticity

Authenticity was first conceptualized in 1973 by MacCannell. Other scholars have offered similar propositions on this concept, concluding that the perception of truthfulness can be described as the degree to which one makes a heavy impression of being authentic by displaying local culture. For example, the cultural tourists' interests are to enjoy that particular culture—the true-life existence of particular historical periods, particular people, and particular regions. In tourism, authenticity refers to an oxymoronic term used to explain how tourists understand or view products and experiences or where consumers interact with products and experiences. Authenticity is an important facet that influences the behaviors of existing people, mainly tourists. It helps people to name many accounts as “artificial elements” in their surrounding environment, leaving a sense of unreality and low desire for acceptance. Thus, authenticity has become another primary source of tourist attraction for those places. Hence, tourist authenticity has a positive effect on his or her experience and revisits intentions for a particular destination brand(Yang et al., 2023).

When tourists come into the zone to meet representatives of different environments, etc., there is a need for ecotourism operators to ensure that they have made genuine attempts at facilitating ecotourism so that the above indicators are achieved and maintained, including ecological conservation, adherence to cultural practices and beliefs of the local people. It also provides positive experiences for the visitor while simultaneously realizing a positive change in perception and behavior toward conserving the environment and communities. In addition, there is still the issue of informing ecotourism destination markets about a region's culture, folklore, natural values, and eco-friendly social standards to appeal to ecologically sensitive tourists.

4.2 Sustainability

Sustainability is another feature that must be considered in developing and establishing the ecotourism brand image and experience. Ecotourism should indeed be adequately planned and utilized to sustain the natural resources and the people benefiting from the tours (Nematollahi et al., 2022). Local governments and ecotourism operators must make proactive plans about utilizing local resources, ensuring their conservation, and setting up the right kind of infrastructure support to carry out ecotourism activities (Thi Khanh & Phong, 2020). This concept of sustainable conservation is helpful as it protects the environment while also giving profits to the local communities so that tourism and conservation can be attained.

4.3 Responsible Management

Responsible management is the third intermediating variable within this ecosystem towards the ecotourism brand experience. In essence, eco-tour operators should ensure that they effectively manage the eco-sites to ensure they are conserved function while at the same time giving the tourists a good view. These involve measures to regulate the behavior of tourists, raising tourists' awareness of environmental conservation and allowing the inclusion of environmental conservation measures in all tourism activities. Responsible management also promotes ecotourism. Therefore, ecotourism marketers are required to be careful about what they portray to potential ecotourists, for the information conveyed has to be at par with a sustainable and genuine form of tourism. From the perspective of the communication strategy, the possibilities of creating a positive image of ecotourism through the focus on its environmental and cultural impacts on the surrounding environment are presented.

Therefore, the strategies of ecotourism branding should stress authenticity, sustainability, and responsible management to be long-lasting and attractive. Thus, the principles of ecotourism can positively promote the enhancement of the natural environment, support communities, and promote tourists' personal and social change (Binangun & Dutha, 2020; Khanh & Phong, 2020; Paul & Brad, 1997; Rezaeinejad & Khaniwadekar, 2021). Forming the specific brand image of ecotourism implies evaluating multiple factors connected with the visitors' desires, perceptions, and attitudes. It has been discovered that the nature-based destination image and the tourists' environmental beliefs were the determining factors in their attitude towards ecotourism. Most ecotourists aim to get close to wildlife, discover more about the indigenous people and their efforts in the conservation of the environment, and opt for environmentally responsible tourism (Sharpley, 2006). However, the degree of realization of these motivations within ecotourism is only sometimes guaranteed and can, therefore, result in the gaps between expectations and authentic experiences.

The marketers of ecotourism must also encounter specific trade-specific issues such as the interaction with local and federal authorities to obtain necessary permits, constant focus on environment-friendly actions, and producing an 'ethic' for eco-tourism that would be appealing to the chosen target market (Paul & Brad, 1997). This chapter connects the responsibility for the successful promotion of ecotourism programs to the range of potential rewards if such initiatives are properly managed depending on the factors that relate to the formation of the brand image in the field of ecotourism.

It is comprehensible that visitors' expectations, motivations, and experiences act as critical components of the overall brand experience related to the ecotourism brand image. Some ecotourists' motivations include appreciating nature, perceiving cultural values and conservation, and best practices on tourists' conduct. However, it is noteworthy that some tourists' motivations may only sometimes be fully met in reality depending on their ecotourism experience; such an area is creating a literature gap in the study of destination brand experience in depth. The perceived image of the nature-based destination affects ecotourists' behavior and perception of ecotourism. This means that policymakers and providers of ecotourism services must deploy adequate thinking and resource protection so that the kind of ecotourism offered meets visitors' expectations and motivation to visit.

Therefore, this chapter establishes a comprehensive understanding of the various factors that define the branding of a specific experience, which in this case is the ecotourism brand experience. The principles of ecotourism state that to fulfill the above expectations of the providers, they must ensure that they capture the exact nature of the needs and trends of this particular market segment to be in a position to offer appropriate and satisfactory experiences in ecotourism (Khanh & Phong, 2020; Paul & Brad, 1997; Roseta et al., 2020; Sharpley, 2006)

5. EVALUATING ECOTOURISM BRAND EXPERIENCE

The subject of ecotourism has its benefits and threats regarding sustainable development and tourists' satisfaction in the corresponding sites. Therefore, the purpose of this research chapter is to identify the consequences of a positive brand experience of an ecotourism destination and its effectiveness on visitors' satisfaction, loyal behavior, willingness to recommend the destination, and purpose of their revisit while also understanding the enhancement of the competitiveness and sustenance of the destination.

Previous studies have revealed that there are possibilities that ecotourism will lead to adverse effects on the economy, society, and the physical environment. For instance, regarding the benefits, the number one impact is that it is overwhelming on infrastructure, damaging to culture, and polluting the environment. These risks must be managed to guarantee the sustainability of ecotourism plans and programs, and proper management strategies must be applied (Buckley, 2009a). However, the literature also proposes that an encouraging ecotourism experience can lead to valuable outcomes for visitors and destinations.

There is evidence that visitors who enjoy the positive brand experience of ecotourism are satisfied with ecotourism destinations because they get the chance to foster interaction with nature and cultural experiences and also participate in the cause of conservation of the natural ecosystems (Agüera, 2014; Buckley, 2009b). This improved satisfaction can be accompanied by improved customer loyalty, where the visitors are likely to revisit the destination and insist that other people also visit the destination. In addition, a positive brand experience makes the visitors change other behaviors by promoting such values and being a precursor to more substantial environmental and social change. From the destination's point of view, the development of a sustainable ecotourism brand can be beneficial to the destination's competitiveness due to the fact that the environment is becoming an essential consideration among tourists. Therefore, the destination would be branded as an ideal tourism destination. It will, in turn, give rise to new spending from visitors, employment and investment opportunities for the local communities, and conservation norms.

Summarizing the results of the literature, it can be stated that although there is scientific evidence of how positive brand experience in ecotourism can have various positive consequences, further research is needed to identify interconnections better and the pros and cons associated with them (Herath, 2002; Kirkby et al., 2011; Kummitha, 2020).

6. DESTINATION BRANDING STRATEGIES FOR ECOTOURISM

Destination image is imperative for ecotourism destinations to appeal to alternative tourism consumers and encourage sustainable tourism practices. Here are some critical strategies for developing an authentic and sustainable brand identity for ecotourism destinations:

6.1 Positioning and Differentiation

Clearly define your destination's unique selling points and position it in the market based on its natural assets, conservation efforts, and authentic cultural experiences. Specifically, market it on the brand's strengths and focus on the following key pillars: sustainability, environmental protection, and the community.

6.2 Storytelling and Authenticity

Develop an appealing brand story of your destination under the theme of outstanding nature, preserving the planet, and culture. Make sure your communication strategy professionally reflects the peculiarities of the destination.

6.3 Stakeholder Engagement

Incorporate the communities and local tourism businesses. In addition to the conservation, the branding process should also reflect the local goals and aspirations. Engage local people and make them act as promoters of the brands and be part of sustainable tourism (Baloch et al., 2023).

6.4 Sustainable Product Development

Promote ecotourism products and programs that incorporate ideas you want to support in your brand, including nature-based activities, learning events, and local people immersion. It should also be noted that it can only be implemented to maximize the products' environmental and societal effects (Baloch et al., 2023).

6.5 Integrated Marketing Communications

Socialize your attractions and promotions through different forms of marketing: social media, content promotion, and associated sustainable tourism travel brands (Baloch et al., 2023). Ensure that your marketing messages are clear, truthful, and in the audience's best interest, which is the environment-friendly tourists. Thus, the application of these strategies can help the destinations of ecotourism to create a substantial grounding and evolutionarily solid image of the brand that would successfully attract the target great number of the clients-sympathizers of the environmental protection that would contribute to a socio-environmental sustainable future of eco destinations.

Apply various marketing communication channels, such as social media, content marketing, and collaboration with eco-friendly travel platforms. This is crucial to endorse your destination's brand identity and sustainability initiatives (Baloch et al., 2023). Confirm that your marketing campaigns are consistent, authentic, and fully integrated with your target audience of eco-conscious travelers. With these strategies, ecotourism destinations can evolve a vivid, authentic, and long-term brand image that fascinates ecotourists. This is how conservation efforts and the sustainability of the destination can be promoted.

7. CASE STUDIES

Here are two case-studies that are selected based on their best practices for generating positive destination brand experiences.

7.1 Case Study: Australia – There is Nothing Like Australia

The campaign started in 2010 and aims to promote Australia as a tourist destination, its features, fauna, and geography.

Strategy: Real-life stories and testimonials of the tourists and people living in the respective areas.

Execution: It also focuses on a combination of advertisements, digital content, and social media presence to promote the aspect of variety in the experience to be offered in Australia, both in cities and in nature.

Best Practices: Authenticity: This involves using real people who are tourists and the locals themselves to create real and tangible material. Diverse Appeal: Emphasizing many more tourist attractions and possibilities for having a good time to meet the demands of different groups of tourists. Interactive Content: Applying web 2.0 tools, digital and social media, and content-generating methods to target probable visitors.

7.2 Case Study: New Zealand - 100% Pure New Zealand

The project, "100% Pure New Zealand," started in 1999. This campaign is one of the longest and most effective destination branding campaigns.

Strategy: The campaign focuses on exploring New Zealand's natural scenery, physical activities, and cultural attractions.

Execution: A combination of consistent messages on most of the media, stunning visuals, and quality storytelling represent New Zealand's landscapes, adventure tourism, and culture.

Best Practices: Consistency: Over the years, consistency in the brand message has helped to remind people of New Zealand's beauty and adventure continuously. Integrated Marketing: Combining old-school advertising with new-school digital and social media to reach as many people as possible. Emotional Connection: This is due to the appeal to emotion, where the concern is formulated based on the desired emotions of adventure and the natural view of prospective guests.

8. KEY CHALLENGES

Here are the key challenges in managing the impact of ecotourism include:

1. **Balancing Conservation and Development:** Ecotourism, in its fundamental form, seeks to preserve the environment. However, in the process of promoting the tourism sector, more facilities and structures will be required, which may be harmful in the long run. Destination managers should address these concerns while at the same time satisfying the above-stated competing objectives.
2. **Controlling Visitor Numbers:** Problems such as congestion at ecotourism sites cause a high population density. This may involve the exploitation of natural resources and negative interference with the locals' social structure. Effective

visitor management is needed to protect the destination's brand image in such circumstances.

3. **Ensuring Equitable Benefits:** However, the opportunity to earn through ecotourism is unavailable to all the people in the community. Local people should also benefit from such avenues, so destination managers should strive to ensure the fair availability of small-scale business opportunities.
4. **Maintaining Authenticity:** Ecotourism has become the buzzword and began as an environmentally friendly method of promoting tourism. It has the potential to turn out most 'un-green,' where destinations may become over-commercialized and start to lose their cultural and natural integrity. Cultural tourism has robust vectors for development since protecting the given place's identity is vital.
5. **Addressing Environmental Impacts:** Even with a greater focus on sustainability, ecotourism has been tragic, with environmental effects like wastewater disposal, water usage, and carbon emissions resulting from transportation. Alleviating these impacts is something that has yet to be done.
6. **Providing Quality Experiences:** Sometimes, ecotourists are highly concerned about their experiences. Hence, destination managers should provide them with quality experience about their destinations.

9. CONCLUSION

This chapter reviewed how the destination brand image and experience are related and grounded on solid theoretical assumptions. Destination brand image can be defined as the cultural and physical elements that make up a destination and the psychological perceptions created in travelers' minds concerning the destination. The destination brand experience covers factors that enable tourists to come, sense, interact, and feel about the destination brand and find the service quality, personal contact, and response in the same stream of brand experiences. That is why, to improve destination brand image and experience, it is necessary to apply complex measures. This encompasses digital marketing communication, narrative, and immersive marketing communication to tell a sequential and consistent story that captures the attention of targeted consumers.

Moreover, concerning brand maintenance, it is significant for companies to be consistent and involved with the stakeholders and incorporate the technology into the brand's process. Those destinations that can assimilate these trends and plan strategic brand image and experience management activities will be better positioned to successfully market and monetize tourists in a more competitive global environment. Consequently, the destination brand experience is a complex and continuously developing phenomenon that strongly depends on the aspects and parameters that define brand attitudes and visitors' experiences. When properly orchestrated, these aspects enhance a destination's brand image within the target market and the sustainable development of a consumer advocacy system after a favorable destination experience.

Therefore, by applying these insights, destination managers can sharpen their understanding and create better and more sustainable branding strategies that attract visitors and ensure they will have a positive perception, build long-term destination loyalty, and act as ambassadors for the destinations. Thus, when organized appropriately, destination brand experience improves competitiveness and sustainability in the global tourism market.

9.1 Managerial Implications

Since the tourism industry is constantly changing, destination managers need to concentrate on the multifaceted character of the destination brand experience. While tangible products can be described as consisting of attributes that can be delivered, destinations provide a list of experiences that might depend on the perception and expectations of the tourist. Destination image, as a part of the overall brand experience or identity, refers to the what, how, and why that represents a tourist destination. Managers must understand that these images are not fixed and can be changed by any factor, from direct or indirect information to associations and natural events (Jebbouri et al., 2022).

Destination branding, on its part, needs to embrace consideration of tourists' perceptions and behavior. Previous evidence suggests that tourists can be attracted to specific destinations through their feelings and perceived satisfaction with the destination itself and the site's physical characteristics (Ip-Soo-Ching et al., 2019). Therefore, destination managers must be empowered to target the right promotional messages and to concentrate on giving tourists superior value than expected. To this end, destination managers must conduct ongoing assessments of tourists' perceptions of the destination in new and traditional media. The chapter is also expected to benefit managers since it reveals how different drivers influence the destination's image and visitors' experiences, which can help managers in their decision-making regarding marketing communication and managing the destination image.

9.2 Future Trends in Ecotourism Management

Ecotourism is gradually transforming into what is being called the tourism of the future, as sustainable tourism and responsible travel have become core aspects of the global tourism industry. Destination management regarding brand experience in the future would involve managing sustainable tourism, increasing the use of big data and artificial intelligence (AI) in marketing the destination brand, and the progressive focus on social media and user content. Contemporary developments in managing ecotourism are motivated by improving technology and increasing community participation to meet the ever-increasing demand for responsible tourism by tourists. Here are the key future trends shaping ecotourism management:

1. **Emphasis on Regenerative Tourism:** Instead of the merely passive approach that seeks to reduce tourism's detrimental effects, this shift is toward proactive renewal and reinvestment in natural and cultural assets. This entails holistic and system-oriented destination management.
2. **Increased Community Involvement:** Effective ecotourism is poised to incorporate the locals into planning, development and management. Such measures empower the communities and ensure fair distribution of returns.
3. **Technological Innovation:** Advanced technologies like digital platforms, data analysis, and renewable energy sources will create innovative ways of managing more and better ecotourism destinations.
4. **Diversification of Ecotourism Experiences:** Ecological tourism is expected to evolve from simply being a typical environmental tourism featuring only nature-based activities into a new and improved type that encompasses cultural, adventurous activities, including relaxation and health resorts.
5. **Stronger Regulations and Certification:** It is expected that destination managers are going to face new pressure to regulate and certify them for the authenticity and sustainability of ecotourism products.
6. **Collaboration and Partnerships:** The best approach to promoting and managing this type of tourism will involve more and closer cooperation between governments, businesses, NGOs, and the local populace.

In order to advance the ecotourism discourses of conservation, local people's political and socio-economic rights, and visitor personal alterations, destination managers should tackle existing problems and adopt those new trends. Further research should, therefore, involve research paradigms of tourism, marketing, environmental science, and sustainability fields to gain a clear and holistic understanding of the visitors' effects and the effects of ecotourism on the destinations (Kummitha, 2020).

REFERENCES

Aro, K., Suomi, K., & Saraniemi, S. (2018). Antecedents and consequences of destination brand love—A case study from Finnish Lapland. *Tourism Management*, 67, 71–81. DOI: 10.1016/j.tourman.2018.01.003

Azinuddin, M., Mohammad Nasir, M. B., Hanafiah, M. H., Mior Shariffuddin, N. S., & Kamarudin, M. K. A. (2022). Interlinkage of Perceived Ecotourism Design Affordance, Perceived Value of Destination Experiences, Destination Reputation, and Loyalty. *Sustainability (Basel)*, 14(18), 11371. DOI: 10.3390/su141811371

Baloch, Q. B., Shah, S. N., Iqbal, N., Sheeraz, M., Asadullah, M., Mahar, S., & Khan, A. U. (2023). Impact of tourism development upon environmental sustainability: A suggested framework for sustainable ecotourism. *Environmental Science and Pollution Research International*, 30(3), 5917–5930. DOI: 10.1007/s11356-022-22496-w PMID: 35984561

Barnes, S. J., Mattsson, J., & Sørensen, F. (2014). Destination brand experience and visitor behavior: Testing a scale in the tourism context. *Annals of Tourism Research*, 48, 121–139. DOI: 10.1016/j.annals.2014.06.002

Binangun, J., & Dutha, I. (2020). Sustainability Concept in Ecotourism on Domestic Tourists of Generation Z. 2nd IConBMT (International Conference on Business, Management, Management, Technology) 2020.

Björk, P. (2000). Ecotourism from a conceptual perspective, an extended definition of a unique tourism form. *International Journal of Tourism Research*, 2(3), 189–202. DOI: 10.1002/(SICI)1522-1970(200005/06)2:3<189::AID-JTR195>3.0.CO;2-T

Buckley, R. (2009). *Ecotourism: Principles and practices*. CABI.

Buckley, R. (2009). Evaluating the net effects of ecotourism on the environment: A framework, first assessment and future research. *Journal of Sustainable Tourism*, 17(6), 643–672. DOI: 10.1080/09669580902999188

Cai, L. A. (2002). Cooperative branding for rural destinations. *Annals of Tourism Research*, 29(3), 720–742. DOI: 10.1016/S0160-7383(01)00080-9

Dekimpe, M. G., Steenkamp, J.-B. E. M., Mellens, M., & Vanden Abeele, P. (1997). Decline and variability in brand loyalty. *International Journal of Research in Marketing*, 14(5), 405–420. DOI: 10.1016/S0167-8116(97)00020-7

Elayouty, A. M. A., Yacout, O. M., & Elgharbawy, A. H. (2023). A Proposed Conceptual Framework for the Mediating Role of Experiential Value between Ecotourism Brand Experience and Tourist Satisfaction. *Journal of Business and Management Review*, 4(12), 952–963.

Herath, G. (2002). Research methodologies for planning ecotourism and nature conservation. *Tourism Economics*, 8(1), 77–101. DOI: 10.5367/000000002101298007

Hosany, S., Ekinci, Y., & Uysal, M. (2006). Destination image and destination personality: An application of branding theories to tourism places. *Journal of Business Research*, 59(5), 638–642. DOI: 10.1016/j.jbusres.2006.01.001

Hosany, S., & Gilbert, D. (2010). Measuring tourists' emotional experiences toward hedonic holiday destinations. *Journal of Travel Research*, 49(4), 513–526. DOI: 10.1177/0047287509349267

Ip-Soo-Ching, J. M., Zyngier, S., & Nayeem, T. (2019). Ecotourism and environmental sustainability knowledge: An open knowledge sharing approach among stakeholders. *Australian Journal of Environmental Education*, 35(1), 62–82. DOI: 10.1017/aee.2018.45

Jebbouri, A., Zhang, H., Imran, Z., Iqbal, J., & Bouchiba, N. (2022). Impact of destination image formation on tourist trust: Mediating role of tourist satisfaction. *Frontiers in Psychology*, 13, 845538. DOI: 10.3389/fpsyg.2022.845538 PMID: 35432069

Junus, S. Z., Hambali, K. A., Iman, A. H. M., Abas, M. A., & Hassin, N. H. (2020). Visitor's perception and attitude toward the ecotourism resources at Taman Negara Kuala Koh, Kelantan. *IOP Conference Series. Earth and Environmental Science*, 549(1), 12088. DOI: 10.1088/1755-1315/549/1/012088

Khanh, C. N. T., & Phong, L. T. (2020). Impact of environmental belief and nature-based destination image on ecotourism attitude. *Journal of Hospitality and Tourism Insights*. DOI: 10.1108/JHTI-03-2020-0027

Kirkby, C. A., Giudice, R., Day, B., Turner, K., Soares-Filho, B. S., Oliveira-Rodrigues, H., & Yu, D. W. (2011). Closing the ecotourism-conservation loop in the Peruvian Amazon. *Environmental Conservation*, 38(1), 6–17. DOI: 10.1017/S0376892911000099

Kladou, S., Giannopoulos, A. A., & Mavragani, E. (2015). Destination brand equity research from 2001 to 2012. *Tourism Analysis*, 20(2), 189–200. DOI: 10.3727/108354215X14265319207399

Konecnik, M., & Gartner, W. C. (2007). Customer-based brand equity for a destination. *Annals of Tourism Research*, 34(2), 400–421. DOI: 10.1016/j.annals.2006.10.005

Krishnapillai, G., & Rehman, M. (2023). Enhancing Brand Equity Through Sustainable Tourism Marketing: A Study on Home-Stays in Malaysia. *Asian Academy of Management Journal*, 28(1), 237–263. DOI: 10.21315/aamj2023.28.1.10

Kummitha, H. R. (2020). Eco-entrepreneurs organizational attitude towards sustainable community ecotourism development. *The Central European Journal of Regional Development and Tourism*, 12(1), 85–101. DOI: 10.32725/det.2020.005

Leroi-Werelds, S., Streukens, S., Brady, M. K., & Swinnen, G. (2014). Assessing the value of commonly used methods for measuring customer value: A multi-setting empirical study. *Journal of the Academy of Marketing Science*, 42(4), 430–451. DOI: 10.1007/s11747-013-0363-4

Li, T., Liu, F., & Soutar, G. N. (2020, December). (Tina), Liu, F., & Soutar, G. N. (2021). Experiences, post-trip destination image, satisfaction and loyalty: A study in an ecotourism context. *Journal of Destination Marketing & Management*, 19, 100547. DOI: 10.1016/j.jdmm.2020.100547

MacCannell, D. (1973). Staged authenticity: Arrangements of social space in tourist settings. *American Journal of Sociology*, 79(3), 589–603. DOI: 10.1086/225585

Nematollahi, S., Afghari, S., Kienast, F., & Fakheran, S. (2022). Spatial prioritization for Ecotourism through applying the Landscape Resilience Model. *Land (Basel)*, 11(10), 1682. DOI: 10.3390/land11101682

Nogueira, S., & Carvalho, J. M. S. (2024). Unlocking the dichotomy of place identity/place image and its impact on place satisfaction for ecotourism destinations. *Journal of Ecotourism*, 23(1), 1–19. DOI: 10.1080/14724049.2022.2106236

Ouboter, D. A., Kadosoe, V. S., & Ouboter, P. E. (2021). Impact of ecotourism on abundance, diversity and activity patterns of medium-large terrestrial mammals at Brownsberg Nature Park, Suriname. *PLoS One*, 16(6), e0250390. DOI: 10.1371/journal.pone.0250390 PMID: 34077471

Paul, H., & Brad, O. (1997). Ecotourism: A guide for marketers. *European Business Review*, 97(5), 231–236. DOI: 10.1108/09555349710179843

Phon, S., Phon, S., & Touch, V. (2024). Factors Influencing the Community-Based Ecotourism Development in Cambodia: Structural Equation Model Analysis. *Utsaha: Journal of Entrepreneurship*, 87–107.

Qu, H., Kim, L. H., & Im, H. H. (2011). A model of destination branding: Integrating the concepts of the branding and destination image. *Tourism Management*, 32(3), 465–476. DOI: 10.1016/j.tourman.2010.03.014

Quynh, N. H., Hoai, N. T., & Loi, N. Van. (2021). The role of emotional experience and destination image on ecotourism satisfaction. *Spanish Journal of Marketing - ESIC, 25*(2), 312–332. DOI: 10.1108/SJME-04-2020-0055

Rezaeinejad, I., & Khaniwadekar, A. (2021). The role of Eco-tourism in sustainable development: case study eco-tourism challenges in Iran. *E3S Web of Conferences, 311*, 2004.

Roseta, P., Sousa, B. B., & Roseta, L. (2020). Determiners in the consumer's purchase decision process in ecotourism contexts: a Portuguese case study. *Geosciences*. https://www.mdpi.com/2076-3263/10/6/224

Sana, C., Chakraborty, S., Adil, M., & Sadiq, M. (2023). Ecotourism experience: A systematic review and future research agenda. *International Journal of Consumer Studies*, 47(6), 2131–2156. DOI: 10.1111/ijcs.12902

Sharma, P., & Nayak, J. K. (2020). Examining experience quality as the determinant of tourist behavior in niche tourism: An analytical approach. *Journal of Heritage Tourism*, 15(1), 76–92. DOI: 10.1080/1743873X.2019.1608212

Sharpley, R. (2006). Ecotourism: A consumption perspective. *Journal of Ecotourism*, 5(1–2), 7–22. DOI: 10.1080/14724040608668444

Stamboulis, Y., & Skayannis, P. (2003). Innovation strategies and technology for experience-based tourism. *Tourism Management*, 24(1), 35–43. DOI: 10.1016/S0261-5177(02)00047-X

Tarigan, M. I., Lubis, A. N., Rini, E. S., & Sembiring, B. K. F. (2023). Antecedents of destination brand experience. *Journal Of Sustainable Tourism And Entrepreneurship*, 4(2), 131–141. DOI: 10.35912/joste.v4i2.428

Thi Khanh, C. N., & Phong, L. T. (2020). Impact of environmental belief and nature-based destination image on ecotourism attitude. *Journal of Hospitality and Tourism Insights*, 3(4), 489–505. DOI: 10.1108/JHTI-03-2020-0027

Torres-Moraga, E., & Barra, C. (2023). Does destination brand experience help build trust? Disentangling the effects on trust and trustworthiness. *Journal of Destination Marketing & Management*, 27, 100767. DOI: 10.1016/j.jdmm.2023.100767

UN Tourism | Bringing the world closer. (2024). Retrieved October 17, 2024, from https://www.unwto.org/

Vargo, S. L., Koskela-Huotari, K., & Vink, J. (2020). Service-dominant logic: foundations and applications. In *The Routledge handbook of service research insights and ideas* (pp. 3–23). Routledge. DOI: 10.4324/9781351245234-1

Yang, L., Hu, X., Lee, H. M., & Zhang, Y. (2023). The impacts of ecotourists' perceived authenticity and perceived values on their behaviors: Evidence from Huangshan World Natural and Cultural Heritage Site. *Sustainability (Basel)*, 15(2), 1551. DOI: 10.3390/su15021551

Chapter 2
Social Media Influencers Shaping Ecotourism Destination Branding

Saqib Rehman
https://orcid.org/0000-0001-6307-7978
Lahore College for Women University, Pakistan

Nabeela Arshad
https://orcid.org/0009-0005-5330-4571
Lahore College for Women University, Pakistan

Aman Ullah
https://orcid.org/0000-0002-6657-9268
University of Melbourne, Australia

Nadia Noor
https://orcid.org/0000-0001-8845-3132
Lahore College for Women University, Pakistan

ABSTRACT

Influencers can use large online followings to create awareness about the destination, answer the tourists' queries, and structure the destination image, environment, and sustainable accommodations while staying in a particular landscape. Moreover, influencers may promote the ecotourists' destination, grab the trust of their followers, and be a carrier of promoting eco-friendly activities at destinations. The theory of planned behaviour sets the direction for this study. It offers a thorough framework for clarifying the factors that may affect or limit persons' intentions to perform certain behaviours. TPB can assist tourists in understanding the motivations behind their choice of destination by analyzing the elements influencing ecotourism.

DOI: 10.4018/979-8-3693-6700-1.ch002

Influencers who engage with ecotourists can shape their perceptions of a region by emphasizing its unique attributes, like captivating natural scenery and sustainable tourism practices.

1. INTRODUCTION

Tourism is a social phenomenon in which people pause their monotonous routines and refresh themselves with diverse lifestyles, experiences, and cultures (Yasin, 2023). Nowadays, tourists' perceptions, destinations' images, and availability of products and services are seeking the ample attention of researchers and academicians (Roy, 2021). Despite the source of entertainment, tourism is one of the key sectors that drives the nation's economy. For instance, Azis et al. (2018), who worked in the Malaysian context, argued that the Malaysian tourism industry ranked fifth-largest and one of the major contributors to economic development.

Ecotourism is one of the key dimensions of tourism, often used for nature-based tourism, and has been acknowledged in the nineties (Rehman et al., 2024). Similarly, Leung et al. (2025) grounded their study on social comparison theory and explored how new travel influencers seek the attention of past or adult tourists. For its broad expansion, studies like Islam et al. (2023) illustrate that growth and continuous development of the tourism sector can be attainable through the adoption of advanced technologies embedded in the public interest to some extent. However, their technological struggles and key findings resolve multiple concerns of tourists. They also highlighted that virtual visits and graphical visuals give a sense and feel of pre-visits and help both first-time visitors and repeaters. Organizations have to deal with frequently changing circumstances and dynamic businesses; where past strategies are almost wrapped up, a dramatic shift has appeared in marketing strategies. Influential marketing is an effective tool that provides consumers with valuable guidance in purchase decisions and engagement (Harrigan et al., 2021). In the current business environment, companies are akin to their full or partial reliance on social media influencers to introduce, advertise, use, and promote products and services (Shuqair, 2024). Thus, following this practice, tourism marketers, players, and organizations rely on influencers for brand promotion.

Almost all businesses i.e., operating in both developed and developing countries, have acknowledged the shift of the conventional market to digital marketing and successfully raised their sales volume (Iswanto et al., 2024). In marketing, influencers may disclose any material information while endorsing a brand. Subsequently, sponsorships of brands significantly calm the influencers in expressing commercial content for their posts, blogs, and reels (Giuffredi-Kähr, 2022). For marketing or promotional activities of products and services, community participation is seen as a significant tool to disburse the companies' insights, customers' experiences and actual responses (Iswanto et al., 2024; Matiza & Slabbert, 2024). Therefore, customers switched or started to use the products or services recommended by their followed influencers (Salouw et al., 2024). Following the same patterns, the study called an influential participation from the local community who have their social media accounts. To target a larger audience and ensure the propagation of responsibility for the required content, influencers with large followings, having a love for natural destinations holding a soft heart towards sustainable practices about tourism destinations and being willing for future survival are called to come forward. This initiative and its continuous practice provide a key edge for the promotion of ecotourism destinations at a larger level by targeting a bigger audience.

While choosing the destination, tourists' centre of attention primarily revolves around the associated risk and trust within their pool of destination places (Ameen et al., 2023). Destination trust of pre-visited or future tourists is a milestone that shortens the current choices of listing concerned spots. Following the findings of the research done by Cao (2020) stated that the entire growth and development of tourism is dependent on tourists' decisions to visit. Therefore, to broaden the zone of tourist destinations, tourist organizations are making their efforts best by adding ecotourist destinations. Tourist organizations are increasingly focusing on creating an environment where tourists take a maximum spot for making the decisions for trips. At present or past functioning tourism organizations have recognized the limitations of the usage of currently available channels while promoting the ecotourists' destinations (Adikaram & Surangi, 2024). Only word of mouth and tourists' experiences are not sufficient enough to answer the entire set of queries visitors have. However, in recent years, most tourists have used social media channels to get an update or even know about the present environment of concerned destinations. Therefore, organizations have switched their traditional marketing to social media platforms for their promotional activities (Ouvrein et al., 2021). In this way, influencers are invited to be part of promotional activities. Influencers having an interest and love for the ecotourists' spots are requested to explore the seldom visited, uneven paths and unknown ways. Next, influencers will express their insights, experiences and thoughts by making blogs, social media posts and online ads, thereby, following the strategy of experiential marketing tourist organizations made their access to massive audiences through the mediums and channelizing of influencers.

Similarly, in the current era of digitalization, people are more interested in exploring the places that are rarely visited. For the promotion or expansion of tourism, especially for virtual visibility of ecotourist destinations, influencers may act as a catalyst and motivate people to provide a preview of particular destinations or spots. Without acknowledging the current significant growth in the usage of social media, tourists cannot find the desirous utility of recreation (Xie-Carson & Benckendorff,

2024). For marketing such destinations, influencers should preferably exercise their existing accounts with many followers and may deliver authentic, valuable, premium, and informative content to future tourists. The study formulated the given set of research questions for its precise assessment.

> **RQ1:** How can ecotourists' destinations be promoted with the involvement of influencers?
> **RQ2:** What would the possible challenges be if the tourism sector made a higher dependence upon influencers?
> **RQ3:** What do tourists learn when they go through the influencers' blogs, experiences and opinions?
> **RQ4:** How do tourists process the influencers' information in deciding on ecotourism destinations?

The study collected the data from the Scopus Database and found 1222 English language scientific articles. The searched articles were studied to determine the current emergence of ecotourism, digital marketing, and social media influencers. The study aims to explore how social media platforms and influencers with large followings can promote ecotourism. More specifically, influencers having a keen interest in natural sciences, focusing on environmental sustainability, promoting eco-friendly activities, developing responsible tourism, and caring about sustainability standards as one of the key ingredients for the destinations are encouraged to work for the tourists' destinations and the local community. Influencers' content regarding answering the maximum queries, and perceptions, and giving insights to people who have never visited ecotourists' spots can promote ecotourism at large.

2. LITERATURE REVIEW

2.1. Role of Influencers in Promoting Ecotourism Destinations

The theory of planned behaviour posits that three primary factors influence an individual's intentions to perform a behaviour (Ajzen, 1985): Attitudes: This is the individual's emotional evaluation towards certain behaviour. In this regard, the ecotourist's perspective on the promoted destination would be evaluated by his or her mind. Subjective Norms: The perceived pressure that exists within a society to either engage in or refrain from engaging in a specific behaviour. This would be the perception that the ecotourist has among their followers, which would influence their decision to visit the location. Perceived Behavioral Control: The degree to which the individual is confident in their ability to execute the behaviour. This would be the ecotourist's overly optimistic assessment of their ability to plan and execute a journey to the destination.

The Theory of Planned Behavior provides a comprehensive and appropriate framework for elucidating the factors that may either influence or restrict individuals' intentions to engage in specific behaviours (Ulker-Demirel & Ciftci, 2020). TPB can help travellers comprehend the reasons why they choose a particular destination for their travels by examining the factors that are at play in the context of ecotourism. Influencers who actively engage with ecotourists can influence how the latter perceive a destination by highlighting the target destination's distinctive characteristics, such as its enticing natural landscapes and responsible tourism practices. The research indicates that potential travellers may be positively influenced by positive representations of the destination (Kilipiri et al., 2023; Pop et al., 2022; Razak & Mansor, 2021). Influencers can publish their experiences alongside the optimistic reactions of other individuals, thereby increasing the visibility of other individuals. It has the potential to foster a sense of social norm consciousness, which in turn reinforces the tradition that a reputable influencer in ecotourism is obligated to promote the destination. Influencers can provide ecotourists with information regarding travel arrangements, accommodation, and other matters that will aid in the enhancement of perceived behavioural control by utilizing knowledge to support habitual practice (Bastrygina et al., 2024). In this scenario, influencers should initially identify potential obstacles and subsequently demonstrate the knowledge and confidence that ecotourists will have to plan and execute the trip.

Lastly, it is important to note that the Theory of Planned Behavior enables the examination of the impact of influencers on ecotourism destinations. The researchers can gain a better comprehension of the factors that can motivate ecotourists and, as a result, improve the investigation of how influencers alter decisions such as attitude, subjective norm, and perceived behavioural control. Influencers established their credibility in viewership and built a large following; they have become crucial components of digital marketing strategies. Their content, shorts, and videos influence a large audience and hit a large pool of people globally (Kirilenko et al., 2023). Due to their large, influential zones, various companies, firms, and tourist organizations use their services for introduction, expansion, usage, and promotion. Similarly, for promoting the ecotourism destinations, enlisted benefits can be taken from such influencers:

2.1.1. Delivering authentic content

Unlike traditional advertisements, influencers have the opportunity to add detailed, authentic, and spiced content that gives a feel of genuine visits. Viewers or the targeted audience may sketch and structure a preview in their minds. As a result, such spots may be added to their list of considerations of choice when they are going to do planning for current or future trips. Further, with the use of social media platforms, influencers share their perceived experiences and real-time information and capture a detailed view of climate and weather situations (Machado Carvalho, 2024). This delivered content is more readily to answer the tourists' narratives. Their pleased views and narratives give an appeal of invitation with a cushion for shaping tourists' perceptions, overcoming prior perceptions, reducing or mitigating perceived fears, and appearing more gracious.

2.1.2. Targeting larger audience

Influential marketing via social media influencers may hit and access a larger audience, and viewers. Unlike traditional advertisement methods, an influential market estimates the number of times a video is being played, the targeted viewership, and the instant reactions of viewers (Bastrygina et al., 2024). Further, the comment sections also help influencers to compile fresh feedback and responses from the public. Thus, more frequent and genuine feedback can be captured through such platforms as the traditional modes lack this ability and remain almost unable while compiling public responses.

2.1.3. Eco-friendly travels

Influencers have a large audience (in the form of their followers) especially, the entire members of the audience almost have a similar type of interest; and are called for influential marketing. Additionally, organizations or individual tourists should look for those influencers who previously held a soft edge for environmental sustainability and eco-friendly travel. Therefore, influencers whose blogs, ads and working for social media posts were a combination of travel and adventure should be chosen as the representatives of ecotourist organizations and destinations (Zhao & Shen, 2024). Along with adventurous trips, influencers have to make a simultaneous effort for eco-friendly activities and sustainable practices and also need to provide the stuff to support the environment that will remain a guiding principle to current and future visitors. Through their content, influencers can transmit the messaging for eco-friendly and sustainable travelling by creating awareness about the prevailing environmental challenges and their adversity to the current and future safety of the environment.

2.1.4. Visual and previews of destinations

With the support of social media tools, e.g., Facebook, Instagram, Twitter, YouTube, Telegram, WhatsApp and TikTok, influencers can provide a detailed view of classic content that attracts visitors' attention. Such platforms are the absolute best and ideal for visually displaying destined beauty, natural charm, paths to move, habituated wildlife, sustainable practices, and destined precautions (Sánchez-Amboage et al., 2024; Tafesse & Wood, 2021). Thereby, such landscapes give an appealing preview to potential travellers and direct them when deciding to visit a particular ecotourist destination.

2.2. Building trust for ecotourism destinations

For travellers, trust is a focal element when visiting ecotourist destinations (Ameen et al., 2023; Meng, Zhang, et al., 2024). Although travellers watch the traditional advertisements for a particular ecotourist's destination, their trust gets stronger with the recommendations and posted comments of people who have done their recent or prior travels. Such reviews and recommendations give ecotourists a piece of relatable and genuine information. Therefore, eco-tourists can build the trust of visitors by:

2.2.1. Developing strong linkages

Influencers holding the exposed to frequent visits and are passionate about the ecotourists' destinations may develop a strong, authentic, and in-depth connection with destinated spots. Without the use of social media, tourist destinations remained almost unexplored among the larger community (Xie-Carson & Benckendorff, 2024). Such connectivity develops strong linkages with certain regions and destinations (Phu, 2024). For regional connectivity, influencers' content, views, and shared experiences can play a significant role in shortening the distances. Therefore, influencers' enthusiasm, genuine concerns, and conversation about the environment gave an appealing call to the larger audience, to zealously visit and explore tourist destinations.

2.2.2. Targeting the environmental influencers

Influencers who have a personal concern about visiting and exploring the destinations are requested to engage with tourist destinations to gain familiarity with unknown paths or recently visited spots. Xie-Carson et al. (2023) reviewed how people get in association with a destination through social media tools and commence to travel there. More specifically, content attributes and visualization of blog and

Instagram posts help people to get ready for a closer view of nature. This measure has dual advantages. At first, it quenches the thirst to explore unknown destinations and spots. Second, it fully allows an influencer to seek fame from the public against it. By availing of both advantages, influencers meet their interest level and generate extra revenue income. In a similar vein, the theoretical evidence of Pham and Khanh (2020) found that directly addressed environmental concerns and dealt with the factors that affect the visitors' attention toward ecotourist's destinations. Moreover, if an influencer sets an agreement of partnership with a particular tourist organization, the development of connection with destinated spots gives an additional income against the visit, promotion, and views.

2.2.3. Travelling with pets

People having tough routines, boring work structures, massive workloads and monotonous routines hinder them from going for recreational activities. Moreover, there is a class of people who are restricted from travelling with their pets. The research work of Meng, Chi, et al. (2024) reported that recently tourists dramatically increasing travelling with their pets. Subsequently, people tried to force the tourist companies to get their pets in. However, the care, handling and medication of pets do not currently allow the tourist companies to carry the pets. Under the current theme and structure of influential marketing, the study realized the dire need to cater the tourists who are reluctant to carry their pets with them. Suggesting the previews and demonstration of the ecotourists' destinations, influencers are requested to do a rehearsal view of visits carrying various pets. Resultantly, visual views for handling, care, medication and vaccination give an obvious idea of looking after the pets at ecotourists' destinations and able to make their trips more enjoyable.

2.2.4. Responsible practices

By adding the ingredient of sustainability, influencers may promote responsible tourism. Influencers have a great cushion in creating content about sustainable measures that can be practised at particular destinations. Responsible practices include eco-friendly accommodations or appropriate use of land (Nahuelhual et al., 2013), ecological security (Sobhani et al., 2023), environmental preservatives (Chakraborty & Ghosal, 2024; Pham & Khanh, 2020), marine preservatives (Lucrezi & Cilliers, 2022), reduction of waste (Hu et al., 2024), collaboration with the local community (Ghaderi et al., 2021; Salouw et al., 2024) and clean environment habits (Sisriany & Furuya, 2024). Such practices develop a sense of responsible tourism which prevents environmental views for current and next generations.

2.2.5. Interaction with strengthened content

Influencers have great connectivity and are tied into a bond with their social media followers. Thereby, influencers tried to cover the maximum concern in their shared posts, reels, and videos (Machado Carvalho, 2024). However, to respond to individual or specific group queries, influencers are encouraged to conduct a few live sessions in the form of live streams. Further, clips of scenes behind the actual shots can also be shared. Question Answer sessions can also be taken. Subsequently, the Frequently Asked Questions (FAQs') section covers the concerns of climate, humidity, accommodations, average rainfall, path steepness, and season change.

4. METHODS

4.1 Keyword analysis

In this section, we presented a few keyword clusters drawn by following the methodology of bibliometric analysis. The manuscript distribution comprised 1222 documents from the Scopus research engine. These documents covered the time from 2000 to 2024. In tourism organizations, ecotourism gets significant importance in the late nineties. That is why the study grouped the documents from 2000 to 2024 so the overall trend and spikes of ecotourism can be seen. Scholars and other researchers have started exploring ecotourism with an equal weightage to general tourism. In the last five years, literature received more than 700 publications that showed a higher acknowledgement of this dimension.

Figure 1 displays a keyword analysis and presents the core keywords used by different authors during their research. This display covers 313 keywords in this area, showing the prime importance of their dimensions, i.e., ecotourism, sustainable tourism travel behaviour, tourism development, and tourism attraction in main tourism.

The top clustered keywords (purple) cover tourism and sustainable tourism. Most developed countries have almost achieved sustainability standards in their tourism sector. A few years back, the United Nations declared 2017 the International Year for Sustainable Tourism for Development; revealing that tourism and hospitality are the catalysts for sustainable development (Prakhar, 2024). In the last 25 years, the publications of sustainable tourism have achieved a growth rate of 19.9%. Here, the study also acknowledged a key contribution of the International Journal of Sustainable Development, which stood first and focused its core attention on sustainable tourism.

Figure 1. All used keywords

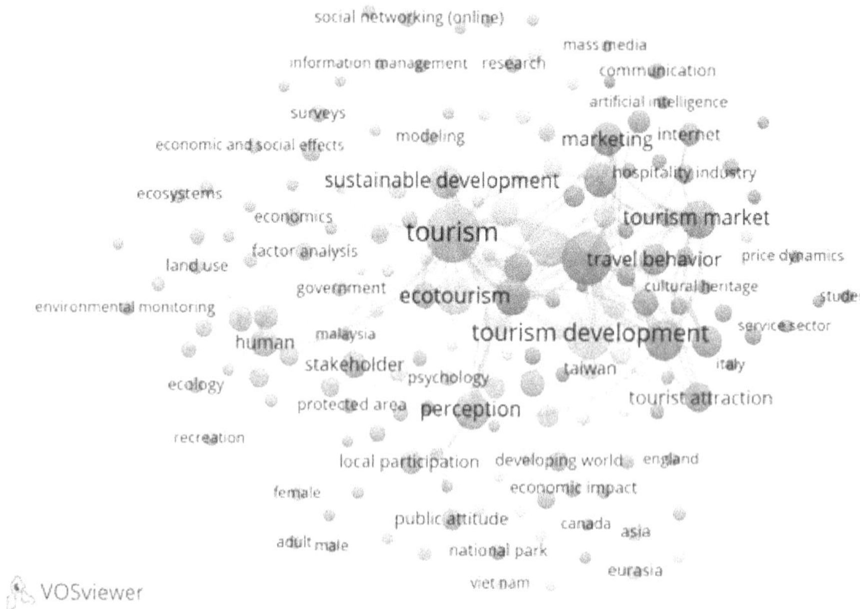

In the current scenario, influencers work with most brands and market their products and services (Tafesse & Wood, 2021). Similarly, tourists' perceptions are highly catered by influencers through their visual recorded videos, displayed in the top-right group of keywords. When the tourists watched such recorded materials, their perceptions, fears, and dilemmas declined. Influencers' content will remain a guiding principle and cover most people's perceptions, queries, ambiguities, and caveats (Iswanto et al., 2024). This communication directly or indirectly promotes tourist attractions, advances the hospitality industry, and develops tourist behaviour. Next, two groups of keywords are putting their core attention on economic contribution, public-owned areas, land use, government support, and local community participation. Together, we must come forward and promote this key dimension of tourism.

Table 1. Top leading countries of tourism

Country	Documents	Citations	Country	Documents	Citations
United States	**198**	**6943**	**Malaysia**	**62**	**858**
China	160	4487	Turkey	59	896
United Kingdom	113	3851	South Korea	46	2234
Australia	91	3749	Iran	44	494
Indonesia	66	302	Taiwan	38	1687

Table 1 presents the top 10 countries keenly contributing their research efforts to the tourism sector and taking great care of ecotourism. From an order of ranking of countries, the USA came first with 198 documents and 6943 citations. China and the UK stood second and third, i.e., (documents = 160; citations 4877) and (documents = 113; citations 3851), respectively. This ranking has attained an equal weightage in both document production and citation. Next, Australia appeared in the fourth position. It just produces 91 documents. However, the quality, authenticity, and generalizability of these 91 research articles gave them 3749 citations.

Compared with Australia, Indonesia's next essential contribution is viewed in 66 documents, and relatively fewer citations were attained (documents = 66; citations 302). Malaysia and Turkey delivered the double-digit documents and sought the triple-digit citations (documents = 62; citations 858) (documents = 59; citations 896), respectively. South Korea contributed another emerging set of 46 papers, and its prime pieces of research received appreciation and acknowledgement with 2234 citations. Next, Iran ranked ninth (documents = 44; citations 494). Taiwan ranked in the tenth position in document production. However, the significance of these 38 documents is genuinely reflected in 1687 citations. Figure 2 displays a view and connectivity of 57 countries.

Figure 2. Top contributing countries

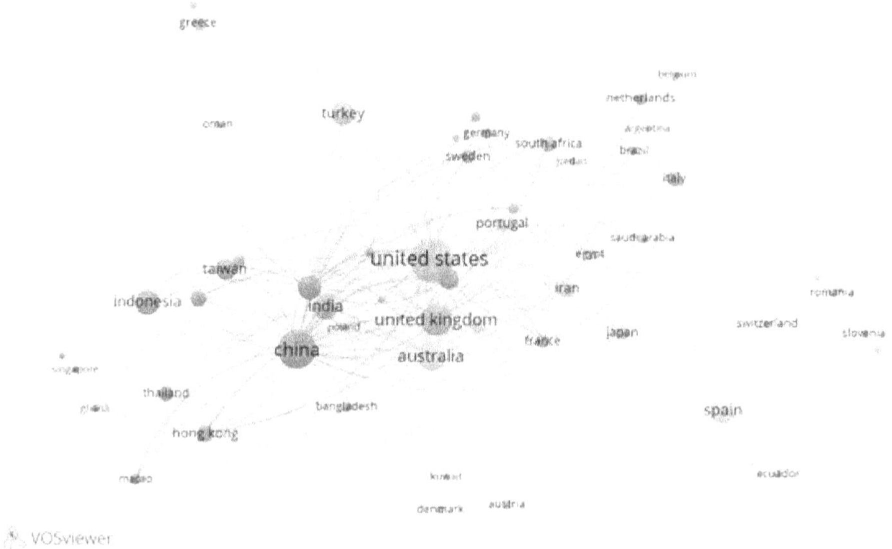

4.1.1 Influential map

Figure 3 gives an influential map and entirely covers the core theme of this chapter. The blue bubbles on the left give an idea of the current trend, past paradigms, and future agendas. Further, it sheds light on the taste, features, and sources of published research articles on tourism. The bottom theme acknowledged the researchers' core dimensions and trends in different time zones. The green cluster holds ample information on tourist and ecotourism spots. This culture covers the history, places, destinations, accommodations, available resources, destinated culture, and landscapes. On the right of the figure, another cluster is given in red, covering the social media and influencers' contributions. It has given all those mediums that resolve the tourists' perceptions, queries, and insights that people may have experienced before their visits.

Figure 3. Influential map

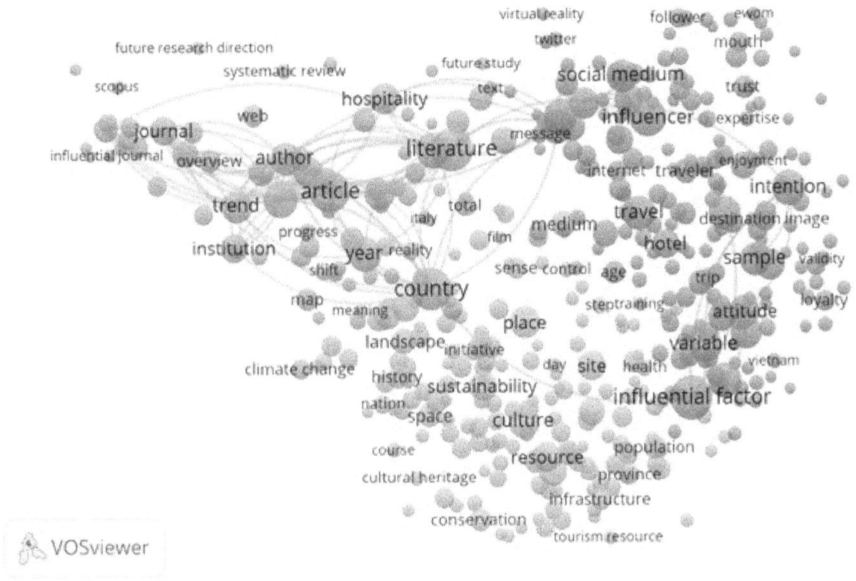

The red culture also covered the tourists' experience, destination image, loyalty, and messaging of tourists. In the view of influencers, it grouped the social media platforms, word of mouth, followers' feedback, and validity of the delivered content (Tafesse & Wood, 2021). Further, it also elaborated and gave an idea about utilizing the influencers' expertise in promoting the ecotourists' spots. Such places are almost unexplored or little explored. Both local and international tourists lack information about it. With the collaboration of influencers, such destinations also appear to have great tourist points and a higher number of annual visits.

Figure 4. Authors' keywords

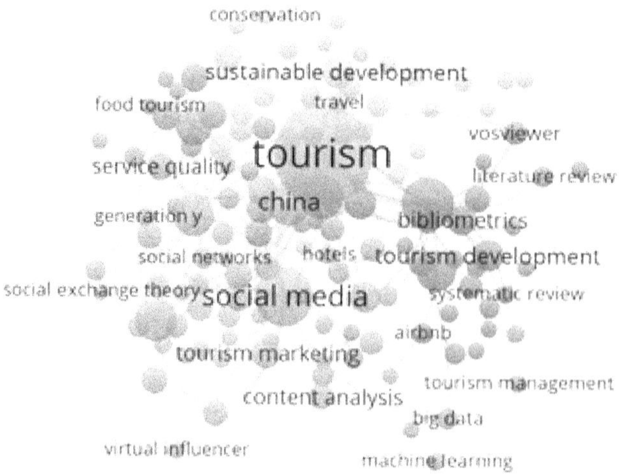

A set of emerging keywords is given in Figure 4. The scholars provide these keywords, which are being reported in their studies. A virtual influencer is given by (Xie-Carson & Benckendorff, 2024); social media is added by Bastrygina et al. (2024) and Yasin (2023); Phu (2024) has given the tourism management; Orea-Giner et al. (2019) directed our attention to tourism development; machine learning in tourism is given by (Arici et al., 2024) and Shuqair (2024) centred its focus to the social exchange through tourism.

Figure 5. Index keywords

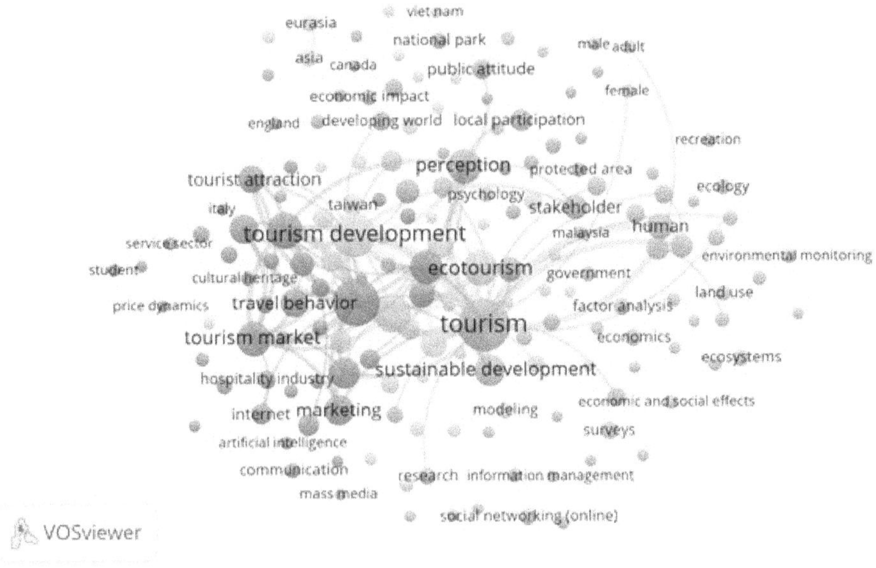

Figure 5 shows the index keywords depicting how tourism remained an emerging concern in academia. Over the decades, it has had the absolute attention of researchers, academicians and policymakers in the fields of economics, the services industry, sustainability and marketing. Further, it also remained one of the key carriers in sharing the culture. A precise sharing of culture including local tradition, customs, norms and local food is mostly done with the acknowledgeable collaboration of the local community. The structuring of index keywords delimitates disruption of the tourism sector at the global level.

Upon view of the figure, it is seen that the entire cluster grouped the academician's contribution from various regions and countries. In index pictorial representation, the countries like USA (United States of America), the United Kingdom, Australia, Canada, Turkey, Indonesia and a few Asian regions are also the part of top countries' list. The ranking of the countries is purely done based on a segment for the research contribution. At the top of the clustered view, bubbles blue in colour depict the economic impact of this sector. The research evidence like Orea-Giner et al. (2019) emphasized the provenance of heritage and antique items and worked for the sustainability of museums. Tourists from all over the world visit museums at various times and get a closer view of the past customs, traditions and uniqueness of lives. Such research attempts gave an ample contribution to the development and emergence of a country's economy. In the same vein, another research named by Ruggeri et al. (2023) suggested to following themes of e-commerce, wine tourism and sustainability. This research made an effort to protect the economies and tourism in cases of global crises. Similarly, Kamruzzaman (2024) offered the key solutions for preserving global businesses in unpredictable and abrupt situations.

At the left corner of the figure, red bubbles delineated a higher attraction to tourism development and its marketing. It gave ample cushion to cultural promotions, internet marketing and the use of AI (Artificial Intelligence) in the promotion of a destination. Through tourism and recreational activities, people share their traditional norms and disburse their cultural heritage to other areas, regions and nations (Yasin, 2023). Next, in the right corner, bubbles purple in colour present the statistical techniques and methodological attempts i.e., survey technique, interview and factor analysis; which were followed in determining the current contribution, existing gaps and needy areas of attention. Simultaneously, it catered to the economic, social and environmental aspects showing the relevance of sustainability. Further, studies conducted at various times fully reported the tracks and paths to attain sustainable standards.

Finally, bubbles with green colour are directing our attention to a leading phenomenon of land usage (Bakri et al., 2022), ecosystem preservation (Azis et al., 2018), ecological measures (Rahmafitria & Kaswanto, 2024) and close monitoring of the environment (Pham & Khanh, 2020).

5. CHALLENGES TO BE ADDRESSED

This study views how influencers can promote ecotourists' destinations with comprehensive social media platforms. As influencers are connected with a larger audience, compared with traditional advertisement, followers rapidly seek new things from influencers. Despite the convenience of the influencers, a few challenges have also been reported.

5.1 Authenticity of the content

The study has set its centres around those influencers who work for environmental sustainability, environment preservation, adventurous moves, eco-friendly accommodations, and responsible tourism. With the collaboration of the tourism organizations and the local community, influencers' content's dual validity and authenticity should also be confirmed. Such verification processes permit the influencers to deliver accurate, authentic, quality-oriented content (Qiu et al., 2024). Virtual views, previews of destinations, and quality of information motivate tourists to visit. Simultaneously, such promotions and destination awareness resolve maximum perceptions and glitches of current and future visitors.

5.2 Make a balance between the promotion and preservation

The social media posts, reels, and videos the influencers share must have the element of environmental preservation. Content that creates only hype of promotion and does not account for the current sustainable practices of the environment should be banned before it is launched. Here, tourist organizations, the local community, past visitors, and influencers need to collaborate mutually so real, genuine, and authentic content may be delivered to the targeted audience.

5.3 Evaluation

Likewise, the assessments of influencers' campaigns are a complex process. The effectiveness, authenticity, and approachability of content usually remain uncalculated and cannot be rated directly. To simplify these complex processes, different evaluation matrices, engagement rate, visits and retention rate, and associations of travels can also be assessed. Therefore, a display of influencers' collaboration can be measured.

6. DISCUSSION

Nowadays, multiple companies ought to adopt digital marketing strategies and say goodbye to the traditional modes of advertisement. In digital marketing, different influencers and social media platforms endorse products and services (Polat et al., 2024). Specifically, influencers having a large pool of followers are working for various companies advertisements and promotions; companies transmit their messages globally and target a large population. Subsequently, through digital marketing, companies are experiencing a remarkable increase in their sales volume and revenues. Simultaneously, digital marketing entered the customers into the system and allowed the companies to compile in-time, spontaneous, and fresh feedback from potential, regular, and walk-in customers. Social media tools and applications enable individuals to easily approach their target market by sharing content with followers (Xie-Carson et al., 2023). Through digital marketing, companies successfully attract unsolicited consumers and expand their businesses considerably.

Execution of digital marketing is incomplete without acknowledging the current contribution of influencers. Influencers are those individuals who structure the content for the introduction, promotion, and trial of a product or service; the nature of the content is formally structured according to the interest or the activity assigned by the company (Iswanto et al., 2024). Their content best cares about the caveats, introduction, usage, features, specifications and precautions of the products and services. This study is an effort to give empirical evidence that contributes its vital contribution to exploring those destinations that were little or seldom explored. Therefore, it is suggested that tourist companies and the local community develop a strong bond with social media influencers, especially engaging influencers working for environmental sustainability, preservation, and natural sciences. To promote a destination, the study calls influencers and requests them to prepare the content for ecotourist destinations.

Generally, most countries have coupled their tourism with sustainability standards and preserving their natural ecosystems. Tourism and courteous hospitality perform as a catalyst for environmental sustainability. Therefore, the United Nations declared 2017 the International Year for Sustainable Tourism for Development. Past studies like Prakhar (2024) shed light on sustainable ecotourism. Thus, this present study also ties a knot of sustainability with ecotourism. For ecotourist destinations, the study gives an open call to influencers who work for a sustainable environment. Their environmental communications and deep interest in preserving the environment prove their sympathy for protecting the natural ecosystem.

This study successfully answered its structured research questions. The study viewed past emergence in the tourism sector as purely the consequence of using social media and digital marketing. The constructive use of social media platforms best manages and organizes the tourism sector. Thus, the study answered the first research question. With the collaboration of social media influencers, we are giving high-quality previews, visuals, and particular clips for ecotourist destinations. Thus, tourists find new places and unexplored paths for their trips. Such influential efforts directly or indirectly resulted in a higher dependence on ecotourism companies, local communities, and tourism organizations. Thereby, the study gave a satisfactory answer to its stated second research question. As mentioned, this current study suggested that tourist companies have to make their promotional dependence on the keen users of social media i.e., influencers and disburse their promotion, advertisements and messages to a larger audience. However, the study listed a few possible future challenges that could happen if the tourism sector has made its entire dependence on social media influencers. Challenges include the recent, upcoming or future possible threats related to content authenticity and its evaluation. Further, the study has emphasized maintaining a distinguishable balance between promotion and preservation. After addressing such current and upcoming challenges, the study remained successful in answering its research question.

In the next research question, the study addressing is about the possible learning of tourists when they watch the influencers' blogs, ads, promotions and posts. With detailed elaboration and realizing the importance of visuals, pre-view and virtual visits to tourists, the study also found the answers to its highlighted research question. Moreover, this elaboration got a little advance in its next research question by demonstrating how tourists can use the information given by influencers. In the classic and authentic delivery of content, influencers made a definite address to the climate, humidity, temperature and seasonal effects. Resultantly, for an individual tourist, this pooled information not only extends the consideration list of places but also gives extensive clearance about choosing and planning the ecotourists' spots.

To resolve their future conflicts, the study suggested settling a few terms and conditions for contracting, promotion, and profit distribution so ecotourism companies, influencers, and the local community work in a calm and collaborative environment. In this way, regulatory bodies, government representatives and policy makers and practitioners have to come forward and structure an appropriate regulatory framework. This practicable measure would address and stop the springing of future conflicts between tourist companies and social media influencers.

Influencers precisely capture destination spots in photos and videos. Their efforts gave a preview of destinations. Influencers' insights, emotions, and recommendations permit people to visit the ecotourist locations. Further, the content attributes of the videos delivered an appealing message for a clean environment and sustainable tourism. Tourists gave significant weight to influencers' remarks and recommendations. This guiding principle expands the exposure for consideration when visiting entirely new destinations.

To study the past literature and trends, the study conducted the keyword analysis from a set of grouped documents from the Scopus website. The keyword clusters visually viewed past trends, paradigms, and current emergence. VOS viewer helps us construct the main themes, where the subthemes and clusters give emerging ideas and principles for promoting ecotourism destinations. Afterwards, it can be concluded that ecotourism can attract more tourists' attention through social media applications and digital marketing techniques.

To preserve the environment and nature's beauty, the study has centred its focus on responsible tourism. Along with other aspects, the study gave equal importance to unexplored destinations and their future expected contribution to the country's economy (Samaddar & Mondal, 2024), sustainability (Orea-Giner et al., 2019) and environmental preservation (Pham & Khanh, 2020). To successfully accept the landscape for ecotourism, the study emphasized carrying the pets to destinations. Carrying pets resolves the many obstacles and thoughts of current and future tourists, resultantly, more people can be part of ecotourism, especially for the exploration of unknown paths.

This present attempt gave a clear route to influencers while promoting the ecotourists' destination. Firstly, destination' previews, demonstration trips and influential marketing play a considerable role in promotion. Further, the quality of delivered content gave an appealing call to the tourists. An informed content with a full brief about weather, conditions i.e., temperature, humidity level, rainfall, and water availability instructing the tourists in planning the trips (Machado Carvalho, 2024). The study suggested joining hands with those influencers who have secured large followings on social media platforms, therefore, their delivered content and compiled information made accessible to a large audience (Bastrygina et al., 2024). Simultaneously, this study put its request to influencers and bound them to disburse the information about the eco-friendly standards (Zhao & Shen, 2024). This step would be an acknowledgeable effort to the sustainability measures.

Influential promotions gave visual visits and previews of the destinations (Tafesse & Wood, 2021). Such promotions priorly secured the tourists' trust, connectivity, sympathy, and charm to the locations. To attain regional connectivity, build memories and develop the environmental association, tourists give a definite visit to a particular destination or set of destinations (Xie-Carson et al., 2023). Continuous, informed, previewed and brief visits develop a sense of responsible tourism among visitors.

Along with the description of influencers' roles, trust-building parameters and possible challenges, the study grouped various sets of keywords that were priorly used in past research attempts. Different pictorial figures of VOS Viewer including *all keywords, authors' keywords* and *index keywords* were presented; simultaneously, we discussed the current and future trends. Moreover, the study reported the top countries (concerning produced documents and secured citations) which were fully captured the emergence of this sector. Within the resident cluster, it successfully presented the possibilities of grouped zones and sub-clusters according to the colours, size and occupancies of bubbles.

6.1 Future agenda

This study significantly contributes to the current literature and calls for future research attempts. The mentioned future directions point out new avenues for young scholars, practitioners, academicians, and researchers. The study openly invites influencers to work to promote ecotourism destinations, but unfortunately, it does not address the measures that are necessary to improve content quality. In the future, researchers are requested to develop a mechanism that assesses the validity and authenticity of delivered content. Second, tourist companies can set partnership agreements with the influencers. Tourists' retention rate, visits, and constructive feedback may help the influencers set the contract terms and conditions. Third, the study tried its best to engage the maximum number of tourists to visit the ecotourist places, therefore, it addresses individuals who are not willing to execute their trips without carrying their pets. In the future, the study gives a call to researchers to conduct a separate study and set its focus to the handling of pets at tourist spots and eco-tourists. Finally, to explore seldom-visited places and destinations of unknown paths, tourist companies are encouraged to create a pool of influencers with high ratings and followers and execute their departure within an influential team.

6.2 CONCLUSION

The chapter attempted to promote ecotourism (a critical dimension of tourism) through digital marketing. In this way, the study involved social media influencers to digitally promote the ecotourist's destinations, therefore, social media influencers are requested to develop the content by visiting such places. Influencers deliver a preview and visual representation of ecotourist places in their social media posts, reels, and videos. This delivered content will cause a definite decline in tourists' fears, insights, and perceptions. Influencers' visits and stays give detailed instructions about the climate, temperature, humidity, rainfall, and precautions to current and future visitors. Simultaneously, this study equally catered to the sustainability standards; influencers working for the natural sciences, environmental sustainability, and preservation need to come forward and collaborate with tourist companies, agents, and the local community. Influencers' environmental conversation, content attributes, and sympathy for the natural ecosystems awaken the element of responsible tourism among people. By grabbing the trust of influencers' followers, eco-friendly activities can be promoted at tourist destinations. Thus, tourists execute their planned trips under the standards of sustainability.

REFERENCES

Adikaram, K. K. N. B., & Surangi, H. A. K. N. S. (2024). Creating opportunities in a challenging environment: Experiential crisis learning behaviour of tourism SMEs in Sri Lanka. *Cogent Business & Management*, 11(1), 2314803. Advance online publication. DOI: 10.1080/23311975.2024.2314803

Ajzen, I. (1985). From intentions to actions: A theory of planned behavior. In *Action control: From cognition to behavior* (pp. 11–39). Springer. DOI: 10.1007/978-3-642-69746-3_2

Ameen, N., Cheah, J.-H., Ali, F., El-Manstrly, D., & Kulyciute, R. (2023). Risk, Trust, and the Roles of Human Versus Virtual Influencers. *Journal of Travel Research*, 63(6), 1370–1394. DOI: 10.1177/00472875231190601

Arici, H. E., Arasli, H., Koseoglu, M. A., Saydam, M. B., & Olorunsola, V. O. (2024). Financial determinants of governance scores in hospitality and tourism enterprises. *Quality & Quantity*. Advance online publication. DOI: 10.1007/s11135-023-01820-7

Azis, S. S. A., Sipan, I., Sapri, M., & Zafirah, A. M. (2018). Creating an innocuous mangrove ecosystem: Understanding the influence of ecotourism products from Malaysian and international perspectives. *Ocean and Coastal Management*, 165, 416–427. DOI: 10.1016/j.ocecoaman.2018.09.014

Bakri, M., Krisjanous, J., & Richard, J. E. (2022). Examining Sojourners as Visual Influencers in VFR (Visiting Friends and Relatives) Tourism: A Rhetorical Analysis of User-Generated Images. *Journal of Travel Research*, 62(8), 1685–1706. DOI: 10.1177/00472875221138975

Bastrygina, T., Lim, W. M., Jopp, R., & Weissmann, M. A. (2024). Unraveling the power of social media influencers: Qualitative insights into the role of Instagram influencers in the hospitality and tourism industry. *Journal of Hospitality and Tourism Management*, 58, 214–243. DOI: 10.1016/j.jhtm.2024.01.007

Cao, J., Zhang, J., Wang, C., Hu, H., & Yu, P. (2020). How far is the ideal destination? Distance desire, ways to explore the antinomy of distance effects in tourist destination choice. *Journal of Travel Research*, 59(4), 614–630. DOI: 10.1177/0047287519844832

Chakraborty, P., & Ghosal, S. (2024). An eco-social exploration of tourism area evolution in mountains through stakeholders' perspective. *Environmental Development*, 49, 100963. Advance online publication. DOI: 10.1016/j.envdev.2024.100963

Ghaderi, Z., Esfehani, M. H., Fennell, D., & Shahabi, E. (2021). Community participation towards conservation of Touran National Park (TNP): An application of reciprocal altruism theory. *Journal of Ecotourism*, 22(2), 281–295. DOI: 10.1080/14724049.2021.1991934

Giuffredi-Kähr, A., Petrova, A., & Malär, L. (2022). Sponsorship Disclosure of Influencers–A Curse or a Blessing? *Journal of Interactive Marketing*, 57(1), 18–34. DOI: 10.1177/10949968221075686

Harrigan, P., Daly, T. M., Coussement, K., Lee, J. A., Soutar, G. N., & Evers, U. (2021). Identifying influencers on social media. *International Journal of Information Management*, 56, 102246. Advance online publication. DOI: 10.1016/j.ijinfomgt.2020.102246

Hu, H., Zhang, Y., Wang, C., & Yu, P. (2024). Factors Influencing Tourists' Intention and Behavior toward Tourism Waste Classification: A Case Study of the West Lake Scenic Spot in Hangzhou, China. *Sustainability (Basel)*, 16(3), 1231. Advance online publication. DOI: 10.3390/su16031231

Islam, M. A., Aldaihani, F. M. F., & Saatchi, S. G. (2023). Artificial intelligence adoption among human resource professionals: Does market turbulence play a role? *Global Business and Organizational Excellence*, 42(6), 59–74. DOI: 10.1002/joe.22226

Iswanto, D., Handriana, T., Rony, A. H. N., & Sangadji, S. S. (2024). Influencers in Tourism Digital Marketing: A Comprehensive Literature Review. *International Journal of Sustainable Development and Planning*, 19(2), 739–749. DOI: 10.18280/ijsdp.190231

Kamruzzaman, L. (2024). Subjective vs. objective assessment of the economic impacts of light rail transit: The case of G:Link in Gold Coast, Australia. *Journal of Transport Geography*, 117, 103883. Advance online publication. DOI: 10.1016/j.jtrangeo.2024.103883

Kilipiri, E., Papaioannou, E., & Kotzaivazoglou, I. (2023). Social media and influencer marketing for promoting sustainable tourism destinations: The instagram case. *Sustainability (Basel)*, 15(8), 6374. DOI: 10.3390/su15086374

Kirilenko, A., Emin, K., & Tavares, K. C. N. (2023). Instagram travel influencers coping with COVID-19 travel disruption. *Information Technology & Tourism*, 26(1), 119–146. DOI: 10.1007/s40558-023-00276-7

Leung, X. Y., Zhong, Y. S., & Sun, J. (2025). The impact of social media influencer's age cue on older adults' travel intention: The moderating roles of travel cues and travel constraints. *Tourism Management*, 106, 104979. Advance online publication. DOI: 10.1016/j.tourman.2024.104979

Lucrezi, S., & Cilliers, C. D. (2022). Factors Influencing marine wildlife voluntourists' satisfaction and post-experience attitudes: Evidence from Southern Africa. *Journal of Ecotourism*, 23(1), 56–80. DOI: 10.1080/14724049.2022.2122983

Machado Carvalho, M. A. (2024). Influencing the follower behavior: The role of homophily and perceived usefulness, credibility and enjoyability of travel content. *Journal of Hospitality and Tourism Insights*, 7(2), 1091–1110. DOI: 10.1108/JHTI-09-2023-0648

Matiza, T., & Slabbert, E. (2024). The Celebrity Influencer: Delineating the Effect of Tourism-Oriented Short Video Marketing on International Tourist Conation. *Journal of Global Marketing*, 37(4), 331–349. DOI: 10.1080/08911762.2024.2377741

Meng, B., Chi, X., Kim, J. J., Kim, G., Quan, W., & Han, H. (2024). Traveling with pets and staying at a pet-friendly hotel: A combination effect of the BRT, TPB, and NAM on consumer behaviors. *International Journal of Hospitality Management*, 120, 103771. Advance online publication. DOI: 10.1016/j.ijhm.2024.103771

Meng, B., Zhang, J., & Choi, K. (2024). The formation of parasocial relationships in tourism social media: A rational and emotional trust-building process. *International Journal of Tourism Research*, 26(3), e2650. Advance online publication. DOI: 10.1002/jtr.2650

Nahuelhual, L., Carmona, A., Aguayo, M., & Echeverria, C. (2013). Land use change and ecosystem services provision: A case study of recreation and ecotourism opportunities in southern Chile. *Landscape Ecology*, 29(2), 329–344. DOI: 10.1007/s10980-013-9958-x

Orea-Giner, A., De-Pablos-Heredero, C., & Vacas Guerrero, T. (2019). Sustainability, economic value and socio-cultural impacts of museums: A theoretical proposition of a research method. *Museum Management and Curatorship*, 36(1), 48–61. DOI: 10.1080/09647775.2019.1700468

Ouvrein, G., Pabian, S., Giles, D., Hudders, L., & De Backer, C. (2021). The web of influencers. A marketing-audience classification of (potential) social media influencers. *Journal of Marketing Management*, 37(13-14), 1313–1342. DOI: 10.1080/0267257X.2021.1912142

Pham, H. S. T., & Khanh, C. N. T. (2020). Ecotourism intention: The roles of environmental concern, time perspective and destination image. *Tourism Review*, 76(5), 1141–1153. DOI: 10.1108/TR-09-2019-0363

Phu, T. N. (2024). Factors Affecting Regional Linkages in Tourism Development, Case Study of A Giang Province and its Surrounding Area in Mekong Delta. *Journal of Sustainability Science and Management*, 19(2), 214–239. DOI: 10.46754/jssm.2024.02.011

Polat, E., Çelik, F., Ibrahim, B., & Gursoy, D. (2024). Past, present, and future scene of influencer marketing in hospitality and tourism management. *Journal of Travel & Tourism Marketing*, 41(3), 322–343. DOI: 10.1080/10548408.2024.2317741

Pop, R.-A., Săplăcan, Z., Dabija, D.-C., & Alt, M.-A. (2022). The impact of social media influencers on travel decisions: The role of trust in consumer decision journey. *Current Issues in Tourism*, 25(5), 823–843. DOI: 10.1080/13683500.2021.1895729

Prakhar, P., Jaiswal, R., & Khan, M. I. A. (2024). Bibliometric Perspectives on Sustainable Tourism and Future Research Agenda. In *Managing Tourism and Hospitality Sectors for Sustainable Global Transformation* (pp. 1–16). IGI Global. DOI: 10.4018/979-8-3693-6260-0.ch001

Qiu, L., Li, X., & Choi, S. (2024). Exploring the influence of short video platforms on tourist attitudes and travel intention: A social–technical perspective. *Journal of Destination Marketing & Management*, 31, 100826. Advance online publication. DOI: 10.1016/j.jdmm.2023.100826

Rahmafitria, F., & Kaswanto, R. L. (2024). The role of eco-attraction in the intention to conduct low-carbon actions: A study of visitor behavior in urban forests. *International Journal of Tourism Cities*, 10(3), 881–904. DOI: 10.1108/IJTC-07-2023-0138

Razak, R. A., & Mansor, N. A. (2021). Instagram influencers in social media-induced tourism: Rethinking tourist trust towards tourism destination. In *Impact of new media in tourism* (pp. 135–144). IGI Global. DOI: 10.4018/978-1-7998-7095-1.ch009

Rehman, S., Arshad, N., & Nasir, A. (2024). Destination Revisit Intention, Continuity, Survival, Success. In *Supporting Environmental Stability Through Ecotourism* (pp. 198-218). https://doi.org/DOI: 10.4018/979-8-3693-1030-4.ch011

Roy, M., & Sharmin, Z. (2021). Consumer Demand for Ecotourism Products and Services in Sajek Valley of Bangladesh. In (pp. 217-244). Tourism Products and Services in Bangladesh: Concept Analysis and Development Suggestions. DOI: 10.1007/978-981-33-4279-8_10

Ruggeri, G., Corsi, S., & Mazzocchi, C. (2023). A bibliometric analysis of wine economics and business research: Insights, trends, and future directions. *International Journal of Wine Business Research*, 36(1), 14–39. DOI: 10.1108/IJWBR-06-2023-0032

Salouw, E., Setiawan, B., Roychansyah, M. S., & Sarwadi, A. (2024). Bibliometric Analysis of Tourism and Community Participation Research: A Comparison of Scopus and Web of Science Databases. *International Journal of Sustainable Development and Planning*, 19(4), 1415–1422. DOI: 10.18280/ijsdp.190419

Samaddar, K., & Mondal, S. (2024). Priming tourists with traditional gastronomic delicacies: Embracing a responsible approach towards sustainable consumption practice. *Consumer Behavior in Tourism and Hospitality*, 19(3), 383–403. DOI: 10.1108/CBTH-03-2023-0026

Sánchez-Amboage, E., Castellanos-García, P., & Crespo-Pereira, V. (2024). Traveler segmentation through Instagram Fashion Influencers. Mirror Tourist as a new segment consumer group. *Journal of Retailing and Consumer Services*, 78, 103735. Advance online publication. DOI: 10.1016/j.jretconser.2024.103735

Shuqair, S., Viglia, G., Costa Pinto, D., & Mattila, A. S. (2024). Reducing resistance to sponsorship disclosure: The role of experiential versus material posts. *Journal of Travel Research*, 63(4), 959–973. DOI: 10.1177/00472875231171668

Sisriany, S., & Furuya, K. (2024). Understanding the Spatial Distribution of Ecotourism in Indonesia and Its Relevance to the Protected Landscape. *Land (Basel)*, 13(3), 370. Advance online publication. DOI: 10.3390/land13030370

Sobhani, P., Esmaeilzadeh, H., Wolf, I. D., Deljouei, A., Marcu, M. V., & Sadeghi, S. M. M. (2023). Evaluating the ecological security of ecotourism in protected area based on the DPSIR model. *Ecological Indicators*, 155, 110957. Advance online publication. DOI: 10.1016/j.ecolind.2023.110957

Tafesse, W., & Wood, B. P. (2021). Followers' engagement with instagram influencers: The role of influencers' content and engagement strategy. *Journal of Retailing and Consumer Services*, 58, 102303. Advance online publication. DOI: 10.1016/j.jretconser.2020.102303

Ulker-Demirel, E., & Ciftci, G. (2020). A systematic literature review of the theory of planned behavior in tourism, leisure and hospitality management research. *Journal of Hospitality and Tourism Management*, 43, 209–219. DOI: 10.1016/j.jhtm.2020.04.003

Xie-Carson, L., & Benckendorff, P. (2024). Insta-fame or insta-flop? The pitfalls of using virtual influencers in tourism marketing. *Journal of Hospitality and Tourism Management*, 60, 116–126. DOI: 10.1016/j.jhtm.2024.06.014

Xie-Carson, L., Magor, T., Benckendorff, P., & Hughes, K. (2023). All hype or the real deal? Investigating user engagement with virtual influencers in tourism. *Tourism Management*, 99, 104779. Advance online publication. DOI: 10.1016/j.tourman.2023.104779

Yasin, A., Raza, S. H., Pembecioglu, N., Zaman, U., Ogadimma, E. C., Khan, A. M., & Khan, S. W. (2023). Modeling the impact of social media influencers on intention to visit ecotourism destinations in the global south. In *Handbook of Research on Deconstructing Culture and Communication in the Global South*. IGI Global. DOI: 10.4018/978-1-6684-8093-9.ch021

Zhao, C., & Shen, H. (2024). The Moderating Effect of Ski Influencer on Ski Tourism Intention. *SAGE Open*, 14(2), 21582440241242318. Advance online publication. DOI: 10.1177/21582440241242318

Chapter 3
Leveraging Social Media for Destination Branding

Muhammad Hamid Murtza
Islamia University of Bahawalpur, Pakistan

Muhammad Imran Rasheed
https://orcid.org/0000-0002-3623-9043
Surrey International Institute, Dongbei University of Finance and Economics, China & University of Surrey, UK

ABSTRACT

This chapter examines and understands social media's significance in destination branding. Social media has become instrumental in shaping perceptions, effectively interacting with and forming destination brands. This section will highlight the critical role of social media in inventing and promoting destination brands, provide a complete analysis of its upshots, and describe theoretical application and support from the literature. With the advent of social media, the methods for advertising destinations have significantly affected customer perceptions. Social media outlets have wide-ranging outreach with interactional features, portraying destinations in previously impossible ways. These outlets can easily express distinctive value propositions to travellers, establishing influential, enduring brands. This chapter will also cover the fundamental concepts and theories related to social media, such as social identity theory and the theory of planned behaviour and its uses and gratifications.

DOI: 10.4018/979-8-3693-6700-1.ch003

INTRODUCTION

This chapter aims to examine and understand the significance of social media in destination branding. Social media has turned out to be very instrumental in shaping perceptions, and effectively interacting with and forming destination brands (Lund, Cohen, & Scarles, 2018). This section will highlight the important role of social media in inventing and promoting destination brands, moreover providing a complete analysis of its upshots along with a description of theoretical application and support from the literature.

With the advent of social media, the methods for advertising destinations have changed significantly affecting customer perceptions. Social media outlets have wide-ranging outreach with interactional features, portraying destinations in ways that were already impossible (Wakefield, 2023). These outlets can easily express distinctive value propositions to travelers, establishing influential, enduring brands. This chapter will also cover the fundamental concepts and theories related to social media, such as social identity theory, the theory of planned behavior, and uses and gratifications. These theoretical frameworks help understand the underlying mechanism explaining the causes and consequences of interacting through social media.

The rationale of the chapter

The tourism sector has witnessed massive growth, in the last two decades, due to the increasing influence of social media platforms. Social media plays a crucial role in shaping brand identity and enhancing visitor engagement through positive word of mouth (WoM). This chapter discusses the important role of social media in promoting tourism destinations and highlights its role in tourism marketing in the digital era. This chapter further elaborates on how various strategies and techniques can be effectively utilized to enhance the destination's image, increase its visibility, and nurture tourist engagement using social media platforms. The chapter presents a holistic approach to integrating social media marketing efforts for tourism marketing and enhancing destination reputation and destination image online. This chapter aims to provide readers with the basic insights for creating, monitoring, and implementing marketing strategy on social media platforms for destination branding.

Significance of the chapter

Social media shapes travel experience and its users like to explore things using digital platforms. An online survey showed that 75% of the tourists are inspired by social media to travel to a particular destination (see Figure 1). During their travel a majority of tourist (57%) also take pictures to share on their social media accounts.

This chapter is very important in understanding the role of harnessing social media for managing destination branding, reputation, and tourist engagement. It provides adequate knowledge about social media management strategies and important tools being utilized for guiding destination marketing on social media platforms.

Figure 1. Social media shapes travel experiences (Statista)

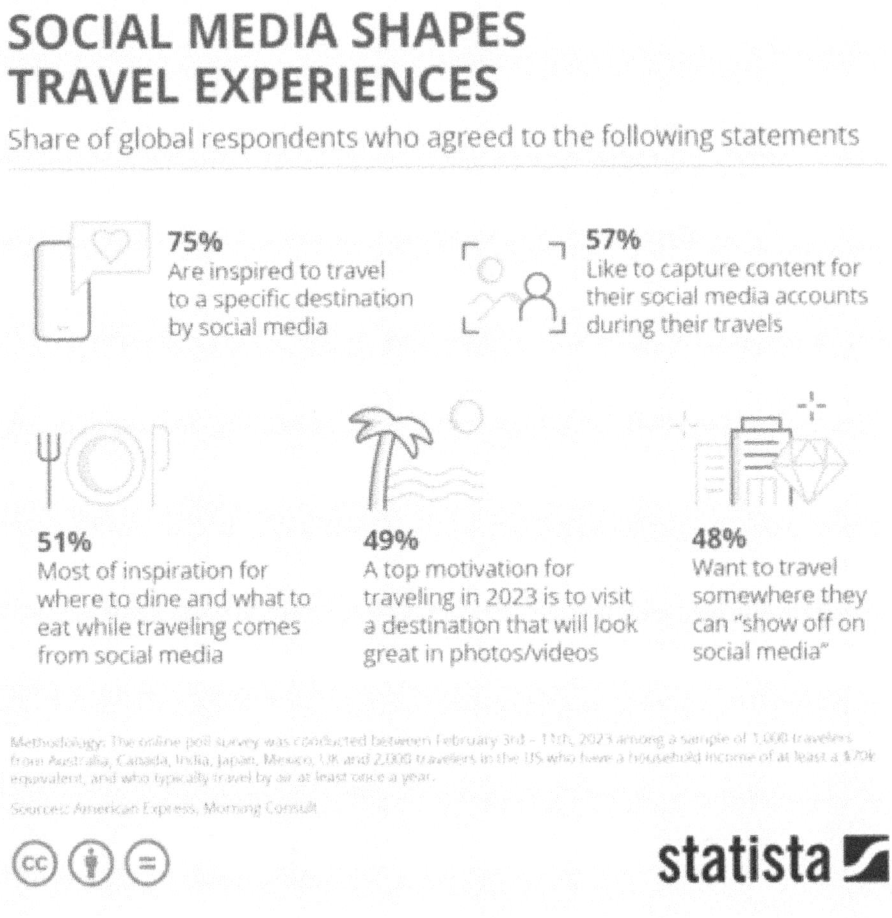

SOCIAL MEDIA SHAPES
TRAVEL EXPERIENCES
Share of global respondents who agreed to the following statements
75%
Are inspired to travel to a specific destination by social media
57%
Like to capture content for their social media accounts during their travels
51%
Most of inspiration for where to dine and what to eat while traveling comes from social media
49%
A top motivation for traveling in 2023 is to visit a destination that will look great in photos/videos
48%
Want to travel somewhere they can "show off on social media"
Methodology: The online poll survey was conducted between February 3rd – 11th, 2023 among a sample of 1,000 travelers from Australia, Canada, India, Japan, Mexico, UK and 2,000 travelers in the US who have a household income of at least a $70k equivalent, and who typically travel by air at least once a year.
Sources: American Express, Morning Consult
statista

1. SOCIAL MEDIA PLATFORMS

The effectiveness of social media platforms in destination branding depends on their demographics, features, and trends. Following we discuss the important social media outlets for destination branding:

1.1 Popular Streams of social media:

I. Instagram

Demographics:

- Mostly utilized by younger audiences, especially those between the ages of 18 and 34.
- Worldwide reach, with a significant presence in both rural and urban regions.

Features:

- Platform with a strong visual component that is perfect for sharing excellent travel images and videos.
- For both short- and long-form video content, use Stories, Reels, and IGTV.
- Using geotags and hashtags will improve discoverability.
- Influencer partnerships to connect with larger audiences.

Trends:

- Reels are being used more often for quick, interesting videos.
- User-generated content (UGC) initiatives to harness actual experiences.
- Integration of e-commerce functionalities to facilitate direct reservations.

II. Facebook

Demographics:

- A large user base that spans age groups with a notable proportion of users in the 25–54 age range.
- A significant presence in markets, both developed and developing.

Features:

- Flexible alternatives for material, such as live streaming, images, videos, and text posts.
- Facebook Pages and Groups for interaction and community building.
- Enhanced choices for ad targeting based on demographics, hobbies, and actions.
- Planning and marketing of events.

Trends:

- Emphasis on live streaming and other forms of video content.
- Facebook Stories are utilized for transient material.
- Expansion of private communities and experiences- and travel-oriented groups.

Iii. YouTube

Demographics:

- Broad appeal, especially among users in the 18–49 age range.
- Substantial worldwide market reach.

Features:

- Long-form video material, perfect for location documentaries, vlogs, and in-depth travel guides.
- Alternatives for monetization via partnerships and advertisements.
- Possibility of live streaming.
- Advantages of SEO with Google search integration.

Trends:

- The rise of influencer collaborations and trip vlogs.
- Usage of travel and how-to videos has increased.
- YouTube Shorts are used to create short, interesting content.

IV. TikTok

Demographics:

- Mostly utilized by younger audiences, particularly those in the 16–24 age range.
- Expanding user base in different areas and age brackets.

Features:

- Short-form video entertainment that emphasizes trends and innovation.
- Possibility of becoming viral with hashtag campaigns and challenges.
- Combining sound and visual effects.
- Opportunities for cooperation with TikTok influencers.

Trends:

- The quick expansion of influencers and material pertaining to tourism.
- Utilizing difficulties and trends to boost participation.
- Users tend to favor information that is genuine and unscripted.

V. Pinterest

Demographics:

- Audience that is primarily female and is heavily represented by users in the 18–49 age range.
- Popular in the United States, but expanding globally.

Features:

- A bookmarking and visual discovery platform.
- Boards and pins to arrange itineraries and ideas for trips.
- For further details and context, use Rich Pins.
- Search features are designed to find novel concepts and fads.

Trends:

- Pinterest is becoming more and more popular for inspiration and organizing trips.
- An increase in narrative and video pins.
- E-commerce features for reservations and transactions are integrated.

VI. Twitter

Demographics:

- Large user base with a notable proportion of users in the 18–49 age range.
- Strong presence among tech-savvy people and in urban regions.

Features:

- Twitter engagement and real-time updates.
- Using hashtags and popular subjects might boost your visibility.
- Twitter Moments: a selection of events and stories.
- Direct communication with users via mentions and answers.

Trends:

- Twitter usage for real-time information and customer support.
- Multimedia content, including pictures and videos, is growing.
- Twitter Spaces are becoming more and more important for live audio chats.

1.2 Social- media and destination branding

Social media platforms are becoming more influential day by day. They have got unmatchable reach, interactive connectivity, and capability to inspire people, therefore their role in destination branding has become crucial. The tourist reliance on social media is growing rapidly making them more dominant in destination branding. Unlike other conventional marketing channels, social media platforms are accessible in every part of the world with ease due to their global reach. The geographical boundaries have shrunk and tourists can access global destinations in real time due to social media. Ease of access to global destinations is key to enhancing their visibility and attraction to international tourists.

Social media plays an important role in destinations due to its visual appeal and storytelling. For example, Instagram is very effective in displaying striking images, beautiful landscapes, cultural fascinations, and food experiences. Visual content connects tourists emotionally motivating them to visit a particular destination. Fostering user-generated content is another important aspect of social media. Tourists share their experiences on social media which enhances the authenticity of their destination. Social media provides more personalization services to target a particular group of the tourist population leading to higher engagement. Social media marketing platforms are more cost-effective maximizing return on investment.

1.3 Analysis of demographics, features, and trends of social media platforms

Given that TikTok and Instagram are visual platforms that appeal to younger audiences with brief, interesting content, they are especially useful for destination branding (Haenlein et al., 2020). For deep and in-depth material, YouTube is perfect, with its extensive travel guides and vlogs, it caters to a wide audience (Chu, 2020). Facebook is a good platform for community development and targeted campaigns because of its adaptability and abundance of advertising possibilities (Cotter et al., 2021). Pinterest is a great place to get materials and inspiration for travel, especially for its mostly female audience (Cario, 2012). For updates and real-time interaction, Twitter is helpful, especially for tech-savvy individuals and those living in cities (Femenia-Serra et al., 2019).

All platforms are showing an increasing preference for video content, according to trends, with short-form videos acquiring a lot of popularity. The integrity and accessibility of destination branding initiatives can also be improved by utilizing influencer relationships and user-generated content.

2. STRATEGY DEVELOPMENT TO CHOOSE THE RIGHT SOCIAL MEDIA PLATFORM

The strategy development for selecting the most suitable platform includes defining destination objectives, selecting an audience, and allocating resources.

2.1 Destination goals

The objectives of destinations must be determined like what you need to achieve through your presence on social media platforms (Tuten, 2023). These may include but are not limited to enhancing brand awareness, boosting website traffic, attracting target audience, and improving event participation. The destination goals should be Specific, Measurable, Achievable, Relevant, and Time-bound (SMART). For example, "increasing website traffic by 10% in next one month".

2.2 Target audience

Effective destination branding necessitates the identification of the demographics of the target audience (Qu, Kim, & Im, 2011). These may include gender, age, education, location, interest, and other behavior patterns. It is also imperative to understand which social media platform is the most popular among your target audience (Van Dijck, & Poell, 2013). For example, various studies highlight that the younger population is more inclined toward TikTok and Instagram while older individuals prefer Facebook (Masciantonio et al., 2021). In addition to this, it is also important to under what motivates users to prefer one social media over others. The objective of the social media user may vary from looking for information, inspiration, entertainment, and interaction.

2.3 Evaluating social media platform

Each social media platform has distinctive features that need to be assessed before starting a marketing campaign (Tuten, 2023). For example, LinkedIn is more professional, Instagram is more Visual-centric, and Twitter is real-time. Your selection of social media platforms solely depends on the type of content you are planning to create for branding (Ashley & Tuten, 2015). Each platform has its potential with respect to engagement and interaction depending upon the type of content i.e. image, article, video, or live streaming.

2.4 Resource allocation

Budget considerations are very important in the selection of social media platforms (Keegan & Rowley, 2017). You need to assess the **number** of resources required for content creation, advertising, and social media management. The human resources or the advertising team should also possess the skill set required for social media marketing. Do you have graphic designers, content creators, and social media managers in your team? In addition to this, the availability of social media management tools is also very important.

2.5 Analyzing competitors

A business must analyze which social media platforms are being used by its competitors for content creation, customer engagement, and business growth. There must be something lacking in the competitors' strategy which may be capitalized for creating a product or service differentiation (Farjoun & Fiss, 2022).

2.6 Selecting a social media platform

Instead of relying on one social media platform a mix of platforms should be selected depending on the target audience and available resources (Kreiss, Lawrence & McGregor, 2020). For instance, Instagram and Facebook may selected for wider reach and engagement, at the same time LinkedIn may be utilized for professional connections, and YouTube for promotional videos. Each platform necessitates a tailored strategy for content creation and dissemination. The marketing team should make sure that branding and messaging are consistent across all the formats.

2.7 Execution and monitoring

Take a start by initiating your presence on the selected platforms, interacting with your customers, and posting consistently according to an already devised content strategy. Performance on social media platforms should be tracked utilizing various analytical tools (Abkenar et al., 2021). The engagement of the targeted audience, website traffic, and business growth shall be monitored. The results of performance monitoring should help refine the overall strategy.

2.8 Adaptation and innovation

The social media trends should be followed to keep the strategy relevant and effective. The feedback from the audience is very crucial to update content and interact more effectively (Zhang, Liu, Wang & Zhao, 2022).

3. CONTENT CREATION

High-quality content creation is imperative to highlight the unique features of any destination making it more appealing and attractive to potential visitors (Ali & Xiaoying, 2021). Content creation requires a mix of appealing visuals, storytelling, technical expertise, and a deep understanding of destinations' unique features. The following techniques may be utilized for content creation:

3.1 Storytelling

Historical background, culture, and landmark features of destinations need to be identified to portray a unique picture of the destination to the visitors (Dedeoğlu et al., 2020). A persuasive story needs to be developed based on these elements. It depends on which aspect of the destination needs many depictions so that the audience may be engaged emotionally. It is important to cover all the necessary details in the story so that no element remains missing.

3.2 Photo and videography

The use of high-definition digital gadgets such as DSLR cameras with a range of lenses may be utilized to capture the beauty of a destination from various angles. The services of professional photographers may be hired so that the basic principles of photography are not compromised. Different angles and perspectives are important for creating appealing and balanced images. The use of drones for capturing aerial views is also very helpful. Video content highlighting the topographical features, layouts, and landscapes plays an important role in showcasing the destination image (Wang et al., 2024).

3.3 People and culture

The involvement of local residents in destination branding is very important (Roxas, Rivera & Gutierrez, 2020). After taking permission and explaining the purpose of their involvement take pictures of the local inhabitants, their routine activities, and interactions. Local products, festivals, ceremonies, and traditional elements need to be documented to add authenticity to the content (Prasiasa, Widari & Susanti, 2023). Some of the destinations have iconic attractions, architectural wonders, and natural phenomena which can stimulate interest and engagement of the target audience. Unseen treasures of beauty and lesser-known spots highlight a different perspective for the niche audience.

3.4 Technological integration and captioning

Most social media platforms support the latest technological advancements like showcasing 360-degree videos and photography for a better and enhanced experience (Chiariotti, 2021). Moreover, virtual reality tours of the destinations are also very common interactive experiences these days. Search engine optimization (SEO) strategy is very important for providing the best descriptions and captions. The social media team should create fascinating captions telling the stories, highlighting context, and containing facts about destinations.

3.5 Consistency in branding and promotion

It is important to keep the tone and style of the content consistent with the brand identity (Alvarado-Karste & Guzmán, 2020). Whether it is the color, font, or whatever aesthetic is followed must be coherent. The brand identity must be kept distinct and discreet using specific logos or watermarks. All type of content needs to be shared on all social media outlets regularly. Each platform has its strengths so the content needs to be customized according to the requirement and target audience. Social media networks work better with collaborations. The partnerships and collaborations with influencers, tourism businesses, and tourism boards will be very helpful in reaching a wider audience. Maximize the interaction and communication with the target audience with live streaming, interact through the comments section, and encourage the audience to share.

3.6 User-generated content (UGC)

Content produced by tourists is recognized as user-generated content. Utilizing user-generated content is also a successful strategy for building authenticity and confidence in your destination (Bandinelli, 2020). There are several ways to motivate tourists to create and utilize content. Various contests can be organized among tourists for the best photography or videography with prize money. The tourist may also be incentivized to share their experiences with specific hashtags. Acknowledging the tourist for their views or sharing their stories on official pages makes them motivated to further share content on social media.

Use of distinctive, and easy hashtags for promotion of the destinations. Tourists may be encouraged to tag their locations in their posts to motivate locals to visit the destination. Real-time uploading of photos and videos has a distinct impact on destination promotion therefore make sure the availability of free WIFI so that real-time experiences may be shared. It is highly recommended to set up some aesthetically pleasant installations for taking photos or selfies for destination branding. Tourist like to share their pleasant photos more on social media (Stsiampkouskaya et al., 2021). Various interactive and unique features provide immersive experiences for the tourist like tourist guides, adventure activities, or cultural performances.

3.7 Utilizing user-generated content

The user-generated content should not be utilized without permission of the tourists. Those who created the content need to be credited therefore they should be asked to mention the intent to use the content so that their rights and privacy are not compromised. Once they agree you are free to post their stories on your website to add authenticity to the destination. Dedicated albums on the website should be created to feature those stories and experiences. Tourists-generated photos and videos may also be utilized for running the awareness or branding campaign of the destination (Tran & Rudolf, 2022). There may be sub-sections of the website showcasing various categories of photos i.e. "best sunset capture" or "mesmerizing hills" highlighting unique features of the destination.

4. ENGAGING COMMUNITY AND MANAGEMENT THROUGH SOCIAL MEDIA

Interacting with users and responding to their comments users is very useful for community engagement. The social media team should also like and comment on those posts that highlight the key features of the destination. This is a great source of encouraging the audience to post and share more content and feel like part of the community (Giertz, et al., 2022). Routine-based sharing the user-generated content on a website or wall improves the visibility of the destination and also encourages the tourists. There must be online forums for the tourists to ask questions, share their ideas, and experiences and remain connected. There should be some events where all these community members may gather. It may be a physical or virtual gathering.

Almost every social media platform provides the service of polls and surveys where the social media team can engage the audience by creating polls or asking questions for immediate response. There may be discussion on issues or opinions about specific topics of mutual interest. Even more detailed responses may be taken using SurveyMonkey and shared on social media platforms. Going live on social media platforms is also very interactive (Evans, Bratton & McKee, 2021). Various interactive posts like fill-in-the-blanks or photo comparisons may engage an audience and increase website traffic.

5. TOOLS FOR FOSTERING ENGAGEMENT AND INTERACTION

Social media marketing tools like Buffer, Hootsuite, and Sprout Social are utilized for scheduling posts, monitoring engagement, and networking with the target audience on various platforms. Implementing chatbots on websites or social media messengers boosts customer interaction and problem-solving. Active engagement of the social media team with the audience on all platforms ensures tracking and monitoring feedback (Drivas et al., 2022). The real-time chat facility on the website provides real-time support to the visitors. Discussion boards and forums help customers share their experiences adding authentic value to the destination.

6. EVALUATING SOCIAL MEDIA PLATFORM PERFORMANCE

The assessment of social media marketing performance is critical for understanding the dissemination of content to the audience, finding new trends, and decision-making (Zhang et al., 2022). Various tools are available to perform this analysis. Some of them are platform-specific tools while others are general. For example, there are built-in analytical tools for Facebook users to check post engagement, page views, or demographic information of the users. Similarly, business accounts on other social media platforms like Instagram provide various matrices, activity graphs, and overall post performance. YouTube and Twitter also provide the facility to check views, impressions, and overall engagement. Google Analytics helps track the audience being driven to the website by social media platforms. You may analyze which social media platform is engaging and driving more audience to the website.

7. TECHNIQUES FOR MONITORING THE SOCIAL MEDIA PLATFORMS

There should be specific key performance indicators (KPIs) for tracking social media performance (Mameli et al., 2022). Engagement rate can be assessed by how much the audience has interacted with your content, by calculating the number of likes, shares, and comments with the number of audience available. Similarly, the reach of the post is identified by identifying new users interacting with the content growth rate of followers available on various social media platforms. The number of clicks on a particular post also measures new impressions. It is also important to understand how much the audience purchases the product after watching social media posts.

Another important technique for monitoring is Benchmarking (Mameli et al., 2022). The performance metrics and analytics may be compared with those of the competitors for product or service improvement. The industry may also provide particular standards which may be utilized for performance evaluation. You may also do experiments with your content to understand its acceptance in the target audience. Various tools available (i.e. Brandwatch) analyze the public sentiment and outreach of your brand to help you redesign your marketing campaign. These tools may be utilized to understand the public sentiment and trends of conversation on all social media platforms.

8. BRAND REPUTATION ON SOCIAL MEDIA

Creating and maintaining an enhanced reputation of the destination on social media is critical for drawing the attention of visitors and promoting a positive image (Baber & Baber, 2023). Here we discuss the effective strategies for enhancing destination image and positive word of mouth.

8.1 Develop a strong brand identity

A consistent tone needs to be established reflecting the distinctive qualities of the destination, whether it is luxury, adventure, cultural, or family-friendly. The color scheme, tone, images, and fonts of content should be distinct and consistent to establish a unified brand image. The top attractions, hidden beauties, and landmarks of the destination should be highlighted on a regular basis differentiating the destination from others.

9. KEY CHALLENGES IN DESTINATION BRANDING THROUGH SOCIAL MEDIA PLATFORMS

Although social media platforms provide several benefits for destination branding and tourism promotion, however, the challenges related to authenticity and data privacy cannot be ignored. These concerns may have a severe impact on the overall success of marketing strategies and the trust of the tourists in the destination brand. It is highly recommended to realize these challenges and tackle them for marketing experts to ensure the credibility of the brand and the privacy of the audience.

9.1 Privacy concerns

Social media platforms mostly depend on utilizing personal data to target individuals for destination branding and providing personalized experiences. These platforms are responsible for privacy and protection of personal data to keep the trust of the users failing which may result in difficulty for the marketing experts. Data privacy laws of the land should be followed to utilize data after users agree to ensure transparency. Tourists are well aware of the data privacy concerns if they find any marketing strategy offensive or there is data privacy concern the trust of potential visitors may be lost.

9.2 Authenticity issues

Providing a genuine experience to the tourists' authenticity of the destination is the most important element of destination branding. Some of the tourist destinations greatly rely on curated content for promoting their attractions. Curated content can be visually engaging but sometimes it appears to be unrealistic. This may lead to dissatisfaction of the tourists upon visiting the destination. Over-curated content can negatively impact the destination image and brand trust.

10. CONCLUSION

Managing a destination's reputation on social media platforms is a strategic multi-dimensional endeavor (Sharmin et al., 2021) which necessitates a pre-emptive and comprehensive approach. By establishing robust brand recognition, actively interacting with the audience, maximizing influence collaboration, and promoting user-generated content, an authentic and positive image of the destination can be created. Addressing feedback from the audience, online monitoring of the destination's reputation, and nurturing a feeling of community are fundamental for future success. Moreover, regular performance evaluation and adaptation to new developments, in terms of technology and trends, surely help keep the destination's social media management strategy effective.

A comprehensive social media marketing strategy can not only establish an enhanced image of the destination but also build a devoted fan base, encourage favorable word of mouth, and build an empathetic story that sounds authentic for both present and potential tourists. In today's highly competitive environment, a careful arrangement of a destination's social media existence can considerably add value to its overall attractiveness and achievement.

11 CASE STUDY: SOCIAL MEDIA DESTINATION BRANDING IN JAPAN

11.1 Introduction

Japan is one of the culturally rich and naturally diversified countries in Asia, that successfully employed social media strategy for uplifting the tourism sector of the country. In this case study we will study how Japan strategically utilized social media for its destination branding which resulted in attracting heaps of tourists from all around the world. This strategy was designed in the years preceding the Tokyo Olympics in 2020 and afterward.

11.2 Background

Japan has been a very popular country for tourists who would love to visit a unique combination of ancient civilization and contemporary modernism at one destination. Yet, recently most of the tourists visiting Japan were either domestic or came from neighboring countries. Acknowledging the possibility of pulling in a larger global viewership, the Japanese tourism leadership started a calculated campaign to boost Japan's global appeal via social media marketing.

The decision of the Japanese government to boost its global image was significant due to the approaching Tokyo Olympics where Japan could utilize this event for projecting their country at the global level. The objective of launching this campaign was promotion Japanese diversified tourist attractions from its humming metropolis to its tranquil countryside, to entice a wide range of tourists encompassing individuals with a passion for adventure, culture, and natural beauty.

11.3 Social media strategy

Establishing a diversified brand identity

The social media branding strategy focused on the diversified destinations of Japan, emphasizing not only the popular cities such as Tokyo and Kyoto but also lesser-known areas and events. The strategy was aimed at showcasing Japan as a location that has enough to offer everyone, whatever their areas of interest—technology, history, environment, or cuisine.

11.4 Main themes

11.4.1 Blend of tradition and modernity

The main theme of Japan's social media strategy was a combination of old and new. Social media platforms showcased a comparison of ancient cultural temples with modern metropolitan cities, demonstrating how innovation and tradition co-existed together in Japan.

11.4.2 Seasonal attractiveness

The four seasons in Japan were primarily focused concentrating on the spring season cherry blossoms, fall foliage, wintertime snow celebrations, and fireworks during summer. Every season was portrayed as a special cause to travel to Japan.

11.4.3 Culinary experiences

World-famous Japanese cuisine was a key component of the branding. Everything from fancy gourmet dining to street food was well covered in the content, showcasing the variety and cultural relevance of Japanese cuisine.

11.4.4 "Enjoy My Japan" drive

In 2018, the Japan National Tourism Organization (JNTO) launched the "Enjoy My Japan" campaign sought to draw in long-haul visitors from continents including Australia, North America, and Europe. An individualistic approach was adopted to attract by producing customized content according to users' interests.

11.5 Key features of the campaign

11.5.1 Personalized planning

The key feature "My Japan Planner" was introduced on the campaign website enabling users to design personalized itineraries according to their interests, including adventure, environment, culture, and cuisine.

11.5.2 Targeted advertisement on social media

Personalized advertisement was made targeting prospective tourists on websites like YouTube, Instagram, and Facebook. Data-driven targeting helped to understand the interests of the international tourist. The advertisement on social media highlighted certain Japanese experiences that aligned with the viewer's interests.

11.5.3 Video content

High-definition videos showcased cultural landmarks, adventure sites, Japanese cities, and the countryside. The video content was created and distributed throughout social media networks, evoking the emotional association of the potential visitors.

11.5.4 Influencer Marketing

Strategic partnerships were made with various influencers comprising Youtubers, travel bloggers, and photographers to reach the global audience. The Japanese government hosted these influencers and gave them firsthand experience and they were asked to share their experiences with their audience. The adventure-seeking influencers were engaged in mountainous areas for pursuits such as trekking, snowboarding, and discovering tiny communities. Similarly, those interested in culture and heritage were given access to traditional events, ceremonies, and trips to sites recognized as UNESCO World Heritage Sites. Influencers with an interest in food and culinary were welcomed to explore the Japanese culinary environment which includes both neighborhood street food markets and restaurants with Michelin stars.

11.5.5 Creating Hashtags and Using User-Generated Content

Exclusive hashtags like #OnlyInJapan, #VisitJapan, and #EnjoyMyJapan were promoted across all social media platforms to motivate tourist to share their experience of visiting Japan. The user-generated content played a significant role in establishing authenticity and online engagement. #OnlyInJapan tag represented activities like bullet train journeys, sumo wrestling, and cherry blossom festivals exclusively available in Japan. #JapanNature focuses natural beauties of Japan encompassing scenic landscapes, and outdoor activities attractive to those who enjoy the outdoors and adventure. The user-generated content was featured on social media pages which helped build a community of tourists and produce a steady flow of authentic content that highlighted the appealing qualities of the nation.

11.5.6 Leveraging Major Events

Japan's social media strategy majorly focused on anticipation of the Tokyo Olympics in 2020. The sports event was promoted showcasing all kinds of tourist attractions evoking interest in culture, traditions, food, and historical sites. The Japanese tourism authorities published a large number of social media posts and videos linking them to the Tokyo Olympics stimulating curiosity and eagerness in prospective guests. The campaign also presented Japanese traditional arts and crafts with the objective to educate international prospective tourists about Japanese culture and heritage in the context of the Olympics.

11.6 Overall Impact of Social Media Campaign

This strategic social media campaign brought substantial achievements for Japan. The anticipated period of the Tokyo Olympics witnessed a constant increase in international tourists. Japan recorded an increase in tourists from 10.4 million in 2013 to a record 31.9 million in 2019. The "Enjoy My Japan" campaign through influencers' partnerships assisted Japan reach out to European, Australian, and North American markets. Social media metrics exhibited high engagement from these regions. Overall Japanese social media campaign achieved huge success in exposing the country as a fascinating, friendly, and diverse place to visit. The Japanese tourism organization conducted surveys that showed a positive image of Japan.

11.7 CONCLUSION

Japan's case study reveals that social media campaigns can significantly impact the overall image and tourism appeal of a country if strategically crafted and well executed. With effective use of social media Japan was able to attract international tourists by focusing on personalized and engaging content, leveraging influencers and event marketing. Japan successfully positioned itself as a top destination for a global audience. The Japanese social media campaign has very important lessons and key insights for similar destinations seeking to use social media to strengthen their brand and draw in more visitors.

Case study information was retrieved from: https://www.japan.travel/en/enjoymyjapan/

REFERENCES

Abkenar, S. B., Kashani, M. H., Mahdipour, E., & Jameii, S. M. (2021). Big data analytics meets social media: A systematic review of techniques, open issues, and future directions. *Telematics and Informatics*, 57, 101517. DOI: 10.1016/j.tele.2020.101517 PMID: 34887614

Ali, D., & Xiaoying, L. (2021). The influence of content and non-content cues of tourism information quality on the creation of destination image in social media: A study of Khyber Pakhtunkhwa, Pakistan. [LASSIJ]. *Liberal Arts and Social Sciences International Journal*, 5(1), 245–265. DOI: 10.47264/idea.lassij/5.1.17

Alvarado-Karste, D., & Guzmán, F. (2020). The effect of brand identity-cognitive style fit and social influence on consumer-based brand equity. *Journal of Product and Brand Management*, 29(7), 971–984. DOI: 10.1108/JPBM-06-2019-2419

Ashley, C., & Tuten, T. (2015). Creative strategies in social media marketing: An exploratory study of branded social content and consumer engagement. *Psychology and Marketing*, 32(1), 15–27. DOI: 10.1002/mar.20761

Baber, R., & Baber, P. (2023). Influence of social media marketing efforts, e-reputation, and destination image on intention to visit among tourists: Application of SOR model. *Journal of Hospitality and Tourism Insights*, 6(5), 2298–2316. DOI: 10.1108/JHTI-06-2022-0270

Bandinelli, C. (2020). The effect of User-Generated Content to promote tourism destinations: the importance of perceived authenticity and trust (Doctoral dissertation).

Cario, J. E. (2012). *Pinterest marketing: An hour a day*. John Wiley & Sons.

Chiariotti, F. (2021). A survey on 360-degree video: Coding, quality of experience and streaming. *Computer Communications*, 177, 133–155. DOI: 10.1016/j.comcom.2021.06.029

Chu, J. (2020). Sustainable Travel on YouTube: Discussion and Perception: How do YouTube travel vlogs discuss sustainable travel? How are they perceived?.

Cotter, K., Medeiros, M., Pak, C., & Thorson, K. (2021). "Reach the right people": The politics of "interests" in Facebook's classification system for ad targeting. *Big Data & Society*, 8(1), 2053951721996046. DOI: 10.1177/2053951721996046

Dedeoğlu, B. B., Van Niekerk, M., Küçükergin, K. G., De Martino, M., & Okumuş, F. (2020). Effect of social media sharing on destination brand awareness and destination quality. *Journal of Vacation Marketing*, 26(1), 33–56. DOI: 10.1177/1356766719858644

Drivas, I. C., Kouis, D., Kyriaki-Manessi, D., & Giannakopoulou, F. (2022). Social media analytics and metrics for improving users engagement. *Knowledge (Beverly Hills, Calif.)*, 2(2), 225–242.

Evans, D., Bratton, S., & McKee, J. (2021). *Social media marketing*. AG Printing & Publishing.

Farjoun, M., & Fiss, P. C. (2022). Thriving on contradiction: Toward a dialectical alternative to fit-based models in strategy (and beyond). *Strategic Management Journal*, 43(2), 340–369. DOI: 10.1002/smj.3342

Femenia-Serra, F., Perles-Ribes, J. F., & Ivars-Baidal, J. A. (2019). Smart destinations and tech-savvy millennial tourists: Hype versus reality. *Tourism Review*, 74(1), 63–81. DOI: 10.1108/TR-02-2018-0018

Giertz, J. N., Weiger, W. H., Törhönen, M., & Hamari, J. (2022). Content versus community focus in live streaming services: How to drive engagement in synchronous social media. *Journal of Service Management*, 33(1), 33–58. DOI: 10.1108/JOSM-12-2020-0439

Haenlein, M., Anadol, E., Farnsworth, T., Hugo, H., Hunichen, J., & Welte, D. (2020). Navigating the new era of influencer marketing: How to be successful on Instagram, TikTok, & Co. *California Management Review*, 63(1), 5–25. DOI: 10.1177/0008125620958166

Keegan, B. J., & Rowley, J. (2017). Evaluation and decision making in social media marketing. *Management Decision*, 55(1), 15–31. DOI: 10.1108/MD-10-2015-0450

Kreiss, D., Lawrence, R. G., & McGregor, S. C. (2020). In their own words: Political practitioner accounts of candidates, audiences, affordances, genres, and timing in strategic social media use. In *Studying Politics Across Media* (pp. 8–31). Routledge. DOI: 10.4324/9780429202483-2

Lund, N. F., Cohen, S. A., & Scarles, C. (2018). The power of social media storytelling in destination branding. *Journal of Destination Marketing & Management*, 8, 271–280. DOI: 10.1016/j.jdmm.2017.05.003

Mameli, M., Paolanti, M., Morbidoni, C., Frontoni, E., & Teti, A. (2022). Social media analytics system for action inspection on social networks. *Social Network Analysis and Mining*, 12(1), 33. DOI: 10.1007/s13278-021-00853-w PMID: 35154503

Masciantonio, A., Bourguignon, D., Bouchat, P., Balty, M., & Rimé, B. (2021). Don't put all social network sites in one basket: Facebook, Instagram, Twitter, TikTok, and their relations with well-being during the COVID-19 pandemic. *PLoS One*, 16(3), e0248384. DOI: 10.1371/journal.pone.0248384 PMID: 33705462

Prasiasa, D. P. O., Widari, D. A. D. S., & Susanti, P. H. (2023). Authenticity and Commodification of Creative Industry Products in The Tourism Sector, Bali. Mudra Jurnal Seni Budaya, 38(3).

Qu, H., Kim, L. H., & Im, H. H. (2011). A model of destination branding: Integrating the concepts of the branding and destination image. *Tourism Management*, 32(3), 465–476. DOI: 10.1016/j.tourman.2010.03.014

Roxas, F. M. Y., Rivera, J. P. R., & Gutierrez, E. L. M. (2020). Mapping stakeholders' roles in governing sustainable tourism destinations. *Journal of Hospitality and Tourism Management*, 45, 387–398. DOI: 10.1016/j.jhtm.2020.09.005

Sharmin, F., Sultan, M. T., Badulescu, D., Badulescu, A., Borma, A., & Li, B. (2021). Sustainable destination marketing ecosystem through smartphone-based social media: The consumers' acceptance perspective. *Sustainability (Basel)*, 13(4), 2308. DOI: 10.3390/su13042308

Stsiampkouskaya, K., Joinson, A., Piwek, L., & Stevens, L. (2021). Imagined audiences, emotions, and feedback expectations in social media photo sharing. *Social Media + Society*, 7(3), 20563051211035692. DOI: 10.1177/20563051211035692

Tuten, T. L. (2023). Social media marketing. Sage publications limited.

Van Dijck, J., & Poell, T. (2013). Understanding social media logic. *Media and Communication*, 1(1), 2–14. DOI: 10.17645/mac.v1i1.70

Wakefield, C. (2023). Exploring Social Media as Engagement in UK Development-led Archaeology (Doctoral dissertation, University of York).

Wang, X., Mou, N., Zhu, S., Yang, T., Zhang, X., & Zhang, Y. (2024). How to perceive tourism destination image? A visual content analysis based on inbound tourists' photos. *Journal of Destination Marketing & Management*, 33, 100923. DOI: 10.1016/j.jdmm.2024.100923

Zhang, H., Zang, Z., Zhu, H., Uddin, M. I., & Amin, M. A. (2022). Big data-assisted social media analytics for business model for business decision making system competitive analysis. *Information Processing & Management*, 59(1), 102762. DOI: 10.1016/j.ipm.2021.102762

Zhang, M., Liu, Y., Wang, Y., & Zhao, L. (2022). How to retain customers: Understanding the role of trust in live streaming commerce with a socio-technical perspective. *Computers in Human Behavior*, 127, 107052. DOI: 10.1016/j.chb.2021.107052

Chapter 4
Building Brand Authenticity and Strategies for Genuine Destination Experiences

Khalid Jamil
https://orcid.org/0000-0003-2106-9173
Beijing University of Technology, China

Aliya Anwar
https://orcid.org/0000-0002-3564-2017
North China Electric Power University, China

Sajjad Ahmad Baig
https://orcid.org/0009-0006-7450-1459
National Textile University, Faisalabad, Pakistan

ABSTRACT

This chapter is devoted to understanding the concept of constructing the destination brand authenticity, focusing on the delicate interplay between tourism and culture. This chapter discusses over-tourism, cultural commodification, environmental degradation, and economic dependency issues based on Bali, Venice, and Kyoto case studies. Every case presented in the paper describes specific actions taken to ensure that genuine values are preserved, including the involvement of the local population, the promotion of ecotourism, the use of the legal framework, cultural conservation, and the diversification of the economy. The measures taken by Bali regarding sustainable tourism, measures taken by Venice in terms of regulatory and artistic support, and measures taken by Kyoto in terms of cultural preserva-

DOI: 10.4018/979-8-3693-6700-1.ch004

tion and implementation of sustainable practices help preserve the true identity of places popular among tourists. The chapter ends by stressing that the approaches discussed should be integrated and dynamic, including community involvement and sustainability.

1. INTRODUCTION

Authenticity is now one of the strategic success factors for destinations in the intensely competitive global tourism industry. Locations must face the challenge of presenting themselves as culturally dense and genuine as tourists opt for strange but significant experiences to become pickier. Thus, this chapter discusses the formation of the real identity of a destination brand. Therefore, the work aims to provide valuable insights and recommendations for all participants in the travel industry. Because people require not only relaxation but also the concept of authenticity in tourism, which has recently been significant, they wish to immerse themselves in the lifestyle, history, and culture of the areas they visit (Chen et al., 2020). Authenticity significantly influences travelers' satisfaction and brand commitment; it determines the schedule and overall experience. Thus, this chapter fills the knowledge gap in the present corpus of research by presenting a comprehensive framework for developing destination brand authenticity (Escobar-Farfán et al., 2024).

With the increased numbers of tourists and the globalization of travel and tourism, authenticity has become one of the cornerstones in marketing and positioning tourism destinations. Given that today's travelers are more inclined to look for experiential and authentic travel experiences, the capacity to create and convey a genuine destination brand has emerged as a critical competitive advantage. This chapter aims to identify the diverse factors involved in constructing destination brand authenticity to present a guide on how tourism players can develop appealing and credible tourist experiences (Kumail et al., 2022).

The remainder of this chapter is organized into several key sections that provide a comprehensive exploration of destination brand authenticity. Following the introduction, Section 3.1 defines destination brand authenticity, focusing on how cultural heritage and traditions play a critical role in shaping a unique and credible brand identity. Section 3.2 delves into the strategies for building authenticity, including the use of storytelling, marketing, and technological integration. This is followed by detailed case studies of Bali, Venice, and Kyoto in Sections 3.3, 3.4, and 3.5, respectively, highlighting both the successes and challenges these destinations face in preserving their brand authenticity amidst growing tourism. Finally, the chapter concludes with a synthesis of best practices and future trends in maintaining authenticity while promoting sustainable tourism development.

2. THE RISING IMPORTANCE OF AUTHENTICITY IN TOURISM

It is, therefore, ironic that while the search for authenticity in tourism is not new, it has become more significant than ever before in the recent past. In the past, the concept of authenticity was considered an add-on when implementing tourism development strategies, and many destinations merely concentrated on constructing iconic landmarks and huge tourism facilities (Jiménez-Barreto et al., 2020). However, today's tourists are more selective and want to touch the soul of the country, its history, folklore, and people. Such a change in travelers' behavior has made authenticity one of the most critical factors of destination branding and marketing. Brand positioning helps be of great significance in the new competitive environment while seeking to position a location when the latter has some comparative advantage in a given environment such as people's cultural background or geographical features of a region. They provide a brief and engaging slogan to sell a tourist destination while creating positive attitudes and associations with a destination stimulate tourist satisfaction among visitors (Chigora et al., 2024). Not only an effective brand for traveling since it leads to increase tourist consumption, employment and investments opportunities in the area. Additionally, it must admit to the fact that effective branding regulates impressions and transforms them: eliminating prejudices, which are no longer topical, and sparking renewed interest in a destination. This article also focuses on the sustainable development by encouraging the use of environmentally friendly products and the encouragement of the use of culture and arts by tourists. Finally, destination branding plays an important role in offering a unique and easily recognizable brand that would help create the firm base and continuity in the process of the formation of sustainable development of the tourism industry.

3. SAMPLE CONTENT FOR KEY SECTIONS

3.1. Defining Destination Brand Authenticity

When applied to destination branding, authenticity means the accurate portrayal of the place's culture, historical background, and people's lifestyle. It explores the core of what makes a place unique and does not limit itself to the topic of sightseeing. Identifying how authenticity has shifted into a critical factor of travel expectations and marketing strategies will advance the analysis of the topic (Khan & Fatima 2021). Destination branding covers the development of a distinct image of a place that sets it apart other places of similar type, whether city, region or country that could attract tourists. It is the intentional dissemination of various promotional features such as marketing communication and image resources including logo, motto, and other materials that project the cultural, historical and generic experience of a place. Destination branding therefore seeks to establish a convincing and powerful image calibrating the tourists' desires so that they can visit often, and in large numbers, for the economic and social progress of the specific destination (Jamil et al., 2022a).

3.2. The Role of Cultural Heritage and Traditions in Destination Branding

Culture and tradition are the most critical components of an essential destination brand. It offers a feeling of location and identity of destinations, thus setting one place apart. Therefore, cultural resources need to be conserved and marketed to support the authenticity of the cultural heritage and build pride among the owners (Loureiro, 2020). This chapter focuses on the strategies destinations can use to build a strong brand story based on cultural capital.

Coined by the author, the physical and abstract components of destination branding are presented below. Concrete components are buildings that are architectural, historical sites, and indigenous foods, while abstract components are mood, legends, and customs of the area (Haq et al., 2024). How all these elements are integrated will assist in generating a brand story that is authentic and logical. It will be easier to combine these elements with the help of bright examples from Kyoto and Tuscany.

3.3. Strategies for Building Authenticity

In order to develop a destination brand that can be relied upon, it is necessary to give considerable consideration to the narrative, the community, and the aspects of environmental sustainability (Shang et al., 2020). In the following section of this article, destination marketers will be provided with helpful advice on how to generate captivating narratives about the region, how to involve people in tourism initiatives, and how to take measures to preserve the region's indigenous culture and natural environment.

- ***Storytelling and Narrative Techniques:*** It is possible to draw a larger audience and differentiate the site from other places by telling anecdotes about the historical events, cultural customs, and customary beliefs that have occurred in the area.
- ***Marketing and Communication:*** Through advertising that is both effective and places an emphasis on these traits, it is possible to contact the members of the target audience of visitors. It is for this reason that the location is promoted across a variety of social media channels, which may involve publish-

ing about actual events that have taken place in the destination (Praswati et al., 2021).

- ***Leveraging Technology:*** When it comes to the preservation of cultural identity, there is no need to be concerned about the utilization of technology because it will assist in the development of virtual tours, augmented reality applications, and mobile applications that will provide visitors with additional information regarding the location.

3.4. Case Study 1: Bali-Indonesia

Bali is one of the Indonesian islands famous for its beautiful views, unique history, and colorful customs. Recently, Bali has developed into one of the most sought-after tourist destinations, with millions of tourists thronging the island yearly. The physical attraction of the island, coupled with its cultural heritage, has been one of its most significant selling points; however, the fast-growing tourism sector has proved to be a challenge in preserving the island's identity (Teng & Chen, 2020). This case study aims to analyze Bali's brand destination authenticity and the factors that have shaped it, measures taken to protect the brand's authenticity, and the current issues Bali faces.

3.4.1. Evolution of Bali's Tourism and Authenticity

Bali, one of the world's famous tourist destinations, started in the 1960s with the establishment of Ngurah Rai International Airport. First, Bali was advertised as an exotic place to visit, with messages referring to beautiful sandy beaches, green rice fields, and ancient temples. The island, which is of Hindu culture and religion, while Indonesia as a whole is predominantly Muslim, was yet another attraction. However, with time and the increase in tourism, the emphasis slowly started moving towards the type of tourism that is mass tourism, and there were significant changes in the infrastructural and hospitality industries (Yuliana et al., 2024). This rapid development introduced economic growth, yet it paved the way for commercializing Bali's cultural and environmental assets. There were signs that conventional dances and other artistic activities, such as ceremonies and rituals, were being done more for the benefit of the visitors rather than spiritually and culturally (Hamdy et al., 2024). Tourism also added pressure to the environmental resources, with problems like littering, water shortage, and traffic jams emerging. Figure 1 represents some highlights of Bali representing it as a brand destination:

Figure 1. Photo of Bali representing it as a brand destination (Bali Tourism Board (BTB))

Figure 2. Photo of Bali representing it as a brand destination (Bali Tourism Board (BTB))

Figure 3. Photo of Bali representing it as a brand destination (Bali Tourism Board (BTB))

Figure 4. Photo of Bali representing it as a brand destination (Bali Tourism Board (BTB))

3.4.2. Weather of Bali

Bali is one of Indonesia's islands which experience tropical weather hot and humid for most of the year. The island experiences two distinct seasons: four months of dry season between April and October, and seven months of wet season between November and March. The dry season of Bali is characterized by abundant sunshine with average temperature of 27°C to 32°c (81°F to 90°F) and low humidity making physical activities ideal. This period is characterized by numerous rainy and thorny storms at times while temperatures range between 25°C – 30°C (77°F – 86°F) and relative humidity of more than 85%. The coastal areas are comparatively hotter in comparison with the other area in Bali and other neighboring place like Ubud is comparatively cooler during the night. The climate of Bali is tropical, and therefore the temperature is warm all over the year no matter whether it is summertime or wintertime.

3.4.3. Factors Influencing the Authenticity of Bali

Several factors have influenced the authenticity of Bali's destination brand:

i. ***Cultural Commodification:*** Many aspects of Balinese art, such as dance, music, and rituals, have been transformed to suit the demand of tourism. Although this has been effective in maintaining and developing Balinese culture to some extent, it has also led to worries about commercialization, for often, the practices are changed to fit the tourists' taste.
ii. ***Environmental Degradation:*** Over the years, the social cost of mass tourism on the environment has been realized. Some of the social impacts of overdevelopment include deforestation, loss of agricultural land, and pollution, evident in the southern part of Bali. The deterioration of natural areas also threatens the essence of the tourist experience people seek.
iii. ***Economic Dependency:*** This implies that the local economy relies hugely on tourism, and in the process, the cultural and natural products are overutilized to the detriment of the community. This economic dependency can hamper the chances of achieving sustainable tourism practices that would benefit the cause of authenticity.
iv. ***Community Involvement:*** The level of locals' participation in decision-making and the planning of tourism activities is the single most significant determinant of authenticity.

3.4.4. Strategies to Preserve Authenticity of Bali

In response to the challenges of maintaining authenticity amidst growing tourism, various strategies have been employed in Bali:

i. ***Cultural Preservation Initiatives:*** Some measures taken to ensure that Balinese culture is as it is preserved include the following. The government, other organizations, and local authorities have provided programs for preserving arts, crafts, and ceremonies. Measures are taken to ensure that cultural shows are executed in their rightful cultural setting and not just for the entertainment of foreigners.
ii. ***Sustainable Tourism Practices:*** Another issue that has received much attention is the use of strategies that will help reduce tourism's effects on the environment. Measures to conserve natural resources include environmentally friendly resort facilities, proper disposal and management of wastes in Bali, and conservation of natural resources. For instance, the Green School Bali is an institution that focuses on nature and the environment and teaches students how to be more environmentally friendly.
iii. ***Community-Based Tourism:*** Promoting community-based tourism has been a major approach to ensuring that tourism impacts favor the locals and respect cultural and physical integrity. This involves the participation of local communities in the development of tourism and allowing them to present an original tourism product. In this regard, there are village tourism activities where tourists can spend their time in native Balinese villages and engage in daily routines.
iv. ***Regulation and Zoning:*** The government of Bali has implemented some measures and policies to curb the growth of tourism facilities. These measures are intended to check uncontrolled growth and development and conserve cultural and natural resources (Le et al., 2024). However, these regulations have not been easily implemented because of enforcement problems and economic factors.

3.4.5. Challenges and Ongoing Efforts in Bali

Despite these strategies, maintaining authenticity in Bali continues to be a complex challenge due to several factors:

i. ***Over tourism:*** That is because many tourists visit Bali, thus exerting pressure on the available resources and facilities in Bali. Many attractions also lead to overcrowding of tourist sites, thereby reducing the quality of tourists' experiences and the feeling of originality. Bali has been grappling with over tourism for years, and the numbers reflect the growing challenge. In 2019, Bali welcomed over 6 million international tourists, and the total number of visitors (including domestic travelers) reached approximately 10 million. Recent data shows that the number of foreign visitors to Bali continues to rise, with I Gusti Ngurah Rai International Airport handling the bulk of these arrivals. The average length of stay for tourists is 8.1 nights, with tourists from various regions contributing to the island's growing visitor count. In 2024, Bali is expected to experience its busiest year yet for tourism. However, this surge has raised concerns among local authorities and communities about the island's ability to sustainably manage the influx, as it strains infrastructure and threatens to disrupt local culture and the environment.

ii. ***Balancing Development and Preservation:*** There is still one of the biggest dilemmas: how can the island continue developing and providing for the tourists' needs without erasing the island's history and people's unique identity and damaging the environment? The question of how to continue the existing process of tourism development while maintaining the non-commercial recreational values that are the basis for creating unique tourism products remains open.

iii. ***Globalization and Cultural Change:*** Globalization has caused several changes in local culture and people's way of life, which in turn erodes the originality of the culture. Because of the influence of globalization, present-day youth may have different attitudes toward the conservation of culture.

iv. ***Economic Pressures:*** This economic reliance on tourism generates the tendency to put economic interests before sustainable and genuine concerns. This may result in choices made in the interest of the many over the few and consequently support mass tourism and development at the expense of culture and nature.

3.4.6. Precautionary Measures to Visit Bali

Thus, there are several guidelines that the Balinese tourist should undertake in order to have a safe trip. First, travelers should always be updated on their vaccines, and other usable vaccines are Hepatitis A, Typhoid, and Rabies depending on the activities to be carried out. As we know that Dengue fever is an issue, it is pertinent to use an insect repellent and dress appropriately to avoid mosquito bites in the months of the wet season. It is hence important that good travel insurance is purchased that will deal with medical contingency, or any other contingency that may occur. Bali's tap water is unfit for consumption so visitors should avoid using it and use bottled water instead; also, it is advised that visitors beware of food especially when preparing it, cook it well. Driving in Bali could be crazy, thus when hiring a scooter make sure you're have an international license that permits you to scooter or ride any other vehicle and put that helmet on. It is also important to contract trustworthy taxis or an application-based transport company. Their calls,

which are natural disasters specific to Bali, it is important that they keep abreast with emergency drills within the area. Furthermore, etiquette especially when visiting temples and dress code and conduct seniority and other cultural aspects should be observed. The final measure relates to the protection of Balinese environment: avoiding use of plastic products and supporting nature conservation and ecotourism projects. These provided precaution reduces the risks and impacts makes it possible for tourist to enjoy and explore Bali.

3.4.7. Conclusion of Case Study 1

Hence, Bali's experience creating and sustaining destination brand authenticity is a testament to the difficulties and issues in a popular tourist spot. The main threats to the islands' identity are the conflict between the image of an exotic tourist paradise and the challenges of a mass tourist destination and globalized culture. Bali has tackled some challenges through cultural preservation activities, sustainable tourism, community-based tourism, and policies. However, there should be a continuous effort and seek balance for Bali to retain its identity and for tourists to have the real Balinese experience. This paper reveals that the case of Bali supports the concept of engaging the locals in planning for tourism and maintaining sustainable practices, as well as coming up with unique ways of developing the tourism sector without compromising the environment. Thus, the problems that Bali encountered on the path of its development may enlighten other tourist destinations about the potential challenges associated with preserving cultural identity due to globalization and the commercialization of tourism.

3.5. Case Study 2: Vince-Italy

Venice, Italy, is one of the world's most famous and written-about places. It is a city built on water with magnificent structures and a long history. However, being a popular tourist destination has ushered the town to some critical challenges, especially regarding the issue of authenticity (Qing et al., 2024). Venice also highlights the development of tourism, the aspects impacting the tourist attraction's authenticity, the approaches taken to maintain the same, and the issues that Venice continues to experience.

3.5.1. Evolution of Venice's Tourism and Authenticity

Venice has been a significant cultural and trading center for centuries. Being a maritime republic, it was a point of contact for different cultures and a trade and art hub during the Renaissance period. In due course, Venice came to be associated with beauty, love, and history, and painters, poets, and travelers flocked to the city. This has been the case since the period of mass tourism in the 20th century, which made Venice one of the most popular destinations in the world. The beauty of the city that distinguishes it by the canals, the age of the buildings, and the art attracts millions of tourists every year. However, what was seen as the key to the rapid increase in tourist numbers was the threat to the heritage and character of the city (Kim et al., 2024). Figure 2 represents some highlights of Venice representing it as a brand destination:

Figure 5. Photo of Venice representing it as a brand destination (Italian National Tourism Board)

Figure 6. Photo of Venice representing it as a brand destination (Italian National Tourism Board)

Figure 7. Photo of Venice representing it as a brand destination (Italian National Tourism Board)

Figure 8. Photo of Venice representing it as a brand destination (Italian National Tourism Board)

3.5.2. Weather of Vince

Specific climate characteristics of the place include: Venice, Italy – has a humid subtropical climate, however it has more distinction towards the seasonal climates. Summer: June to August is hot and humid with average temperature of between 25 and 30 degrees Celsius and humidity above 70% thus the atmosphere is sultry. Winter is from December to February and is characterized by cold and damp with temperature between 0°C and 7°C (32°F to 45°F) the cold is worsened by high humidity and occasional fog during the dawn. Summer ranges from June to August, with higher temperatures fluctuating between 24°C and 34°C (75°F and 93°F); Autumn covers September and October and the temperature ranges from 10°C to 20°C (50°F and 68°F] Rainy season is during November and December and temperatures range between 0°C and 10°C (32°F and 50°F] The best time to visit Venice is in spring, Summer is characterized by the period between June to August, while the temperature range is between 10°C (50°F) to 22°C (72°F) the humidity rises hence once in a while is known to cause "Acqua Alta" meaning high water or flood time. Rainfall is more or less spread throughout the year in Venice besides the high degree of humidity throughout the year, is even higher during the summer.

3.5.3. Factors Influencing the Authenticity of Venice

Several factors have influenced the authenticity of Venice's destination brand:

i. ***Over tourism:*** Over tourism is a significant challenge in Venice, where the rate of annual visitors outweighs that of residents. This has implied overcrowded streets, crowded canals, and pressure on the infrastructure, which has changed the daily lives of the Venetians. For instance, Venice Italy has been receiving a very large number of tourists through word of mouth and this has greatly affected the infrastructure of the country and residents. This trend at a given year the city received nearly 4.6 million tourists Architecturally, there were even months that recorded very high visitor traffic of up to 580000 in a month like July. This causes very high traffic especially during times when about 60,000 visitors per day may be recorded more than the approximately 49,000 residents of the island. Such inequality not only exerts pressure on resource but also leads to environmental problems, including canal erosion and pollution, waste problem, and housing accessibility or unaffordability.

ii. ***Environmental Degradation:*** The physical environment that hosts Venice is very sensitive due to the establishment of the city on a lagoon, which makes it vulnerable to destruction due to the effects of mass tourism. Like many coastal cities, motorized boats, pollution, and rising sea levels have compounded problems such as erosion, flood, locally called acqua alta, and deterioration of the historical bases of structures.

iii. ***Cultural Erosion:*** Tourism in Venice has resulted in the formation of a culture industry, where Venice's culture has been turned into a commercial product. The manifestations of culture and entertainment events like carnival in Venice and traditional professions like Murano glass makers have gradually begun to pander to the tourist's eye and need, often compromising with the traditional essence of the art form.

iv. ***Economic Dependency:*** The concentration has shifted towards the service industry, particularly tourism; many stores and services cater to tourists but are fewer for Venetians. These economic changes have pushed the locals out and projected the population, lessening the chances of maintaining authentic culture.

3.5.4. Strategies to Preserve the Authenticity of Venice

In response to the challenges of maintaining authenticity amidst growing tourism, various strategies have been employed in Venice:

i. ***Regulation of Tourism Activities:*** Due to the increased flow of tourists to Venice, the government of Venice has taken measures to control the number of tourists. These range from controlling the access of cruise ships to the lagoon to controlling visitor access to public areas and advocating for off-peak tourism to spread the load of visitors throughout the year.

ii. ***Cultural Preservation Initiatives:*** Venice has not been left behind when it comes to preserving cultural history in its genuine state. The city has subsidized and promoted local artisans and traditional crafts in the region. Despite all the trends, festivals and cultural events are being held with the primary concern of preserving their authenticity and the participation of local people.

iii. ***Sustainable Tourism Practices:*** Reducing negative environmental impacts has been a major approach to supporting tourism. Measures range from advocating for the adoption of environmentally friendly transport to providing means of dealing with waste and adopting an environmentally friendly approach in the restoration processes (Tanaka et al., 2024).

iv. ***Community Involvement:*** Tourism planning and decisions should involve the locals to maintain the originality of the tourism activity. This has also facilitated the development of community-based tourism policies to the extent that a specific community will benefit economically and socially while at the same time being culturally sensitive (Lin et al., 2024).

v. ***Promoting Lesser-Known Attractions:*** To decrease congestion at locations such as St. Mark's Square and Rialto Bridge, attempts are made to introduce and popularize less visited places and districts. This strategy is beneficial as it prevents overcrowding in some areas while enabling tourists to get a real feel of Venice.

3.5.5. Successes Stories of Venice and Challenges

Successes Stories of Venice

i. **Regulation of Cruise Ships:** Another crucial measure adopted by Venice was to control the access of the big ships, mainly cruise ships, in the lagoon area. These ships pollute the environment and cause overcrowding. Some of the measures that have been taken by Venice include changing the direction of the cruise ship traffic and admitting fewer ships to the city; this has gone a long way in protecting the environment as well as easing the pressure on the archaic structures in the region.

ii. ***Support for Local Artisans:*** It has launched programs that encourage local craftsmen and the development of cultural products. The "Artisan's Venice" project is designed to preserve and develop the activity of the masters of the craft so that the city's guests receive not a set of ready-made souvenirs but products made by Venetian masters.

iii. ***Sustainable Practices:*** The following successful measures have been adopted in Venice to minimize the adverse effects of tourism: For instance, the "Venice Resilient" initiative aims to address climate change and sustainable cities, addressing the problem of increasing sea levels and environmental decline in Venice.

Challenges

i. ***Resident Exodus:*** According to experts, one of the most critical issues Venice has to deal with is population drain. Tourism has inflated the prices of goods and services and skyrocketed property prices, pushing Venetians out of their city. This depopulation threatens Venice's cultural and social life since it becomes almost impossible to support real community life.
ii. ***Balancing Development and Preservation:*** As a result, the attempts and measures taken to provide modern facilities for tourism and, at the same time, to maintain the historical and cultural characteristics of the city are still an issue. The proposed development projects, for instance, new hotels or other tourist facilities, are usually resisted by archaeologists, other conservationists, and local people who want the area to retain its originality.
iii. ***The commodification of Culture:*** The principle of cultural tourism is that while cultural events and traditional crafts are encouraged, their commercialization is always possible. Sustaining the integrity of these traditions as living and not just showpieces is a tricky proposition.
iv. ***Enforcement of Regulations:*** Therefore, regulating tourism activities and enforcing these measures are challenging processes that require constant effort. To be effective, compliance from both tourists and businesses is mandatory in this case.

3.5.6. Future Trends and Strategies

Maintaining authenticity in Venice requires ongoing efforts and innovative strategies to address the challenges posed by mass tourism and globalization. Future trends and techniques that could support the preservation of Venice's authenticity include:

i. ***Technological Integration:*** It is thus important to use technology in regulating tourist flows and improving visits. Intelligent tourism solutions, for instance, applications that monitor the number of tourists in crowded places and recommend less crowded and less popular sites, can assist in sharing the load.

ii. ***Collaborative Governance:*** Engaging all stakeholders, including the local government, residents, business people, and tourists, in tourism management results in more appropriate solutions. Integrative strategies ensure that the multiple stakeholders' concerns are addressed in tourism development and management.
iii. ***Education and Awareness:*** In this case, tourists need to be made aware of the need to protect Venice's culture and environment. Public awareness programs can change tourists' behavior, implying responsible attitudes toward destinations' cultural, environmental, and economic realities.
iv. ***Diversification of the Economy:*** The accommodation problem is solved by diversifying the economy from tourism, which decreases the number of individuals dependent on this field for their income. Developing other sectors, such as the tech sector, education sector, and creative industries, offers different sources of income apart from tourism.
v. ***Monitoring and Evaluation:*** The two implications are the constant assessment and evaluation of tourism's impacts and the efficiency of preservation measures. Flexible strategies could be applied, changing the measures depending on the feedback and information received to guarantee their efficiency in the future (Rini et al., 2024).

3.5.7. Precautionary Measure while visiting Vince

Some dos and don'ts that may be of help tp any visitors intending to visit Venice Italy include: Since the city sits on the water, it experiences what is called the 'Acqua Alta' which is high water and is more frequent in the autumn and winter season, one needs to check the weather forecast regularly and takes waterproof shoes to move around on a flooded area. Custom local ordinances apply; do not sit on any bridge or piazza, and swimming is prohibited within the Venetian canals. There is always a high incidence of persons using crowd indoctrination techniques to steal from tourists, especially at fixed places like Piazza San Marco and the Rialto Bridge, so travelers must ensure the safety of their belongings. When you use public transportation, especially the vaporetto, it is wise to purchase your tickets early and except to be squeezed when heading for the vaporetto especially in the rush hours. During summer, it important to take extra precaution as the weather is hot and humid; do not forget to take water and apply sunscreen. Also, since Venice is a city with many crossing bridges it is advisable to travel with minimal luggage all through the city. Finally, I suggest picking up a few basic Italian phrases to enjoy your vacation and not offend the locals. What has been said above should help make the visit to Venice safer and more enjoyable.

3.5.8. Conclusion of Case Study 2

In its endeavor to sustain destination brand sincerity, the case of Venice demonstrates the dynamics and issues a famous tourist place encounter. The city has always been popular and still has millions of tourists visiting it. However, the problems of over-tourism, deterioration of the environment, and the commercialization of culture still need to be addressed for an authentic city (Hamdy et al., 2024). Some of the measures that Venice has taken to overcome these challenges are regulation, cultural conservation, tourism sustainability, and community participation. However, constant endeavors and ideas are the key factors that must be invested to save Venice's identity and provide the tourists with an authentic experience. To avoid Venice's mishap, other destinations need to understand the challenges of preserving the originality of tourism in an environment that continues to be commercialized and globalized. The case of Venice demonstrates that economic development should be created hand in hand with preserving historical and cultural sites, citizens' engagement in tourism development, and the support of sustainable initiatives. Thus, it can be considered a successful model for other places that have to maintain their identity while simultaneously meeting the needs of the modern tourist.

3.6. Case Study 3: Kyoto-Japan

Kyoto is a beautiful city in Japan well known for its cultural landmarks, traditional buildings, and history. Kyoto is another city that was once the imperial capital of Japan, and to this day, one can still see numerous historical sights. However, like many other cities that become tourist attractions, Kyoto is not immune to the issues connected with the preservation of the genuine spirit of the city. This chapter aims to discuss the Kyoto process that has been trying to preserve its destination brand authenticity and learn about the factors that affected it, the actions Kyoto has taken to maintain its authenticity, and the challenges it faced.

3.6.1. Evolution of Kyoto's Tourism and Authenticity

Kyoto is over a thousand years old and was Japan's imperial capital from 794 to 1868. Taí has many UNESCO World Heritage sites, including temples, shrines, and traditional Japanese gardens. This is why Kyoto is unique and is famous for its cultural heritage and the attempt to keep and develop classical Japanese arts, crafts, and customs. Kyoto tourism dates back to the early twentieth century when there was a massive flow of tourists from within Japan and other parts of the world. The city's attractions are the historical buildings, a tea ceremony, geisha, traditional culture, and the views of cherry blossoms and autumn leaves. Nonetheless, the growth and particularly the modernization of tourism in the past decades has posed several problems in preserving the actual historical character of the city. Figure 3 represents some highlights of Kyoto representing it as a brand destination:

Figure 9. Photo of Kyoto representing it as a brand destination (Kyoto City Tourism Association)

Figure 10. Photo of Kyoto representing it as a brand destination (Kyoto City Tourism Association)

Figure 11. Photo of Kyoto representing it as a brand destination (Kyoto City Tourism Association)

Figure 12. Photo of Kyoto representing it as a brand destination (Kyoto City Tourism Association)

3.6.2. Weather of Kyoto

Kyoto city is situated in Japan and has a humid-sub tropical climate just as most parts of asia but the climate has well defined seasons. Summers are hottest and wettest in the season between June and August with maximum temperature reaching 27- 35 degree Celsius and humidity marks touching 75 percent and above. Late autumn from December to February is comparatively cold, the temperature varies between 0°C and -10°C (32°F to 50°F), though snowfalls are rare, sometimes you may find fog or light snow. While is one of the favored seasons in Japan, there is still a slight chance of rain and it is chilly between 10 °C and 20 °C (50°F to 68°F) depending on the year for the cherry blossom or Samurai season in April. The autumn begin in September and last until November with an average temperature at 10 to 25 degrees Celsius (50-to-77-degree Fahrenheit) and low humidity is preferable for viewing the autumn leaves. Kyoto receives the most tourists during the spring and autumn because the climate is favorable and the natural surroundings are most picturesque.

3.6.3. Factors Influencing the Authenticity of Kyoto

Several factors have influenced the authenticity of Kyoto's destination brand:

i. ***Cultural Commodification:*** Kyoto is facing the problem of commodification of its culture due to the commercialization of cultural heritage for tourists. There are often cases when geisha performances, tea ceremonies, and traditional crafts are altered to fit tourists' expectations; their genuine essence is thus compromised.
ii. ***Over tourism:*** A direct consequence of increased tourism, and international tourists in particular, is congestion, delays, and mounting pressure on physical infrastructure. Places such as the bamboo forest in Arashiyama, Fushimi Inari shrine, and the Kinkaku-ji temple attract many people and, at times, flood the areas, thus affecting the experience of the visitors and the inhabitants.
iii. ***Environmental Impact:*** The environment is threatened by the effects of mass tourism, such as the management of waste, the wearing out of historical sites, and pollution.
iv. ***Economic Dependency:*** Tourism has economic effects on the positive side, but this sector's dependency has negative effects on the economy. It can also increase the cost of living and the price of real estate, making it hard for a local population to sustain preindustrial standards of living and commerce.
v. ***Community Involvement:*** The degree of integration of local communities in the planning and management process of tourist activities determines the issue of authenticity to a large extent (Majeed et al., 2024). The following analysis supports the argument that tourism should positively impact the economic and social well-being of Kyoto's citizens in order to protect the city's culture (Jamil et al., 2022b).

3.6.4. Strategies to Preserve Authenticity

In response to the challenges of maintaining authenticity amidst growing tourism, various strategies have been employed in Kyoto:

I. ***Regulation of Tourism Activities:*** Kyoto city government has implemented the following measures to curtail the flow of tourists: off-peak tourism, limitation on the number of visitors to certain areas, and use of tickets to control crowds. Also, controls on the extent of business activities that can be carried out within historic areas aid in maintaining the historic character of the places.
II. ***Cultural Preservation Initiatives:*** It is noteworthy that attempts have been made to keep Kyoto in its original design and feel. This ranges from subsidies to traditional arts and crafts to workshops and other promotional activities. Organizations such as the Kyoto Cultural Association are involved in the preservation and promotion of cultural aspects as they are relevant to society.

III. ***Sustainable Tourism Practices:*** One approach that has been encouraged in relation to the environmental question in tourism is sustainable tourism. Measures include promoting the use of public transport, environmentally friendly waste management practices, and the sustainable development of accommodations in the region by business establishments (Wang et al., 2024).
IV. ***Community-Based Tourism:*** Thus, it is vital to include local communities in the tourism planning process and give them a chance to share the best of their hospitality with tourists. Activities like cultural tours led by local people and homestays give tourists an opportunity to get a closer look at the culture of Kyoto.
V. ***Promoting Lesser-Known Attractions:*** Hence, attempts have been made to diversify demand from overcrowded sites and areas and turn visitors' attention to other attractions and districts. This strategy allows further distribution of tourist traffic within the city, which helps to prevent overcrowding and encourages Kyoto tourists to explore more places with cultural significance.

3.6.5. Success Factors of Kyoto and Challenges

Successes Factors

i. ***Regulation of Short-Term Rentals:*** Due to the unfavorable effects of short-term lettings on communities, Kyoto cracked down on Airbnb and similar services. These regulations aim to prevent overcrowding of residential areas with tourists and keep housing prices affordable.
ii. ***Support for Traditional Crafts:*** Kyoto is well known for its culture of craft products, such as Nishijin weaving, Kiyomizu pottery, Kyoto lacquerware, and so on. The city encourages these crafts through subsidies, training, and promotion activities. An annual festival known as the "Kyoto Traditional Crafts Fair" brings together the local craftsmen and their products, supporting the continuation of such traditions.
iii. ***Sustainable Practices:*** Kyoto has embraced sustainable tourism, as discussed earlier. The city supports measures to promote public transportation; bicycle rental is available, and some areas are designed especially for pedestrians. Furthermore, most classical inns (ryokan) and restaurants have changed their policies and practices to save the earth, including waste disposal and using organic foods and vegetables produced in Japan.

Challenges

i. ***Over tourism:*** Thus, over tourism can still be considered a major problem even if there are attempts to control it. This is because public sites are still bearing the brunt of overcrowding, which in turn affects the guest experience and the people living in the area. Control and distribution of tourists' flow and the balance of tourism and ordinary life in Kyoto are still issues. Kyoto in Japan is a classic example a world heritage site that has been struggling and suffering from over tourism during the seasonal periods like cherry blossom festivals, and autumnal colors. The tourist influx to Kyoto is relatively high, and in 2019 when the pandemic had not yet hit the country, it received about 53 million tourists. This has put a lot of pressure on the city and tourism alone accounts for about 12% of Kyoto's GDP. However, due to increased traffic flow, crowded tourist attractions increase problems for inhabitants of the country as well as the service sector and the edifice structure in the country such as Fushimi Inari Shrine and Gion district. Successful measures for controlling over tourism have been implemented; these are crowd forecasting and off-peak visits, and 52% of tourists will change their next trips avoiding crowds. However, there are some concerns for interests of people, mainly the quality of their life is affected by tourism and despite of the economic effects of tourism is felt. Although COVID-19 led to a decline of tourists in 2020, with reference to the statistical data of 2024 the flow of tourists is growing, and the problems of overcrowding and the control of tourists'' streams have become relevant for the city again.

ii. ***Cultural Commodification:*** Nevertheless, cultural production and tourism continue to entail the commercialization of culture for the consumption of foreign travelers. The challenge of preserving the originality of such ceremonies, dances, weaving, mosaics, and other arts so as not to make them a mere tourist attraction is tricky.

iii. ***Resident Exodus:*** However, high costs of living, such as those occasioned by the growth of the tourism sector, have seen the local people move out in large numbers. Most of the young people relocate to other areas characterized by lower costs of living. Thus, the population becomes elderly, and they lose culturally appropriate ways of living. This demographic change presents difficulties to the continuation of genuine cultural practices.

iv. ***Balancing Modernization and Preservation:*** It is not easy to update facilities to accommodate tourists while respecting Kyoto's historical and cultural values. New constructions like hotels and tourism facilities, for instance, will always encounter resistance from those who hold conservationist ideals or people of the area who are likely to lose their cultural identity.

3.6.6. Future Trends and Strategies for Kyoto

Maintaining authenticity in Kyoto requires ongoing efforts and innovative strategies to address the challenges posed by mass tourism and globalization. Future trends and techniques that could support the preservation of Kyoto's authenticity include:

i. ***Smart Tourism Management:*** Technology can be useful in regulating tourist flows and improving visitors' experiences. For example, real-time monitoring of tourist numbers in hotspots and mobile apps containing recommendations for non-popular sights can encourage tourists to spread out more and thus avoid crowds.
ii. ***Collaborative Governance:*** Community participation in tourism management entails the government, the locals, the entrepreneurs, and the visitors coming up with sustainable measures. Cooperative strategies help to maintain the balance of stakeholder's needs and wants in the development and management of tourism.
iii. ***Education and Awareness:*** Tourists should know how they can contribute to the conservation of culture and physical features of Kyoto. Awareness campaigns can make the target population sensitive and guarantee proper conduct in the tourist destination.
iv. ***Diversification of the Economy:*** Another way to protect authenticity is to decrease the locals' reliance on the tourism industry by diversifying their economy. Thus, diversification can create new streams of income other than tourism with the help of supporting technology, education, or creative industries.
v. ***Monitoring and Evaluation:*** The assessment of tourism's impacts and the efficiency of preservation measures should be conducted ceaselessly. The best solution is adaptive management practices, which means that measures should be adjusted depending on the outcomes and feedback received.

3.6.7. Precautionary Measures while visiting Kyoto

There are some few important precautions that any visitor who intends to tour Kyoto, Japan should consider when planning to tour the country. It is necessary to dress according to the climate: loose informal T-shirts and trousers, caps and sunblock for hot summer as well as; warm thick clothes, cap, gloves, and scarves to protect from chilling winter that requires defrosting to 0+ Celsius. When in temples and shrines wear appropriate clothing, do not wear shoes were prohibited and be considerate. This common tourist attraction can also be very busy during the cherry blossom season or autumn maples and therefore, it is suggested to arrive before opening time, later or towards the evening. Although in the public transport system everyone has to adhere to the timetable, there are some general manners that people should remember, for example, do not push themselves to the front or raise their voices. Japanese land is seismically active – acquaint yourself with the safety practices and general emergency plans. Always have some cash on you because some bureaus, restaurants or shops do not accept credit cards, and be polite to the local environment: do not litter and stay away from protected areas. Professionally, obeying these rules shall enable any person to have a positive experience throughout their visit to Kyoto.

3.6.8. Conclusion of Case Study 3

This case study has outlined the case of Kyoto and its progression in preserving the destination brand's genuineness, which proves how culturally historic cities are vulnerable to the issues and difficulties they encounter. Tourism has remained a major attraction due to the town's architectural design, culture, and tradition (Lonardi et al., 2024). However, matters concerning over-tourism, commercialization of culture, and cultural impact on the environment are real and have severe consequences. It is necessary to continuously implement new approaches to guarantee that this city will remain a cultural tourist destination with genuine experiences. Thus, Kyoto's experience can be a reference point for understanding how other destinations can sustain their authenticity in a globalizing and commercializing world. Kyoto again shows that it is possible to develop and preserve, consider locals in tourism planning, and encourage sustainability. Thus, it becomes a perfect reference for other places that want to maintain their locations' cultural and historical identity while satisfying the new generation of tourists' requirements.

3.7. Conclusion

Therefore, the output of this chapter suggests that when it comes to establishing destination brand authenticity, the issue of development versus the preservation of cultural heritage must be addressed: the case of Bali, Venice, and Kyoto. Every place is vulnerable to problems such as overcrowding, cultural exploitation, and environmental deterioration. The identified strategies include the following: community participation, sustainability, legal frameworks, culture conservation, diversification of the economy, awareness, and constant assessment. Balinese care about sustainable tourism and community involvement, Venetian actions and support of local artists and artisans, and Kyoto's cultural conservation and environmental-friendly practices prove the necessity of integrated and evolutionary strategies. From these cases, other destinations can avoid various pitfalls in tourism development and conservation to remain faithful to the cultures and give tourists a real taste of the places.

REFERENCES

Chen, R., Zhou, Z., Zhan, G., & Zhou, N. (2020). The impact of destination brand authenticity and destination brand self-congruence on tourist loyalty: The mediating role of destination brand engagement. *Journal of Destination Marketing & Management*, 15, 100402. DOI: 10.1016/j.jdmm.2019.100402

Chigora, F., Ndlovu, J., & Nyagadza, B. (2024). Building positive Zimbabwean tourism festival, event and destination brand image and equity: A systematic literature review. *Cogent Social Sciences*, 10(1), 2318867. DOI: 10.1080/23311886.2024.2318867

Escobar-Farfán, M., Cervera-Taulet, A., & Schlesinger, W. (2024). Destination brand identity: Challenges, opportunities, and future research agenda. *Cogent Social Sciences*, 10(1), 2302803. DOI: 10.1080/23311886.2024.2302803

Hamdy, A., Zhang, J., & Eid, R. (2024). Does destination gender matter for destination brand attachment and brand love? The moderating role of destination involvement. *Marketing Intelligence & Planning*, 42(1), 120–148. DOI: 10.1108/MIP-05-2023-0211

Hamdy, A., Zhang, J., & Eid, R. (2024). Does destination gender matter for destination brand attachment and brand love? The moderating role of destination involvement. *Marketing Intelligence & Planning*, 42(1), 120–148. DOI: 10.1108/MIP-05-2023-0211

Haq, M. D., Tseng, T. H., Cheng, H. L., Chiu, C. M., & Kuo, Y. H. (2024). This country is Loveable: A model of destination brand love considering consumption authenticity and social experience. *Journal of Destination Marketing & Management*, 32, 100878. DOI: 10.1016/j.jdmm.2024.100878

Jamil, K., Dunnan, L., Gul, R. F., Shehzad, M. U., Gillani, S. H. M., & Awan, F. H. (2022a). Role of social media marketing activities in influencing customer intentions: A perspective of a new emerging era. *Frontiers in Psychology*, 12, 808525. DOI: 10.3389/fpsyg.2021.808525 PMID: 35111111

Jamil, K., Hussain, Z., Gul, R. F., Shahzad, M. A., & Zubair, A. (2022b). The effect of consumer self-confidence on information search and share intention. *Information Discovery and Delivery*, 50(3), 260–274. DOI: 10.1108/IDD-12-2020-0155

Jiménez-Barreto, J., Rubio, N., & Campo, S. (2020). Destination brand authenticity: What an experiential simulacrum! A multigroup analysis of its antecedents and outcomes through official online platforms. *Tourism Management*, 77, 104022. DOI: 10.1016/j.tourman.2019.104022

Juliana, J., Syiva, A. N., Rosida, R., Permana, E., Zulfikar, R. M., Abduh, M., & Inomjon, Q. (2024). Revisit Intention Muslim Tourists to Halal Tourism in Yogyakarta: Analysis of Facilities, Promotion, Electronic Word of Mouth, and Religiosity. *Review of Islamic Economics and Finance*, 7(1), 1–22.

Khan, I., & Fatma, M. (2021). Online destination brand experience and authenticity: Does individualism-collectivism orientation matter? *Journal of Destination Marketing & Management*, 20, 100597. DOI: 10.1016/j.jdmm.2021.100597

Kim, S. I., Al-Ansi, A., Lee, J. S., Chua, B. L., Phucharoen, C., & Han, H. (2024). Wellness tourism experience and destination brand love. *Journal of Travel & Tourism Marketing*, 41(7), 988–1004. DOI: 10.1080/10548408.2024.2369752

Kumail, T., Qeed, M. A. A., Aburumman, A., Abbas, S. M., & Sadiq, F. (2022). How destination brand equity and destination brand authenticity influence destination visit intention: Evidence from the United Arab Emirates. *Journal of Promotion Management*, 28(3), 332–358. DOI: 10.1080/10496491.2021.1989540

Le, T. H., Novais, M. A., Arcodia, C., Berchtenbreiter, R., Humpe, A., & Nguyen, N. (2024). How authenticity in events fosters social sustainability: Towards an authenticity ecosystem and implications for destination management. *Tourism Management Perspectives*, 51, 101222. DOI: 10.1016/j.tmp.2024.101222

Lin, S., Xu, S., Liu, Y., & Zhang, L. (2024). Destination brand experience, brand positioning, and intention to visit: A multi-destination comparison study. *Journal of Vacation Marketing*, 30(3), 599–614. DOI: 10.1177/13567667231155646

Lonardi, S., Scholl-Grissemann, U., Peters, M., & Messner, N. (2024). Leveraging minority language in destination online marketing: Evidence from Alta Badia, Italy. *Journal of Destination Marketing & Management*, 31, 100857. DOI: 10.1016/j.jdmm.2024.100857

Loureiro, S. M. C. (2020). How does the experience and destination authenticity influence "affect"? *Anatolia*, 31(3), 449–465. DOI: 10.1080/13032917.2020.1760903

Majeed, S., Zhou, Z., & Kim, W. G. (2024). Destination brand image and destination brand choice in the context of health crisis: Scale development. *Tourism and Hospitality Research*, 24(1), 134–151. DOI: 10.1177/14673584221126798

Praswati, A. N., Wardani, N. M., & Rohim, M. (2021). The Impact of Online Destination Brand Experience, Destination Brand Authenticity and Tourist Destination Image on Behavioral Intentions. *Journal of Indonesian Tourism and Development Studies*, 9(3), 145–152. DOI: 10.21776/ub.jitode.2021.009.03.01

Qing, W., Safeer, A. A., & Khan, M. S. (2024). Influence of social media communication on consumer purchase decisions: Do luxury hotels value perceived brand authenticity, prestige, and familiarity? *Journal of Hospitality and Tourism Technology*, 15(3), 465–478. DOI: 10.1108/JHTT-09-2023-0282

Rini, E. S., Rombe, E., & Tarigan, M. I. (2024). Brand destination loyalty: The antecedents of destination brand experience. *Cogent Business & Management*, 11(1), 2320992. DOI: 10.1080/23311975.2024.2320992

Shang, W., Yuan, Q., & Chen, N. (2020). Examining structural relationships among brand experience, existential authenticity, and place attachment in slow tourism destinations. *Sustainability (Basel)*, 12(7), 2784. DOI: 10.3390/su12072784

Tanaka, S., Kim, C., Takahashi, H., & Nishihara, A. (2024). Impact of brand authenticity on word-of-mouth for tourism souvenirs. *Cogent Business & Management*, 11(1), 2290222. DOI: 10.1080/23311975.2023.2290222

Teng, H. Y., & Chen, C. Y. (2020). Enhancing celebrity fan-destination relationship in film-induced tourism: The effect of authenticity. *Tourism Management Perspectives*, 33, 100605. DOI: 10.1016/j.tmp.2019.100605

Wang, D., Shen, C. C., Tseng, T. A., & Lai, C. Y. (2024). What is the most influential authenticity of beliefs, places, or actions on the pilgrimage tourism destination attachment? *Sustainability (Basel)*, 16(1), 431. DOI: 10.3390/su16010431

Yuliana, Y., Rini, E. S., Situmorang, S. H., & Silalahi, A. S. (2023). Mediating role of authenticity in the relationship between destination image and destination loyalty. *Innovative Marketing*, 19(4), 14–25. DOI: 10.21511/im.19(4).2023.02

Zhou, Z., Wang, Y., & Zhou, N. (2023). Effects of multidimensional destination brand authenticity on destination brand well-being: The mediating role of self-congruence. *Current Issues in Tourism*, 26(21), 3532–3546. DOI: 10.1080/13683500.2022.2134985

Chapter 5
Destination Branding and Luxury Experiences in the Digital Age

Mario Sierra Martin
https://orcid.org/0009-0004-1044-1851
Universidad de Málaga, Spain

Marisol de Brito Correia
https://orcid.org/0000-0002-1788-6114
University of Algarve, Portugal

Nelson da Silva deMatos
https://orcid.org/0000-0002-6263-5007
University of Algarve, Portugal

Álvaro Díaz Caquero
https://orcid.org/0000-0001-7396-1003
Universidad de Málaga, Spain

Pilar Alarcón Urbistondo
Universidad de Málaga, Spain

ABSTRACT

In an era where the digital image of a destination can be as influential as actual experiences, this chapter will evaluate how Spain and Portugal use digital platforms to cultivate and promote their identities as luxury destinations. Through a methodology that combines quantitative and qualitative analysis, the effectiveness of the digital marketing techniques employed will be examined, including content management on social media, user interaction, and the adaptation of marketing

DOI: 10.4018/979-8-3693-6700-1.ch005

strategies to changes in consumer preferences and behaviours. Additionally, our research leverages user-generated content, specifically comments extracted from TripAdvisor, to gauge perceptions of luxury hotels in both countries. By analyzing these comments, we gain insights into customer satisfaction, expectations, and the overall reputation of the hotels. This comprehensive approach allows us to assess the strategies deployed by these destinations and their real-world impact on the luxury tourism market.

INTRODUCTION: SIGNIFICANCE OF RESEARCH IN THE CONTEXT OF LUXURY TOURISM

Digitalization has usefully matured to adapt to modern times. This has revolutionized the panorama and the rules of the game in the tourism sector. It has been mainly in the last decades that the category has been transformed most notably as, in addition to the advances and modifications developed, there has also been a greater awareness of this segment by society (Cheng et al., 2023; Cuomo et al., 2021). We could thus affirm that both tourist destinations and travelers have changed not only the way they communicate, but also the way they promote themselves, plan trips, live experiences, share their opinions, drawing more inspiration from a concept of smart destinations through the use of technological tools to improve both the visitor experience and the quality of service (Sharmin et al., 2015).

With the democratization of Internet access and its widespread use by society as a whole through mobile devices, tourists have at their fingertips all kinds of real-time information on destinations, hotels, tourist attractions, etc. (Kumar et al. 2023). This factor has propelled the market penetration of digital platforms such as social networks, where there is a meeting point between different travelers looking to share experiences and recommend other users about their stay and accommodation.

There are a multitude of different platforms on the market, with TripAdvisor and Booking.com being the most popular worldwide. These tools have become fundamental for decision making in travel planning (Martin-Fuentes et al., 2020). Travelers can read reviews and opinions of other travelers who relate their hotel stay detailing their opinions about each of the services offered by the hotels. It is in this way that these platforms have become safe tools for other users, who, through their mobile devices and before committing to a reservation, browse to see the opinions and comments of other users in search of the best option for their stay. This democratization of information has empowered tourists, which in turn has raised the quality standards of hotels as they are continually exposed by their travelers. Thanks to these platforms, more transparency, authenticity and quality in tourism experiences are now expected (Madrigal-Moreno et al., 2020).

The manner the aforementioned travelers interact has evolved significantly due to the aforementioned digitalization of the industry. Global tourists use the Internet as their principal source of information to plan and book their trips. This is in addition to the comparison of different opinions among the user community (Vallejo et al.,2017). Before making their final purchase decision, 90% of consumers consider electronic word of mouth (eWOM) (Akhtar et al., 2019). In this way, customers can make sounder decisions quickly and effectively thanks to this immediate accessibility to a variety of experiences and opinions of other users who have already had contact with these companies. Therefore, from a marketing point of view, effective online reputation management has become essential for hotel establishments and tourist destinations. In such a competitive market, proactively managing online reviews and comments not only has a positive impact on tourists' booking decisions, but also allows destinations to meet the progressively demanding expectations of voyagers.

Nevertheless, scaling attendance quality in the tourism sector, especially in luxury hotels, can be complicated by its intangible and subjective nature. Whereas online reviews supply us with invaluable information about guests' experiences, interpreting this data requires special care and caution. Personal expectations and personal observations play a decisive role in the assessment of service quality. This means that the same hotel can receive very different ratings depending on the individual experience of each guest. On account of that it is of particular interest to have analytical methods to identify meaningful patterns of behavior due to the large amounts of data generated on these digital platforms.

In the strongly competitive hotel segment, quality has become a crucial component for both large and smaller companies. Customer demand for quality service has increased due to factors such as adventure tourism, collaborative tourism, interest in the environment and the request for unique experiences (Rabadán-Martín et al., 2019). This similarly means that hotel companies can also provide a catalogue of experiences to complete their guests' journey. This increase in competition, which has been on the rise for decades, has led hotel companies to recognize quality as an important origin of competitive advantage, which is why guest reviews have become even more relevant.

Travelers can not only quickly access a wide range of experiences and reviews from other users through the use of digital platforms such as TripAdvisor and Booking.com, but they can also effortlessly compare a variety of accommodation preferences before making booking decisions and can also rely on real feedback from other guests. As a result, the online reputation of hotels has had a significant impact on the brand image of a destination; this has a direct impact on the preferences and decisions of luxury tourists (Kladou & Eleni Mavragani, 2015). Therefore, a key strategy to ensure a lasting competitive advantage in a globalized and demanding market is the ability of destinations and hotel establishments to effectively succeed in their digital presence and proactively respond to reviews and comments.

In an era where the digital image of a destination can be as prominent as the actual experiences, this chapter will assess how Spain and Portugal use digital platforms to cultivate and promote their identities as luxury destinations. Through a methodology that combines quantitative and qualitative analysis, it will examine the effectiveness of the digital marketing techniques employed, including social media content management, interaction with users and the adaptation of marketing strategies to changes in consumer preferences and behaviors.

Digitalization in the Tourism Category

Digitalization has completely modified the travel sector, transforming both site promotion and travel planning and enjoyment (Cuomo et al., 2021). By using the Internet to harness its power, digital technology has drastically changed the travel industry and thus improved the accessibility of travel planning and booking systems. The digital revolution has made a wealth of current knowledge available to customers, helping them to make educated and personalized selections.

Due to the rise of reviews in all sectors, online hotel booking companies such as Airbnb and Booking.com have made accommodation reviews more important as well as incorporating more booking options available to a larger audience, allowing visitors to quickly compare prices, read reviews and book from wherever being in the world (Balagué et al., 2016). The fact that digital platforms will account for 88% of travel bookings by 2022, as reported by Statista (2023), demonstrates the widespread use of these technologies in the business sector.

Social media in this regard plays an important role as it has enabled customers to share their opinions and experiences on a personal basis with the digital community (Curlin et al., 2019). All this makes for two-way communication in the sector allowing tourism businesses to interact directly with their customers, respond to comments and change their offers according to the feedback received. In recent years, there has been a trend towards personalizing the traveller experience thanks to artificial intelligence (AI) (García-Madurga & Grilló-Méndez, 2023). Companies can predict tourists' preferences and make personalized recommendations based on the analysis of usually large amounts of data. By resolving passengers' questions quickly and correctly, AI-powered virtual assistants and chatbots increase the efficiency of customer service, thereby improving consumer satisfaction and the travel experience (revfine.com, 2019).

Ultimately, digital has helped tourism businesses become more competitive and efficient, as well as how guests plan and enjoy their trips. For tourism destinations to remain interesting and relevant in the ever-changing global market, the adoption of digital technologies is essential.

The evolution of digital in tourism

Since the 1950s, hotels have been automating their operations to stay ahead of the curve and provide the best services. They have benefited from the global distribution systems of airlines to increase their global reach (Buhalis, 1998) to connect travelers from different parts of the world. In the 1990s, hotels were already digitizing and selling directly to customers through their own websites using a proprietary reservation system. When OTAs emerged, hotels started to use them as additional channels to simplify processes (Ackerman, 2016), until the hotel industry realized that OTACs increased hotel distribution costs.

Today, to join the hotel distribution battle in the digital environment, previously non-competing platforms such as Booking and TripAdvisor are expanding their business models by incorporating new systems that are revolutionizing the industry.

Thus, we can see how disruptors such as Airbnb and HomeAway, which have also used the collaborative economy, are now competing for a share of hotel occupancy and with a strong relationship based on their review ratings. The future is bright and there is a glimpse of how it can continue to digitize all its services with further disruptions such as blockchain and other technological innovations (Quimby, 2018).

Since its inception, digitization has led to improvements in online reputation management, an essential aspect of the tourism industry. In order to maintain a positive and competent image in the market, it is essential to efficiently manage these reviews and use the feedback to continuously improve services of record quality.

The impact of technology on consumer demeanor

The way consumers behave in the tourism sector has changed significantly thanks to technology, from pre-trip planning and booking to the destination experience (Shin & Jeong, 2022).

Changes in the accessibility of information have influenced both consumers and institutions. Social networks have incorporated a different form of communication, and the exchange of information and the importance of social networks have increased. In order to improve corporate reputation, it is interesting to conduct market research by assessing customer experience; these sources of information can provide ideal opportunities for marketing, branding, product development and positioning. At the same time, these platforms can help consumers to identify their needs, analyze their choices and guide other consumers (Mazzarol et al., 2007; Nardi et al., 2007; Gretzel & Yoo, 2008).

The emergence of many valuable applications for travelers and the creation of digital platforms that enable communication between customers and service providers has been driven primarily by the expansion of Internet access (Benaddi et al., 2024). It is therefore essential to understand how these technologies have affected consumers and how they enable them to access detailed information, share opinions and personalize their experiences.

Planning step.

Users often turn to social media for inspiration. For ideas about experiences and destinations, users often turn to trending social networks or influencers to share their point of view. Users can find both visual inspiration through photos and videos shared by other users, and emotional inspiration by discovering different places through the same photos and videos shared by other travelers on platforms such as Instagram, Pinterest and YouTube.

This first stage of travel planning is being disrupted by technology. Travelers can find and compare effective options for flights, accommodation and activities through online price comparison sites and online booking platforms. Search engines and mobile apps are tools and resources that help travelers plan every aspect of their trip accurately and conveniently.

Stage Booking Process.

The booking process has become almost entirely digital through the influence of platforms such as Booking.com, Airbnb and Expedia. In addition to providing greater transparency and trust, these platforms allow for quick and secure bookings. In addition, reviews from other users are plentiful, further incentivizing bookings.

Sharing experiences and feedback.

Technology allows users to express their opinions after the trip through platforms such as TripAdvisor. This feedback provides important information for tourism service providers to adapt and improve their offerings, and it is also useful for other travelers.

The constant influence of user reviews on customer behavior is evident, we can see how a large number of both positive and negative reviews are generated on a daily basis and that hotel companies really need to pay attention to maintain a good brand image.

- Customer satisfaction and personalization.

Personalizing the travel experience relies heavily on big data and artificial intelligence (AI), as we discussed earlier. By analyzing users' behavioral data and preferences, companies can provide individualized recommendations and services tailored to each customer's specific needs. AI-based virtual assistants and chatbots improve customer service and respond quickly and accurately to travelers' queries, increasing customer satisfaction and enhancing the travel experience, which can then translate into positive reviews in digital media.

Based on this, tourists can easily gain insight into their purchasing decisions by relying on feedback and information posted by other users on these platforms (Liu & Park, 2015). For this reason, it is important for tourism professionals to understand these stages and see at what stage each review occurred.

The impact of TripAdvisor reviews on consumers

TripAdvisor is an online review network that has transformed the way consumers evaluate and select tourism services that best suit their needs. These platforms provide a space for users to share their experiences, which in turn significantly influences the decisions of future travelers. The information provided in these reviews benefits businesses, managers and potential guests alike, allowing them to better understand consumer preferences and improve their offerings (Yilmaz, 2020).

In today's digital context, online reviews have become a critical component for consumers when booking hotels. Different age groups respond differently to review features, providing a unique opportunity for hotels to tailor their marketing strategies to the specific needs of each generation.

The literature has extensively explored the impact of these reviews, highlighting how both positive and negative comments can have a profound effect on the tourism industry. Numerous studies recognize that digital channels influence consumers and that their online behavior develops early (Law, 2006; Briggs et al., 2007; Chung & Buhalis, 2008; Yoo & Gretzel, 2009; Stringam et al., 2010).

Advanced review sites such as TripAdvisor are increasingly dependent on the ability of businesses to continuously update and improve their services due to the need for long-term sustainability and competitiveness, changing consumer demands and rapidly evolving technologies. TripAdvisor should continue to innovate, explore cutting-edge resources and drive value creation. To reach a global audience, it will be critical for the company to develop its social media capabilities, enhance its service offerings and optimize its use of mobile technology. In addition, by integrating rich travel content, the company can expand and enhance its production capabilities.

TripAdvisor's ability to educate its users and potential customers and significantly influence the thoughts and comments expressed has cemented its dominant position among travel blogs (Gretzel & Yoo, 2008; Dahlander & Gann, 2010).

The importance of tourism in Southern Europe

The economies of the Costa del Sol in Spain and the Algarve in Portugal, two of the most famous and popular places in Southern Europe, are heavily dependent on tourism. In addition to their favorable climate and natural beauty, these areas are characterized by a first-class tourist infrastructure, including a wide range of 5-star hotels.

With their significant contribution to the economic development and worldwide recognition of both regions as world-class tourist destinations, these luxury establishments play a key role in attracting tourists with high purchasing power.

The 5-star hotels have played a key role in the development of tourism on the Costa del Sol, especially in Malaga. Tourism in the province of Malaga has been a record year, with a notable increase in the supply of accommodation and a high overall demand, according to the 'Balance of the Tourism Year 2023'. Guests at these hotels are mainly from Nordic countries, Germany, France and the United Kingdom. To attract and retain these visitors and ensure that tourists' experiences are positive and satisfying, effective online reputation management through platforms such as TripAdvisor has been essential.

In Portugal, the luxury hotel sector has experienced a similar increase in the Algarve. British and German tourists have significantly increased bookings in 5-star hotels in this area. In compliance with the 'Bulletin of September 2019', luxury hotels in the Algarve have maintained a high occupancy rate and a prolonged average stay of tourists. Online reviews on sites such as TripAdvisor, which provide an honest and detailed assessment of the quality of service, are essential for tourists to decide on their accommodation, as they are on the Costa del Sol.

The relevance of 5-star hotels, both as representatives of the quality and luxury of these places, is evident in the comparison between the Costa del Sol and the Algarve. Proactive online reputation management and the ability to adapt to the changing demands of tourists are essential to maintain their competitiveness in the global market, as demonstrated by both markets. The impact of TripAdvisor reviews on the perception and selection of 5-star hotels in these two regions will be examined in detail. The implications for consumer behavior and the economic success of the destinations will be highlighted.

Tourism balance of the Costa del Sol hotel sector (Malaga)

There has been remarkable growth in the 5-star hotel sector in the Costa del Sol. According to the "Balance of the Tourism Year 2023", the regulated supply of tourist accommodation in the province of Malaga has reached record levels, with more than 584,000 beds available in December 2023, an increase of 14.7% over the previous year.

Five-star hotels have played a key role in this growth. These high-end establishments attract not only domestic tourists, but also a significant number of international visitors. In fact, the international market showed a remarkable increase, with a 19.8% increase in the number of international travelers and an 18.1% increase in international overnight stays compared to the previous year.

In terms of tourist origin, the main source markets for tourists staying in the Costa del Sol's 5-star hotels are the UK, Germany, France and the Nordic countries. These visitors not only represent a significant volume of voyagers, but also contribute to a high number of overnight stays, extending their stay to enjoy the region's diverse tourism offer.

To maintain and improve the competitiveness of these luxury hotels, the relevance of online reviews, especially on platforms such as TripAdvisor, is crucial. User reviews and ratings significantly influence the decisions of future guests. The experiences shared on these platforms not only provide an authentic assessment of service quality, but also help hotels identify areas for improvement and proactively respond to customer needs and expectations.

In summary, hotel tourism on the Costa del Sol, particularly in the 5-star segment, has experienced remarkable growth, driven by strong international demand and an increase in the supply of quality accommodation. Effective online reputation management through platforms such as TripAdvisor is essential to maintain this positive momentum, ensuring that the tourist experience remains satisfactory and attractive to new visitors.

Tourism balance of the hotel sector in the Algarve (Portugal)

In the Algarve tourism market in Portugal, 5-star hotels play a crucial role in attracting international tourists. The occupancy rate of 5-star hotels has increased significantly compared to previous years, reaching an average of 87.9% in September 2019, according to the Boletim de September 2019. This growth highlights the importance and high demand for luxury accommodation in the region.

Tourists visiting 5-star hotels in the Algarve are mainly from the UK, followed by Germany, Portugal and other European countries. In terms of overnight stays, the British account for the largest share with 32.7% of hotel nights, followed by the Portuguese with 21.0%, the Germans with 10.1% and the Irish with 6.7%. These figures reflect the Algarve's heavy reliance on the northern and central European source markets, in particular the UK and Germany, to fill its high-quality accommodation.

The increase in occupancy of 5-star hotels also translates into an increase in the number of overnight stays.

The average length of stay per person in these hotels was 4.7 nights, with Dutch and Belgian tourists staying the longest at 6.1 and 5.8 nights respectively. These stay patterns are indicative of a tourism that is not only looking for quality and luxury, but also for extended experiences in the destination.

The importance of online reviews, especially on platforms such as TripAdvisor, is crucial for 5-star hotels in the Algarve. User reviews and ratings have a significant impact on the decisions of future guests. Shared experiences provide an authentic and detailed assessment of service quality, helping other travelers to make informed decisions. In addition, effective online reputation management enables hotels to address negative comments in a constructive manner, thereby improving overall perception and customer satisfaction.

In summary, 5-star hotels in the Algarve have experienced growth in occupancy and room nights, driven by strong international demand, particularly from British and German tourists. Online reputation management through reviews on platforms such as TripAdvisor is fundamental to maintaining and building on this positive momentum. It ensures that tourists' experiences remain satisfactory and attractive to new holidaymakers.

Analyzing the mood of 5-star hotels in southern Spain and southern Portugal

A sentiment analysis of reviews of five-star hotels in southern Spain and southern Portugal is presented in this study. Ten hotels were selected from each region, and the most recent 25 reviews of each hotel were obtained from TripAdvisor, resulting in a total of 250 reviews for Southern Spain and 250 reviews for Southern Portugal, each with their respective titles. The study was carried out with data updated until June 2024.

For the descriptive data analysis, these were separated into review titles and review content, in order to study them separately. In each dataset (titles of reviews from Spain, content of reviews from Spain, titles of reviews from Portugal and content of reviews from Portugal), the respective tokenization of the data was performed for the sentiment analysis and the following analysis.

Table 1. Summary

Analysis	Software
Word Frequency and Word Cloud (Frequency)	KH coder3 and Python
Polarity of the Words	Python
Frequency of Words by Their Polarity (Negative or Positive)	Python
Co-occurrence network	KH coder3

Source: Own elaboration (2024)

Descriptive Analysis of 5 Five-Star Hotels in Southern Spain

Analysis of review titles:

The following descriptive analysis of the review titles of 10 five-star hotels in southern Spain begins by noting that the 5 most frequent words are hotel, great, experience, and best as shown in the following frequency graph and word cloud of repeated words:

Figure 1. Frequency graph in five-star hotels in titles. Southern Spain (Own elaboration, 2024)

Figure 2. Word cloud in titles. Southern Spain (Own elaboration, 2024)

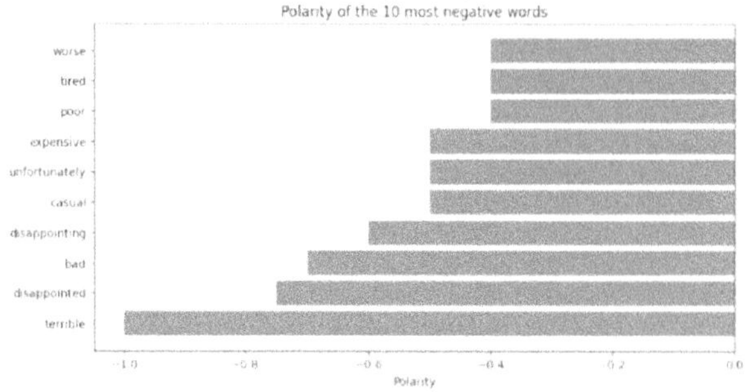

Now let's observe the polarity of the words in the titles: In the following graph, we can see that some of the words with negative polarity are terrible, bad, and expensive.

Figure 3. Negative polarity in titles. Southern Spain (Own elaboration, 2024)

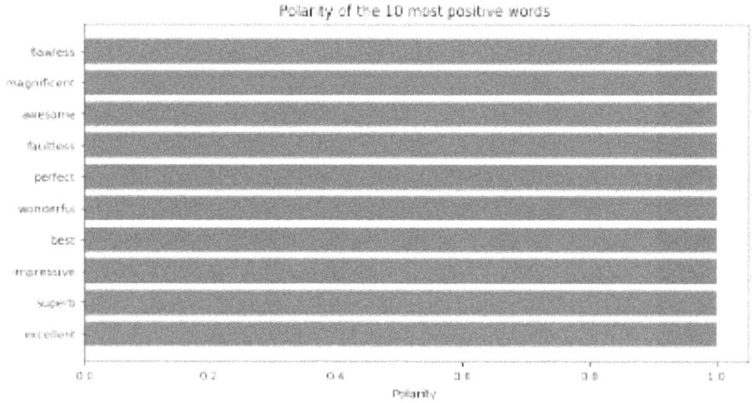

Some words with positive polarity are excellent, best, and perfect. See the following graph.

Figure 4. Positive polarity in titles. Southern Spain (Own elaboration, 2024)

List

#	Palabra	POS / Corr.	Frecuencia
1	hotel	Noun	25
2	excellent	Adj	8
3	great	Adj	8
4	location	Noun	6
5	staff	Noun	6
6	stay	Noun	6
7	fabulous	Adj	5
8	holiday	Noun	5
9	experience	Noun	4
10	family	Noun	4
11	good	Adj	4
12	service	Noun	4
13	superb	Adj	4
14	terrific	Adj	4
15	amazing	Adj	3
16	beautiful	Adj	3
17	friendly	Adj	3
18	lovely	Adj	3
19	relax	Verb	3
20	room	Noun	3
21	wonderful	Adj	3
22	[illegible]	Noun	2
23	algarve	Noun	2
24	beach	Noun	2
25	break	Noun	2
26	come	Verb	2
27	need	Verb	2
28	place	Noun	2
29	portugal	Adj	2
30	short	Adj	2
31	stay	Verb	2
32	time	Noun	2
33	[illegible]	Noun	2

To better visualize the most repeated positive and negative words, we can use a word cloud for each category as follows:

- Positive word cloud

Figure 5. Positive word cloud in titles. Southern Spain (Own elaboration, 2024)

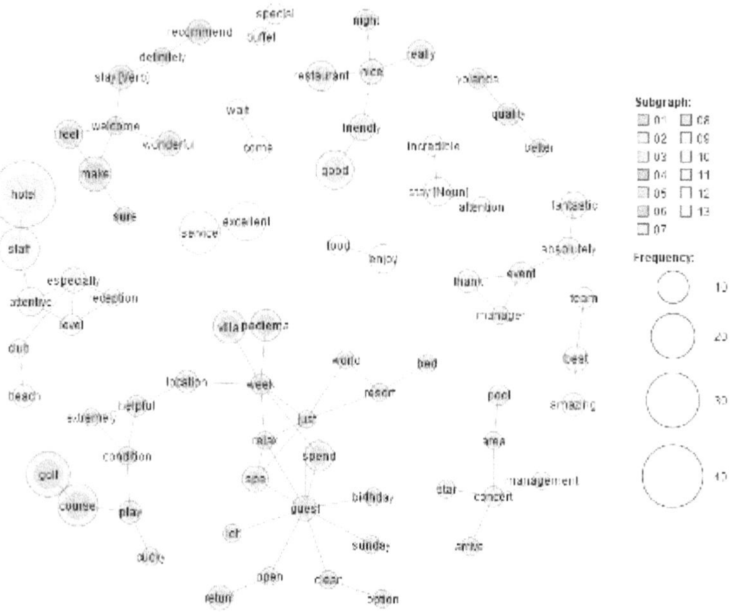

Figure 6. Negative word cloud in titles. Southern Spain (Own elaboration, 2024)

It is worth noting that words with the most positive polarity, such as excellent, best, superb and delicious, are among the most recurrent. This suggests that the positive review titles were written with a very positive sentiment. On the other hand, when looking at the most repeated negative words, the word terrible stands out, with a polarity score of -1. This means that the majority of negative titles contained this word, indicating that they were very negative. Finally, it is worth noting that the number of negative titles is small, as evidenced by the fact that the word "terrible" does not appear in the frequency graph of the 33 most mentioned words, indicating a minimal number of negative titles.

Co-occurrence network: next, we will have a graphical representation of which words are related, that is, which words have been written in the same title.

Figure 7. Co-occurrence network in titles. Southern Spain (Own elaboration, 2024)

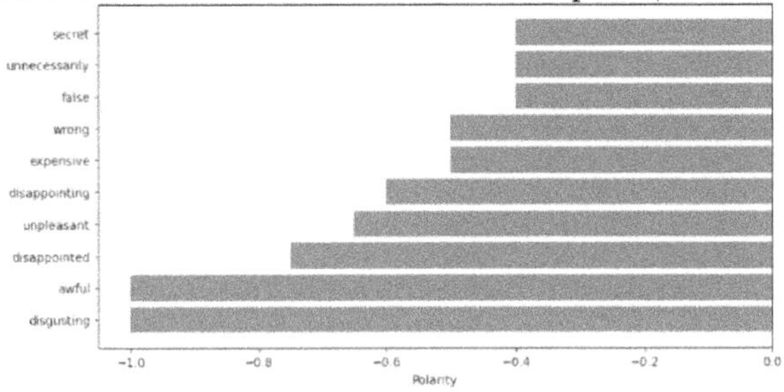

Noting that the review titles show that the hotel staff are friendly, we can see a relationship between friendly and staff. We can also see that bathroom is related to disappoint, indicating that there were titles that reviewed the bathrooms negatively. On the other hand, we can see that the word best is strongly associated with Marbella, showing that many comments attributed the five-star hotels in the Marbella area as the best, indicating overall satisfaction with the five-star hotels in Marbella.

- Analysis of review content:

the following descriptive analysis of the review content of 10 five-star hotels in southern Spain starts with the fact that the 5 most frequent words are hotel, golf, service and staff, as shown in the frequency graph and word cloud of repeated words below:

Figure 8. Analysis of review content. Southern Spain (Own elaboration, 2024)

List

#	Palabra	POS / Conj	Frecuencia
1	hotel	Noun	65
2	Great	ProperNoun	18
3	experience	Noun	16
4	best	Adj	14
5	excellent	Adj	14
6	Marbella	ProperNoun	14
7	service	Noun	14
8	staff	Noun	14
9	wonderful	Adj	14
10	stay	Noun	11
11	good	Adj	10
12	great	Adj	10
13	location	Noun	10
14	Malaga	ProperNoun	10
15	place	Noun	10
16	amazing	Adj	9
17	beautiful	Adj	8
18	Stay	ProperNoun	8
19	Hotel	ProperNoun	7
20	perfect	Adj	7
21	stay	Verb	7
22	friendly	Adj	6
23	Fabulous	ProperNoun	5
24	fantastic	Adj	5
25	nice	Adj	5
26	recommend	Verb	5
27	resort	Noun	5
28	star	Noun	5
29	superb	Adj	5
30	customer	Noun	4
31	EXCEPTIONAL	ProperNoun	4
32	Fantastic	ProperNoun	4
33	food	Noun	4

Figure 9. Word Cloud of review content. Southern Spain (Own elaboration, 2024)

Now let's look at the polarity of the words in the reviews: in the graph below, some of the words with negative polarity are disgusting, horrible and worst.

Figure 10. Polarity of the 10 most negative words of review content. Southern Spain (Own elaboration, 2024)

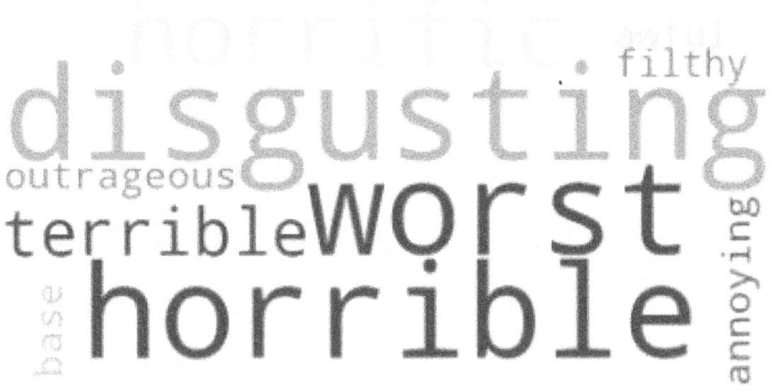

Some words with positive polarity are delightful, awesome, and impressed. See the following graph:

Figure 11. Polarity of the 10 most positive words of review content. Southern Spain (Own elaboration, 2024)

List

#	Palabra	POS / Conj	Frecuencia
1	hotel	Noun	45
2	golf	Noun	21
3	course	Noun	18
4	service	Noun	18
5	staff	Noun	18
6	room	Noun	16
7	excellent	Adj	15
8	good	Adj	15
9	great	Adj	12
10	make	Verb	12
11	villa	Noun	11
12	paderna	Noun	10
13	breakfast	Noun	9
14	place	Noun	9
15	restaurant	Noun	9
16	spend	Verb	9
17	attentive	Adj	8
18	enjoy	Verb	8
19	feel	Verb	8
20	stay	Noun	8
21	time	Noun	8
22	beautiful	Adj	7
23	fantastic	Adj	7
24	friendly	Adj	7
25	really	Adv	7
26	spa	Noun	7
27	best	Adj	6
28	come	Verb	6
29	especially	Adv	6
30	guest	Noun	6
31	nice	Adj	6
32	recommend	Verb	6
33	return	Verb	6

To better visualize the most repeated positive and negative words, we can use a word cloud for each category as follows:

- Positive word cloud

Figure 12. Positive word cloud of review content. Southern Spain (Own elaboration, 2024)

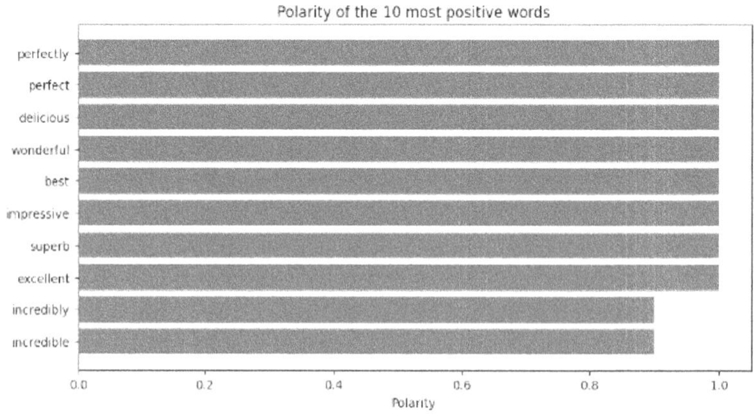

- Negative word cloud

Figure 13. Negative word cloud of review content. Southern Spain (Own elaboration, 2024)

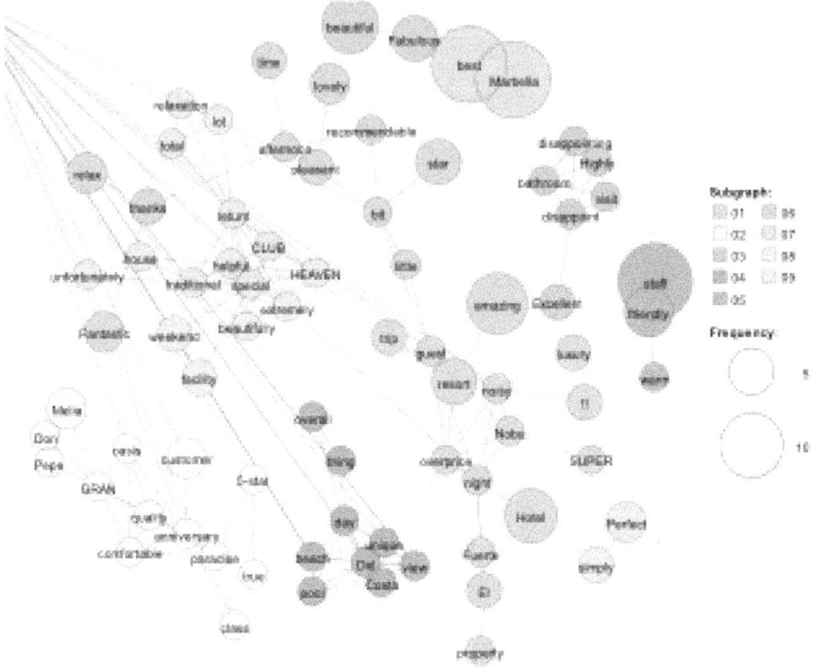

It can be seen that words with the most positive polarity, such as magnificent, delicious, exquisite and impressed, are among the most repeated. This is an indication that positive reviews are predominantly the result of very positive sentiments. On the other hand, the most repeated negative words include disgusting and horrible, which have a polarity of -1. This means that most negative reviews contained these words, which means that they were very negative. Finally, it's worth noting that the number of negative reviews is limited, as evidenced by the fact that the words disgusting and horrible do not appear in the frequency graph of the top 33 words, indicating a minimal number of negative reviews.

Network of co-occurrence: the next step is to have a look at the graph to see which words are related to each other, that is, which words have been in the same review.

Figure 14. Network of co-occurrence in the same review. Southern Spain (Own elaboration, 2024)

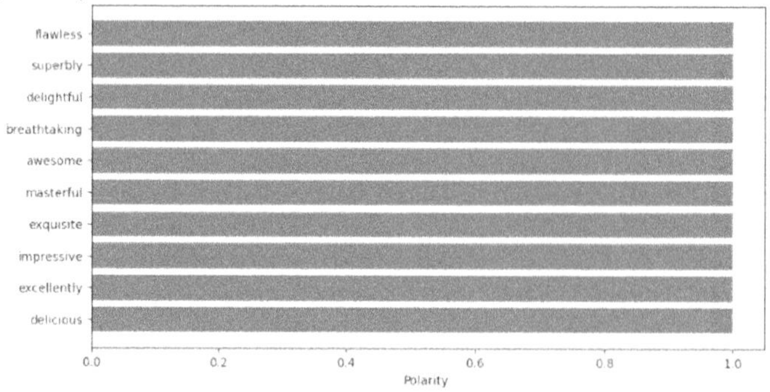

Let's look at the relationship between words like staff and reception with attentive or service and excellent, which shows good service and attention in general in the reviews. Also, the relationship between food and enjoy shows that the food in these restaurants is appealing. Note that there are no negative words with relationships, this shows that the service was generally excellent in the five-star hotels in southern Spain.

Descriptive analysis of 5-star hotel in southern Portugal

Analysis of review titles: the following descriptive analysis of the review titles of 10 five-star hotels in Southern Portugal starts with the observation that the 5 most frequent words are hotel, excellent, great and location, as shown in the frequency graph and word cloud of repeated words below:

Figure 15. Frequency graph in titles. Southern Portugal (Own elaboration, 2024)

Figure 16. Word cloud in titles. Southern Portugal (Own elaboration, 2024)

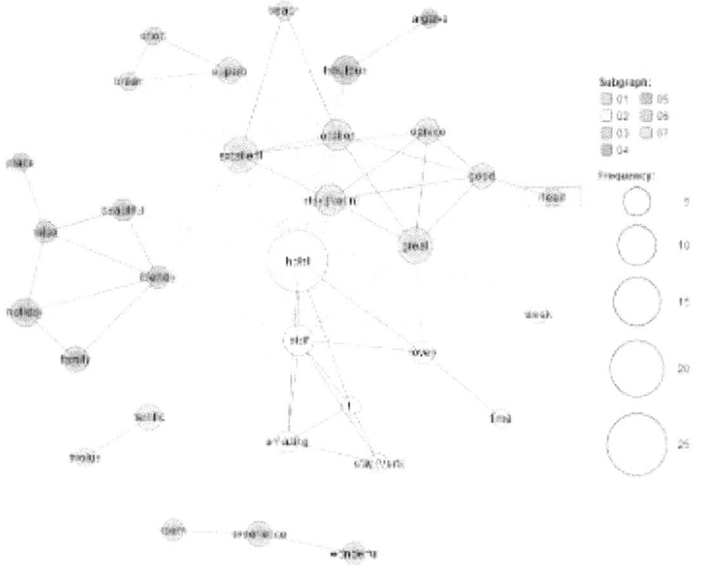

Now let's look at the polarity of the words in the headings: Let's see in the following graph that some of the words with negative polarity are disgusting, awfully disappointed.

Figure 17. Polarity of the 10 most negative words in titles. Southern Portugal (Own elaboration, 2024)

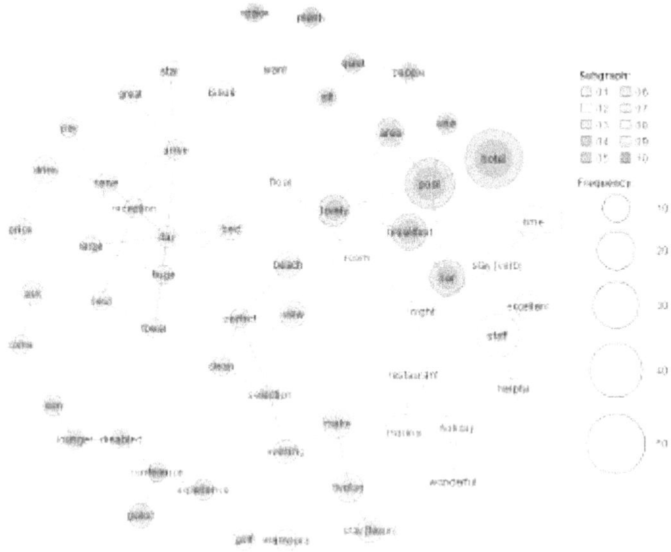

Some words with positive polarity are flawless, awesome, and magnificent. See the following graph.

Figure 18. Polarity of the 10 most positive words in titles. Southern Portugal (Own elaboration, 2024)

To better visualize the most repeated positive and negative words, we can use a word cloud for each category as follows:

- Positive word cloud:

Figure 19. Positive word cloud in titles. Southern Portugal (Own elaboration, 2024)

- Negative word cloud:

Figure 20. Negative word cloud in titles. Southern Portugal (Own elaboration, 2024)

We observe that words with the most positive polarity, such as superb, excellent and flawless, are among the most frequently repeated. This is an indication that positive reviews are predominantly the outcome of very positive sentiment. On the other hand, the most repeated negative words are disgusting and awful, which have a polarity of -1. This means that most negative reviews contain these words, which means that they were very negative. Finally, it is worth noting that the number of negative reviews is small, as evidenced by the fact that the words disgusting and awful do not appear in the frequency graph of the 33 most mentioned words, indicating a minimal number of negative reviews.

Co-occurrence network: in the next step, we will graphically examine which words are related to each other, i.e. which words appear in the same title.

Figure 21. Co-occurrence network in the same title (Own elaboration, 2024)

We can distinguish a relationship between amazing and staff, indicating a positive predilection in the titles regarding the staff, as well as a similar attitude towards the words wonderful and room. On the other hand, there are no negative words, which shows that the titles were generally positive.

Analysis of the reviews:

The following indicative analysis of the review content of 10 five-star hotels in southern Portugal begins by noting that the 5 most frequent words are hotel, pool, room, and staff, as shown in the following frequency graph and word cloud of repeated words:

Figure 22. Analysis of the review content of 10 five-star hotels in southern Portugal (Own elaboration, 2024)

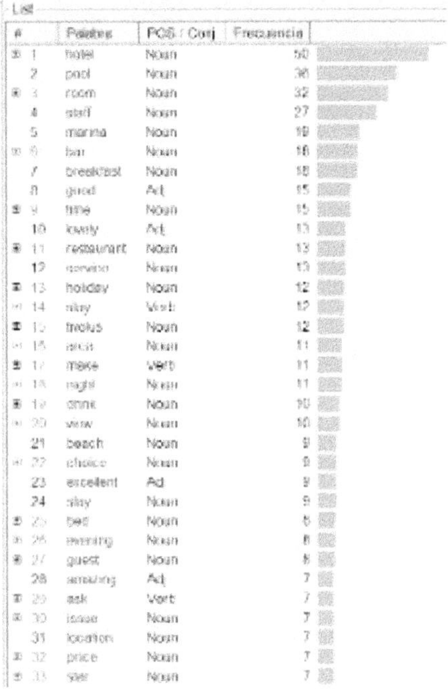

List

#	Palabra	POS / Conj	Frecuencia
1	hotel	Noun	50
2	pool	Noun	38
3	room	Noun	32
4	staff	Noun	27
5	marina	Noun	19
6	bar	Noun	16
7	breakfast	Noun	16
8	good	Adj	15
9	time	Noun	15
10	lovely	Adj	13
11	restaurant	Noun	13
12	service	Noun	13
13	holiday	Noun	12
14	stay	Verb	12
15	[illegible]	Noun	12
16	[illegible]	Noun	11
17	make	Verb	11
18	night	Noun	11
19	drink	Noun	10
20	view	Noun	10
21	beach	Noun	9
22	choice	Noun	9
23	excellent	Adj	9
24	stay	Noun	9
25	bed	Noun	8
26	evening	Noun	8
27	guest	Noun	8
28	amazing	Adj	7
29	ask	Verb	7
30	issue	Noun	7
31	location	Noun	7
32	price	Noun	7
33	star	Noun	7

Figure 23. Word cloud of the review content. Southern Portugal (Own elaboration, 2024)

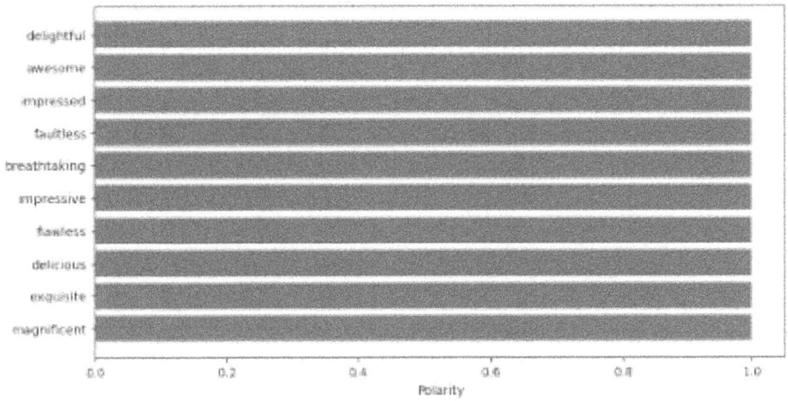

Now let's have a look at the polarity of the words in the reviews: In the following graph, we can see that some of the words with negative polarity are terrible, miserable, and dreadful.

Figure 24. Negative polarity of the review content. Southern Portugal (Own elaboration, 2024)

Figure 1: Summary Table

Analysis	Software
Word Frequency and Word Cloud (Frequency)	KH coder3 and Python
Polarity of the Words	Python
Frequency of Words by Their Polarity (Negative or Positive)	Python
Co-occurrence network	KH coder3

Source: Own elaboration (2024)

Some words with positive polarity are delightful, awesome, and impressed. See the following graph:

Figure 25. Positive polarity of the review content. Southern Portugal (Own elaboration, 2024)

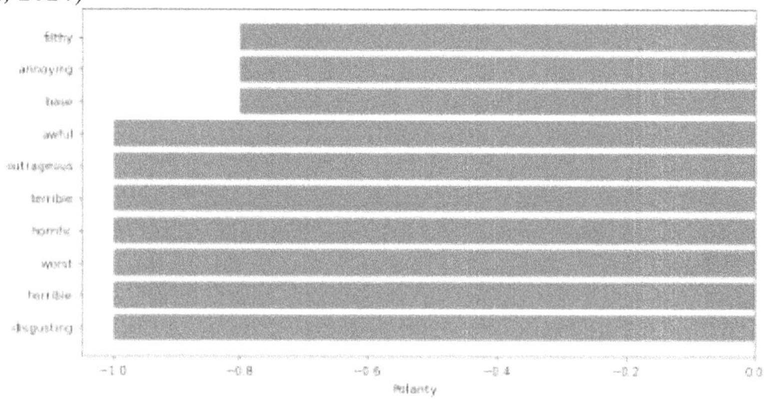

To better visualize the most repeated positive and negative words, we can use a word cloud for each category as follows:

- Positive word cloud:

Figure 26. Positive word cloud of the review content. Southern Portugal (Own elaboration, 2024)

- Negative word cloud:

Figure 27. Positive word cloud of the review content. Southern Portugal (Own elaboration, 2024)

We observe that words with the most positive polarity, such as magnificent, delicious, and flawless, are among the most repeated. This indicates that positive reviews were predominantly written with a very positive sentiment. On the other hand, the most repeated negative words include worst and horrific, which have a polarity score of -1.

In other words, the majority of negative reviews had these words in them, which is an indication that they were very negative. Finally, it is worth noting that the number of negative reviews is small, as evidenced by the fact that the words worst and horrific do not appear in the frequency graph of the top 33 words, indicating a minimal number of negative reviews.

Co-occurrence network: The next step is to examine graphically which words are related to each other, that is, which words have appeared in the same review.

Figure 28. Co-occurrence network which words in the same review. Southern Portugal (Own elaboration, 2024)

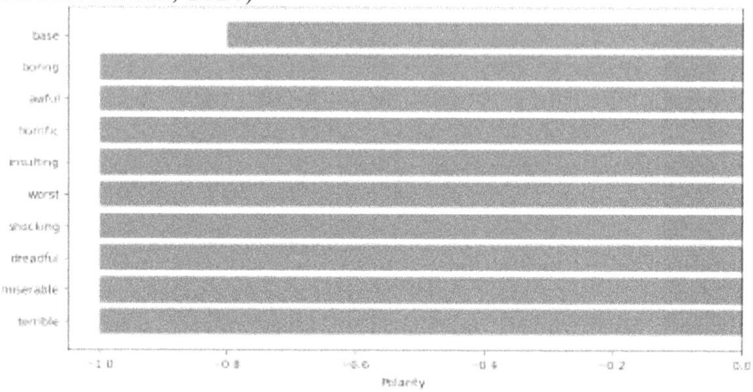

Figure 29. Negative word cloud of the review content. Southern Portugal (Own elaboration, 2024)

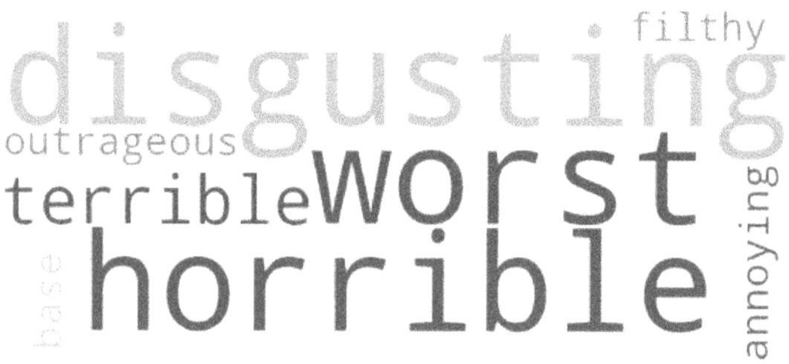

We visualize a relationship between words such as staff with excellent and helpful, as well as the relationship between restaurant and wonderful. These connections generally indicate that the five-star hotels in southern Portugal are highly rated attractions according to their users.

FUTURE RESEARCH DIRECTIONS

Luxury tourism, especially in destinations such as the Costa del Sol and the Algarve, is set to change as consumer expectations and technology continue to evolve. For a deeper understanding of this phenomenon, it is essential to identify potential areas for future research and analysis of emerging trends that could have an impact on the sector in the coming years.

Customer experience innovation is a fundamental aspect of business strategy today.

One of the key research areas focuses on customer experience innovation. The increasing use of emerging technologies such as Artificial Intelligence (AI), Virtual Reality (VR) and Augmented Reality (AR) has created great potential to more effectively enhance and personalize the customer experience in high-end hotels. Future research could focus on the effective integration of these technologies into hotel services to create more immersive and satisfying experiences.

Sustainability and responsible travel

The concept of sustainability in the tourism industry refers to the ability to meet the current needs of tourists and the industry without compromising the ability of future generations to meet their own needs. Responsible tourism involves minimizing negative impacts on the environment, culture and local economy, while at the same time lessening negative effects on the environment, culture and local economy.

Another important aspect to consider is sustainability and responsible tourism. In the current context of growing concern about climate change and environmental protection, it is interesting to note that superior hotels are implementing measures that promote sustainability. Future research could investigate best practices to reduce hotel carbon emissions, increase energy efficiency and promote sustainable tourism while ensuring service quality. Assessing the impact of sustainable practices on consumer perceptions and booking decisions will be critical to the successful implementation of these initiatives.

The impact of online reviews and digital reputation

Further research into the dynamics of digital interactions on platforms such as TripAdvisor is essential given the significant impact of online reviews in this context. Future research could analyse the evolution of reputation management strategies in the context of new technologies. It could also explore how hotels can use advanced data and analytics to more effectively anticipate and respond to trends in consumer reviews. Investigating the impact of influencers and digital marketing strategies on building the online reputation of high-end hotels is a promising area of research.

Personalization and big data

Online personalization has become a key strategy for businesses in the digital age. The use of big data has enabled organizations to collect and analyze large amounts of user data, allowing them to personalize their products and services according to individual consumer preferences and behaviors.

Personalization remains a fundamental aspect of the luxury travel industry. Hotels can deliver highly individualized experiences by using big data to collect and scrutinize information about customer preferences and behaviors. Future research could focus on how hotels can ethically and effectively use the information collected to anticipate customer needs and increase guest satisfaction.

New Business Models

Technological advances have led to the emergence of new business models in today's business environment.

It is crucial to explore new business models in the high-end hotel industry. In this new context, it is crucial to analyze the ability of 5-star hotels to adjust and remain competitive in the face of the emergence of new modalities such as collaborative tourism and shared accommodation platforms. Research could focus on the integration of complementary services, the generation of unique experiences and cooperation with other industry sectors in order to provide more attractive and varied tourism packages.

CONCLUSIONS

In conclusion, this study provides an in-depth analysis of how Spain and Portugal utilize digital platforms to establish their identities as luxury destinations, emphasizing the impact of online reviews and user-generated content on the perception of luxury hotels. This analysis is particularly valuable for marketing professionals and hotel managers who work on enhancing the brand image as a tourism destination. By examining data from platforms such as TripAdvisor, the research offers valuable and real-world insights into customer satisfaction, expectations, and the overall reputation of these establishments. The findings underscore the critical role that effective online reputation management plays in influencing booking decisions and maintaining a competitive edge in the luxury tourism sector. Moreover, the study reveals that while positive reviews significantly enhance a hotel's reputation, negative feedback must be addressed proactively to mitigate its potential impact. This comprehensive approach not only evaluates the effectiveness of digital marketing strategies but also demonstrates their tangible effects on the luxury tourism market in Southern Europe.

Future Decisions

Based on the findings, it is recommended that luxury hotels in Spain and Portugal continue investing in robust strategies for managing their online reputation, leveraging advanced data analytics to effectively anticipate and respond to consumer reviews. The integration of emerging technologies such as artificial intelligence and big data will be crucial in providing personalized and immersive experiences that meet the evolving expectations of high-end travelers. Additionally, sustainable tourism practices should be prioritized to align with the growing consumer demand for environmentally responsible options. These strategies will not only enhance guest satisfaction but also strengthen the position of these destinations in the global luxury tourism market. Future research should focus on exploring new business models that incorporate collaborative tourism and shared accommodation platforms, as well as the influence of digital influencers on destination branding. This approach will enable the sector to remain adaptable and resilient in a rapidly changing digital landscape.

REFERENCES

Akhtar, N., Sun, J., Akhtar, M. N., & Chen, J. (2019). How attitude ambivalence from conflicting online hotel reviews affects consumers' behavioural responses: The moderating role of dialecticism☆. *Journal of Hospitality and Tourism Management*, 41, 28–40. DOI: 10.1016/j.jhtm.2019.09.003

Al Balushi, M. K., Soliman, M., Kennedy, R. E., & Palla, A. H. (2024). Shifts in tourism knowledge: HEI contributions to destination branding and economic development. In *Shifts in Knowledge Sharing and Creativity for Business Tourism* (pp. 145–162). IGI Global.

Arriaga Navarrete, R., & González Pérez, C. R. (2019). The tourism sector and its productive linkages: An input-output analysis and endogenous consumption. *Revista de economía*, 36(92), 94–128.

Balagué, C., Martin-Fuentes, E., & Jesús Gómez, M. (2016a). Reliability of authenticated versus non-authenticated hotel reviews: TripAdvisor and Booking.com case. *Cuadernos de Turismo*, 38, 63–82. DOI: 10.6018/turismo.38.271351

Balagué, C., Martin-Fuentes, E., & Jesús Gómez, M. (2016b). Reliability of authenticated versus non-authenticated hotel reviews: TripAdvisor and Booking.com case. *Cuadernos de Turismo*, 38, 63–82. DOI: 10.6018/turismo.38.271351

Barnes, , Mattsson, J., & Sørensen, F. (2014). Destination brand experience and visitor behavior: Testing a scale in the tourism context. *Annals of Tourism Research*, 48, 121–139. DOI: 10.1016/j.annals.2014.06.002

Buhalis, D., & Main, H. (1998). Information technology in peripheral small and medium hospitality enterprises: Strategic analysis and critical factors. *International Journal of Contemporary Hospitality Management*, 10(5), 198–202. DOI: 10.1108/09596119810227811

Cheng, X., Xue, T., Yang, B. and Ma, B. (2023), "A digital transformation approach in hospitality and tourism research", International Journal of Contemporary Hospitality Management, Vol. ahead-of-print No. ahead-of-print, .DOI: 10.1108/IJCHM-06-2022-0679

Cuomo, M. T., Tortora, D., Foroudi, P., Giordano, A., Festa, G., & Metallo, G. (2021). Digital transformation and tourist experience co-design: Big social data for planning cultural tourism. *Technological Forecasting and Social Change*, 162, 120345. DOI: 10.1016/j.techfore.2020.120345

Curlin, T., Jaković, B., & Miloloža, I. (2019). Twitter usage in Tourism: Literature Review. In Business Systems Research (Vol. 10, Issue 1, pp. 102–119). Sciendo. DOI: 10.2478/bsrj-2019-0008

da Silva, M. B. D. O., Moreira, M. C. D. S., de Souza, Á. G. R., Arruda, D. D. O., & Mariani, M. A. P. (2019). Gastronomy on TripAdvisor: what tourists comment about restaurants in Bonito-MS-Brazil?.

Filieri, R., Acikgoz, F., Ndou, V., & Dwivedi, Y. (2021). Is TripAdvisor still relevant? The influence of review credibility, review usefulness, and ease of use on consumers' continuance intention. *International Journal of Contemporary Hospitality Management*, 33(1), 199–223. DOI: 10.1108/IJCHM-05-2020-0402

García-Madurga, M. Á., & Grilló-Méndez, A. J. (2023). Artificial Intelligence in the Tourism Industry: An Overview of Reviews. In Administrative Sciences (Vol. 13, Issue 8). Multidisciplinary Digital Publishing Institute (MDPI). https://doi.org/ DOI: 10.3390/admsci13080172

Gretzel, U., & Yoo, K. H. (2008). Use and Impact of Online travel Reviews. *Information and Communication Technologies in Tourism*, 1(1), 35–46. DOI: 10.1007/978-3-211-77280-5_4

Hassan, . (2010). Perception of destination branding measures: A case study of Alexandria destination marketing organizations. *International Journal of Euro-Mediterranean Studies*, 3(2), 269–288.

Herrero Amo, M. D., & De Stefano, M. C. (2019). Public–private partnership as an innovative approach for sustainable tourism in Guanacaste, Costa Rica. *Worldwide Hospitality and Tourism Themes*, 11(2), 130–139. DOI: 10.1108/WHATT-11-2018-0078

Hudson, S., & Ritchie, J. B. (2009). Branding a memorable destination experience. The case of 'Brand Canada'. *International Journal of Tourism Research*, 11(2), 217–228. DOI: 10.1002/jtr.720

Jaboob, . (2023). Digital Technologies as a Key Driver of Sustainable Global Higher Education. In *Technologies for Sustainable Global Higher Education* (pp. 77–94). Auerbach Publications. DOI: 10.1201/9781003424543-5

Kladou, S., & Mavragani, E. (2015). Assessing destination image: An online marketing approach and the case of TripAdvisor. *Journal of Destination Marketing & Management*, 4(3), 187–193.

Koncul, N. (2012). Wellness: A new mode of tourism. In Ekonomska Istrazivanja (Vol. 25, Issue 2, pp. 525–534). Faculty of Economics and Tourism "Dr. Mijo Mirkovic." https://doi.org/DOI: 10.1080/1331677X.2012.11517521

Liu, Z., & Park, S. (2015). What makes a useful online review? Implication for travel product websites. *Tourism Management*, 47(1), 140–151. DOI: 10.1016/j.tourman.2014.09.020

Londoño, M. P. L., & Hernandez-Maskivker, G. (2016). Green practices in hotels: The case of the GreenLeaders Program from TripAdvisor. *Sustainable Tourisim VII*, 1, 1–13. DOI: 10.2495/ST160011

Madrigal-moreno, S., Madrigal-moreno, F., & Juárez-lópez, B. (2020). Internet y redes sociales en la construcción de la reputación digital de la organización del sector turístico. Revista Espacios, 41(14).

Martin-Fuentes, E., Mateu, C., & Fernandez, C. (2020). The more the merrier? Number of reviews versus score on TripAdvisor and Booking.com. *International Journal of Hospitality & Tourism Administration*, 21(1), 1–14. DOI: 10.1080/15256480.2018.1429337

Mazzarol, T., Sweeney, J., & Soutar, G. (2007). Conceptualizing word-of-mouth activity, triggers and conditions: an exploratory study.

Morando, M., & Platania, S. (2022). Luxury Tourism Consumption in the Accommodation Sector: The Mediation Role of Destination Brand Love for Potential Tourists. *Sustainability (Basel)*, 14(7), 4007. Advance online publication. DOI: 10.3390/su14074007

Motoki, K., Park, J., Pathak, A., & Spence, C. (2023). Creating luxury brand names in the hospitality and tourism sector: The role of sound symbolism in destination branding. *Journal of Destination Marketing & Management*, 30, 100815. Advance online publication. DOI: 10.1016/j.jdmm.2023.100815

Nardi, B. A., Schiano, D. J., Gumbrecht, M., & Swartz, L. (2007). Why we blog. *Communications of the ACM*, 47(12), 41–46. DOI: 10.1145/1035134.1035163

Rabadán-Martín, I., Aguado-Correa, F., & Padilla-Garrido, N. (2019). Facing new challenges in rural tourism: Signaling quality via website. *Information Technology & Tourism*, 21(4), 559–576. DOI: 10.1007/s40558-019-00157-y

Sharmin, F., Sultan, MT, Badulescu, D., Badulescu, A., Borma, A. y Li, B. (2021), "Ecosistema de marketing de destino sostenible a través de las redes sociales basadas en teléfonos inteligentes: la perspectiva de aceptación de los consumidores",Sustainability, Vol.13No.4,2308, .DOI: 10.3390/su13042308

Shin, H. H., & Jeong, M. (2022). Redefining luxury service with technology implementation: The impact of technology on guest satisfaction and loyalty in a luxury hotel. *International Journal of Contemporary Hospitality Management*, 34(4), 1491–1514. DOI: 10.1108/IJCHM-06-2021-0798

Tuominen, P. (2011). The influence of TripAdvisor consumer-generated travel reviews on hotel performance.

Vallejo, G., Gonzalo, F., Rafael, M., Genaro, O., Nuria, M., & Fernando, C. (2017). *Usos, actitudes y tendencias del consumidor digital en la compra y consumo de viajes*. Observatorio Digital IAB Spain.

Van Laer, T., Edson Escalas, J., Ludwig, S., & Van Den Hende, E. A. (2019). What happens in Vegas stays on TripAdvisor? A theory and technique to understand narrativity in consumer reviews. *The Journal of Consumer Research*, 46(2), 267–285.

Wang, C. N., Tran, K. M., Huang, C. C., Wang, Y. H., & Dang, T. T. (2022). Supporting Luxury Hotel Recovered in Times of COVID-19 by Applying TRIZ Method: A Case Study in Taiwan. *Systems*, 10(2), 33. Advance online publication. DOI: 10.3390/systems10020033

Wichels, S. (2014). Nuevos desafíos en Relaciones Públicas 2.0: La creciente influencia de las plataformas de online review en Turismo / New Challenges in Public Relations 2.0: The growing influence of online review platforms in Tourism. DOI: 10.5783/RIRP-7-2014-12-197-216

Xiang, Z., Wöber, K., & Fesenmaier, D. R. (2008). Representation of the online tourism domain in search engines. *Journal of Travel Research*, 47(2), 137–150. DOI: 10.1177/0047287508321193

ADDITIONAL READING

Neves, M. S. (2019). EXPLORING CUSTOMER INTERACTION AND MANAGEMENT RESPONSE IN LUXURY HOSPITALITY THROUGH ONLINE REVIEWS IN SOCIAL MEDIA.

Park, J. Y., & Lee, H. E. (2024). How Consumer Photo Reviews and Online Platform Types Influence Luxury Hotel Booking Intentions Through Envy. *Journal of Travel Research*, 00472875241247317. Advance online publication. DOI: 10.1177/00472875241247317

Ríos-Martín, M. Á., Folgado-Fernández, J. A., Palos-Sánchez, P. R., & Castejón-Jiménez, P. (2020). The impact of the environmental quality of online feedback and satisfaction when exploring the critical factors for luxury hotels. *Sustainability (Basel)*, 12(1), 299. Advance online publication. DOI: 10.3390/su12010299

Song, J., Jai, T. M., & Li, X. (2020). Examining green reviews on TripAdvisor: Comparison between resort/luxury hotels and business/economy hotels. *International Journal of Hospitality & Tourism Administration*, 21(2), 165–187. DOI: 10.1080/15256480.2018.1464418

KEY TERMS AND DEFINITIONS:

Artificial Intelligence (AI): Artificial intelligence (AI) is a field of computer science that focuses on creating systems capable of performing tasks that normally require human intelligence. These tasks include speech recognition, decision making, language translation and data analysis. In the hospitality industry, AI is used to improve customer service through chatbots, personalize service recommendations and optimize internal operations.

Online Reputation: Online reputation refers to the public perception of a company or individual in the digital environment. This perception is influenced by the opinions and comments left by users on review platforms, social media and other websites. For luxury hotels, managing online reputation is crucial, as positive reviews can attract more customers, while negative reviews can deter potential guests. Online reputation directly affects consumers' trust and purchasing decisions.

Sustainable tourism: Sustainable tourism is an approach to tourism that seeks to minimize negative environmental, social and economic impacts while maximizing the well-being of local communities and the conservation of natural resources. This includes practices such as reducing carbon footprint, using resources efficiently, promoting local culture and ensuring economic benefits for host communities.

Virtual Reality (VR): Virtual reality (VR) is a technology that creates a simulated digital environment in which users can interact in an immersive way. In tourism, VR allows potential tourists to explore destinations and accommodation from the comfort of their homes, which can influence their booking decisions. Hotels can use VR to offer virtual tours of their facilities, thus enhancing the user experience and highlighting their services.

Chapter 6
Artificial Intelligence and Destination Branding

Maha Khamis Al Balushi
https://orcid.org/0000-0002-5897-9800
Sultan Qaboos University, Oman

Mohammad Soliman
https://orcid.org/0000-0002-9359-763X
Sultan Qaboos University, Oman

Mohammed S. Al Hosni
https://orcid.org/0009-0000-4069-1182
Sultan Qaboos University, Oman

Amal Al Mamari
https://orcid.org/0009-0007-9173-5916
Sultan Qaboos University, Oman

ABSTRACT

Artificial intelligence (AI) has become a significant focus of research and practical applications within the tourism industry. Tourism researchers and practitioners have recently changed their methods by incorporating AI tools, resulting in new approaches to generate and use insights. These AI-driven developments hold great potential for enhancing destination branding. The current chapter aims to showcase the main benefits of using AI in destination branding, examine how AI helps create and implement effective branding strategies, identify the key challenges and complexities of integrating AI tools for this purpose, and highlight the crucial ethical considerations that need to be addressed when using AI in destination branding. This chapter presents several theoretical implications and helpful practical recommendations for using AI in destination branding.

DOI: 10.4018/979-8-3693-6700-1.ch006

1. INTRODUCTION

Artificial intelligence (AI) is known as the simulation of human-linked intelligence and cognitive capacities by machines (Lv et al., 2022). AI encompasses the capacity to deploy intricate activities, understand human emotions, and arrive at rational conclusions (Korteling et al., 2021). AI stands out for its capacity to provide knowledge that can be put to use, making it a valuable instrument for growing productivity in a variety of sectors. AI could therefore become a crucial tool to be deployed for destination branding, assisting destination marketers in developing customised and data-driven brand features that present the ideal site to the ideal tourist (Paolanti et al., 2021). However, the key perspectives concerning AI adoption in destination branding should be considered because of the complex nature of destination branding.

The AI field is rapidly evolving, with numerous significant AI models introduced annually. In 2022, several major AI models were launched, particularly impacting the service sector with applications in customer service analytics and segmentation (Maslej et al., 2023). AI models like ChatGPT are widely accessible, facilitating their use in different industries such as tourism and marketing (Megahed et al., 2024). Companies in the tourism sector, such as Tripadvisor, Airbnb, and Skyscanner, are integrating AI tools into their digital infrastructures (Filieri et al., 2021).

A destination can be perceived in several ways, from a familiar physical space to a conceptual identity shaped by people's personalities, past experiences, destination knowledge, travel experiences, and visiting purposes (Buhalis, 2000). Destination branding involves collaboration between and contributions from multiple stakeholders to develop a destination brand image that attracts more potential tourists (Al Balushi et al., 2013). Destination branding aims to create a unique identity for the destination by capturing its essence, vision, and meaning to attract tourists and maximise the destination's value (Hassan et al., 2010). With technological advancement, particularly the growth of generative AI (GenAI) and the increased use of social media by tourists, research in destination branding has expanded to include new dimensions such as promotion, engagement, and building and enhancing the tourist experience within a digital destination marketing framework (Confetto et al., 2023; Soliman et al., 2024). As a highly competitive field, destination branding requires an omnichannel approach, involving multiple marketing channels while simultaneously and rapidly adapting to both global and local environments (Confetto et al., 2023; Escobar-Farfán et al., 2024). As a result, destination management organizations dedicate substantial time and resources to analysing destination information, aiming to create strategies that promote a positive image to attract potential tourist target markets (Confetto et al., 2023; Hanna et al., 2021).

AI tools can analyse unstructured data from sources, involving images, videos, text, and behavioural trends (e.g., online browsing and app usage). As AI continues to evolve, it is being applied in industries like hospitality, tourism, and marketing, where understanding human behaviour and perception is key to effective communication (Ku & Chen, 2024; Law et al., 2024). In this vein, AI-driven tools could engage with consumers and analyse customer experiences and preferences to accomplish certain objectives such as improving service, fostering stronger connections, and capturing customer value (Huang et al., 2024).

Consequently, AI can be incorporated into the process of destination branding to improve, create, facilitate, and optimize tasks that rely on human cognitive effort (Law et al., 2024; Soliman & Al Balushi, 2023). AI could be adopted by DMOs (Huang et al., 2024) and other tourism-related stakeholders to build digital brands for tourist destinations (Confetto et al., 2023) and to enhance competitiveness through the utilization of destination brand experience data (Calderón-Fajardo et al., 2024). In this respect, Australia analysed online images to enhance its destination image (Wang et al., 2020). Additionally, AI techniques have been adopted to analyse Instagram posts from visitors to Foça, Turkey, identifying key factors forming the destination image (Koruyan & Akatas, 2022).

On the other hand, the growing popularity of social media, a diversification of marketing channels, and the worldwide significance of marketing initiatives have brought about both complexity and breadth to the retail base of consumers (Filieri et al., 2021). The competition for destination branding specialists has increased as a result, and to stay relevant, they have to constantly revamp their brand identity. To do this, DMOs and stakeholders need to collaborate closely together, devote a significant number of resources, and sift through massive amounts of data to produce insightful analyses that will draw in vacationers (Al Balushi, Soliman, et al., 2024).

Recently, AI has emerged as an essential tool to support DMOs and policy-makers in creating personalised destination marketing campaigns (Paolanti et al., 2021) moving away from static segment-based campaigns. For the supply side, AI provides personalised recommendations, customer service chatbots, and predictive analytics. Furthermore, generative ML algorithms, such as ChatGPT, can analyse users' preferred activities, demographics, and behaviour patterns to provide tailored recommendations (Soliman & Al Balushi, 2023). For example, DMOs and policymakers in Southern Italy used insights from ML-AI that analysed complex geotagged Twitter posts in different languages, with spelling errors, abbreviations, and special characters to determine tourist sentiments toward the destination (Camacho-Ruiz et al., 2023). Regarding the demand side, AI can suggest specific destinations, attractions, and unique experiences. AI-driven destination branding offers numerous benefits, such as transforming vast amounts of data into actionable insights, enhancing destination brand competitiveness, and providing cost-efficient resource management and flexibility (Soliman & Al Balushi, 2023). Recent trends indicate increased interaction between customers and AI through AI-driven chatbots, AI-based robotics, AI-integrated virtual and augmented reality applications, AI-based search travel recommendation systems, and virtual influencers (Kim et al., 2024). These emerging technologies are redefining how destinations engage with potential tourists.

Research indicates that an increasing number of hospitality and tourism businesses, especially hotels, are interested in partnering with technology companies and AI-based startups to use AI applications such as chatbots, hotel recommendations and contactless communication (Kim et al., 2024). As AI and destination branding evolve, their intersection offers numerous benefits, including personalised marketing, enhanced brand competitiveness, and efficient resource management (Soliman & Al Balushi, 2023). However, using AI presents some challenges for destination marketers (Huang *et al.*, 2022). For example, adopting AI tools in destination branding poses challenges in creating relevant content that captures a destination's unique identity and authenticity (Kong et al., 2023).

Using AI in destination branding also raises ethical imperatives such as privacy, bias, fairness, and security (Escobar-Farfán et al., 2024). As tourists provide personal information at each stage of their travel, a range of demographic, social, behavioural and geographic data is accessible to these destinations, airlines and travel agencies. If adequate measures are not taken, the privacy of those travellers could be compromised. Using AI in destination branding also raises questions about how tourists perceive interaction with AI agents that can demonstrate inauthentic emotions while being pleasant. There is also a question of how the tourists' demographics determine their trust or distrust of AI. Another ethical imperative is the potential of AI to change job roles and automate tasks, displacing human jobs and significantly impacting employment in the tourism and hospitality sectors (Kim et al., 2024).

Furthermore, since various stakeholders are involved in destination branding, their knowledge about AI's use cases, challenges, and impact is essential to share the destination brand image efficiently and effectively. As an emerging field, AI-driven destination branding is rapidly expanding and requires frequent re-evaluation to capture advancement on both fronts. Thus, as AI and destination branding evolve, so does their nexus.

2. THEORETICAL BACKGROUND

AI has been integrated into various industries (Ivanov et al., 2024; Kamila & Jasrotia, 2023), including destination branding within the tourism and marketing sectors, as evidenced by scholarly literature (Doborjeh et al., 2022; Filieri et al.,

2021; Ivanov & Soliman, 2023; Ku & Chen, 2024; Maslej et al., 2023). AI's ability to analyse massive amounts of data, handle human interaction across stakeholders, and make informed decisions supports the dynamic updates required for destination branding to remain relevant and competitive. However, the adoption of AI in destination branding poses key challenges due to AI's inherent limitations and ethical imperatives, which are still being researched.

2.1 Benefits of AI-driven Destination Branding

Given the preceding discussion, this section highlights the key benefits derived from using AI in destination branding.

A. Enhancing destination brand competitiveness

According to marketing theory, a brand's intended level of customer satisfaction is achieved through its strategic positioning (Al Balushi, Hussain, et al., 2024). In this vein, destinations are becoming extremely competitive as they strive to attract more tourists and investors, making destination branding crucial for competitiveness (Song et al., 2024; Xu & Au, 2023). Destination branding plays a pivotal role in this by providing uniqueness and feasibility of the destination via various brand determinants (Miličević et al., 2017). AI could reinforce the destination competitiveness and its branding (Miličević et al., 2017). Many destination branding marketers have used AI effectively to increase their competitiveness by identifying and leveraging the destinations' unique selling points by analysing competitive landscape and tourist data. For example, a study utilized AI big data to determine the competitiveness of three destinations: Crete (Greece), Belek (Turkey), and Mallorca (Spain), by analysing their satisfaction levels through their comments on a social media platform (Cimbaljević et al., 2019). The study suggested that policymakers and DMOs can benefit significantly by harvesting customer data to understand their destination's competitive position, which, in turn, can help them design and implement their services competitively (Cimbaljević et al., 2019). Similarly, another study used AI to explore the experiences of residents and visitors in 20 Nordic cities by analysing their tweets. Using the themes extracted from the analysis, the researchers produced marketing elements such as logos, slogans and campaign names through generative AI tools such as Midjourney and ChatGPT.

AI can analyse large quantities of visitors' data, including text, images, videos, and voice recordings as well as their digital activity, and use that analysis to help in identifying target groups, analysing competition, conducting SWOT analysis and communicating the brand image (Penpece Demirer & Büyükeke, 2024). The data is gathered through ML and analysed by AI to identify patterns that humans are not able to recognize (Haleem, Javaid, et al., 2022). For example, it can analyse which Facebook posts people liked to predict their personality traits. Similarly, by analysing past data, AI can predict which customers will leave a digital platform and which online content will bring them back. Furthermore, facial recognition software, using AI, can track tourists' store visits and connect the data to their social media profiles, which can then be used to send customized notifications to tourists.

AI can be used to identify tourists' thoughts and emotions by analysing their social media activity. Destinations can use that data to form a brand identity that resonates with their visitors (Haleem, Javaid, et al., 2022) and create emotionally appealing advertisement content (Soliman, Al-Shanfari, et al., 2023) as people like to watch advertisements that they can relate to (Haleem, Javaid, et al., 2022). Khumtaveeporn and Wattanasuwan (2023) conducted a sentiment analysis on online reviews by tourists concerning a popular tourist destination, Buriram, Thailand. Their study found that a destination could emphasize its archaeological sites and sports in its branding to attract tourists. Another study analysed Google Maps reviews of thematic and non-thematic parks in Bandung, Indonesia. It is revealed that thematic parks received substantially greater ratings from visitors and could therefore be highlighted in the city branding to attract more visitors (Munawir et al., 2019).

Thus, it is essential to apply AI models to destination branding; given their benefits such as the ability to estimate consequences using data from multiple sources (Song et al., 2024). Such sources consist of tourists' online reviews, posts on social media, digital engagement, and competitors' marketing campaign metrics (Maslej et al., 2023). AI can then suggest appropriate attributes like the right price for an offering, the best time to post content, the best destination to recommend for tourists, the right ad content relevant to the target customers, and which customers should be excluded from the campaign (Haleem, Mohd, et al., 2022). These insights are then utilized by people to decide or request AI to execute the decision. In addition, destinations can alert and welcome visitors, using AI-powered notifications (Haleem, Javaid, et al., 2022).

B. Cost efficiency and resource management

Using AI in destination branding can reduce costs and resource requirements of human capital, physical space and content creation. Many AI models can be used online for a small subscription fee, which eliminates the requirement for high-end computing, maintenance, and software engineers within DMOs (Seyyedamiri et al., 2022).

AI models (e.g., ChatGPT) can perform activities such as developing SWOT analysis, market segmentation and even creating marketing campaigns based on competitors' marketing materials and online reviews. This reduces or eliminates the need to hire employees for various marketing tasks, leading to lowering costs (Arman & Lamiyar, 2023; Carvalho & Ivanov, 2024). Also, AI models make it possible for DMOs to create several versions of elements in destination branding marketing and refine them using natural language without requiring them to have skills in data management and information processing. In addition, AI-based destination branding aids in managing resources and decision-making in different aspects, complementing the marketing teams in performing tactical tasks (Carvalho & Ivanov, 2024).

C. Enhancing user experiences

It is noticeable that integration of the AI with other technologies such as AR and VR enables more amount of control for tourists in terms of their engagements with their destinations in every decision-making stage. In executing the dreaming phase as suggested by Ammirato et al. (2018), potential tourists can explore and select different attractions and services using VR. Marriott Caribbean & Latin America Resorts employ AR to let a tourist virtually `step into' a resort and be persuaded to book a stay in this resort. Similarly, people can experience virtual tours of key destinations and attractions in Dubai, UAE (Ghandour et al., 2021). Moreover, tourists could post and tag photos through AR applications linked to social media accounts. It provides them with an opportunity to communicate with and recommend products to other visitors which in turn enhances confidence and awareness of prospective visitors (Ghandour et al., 2021).

AI can help enhance tourists' experience during the trip planning and booking phase (Ammirato et al., 2018). This could be achieved by using Tourism Recommender Systems (TRS) which provide personalised recommendations by analysing tourists' behaviour, personal preferences, and demographic data using algorithms (Virutamasen et al., 2024). Additionally, TRS can connect environmentally conscious visitors to less famous, cultural or heritage destinations (Virutamasen et al., 2024), helping promote those destinations while achieving ecological targets (Arora & Chandel, 2024). Moreover, AI can be used with interactive technologies to elevate tourists' experiences during the experiencing phase (Ammirato et al., 2018). Furthermore, AI-based data can be utilized by hotels to increase visitors' satisfaction by customizing the "room temperature, amenities, dining options" and other options as per their preferences. This can help increase their loyalty, eventually increasing revenue (Bulchand-Gidumal et al., 2024).

D. AI success in destination branding

Prior research demonstrated the benefits of using AI to promote the uniqueness of destinations at various stages of DMO efforts (Ruiz-Real *et al.*, 2020). Studies have also examined the use of ML to conduct market segmentation based on perceived destination characteristics (Doborjeh et al., 2022). Other studies have articulated the application of AI to make a destination look more visually appealing by analysing tourists' responses to the destination's image and adjusting that image based on those insights (Zhang *et al.*, 2023). Recently, a study used psychophysiology techniques such as eye tracking (ET) and Galvanic Skin Response (GSR) to analyse consumers' response to AI-generated brand logos. This study found that consumers' responses were in line with brand personality attributes such as sincerity, excitement and competence (Calderón-Fajardo et al., 2024).

AI models can also identify trends by analysing past and current global events (Zhang et al., 2019). This can assist destination marketers in emphasizing destination attributes that satisfy their tourists' needs and can strengthen the destination's brand identity (Calderón-Fajardo et al., 2024). Furthermore, AI models can adapt to the vast amount of information coming from a surge of competing destination brands and social media activity, with minimum human intervention. Hence, by leveraging data analytics, AI can enhance marketing effectiveness in destination branding.

AI models have changed destination branding efforts in two stages: generating destination brand identity stage and the feedback stage to respond to the current competitive market. At the generation stage, AI models have enabled destinations to generate brand marketing elements without the need for humans to label and analyse data from various sources that are available publicly (Seyyedamiri et al., 2022). For example, generative AI was used to analyse 1.9 million tweets related to Nordic cities and develop new branding materials for them (Doborjeh et al., 2022). At the feedback stage, AI models help destination marketers evolve their brand identity to cater to tourists' expectations and needs by providing input based on their analysis of tourists' experiences with the destination.

2.2. Challenges of Adopting AI in Destination Branding

This part represents the essential challenges related to the adoption of AI in destination branding.

A. Maintaining the relevance of AI-driven destination branding

One of the key concerns comes from the fact that AI models are fundamentally generative, meaning that they rely almost exclusively on the dataset used to train an AI. Such datasets could be scarce, biassed or flooded with excessive or closely peripheral data. In the past, generative models have been applied and then later dismantled because of considerable data bias. For instance, Microsoft's chatbot Tay which went online in 2016 to be 'retired' after a mere 16 hours of its initial response when it began to post blatantly obscene tweets (Maslej et al., 2023). This challenge threatens to put free-roaming AI models in danger of producing unrelated destination brand marketing content materialism with little to no subject-matter expert control over the content (Belanche et al., 2024). Besides, AI models also have a weakness in verifying and excluding fake data (Dwivedi et al., 2024), which could then infiltrate and influence the content of marketing messages and at some point, need an expert to debug them using processes such as inductive bias which involves laying down critical roles and boundaries for AI-generated content (Lv et al., 2022).

An initial issue when applying AI in the branding of destinations is preserving the attributes of brand genuineness, distinctiveness and storytelling, which might appeal to potential tourists. As previously elaborated, authenticity greatly depends on distinct and humanised destination portrayal, which is severely affected by AI. AI tools or models are very effective in data analysis and personalization but have no native feel of the culture and traditions that help preserve the identity of the destination (Maslej et al., 2023). If much content is sourced through AI, then, there is a potential for content to provide but a generic view of a destination which defeats the purpose of travelling to have an authentic experience in the next best destination. Therefore, the integration of AI to create the content must be carefully controlled so as not to spike while maintaining its continuity in reflecting the cultural identity of the destination (Escobar-Farfán et al., 2024; Sharma, 2022). This balance can be achieved by using credible data that is reviewed for inconsistencies.

Brand image or identity sets a destination apart from competitors because it defines the essence of the destination effectively (Escobar-Farfán et al., 2024). However, if marketers rely on the evaluation AI models to define the identity of a destination brand through analytics, then the terminal brand identity will be generalised and watered down. AI may have a missing plot over a certain place and its culture, sentiment, and all the other perceivable elements because, by design, the AI program is a tool that looks for these features based on the data it was fed with (Soliman & Al Balushi, 2023). Hence, it may lack in portraying the diverse events in a destination, which may be less highlighted, or considered as sensitive (Yen et al., 2020). However, to maintain the credibility and accuracy of the AI-generated narrative, there is a need for human interaction when filtering any of the generated narratives to suit the brand identity that is within the established core attributes.

B. AI regulations and acceptance

Due to the complexity of AI, existing AI models are largely unregulated or lack proper oversight, making the regulation of AI an ongoing topic of discussion and debate (Maslej et al., 2023). Several existing AI solutions are cloud-based and may necessitate sharing sensitive data with third parties, posing privacy issues that could jeopardize the competitive advantage envisioned from employing AI-enabled destination branding. Therefore, integrating AI in destination branding can be a difficulty for DMOs and government bodies because of either a lack of legislation or strict limitations on the usage of cloud-based services (Smuha, 2021).

As DMOs use AI models to approach and interact with potential tourists for destination brand development, another challenge they face is guiding AI algorithms to present content optimally based on customers' personalities and their perceived visual responses and emotions from interacting with AI-generated content (Calderón-Fajardo et al., 2024; Smuha, 2021). Furthermore, DMOs may face resistance from groups with a negative view of AI and prefer authentic human interactions. This resistance can extend to perceptions of AI-generated marketing elements, such as slogans, images, and interactive features, that are perceived to be inferior to human-generated marketing communication, especially if they lack empathetic elements (Chi et al., 2022), hindering the destination brand impact. Moreover, improper use of AI by DMOs without the right frequency and type of communication could overwhelm tourists with information, leading to negative sentiments towards the destination (Lv et al., 2022). It is critical to highlight the relative nature of many of the challenges and complexities involved in integrating AI tools for destination branding due to the rapid advancement in AI, researchers' adaptability with AI tools, and the enormous knowledge created in scholarly research to overcome those challenges (Chi et al., 2022; Grundner & Neuhofer, 2021).

2.3. Ethical imperatives of adopting AI in destination branding

AI tools offer innovative methods in destination branding to attract tourists and investors. However, recent research underscores potential cons (e.g., job displacement, privacy issues, ethical dilemmas, security risks, and adverse outcomes associated with AI) (Grundner & Neuhofer, 2021). To implement AI in destination branding, these ethical considerations must be addressed to ensure that the practices are operationally effective and responsibly aligned with the core values of tourists and host communities (Grundner & Neuhofer, 2021). Implementing AI in destination branding initiatives involves several critical ethical considerations to be addressed ensuring responsible and effective usage of AI. These include:

A. Privacy and data security

AI relies on big data that includes important and intimate details of users, thus sowing worry over the privacy and security of information. The use of AI services, which include service robots, automated data analytics, voice assistants, and facial recognition among others, also brings ethical and privacy concerns in operations and decisions making a profound way affecting customers' trust (Grundner & Neuhofer, 2021). The initial driving forces it points out for the adoption of AI in destination branding refers to the need to make moral right decisions as well as to ensure that the data used is correct thus making a rational decision regarding the use of tools based on AI (Law et al., 2024). There is a necessity to use protection settings for user data in connection with ethical considerations. The measures include proper custody of data, acknowledging codes, users' passwords on data and stringent access control measures to discourage or restrict entry into the data to unauthorized individuals or firms (Law et al., 2024). Adopting AI technologies in destination branding calls for commitment to the cardinal principles of ethically handling big data while putting into consideration the rights of individuals. Possible solutions could be to use such technologies if there is informed consent on how such technologies would be used, including making the people fully aware of such use (Kaushik et al., 2024).

B. Transparency and accountability

Customers need to fully understand and be able to control their data being utilised and processed by AI. This brings attention to transparency something that must adhere to fundamental tenets like fairness as well as respect of their self-governance. In fact, this also highlights the importance of their privacy protection. By making privacy policies understandable and available to users, it is possible to guarantee accountability and transparency. Getting consumers' express agreement is essential before collecting their data. For users to comprehend the possible risks of sharing their data, they also need to be properly informed about the extent to which AI systems would gather, process, and use it (Aldboush & Ferdous, 2023; Kamila & Jasrotia, 2023). By being transparent about how data is handled, the company will foster user trust by letting them know they have control over their personal data.

Deploying AI for destination branding requires setting up distinct accountability procedures by firms, which in turn, are held responsible for data processing practices when consent processes are transparent. Having unambiguous records of user permission facilitates the formulation of liability in cases of undesirable actions (e.g., breaches or violations) and allows for responsible behaviours. Accountability frameworks are necessary to stop AI from being abused and misused. They entail assigning blame to certain people for decisions made by AI and setting up procedures to deal with unfavourable results. It is necessary to clearly define the roles and responsibilities of different stakeholders to properly create and use AI technology (Kamila & Jasrotia, 2023).

C. Bias and fairness

There are ethical concerns to be outlined since AI tools have the likelihood to unintentionally reinforce bias while developing destination branding (Kishan et al., 2024). This comprises the culmination of inappropriate consequences or instances of discrimination, such as the unfair targeting or exclusion of particular people from the initiatives related to destination branding (Kamila & Jasrotia, 2023).

As a result, adopting ethical data-processing procedures is crucial to diminish and/or prevent bias in AI-driven branding-based activities (Varsha, 2023). Such methods contain thorough audits of AI tools to find and fix biases. Using representative and diverse training data is regarded as one of the effective ways to diminish the possibility of biased outcomes in AI. Aldboush and Ferdous (2023) illustrated that conducting routine monitoring of AI tools is vital to guarantee their fairness and transparency. Besides, this approach helps tackle any emergent ethical concerns with the AI application. Fairness is cultivated in software and professional services organizations through the promotion of inclusivity, diversity, and equality (Kishan et al., 2024).

D. Human–AI interaction

Considering its influence, the incorporation of AI tools into multiple aspects has recently raised ethical concerns, referring to AI-human interactions (Kishan *et al.*, 2024). Despite the fact that AI can streamline numerous operations, human intervention remains crucial. This leads to guaranteeing the responsible and efficient adoption of AI and verifying that AI-produced branding components accurately capture the core of the destination. In this respect, service robots and other AI-powered devices could match or surpass human capabilities in several tasks, but they are not without flaws (Balasubramaniam et al., 2022).

In addition, AI systems could potentially take over human decision-making in certain areas, which could affect human autonomy and control. This raises concerns about the future influence of AI on decision-making by humans. In order to ensure that technology enhances rather than diminishes the human element in marketing practices, the integration of AI and marketing requires a strategic approach and human intuition (Kamila & Jasrotia, 2023).

Destination branding necessitates a balance between AI-based tools and human interaction, with AI boosting the efficiency and personalization of tactics used by human destination evangelists (Kumar et al., 2024). Destination marketers and concerned stakeholders should evaluate AI-driven choices, generated media, and customer interactions in light of the current ethical imperatives in AI adaptation. Also, they ought to ensure that AI tools enhance human decision-making rather than swap out it.

3. CONCLUSIONS

Technological progress has revolutionized various businesses, involving the tourism-related sector. This is an improvement in the machinery (e.g., cutting-edge self-service technologies, ML, GenAI, software, or algorithms) (Ivanov et al., 2024; Wirtz & Pitardi, 2023). Recent advancements in AI for complex human cognitive tasks have made significant progress, driving innovative applications across various fields, including destination marketing and branding. In this regard, AI tools are crucial for creating distinctive narratives that convey the essence of a destination (Fusté-Forné & Orea-Giner, 2023). The use of AI is bound to occur in business, economic, and educational fields, and the adoption of AI is now commonly producing content in many fields. As a result, generative AI tools can create compelling content that enhances destination branding (Soliman & Al Balushi, 2023).

AI integration in numerous settings and uses has quickly advanced in the fourth industrial revolution, revolutionising virtually all basic human activities and existence (Soliman, Al-Shanfari, et al., 2023). AI has gone almost everywhere in terms of its applicability; it has found its niche in business, tourism, and people's everyday lives (Grundner & Neuhofer, 2021). AI has received significant attention in both academic and practical tourism and hospitality contexts (Knani et al., 2022). Thus, AI tools have enhanced the research methodologies by incorporating their view in different fields of study, especially within tourism options (Soliman, Al-Shanfari, et al., 2023). Overall, the innovations prescribed by AI have significantly shifted the process of creating and using knowledge within these fields, thus showcasing an enormous opportunity to use such tools to achieve the aim of destination branding.

Consequently, this chapter offers substantial contributions from both theoretical and practical viewpoints. Theoretically, the present endeavour enhances knowledge in several ways and focuses primarily on tourism, AI, and marketing. It enhances the knowledge base in AI applied to tourism destination marketing, as the latter sub-discipline of tourism marketing is still in its infancy in academic research. In addition, it is evident that recent studies have highlighted the utilisation of AI tools in diverse tourism-related areas, such as gastronomy in tourism (Fusté-Forné & Orea-Giner, 2023), destination evangelism (Soliman & Al Balushi, 2023), sensory marketing for accessible tourism (Soliman, Al-Shanfari, et al., 2023), tourism education and research (Ivanov & Soliman, 2023), etc. However, it is still possible to single out the lack of attention in empirical studies concerning the application of AI-based tools within the context of destination branding. Indeed, this chapter effectively addresses this gap, which constitutes a significant theoretical contribution as it provides a sound understanding of using AI techniques in this specific framework. In addition, the current chapter clearly establishes that AI harbours many benefits in destination branding. In it, the authors systematically discuss how selected AI technologies can help build and implement a sound destination brand management framework. This could complement the current literature on the possibilities of applying AI in destination branding. Moreover, this chapter is devoted to identifying the significant issues and difficulties of integrating AI tools into the development of destination branding, which encompasses the necessity to keep the AI branding relevant, along with the concerns regarding AI regulations and acceptance. This paper also discusses the implementation problem of cost and resources for AI, which is a challenge for most organisations. However, the present chapter also powerfully highlights the ad hoc ethical question that has to be solved when using AI in destination branding. There is a call to establish a code of ethics and best practices to avoid the misuse of technologies, the violation of individual rights, and the worsening of existing social injustice.

Practically, the current work offers valuable managerial contributions and actionable insights for key stakeholders, including destination managers and marketers, focusing on the essential elements of incorporating AI into destination branding. To begin with, this paper emphasises the significant benefits that AI can bring to destination branding efforts. These benefits include enhancing destination brand competitiveness, cost efficiency and resource management, and AI success in destination branding. In addition, AI can analyse large amounts of data, making it possible for destination managers to understand visitors' preferences and behaviour patterns better and, therefore, target their marketing strategies more accurately. Moreover, this research outlines the significant issues and ethical considerations concerning AI's application in destination branding. It discusses concerns like the challenges of implementing AI technologies, the requirement of constant data updates to keep its accuracy, and the question of technological advances. These issues reveal critical factors for the proper, conceptually developed implementation approach and the continuous training of the staff to integrate AI systems properly. Thus, the completed research outlines the steps that he/she and other stakeholders should follow to overcome these challenges and efficiently incorporate AI solutions into branding processes.

Considering the preceding discussion, the present conceptual work provides several directions for future research. To begin with, future research could conduct a systematic review or bibliometric study to map the field of AI and destination branding based on different metrics that have been applied in prior studies within various contexts (Au-Yong-Oliveira et al., 2021; de Bruyn et al., 2023; Meyer et al., 2023; Soliman, Fatnassi, et al., 2023; Soliman, Gulvady, et al., 2023). This approach would entail cataloguing the available literature to highlight the significant patterns, authors, and studies most prevalent in this field. Additionally, this can positively contribute to future studies of the current and future trends in the usage of AI applications in improving destination branding strategies and their effects. Next, future research is suggested to conduct an empirical study with varied objectives across different sectors and regions. In this vein, the empirical investigation of the key drivers and challenges of adopting AI in destination branding could be a valuable avenue for further work. Furthermore, future work could conduct qualitative approach-based research, employing interviews, to unveil the perceptions and attitudes of destination managers and marketers toward adopting AI for destination branding. Moreover, future research could focus on the ethical concerns associated with AI applications in destination branding to enhance destination branding through AI applications and protect stakeholders' interests.

REFERENCES

Al Balushi, M., Butt, I., & Al Siyabi, K. (2013). Review of awareness and views on branding Oman as a nation. *International Journal of Business and Economics*, 5(1), 7–19.

Al Balushi, M. K., Hussain, K., & Al Mahrouqi, A. N. (2024). Strategic University Positioning: Fostering Student Satisfaction and Well-being. *Current Psychology (New Brunswick, N.J.)*, 43(29), 1–13. DOI: 10.1007/s12144-024-06104-3

Al Balushi, M. K., Soliman, M., Kennedy, R. E., & Palla, A. H. (2024). Shifts in tourism knowledge: HEI contributions to destination branding and economic development. In *Shifts in Knowledge Sharing and Creativity for Business Tourism* (pp. 145–162). IGI Global., DOI: 10.4018/979-8-3693-2619-0.ch009

Aldboush, H. H., & Ferdous, M. (2023). Building trust in fintech: An analysis of ethical and privacy considerations in the intersection of big data, AI, and customer trust. *International Journal of Financial Studies*, 11(3), 90. DOI: 10.3390/ijfs11030090

Ammirato, S., Felicetti, A. M., Della Gala, M., Raso, C., & Cozza, M. (2018). Smart tourism destinations: can the destination management organizations exploit benefits of the ICTs? Evidences from a multiple case study. Collaborative Networks of Cognitive Systems: 19th IFIP WG 5.5 Working Conference on Virtual Enterprises, PRO-VE 2018, Cardiff, UK, September 17-19, 2018, Proceedings 19, Arman, M., & Lamiyar, U. R. (2023). Exploring the implication of ChatGPT AI for business: Efficiency and challenges. *International Journal of Marketing and Digital Creative*, 1(2), 64–84. DOI: 10.31098/ijmadic.v1i2.1872

Arora, M., & Chandel, M. (2024). Role of Artificial Intelligence in Promoting Green Destinations for Sustainable Tourism Development. In *The Role of Artificial Intelligence in Regenerative Tourism and Green Destinations* (pp. 247–260). Emerald Publishing Limited., DOI: 10.1108/978-1-83753-746-420241016

Au-Yong-Oliveira, M., Pesqueira, A., Sousa, M. J., Dal Mas, F., & Soliman, M. (2021). The potential of big data research in healthcare for medical doctors' learning. *Journal of Medical Systems*, 45(1), 13. DOI: 10.1007/s10916-020-01691-7 PMID: 33409620

Balasubramaniam, N., Kauppinen, M., Hiekkanen, K., & Kujala, S. (2022). Transparency and explainability of AI systems: Ethical guidelines in practice. *Information and Software Technology*, 159, 3–18. DOI: 10.1016/j.infsof.2023.107197

Belanche, D., Belk, R. W., Casaló, L. V., & Flavián, C. (2024). The dark side of artificial intelligence in services. *Service Industries Journal*, 44(3-4), 149–172. DOI: 10.1080/02642069.2024.2305451

Buhalis, D. (2000). Marketing the competitive destination of the future. *Tourism Management*, 21(1), 97–116. DOI: 10.1016/S0261-5177(99)00095-3

Bulchand-Gidumal, J., William Secin, E., O'Connor, P., & Buhalis, D. (2024). Artificial intelligence's impact on hospitality and tourism marketing: Exploring key themes and addressing challenges. *Current Issues in Tourism*, 27(14), 2345–2362. DOI: 10.1080/13683500.2023.2229480

Calderón-Fajardo, V., Anaya-Sánchez, R., & Molinillo, S. (2024). Understanding destination brand experience through data mining and machine learning. *Journal of Destination Marketing & Management*, 31, 100862. DOI: 10.1016/j.jdmm.2024.100862

Camacho-Ruiz, M., Carrasco, R. A., Fernández-Avilés, G., & LaTorre, A. (2023). Tourism destination events classifier based on artificial intelligence techniques. *Applied Soft Computing*, 148, 110914. DOI: 10.1016/j.asoc.2023.110914

Carvalho, I., & Ivanov, S. (2024). ChatGPT for tourism: Applications, benefits and risks. *Tourism Review*, 79(2), 290–303. DOI: 10.1108/TR-02-2023-0088

Chi, O. H., Gursoy, D., & Chi, C. G. (2022). Tourists' attitudes toward the use of artificially intelligent (AI) devices in tourism service delivery: Moderating role of service value seeking. *Journal of Travel Research*, 61(1), 170–185. DOI: 10.1177/0047287520971054

Cimbaljević, M., Stankov, U., & Pavluković, V. (2019). Going beyond the traditional destination competitiveness–reflections on a smart destination in the current research. *Current Issues in Tourism*, 22(20), 2472–2477. DOI: 10.1080/13683500.2018.1529149

Confetto, M. G., Conte, F., Palazzo, M., & Siano, A. (2023). Digital destination branding: A framework to define and assess European DMOs practices. *Journal of Destination Marketing & Management*, 30, 100804. DOI: 10.1016/j.jdmm.2023.100804

de Bruyn, C., Said, F. B., Meyer, N., & Soliman, M. (2023). Research in tourism sustainability: A comprehensive bibliometric analysis from 1990 to 2022. *Heliyon*, 9(8), e18874. Advance online publication. DOI: 10.1016/j.heliyon.2023.e18874 PMID: 37636413

Doborjeh, Z., Hemmington, N., Doborjeh, M., & Kasabov, N. (2022). Artificial intelligence: A systematic review of methods and applications in hospitality and tourism. *International Journal of Contemporary Hospitality Management*, 34(3), 1154–1176. DOI: 10.1108/IJCHM-06-2021-0767

Dwivedi, Y. K., Pandey, N., Currie, W., & Micu, A. (2024). Leveraging ChatGPT and other generative artificial intelligence (AI)-based applications in the hospitality and tourism industry: Practices, challenges and research agenda. *International Journal of Contemporary Hospitality Management*, 36(1), 1–12. DOI: 10.1108/IJCHM-05-2023-0686

Escobar-Farfán, M., Cervera-Taulet, A., & Schlesinger, W. (2024). Destination brand identity: Challenges, opportunities, and future research agenda. *Cogent Social Sciences*, 10(1), 2302803. DOI: 10.1080/23311886.2024.2302803

Filieri, R., D'Amico, E., Destefanis, A., Paolucci, E., & Raguseo, E. (2021). Artificial intelligence (AI) for tourism: An European-based study on successful AI tourism start-ups. *International Journal of Contemporary Hospitality Management*, 33(11), 4099–4125. DOI: 10.1108/IJCHM-02-2021-0220

Fusté-Forné, F., & Orea-Giner, A. (2023). Gastronomy in tourism management and marketing: an interview with ChatGPT. *ROBONOMICS: The Journal of the Automated Economy, 4*, 42-42. https://www.journal.robonomics.science/index.php/rj/article/view/42

Ghandour, A., Kintonova, A., Demidchik, N., & Sverdlikova, E. (2021). Solving tourism management challenges by means of mobile augmented reality applications. [IJWLTT]. *International Journal of Web-Based Learning and Teaching Technologies*, 16(6), 1–16. DOI: 10.4018/IJWLTT.293280

Grundner, L., & Neuhofer, B. (2021). The bright and dark sides of artificial intelligence: A futures perspective on tourist destination experiences. *Journal of Destination Marketing & Management*, 19, 100511. DOI: 10.1016/j.jdmm.2020.100511

Haleem, A., Javaid, M., Qadri, M. A., Singh, R. P., & Suman, R. (2022). Artificial intelligence (AI) applications for marketing: A literature-based study. *International Journal of Intelligent Networks*, 3, 119–132. DOI: 10.1016/j.ijin.2022.08.005

Haleem, A., Mohd, J., Mohd, A. Q., Sindh, R. P., & Rajiv, S. (2022). Artificial intelligence (AI) applications for marketing: A literature-based study. *International Journal of Intelligent Networks*, 3, 119–132. DOI: 10.1016/j.ijin.2022.08.005

Hanna, S., Rowley, J., & Keegan, B. (2021). Place and destination branding: A review and conceptual mapping of the domain. *European Management Review*, 18(2), 105–117. DOI: 10.1111/emre.12433

Hassan, S. B., Soliman, M., & Al Bohairy, H. (2010). Perception of destination branding measures: A case study of Alexandria destination marketing organizations. *International Journal of Euro-Mediterranean Studies*, 3(2), 271–288. https://emuni.si/wp-content/uploads/2019/02/3_269-288.pdf

Huang, A., Ozturk, A. B., Zhang, T., de la Mora Velasco, E., & Haney, A. (2024). Unpacking AI for hospitality and tourism services: Exploring the role of perceived enjoyment on future use intentions. *International Journal of Hospitality Management*, 119, 103693. DOI: 10.1016/j.ijhm.2024.103693

Ivanov, S., & Soliman, M. (2023). Game of algorithms: ChatGPT implications for the future of tourism education and research. *Journal of Tourism Futures*, 9(2), 214–221. DOI: 10.1108/JTF-02-2023-0038

Ivanov, S., Soliman, M., Tuomi, A., Alkathiri, N. A., & Al-Alawi, A. N. (2024). Drivers of generative AI adoption in higher education through the lens of the Theory of Planned Behaviour. *Technology in Society*, 77, 102521. DOI: 10.1016/j.techsoc.2024.102521

Kamila, M. K., & Jasrotia, S. S. (2023). Ethical issues in the development of artificial intelligence: recognizing the risks. *International Journal of Ethics and Systems*(ahead-of-print). https://doi.org/DOI: 10.1108/IJOES-05-2023-0107

Kaushik, K., Khan, A., Kumari, A., Sharma, I., & Dubey, R. (2024). Ethical Considerations in AI-Based Cybersecurity. In *Next-Generation Cybersecurity: AI, ML, and Blockchain* (pp. 437-470). Springer. https://doi.org/DOI: 10.1007/978-981-97-1249-6_19

Khumtaveeporn, I., & Wattanasuwan, K. (2023). AI Sentiment Analysis for Destination Branding: A Case Study of Buriram, Thailand. *Journal of Business Administration*, 46(180), 50–74.

Kim, H., So, K. K. F., Shin, S., & Li, J. (2024). Artificial intelligence in hospitality and tourism: Insights from industry practices, research literature, and expert opinions. *Journal of Hospitality & Tourism Research (Washington, D.C.)*, 10963480241229235, 10963480241229235. Advance online publication. DOI: 10.1177/10963480241229235

Kishan, K., Mishra, A., Tiwari, V., & Vemuri, V. P. (2024). Artificial Intelligence: The Next Frontier for Marketing in the Tourism Industry. *Academy of Marketing Studies Journal*, 28(1).

Knani, M., Echchakoui, S., & Ladhari, R. (2022). Artificial intelligence in tourism and hospitality: Bibliometric analysis and research agenda. *International Journal of Hospitality Management*, 107, 103317. DOI: 10.1016/j.ijhm.2022.103317

Kong, H., Wang, K., Qiu, X., Cheung, C., & Bu, N. (2023). 30 years of artificial intelligence (AI) research relating to the hospitality and tourism industry. *International Journal of Contemporary Hospitality Management*, 35(6), 2157–2177. DOI: 10.1108/IJCHM-03-2022-0354

Korteling, J., van de Boer-Visschedijk, G. C., Blankendaal, R. A., Boonekamp, R. C., & Eikelboom, A. R. (2021). Human-versus artificial intelligence. *Frontiers in Artificial Intelligence*, 4, 622364. DOI: 10.3389/frai.2021.622364 PMID: 33981990

Koruyan, K., & Akatas, E. (2022). Destination Image Analysis with User-Generated Content: A Computer Vision and Machine Learning Approach. *Journal of Tourism & Gastronomy Studies*, 10(3), 2126–2143. DOI: 10.21325/jotags.2022.1085

Ku, E. C., & Chen, C.-D. (2024). Artificial intelligence innovation of tourism businesses: From satisfied tourists to continued service usage intention. *International Journal of Information Management*, 76, 102757. DOI: 10.1016/j.ijinfomgt.2024.102757

Kumar, V., Ashraf, A. R., & Nadeem, W. (2024). AI-powered marketing: What, where, and how? *International Journal of Information Management*, 77, 102783. DOI: 10.1016/j.ijinfomgt.2024.102783

Law, R., Lin, K. J., Ye, H., & Fong, D. K. C. (2024). Artificial intelligence research in hospitality: A state-of-the-art review and future directions. *International Journal of Contemporary Hospitality Management*, 36(6), 2049–2068. DOI: 10.1108/IJCHM-02-2023-0189

Lv, X., Yang, Y., Qin, D., Cao, X., & Xu, H. (2022). Artificial intelligence service recovery: The role of empathic response in hospitality customers' continuous usage intention. *Computers in Human Behavior*, 126, 106993. DOI: 10.1016/j.chb.2021.106993

Maslej, N., Fattorini, L., Brynjolfsson, E., Etchemendy, J., Ligett, K., Lyons, T., Manyika, J., Ngo, H., Niebles, J. C., & Parli, V. (2023). Artificial intelligence index report 2023. *arXiv preprint arXiv:2310.03715*. https://doi.org//arXiv.2310.03715DOI: 10.48550

Megahed, F. M., Chen, Y.-J., Ferris, J. A., Knoth, S., & Jones-Farmer, L. A. (2024). How generative AI models such as ChatGPT can be (mis) used in SPC practice, education, and research? An exploratory study. *Quality Engineering*, 36(2), 287–315. DOI: 10.1080/08982112.2023.2206479

Meyer, N., Ben Said, F., Alkathiri, N. A., & Soliman, M. (2023). A scientometric analysis of entrepreneurial and the digital economy scholarship: State of the art and an agenda for future research. *Journal of Innovation and Entrepreneurship*, 12(1), 70. DOI: 10.1186/s13731-023-00340-w

Miličević, K., Mihalič, T., & Sever, I. (2017). An investigation of the relationship between destination branding and destination competitiveness. *Journal of Travel & Tourism Marketing*, 34(2), 209–221. DOI: 10.1080/10548408.2016.1156611

Munawir, K., Koerniawan, M. D., & Dewancker, B. J. (2019). Visitor Perceptions and effectiveness of place branding strategies in thematic parks in Bandung City using text mining based on Google Maps user reviews. *Sustainability (Basel)*, 11(7), 2123. DOI: 10.3390/su11072123

Paolanti, M., Mancini, A., Frontoni, E., Felicetti, A., Marinelli, L., Marcheggiani, E., & Pierdicca, R. (2021). Tourism destination management using sentiment analysis and geo-location information: A deep learning approach. *Information Technology & Tourism*, 23(2), 241–264. DOI: 10.1007/s40558-021-00196-4

Penpece Demirer, D., & Büyükeke, A. (2024). Unravelling tourism destination's competitiveness using big data analytics: A comparative analysis. *Kybernetes*. Advance online publication. DOI: 10.1108/K-12-2023-2580

Seyyedamiri, N., Pour, A. H., Zaeri, E., & Nazarian, A. (2022). Understanding destination brand love using machine learning and content analysis method. *Current Issues in Tourism*, 25(9), 1451–1466. DOI: 10.1080/13683500.2021.1924634

Sharma, P. (2022). Understanding destination evangelism: A social media viewpoint. *Marketing Intelligence & Planning*, 40(1), 72–88. DOI: 10.1108/MIP-04-2021-0128

Smuha, N. A. (2021). From a 'race to AI'to a 'race to AI regulation': Regulatory competition for artificial intelligence. *Law, Innovation and Technology*, 13(1), 57–84. DOI: 10.1080/17579961.2021.1898300

Soliman, M., & Al Balushi, M. (2023). Unveiling destination evangelism through generative AI tools. *ROBONOMICS: The Journal of the Automated Economy, 4*(54), 1. https://journal.robonomics.science/index.php/rj/article/view/54

Soliman, M., Al Balushi, M. K., & Kennedy, R. (2024). Digital marketing for cruise tourism in Oman: Opportunities and challenges. *Social Media Strategies for Tourism Interactivity*, 106-131. https://doi.org/DOI: 10.4018/979-8-3693-0960-5.ch005

Soliman, M., Al-Shanfari, L. S., & Gulvady, S. (2023). Sensory marketing and accessible tourism: An AI-generated article. *ROBONOMICS: The Journal of the Automated Economy*, *4*, 53. https://journal.robonomics.science/index.php/rj/article/view/53

Soliman, M., Fatnassi, T., Elgammal, I., & Figueiredo, R. (2023). Exploring the major trends and emerging themes of artificial intelligence in the scientific leading journals amidst the COVID-19 era. *Big Data and Cognitive Computing*, 7(1), 12. DOI: 10.3390/bdcc7010012

Soliman, M., Gulvady, S., Lyulyov, O., & Pimonenko, T. (2023). Research trends and themes in the top-tier tourism, leisure and hospitality journals: A bibliometric and network analysis before and during the COVID-19 era. *International Journal of Hospitality and Tourism Systems*, 16(1). http://www.publishingindia.com/ijhts/24/research-trends-and-themes-in-the-top-tier-tourism-leisure-and-hospitality-journals-a-bibliometric-and-network-analysis-before-and-during-the-covid-19-era/32022/76862/

Song, M., Chen, H., Wang, Y., & Duan, Y. (2024). Can AI fully replace human designers? Matching effects between declared creator types and advertising appeals on tourists' visit intentions. *Journal of Destination Marketing & Management*, 32, 100892. DOI: 10.1016/j.jdmm.2024.100892

Varsha, P. (2023). How can we manage biases in artificial intelligence systems–A systematic literature review. *International Journal of Information Management Data Insights*, 3(1), 100165. DOI: 10.1016/j.jjimei.2023.100165

Virutamasen, P., Ahadi, N., Wang, J., Zanjanab, A. G., Wongpreedee, K., & Sohaee, N. (2024). Contextual Based E-Tourism Application: A Personalized Attraction Recommendation System for Destination Branding and Cultivating Tourism Experiences. 2024 5th Technology Innovation Management and Engineering Science International Conference (TIMES-iCON), Wang, R., Luo, J., & Huang, S. S. (2020). Developing an artificial intelligence framework for online destination image photos identification. *Journal of Destination Marketing & Management*, 18, 100512. DOI: 10.1016/j.jdmm.2020.100512

Wirtz, J., & Pitardi, V. (2023). How intelligent automation, service robots, and AI will reshape service products and their delivery. *Italian Journal of Marketing*, 2023(3), 289–300. DOI: 10.1007/s43039-023-00076-1

Xu, J., & Au, T. (2023). Destination competitiveness since 2010: Research themes, approaches, and agenda. *Tourism Review*, 78(3), 665–696. DOI: 10.1108/TR-10-2022-0494

Yen, C.-H., Teng, H.-Y., & Chang, S.-T. (2020). Destination brand identity and emerging market tourists' perceptions. *Asia Pacific Journal of Tourism Research*, 25(12), 1311–1328. DOI: 10.1080/10941665.2020.1853578

Zhang, K., Chen, Y., & Li, C. (2019). Discovering the tourists' behaviors and perceptions in a tourism destination by analyzing photos' visual content with a computer deep learning model: The case of Beijing. *Tourism Management*, 75, 595–608. DOI: 10.1016/j.tourman.2019.07.002

Chapter 7
Analyzing Destination Branding Themes Using Co-Word Analysis

Hamid Derviş
https://orcid.org/0000-0002-9069-571X
Kastamonu University, Turkey

ABSTRACT

The chapter provides practical strategies for leveraging Social Network Analysis (SNA) in destination branding, offering insights on using interconnected keywords to create a cohesive brand identity extracted from Clarivate Analytics Web of Science (WOS). Using Istanbul, Konya, and Kastamonu showcased as destination brands, the chapter demonstrates how SNA can be applied in real-world contexts, providing insights into the benefits of a strategic branding approach through SNA. The author emphasizes the significance of a connected keyword network and offers practical strategies for leveraging these connections to establish a sustainable destination brand identity. The findings serve as a guide for tourism and hospitality practitioners, assisting them in creating compelling, sustainable destination brands. Similarly, this methodology can be applied to investigate the complex relationships among stakeholders, including local communities, businesses, government agencies, and tourists.

INTRODUCTION

The co-word analysis method allows us to identify key terms and their associations, illuminating insights into the intellectual structure and evolution of the tourism realm. Co-word analysis reveals the temporal development in a specific realm,

DOI: 10.4018/979-8-3693-6700-1.ch007

adapted to analyze the relationships between words or terms within a text corpus. The analytical technique can reveal how different destination branding elements are interconnected and help identify emerging trends and patterns within the field. Vila-López, Kuster-Boluda, Mora-Pérez, and Sarabia Sanchez (2024) applied co-word analysis to uncover patterns, structures, and critical concepts in keywords in the research on the relationship between sports and destination image. Their studies revealed that the keywords used in 2003-2013 were event and attitude, whereas those used in 2013–2022 were image, loyalty, football, brand, destination, and consumers. They concluded that sports use in destination branding has focused on countries like Brazil, the USA, China, and Israel, often due to major sporting events or efforts to restore a country's image through sports diplomacy. Applying social network analysis (SNA) methods, particularly co-word analysis, to destination branding, one can uncover complex relationships and trends essential for understanding how these brands are formed and perceived. Collaborative destination branding involves stakeholders, such as tourists, residents, and businesses, who collaboratively shape the brand's identity through interactions and shared experiences. Saraniemi (2011) highlights that the brand identity emerges from these stakeholder interactions, emphasizing that it represents a comprehensive identity shaped by both the supply and demand sides, which aligns with service co-production principles. Giannopoulos et al. further support this collaborative process, pointing out that participants' shared resources and brand values foster a sustainable branding strategy, affirming that destination branding is a joint effort (Giannopoulos et al., 2020).

The chapter follows: first, we define and explain the fundamentals of social network analysis and its historical development until the present as a methodology; second, Istanbul, Konya, and Kastamonu as a destination brand and their touristic significance will be presented; third, some challenges destination brands are facing will be given; fourth, the rational of study will be discussed, and finally the last sections are: data collection, methods, and results of the research followed by conclusion and remarks.

Social Network Analysis (SNA) as a Methodology

Social network analysis (SNA) is a technique from sociology that studies social structures through graph theory and social structure. It represents networked structures in terms of nodes (representing individuals or entities within the network) and edges (representing relationships or interactions between these entities). Similarly, Co-word analysis, a technique in social network analysis (SNA), examines the relationships and patterns among words in various texts, including scientific articles. Co-word analysis aligns with the SNA approach in several distinguish ways:

1. **Nodes and Edges:** nodes present individuals or items, and edges represent their relationships or interactions. In co-word analysis, the nodes are words or terms, and the edges represent the co-occurrences of these words within the same documents.
2. **Network Structure:** Co-word analysis and SNA involve analyzing the network structure to understand node connections and relationships. Co-word analysis helps identify clusters of related terms and the overall structure of the knowledge domain.
3. **Centrality Measures:** SNA uses centrality measures to identify essential nodes within a network (FasterCapital, n.d.).
4. Similarly, co-word analysis can identify key terms central to the field using metrics like:
   - **Degree centrality**, which measures the number of direct connections a node has (Freeman 1979).
   - **Betweenness centrality** measures the location of a node on the shortest paths connecting other nodes in a network. Nodes with high betweenness can control the flow of information (Freeman 1977).
   - **Closeness centrality** measures how close a node is to all other nodes in the network. It represents the ability of a node to spread information efficiently through the network (Freeman, 1977).
5. **Clusters and Communities:**

SNA often identifies clusters or communities within a network. Co-word analysis can similarly reveal clusters of terms that frequently co-occur, indicating themes or topics within the research area. Path is a sequence of edges connecting two nodes, and Geodesic Distance is the shortest path between two nodes.

6. **Dynamic Network Analysis:**

Studies the changes in the network over time, including how nodes and edges are added or removed and how these changes affect the overall network structure.

7. **Network Visualization:**

Visual tools are used to create graphs that represent the network, making it easier to see patterns and relationships.

8. **Social Capital:**

Refers to the resources available to individuals or groups through their network connections. It can be divided into bonding social capital (within a group) and bridging social capital (between groups)

9. **Path Length and Connectivity:** Metrics such as average path length, network density, and transitivity, commonly used in SNA, are also applied in co-word analysis to understand the connectivity and cohesion of the term network. Density indicates the overall level of connectedness in the network. High density means that many nodes are connected, suggesting a tightly-knit network (Wasserman & Faust, 1994; Scott, 2017; Borgatti, Everett, & Johnson, 2018).

Historical Development of Social Network Analysis

Social Network Analysis (SNA) and tourism intersect in several exciting ways, offering insights into how individuals and groups interact and influence tourism activities. Social Network Analysis (SNA) is a methodological approach to understanding social structures through the use of networks and graph theory. It has evolved over the years, integrating concepts from sociology, anthropology, psychology, and more recently, computer science. This development can be traced through several key phases.

Early Foundations: Georg Simmel a German sociologist, introduced the concept of social circles and the importance of understanding social interactions. His work laid the groundwork for viewing society as a web of relationships rather than just individual entities. Jacob Moreno a psychiatrist and sociologist, developed sociometry, a precursor to SNA. He used sociograms to map the relationships within small groups, particularly in his studies of classroom dynamics (Moreno, 1943, 1938).

Formative Years (1930s-1950s)

Harvard Human Relations Group under the leadership of Elton Mayo and W. Lloyd Warner, the group conducted the famous Hawthorne Studies, which emphasized the importance of informal social relationships in the workplace (Roethlisberger & Dickson, 1939). Kurt Lewin's work on group dynamics and his development of field theory further contributed to the understanding of social networks. He introduced concepts such as "group cohesion" and "social forces." Solomon Asch's experiments on conformity highlighted the influence of social networks on individual behavior, demonstrating how group pressure can affect opinions and actions (Lewin, 1947).

Structuralism and the Role of Networks (1960s-1980)

During this period, scholars like Harrison White and Mark Granovetter began formalizing the study of social structures (Granovetter, 1973). White's "Harvard structuralists" emphasized the importance of analyzing social networks in understanding social behavior. Stanley Milgram's Small-World experiment demonstrated the "six degrees of separation" phenomenon, showing that individuals are connected by short chains of acquaintances (Milgram, 1967 & Watts, 2003). This experiment popularized the concept of the small-world network. Mark Granovetter's "The Strength of Weak Ties " Granovetter's seminal paper highlighted the importance of weak ties in social networks, arguing that they play a crucial role in the diffusion of information and innovation. Linton Freeman's work on centrality measures provided tools to quantify the importance of nodes within a network, enhancing the analytical capabilities of SNA (Freeman, 1978).

Computational and Technological Advances (1990s-Present)

The advent of powerful computing technologies and the rise of the internet allowed for the collection and analysis of large-scale social network data. Scholars like Duncan Watts and Steven Strogatz formalized the study of small-world networks paper (Watts & Stragatz, 1988). Albert-László Barabási work on scale-free networks revealed that many real-world networks, including social networks, follow a power-law distribution. His book "Linked" brought network science to a broader audience (Barabási, 2003). Emergence of Social Media and the rise of social media platforms like Facebook, Twitter, and LinkedIn revolutionized SNA by providing massive datasets on social interactions. Researchers began exploring new phenomena such as online social influence, viral marketing, and digital communities. Proliferation of big data and advancements in machine learning further transformed SNA. Techniques from artificial intelligence and data mining were integrated into SNA, allowing for more sophisticated analysis of complex networks. Presently, SNA is used across various fields, including epidemiology, criminology, organizational studies, and marketing. It continues to evolve with the development of new analytical tools and the increasing availability of diverse data sources.

The Social Network Analysis's evolution reflects a journey from early theoretical insights to a robust, interdisciplinary methodology. As technology advances and the world becomes increasingly interconnected, SNA will continue providing valuable insights into social relationships' structure and dynamics.

In the following sections, we explain the three cities: Istanbul, Konya, and Kastamonu. First, several research articles on Istanbul will be discussed; Second, Konya hosted the first Islamic Games, brand destination; Third, the city of Kastamonu, as a brand destination, will be briefly introduced—the chapter counties with the rationale of the research, data collection, methods, and conclusion.

Istanbul as a Destination Brand

Istanbul, straddling two continents and a melting pot of cultures, is rich in history, diversity, and beauty. As a destination brand, Istanbul encompasses a mixture of the ancient and the contemporary, the East and the West. Oğuztimur (2017, p 1) approached the Istanbul as a brand destination form two main attributes: professional who manage the touristic places, and particularly tourists. In his essay concludes that "basic branding strategies accepted for İstanbul should encapsulate, (1) tourism variability and geographic wideness, (2) originality and character, (3) interaction and communication, (4) global effect, (5) strong infrastructure and high quality of life, (6) the spirit of the city, and (7) the symbol attributed to the city." Istanbul's history is a testament to its enduring allure. Formerly known as Byzantium and later Constantinople, and now Istanbul, the city has been the capital of three major empires: Roman, Byzantine, and Ottoman. Istanbul as a city brand should be look upon from three interrelated phases: Self-Orientalism, the City of Religions and the Multi-Faceted City (Uysal, 2017, p. 1). Although the key historical landmarks such as the Hagia Sophia, Topkapi Palace, and the Blue Mosque are iconic symbols of Istanbul's storied past, local restaurants as an image brands become an integral part tourists attraction. These local restaurants are not only just tourist attractions but also narrative tools that impact the story of a city at the crossroads of civilization for centuries. Although the key historical landmarks such as the Hagia Sophia, Topkapi Palace, and the Blue Mosque are iconic well, well-known symbols of Istanbul's storied past, contemporary restaurants as an image brand play an integral part in engaging tourist attractions. Karagöz et al. Demirçiftçi, and Erkmen (2022, p 323) surveyed the tourists attending the restaurants near the Eminonu, Beyazit, and Sultanahmet, the most visited tourist places in Istanbul. Their findings pointed out that restaurants should pay attention to the atmosphere and physical environment of the restaurant setting. That is, the restaurant's interior design and ambiance should reflect the local culture of the destination to satisfy the entertainment dimension of the restaurant experience. Second, local restaurants should enable customers to learn about new food items and cultures regarding education. With this in mind, service employees must be well-trained to provide detailed explanations about menu items. Third, local restaurants play an essential role in destination attractiveness and return to a destination. Thus, restaurant executives need to work with destination marketing organizations to promote their restaurants (Karagöz et al., 2022, p 323).

Cities utilize marketing strategies to rejuvenate campaigns, partnerships, and broader audiences locally and internationally. Istanbul's marketing branding strategy involves cultural tourism to elevate tourism and attract entrepreneurship. Uysal and Özden (2011) stated that cultural tourism facilitates the restoration of particular churches and mosques, which are the valuable assets of Istanbul's destination brands. Lastly, the illumination or digitization of monumental buildings with architectural, technical, economic, and ecological sensitivity is crucial to destination brand-making. For example, Istanbul attracts more potential visitors by illuminating Istanbul's monumental landmarks, such as Maiden's Tower (Güngör & Akar, 2022).

Konya as a Destination Brand

Konya is one of the oldest cities in Türkiye in terms of history, culture, spirituality, religious significance, and distinctive cultural landscape, which offers a unique experience to travelers and tourists from local and global populations. Recently, Konya held its first Islamic Games in 2024, which was its first kind. Researchers took this opportunity to survey the spectators at this event. Akkaya et al. assessed the spectator's perception regarding "event quality, host city evaluation, place attachment, and destination brand equity." Their results revealed that in "strategic marketing and branding communication, destinations can promote their unique hospitality, historical and cultural heritage, natural beauty, museums, and other attractions, thus fostering strong brand associations and destination positioning (Akkaya et al., 2024)." In another study, Sakar (2022) studied brands in terms of self-personality and how the destination image is associated with tourist self-image, and based on the results of the study, clues about destination marketing of the province are obtained.

Kastamonu as a Destination Brand

Kastamonu, a historically rich city in Turkey's Black Sea region, is a hidden gem known for its historical landmarks, stunning landscapes, and traditional Turkish culture, attracting domestic and international tourists. Kastamonu offers its natural natural beauty, historical significance, and cultural features, making it an excellent destination for culture and belief tourism. Kastamonu Despite offering various tourism options, such as coastal tourism, eco-tourism, and religious tourism, these resources still need to be fully utilized. There is a growing demand for alternative tourism destinations globally and within our city. Considering Kastamonu's tourism potential, showcasing its facilities on national and international platforms is essential. Ibret et al. (2015) stated that from the Neolithic period to the present, Kastamonu has been home to various civilizations and states, and after, Kastamonu became a cultural and religious hub through Islamization within Anatolia. The city's historical structure has maintained its spiritual ambiance, enhancing the culture and belief tourism within Kastamonu.

Historically, Kastamonu is rich in historical heritage, featuring sites from the Byzantine and Ottoman eras. The Byzantine-era Kastamonu Castle provides panoramic views of the city and reflects its ancient roots. Additionally, the well-preserved Ottoman architecture, including the Nasrullah Mosque and the Liva Paşa Mansion Ethnography Museum provide insight into the city's rich history. Kastamonu, surrounded by lush forests, rivers, and mountains, is a paradise for nature lovers. Ilgaz Mountain National Park is ideal for winter sports like skiing, while Valla Canyon and Ilıca Waterfall provide breathtaking views and excellent hiking and photography opportunities. The UNESCO-recognized Küre Mountains National Park is notable for its biodiversity and scenic beauty.

The city's cultural fabric is enriched with traditional Turkish customs. Visitors can explore local crafts like hand-woven textiles and copperwork in Kastamonu's marketplaces. The Kastamonu Turkish Bath (Kastamonu Hamamı) and regional specialties, such as the renowned Kastamonu bread and meat dishes, offer an authentic taste of the area's culture. From ancient civilizations to the present, Kastamonu has established itself as a destination brand uniquely combining history, nature, and culture. The ancient city of Pompeipolis within Kastamonu depicts its historical richness from the past, which appeals to travelers looking for adventure and tradition (Cetin, 2015). Pompeipolis' exhibition and archaeological site preservation are touristic, attracting many potential tourists from Türkiye, locally and globally.

Destination Brand and Challenges

One of the primary challenges in destination branding is ensuring sustainability while managing environmental impacts (Tulasi et al., 2024, p. 1). Authors examined the role of aesthetics in tourist satisfaction in the Ghanaian hospitality industry, they argued that "Ghanaian hospitality sector should push creativity to new heights by ensuring that venues change their appearance and ambiance through the use of creative lights, music, and food setups" (Tulasi et al., 2024, p. 1). Moreover, the destination's food image is considered one of the variables in promoting the brand destination; for instance, researchers found UNESCO's seven themes "crafts and folk art, design, film, gastronomy, literature, media arts, and music" (MENA Report,

2017), in the gastronomy tourism context in City of Gaziantep, Türkiye is crucial in destination branding (Yilmaz et al., 2020).

Another challenge that destination brands face is over-tourism, which is driven by increased travel accessibility due to budget airlines and global connectivity, the rapid popularity of destinations through social media and marketing, and economic incentives that attract more visitors. Additionally, destinations with unique attractions, major events, or cruise tourism can experience significant overcrowding. Poor planning, lack of regulation, seasonal peaks, and the concentration of tourists in popular spots further exacerbate the issue. Effective management and regulation are essential to balance the benefits of tourism with the well-being of local communities and the sustainability of destinations. Many popular tourist destinations need help with over-tourism, where the sheer number of visitors exceeds the area's capacity, leading to environmental degradation, pollution, and strain on local resources. Balancing the influx of tourists with preserving natural habitats and cultural heritage sites is crucial. Implementing sustainable tourism practices, such as promoting eco-friendly travel options and enforcing strict environmental regulations, can help mitigate these issues but requires significant effort and cooperation from local authorities, businesses, and tourists.

According to the literature, welcoming nature in tourism is crucial for enhancing tourists' experiences and strengthening destination branding. Friendly and hospitable resident interactions create positive memories, encouraging repeat visits and favorable word-of-mouth recommendations. This welcoming attitude supports sustainable tourism by fostering responsible behavior and appreciation for local cultures while driving economic benefits through increased tourist spending. Furthermore, it garners community support for tourism initiatives, facilitates meaningful cultural exchange, and helps reduce conflicts between tourists and locals. Overall, a welcoming nature contributes to a more enriching travel experience and supports destinations' economic and social well-being. Wang et al. (2021) demonstrated a strong link between resident attitudes and destination branding, highlighting how interactions between residents and tourists can enhance brand support and address perceptions of over-tourism in China's rural areas. Economic factors also pose significant challenges in destination branding. Over-reliance on tourism can make local economies vulnerable to fluctuations caused by seasonal variations, economic downturns, or global crises such as pandemics. Destinations must diversify economies to reduce this dependency and promote year-round tourism to stabilize income streams. Additionally, developing robust infrastructure that can support tourism without compromising the quality of life for residents is essential. This includes investing in transportation, accommodation, and other essential services while ensuring the local community benefits from tourism revenues.

In today's globalized world, cultural intelligence has become a critical skill for expats professionals. Building on the importance of cross-cultural training, expatriates must also develop solid cultural intelligence to navigate their new surroundings effectively. Building on the importance of cross-cultural training, expatriates must also develop strong cultural intelligence to navigate their new surroundings effectively. In other words, how can expatriates effectively adapt to a new cultural environment?

Aktan, Zaman, and Nawaz (2021) examined destinations' personalities and brand equity through the lens of expats living abroad. Their study highlights expatriate communities' pivotal role in tourism destination branding, focusing on 307 expatriates from Korea and Turkey. Their findings offer valuable insights for marketers assessing the vital role of global expatriates in strengthening tourism destination branding. Destination branding efforts must prioritize preserving and celebrating local cultures and involving communities in the tourism planning process. Encouraging cultural tourism that respects and highlights local traditions can enhance the tourist experience while safeguarding the cultural identity of the destination.

Rational of Study

The objectives of a study using co-word analysis, a type of social network analysis (SNA) approach, are to systematically explore and map the intellectual structure of a specific research domain. Previous studies done using co-word analysis indicated the significance of the technique and its contribution to the vast field of tourism. One of the seminal co-word applications in tourism research was made by Singh et al. (2011) to perform a bibliometric assessment in the " Journal of Quality Assurance in Hospitality & Tourism." Also, Ülker et al. employed co-word analysis to identify the most frequently used keywords in tourism and hospitality studies, demonstrating how specific terms like "bibliometric analysis," "tourism," and "hospitality" often co-occur, thus indicating prevalent themes in the literature (Ülker et al., 2022). In another study, Kusumaningrum's bibliometric analysis showed that sustainability research in destination branding is developing, with co-word analysis being a significant tool for mapping research trends and opportunities (Kusumaningrum, 2023). Long et al. also, in support of Kusumaningrum, argued that the importance of co-occurrence through social commerce significantly enhances destination brand equity, highlighting the role of tourists in sharing their experiences and recommendations (Long et al., 2022). To our knowledge, all previous studies mainly applied bibliometric methods in their articles; therefore, in this exploratory approach, the co-word technique is applied from a social network analysis perspective.

The study aims to identify and visualize the main themes, trends, and relationships among key concepts by examining the co-occurrence patterns of keywords within a destination brand of academic publications. This approach helps uncover the underlying structure and evolution of the field, highlighting emerging topics, influential research areas, and potential gaps in the literature. Additionally, the study seeks to understand the interconnectedness and clustering of co-word. Co-word analysis can provide insights into how knowledge is organized and disseminated within destination branding, ultimately contributing to a deeper understanding and more informed strategic decisions for future research directions. This chapter will utilize SNA methodology to address the following research questions:

- What are the most frequently co-occurring keywords in the selected research domain, and how are they interconnected?
- Does the network of co-occurring keywords exhibit small-world properties?
- Which keywords serve as bridges between different clusters within the network, and what role do they play in the integration of diverse research themes?

Data Collection

To this end, WoS reports that there are about 2800 publications in their core collection on "Tourism" and "Destination Branding" (see Fig. 1). Publication on destination branding started slowly. However, the number of articles gradually increased during 2020 to 321.

Figure 1. Destination branding publications from 1999 to 2024 as of 17.07.2024.

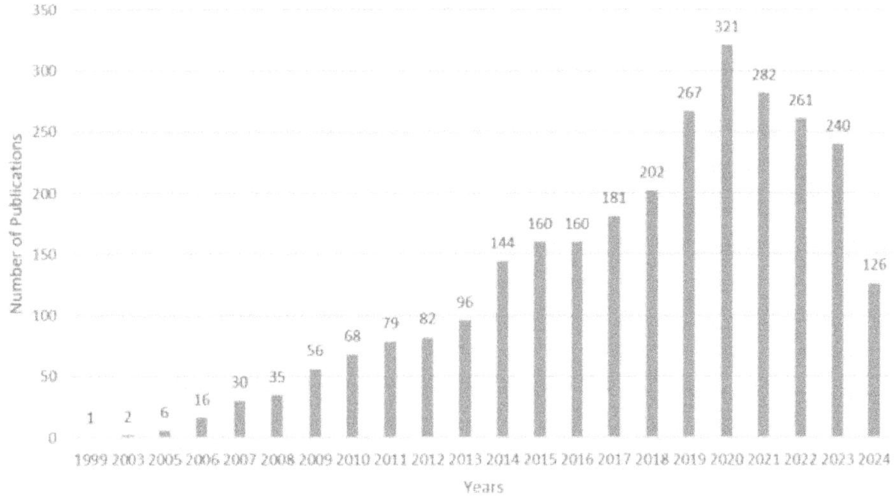

Methods

Web of Science (WoS) is considered trustworthy because of its rigorous selection process for including journals and articles. WoS uses a comprehensive set of criteria to evaluate the quality and impact of journals, ensuring that only high-quality, peer-reviewed publications are indexed. Therefore, we selected only 150 records to access and map the network structure of the scientific articles and clarify the visualization (See Fig. 2). Bibliometrix (Aria & Cuccurullo, 2017) an R software package that operates within R-Studio, was used.

Results

A keyword co-occurrences network analysis also shows a conceptual structure of the destination branding scientific domain. Following are answer the research's questions,

- What are the most frequently co-occurring keywords in the selected research domain, and how are they interconnected?

Red Cluster (Left) encompasses Satisfaction, Place, Trust, Management, Behavior, Loyalty, Travel, Consumption, Antecedents, Destination Brand, and Place Attachment, emphasizing how these factors influence consumer satisfaction and behavior. In contrast, the Blue Cluster (Right) holds Model, Perceptions, Impact, Experience, Involvement, Quality, Customer-Based Brand, Australia, and Dimensions.

Figure 2. Network structure of the keyword co-occurrences

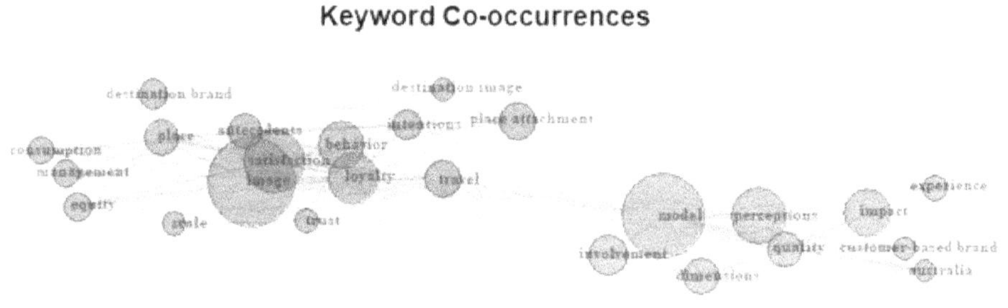

A total of 320 keywords was formed the network structure with a density of 0.045 which indicate that all the nodes are not connected with each other. In the other word, density value of 0.045 in a co-word occurrence network indicates a sparse network with low connectivity among keywords, reflecting that the majority of terms do not frequently co-occur. This can point to a research field with many distinct or loosely connected topics (See Table 1).

Table 1. Measures of the co-word structure

Main statistics about the network	
Size	320
Density	0.045
Transitivity	0.304
Diameter	5
Degree Centralization	0.397
Average path length	2.417

A transitivity value of 0.304 in a co-word occurrence network suggests a moderate level of interconnectedness among keywords, highlighting the presence of some cohesive clusters and areas with weaker connections. A transitivity can help understand the main themes and sub-themes within the analyzed research area. In addition, a diameter 5 in a co-word occurrence network indicates moderate connectivity and spread among the terms. A diameter 5 suggests a well-integrated network where even the most distant terms are relatively close regarding their co-occurrence relationships. A network with a degree centralization of 0.397 in a co-word occurrence network indicates a moderate level of centralization, with several essential terms playing a central role in connecting the network, but not to the extent that the network is dominated by a single or a few terms. Degree centrality reflects a balanced structure with both influential and peripheral terms (See Table 1).

- Does the network of co-occurring keywords exhibit small-world properties?

The measure obtained from the network indicates that network structures share small-world properties. The network features a modular structure characterized by tightly-knit clusters and numerous inter-cluster connections, indicating small-world properties. This arrangement facilitates efficient information dissemination throughout the network. The overall structure of the network has high clustering and short path lengths, which indicate small-world attributes. In another words, Networks with short average path lengths often display the small-world phenomenon, where most nodes can be reached from any other node through several steps (See Figure2).

- Which keywords serve as bridges between different clusters within the network, and what role do they play in integrating diverse research themes?

An average path length of 2.41 in a co-word occurrence network indicates that the network is well-connected and that most terms are relatively close, reflecting a cohesive and integrated structure of the analyzed research area. Keywords like "satisfaction," "trust," and "management" from the red cluster, along with "model," "perceptions," and "quality" from the blue cluster, likely act as bridges. They connect various research themes, integrating consumer behavior discussions with theoretical models and quality perceptions. For example, "Satisfaction" bridges consumer behavior and place-related studies with broader discussions on destination branding and management strategies. The word "Model" connects empirical studies on perceptions and impact with theoretical frameworks, facilitating a comprehensive understanding of the research domain, and "Quality" gates discussions on customer-based brand metrics with experiential and involvement-related themes, highlighting its role in perceived brand value and consumer experiences (See Figure2).

The conceptual structure of a field is the organization and relationships of key concepts, theories, and themes within an academic or research area. It serves as a framework for understanding these elements' interconnections and contributions to the overall body of knowledge (See Figure 3).

Figure 3. The conceptual structure of the destination branding based on the title and abstract of the scientific articles from WoS

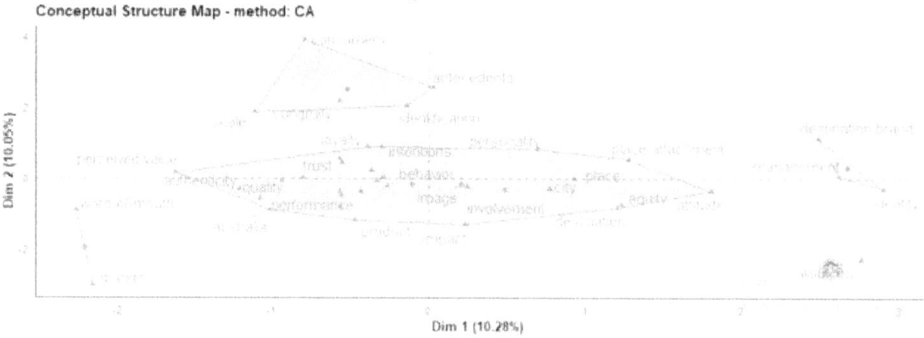

The above image is a Conceptual Structure Map generated using Correspondence Analysis (CA). The conceptual map helps to visualize the relationships among various concepts within destination branding. The image is a Conceptual Structure Map generated using Correspondence Analysis (CA). The conceptual map helps to visualize the relationships among various concepts within destination branding. The map consists of three parts; one can interpret the map as follows:

Red Cluster (Top left) encompasses Scale, Congruity, Identification, Antecedents, and Consumers. This cluster focuses on the relationships between consumers and the factors influencing their identification and perception of congruity with various scales and antecedents. Green Cluster (Left center) comprises Market, Word-of-Mouth, and Perceived Value. This cluster is centered around market-related concepts and highlights the importance of perceived value and word-of-mouth in the market context.

Blue Cluster (Center) includes Australia, Authenticity, Quality, Trust, Loyalty, Intentions, Behavior, Product, Image, Impact, Performance, Equity, Place Attachment, Personality, Involvement, City, Destination. This central cluster represents various concepts related to destination branding, consumer behavior, and place attachment. It indicates the multifaceted nature of the research area, encompassing aspects of product performance, quality, trust, and the impact on destinations.

Yellow Cluster (Right) shows the Destination Brand, Management, and Identity. This cluster focuses on destination branding and its management, highlighting the role of identity in shaping destination brands. Finally, Purple Point (Bottom right) depicts Alliances. This concept is more isolated but indicates the importance of strategic alliances in the overall conceptual structure.

An overall interpretation indicates that the central blue cluster signifies the core concepts in the field, such as consumer behavior, place attachment, and destination branding. Peripheral Themes (red, green, yellow, and purple) represent more specific or ancillary themes that support or influence the central concepts. The proximity of interconnections concepts within the same cluster indicates a strong relationship or association between them. For instance, trust, loyalty, and behavior are closely related and form part of the central cluster (See Fig. 3).

CONCLUSION AND REMARKS

This exploratory study analyzes destination branding using the social network analysis method, particularly co-word analysis. We extracted scientific articles from the Clarivate Web of Science (WoS) to undertake the task using a textual query. We mentioned that co-word analysis is a method within the broader social network analysis framework (SNA). Therefore, the same principle and metrics of SNA can be applied to nodes within a network structure of authors, countries, stakeholders, citations, journals, institutions, destinations, and themes, to name a few, to delve into destination branding within tourism as a research field. Scholarly communications about Istanbul, Konya and Kastamonu as destination brands were discussed and described in terms of history, culture.

We utilized social network analysis (SNA) methods like co-word analysis, which can help us understand and evaluate destination tourism brands by examining how different keywords associated with a destination are interconnected in research papers, social media posts, or reviews. Scientific articles within destination branding were selected from WoS. Co-word analysis involves creating a network where keywords are nodes, and their co-occurrences (how often they appear together) are edges. By analyzing the network, we can identify key themes and concepts that define the destination's brand. For example, if keywords like "historic sites," "culinary experiences," and "cultural festivals" frequently co-occur about a city, these elements are likely central to its tourism brand. This approach helps us see the strengths, unique attributes, and overall perception of the destination in a structured and data-driven way. The network exhibits characteristics suggesting it possesses small-world properties, tightly-knit clusters, and numerous connections.

This structure facilitates efficient information dissemination across the destination brands' research domain, promoting interdisciplinary collaboration and integrating diverse themes. High centrality keywords within each cluster, such as "satisfaction" and "model," are crucial in connecting their respective thematic areas and serve as bridges linking different clusters (see Fig. 2). These bridge keywords enhance the overall coherence of the research field by connecting empirical studies on consumer behavior with broader theoretical discussions on branding and quality perceptions. A conceptual Structure Map was generated using Correspondence Analysis (see Fig. 3), which implies the relationships among various concepts within a given field, such as destination brands. It highlights the central themes of consumer behavior, destination branding, and place attachment, along with ancillary themes like market dynamics, consumer identification, and strategic alliances. The map helps practitioners understand how these concepts interact and contribute to the field of destination brands in tourism.

As a destination brand, we showcase three cities in Türkiye, each with a significant tourism brand, such as Istanbul, Konya, and Kastamonu. Istanbul, Turkey's largest city, enchants visitors with its rich history, cultural diversity, and strategic position between Europe and Asia. The city's identity is deeply embedded in its storied past as the heart of the Byzantine and Ottoman Empires, showcased by landmarks such as the Hagia Sophia, Topkapi Palace, and the Blue Mosque. These sites draw countless tourists annually and reflect Istanbul's profound cultural heritage and architectural magnificence. Additionally, the bustling bazaars and vibrant neighborhoods like Beyoğlu and Kadıköy highlight the city's dynamic blend of tradition and modernity. Istanbul also serves as a global business hub, hosting international conferences and festivals, and its culinary scene offers everything from traditional delights to innovative fusion cuisine, all set against the picturesque backdrop of the Bosphorus Strait.

Konya and Kastamonu offer distinct yet equally compelling attractions. Konya is celebrated for its spiritual and cultural significance as the home of Rumi and the Whirling Dervishes, with the Mevlana Museum and the city's serene atmosphere, drawing visitors seeking spiritual enrichment. The city harmoniously blends its historical and religious heritage with modern developments, maintaining its unique character. Kastamonu, on the other hand, is known for its well-preserved Ottoman architecture and natural beauty. The city's historical buildings, such as Kastamonu

Castle and Nasrullah Mosque, offer a glimpse into its Ottoman past. At the same time, the surrounding Ilgaz Mountain National Park provides massive opportunities for outdoor activities. Konya and Kastamonu showcase Turkey's diverse offerings, from spiritual journeys and historical exploration to natural retreats and adventure.

However, the journey to successful destination branding is fraught with challenges. Sustainability is a significant concern, managing environmental impacts and balancing visitor numbers to prevent over-tourism. Economic factors also play a significant role, as destinations must avoid over-reliance on tourism and address the seasonal fluctuations that can destabilize local economies. This calls for diversified investment and infrastructure development to support year-round tourism and enhance the local economy's resilience.

Generally speaking, a firm destination branding policy must emphasize authenticity, sustainability, and community engagement, highlighting the area's actual cultural, historical, and natural features while ensuring environmentally friendly tourism practices that bolster local economies. This policy should involve local stakeholders, including residents and businesses, in the branding process to reflect their perspectives and needs. Further, It should highlight responsible tourism practices that reduce environmental impact and protect cultural heritage. Transparent communication and consistent monitoring are crucial for adapting the branding strategy based on feedback and evolving conditions, fostering a balanced and holistic approach to destination development.

REFERENCES

Akkaya, Ö., Arslan, Ö., & Zerenler, M. (2024). Revisiting the host city: Examining event quality, host city evaluation, place attachment and destination brand equity from the spectators at the Konya Islamic Games 2022. *Journal of Convention & Event Tourism*, •••, 1–29. DOI: 10.1080/15470148.2024.2382145

Aktan, M., Zaman, U., & Nawaz, S. (2021). Examining destinations' personality and brand equity through the lens of expats: Moderating role of expat's cultural intelligence. *Asia Pacific Journal of Tourism Research*, 26(8), 849–865. DOI: 10.1080/10941665.2021.1925314

Aria, M., & Cuccurullo, C. (2017). Bibliometrix: An R-tool for comprehensive science mapping analysis. *Journal of Informetrics*, 11(4), 959–975. DOI: 10.1016/j.joi.2017.08.007

Barabási, A.-L. (2003). *Linked: How Everything is Connected to Everything Else and What It Means for Business, Science, and Everyday Life*. Plume.

Borgatti, S. P., Everett, M. G., & Johnson, J. C. (2018). *Analyzing Social Networks* (2nd ed.). SAGE Publications.

Cetin, M. (2015). Evaluation of the sustainable tourism potential of a protected area for landscape planning: A case study of the ancient city of Pompeipolis in Kastamonu. *International Journal of Sustainable Development and World Ecology*, 22(6), 490–495. DOI: 10.1080/13504509.2015.1081651

FasterCapital. (n.d.). *Centrality measures in social network analysis*. Retrieved October 17, 2024, from https://fastercapital.com/topics/centrality-measures-in-social-network-analysis.html

Freeman, L. C. (1977). A set of measures of centrality based on betweenness. *Sociometry*, 40(1), 35. DOI: 10.2307/3033543

Freeman, L. C. (1978). Centrality in social networks conceptual clarification. *Social Networks*, 1(3), 215–239. DOI: 10.1016/0378-8733(78)90021-7

Freeman, L. C. (1978). Centrality in social networks: Conceptual clarification. *Social Networks*, 1(3), 215–239. DOI: 10.1016/0378-8733(78)90021-7

Granovetter, M. S. (1973). The Strength of Weak Ties. *American Journal of Sociology*, 78(6), 1360–1380. DOI: 10.1086/225469

Güngör, G., & Akar, T. (2022). Kentin Simgesini Görünür Kılmak: Kızkulesi'nden Kızkalesi'ne Bir Aydınlatma Diyaloğu. *The Turkish Online Journal of Design Art and Communication*, 12(2), 300–315.

İbret, Ü., Aydınözü, D., & Uğurlu, M. (2015). KASTAMONU ŞEHRİNDE KÜLTÜR VE İNANÇ TURİZMİ. *Marmara Coğrafya Dergisi*, 0(32), 239–269. DOI: 10.14781/mcd.00582

Karagöz, H. A., Demirçiftçi, T., & Erkmen, E. (2022). Local Restaurants' Effect on Tourist Experience: A Case from Istanbul. *Journal of Economy Culture and Society*, 0(65), 313–327. DOI: 10.26650/JECS2021-1007826

Kasapoğlu, C., Aksoy, R., & Başkol, M. (2023). Assessing Destination Brand Associations on Twitter: The case of Istanbul. [AHTR]. *Advances in Hospitality and Tourism Research*, 11(4), 443–475. DOI: 10.30519/ahtr.1116172

Kusumaningrum, S. D. (2023). Sustainability and destination branding: A review of research trends. *Turisztikai És Vidékfejlesztési Tanulmányok*, 7(4), 110–127. DOI: 10.15170/TVT.2022.07.04.08

Lewin, K. (1947). *Field Theory in Social Science: Selected Theoretical Papers*. Harper & Row.

Long, P. H., Woyo, E., Pham, T. H., & Dao, T. X. T. (2022). Value co-creation and destination brand equity: Understanding the role of social commerce information sharing. *Journal of Hospitality and Tourism Insights*, 6(5), 1796–1817. DOI: 10.1108/JHTI-04-2022-0123

Milgram, S. (1967). The small world problem. *Psychology Today*, 1(1), 61–67.

Moreno, A., Jabreel, M., & Huertas, A. (2015). Automatic analysis of the communication of tourist destination brands through social networks. In *10th International Conference on Intelligent Systems and Knowledge Engineering (ISKE)* (pp. 546-553). IEEE. https://doi.org/DOI: 10.1109/ISKE.2015.22

Moreno, J. L. (1934). *Who Shall Survive?* Beacon House.

Moreno, J. L., & Jennings, H. H. (1938). Statistics of social constellations. *Sociometry*, 1(3), 342–374. DOI: 10.2307/2785588

Morgan, N. J., Pritchard, A., & Piggott, R. (2003). Destination branding and the role of the stakeholders: The case of New Zealand. *Journal of Vacation Marketing*, 9(3), 285–299. Advance online publication. DOI: 10.1177/135676670300900307

Oğuztimur, S. (2017). *Modeling a City's Branding Tools: The Case of Istanbul*. InTech., DOI: 10.5772/intechopen.69269

Pike, S. (2005). Tourism destination branding complexity. *Journal of Product &Amp. Journal of Product and Brand Management*, 14(4), 258–259. DOI: 10.1108/10610420510609267

MENA Report. (2017). Canada: Toronto designated a UNESCO Creative City of Media Arts. *MENA Report*

Roethlisberger, F. J., & Dickson, W. J. (1939). *Management and the Worker*. Harvard University Press.

Sakar, A. S. (2022). The Brand Personality of Konya City As a Touristic Destination. *Selçuk Turizm Ve Bilişim Araştırmaları Dergisi*, 1(2), 25–31.

Saraniemi, S. (2011). From destination image building to identity-based branding. *International Journal of Culture, Tourism and Hospitality Research*, 5(3), 247–254. DOI: 10.1108/17506181111156943

Scott, J. (2017). *Social Network Analysis: A Handbook* (4th ed.). SAGE Publications. DOI: 10.4135/9781529716597

Singh, R., Sibi, P. S., Sharma, P., Tamang, M., & Singh, A. K. (2021). Twenty years of journal of quality assurance in hospitality & tourism: A bibliometric assessment. *Journal of Quality Assurance in Hospitality &Amp. Tourism (Zagreb)*, 23(2), 482–507. DOI: 10.1080/1528008X.2021.1884931

Tulasi, E. E., Ashiaby, O. E., Kodua, P., Ahlijah, B., & Agyeman-Duah, M. O. (2024). The role of aesthetics in tourist satisfaction in the Ghanaian hospitality industry. *Heliyon*, 10(1), e32944. DOI: 10.1016/j.heliyon.2024.e32944 PMID: 38994054

Ülker, P., Ülker, M., & Karamustafa, K. (2022). Bibliometric analysis of bibliometric studies in the field of tourism and hospitality. *Journal of Hospitality and Tourism Insights*, 6(2), 797–818. DOI: 10.1108/JHTI-10-2021-0291

Uysal, Ü. (2017). A brief history of city branding in istanbul., 117-131. https://doi.org/DOI: 10.4018/978-1-5225-0576-1.ch006

Uysal, Ü., & Özden, P. (2011). *Cultural tourism as a tool for urban regeneration in İstanbul*. WIT Press., DOI: 10.2495/ST110351

Vila-López, N., Kuster-Boluda, I., Mora-Pérez, E., & Sarabia Sanchez, F. (2024). The role of sports on destination branding: A bibliometric study. *Journal of Vacation Marketing*, 13567667241272811. Advance online publication. DOI: 10.1177/13567667241272811

Wang, H., Xiong, L., & Gage, R. (2021). Cultivating destination brand ambassadors in rural China: Examining the role of residents' welcoming nature. *International Journal of Tourism Research*, 23(6), 1027–1041. DOI: 10.1002/jtr.2460

Wasserman, S., & Faust, K. (1994). *Social Network Analysis: Methods and Applications*. Cambridge University Press. DOI: 10.1017/CBO9780511815478

Watts, D. (2003). *Six Degrees: The Science of a Connected Age*. W. W. Norton & Company.

Watts, D. J., & Strogatz, S. H. (1998). Collective dynamics of 'small-world' networks. *Nature*, 393(6684), 440–442. DOI: 10.1038/30918 PMID: 9623998

Yilmaz, G., Kilicarslan, D., & Caber, M. (2020). How does a destination's food image serve the common targets of the UNESCO creative cities network? *International Journal of Tourism Cities*, 6(4), 785–812. DOI: 10.1108/IJTC-07-2019-0115

ADDITIONAL READING

Elizabeth, A., T.O, F., & M.O., À. (. (2023). The impact of destination brand image on entrepreneurial development in the tourism host communities in the south-west region of nigeria. *International Journal of Research Publication and Reviews*, 4(7), 1773–1780. DOI: 10.55248/gengpi.4.723.17731780

Ouda, N., Ezzat, M., & Abu-El Gheit, N. (2023). Applicability of reputation marketing to the branding of luxor as a tourist destination. *International Journal of Tourism and Hospitality Management*, 6(2), 1–18. DOI: 10.21608/ijthm.2023.327203

Son, V. H. and Thao, N. V. H. (2023). Bibliometrics of destination marketing research: cocitation and bibliographic coupling analyses. *T p Chí Nghiên C u Tài Chính - Marketing*, 116-126. https://doi.org/DOI: 10.52932/jfm.vi6.436

Tiago, F., Correia, P. Á. P., Briciu, V., & Borges-Tiago, T. (2021). Geotourism destinations online branding co-creation. *Sustainability (Basel)*, 13(16), 8874. DOI: 10.3390/su13168874

KEY TERMS AND DEFINITIONS

Bibliomertix: Bibliometrix is a software written in R that runs in RStiduo to conduct bibliometric analysis.

Co-word analysis: Co-word analysis measures the co-occurring words in a set of documents within an article or abstract of the article.

Degree Centrality: Degree centrality measures a network's properties based on nodes' location and edges as the relation between them in Closeness, Betweenness, and Degree.

Destination Brands: Destination brands create and advertise tourist destinations in any form to attract tourists from local or global populations.

Kastamonu: The City of Kastamonu is a tourist palace located northeast of Anatolia, Türkiye, with a castle dating back to the Roman era.

Konya: The City of Konya is a tourist palace located in central Anatolia, Türkiye, which has witnessed many Empires, including Hetits, Romans, Selcuks, and Ottamans.

Social Network Analysis(SNA): Social network analysis is a methodology that measures entities in the context of nodes and relationships among them.

Chapter 8
Eco-tourism Branding Balancing Conservation and Community

Uma Pandey
https://orcid.org/0000-0002-8817-1546
Jagran Lakecity University, India

Hafizullah Dar
https://orcid.org/0000-0003-2388-9474
Lovely Professional University, India

ABSTRACT

Balancing conservation and community development is a significant challenge, especially where natural resources are protected and serve as livelihoods for locals. This study focuses on Kanha National Park in central India, which conserves diverse flora and fauna, including tigers and swamp deer. Conservation efforts often conflict with the livelihoods of locals living in buffer zones, leading to socioeconomic issues. Eco-tourism offers an alternative income source, leveraging the park's natural beauty and biodiversity. This chapter analyzes Kanha's eco-tourism branding, highlighting sustainable tourism practices and their ecological importance. Sustainable measures, like eco-friendly lodging and income reinvestment in community projects, align local interests with conservation goals. Despite challenges, the chapter suggests Kanha's model as an example of effective eco-tourism branding, promoting conservation and regional development through inclusive management.

DOI: 10.4018/979-8-3693-6700-1.ch008

1. INTRODUCTION

The initial idea of establishing Protected Area (PA) was based on the need for biodiversity conservation (Saout et al., 2013). However, the strict conservation policies enforced in and around these PAs impact the livelihoods of local communities that depend on them. The biggest challenge for policymakers and conservationists worldwide is that they should balance environmental conservation and the socioeconomic development of these local communities. Even though proper management of PAs requires the conservation of natural ecosystems for their long-term sustainability, it does not mean that the welfare of individuals living in such environments for generations should be compromised. The establishment of PAs may hurt local communities (Andrade & Rhodes, 2012; Abukari & Mwalyosi, 2020). A study by Bonye et al. (2023) suggests that most residents lose their traditional means of livelihood due to inadequate access to forest resources, which increases their poverty and food insecurity. The jobs in and around the PAs in the form of tourism or park management are few and, hence, usually cannot compensate for the loss from their traditional sources of income. This results in poverty and marginalization because most people have no alternate livelihoods. In such areas, education and health facilities are also underdeveloped, deepening the community's backwardness. Their youth have limited skill development and employment opportunities, so they migrate to urban areas for better prospects for jobs and facilities. This socioeconomic exclusion fuels resentment toward conservation policies and poses a significant challenge to harmonious coexistence between the success of conservation efforts and community well-being (Montenegro-Pazmiño & Muñoz, 2024). Therefore, authorities in such PAs must maintain a proper balance between conservation and community interests. This balanced approach is essential to involve local communities which is needed for the success of any conservation activity. Conservation goals may be more coherently connected with community welfare if community perspectives are considered throughout the planning process and sustainable livelihood choices are considered. PAs should be managed inclusively and collaboratively, and the local community should be engaged to meet the ecological and human needs together to ensure that local community interests are balanced. Fundamentally, PA management depends on the cooperation and support of locals living within or near these areas to succeed in sustainable conservation.

1.1. Conflict

The establishment of the PAs is an essential process in preserving the biodiversity that brings considerable conflicts like the use of resources, human-wildlife conflict, and policy implementation issues between the objectives of conservation and the means of livelihood for local communities (Samal & Dash, 2023). The reason for such conflicts is the restrictions placed on traditional uses of forest resources that may affect the socio-economic welfare of local communities living within or around these PAs if not appropriately regulated. However, the preservation of the biodiversity of the PAs, along with the protection of endangered species, is of prime concern; the well-being and socio-economic development of the local communities should not be brushed aside. The major conflicts in PAs are discussed below:

1.1.1. Use of Resources

For generations, local indigenous communities have dwelled in and around PAs. These local communities' lives are culturally and spiritually connected with the forest as they believe that their deity resides in the forest. The forest also provided them with food, fuel, fodder, and medicinal plants. Their livelihoods have depended on shifting cultivation, raising livestock, harvesting Non-Timber Forest Products (NTFPs), and practicing small-scale agriculture for generations (Luz & Ruiz-Mallén, 2020; De Bruyn et al., 2022). However, this relationship changed drastically with the strict conservation measures that followed the establishment of PAs. The authorities put stringent restrictions on resource extraction and land use both in and around the PAs to ensure the integrity of the PA's ecological systems and protect its focal species. These conservation measures have created conflict between the local communities dependent on forest resources for their livelihoods and conservation authorities.

1.1.2. Conservation vs. Livelihoods

Restrictions on traditional livelihood practices like NTFP collection, and grazing cattle have resulted in several challenges, the most significant of which are decreased income and food security for many communities. Because these communities have limited access to conventional resources, they struggle with poverty and unstable economies. The displacement and resettlement of some communities because of conservation initiatives have made the challenge worse (Cernea & Schmidt-Soltau, 2006; Lasgorceix & Kothari, 2009; Miller et al., 2022; Bontempi et al., 2023). It is challenging for resettled families to cope with the new environment and to obtain alternate livelihoods. One or more males in every household migrate to other towns for employment to survive. In many cases, the government fails to provide sufficient compensation and help for the resettlement process, which has caused resentment against the conservation authorities (Sarma & Barpujari, 2022).

1.1.3. Human-Wildlife Conflicts

The other major conflict around PAs is related to human-wildlife interactions (Chaplin-Kramer et al., 2023). Since local communities have limited access to PA resources, they generally encroach into buffer areas and even into core areas of the PA to fulfill their needs. They get involved in the illegal trading of forest resources, which may involve the killing of wild animals. The killing of wildlife in retaliation by angry villagers further heightens tension between conservation goals and local livelihoods. Animals, as they know no boundaries, often come to human settlements and damage the crops, prey on their livestock, and, in some cases, even threaten human safety. These conflicts have a sizeable economic impact on the local communities, who generally incur losses. In an attempt to mitigating human-wildlife conflicts, attempts, like compensation schemes or barrier building, deliver mixed results that bring out the complications in finding practical solutions.

Eco-tourism has been presented as a plausible answer to boosting conservation with community development (Samal & Dash, 2022; Zhang et al., 2023). It stresses low-impact activities in the natural environment, such as guided nature walks, homestays run by the community, and cultural events. The way these activities are carried out minimizes environmental impact while maximizing residents' financial benefits. It also actively engages the local community while offering tourists an immersive experience. In addition to providing alternate sources of income, ecotourism makes locals feel proud and gives them a sense of ownership towards conservation efforts.

1.2. Understanding Eco-Tourism

Eco-tourism is sustainable tourism that supports responsible travel to natural areas, allowing the conservation of the environment while supporting the well-being of local communities and provision of education to both hosts and tourists. Ceballos-Lascuráin (1996) was the first to coin the word “eco-tourism”. He defined it as environmentally responsible travel to relatively undisturbed natural areas to enjoy and appreciate nature, promoting conservation with low visitor impact and encouraging active socio-economic involvement of local populations. According to Fennell (1999), it is a form of tourism that focuses on the experience and appreciation of nature, but at the same time is sustainable. Honey (2009) refers to it as tourism which includes conservation, communities, and sustainable travel in responsible travel to natural sites that conserve the environment and uplift well-being among the people at the location. The International Eco-Tourism Society (2015) also has a similar definition of eco-tourism, which says that eco-tourism is responsible travel to natural areas that conserve the environment, supports the well-being of local people, and involves interpretation and education.

1.3. Principles of Eco-Tourism

1.3.1. Minimization of Impact: The first principle of eco-tourism is to minimize the adverse impacts of tourism on both the environment and society (Shasha et al., 2020). Therefore, the willing PAs which intend to introduce eco-tourism should avoid all forms of destruction and disruption that may be done to wildlife habitats and reduce waste in the ecosystem, control pollution, and resources should be used carefully.

1.3.2. Building Environmental and Cultural Awareness and Respect: The second principle of eco-tourism is that education of the tourists, local communities, and other stakeholders on the importance of conserving the environment and cultural heritage is highly crucial (Keitumetse, 2009). Awareness-raising activities among stakeholders should be done in PAs planning to go for eco-tourism.

1.3.3. Pleasant Experience for Tourists and Hosts: The third principle of eco-tourism suggests that it is absolutely necessary to ensure that both the tourist and the local community have enjoyable experiences (Paul & Roy, 2023). If PAs wish to adopt the eco-tourism model, they should ensure pleasurable experiences for tourists and local communities. It will promote a healthy relationship between the tourists and the locals through mutual respect and support.

1.3.4. Monetary Support for Conservation: The fourth principle of eco-tourism requires that the revenues generated from eco-tourism be utilized in conserving the areas (Stronza, 2007). In this case, PAs seeking to utilize the gains from the use of eco-tourism have to ensure that the returns derived from the tourism activities are used to manage the area and support wildlife conservation and environmental education.

1.3.5. Financial Benefits and Empowerment for Local People: The last principle of eco-tourism requires that authorities need to guarantee that the local community receives financial benefits. This can be done by providing them with employment opportunities and supporting them with local businesses (Snyman, 2020). PAs willing to adopt the approach of eco-tourism should first empower such communities through active involvement in policy decisions and help them financially.

1.4. Research Objectives:

The chapter aims to analyse how KNP eco-tourism branding balances conservation with
community interests. Its objectives are to:

- Evaluate the different conservation measures taken within KNP.
- Assess the involvement of communities in and benefits from eco-tourism activities. Examine the eco-tourism branding and marketing of KNP.

- Outline the main challenges to balancing conservation and community interests and potential opportunities for developing eco-tourism initiatives.

The research objectives will be achieved by discussing the case of KNP. It will include
review of relevant literature, and interviews with tourists who visited KNP.

1.5. Significance:

This chapter stresses the need for an eco-tourism destination brand to balance conservation and community development properly. The chapter will give information on how destinations can develop themselves as an eco-tourism brand and provide strategies for balancing environmental preservation and socio-economic development for local communities, thus minimizing conflicts between conservation authorities and locals worldwide. The chapter will also provide important information about eco-tourism practices to policymakers, conservationists, and tourism developers. This information will be appropriate for repositioning conservation objectives with the welfare of local communities.

2. LITERATURE REVIEW

2.1. Eco-tourism Benefits:

Eco-tourism benefits stakeholders in different ways. It has to create value for the environment, local people, tourists, and other stakeholders on the same level. Eco-tourism contributes to environmental conservation as it generates the revenues required to manage and protect the natural areas (Zhou et al., 2021). Besides this, ecotourism raises environmental awareness related to biodiversity's value and promotes its conservation ethics among tourists and the local people (Guri et al., 2020). It acts as a tool to create income-generating avenues for local communities, including employment and local enterprises (Anwar et al., 2023). Additionally, it can promote community development by providing funds for infrastructure improvements such as power, education, and medical facilities (Snyman, 2016). It promotes cultural exchange and understanding between tourists and local communities (Gumede and Nzama, 2022). It can help preserve cultural heritage by promoting traditional cultural practices and crafts as tourist attractions (Oladeji et al., 2021).

2.2. Conservation Efforts in Protected Areas:

PAs form an integral resource in the conservation of biodiversity worldwide. They allow the maximum number of species to be afforded shelter but, at the same time, ensure the conservation of the necessary characteristics of the environment. Worldwide, eco-tourism is being used by various PAs to manage their areas (Ioppolo et al., 2013; Maksanova et al., 2023; Sharma, 2011). Such PAs should adopt the best eco-tourism practices with stakeholder involvement and adaptive planning. Tourism activities in such PAs should be regulated strictly to harmonize with conservation objectives and mitigate negative impacts. In addition, they should safeguard the interests of different stakeholder groups involved in tourism. They should collaborate with stakeholders, including government agencies, NGOs, local communities, park authorities, and commercial sector players (Ioppolo et al., 2013). It can help to develop a sense of ownership and responsibility among stakeholders, which leads to increased support for conservation activities (Sterling et al., 2017).

Eco-tourism ventures have helped protect the environment in several case worldwide. Eco-tourism ventures are regulated, hence minimizing their contribution to the destruction of the environment while educating the tourists on their contribution to the ecosystem. For example, Miller et al. (2023) wrote that implementing eco-tourism in Costa Rica prevented the rainforest from being destroyed, along with the diversity of its species. The country has used its great biodiversity to foster a performing eco-tourism sector that finances the conservation programs. Several African countries, including Kenya, Tanzania, and Botswana, have turned to eco-tourism to conserve wildlife. These countries have placed community-based conservation policies where the locals are responsible for managing PAs and empowering them with tourism opportunities (Turner, 2004). Maasai Mara National Reserve in Kenya was able to strike a balance between eco-tourism and community development to contribute to proper conservation (Tubey et al., 2020). In Australia, institutionalized eco-tourism generates revenue for preserving the reef and creates the consciousness of the need to conserve marine life. Eco-tourism businesses that are regulated minimize their impact on the environment while educating tourists about the ecological significance of the reef (Ewart et al., 2024).

2.3. Community Involvement in Eco-Tourism:

Eco-tourism cannot be successful without community involvement at the local level. It ensures that there is appropriate sharing of benefits accruing from tourism and that local people have a stake in the conservation effort (An & Park, 2023). The community can be involved through employment and entrepreneurship, making them participate in decision-making or management. Getting local communities involved in eco-tourism, provides a number of benefits like economic empowerment, conservation support, and cultural preservation (Anwar et al., 2023). The income generated by eco-tourism can reduce the poverty of local people and enhance their livelihood. Engaging with the local communities and sharing a specific interest within an eco-tourism destination will increase conservation support, as they will be more motivated to protect the natural resources that provide them great economic benefits (Stronza & Gordillo, 2008). Community-based models are very successful in producing local stewardship and improving conservation outcomes. The other advantage of community involvement is that it might help in cultural preservation. Eco-tourism will aid in the conservation of cultural heritage through the promotion of traditional practices and crafts as tourist attractions, thus leading to pride among the members of the community (Altassan, 2023).

2.4. Branding in Eco-Tourism:

Efficient branding of a destination as an eco-tourism destination can help it to be distinguishable among other destinations and ensures that environmentally conscious tourists get the values and experiences that such a destination intends to provide them (Insch, 2011). Branding of eco-tourism destinations is essential as it can aid in developing positive tourist perceptions and behavior so that they can contribute to raising funds for conservation (Batool et al., 2024). It can also help prospective tourists to choose their destinations and activities. A study by Wallace (2019) suggests that eco-tourism branding can draw travelers interested in eco-friendly and responsible travel by differentiating itself based on certain ecological and cultural aspects of the place. It considers various aspects such as sustainability, conservation, and cultural authenticity. Destinations can highlight their environmental protection initiatives, biodiversity, and local customs and traditions (Neto, 2003). It can help raise awareness and funds for conservation in protected areas. By highlighting tourism's value-oriented towards conservation, branding can attract tourists ready to spend on conservation processes, which will improve the economic viability of eco-tourism destinations to ensure long-term conservation (Shoo & Songorwa, 2013; Boley & Green, 2015).

Moreover, eco-tourism branding can foster a sense of stewardship among tourists so that they may wish to behave in an environmentally friendly manner during and after their visit. Educating travelers about a place's ecological and cultural qualities through ecotourism branding may give traveler experiences more purpose and respect and matters about conservation. This type of approach draws visitors and broadens their understanding of cultural heritage preservation. There are drawbacks to eco-tourism branding in addition to its possible advantages. Branding should reflect values and 'real life' at a destination. Misleading or exaggerated branding may result in dissatisfied tourists, which may further harm the reputation of a destination. Another crucial challenge the dilemma between the commercial interest and sustainability. However, branding improves tourism revenues, such revenues cannot be at the expense of the environment or social responsibility. The maintenance of high standards and authenticity is essential in eco-tourism branding.

3. METHODOLOGY

3.1. Research Design: This chapter employs a case study approach where eco-tourism branding of KNP is analyzed. Case study approach provides the researchers with the capacity for in-depth examination of complex issues within a particular context.

3.2. Data Collection:

Document Sources: Promotional brochures, websites, social media campaigns, reports and formal policy documents available online.

Interviews: The primary data was collected through telephonic interviews with tourists who have visited KNP to explore their experiences and behaviors related to its eco-tourism branding. Interviews are best tool to provide deep insights about participant's experiences and behaviour for understanding.

3.2. Methods:

Document Analysis: Various documents were examined to get insights about KNP eco-tourism branding strategies. The analysis helps to find key concepts, messages, and techniques utilized in creating the park's brand identity

Theme analysis: Telephonic interviews of tourists were analyzed to develop themes to gain ideas about tourists' perceptions and experiences. Theme analysis allows to find key areas, uncover patterns, and interpret underlying meanings.

3.4. Study Area: KNP, situated right in the heart of Madhya Pradesh, is one of India's well-known PAs. The park, which has an area of approximately 940 square kilometers, was set up in 1955 and declared a tiger reserve under Project Tiger in 1973.

Figure 1. Map of Kanha National Park (ntca.gov.in)

Table 1. Basic information about Kanha National Park

Longitude: 80°26' 10" E to 81° 04' 40" E
Latitude: 22° 01' 05" N to 22° 27' 48"
Elevation: 450m to 900m (above MSL)
Annual Rainfall: 1400 mm
Temperature: Summer 11°C to 43°C,
Winter -2°C to 29°C

Information Source: ntca.gov.in

The reserve area, including the surrounding buffer zones, occupies nearly 2,074.31 square kilometers ("Tiger Conservation Plan for the Buffer Zone of the Kanha Tiger Reserve," n.d.). According to the official website of Kanha National Park, there are around 850 species of 10 types of Angiosperms from 506 genera and

134 families, as well as 22 species of Pteridophytes from 14 genera and 14 families. The floral diversity mentioned above includes two species of gymnosperms from two genera and two families. In addition, there are about 50 kinds of water plants and 18 uncommon plant species in the flora mentioned above. Kanha is known for thousands of ungulates of at least nine significant species, including tigers, leopards, and wild dogs: chital (*Axis axis*), sambar (*Cervus unicolor*), barasingha (*Rucervus duvaucelii branderi),* barking deer (*Muntiacus muntjak*), chousingha (*Tetracerus quadricornis*), gaur (*Bos gaurus*), nilgai (*Boselaphus tragocamelus*), wild pig (*Sus scrofa*), and the recently reintroduced blackbuck. About 325 species of birds, 18 species of smaller mammals, 39 species of reptiles, over 500 insect species, 114 species of spiders, and approximately 150 species of butterflies are also known to exist. Some rare animals, such as the mouse deer, rusty spotted cat, and little Indian civet, have also been caught via camera traps (www.kanhatigerreserve.org, n.d.) The Park's diversity of avifauna includes raptors, waterfowl, and a string of colorful passerines. The different landscapes of Kanha—from dense Sal forests to extensive grasslands and riverine habitats—provide a crucial haven for a wide variety of flora and fauna. The park is well-known for its high conservation value, more in terms of perpetuating the Bengal Tiger (*Panthera tigris tigris*) and the hardground Barasingha (*Rucervus duvaucelii branderi*), the latter being Kanha's flagship species. The Swamp Deer, or Barasingha, was nearly wiped off the face of Earth during the 1960s but has since staged an inspiring comeback because of the extensive conservation programs. Today, KNP is known for Barasinghas's largest and most healthy population, together with other endangered species like tigers, hence making it a primary habitat for them that is under constant monitoring for India's wildlife conservation effort. It implements various conservation measures over these varied ecosystems, which vary in habitat management, anti-poaching activities, and scientific research. Habitat management includes the management of grasslands and water bodies essential for the survival of key species such as the Barasingha and the Tiger (Rawat & Adhikari, 2015). Poaching and illegal activities are curbed through anti-poaching activities undertaken regularly through monitoring and patrolling. In addition, park authorities employ advanced technologies such as camera traps and GPS tracking. Scientific research plays a vital role in informing the policies and practices of conservation. Studies of wildlife behavior, population dynamics, and habitat use help devise effective management plans (McLane et al., 2011; Matthiopoulos et al., 2015).

We have chosen KNP for the following reasons:

- **Richness in Biodiversity and Conservation:** It is considered the benchmark park for Tigers and Barasinghas conservation. It will provide us with a great platform to investigate how eco-tourism may contribute to preserving biodiversity.

- **Community Involvement:** It has been involving local people in its initiatives of eco-tourism, making it a place with much potential to be explored for community involvement in sustainable tourism.
- **Eco-Tourism Branding**: The park has become one of India's top ecotourism destinations because to its distinctive brand identity. Its branding techniques aid in determining how marketing affects tourism and conservation results.

4. ECO-TOURISM BRANDING IN KANHA NATIONAL PARK

KNP approaches eco-tourism branding strategically in order to highlight sustainability, conservation, and cultural authenticity. It has a strong brand image and is one of India's top wildlife destinations, drawing eco-aware tourists from all over the world. The section that follows examines marketing channels and promotional activities, assesses the methods employed to position KNP as an eco-tourism destination, and looks at how visitors feel about the branding and overall experience.

4.1. Eco-Tourism Branding Strategies

Branding is essential in distinguishing eco-tourism destinations from other available destinations by clearly conveying its value propositions (Ashton, 2015; Hudson & Ritchie, 2009; Rivera & Croes, 2010). The branding strategies deployed by KNP emphasize three key elements: conservation, community involvement, and cultural heritage.

4.1.1. Conservation focussed Branding

The KNP has established its brand image as a wildlife conservation leader for the Bengal tiger and the Barasingha (swamp deer). It is the only park in India with a mascot called 'Bhoorsingh the Barahsingha." The park, also called the Kanha Tiger Reserve, is meant strictly for the conservation of tigers. As a tiger reserve, it focuses on successful conservation efforts that elevate the number of tigers. Other than tigers, the park also accommodates such as the Indian wild dog (dhole), Indian leopard, sloth bear, gaur (Indian bison), and thousands of birds and other reptilian species, like the Indian python, except for the Indian peafowl and crested serpent eagle. KNP also offers a variety of flora, including sal and bamboo trees, grasslands, and aquatic habitats, making KNP an essential site for biodiversity conservation. It attracts the attention of wildlife enthusiasts as well as tourists interested in financially contributing to conservation efforts.

4.1.2. Community Involvement focussed Branding

Community involvement is another critical part of Kanha's branding strategy. The park engages local communities in its eco-tourism initiatives and emphasizes that tourism directly benefits the people living in or around the park area. This is evident through their branding messages, which display community-driven initiatives in tourism-based activities like guided village tours, handicraft demonstrations, and cultural performances. By discouraging mass tourism, KNP is a socially responsible destination that empowers the area's local community. It attracts tourists who are sensitive towards the authenticity of cultures and adds to the positive image of the park as a destination for socially responsible tourism. In KNP, an Eco-tourism Development Committee (EDC) is also constituted, involving locals and other stakeholders. This committee is responsible for making decisions related to conservation and tourism in the park.

4.1.3. Cultural Heritage focussed Branding

The branding of Kanha also reflects the rich cultural heritage of the region. Being culturally diverse and the land of indigenous tribes like Gonds and the Baigas, KNP is home to some of the most vibrant traditions. Almost every brand carries a small quantity of culture in the form of traditional music, dance forms, and art. Images of festivals in local villages, tribal arts, and traditional clothes are shown in marketing material, thereby ultimately linking nature with culture. This orientation in culture makes the park more attractive to tourists who seek both natural and cultural attractions, hence making KNP a place that offers the perfect holistic eco-tourism experience. To host traditional ethnic performances for the guests, the corresponding EDCs are asked to have sturdy platforms/stages built in Khatia, Manjitola, and Sarhi villages. For the dance performances, which feature the karma, saila, and gendi dances, the EDCs are in charge of setting up appropriate costumes and musical equipment.

4.2. Marketing and Promotion

KNP uses various marketing channels and promotional activities to reach the target audience and deliver the branding message. All these efforts are made to increase awareness, attract more tourists, and establish it as a famous eco-tourism destination brand.

4.2.1. Digital Marketing

One such promising means of promoting KNP to the global audience as eco-tourism destination brand is digital marketing. In this direction, the park has an official website and promotional materials on the web, including social media and travel portals. Digital marketing strategies include:

- **Website:** The official website of Kanha is a one-stop guide to knowledge regarding the park, its wildlife, conservation and community efforts, and tourist experiences. More information may be obtained at Madhya Pradesh Tourism's website. The state tourism website has high-resolution photographs, videos, and blogs, making it more engaging and informative for visitors.
- **Social media:** The KNP is active on several social media platforms, including Facebook, Instagram, and Twitter. These platforms are used to keep followers informed, promote events, and reply to their comments. This allows the park to reach a larger number of people while also fostering a feeling of community among ecotourism enthusiasts. Documentaries are being created and shared on YouTube to raise awareness of the park.
- **Online Travel Portals:** KNP also partners with online travel portals like TripAdvisor and Booking.com. Many tourists look for eco-destinations through these websites. These websites act as platforms for user reviews, ratings, and recommendations to gain better visibility and credibility.

4.2.2. Alliances and Partnerships

KNP collaborates with various organizations to advance the brand of eco-tourism for the park. It has partnerships with conservation NGOs, travel agencies, and government which helps in amplifying the messages and spreading the word.

- **Conservation NGOs:** The partnerships with the conservation organizations increases credibility of the park as eco-tourism destination brand and its commitment to conservation. In most cases, this involves shared campaigns, education, and research programs that highlight conservation initiatives of the park.
- **Eco-Travel Agencies:** Kanha collaborates with eco-tourism travel agencies for designing tour packages reflecting themes of sustainable travel. The park is branded as responsible travel destination, which helps attract eco-sensitive tourists.
- **Government Departments:** KNP also liaise with various government entities such as the Ministry of Tourism, the Madhya Pradesh Tourism Board,

and the Ministry of Environment, Forest and Climate Change to promote itself in national and international tourism fairs. Such affiliations allow the park to be project and present its eco-tourism initiatives to the concerned stakeholders of that particular industry.

4.2.3. Advertisement Campaigns

KNP runs various promotional campaigns for better awareness among tourists. The promotional campaign always focusses on a particular theme of the park, whether it is wildlife conservation, cultural heritage, or any other form of community involvement. These campaigns would assist in creating a better awareness of the destination to attract prospective tourists.

- **Wildlife Photography Competitions:** Visitors are encouraged to use photography to capture their experiences and share them with others by participating in the park's wildlife photography competitions. This approach generates user-generated content, which will be utilized in promotional materials to showcase the biodiversity and beauty of the surrounding environment.
- **Eco-Tourism Events:** A variety of events on eco-tourism are organized at KNP, such as guided nature walks, bird-watching tours, and festivals that reflect regional culture. Each one of these has, over the years, acted to engage tourists and showcase something about what the park has to offer. This is promoted through various channels as a means of attracting tourists who desire far more immersive experiences.
- **Educational Programs:** To educate people about the fundamentals of eco-tourism, the park offers educational programs to corporations, colleges, and educational institutions. As an environmental educator and a responsible eco-tourism destination, this initiative enhances the park's brand value.

4.3. Tourists Perception and Experience

It is very important to understand how tourists perceive KNP as an eco-tourism destination brand. For this we need to know their response if an evaluation of the effectiveness of branding strategies adopted by the park has to be made, along with identifying areas of improvement. The perception and experience of the tourist are shaped by many factors, which include the marketing messages of the destination, on-site experiences, and interactions with staff and the community locals (Cox & Wray, 2011). For getting an idea about tourist perception, we telephonically interacted with 15 tourists who have visited KNP and a thematic analysis according to their responses is discussed below.

Overall, the brand image of the park, according to the tourists, is very positive. The tourists respect the fact that KNP is primarily conservation-oriented, socially involved, and culturally genuine. Interviews have been analyzed, which further stipulate the fact that tourists are attracted to the reputation of Kanha as the best eco-tourism destination with regard to issues such as sustainability and social responsibility. Following sections presents the perception of tourists about crucial aspects of eco-tourism at the park.

- **Conservation Messaging:** Tourists appreciate the conservation efforts taken by the park. Specifically, they are impressed by Kanha's effective conservation of tigers. A good number of tourists mentioned that they visited Kanha with a view to supporting the conservation effort and seeking information on wildlife preservation.
- **Community Involvement:** Many tourists mentioned how their engagement in the local community added value to their experiences. Working with local tour guides, craftspeople, or entertainers improved the cultural experience and strengthened ties to the location.
- **Cultural Heritage:** Many tourists also appreciate the park's cultural heritage around traditional music, dance, and crafts. The cultural aspects bring fullness to the experience of tourists and add depth and diversity to the attractions in the park.
- **Wildlife Viewing:** For so many tourists, tigers, leopards, and other iconic species like these would be a highlight. Safaris rank highly in the experiences of tourists owing to their knowledge regarding the guidance of safaris and sustainable practices. In addition, tourists are encouraged to adhere to precautionary measures and safety standards within the park, such as remaining inside vehicles during safaris and following designated routes. The park management provides guidelines to ensure the safety of both tourists and wildlife.
- **Accommodation and Facilities:** Eco-friendly tourist accommodations and facilities within the park seem adequate to tourists, though some note the requirement for infrastructural and other improvements for better comfort and accessibility. They also advise potential tourists to make prior bookings, as it guarantees better accommodation choices and helps avoid peak season overcrowding. Prior bookings also provide benefits like discounted package deals and guided tour options. Nearby restaurants and accommodations in the vicinity of the park offer traditional cuisine and comfortable stays, ensuring an authentic experience for both local and international tourists.

- **Educational Activities:** Tourists appreciate the educational activities taken within the park, like nature walks, workshops, and interpretive centres. These activities are very informative in regard to the ecological and conservation perspectives of the park.
- **Challenges and Improvements:** Some of these tourists feel that overcrowding is a major cause for worry, especially in peak seasons, killing the serenity and immersion associated with eco-tourism. Therefore, it is important to deal with these challenges to keep its brand image as eco-tourism destination.
- **Climate, Temperature, and Seasons:** Tourists advise others to plan their trips according to different climatic conditions, ensuring the best experience. KNP experiences three main seasons: winter (October to March), summer (April to June), and the monsoon (July to September). Winter is the best time to visit, with temperatures ranging from 11°C to 25°C, while summer temperatures can reach up to 40°C. The monsoon season brings heavy rains and higher humidity levels, making some areas inaccessible.
- **Tourist Vehicles:** Tourists support that for visiting Kanha, they are required to use park-approved safari vehicles, which are specially designed to navigate the terrain of different zones within the park. They highlighted that private vehicles are not allowed for safaris; standard vehicles can be used to reach designated entry points. The park's safari vehicles are equipped to handle rough, undulating terrain and diverse climates across the different zones.
- **Package Deals:** Tourists were happy with various eco-tourism package deals that cater to different preferences. These packages include safari experiences, cultural activities, and guided tours, allowing tourists to engage with the park's natural and cultural heritage at various price points. Special discounts are also available for early bookings and off-peak season visits, providing added value.

5. BALANCING CONSERVATION AND COMMUNITY INTERESTS IN KANHA NATIONAL PARK

In PAs, an important consideration is effective management practices to strike a balance between conservation and community concerns. KNP adopts various strategies for same which include:

5.1. Zoning and Land-Use Planning: Zoning and land-use planning are required before assigning tourism activities in order to avoid undermining conservation goals. Zoning can help establish places for tourism, conservation, and community usage, thereby minimizing conflicts and lowering consequences. The KNP has established zoning measures to segregate tourism and conservation zones, thereby protecting delicate environments from human interference.

5.2. Monitoring and Evaluation: Monitoring provides early indicators of emerging issues, enabling the development of adaptive management strategies. In KNP, monitoring programs help track the effects of tourism on wildlife populations, community benefits, and tourism-related impacts, allowing for timely and appropriate adjustments to management approaches as needed. Regular monitoring and evaluation are essential to assess the impacts of tourism operations that strive to align closely with sustainability goals.

5.3. Revenue-sharing and Benefit-sharing Mechanisms: To ensure that the local community gets a fair share of the economic benefits made from eco-tourism, there needs to be the implementation of proper revenue-sharing strategies. Some of these include direct payments, community development funds, or support for local enterprises (Mbaiwa, 2005). In this regard, KNP has instituted revenue-sharing programs that give a portion of the tourism revenue to community-based development projects, including schools, health centers, and infrastructure. They also have a fund called as Kanha Vikas Nidhi which is used for upliftment of the rural community. The management also started a school for young children of remote staff and nearby villages to lay a strong educational foundation for them. The school serves as both a daycare for children and a tutoring center for those who have dropped out. This project began in the summer of 2017. The school is at Mukki and established for staff's children who qualify for nursery, LKG, UKG, Class-I, and II, which government schools do not provide.

5.4. Capacity Building and Training: Capacity building and training programs are important in enhancing the skills and knowledge of local communities and their effective involvement in eco-tourism initiatives. Training can be given on issues such as tourism management, hospitality, guiding, etc., and, more importantly, environmental education. The management has initiated a scheme to assure jobs for the youths from the tiger reserve. It has started a hospitality training course at the Khatia hospitality centre, in partnership with the Indian Hotel Company Ltd. and PRATHAM Education Foundation. The district administration-funded programme has trained many youths so far, and many more are in the pipeline to improve their career prospects. The Kanha management is also getting the youths prepared for trades like mechanics and electricians and looking for additional funding to support these activities. The security training is being availed through tie-ups with a New Delhi security firm and retired army officers. Similarly, the masonry and electrical training programs have helped the participants find employment across various states. The KNP organizes training workshops for enhancing the capacities of locals and improving their involvement in tourism activities.

5.5. Conflict Resolution Mechanisms: To sustain tourism operations, effective conflict resolution processes must be in place to reconcile conservation goals with community interests. These methods could include dialogue platforms, mediation procedures, and grievance resolution systems. The KNP has implemented conflict resolution mechanisms that include stakeholders in communication and negotiation in order to manage problems and create confidence among different groups.

6. CHALLENGES AND OPPORTUNITIES

It's a challenge, and yet, there is an opportunity to balance conservation interests with community interests. KNP is diverse in wildlife, rich in cultural background, and depends entirely on local economies, making managing its needs especially challenging. Recognizing the challenges and seizing opportunities are central to the balance of conservation effort These would, in turn, ensure the sustainability of the eco-tourism projects for the community and other stakeholders.

6.1. Challenges

6.1.1. Conflicting Land Use Needs: Eco-tourism at KNP should address land use conflicts. The establishment of the park has restricted local's access to forests and other natural resources. The forest was traditionally used for their livelihoods, such as grazing, firewood, and NTFP collection. This leads to resentment among local community who feel that using forest resources is their customary rights and their rights and interests are being sacrificed for conservation purposes. Hence, it can be challenging to deal with them and make them friendlier towards tourists.

6.1.2. Economic Inequalities: While eco-tourism can bring economic benefits to a region, there is a great challenge in equally distributing these benefits among all stakeholders. External operators and investors receive a substantial amount of tourism earnings, leaving the locals with little to no profit. This inequal distribution exacerbate existing socioeconomic imbalances and reduce community support for conservation efforts, as residents may see no clear benefits from tourism activities.

6.1.3. Environmental Degradation: Eco-tourism can result in degradation if it is not managed well. This increased tourist footfall can result in habitat disturbance, pollution and wildlife stress which may actually work in contradiction to the objectives of conservation. The tourism infrastructure like roads, hotels, and other relevant facilities can impact negatively on the environment if not designed and managed sustainably.

6.1.4. Cultural Commodification: Commercialization of cultural heritage in tourism can result in the loss of authenticity of local traditions. This has also been referred to as the 'commodification' of culture. Communities might find themselves under pressure to change their cultural practice to tourist expectations, thus contributing to cultural erosion and dissatisfaction among the local people who value their cultural identity and heritage.

6.1.5. Policy and Management Challenges: It is extremely challenging to translate these complicated issues into management strategies and regulations that strike a balance between community interests and conservation. Effective governance and flexible management techniques are necessary to guarantee benefit-sharing, stakeholder cooperation, and dispute resolution. Inadequate resources, bureaucracy, and a lack of coordination among stakeholders can all impede the creation and execution of successful policies.

6.2. Opportunities

6.2.1. Community Empowerment and Participation: Kanha offers considerable scope for developing eco-tourism through the empowerment of local communities and involving them in the tourism management and planning process. Community-based tourism can provide locals with voice and decision-making powers and ensure that they receive their rightful share from tourism ventures. Community empowerment may foster a sense of ownership and responsibility, thereby leading to enhanced support from it for the conservation process.

6.2.2. Sustainable Tourism Practices: The adoption of sustainable tourism practices from low-impact accommodations to renewable energy sources to well-established waste management systems reduces the impact of tourist activities on the environment, which will add to this park's reputation as a premier eco-tourism destination. This means that the practice will attract more environmentally conscious travelers who are willing to pay a premium for these kinds of experiences.

6.2.3. Educational and Interpretive Programs: Educational and Interpretive Programs can be enhanced to reach a wider audience and to sensitize them and local communities on the need to conserve flora, fauna, and cultural heritage. This facility will enhance the tourists' experience through the provision of information that increases their understanding of the biodiversity within the park and what is being undertaken for its conservation and the local culture. Environmental education may foster an attitude of conservation ethics in both tourists and locals within the park, thereby creating responsible behavior.

6.2.4. Diversification of Economic Opportunities: KNP should generate better and diverse income opportunities for local communities. Opportunities for entrepreneurship support and capacity building strengthen the economic options for local people. It stimulates the development of complementary sectors linked to handicrafts, cultural performances, and local cuisine. By offering the chance to promote local products and services, supplementary livelihood options are opened up for communities, all with reduced dependence on unsustainable uses of resources.

6.2.5. Strengthening Policy Frameworks: Improving conservation and community benefits can be achieved by strengthening policies that can facilitate balanced eco-tourism. An environment that is favorable to the implementation of eco-tourism initiatives is created by policies that support stakeholder engagement and fair benefit sharing with sustainable development. The park's ability to manage for sustainable purposes may be enhanced by removing bureaucratic red tape and encouraging increased collaboration between governmental organizations, non-profits, and private industry.

7. CONCLUSION

This chapter gives some crucial insights about balancing conservation and community interests. Through the case study approach, a clear understanding is developed regarding how eco-tourism can support biodiversity conservation with improved local community welfare. KNP, here presents an excellent example how through eco-tourism, it has generated tremendous economic benefits to the local communities by providing employment and supporting locally based businesses. It supports community-based tourism, which gives locals an active role in decision making in tourism activities and makes sure they get the benefited from tourism. The eco-tourism has led to the successful conservation of Kanha's biodiversity concerning the Bengal tiger and Barasingha. Eco-tourism also plays a crucial role in financing various conservation activities, including habitat restoration, anti-poaching efforts, and wildlife monitoring. Though KNP has been at the frontline so far as eco-tourism is concerned, it also brings on board some challenges in meeting the twin interests of conservation and community. The significant challenges include conflicts over access to resources, economic disparities, and cultural commodification that must be addressed to ensure the sustainability of eco-tourism initiatives. Various strategies should be adopted to reduce negative effects on the environment and local communities like implementing low-impact infrastructure, effective tourist management, and stakeholder participation. At KNP we can see that these strategies are beneficial to a large extent in maintaining a balance between tourism development and conservation objectives.

This study has important implications for eco-tourism policy and practice, especially in PAs like KNP. Policies in other PAs should focus on including local communities and ensuring that eco-tourism ventures share benefits fairly. National and regional guidelines need to clearly emphasize involving local communities in tourism planning and management to make sure their needs and interests are considered. Building skills in local communities is also essential, and investing in such programs will help them gain the abilities needed for successful eco-tourism activities. This can include training in tourism management, hospitality, tour guiding and other skills which can help them to earn a living. It is also important to have effective strategies to resolve various conflicts between conservation and community interests. PAs should regular monitor and evaluate tourism activities to understand their environmental impacts and to make sure they align with sustainability goals. Monitoring should keep track of tourist impacts, wildlife populations, and the benefits to local communities and management practices should be adjusted as needed. However, KNP is doing well through eco-tourism, based on the findings, our study offers some recommendations. To improve KNP's eco-tourism branding, it's important to present the park not only as a leader in wildlife conservation but also as a model for sustainable practices like community involvement. Successful eco-tourism branding must balance conservation goals with real benefits for local residents, which can help build the park's reputation as an establishment which is socially responsible and environmentally sustainable. The following recommendations are presented which aim at achieving this balance while reinforcing Kanha's eco-tourism brand:

Encourage Greater Community Participation: The park has policies like forming eco-tourism development committee which should include locals and involve them in various activities related to tourism. It is recommended that the locals should be encouraged and educated about their participation in eco-tourism. It should continue actively engaging the local residents in planning and decision-making on eco-tourism. Their increased engagement will contribute in positioning KNP as an eco-tourism destination brand that respects and includes community in its efforts towards conservation.

Ensure Fair Revenue Sharing: The park has a fund named as Kanha Vikas Nidhi Fund which focuses on using the revenue generated from tourism in infrastructure development. It is recommended that the authorities should ensure that revenues generated by tourism are equitably shared among local communities. Also, the locals should get suitable jobs in the park and supported for establishing their businesses. It will establish KNP as an eco-tourism destination brand promoting economic equitability and social sustainability.

Implement Sustainable Tourism Practices: The park has set guidelines to minimize the impact on environment and locals like only permitted vehicles entering the park, involving locals. It is recommended that more sustainable practices in tourism like going for low-impact infrastructure, effectively managing tourist activities, and collaborating and raising awareness among all stakeholders should be followed that can help KNP in building a brand image associated with environmental responsibility.

Establish Conflict Resolution Mechanisms: The park has various strategies to resolve conflict like compensation for the loss or injury to life by wild animals, designated different areas for wild and locals, providing alternate livelihood means etc. It is recommended that park should institutionalise conflict resolution and equitable sharing of rewards among communities and conservation which will help KNP to be an eco-tourism destination brand that balances local interest with environmental conservation.

Support Conservation Initiatives: Conservation is the park's top priority, and it has already employed various strategies like animal monitoring, habitat restoration, and anti-poaching efforts. However, these initiatives need financial support. It's recommended that the park should promote eco-tourism through different channels and use the funds generated to strengthen these conservation efforts. This would help position Kanha as a leading eco-tourism destination, known for its commitment to wildlife protection and long-term sustainability.

Market itself as an Eco-tourism Destination Brand: While KNP is well-known as a national park, it should be marketed and promoted as an eco-tourism destination brand. This will help to attract tourists interested in eco-tourism activities, improving the park's image and attractiveness in the eco-tourism industry. Kanha may thereby attract environmentally conscious visitors and establish itself as a prominent actor in responsible tourism.

These strategies will not only support conservation efforts but also help KNP to establish itself as a strong eco-tourism brand that resonates with tourists seeking meaningful and sustainable travel experiences. However, this chapter presents valuable insights on establishing KNP as Eco-Tourism Brand, future longitudinal studies should focus on the impacts of eco-tourism branding on conservation and community development. The information shared through such studies can be used to effectively demonstrate the sustainability and effectiveness of eco-tourism branding initiatives. Future studies may also focus on comparative analyses of eco-tourism branding initiatives in different PAs which can help to identify best practices and lessons learned. Successful initiatives can highlight effective strategies. Furthermore, research on how tourists behave and view eco-tourism might shed light on their reasons for visiting, satisfaction, and intention to support conservation. These results can be used to create marketing strategies and educational initiatives that will encourage responsible travel. It is also important to look at how climate change is impacting eco-tourism, especially considering the conservation efforts in protected areas. Identifying ways to adapt will help keep eco-tourism strong as conditions change. More research on this will help us better understand how eco-tourism supports conservation and community development, providing useful insights for policymakers, practitioners, and others involved in sustainable tourism.

REFERENCES

Abukari, H., & Mwalyosi, R. B. (2020). Local communities' perceptions about the impact of protected areas on livelihoods and community development. *Global Ecology and Conservation*, 22, e00909. DOI: 10.1016/j.gecco.2020.e00909

Altassan, A. (2023). Sustainability of Heritage Villages through Eco-Tourism Investment (Case Study: Al-Khabra Village, Saudi Arabia). *Sustainability (Basel)*, 15(9), 7172. DOI: 10.3390/su15097172

An, S., & Park, H. (2023). Factors driving community engagement through social capital formation - focusing on community-based eco-tourism in Dongbaek Village, Jeju, Korea. *International Journal of Global Environmental Issues*, 22(4), 355–374. DOI: 10.1504/IJGENVI.2023.136294

Andrade, G. S. M., & Rhodes, J. R. (2012). Protected Areas and Local Communities: An Inevitable Partnership toward Successful Conservation Strategies? *Ecology and Society*, 17(4), art14. Advance online publication. DOI: 10.5751/ES-05216-170414

Anwar, R. K., Saepudin, E., & Rukmana, E. N. (2023a). Eco-tourism and economic striving of the locals: From participation to empowerment. *Journal of Infrastructure Policy and Development*, 8(2). Advance online publication. DOI: 10.24294/jipd.v8i2.3038

Anwar, R. K., Saepudin, E., & Rukmana, E. N. (2023b). Eco-tourism and economic striving of the locals: From participation to empowerment. *Journal of Infrastructure Policy and Development*, 8(2). Advance online publication. DOI: 10.24294/jipd.v8i2.3038

Ashton, A. S. (2015). Developing a Tourist Destination Brand Value: The Stakeholders' Perspective. *Tourism Planning & Development*, 12(4), 398–411. DOI: 10.1080/21568316.2015.1013565

Batool, N., Wani, M. D., Shah, S. A., & Dada, Z. A. (2024). Tourists' attitude and willingness to pay on conservation efforts: Evidence from the west Himalayan eco-tourism sites. *Environment, Development and Sustainability*. Advance online publication. DOI: 10.1007/s10668-024-04679-2

Boley, B. B., & Green, G. T. (2015). Ecotourism and natural resource conservation: The 'potential' for a sustainable symbiotic relationship. *Journal of Ecotourism*, 15(1), 36–50. DOI: 10.1080/14724049.2015.1094080

Bontempi, A., Venturi, P., Del Bene, D., Scheidel, A., Zaldo-Aubanell, Q., & Zaragoza, R. M. (2023). Conflict and conservation: On the role of protected areas for environmental justice. *Global Environmental Change*, 82, 102740. DOI: 10.1016/j.gloenvcha.2023.102740

Bonye, S. Z., Yiridomoh, G. Y., & Nsiah, V. (2023). Our forest, our livelihood: Natural resources' use controversies and community livelihood sustainability in the Mole National Park, Ghana. *Land Use Policy*, 127, 106589. DOI: 10.1016/j.landusepol.2023.106589

Ceballos-LascuráIn, H. (1996). *Tourism, Ecotourism, and Protected Areas: The State of Nature-Based Tourism Around the World and Guidelines for Its Development.* http://ci.nii.ac.jp/ncid/BA32002622

Cernea, M. M., & Schmidt-Soltau, K. (2006). Poverty Risks and National Parks: Policy Issues in Conservation and Resettlement. *World Development*, 34(10), 1808–1830. DOI: 10.1016/j.worlddev.2006.02.008

Chaplin-Kramer, R., Neugarten, R. A., Gonzalez-Jimenez, D., Ahmadia, G., Baird, T. D., Crane, N., Delgoulet, E., Eyster, H. N., Kurashima, N., Llopis, J. C., Millington, A., Pawlowska-Mainville, A., Rulmal, J., Saunders, F., Shrestha, S., Vaughan, M. B., Winter, K. B., Wongbusarakum, S., & Pascual, U. (2023). Transformation for inclusive conservation: Evidence on values, decisions, and impacts in protected areas. *Current Opinion in Environmental Sustainability*, 64, 101347. DOI: 10.1016/j.cosust.2023.101347

Cox, C., & Wray, M. (2011). Best Practice Marketing for Regional Tourism Destinations. *Journal of Travel & Tourism Marketing*, 28(5), 524–540. DOI: 10.1080/10548408.2011.588112

De Bruyn, L. L., Duong, T. M. P., Kristiansen, P., Marshall, G. R., & Wilkes, J. (2022). The Role of Livelihood Initiatives in Reducing Non-wood Forest Product Reliance in Protected Areas of Southern Vietnam: Opportunities and Challenges. In *Sitra* (pp. 221–251). DOI: 10.1007/978-3-030-99313-9_10

Ewart, M., Scherrer, P., & Dimmock, K. (2024). Managing commercial tourism for conservation and sustainable use: Policy instrument interactions in Cape Byron Marine Park, Australia. *Marine Policy*, 166, 106233. DOI: 10.1016/j.marpol.2024.106233

Fennell, D. A. (1999). *Ecotourism: An Introduction.* http://ci.nii.ac.jp/ncid/BA4004316X

Gumede, T. K., & Nzama, A. T. (2022). Approaches toward Community Participation Enhancement in Ecotourism. In *IntechOpen eBooks*. DOI: 10.5772/intechopen.100295

Guri, E. A., Osumanu, I. K., & Bonye, S. Z. (2020). Eco-cultural tourism development in Ghana: Potentials and expected benefits in the Lawra Municipality. *Journal of Tourism and Cultural Change*, 19(4), 458–476. DOI: 10.1080/14766825.2020.1737095

Honey, M. (2009). Ecotourism and sustainable development: Who owns paradise? *Choice (Chicago, Ill.)*, 46(06), 46–3341. DOI: 10.5860/CHOICE.46-3341

Hudson, S., & Ritchie, J. R. B. (2009). Branding a memorable destination experience. The case of 'Brand Canada.'. *International Journal of Tourism Research*, 11(2), 217–228. DOI: 10.1002/jtr.720

Ioppolo, G., Saija, G., & Salomone, R. (2012). From coastal management to environmental management: The sustainable eco-tourism program for the mid-western coast of Sardinia (Italy). *Land Use Policy*, 31, 460–471. DOI: 10.1016/j.landusepol.2012.08.010

Keitumetse, S. O. (2009). The Eco-tourism of Cultural Heritage Management (ECT-CHM): Linking Heritage and 'Environment' in the Okavango Delta Regions of Botswana. *International Journal of Heritage Studies*, 15(2–3), 223–244. DOI: 10.1080/13527250902890811

Lasgorceix, A., & Kothari, A. (2009). Displacement and relocation of protected areas: a synthesis and analysis of case studies. *Economic and Political Weekly/ Economic & Political Weekly, 44*(49), 37–47. https://kalpavriksh.org/images/CLN/Media_Displacement%20from%20PAs_EPW_5Nov.pdf

Luz, A. C., & Ruiz-Mallén, I. (2020). Community-Based Management and Research to Forest Conservation. In *Encyclopedia of the UN sustainable development goals* (pp. 148–161). DOI: 10.1007/978-3-319-71065-5_133-1

Maksanova, L., Bardakhanova, T., Budaeva, D., Mikheeva, A., Lubsanova, N., Sharaldaeva, V., Eremko, Z., Andreeva, A., Ayusheeva, S., & Khrebtova, T. (2023). Ecotourism Development in the Russian Areas under Nature Protection. *Sustainability (Basel)*, 15(18), 13661. DOI: 10.3390/su151813661

Matthiopoulos, J., Fieberg, J., Aarts, G., Beyer, H. L., Morales, J. M., & Haydon, D. T. (2015). Establishing the link between habitat selection and animal population dynamics. *Ecological Monographs*, 85(3), 413–436. DOI: 10.1890/14-2244.1

McLane, A. J., Semeniuk, C., McDermid, G. J., & Marceau, D. J. (2011). The role of agent-based models in wildlife ecology and management. *Ecological Modelling*, 222(8), 1544–1556. DOI: 10.1016/j.ecolmodel.2011.01.020

Miller, A. B., Cox, C., & Morse, W. C. (2023). Ecotourism, wildlife conservation, and agriculture in Costa Rica through a social-ecological systems lens. *Frontiers in Sustainable Tourism*, 2, 1179887. Advance online publication. DOI: 10.3389/frsut.2023.1179887

Miller, F., Ha, T. T. P., Van Da, H., Thuy, N. T. T., & Ngo, B. H. (2022). Double displacement – Interactions between resettlement, environmental change and migration. *Geoforum*, 129, 13–27. DOI: 10.1016/j.geoforum.2021.12.016

Montenegro-Pazmiño, E., & Muñoz, G. (2024). Unveiling Social Dynamics in People's Perception of Raptors to Guide Effective Conservation Strategies. *Journal of Ethnobiology*, 44(2), 112–128. DOI: 10.1177/02780771241250117

www.kanhatigerreserve.org. (n.d.). kanhatigerreserve.org. Retrieved September 28, 2024, from https://www.kanhatigerreserve.org/flora-and-fauna

Neto, F. (2003). A new approach to sustainable tourism development: Moving beyond environmental protection. *Natural Resources Forum*, 27(3), 212–222. DOI: 10.1111/1477-8947.00056

Oladeji, S. O., Awolala, D. O., & Alabi, O. I. (2021). Evaluation of sustainable ecotourism practices in Oke-Idanre Hills, Ondo-State, Nigeria. *Environment, Development and Sustainability*, 24(2), 2656–2684. DOI: 10.1007/s10668-021-01550-6

Paul, I., & Roy, G. (2023). Tourist's engagement in eco-tourism: A review and research agenda. *Journal of Hospitality and Tourism Management*, 54, 316–328. DOI: 10.1016/j.jhtm.2023.01.002

Rawat, G. S., & Adhikari, B. S. (2015). Ecology and management of grassland habitats in India. In *ENVIS Bulletin: Wildlife & Protected Areas*. ENVIS Bulletin: Wildlife & Protected Areas.

Rivera, M. A., & Croes, R. (2010). Ecotourists' loyalty: Will they tell about the destination or will they return? *Journal of Ecotourism*, 9(2), 85–103. DOI: 10.1080/14724040902795964

Samal, R., & Dash, M. (2022a). Ecotourism, biodiversity conservation and livelihoods: Understanding the convergence and divergence. *International Journal of Geoheritage and Parks*, 11(1), 1–20. DOI: 10.1016/j.ijgeop.2022.11.001

Samal, R., & Dash, M. (2022b). Ecotourism, biodiversity conservation and livelihoods: Understanding the convergence and divergence. *International Journal of Geoheritage and Parks*, 11(1), 1–20. DOI: 10.1016/j.ijgeop.2022.11.001

Saout, S. L., Hoffmann, M., Shi, Y., Hughes, A., Bernard, C., Brooks, T. M., Bertzky, B., Butchart, S. H. M., Stuart, S. N., Badman, T., & Rodrigues, A. S. L. (2013). Protected Areas and Effective Biodiversity Conservation. *Science*, 342(6160), 803–805. DOI: 10.1126/science.1239268 PMID: 24233709

Sarma, U. K., & Barpujari, I. (2022). Realizing a rights-based approach to resettlement from protected areas: Lessons from Satpura Tiger Reserve, Madhya Pradesh (India). *Land Use Policy*, 125, 106494. DOI: 10.1016/j.landusepol.2022.106494

Sharma, R. A. (2011). Co-Management of Protected Areas in South Asia with Special Reference to Bangladesh. *Asia-Pacific Journal of Rural Development*, 21(1), 1–28. DOI: 10.1177/1018529120110101

Shasha, Z. T., Geng, Y., Sun, H., Musakwa, W., & Sun, L. (2020). Past, current, and future perspectives on eco-tourism: A bibliometric review between 2001 and 2018. *Environmental Science and Pollution Research International*, 27(19), 23514–23528. DOI: 10.1007/s11356-020-08584-9 PMID: 32307679

Shoo, R. A., & Songorwa, A. N. (2013). Contribution of eco-tourism to nature conservation and improvement of livelihoods around Amani nature reserve, Tanzania. *Journal of Ecotourism*, 12(2), 75–89. DOI: 10.1080/14724049.2013.818679

Snyman, S. (2016). The role of private sector ecotourism in local socio-economic development in southern Africa. *Journal of Ecotourism*, 16(3), 247–268. DOI: 10.1080/14724049.2016.1226318

Snyman, S. (2020). The role of private sector ecotourism in local socio-economic development in southern Africa. In *Routledge eBooks* (pp. 47–68). DOI: 10.4324/9780429423437-4

Sterling, E. J., Betley, E., Sigouin, A., Gomez, A., Toomey, A., Cullman, G., Malone, C., Pekor, A., Arengo, F., Blair, M., Filardi, C., Landrigan, K., & Porzecanski, A. L. (2017). Assessing the evidence for stakeholder engagement in biodiversity conservation. *Biological Conservation*, 209, 159–171. DOI: 10.1016/j.biocon.2017.02.008

Stronza, A. (2007). The Economic Promise of Ecotourism for Conservation. *Journal of Ecotourism*, 6(3), 210–230. DOI: 10.2167/joe177.0

Stronza, A., & Gordillo, J. (2008). Community views of ecotourism. *Annals of Tourism Research*, 35(2), 448–468. DOI: 10.1016/j.annals.2008.01.002

The International Ecotourism Society. (2015). *What Is Ecotourism?* ecotourism.org. Retrieved September 28, 2024, from https://ecotourism.org/what-is-ecotourism/

Tiger Conservation Plan for the Buffer Zone of the Kanha Tiger Reserve. (n.d.). In www.mpforest.gov.in. Retrieved September 28, 2024, from https://www.mpforest.gov.in/img/files/Kanha_TCP_Buffer.pdf

Tubey, W. C., Kyalo, D. N., & Mulwa, A. S. (2020). Environmental conservation strategies and sustainability of community-based tourism in Kenya: A case of Maasai Mara conservancies. *International Journal of Tourism Policy*, 10(2), 123. DOI: 10.1504/IJTP.2020.110864

Turner, R. L. (2004). COMMUNITIES, WILDLIFE CONSERVATION, AND TOURISM-BASED DEVELOPMENT: CAN COMMUNITY-BASED NATURE TOURISM LIVE UP TO ITS PROMISE? *Journal of International Wildlife Law and Policy*, 7(3–4), 161–182. DOI: 10.1080/13880290490883232

Wallace, R. (2019). Ecotourism in Asia. In *Advances in hospitality, tourism and the services industry (AHTSI) book series* (pp. 192–211). DOI: 10.4018/978-1-5225-7253-4.ch009

Zhang, H., Liang, Q., Li, Y., & Gao, P. (2023). Promoting eco-tourism for the green economic recovery in ASEAN. *Economic Change and Restructuring*, 56(3), 2021–2036. DOI: 10.1007/s10644-023-09492-x

Zhou, W., Zheng, B., Zhang, Z., Song, Z., & Duan, W. (2021). The role of eco-tourism in ecological conservation in giant panda nature reserve. *Journal of Environmental Management*, 295, 113077. DOI: 10.1016/j.jenvman.2021.113077 PMID: 34146778

Chapter 9
Balancing Bias and Sustainability in Heritage Tourism

Aditi Nag
https://orcid.org/0000-0002-0604-6945
Manipal University Jaipur, India

Anurag Singh Rathore
https://orcid.org/0009-0004-0112-5478
Indira Gandhi National Open University, India

ABSTRACT

This paper examines the complex dynamics of biases in ecotourism and destination branding within the context of heritage site management. It explores how these biases influence perceptions, visitor experiences, and sustainable practices at iconic destinations such as the Taj Mahal, Machu Picchu and Serengeti National Park. The study identifies critical challenges and opportunities in promoting inclusive, authentic, and sustainable tourism by integrating insights from predictive analytics, cultural sensitivity, and ethical considerations. Drawing on case studies and theoretical frameworks, the paper offers practical implications for mitigating biases, enhancing visitor engagement, and safeguarding cultural and natural heritage. It concludes by advocating for integrated strategies that balance effective branding with responsible stewardship to ensure the long-term preservation and equitable enjoyment of heritage sites worldwide.

DOI: 10.4018/979-8-3693-6700-1.ch009

1 INTRODUCTION

In tourism, brands have become invaluable competitive assets representing value and differentiation (Aaker, 1991; Kotler and Gertner, 2007; Ryan, 2015). This trend is particularly pronounced in the tourism sector, where the emergence of numerous destination brands has been notable in recent years (Balakrishnan, 2009; Ryan, 2015). The 'World Heritage Site' (WHS) designation, as noted by Ryan and Silvanto (2009, 2010) and Hall and Piggin (2003), has evolved into a significant destination brand of growing prominence. It is increasingly utilised to promote and differentiate various locations (Ryan, 2015). This growing prominence of the WHS brand aligns with a paradigm shift in heritage protection and preservation, extending World Heritage Status from tangible natural and cultural sites to intangible cultural heritage (ICH), such as living cultural practices and traditions (Ahmad, 2006; Ryan, 2015). UNESCO's adoption of the Convention for the Safeguarding of Intangible Cultural Heritage in 2003, which took effect in 2006 following approval by 30 state parties (UNESCO, 2012), underscored the importance of intangible heritage. This new convention equated the protections for intangible cultural heritage with those provided for cultural and natural heritage sites by the 1972 UNESCO World Cultural Convention (UNESCO, 2012). This significant expansion of the heritage universe allows tourism professionals to use the World Heritage designation more effectively for branding, promoting, and differentiating destinations (Ruggles and Silverman, 2009; Ryan, 2015).

Initially intended for preserving natural and cultural patrimony, the WHS designation has transformed over four decades into a coveted brand and a mark of quality for tourism planners and professionals (Ryan and Silvanto, 2009, 2010; Hall and Piggin, 2003; Ryan, 2015). A key instrument in destination marketing and promotion, this certification attests to a site's quality and distinctiveness (Ryan and Silvanto, 2009, 2010; Ryan, 2015). As Baker and Cameron (2008) emphasise, branding is crucial to developing effective tourism strategies and plans. A developing location may increase local revenue and tourists by developing a strong tourism brand. Research in the past two decades highlights the importance of image in helping tourists comprehend and value a place. Historically, researchers like Fakeye and Crompton (1991) and Ryan (2015) have been focusing on the stimulus of topographical distance in the development of destination perception and the impact of travel time on the stay duration, which is usually measured by distance. Nevertheless, tourism products include the experience of visiting a destination and the process of ultimately selecting it (Ritchie and Crouch, 2003, 2010).

For decades, researchers like Morgan, Pritchard, and Pride (2007) have suggested using destination branding to determine the attitudes and views of potential tourists, specifically for heritage sites. However, the perspectives get distorted and blurred due to the several biases in the present nature of ecotourism. These biases, which can include preconceived notions about the environmental impact of tourism or cultural stereotypes, make administrating and promoting heritage destinations challenging. In an attempt to unpack a few of these biases inherent in ecotourism, the study expounds on the repercussions of such perceived biases for destination branding and heritage site management (HSM). To match sustainable and inclusive tourism principles, heritage sites can confront any such bias to improve their branding strategies. Fennell (2020) asserts that familiar stakeholders perceive ecotourism as an environmentally sensitive by-product of tourism, designed to promote the improvement of the environment whilst additionally benefiting local communities by gaining tremendous mileage. Hatma Indra Jaya, Izudin, and Aditya (2024), however, discuss that the attitudes and behaviours of tourists get considerably altered due to social, cultural, and environmental predispositions. Through a preliminary theoretical exploration of destination branding and ecotourism, heritage site-specific case studies and suggestive measures for bias mitigation, the study combines predictive analytics, cultural sensitivity, and ethics, ultimately introducing a holistic approach to promoting heritage tourism in terms of efficiency and inclusivity. Therefore, interplays between destination branding and HSM have been established as cornerstones for promoting sustainable tourism practices (STP). Exploring ecotourism biases is essential to further the efforts in destination branding. Unsurprisingly, it is necessary to formulate inclusive, sustainable, and successful tourism initiatives for which heritage site managers and tourism professionals need guidance to work further.

2 LITERATURE REVIEW

Domains – ecotourism, destination branding, and HSM – are extensive and multi-dimensional in appeal because of the complexity and inter-connectedness of these concepts. This study explores key themes, theoretical frameworks, and case studies related to these topics to ensure that all aspects are adequately explored and to provide an adequate understanding of the implications for improving sustainable and inclusive heritage tourism.

2.1 Ecotourism and Its Biases

Ecotourism has been attracting much attention in the last few decades due to its benefits to both the environment and locals, much like sustainable tourism. Conversely, the biases concomitant with ecotourism can drastically alter its impact and result. Researchers (Hvenegaard and Dearden, 1998; Holder et al., 2024) have been unceasingly attempting to establish a connection between the respective backgrounds and preferences of tourists and the effects cultural biases can create in their expectations and experience. Similarly, as per Le Corre et al. (2024), social biases can influence tourist behaviour and sanction stereotypes or exclusions towards tourists centred upon prevailing norms and expectations. Equally, a significant influence on tourist perceptions is based on the destination's conditions and sustainability practices triggered by environmental biases. In a collective set-up, the implications of these biases accentuate the salience of shifting towards ecotourism in a more elusive fashion as a tangible echo of policy provisions. According to Fennell, Moorhouse, and Macdonald (2024), Plesa (2024), and Gade, Johnpaul, and Miryala (2024), the development of inclusive and sustainable ecotourism necessitates emphasising cultural sensitivity and ethics as auxiliary principles. These works establish the coherent relationship between tourist satisfaction and the overall success of ecotourism projects where these biases go hand-in-hand. Every cultural tourist group differs regarding expectations and perceptions of ecotourism experiences (Le Corre et al., 2024). These behaviours can also be elucidated through societal influences due to contradictory habits of relishing and appreciating ecotourism activities (Karayazi, Dane and Arentze, 2024). Pollution, overcrowding, or other environmental conditions can hurt tourist experiences and perceptions (Cook, 2024).

2.2 Destination Branding

Destination branding, aka strategic place creation for tourist attraction with distinct image quality, has critical elements like brand identity, brand image, and brand equity, as stated by Morgan, Pritchard and Pride (2007) and Wang, Cao and Cai (2024). Pike et al. (2024) suggest that a destination's specific attributes and personality create its brand identity, whereas how a prospective tourist perceives it is brand image, while the incremental value an effective brand brings to the table refers to brand equity, informing tourist loyalty and preference (Alagarsamy, Mehrolia and Paul, 2024). The academia depicts destination branding as a critical step for shaping tourist perceptions and experiences. As argued by Kavaratzis and Ashworth (2005) and Anholt (2006), the need for a coherent and authentic brand emerges that resonates with the tourists and reflects on the distinct attributes of the destination, emphasising the prominence of destination branding. It has been well-established in past research how destination branding can effectively create attractive and competitive destinations whilst sharpening them for the current market, calling forth positive perceptions and action among tourists through good brand image about a particular destination, henceforth increasing the satisfaction level and loyalty towards a particular destination as widely proven by various researchers (Ekinci and Hosany, 2006; Casado-Aranda, Sánchez-Fernández, and Ibáñez-Zapata, 2023).

2.3 Heritage Site Management (HSM)

Balancing the preservation of physical and cultural integrity in heritage sites through the management of tourism with tourist demand necessitates the integration of three core elements, namely conservation, community involvement and sustainability (Timothy and Boyd, 2003). While conservation protects a site from historical and cultural importance, inclusive, participatory planning of local communities in tourism development and management calls for community engagement. Nevertheless, it is challenging to involve communities with the tourism product and its development, as asserted by researchers like Cleere, McKercher and du Cros (2002), Chhabra, Healy and Sills (2003), Aas, Ladkin and Fletcher (2005). Sustainability is the task of long-term survival of environmental components alongside the interests of tourists and local communities. At the same time, its crux is penetrating responsible practices concerning the three constituents: local communities, tourists, and the environment. Using several frameworks to conserve and advance destinations with outstanding universal value, labelling destinations as WHS has transformed HSM. Ruggles and Silverman (2009), promoters of WHS, have noted that heritage sites become more appealing and highly visible once labelled as WHS to prospective tourists, enhancing tourism and economic activities. Meanwhile, converting the WHS brand as a threat through the opportunity for increased popularity. Suitable management measures for mitigating detrimental effects are necessary, as mass tourism can put too much stress on a destination's infrastructures (Pedersen, 2002; Nag and Mishra, 2024a, 2024b, 2024c, 2024d). Harmonising the contribution through preservation and demand by the tourists necessitates proper management of heritage sites. Studies indicate that the participation of local communities can raise tourism authenticity and sustainability in heritage sites' management and marketing (Chhabra, Healy and Sills, 2003), allowing for better heritage integrity protection while tourist experience enhancement pursues sustainable tourism behaviour by minimising the adverse environmental effects and dealing with low tourist numbers (Garrod and Fyall, 2000). While implementing adaptive management practices, cultural sensitivity must be coupled with ethical concerns to meet the requirements of balancing conservation and tourism development in the management process of a heritage destination (Throsby, 2012; Smith, 2020; Nag and Mishra, 2024b).

2.4 Addressing Biases and Enhancing Inclusivity

Balancing ecotourism and destination branding (EDB) is a retrospective term involving predictive analytics, cultural sensitivities, and ethical considerations. Allowing heritage destinations to be aware of tourist behaviour and preferences entails predictive analytics to be able to adjust branding strategies for bias combat

(Gretzel et al., 2006; Chen, Chiang and Storey, 2012; Nag, 2022, 2023; Nag and Mishra, 2024b). To construct resilient brands through cultural, social, and environmental data, heritage destinations require bias minimisation and forging better tourist experiences (Wu, 2013; Davenport et al., 2007). Prediction of trends, facing potential challenges before they happen, and developing specific marketing tactics are goals served by predictive analytics to tourism professionals (Chen, Chiang, and Storey, 2012; Waller and Fawcett, 2013). Kim and Fesenmaier (2008) argue that cultural, social, and environmental knowledge aids in tourist target-specific marketing strategies. Cultural and social consciousness is the foundation of understanding tourist origin sources and their differentiating tastes, guaranteeing their uptake by creating different tourism practices (Richards, 2007). The integral components of EDB are ethical considerations, including tourists' right to privacy, transparency, and responsible representation of cultural heritage (D'Hauteserre, 2004; Nag and Mishra, 2024c). Responsible exemplification of authentic and respectful cultural heritage interpretation at heritage destinations entails responsibilities balancing effective branding (Hede, 2008). Another viewpoint from the ethical dimension within sustainable activities considers local community and environment benefits at ecotourism destinations (Weaver, 2001; Hudson and Miller, 2005; Wheeler, Frost and Weiler, 2011).

Focusing on sustainability and inclusiveness through a blend of these aspects can produce a rich branding of the heritage destination, consisting of rudimentary frames of long-term goals toward conservation, community involvement, and adaptive management. Reducing bias and cultivating cultural sensitivity at heritage destinations can magnify a more inclusive and sustainable tourism industry (Harrison and Campus, 2004; Sharpley, 2009). The development of tourism is, therefore, consistent with the values of community welfare, cultural preservation, and environmental protection (Hall and Richards, 2000; Mowforth and Munt, 2015). Studies like Nag (2023) and Nag and Mishra (2024a), among others, have empirically validated that sustainable tourism activities upsurge tourist satisfaction and loyalty meanwhile conserving the cultural and natural heritage of the nation, thus underlining the requirement for conservation, community involvement, and adaptive management for effective HSM through sustainability in the long-run (Garrod and Fyall, 2000).

Literature on ecotourism, destination branding, and HSM further provides ideas about the challenges and opportunities for heritage tourism development. Future research is essential for navigating diverse dynamics by shedding light on the best practices in managing and promoting heritage sites concerning cultural diversity and support of sustainable development.

2.5 Integration of Theoretical Frameworks in Ecotourism and Destination Branding (EDB)

Analysing EDB concepts demands the integration of established theoretical frameworks, which can inform the practices in their domain of ecotourism, inspiring one to contemplate strategies in destination branding, as presented in Table 1. Emerging trends and themes of absolute prominence in HSM can be understood through stakeholders' consumer relations and tourism and environment communication. Reshaping of EDB assumes the significance of foregrounding emerging trends and contemporary issues alongside established theoretical foundations, reflecting the ever-changing dynamics of tourism, thus introducing challenges and opportunities and demanding adaptive strategies (Lee and Jan, 2018).

Table 1. Theoretical frameworks, emerging trends and issues and their relevance to EDB

		Description	Relevance to EDB
Framework	Service-Dominant Logic	Emphasises co-creation of value through interactions between providers and consumers.	Highlights the importance of engaging local communities and tourists in creating shared experiences.
	Stakeholder Theory	Focuses on relationships between organisations and various stakeholders.	Assists in balancing the interests of local communities, tourists, governments, and conservationists.
	Social Exchange Theory	Suggests the exchange of tangible and intangible resources forms human relationships.	Helps understand tourist satisfaction based on perceived benefits versus the costs of the experience.
	Cultural Dimensions Theory	Examines how cultural differences influence behaviour and expectations.	Provides insights into tailoring branding strategies for diverse tourist demographics and cultural backgrounds.
	Systems Theory	Analyses complex interrelationships within systems, emphasising holistic approaches.	Encourages a comprehensive view of tourism as interconnected with environmental sustainability and community needs.

continued on following page

Table 1. Continued

		Description	Relevance to EDB
Emerging Trends and Contemporary Issues	Digital evolution	Qu, Kim and Im (2011) suggest that social media and online platforms have revolutionised destination branding by utilising digital content, user-generated reviews, and online influencers to evolve tourist perceptions.	A mass utilisation of said platforms creates broader audience reach, tailored marketing efforts, and enhanced tourist' interaction before, during, and after visitation.
	Effects of Climate Change	Impacts tourists' perception of destinations, necessitating adaptive branding strategies and balancing sustainability with heritage site preservation (Lee and Jan, 2018).	Tourists' sensitivity towards themselves and nature requires an equilibrium between sustainability and preservation of heritage sites.
	Cultural Sensitivity	Misrepresentation or commercialisation of culture can create conflict between tourists and residential communities.	Respectful reflection of local culture in core branding is required through an all-inclusive approach (Quoquab, Mohammad, and Mohd Sobri, 2021).

(Source: Authors' compilation)

Collective utilisation of these theories and emerging trends conceptualizes more holistic approaches towards EDB with better situational insights, further systematically anchoring research by exploring the complexities involved. Furthermore, an impression of making branding strategies relevant, responsive, and effective in today's vibrant tourism environment rests on the dilemmas of the contemporary world encompassing digital transformation, climate change, and cultural sensitivity. Theoretical bases can support a structured analysis for deconstructing critical themes and trends encompassing practical insights into how destinations can improve branding at heritage sites.

2.6 Critical Themes and Issues in EDB

Key themes, including sustainability, community involvement, and cultural sensitivity, emerge in Table 2 about EDB through the literature review, diving into contemporary issues faced by tourism today, such as climate change and technological advancement in informational aspects. Thus, ecotourism is driven by communities, data ethics, privacy, and bias reduction in predictive analytics pragmatic to the tourism industry, advocating for a highly integrative discursive approach. The challenges forge the landscape of ever-evolving heritage tourism dynamics, requiring opportunistic, adaptive, and forward-looking approaches to destination branding and management.

Table 2. Key themes, contemporary issues and their relevance to EDB

		Description	Relevance to EDB
Theme	Sustainability	Focuses on minimising environmental impacts while promoting economic and social benefits.	Ensures tourism practices do not degrade natural resources or local cultures, which is crucial for the long-term viability of heritage sites.
	Community Engagement	Involves local populations in tourism planning and decision-making.	Enhances authenticity and fosters local ownership, leading to sustainable and responsible tourism practices.
	Cultural Sensitivity	Recognises and respects the diverse cultural backgrounds of tourists and host communities.	Promotes inclusive tourism experiences, celebrating local heritage while aligning with diverse tourist expectations.
		Impact on EDB	
Contemporary issues	Impact of climate change	Rising sea levels, extreme weather, and coral bleaching directly affect natural and cultural heritage (Nabilah and Safitri, 2024). Necessitates adaptive management for sustainability and long-term preservation.	
	Role of Technology	Social media, mobile apps, and virtual reality (VR) enhance tourist experiences. Increases visibility and tailors experiences to diverse audiences (Wallace, 2019). Creates deeper connection spaces, enhancing tourist engagement.	
	Privacy and Data Ethics	Questions were raised on data privacy, ethics, and bias in predictive analytics. Transparency and fairness in tourist data collection and usage are crucial for heritage sites. Building trust through ethical data use and ensuring branding doesn't invade tourist privacy are key (Li, Liu and Soutar, 2021).	

(Source: Authors' compilation)

2.6.1 Overcoming Biases in Predictive Analytics

Recent scholarly evidence shows that predictive analytics strengthens the tourist experience and strengthens destination branding, although it can potentially induce bias and ethical concerns. Thus, to eliminate biases in the execution of a destination's branding strategy for fair policy, the study implores several areas in need of improvement.

1. **Community-led Ecotourism:** Mastika and Nimran (2020) imply that community-led ecotourism has the potential to foster the integration of locals in decision-making to help cultural sensibility and authenticity in heritage sites, therefore building tourism practices reflecting on authentic traditions and values of the place to create meaningful tourist experiences.

2. **Climate Change and Heritage Tourism:** Various cases around the world, like Venice or the Great Barrier Reef, specifically discuss the impacts of climate change on heritage tourism, showing climate-related difficulties breaking natural and cultural heritage whilst showing a strong need for the development of sustainable tourism solutions (Jopp et al., 2015).
3. **Ethical Data Use in Predictive Analytics:** As predictive analytics increasingly comes into play in tourism, ethical issues regarding the use, privacy, and potential discrimination of data need to be developed for the responsible use of tourist data in non-discriminatory ways. Unless such rules build tourist trust, neither fair nor inclusive branding practice is ensured.

Scrutinising imperative issues in EDB makes it evident that community involvement, sustainability, and cultural sensitivity are closely related, becoming the defining factors for sustainable tourism policy, advocating for no harm to the tourist experience whilst protecting heritage and nurturing local communities. Sustainability, being the core goal, focuses on tourism being able to induce economic upliftment without inducing damage to the local environment. While community involvement is a pillar of cultural originality, their cultural sensitivity ensures that tourism activities respect and promote the rich diversity of tourists and host communities. Contemporary input of relevance and aptness of issues involved can be enhanced through Modern issues to further effective HSM and destination branding.

2.7 Enhancing Comprehensive Coverage in EDB

The discourse of EDB requires an interceded approach between significant themes and core aspects focusing on three significant domains – involvement of the local community, climate change and environmental sustainability, and digital and virtual tourism – to gain a holistic overview of the challenges and opportunities faced by this dynamic sector.

2.7.1 Local Community Involvement

An STP calls for proper local involvement in the planning process of tourism, correlating cultural values and community needs beyond merely giving ownership feelings to the local population by adding value to the overall design. Local community involvement allows locals to control the management of their cultural and natural resources through community-led ecotourism, thus ensuring a thought-provoking approach that enhances their sensitivity and development of sustainable tourism use (Mastika and Nimran, 2020). Costa Rica's community-based ecotourism is the most vibrant representation of local-led leadership for actualising better environmental outcomes and authentic cultural experiences for tourists, emphasising economic benefits among locals.

2.7.2 Climate Change and Environmental Sustainability

Bidirectional discussion between climate change and environmental sustainability can be facilitated by heritage tourism to emphasise climate change and environmental sustainability, two of the biggest challenges to the long-term protection of heritage sites. Jopp et al. (2015) argue that climatic change directly threatens the impact on heritage tourism through the physical integrity of the tourist experience at heritage sites. Cases like Venice, where rising sea levels pose a threat to the fragile heritage city, and the Great Barrier Reef, where coral bleaching is threatening one of the world's most important natural heritage sites, ask for urgent adaptive strategies to sustain the destinations rather than harm cultural and natural heritage. Mastika and Nimran (2020) suggest a strategic adaptive management approach to mitigate the adverse effects of climate change, including responsible waste, control of tourist numbers, and conservation investments to balance tourism demands with the preservation of the environment and cultural resources.

2.7.3 Digital and Virtual Tourism

EDb also shares a link with digital and virtual tourism. However, digital technological advances have transformed how destinations market themselves while interacting with potential tourists. Social media, mobile applications, and VR experiences have become the go-to avenues for destination brands for immersion creation, attracting more consumers, and establishing relationships and communication between brands and travellers in increasingly competitive tourism markets. This has also been rushed due to the onset of the pandemic, calling for digitisation and contact-free solutions like virtual tours and digital engagements to retain tourists' interests. Nabilah and Safitri (2024) argue that sustaining long-term interest in heritage sites through a global audience can be provided through virtual tourism and its new value elements.

Sustainability requires comprehensive discussions on EDB through inclusive approaches of local communities, climate change and digital tourism for authenticating any service that does not offend the cultural values and through direct equity distribution to the local populations based upon strategies to protect heritage sites from environmental degradation while promoting sustainable tourism. The growing changes in the tourism industry through digital and virtual parts of tourism are opening new communication channels while, at the same time, enhancing the global image of heritage destinations, especially in the context of post-pandemic attributes.

3 METHODOLOGY

The study uses a mixed-method approach, with a literature review to collect data about the biases and strategies related to ecotourism in enhancing destination branding at heritage sites, while supplemented by case studies of three heritage destinations to create a multi-dimensional relative to the research problem. The literature review focuses on keywords including 'ecotourism biases', 'destination branding' and 'heritage site management', selecting peer-reviewed articles and omitting grey literature. The trends, challenges, and best practices currently being developed have been studied using the core themes to provide an overall understanding of the theoretical and practical dimensions of the study. The case studies complement the literature by focusing on the implementation of branding strategies and ecotourism practices, selected due to their relevance and the availability of data on secondary data sources like tourism reports and site management documents. Following these steps, an analysis phase was conducted, and findings from the literature review and case studies were integrated to identify critical trends, challenges, and best practices through categorisation and interpretation using thematic analysis. This analysis focused on the identification of how cultural, social, and environmental biases influence tourist behaviour and site management, what role destination branding strategies play in the promotion of destination image, tourist satisfaction and overall economic benefits, and the effectiveness of conservation, community engagement, and sustainability practices in creating resilient tourist experience with proper protection and promotion of heritage sites. The research process incorporates ethical considerations, including data transparency, stakeholder engagement, and cultural and environmental sensibility, whilst ensuring the provision of robust and reliable research to benefit tourism professionals and heritage site managers.

4 CASE STUDIES

This section elaborates on real-world cases of ecotourism bias effects on the branding and management of heritage sites, identifying subtle, insidious ways in which cultural, social, and environmental biases manifest to impact tourist perception and behaviour. The case studies were selected based on specific issues and strategies adapted to overcome the same bias towards implementing more sustainable and inclusive tourism development. Based on such understanding from case studies, best practices and strategic recommendations are derived concerning bettering destination branding and HSM.

4.1 Case Study 1: The Taj Mahal, India

The WHS Taj Mahal investigates how tourist bias, destination branding, and HSM affect people's perception and interaction with this iconic landmark. Table 3 highlights the opportunities and challenges in promoting and administering the Taj Mahal by examining solutions for improving tourist services, STP, and cultural sensitivity, emphasising how crucial it is to comprehend the complexities of historic tourism.

Table 3. Branding, biases, and management strategies for the Taj Mahal

Category	Aspect	Description	References
Branding Strategies – The branding efforts focus on the following aspects	Historical Significance	The Taj Mahal is celebrated as an epitome of Mughal architecture and a symbol of India's rich history. This narrative is consistently reinforced in promotional materials, including brochures, websites, and travel guides.	Akhtar and Anjum, 2022; Kainthola Tiwari and Chowdhary, 2021;
	Architectural Excellence	Emphasising the Taj Mahal's intricate design and craftsmanship, branding materials often showcase its marble domes, minarets, and elaborate inlay work, drawing attention to its aesthetic and engineering marvel.	
	Romantic Symbolism	The story of Emperor Shah Jahan building the Taj Mahal in memory of his beloved wife, Mumtaz Mahal, is central to its brand. This romantic narrative appeals to a broad audience, enhancing its allure as a must-visit destination.	Majumder et al., 2021; Kumari, 2021;
Biases Identified – Several biases influence tourist perceptions and experiences at the Taj Mahal.	Cultural Biases	Tourists from different cultural backgrounds often have varying expectations and interpretations of the Taj Mahal's significance. Western tourists may primarily view it as an architectural wonder, while Indian tourists might connect more deeply with its historical and cultural context.	
	Social Biases	Social norms and expectations can shape tourist behaviour. For example, emphasising the Taj Mahal as a romantic destination might influence couples to visit, potentially overshadowing other aspects of its heritage.	Suklabaidya and Aggarwal, 2020;
	Environmental Biases	The environmental conditions surrounding the Taj Mahal, such as pollution from nearby industries and heavy tourist traffic, can impact tourist experiences. Perceptions of the site's cleanliness and conservation efforts play a significant role in shaping overall satisfaction.	

continued on following page

Table 3. Continued

Category	Aspect	Description	References
Management Implications – Addressing these biases requires a multifaceted approach to ensure the Taj Mahal's sustainable and inclusive promotion and management.	Cultural Sensitivity	Diverse Narratives: Incorporating diverse narratives that resonate with various cultural groups can enhance the inclusivity of the Taj Mahal's branding. For instance, highlighting stories from different historical periods and cultural perspectives can enrich tourist understanding and appreciation.	Hameed and Khalid, 2018; Kamat, 2013; Parwez, 2013;
		Multilingual Resources: Providing information in multiple languages and formats can help cater to a global audience, making the site more accessible and engaging for international tourists.	
	Sustainable Tourism Practices	Tourist Management: Implementing measures to control tourist numbers, such as timed entry tickets and restricted access during peak hours, can help reduce overcrowding and minimise environmental impact.	Arunmozhi and Panneerselvam, 2013
		Pollution Control: Collaborating with local authorities to address pollution sources and promote eco-friendly practices can improve the site's environmental conditions. Initiatives like green transportation options and waste management programs can significantly enhance tourist experiences.	
	Enhanced Tourist Services	Educational Programs: Offering guided tours, workshops, and interactive exhibits can give tourists a deeper understanding of the Taj Mahal's historical and cultural context. Educational programs tailored to different age groups and interests can enrich the tourist experience.	
		Facilities Improvement: Upgrading tourist amenities, such as restrooms, seating areas, and information centres, can improve comfort and convenience, contributing to higher satisfaction levels.	

4.2 Case Study 2: Machu Picchu, Peru

Machu Picchu, an iconic tourist destination in Peru, is a branding model that manages and experiences heritage sites globally. Social, environmental, and cultural aspects influence its management and branding. UNESCO has recognised Machu Picchu as a WHS, and its study provides valuable lessons on community involvement, STP, and cultural sensitivity (refer to Table 4).

Table 4. Branding, biases, and management strategies for Machu Picchu

Category	Aspect	Description	References
Branding Strategies	Historical Significance	Emphasising Machu Picchu as an archaeological marvel, showcasing its intricate stone structures, terraces, and importance as a historical site.	Selcuk et al., 2023; Sotomayor and Guillén, 2022;
	Cultural Heritage	Highlighting the Incan civilisation's ingenuity, spirituality, and architectural prowess are integral to the site's identity.	
	Natural Beauty	Promoting the breathtaking natural surroundings, including the lush, mountainous landscape and the region's biodiversity.	Huamanchumo, Flores and Barrantes, 2020;
Biases Identified – Several biases impact tourist perceptions and behaviours at Machu Picchu	Social Biases	Perceptions of exclusivity and the influence of global travel trends affect tourist behaviour. Many tourists view Machu Picchu as a 'must-see' destination, leading to high expectations and sometimes unrealistic perceptions of the site.	
	Environmental Biases	The site's fragility and the impact of climate change significantly influence tourist experiences. Tourists' perceptions can be affected by weather conditions, the physical state of the site, and the environmental policies in place.	Pavelka, 2016; Larson and Poudyal, 2012;
	Cultural Biases	Tourists from different cultural backgrounds may have varying interpretations and appreciations of Machu Picchu's historical and cultural significance, leading to diverse tourist experiences and expectations.	Ypeij, 2012; Richter and Tveteras, 2012;
Management Implications – The management of Machu Picchu must address these biases to enhance tourist experiences and ensure the site's sustainability.	Promoting Community Involvement	Engaging local communities in tourism development can help mitigate social biases. This approach fosters a sense of ownership and inclusivity, ensuring that tourism benefits are shared locally and that the community plays a role in preserving the site.	Carlson, 2012; Maxwell, 2012, 2009;
	Sustainable Tourism Practices	Implementing strategies to manage tourist numbers, reduce environmental impact, and protect the site's integrity is crucial. Limiting daily tourists, enforcing strict environmental regulations, and promoting eco-friendly practices can address environmental biases.	
	Cultural Sensitivity	Enhancing the cultural sensitivity of promotional materials and tourist services can help mitigate cultural biases. Providing comprehensive and accurate information about the site's historical and cultural context can enrich tourist understanding and appreciation.	Arellano, 2011; Johnston, 2000

Machu Picchu's management can counter tourist bias through community involvement, STP, and cultural sensitivity improvement, demonstrating that HSM is wholesome and not harmful to preservation but supports tourist satisfaction and community benefit.

4.3 Case Study 3: Serengeti National Park, Tanzania

Serengeti National Park, a UNESCO WHS in Tanzania, showcases the challenges and opportunities of heritage tourism, with global significance, high tourist traffic, and complex social, environmental, and cultural factors influencing its management and branding strategies. Table 5 explores community involvement, sustainability, and cultural sensitivity, highlighting the importance of conservation.

Table 5. Comprehensive overview of branding, biases, and management strategies for Serengeti National Park

Category	Aspect	Description	References
Branding Strategies	Wildlife Conservation	Emphasising the park's role in protecting diverse wildlife and ecosystems.	Kaiza-Boshe, 2024; Mwaibofu, 2021; Bakari, 2021;
	Adventure Tourism	Promoting safari experiences and adventure activities to attract thrill-seekers.	
	Cultural Heritage	Highlighting the Maasai culture and traditions to enhance the tourist experience.	
Biases Identified	Social Biases	Perceptions of exclusivity can affect tourist expectations; some may feel alienated by luxury offerings.	Nsemwa, 2020; Gardner, 2016;
	Environmental Biases	Climate change impacts and park fragility can influence tourist experiences; visible environmental conditions shape perceptions.	
	Cultural Biases	Different cultural backgrounds lead to varied interpretations of the park's significance.	
Management Implications	Promoting Community Involvement	Engaging local Maasai communities in tourism development fosters ownership and enhances cultural sensitivity.	
	Sustainable Tourism Practices	Implementing measures to manage tourist numbers and protect ecosystems is crucial for sustainability.	
	Cultural Sensitivity	Multilingual resources and educational programs can enrich tourists' understanding of local cultures.	

Serengeti National Park faces challenges due to destination branding and tourist biases. Community involvement, STP, and cultural sensitivity can counterbalance these biases, highlighting the need for integrated management.

5 DISCUSSION

This section explores the impact of biases in EDB on managing heritage sites, focusing on the three case studies – Taj Mahal, Machu Picchu, and Serengeti National Park – highlighting the need for engagement between cultural sensitivity, predictive analytics, and ethical considerations in promoting of sustainable, inclusive, and culturally respectful tourism experiences. While addressing challenges in branding strategies and biased narratives in tourism economies concerning heritage site integrity, local community benefits and service ecosystems, the study proposes strategies to reduce biases, authenticity, and tourist engagement. This section contributes to the ongoing dialogue on sustainable management of heritage sites and responsible tourism practices in a changing world.

5.1 Integrating Predictive Analytics

Heritage destinations can market tourist experiences through the application of predictive analytics integrated into destination branding by acquiring an opportunity for a fundamental transformation. Since predictive analytics relies on historical data, machine learning algorithms, and statistical techniques for behaviour prediction, heritage destinations can leverage them to provide insightful information about tourist behaviours and preferences for more strategic and directed branding efforts.

5.1.1 Understanding Tourist Behaviors and Preferences

Social media, tourist surveys, booking patterns, and environmental sensors have proved remarkably effective in tracking enormous amounts of data for predictive analytics. Merely gleaning the patterns and trends from this data can drastically improve understanding of tourist behaviours and preferences for heritage destinations. Moreover, uncovering which cultural experiences are most in demand with different demographic groups through predictive models can bring peak attraction attendance by determining what drives tourist satisfaction, as shown in Table 6.

Table 6. Analyzing data sources and identifying patterns and trends for heritage sites

Category	Aspect	Description	Example	References
Analysing Data Sources	Social Media	Social media platforms are a goldmine for understanding tourist sentiments and preferences. By analysing posts, comments, and interactions related to a heritage destination, predictive models gauge public perception and identify trending topics.	The Louvre Museum in Paris uses social media analytics to understand tourist feedback and preferences, helping them tailor their exhibits and marketing strategies accordingly.	Kefi et al., 2024; Corona, 2021; Coman et al., 2020
	Tourist Surveys	Surveys provide direct feedback from tourists about their experiences. Analysing survey data helps identify areas of improvement and understand what aspects of the heritage site are most appreciated.	The National Park Service in the United States regularly conducts tourist surveys to collect data on tourist satisfaction, which informs their management and promotional strategies.	Liang et al., 2022; Miller-Rushing et al., 2021
	Booking Patterns	Analysing booking data reveals trends in tourist behaviour, such as peak booking times, average stay duration, and preferred types of accommodations.	Predictive analytics used by Disney Parks help optimise tourist flow and reduce wait times by analysing booking and attendance patterns, ensuring a better tourist experience.	Zhang et al., 2022; Guo et al., 2022
	Environmental Sensors	Sensors placed around heritage sites provide real-time data on tourist movement and density. This information helps manage crowds and enhance the tourist experience.	Venice uses environmental sensors to monitor tourist numbers and manage overcrowding in popular areas like Piazza San Marco.	Campagnaro et al., 2024; Salerno and Russo, 2022

continued on following page

Table 6. Continued

Category	Aspect	Description	Example	References
Identifying Patterns and Trends	Popular Cultural Experiences	Predictive analytics identifies which cultural experiences resonate most with different demographic groups.	Data shows that younger tourists prefer interactive and digital exhibits, while older tourists favour traditional guided tours. The British Museum in London has used such insights to develop targeted exhibits and programs that cater to diverse tourist preferences.	King et al., 2021; Choi, Berridge and Kim, 2020
	Peak Attendance Times	Predictive models forecast peak visiting times by analysing historical attendance data, allowing heritage sites to prepare accordingly.	Predictive analytics at the Smithsonian Institution in Washington, D.C., helps manage tourist flow during peak tourist seasons, ensuring a smoother experience.	Wu, 2023; Thompson, 2022
	Tourist Satisfaction Factors	Understanding what factors influence tourist satisfaction helps in enhancing the overall experience. Predictive models analyse feedback from surveys and social media to identify key satisfaction drivers.	The Rijksmuseum in Amsterdam uses tourist feedback to continually improve its services, from exhibit layouts to tourist amenities.	Santen, 2023; Alexandrou, 2020

Disney Parks in the USA implemented a system called "MyMagic+" to predict tourist behaviour and optimise park operations, improving satisfaction by 20%. The Louvre Museum in France used social media analysis to track real-time opinions and feedback from tourists, identifying and addressing issues in real time. The National Park Service in the USA used Predictive Analytics to manage tourist traffic in parks like Yellowstone, guiding entry times and resource utilisation decisions. Venice in Italy developed an advanced predictive analytic system to manage tourist flow, reducing overcrowding by up to 15% in key tourist areas. The Rijksmuseum in the Netherlands also used data- and tourist-centric approaches to design exhibitions and services based on feedback from tourists, focusing on engaging presentations and accessible information. These strategies have helped improve tourist satisfaction and ensure a more enjoyable and satisfactory visit experience. Thus, predictive analytics holds the potential to improve heritage destinations by analysing tourist behaviour and preferences, enhancing experiences and branding strategies through the utilisation of data from various sources, in turn creating more exciting, satisfying, and personalised tourist experiences, preserving heritage destinations, and making them attractive to future generations.

5.1.2 Personalization of branding strategy

Through its capability to inform branding strategy for a more personalised approach to tourists' needs and preferences, predictive analytics has gained a proper footing in the current market, at times through models that can indicate the interest of younger tourists in terms of interactivity and immersiveness of experience types. Using these can aid destinations in developing market-influential active-experience-based strategies, suggesting possible avenues for tourist attraction, be it locally or internationally (refer to Table 7).

Table 7. Tailoring branding strategies using predictive analytics for heritage sites

Strategy	Insight from Predictive Analytics	Implementation	Case Study/Example	Outcome
Developing and Promoting Interactive and Immersive Experiences	Younger tourists prefer interactive and immersive experiences.	Develop interactive exhibits, VR tours, and AR experiences.	Smithsonian American Art Museum: VR experience of artworks.	20% increase in engagement among younger tourists.
Emphasising Cultural Narratives in Marketing Campaigns	Certain cultural narratives resonate more with international tourists.	Highlight these narratives in marketing campaigns.	The Louvre Museum: Focus on iconic artworks like the Mona Lisa.	15% increase in international tourists.
Optimising Tourist Experiences	Families with children prefer educational and interactive activities; older tourists prefer guided tours and historical exhibits.	Develop family-friendly tours and interactive exhibits.	The British Museum: Family-friendly tours and interactive exhibits.	25% increase in family visits.
Enhancing Global Marketing Campaigns	Understand the preferences and cultural sensitivities of tourists from different regions.	Create targeted promotional materials.	The Great Wall of China: Focus on historical significance for European and North American tourists.	12% increase in international visits.
Enhancing Global Marketing Campaigns	Preferences of Japanese tourists include detailed historical narratives and cultural insights.	Develop guided tours and promotional content in Japanese.	Machu Picchu: Tailored content and tours for Japanese tourists.	10% increase in tourists from Japan.

5.1.3 Mitigating Biases

Although predictive analytics has numerous potential advantages, bias neutralisation in ecotourism is the most prominent over traditional branding, which reflects biased cultural, social, or environmental aspects, thus influencing the image of the heritage site adversely. Having various sources and data sets, it proposes a more inclusive branding approach (Liang et al., 2022; Miller-Rushing et al., 2021), revealing aspects beyond the 'conventional branding strategies'. For instance, if, for example from data analysis, certain practices of intangible cultural heritage are poorly represented, branding for that destination may be so designed to bring out those things more (Wu, 2023; Thompson, 2022)—for instance, promotion of traditional crafts and rituals in Kyoto, Japan. Predictive analytics proved a need to delve into the culture. With this in mind, the marketing campaign for the city targeted its efforts on conducting tea ceremonies, wearing traditional kimonos, and more to make other original crafts. Translation led to an influx of 15% of cultural tourists (Prough, 2022). Predictive analytics can also help unravel and neutralise ecotourism branding biases towards the environment (Alexandrou, 2020). For example, predictive models indicated that while beaches remained much more promoted in Costa Rica, the nation's vital biodiversity and conservation practices became less of a marketing tool. By rebranding tourism from national parks and biodiversity, Costa Rican tourism grew with an increase of 20% of eco-tourists identified with the importance of preservation and cultural assets (Dimitrijevic, Silic and Silic, 2022).

Predictive analytics will help end social biases. Data in South Africa reported that Indigenous stories are underrepresented during tourism marketing, according to Abebe et al., 2021. Branding strategies in South Africa adopted the findings to present a more fluid narrative based on Indigenous heritages and practices, leading to a diverse population of tourists with a higher appreciation for their cultures. Predictive analytics also allows real-time branding strategy adjustments based on prevailing trends and tourist comments, respectively (King et al., 2021; Choi, Berridge and Kim, 2020). The Galápagos Islands embraced predictive analytics to monitor the different tourists' interests and modify their ecotourism activities based on the same. The tourist boards of these islands increased snorkelling and diving tour sales, as it was learned that there was increased interest in marine conservation, thus increasing tourist satisfaction levels by 12% (Cajiao et al., 2020). Predictive analytics can aid heritage destinations in creating more holistic and diverse branding policies. This approach will ensure that all the cultural, social, and environmental aspects are relatively well represented and will further increase tourists' engagement in interests diversified towards a grander scale. Predictive analytics reduces biases yet enhances the general tourist experience and fosters STP.

5.1.4 Improving Tourist's Experience

Predictive analytics not only enhances effective branding but also the general tourist experience. For example, they will help predict tourist needs and preferences for delivering more customised and fulfilling experiences. For example, predictive models may help manage tourist flow to avoid crowded destinations, suggesting visit times with optimum crowding and customised tours based on tourist interests. This would increase satisfaction levels among tourists to a great extent and aim to make repeat visits (Refer to Table 8).

Table 8. Improving tourist experiences using predictive analytics for heritage sites

Aspects	Details	Examples
Managing Tourist Flow	Predictive models analyse tourist data to forecast future flows and manage crowds.	**Louvre Museum, Paris**: Uses predictive analytics to suggest less busy times for visiting, reducing overcrowding, and enhancing tourist satisfaction.
Recommending Optimal Visit Times	Analyses tourist patterns, weather, and events to recommend the best visit times.	**Alhambra, Spain**: Advises tourists on the best times to visit different parts of the complex, ensuring a more enjoyable experience by evenly spreading the influx of tourists.
Personalised Itineraries	Creates personalised itineraries based on tourist interests and preferences.	**Disney World**: Offers tailored recommendations for attractions, dining, and entertainment, enhancing the tourist experience by aligning with individual interests.
Enhancing Tourist Satisfaction	Provides customised experiences, meeting tourist expectations effectively, leading to higher satisfaction.	**British Museum**: Uses tourist feedback and behaviour data to continuously improve the tourist experience, resulting in higher satisfaction scores and increased repeat visits.
Encouraging Repeat Visits	Personalisation encourages tourists to return by catering to their needs and preferences.	**Metropolitan Museum of Art, New York**: Employs predictive analytics to optimise exhibits and services based on tourist preferences, leading to increased satisfaction and a higher rate of repeat visits.

5.1.5 Case Studies and Best Practices

Predictive analytics will make a difference in branding and the effective management of heritage sites. Heritage sites can obtain much-needed information about tourist behaviour and preferences by applying data from various sources such as social media, surveying tourists, booking patterns, and sensors within environments. Such information would facilitate branding that is finely tailored to tourists' needs. Predictive analytics will contribute much more to tourists, such as recommendations, avoidance of crowding, and sustainable management at the site. Examples of the

Taj Mahal, Machu Picchu, and Serengeti National Park are presented, which help in understanding better practical applications, possibilities of implementation and the recommended policies on integrating predictive analytics into HSM (Refer Table 9).

Table 9. Utilizing predictive analytics for HSM

Heritage Site	Application of Predictive Analytics	Implementation Prospects	Policy Recommendations	Details	Benefits
The Taj Mahal, India	Managing Crowds: Predict peak visiting times and allocate resources effectively. Tailoring Marketing Strategies: Identify tourist preferences for cultural narratives and highlight these in promotions.	• Use real-time tourist data and historical trends to develop predictive models. • Implement dynamic scheduling of staff and guides based on predictions. • Enhance marketing efforts to focus on preferred cultural narratives, utilising data from tourist feedback and social media analytics.	• Establish a centralised data collection and analysis unit to monitor tourist trends continuously. • Develop flexible staffing policies to accommodate dynamic tourist flow management. • Implement targeted marketing campaigns emphasising cultural narratives identified through predictive analytics.	Real-time data from social media and tourist surveys help predict peak times and tourist preferences.	Optimises resource allocation, reduces overcrowding, enhances tourist satisfaction, and increases marketing effectiveness.
Machu Picchu, Peru	Protecting the Site: Forecast tourist numbers to implement protective measures against over-tourism. Guided Tours: Develop guided tours that minimise environmental impact.	• Use predictive models to forecast tourist numbers and set daily tourist caps. • Design and implement guided tours based on predictive analysis to manage tourist flow. • Employ real-time monitoring to adjust tour schedules dynamically.	• Introduce timed entry tickets based on tourist forecasts to manage peak times. • Create comprehensive guided tour schedules to distribute tourists across the site evenly. • Develop a real-time monitoring system to adapt tourist management strategies promptly.	Predictive analytics provides accurate tourist forecasts and helps design eco-friendly guided tours.	Protects the site, prevents overcrowding, ensures sustainable tourism, and enhances the tourist experience.

continued on following page

Table 9. Continued

Heritage Site	Application of Predictive Analytics	Implementation Prospects	Policy Recommendations	Details	Benefits
Serengeti National Park, Tanzania	Managing Wildlife Interactions: Predict animal movements and optimise safari routes for minimal disturbance.	• Utilize GPS tracking data from wildlife to develop predictive models of animal movements. • Implement dynamic routing for safari vehicles based on real-time wildlife location data. • Analyze historical patterns to enhance wildlife viewing experiences while minimising ecological impact.	• Establish partnerships with conservation organisations for data sharing. • Develop guidelines for safari operators based on predictive insights. • Implement educational programs about wildlife behaviour for tourists.	Real-time tracking of wildlife movements provides insights into optimal viewing opportunities while protecting habitats.	Enhances wildlife viewing experiences, minimises ecological disturbance, and promotes sustainable practices among safari operators.

5.1.6 Challenges and Considerations

Predictive analytics offers benefits in heritage destination management but also carries risks, such as data privacy and ethical standards. The collection and analysis of tourist data must comply with privacy regulations and ethical guidelines to protect people's rights and maintain trust. The accuracy of predictive models depends on the quality and depth of data used. Proper collection mechanisms and systems are essential for exploitation, ensuring comprehensive, credible, and appropriate information. Heritage destinations can use predictive analytics to optimise resource management, enhance tourist experiences and contribute to sustainable heritage preservation and development.

Predictive analytics in destination branding can improve marketing and tourist experience by focusing on tourist preferences, counteracting biases, and providing tailored experiences using data-driven insights. As heritage sites develop rapidly, tourism will benefit from the optimisation and ease of predictive analytics, enabling them to navigate risk and achieve sustainable growth.

5.2 Ethical Considerations

One should note that worries regarding ethical considerations in EDB are particularly critical, particularly in the context of heritage sites. Transference, tourist privacy protection, and inclusiveness are considered (Khaokhrueamuang, 2020). Cultural heritage sites should strike a balance between effective branding and the duty of preserving the original forms of the cultural heritage (Choi, Berridge and Kim, 2020; Alexandrou, 2020; Miller-Rushing et al., 2021; King et al., 2021; Liang et al., 2022; Thompson, 2022; Salerno and Russo, 2022; Zhang et al., 2022; Guo et al., 2022; Wu, 2023; Santen, 2023; Campagnaro et al., 2024).

5.2.1 Transparency

Transparency is crucial in building trust among tourists and stakeholders, especially in heritage sites like the Taj Mahal, Machu Picchu, and Serengeti National Park. False claims and exaggerations can damage a place's reputation and reduce its trust factor. Heritage sites should present truthful information about their historical and cultural significance, including what tourists can see and experience, and in-depth details about their historical and architectural significance. This will enable tourists to appreciate the actual value of the sites and understand the effort put into maintaining them. Transparency also involves the openness of concerns about conserving the site, managing tourists, and protecting it from tourism activities. For example, the management of these sites publicly declared that hosting too many tourists and their impact on the site became a nightmare. This information can make tourists aware of developing a sense of responsibility for responsible tourism. The campaign with the Taj Mahal, Machu Picchu, and Serengeti National Park epitomises the principle of transparency. The management of these sites provides extensive information about their historical and cultural value, architectural miracles, and current preservation efforts. They openly declare restraints and regulations within the site to preserve them, including controls on tourists and set routes to reduce degradation. Transparent communication helps tourists gain confidence in the sites, leading to higher tourist satisfaction rates, repeat visits, and positive word-of-mouth recommendations. Effective promotional strategies should be founded on transparency, using available media to disseminate factual information, such as brochures, websites, guided tours, and educational programs. All promotional materials must be updated at heritage sites in light of current conservation or tourist management changes. Engagements with stakeholders, including local communities, conservation organisations, and government agencies, also contribute to transparency. Involving these groups in policy determination and involving transparent and open information about management practices can lead to more efficient conservation strategies and better cultural preservation.

5.2.2 Tourist Privacy

Advanced predictive analytics is crucial for tailoring branding strategies and understanding tourist behaviour, preferences, and trends. However, this data must be handled responsibly and ethically, following the privacy act and regulations, such as Europe's General Data Protection Regulation (GDPR). Heritage sites must ensure that their tourist information is kept safe through proper data protection. Compliance with privacy laws, such as the GDPR, is essential for heritage sites. They must obtain explicit consent from tourists to collect data and provide information about the purpose. Data must be anonymised where possible to protect tourist identities and prevent risks of data breaches and unauthorised access. Transparency is also essential for heritage sites, as it establishes trust with tourists and commitment to ethical handling. This can be achieved through clear communication on the site, an easily accessible privacy policy, and regular updates on data usage. For example, the British Museum used predictive analytics to collect data about exercise for family-friendly tours and interactive exhibitions, ensuring the data was treated with utmost privacy. This responsible approach ensures effectiveness in branding strategies and respect for the trust and privacy of tourists, ensuring a positive and ethical approach to data handling.

5.2.3 Promoting Inclusivity

Heritage sites must prioritise inclusivity in branding and ecotourism practices to ensure that every tourist, regardless of background or ability, can fully immerse themselves in the heritage experience. This can be achieved by recognising and accommodating tourists' diverse needs and desires, such as those with disabilities, age, gender, and ethnic background. Physical accessibility should be a priority, offering accommodations such as ramps for wheelchairs, tactile paths, Braille signage, audio guides, and multimedia with captioning. These measures enable people to move and visit the site autonomously without waiting for assistance, ensuring a better overall experience. Inclusive programming is crucial for involving diverse audiences in the attitudes of belonging and participation, including exhibitions, interactive exhibits, storytelling, and accessible heritage trails. Diversity enriches content representations at the site by promoting tourists' experiences by presenting various perspectives across different cultures, histories, and contributions. This approach promotes dialogue and cross-cultural understanding between tourists while valuing human heritage. The Smithsonian Institution is an example of a commitment to inclusivity, developing tactile tours for tactile learners, distributing materials in Braille and audio guides, and designing exhibits accessible to ensure full participation and appreciation for cultural heritage. These locations may create unforgettable experiences aimed at a wider global audience by adopting diversity in branding and ecotourism practices, making them more friendly and inclusive.

5.2.4 Balancing Authenticity and Respect

Heritage sites face a significant challenge in balancing efficient branding creation and responsibility towards authenticity and respect in the presentation of cultural heritage. This requires close cooperation with local communities and other actors to ensure that cultural heritage is represented honestly, respectfully, and beneficially for both parties. Authentic branding ensures the cultural heritage remains intact while tourists can appreciate its features more wholly and profoundly. Local people should collaborate with heritage sites to perceive heritage correctly through uncommunicated knowledge, traditions, and stories about heritage sites. Involving these communities in tourism activities ensures that cultural heritage presentations echo authentically with locals and tourists. A key feature of sustainable tourism is the fair sharing of the benefits secured from tourism. Heritage sites must ensure equitable distribution of tourism's economic and social benefits among concerned stakeholders and nearby local communities. This can be achieved through revenue-sharing programs, community-based tourism projects, training mechanisms for entrepreneurs, community infrastructure and development investments, and improvements to local amenities and facilities. Sustainable tourist practices are vital to cultural sustainability, and environmentally friendly and culturally sensible practices when visiting heritage sites are recommended. Tourist education about the value of heritage sites and motivating them towards responsible behaviour can significantly spread the word about sustainability efforts. In Agra, with the Taj Mahal, working with artisans and craftspeople of the local area coordinates work to heighten the authentic tourist experience level. Community-based tourism projects ensure equitable sharing of the economic benefits of tourism. Revenue-sharing programs can support local development projects, while capacity-building workshops help entrepreneurs upgrade their skills and services. In Machu Picchu, heritage sites can create employment, benefiting the local population by promoting ecotourism among vulnerable communities. Heritage sites can promote cooperation, sustainability, and respect for cultural heritage by collaborating with local people through equitable benefit distribution, best practices in sustainable tourism, and a dedication to inclusivity. By putting these ideas into practice, Agra and Machu Picchu will significantly improve the visitor experience while maintaining the authenticity and integrity of these places.

5.2.5 Addressing Cultural Sensitivities

Ethical branding is crucial in promoting cultural heritage and avoiding commodification or misrepresentation. It involves treating cultural narratives and symbols with respect and authenticity, ensuring they are used in marketing campaigns that honour their true meaning and significance. This involves consultation with cultural experts, community leaders, and other stakeholders to ensure that all portrayed elements meet authenticity in subtleties, values, and beliefs. Cultural involvement in ethical branding involves proper dialogue and consent from people regarding their views and wishes on how their culture will be used and shared. This ensures ownership and respect for their culture. For example, promoting Indigenous cultural heritage in Australia involves an Aboriginal community-led collaboration, which respects and gets Aboriginal cultural rights. In the case of Machu Picchu, ethical branding involves engaging with local Quechua communities, such as leaders, historians, and custodians of culture, to make their stories and symbols more authentic and subtle. Initiatives such as community-based tourism projects and workshops on traditional practices can engage tourists in authentic experiences, leading to cross-cultural understanding and respect. Ethical branding of heritage sites like the Taj Mahal, Machu Picchu, and Serengeti National Park should be carried out with particular consideration of local historians, cultural experts, and communities in policymaking. Authentic accounts, symbols, and insights from cultural custodians and experts are helpful, and thoughtful choice and presentation of themes on the symbolism of cultural heritage and architectural excellence ensure that the presentation does not remain shallow or commercialised. Cultural exchange programs and workshops with local artisans, historians, and others can educate tourists about Mughal culture, Incan heritage, and the ecological significance of Serengeti. Touring projects focusing on crafting local arts and traditional practices can add more experiences to tourists' tables, creating economic value for the locality. Sensitive, authentic, and collaborative applications of cultural branding empower heritage sites to promote positive cultural relations, cross-cultural understanding, and proper preservation and appreciation of cultural heritage. If strictly applied in heritage sites like Machu Picchu, the Taj Mahal, and Serengeti National Park, the tourist experience will soar sky-high while maintaining and preserving cultural heritage in the long run.

5.2.6 Sustainable Practices

Sustainability is an ethical imperative in branding and ecotourism practices, focusing on environmental conservation, minimising ecological footprints, and encouraging responsible tourist behaviour. Heritage sites must take proactive measures to minimise their ecological footprint, natural habitats, and biodiversity, ensuring they maintain their natural and cultural heritage for future generations. STPs focus on conserving and restoring natural habitats, protecting wildlife species, and managing resources sustainably. The Galápagos Islands are considered good practices for ethical branding and sustainable ecotourism, with tourist numbers controlled to avoid impacts on the fragile ecosystem. Tourist education on the value of preserving heritage and sustainability practices is essential. It can be complemented by interpretive signage, guided tours, educational programs, and interactive exhibits on environmental challenges and their solutions. Incorporating sustainability into branding and ecotourism practices at heritage destinations like Machu Picchu, Taj Mahal, and Serengeti National Park can lead to several easy-to-implement actions. For Machu Picchu, applying tourist management plans that limit visitors to the site per time and providing responsible tourism guidebooks can help reduce environmental damage while offering a sustainable tourism experience. For the Taj Mahal, arranging eco-friendly transport facilities and waste management programs can minimise tourism impacts. For Serengeti National Park, developing wildlife management plans that follow population monitoring and suitable routes with adequate distance between humans and animals can meet environmental preservation. Educational programs for tourists can heighten understanding and appreciation of local ecosystems and conservation efforts. The site is committed to environmental stewardship and conserving and valuing the natural and cultural legacy for future generations by integrating sustainability into its branding and ecotourism activities. Since it guarantees transparency, safeguards visitor privacy, and respects cultural sensitivity while providing a pro-consumerist travel experience, ethical consideration is exceptionally pertinent to EDB. In addition to improving customer pleasure, this strategy helps to preserve and honour cultural heritage.

5.3 Long-term Sustainability

Sustainable destination branding is a sustainable approach that emphasises long-term goals, such as conservation, community involvement, and adaptive management, rather than quick returns. It aims to preserve natural and cultural heritage, ensuring that heritage is maintained for extended periods and used over time. Local communities are also crucial in sustainable destination branding, as they involve stakeholders, indigenous groups, and residents in decision-making processes, promoting equitation and ownership. Adaptive management approaches are essential in sustainable destination branding, involving continuous monitoring, evaluation, and adjustment of tourism practices based on environmental, social, and economic feedback. This approach enhances resilience and sustainability at destinations, allowing for flexibility and responsiveness. Ethical destination branding also addresses the issue of bias and stereotypes in tourism narration and marketing strategies. This assignment focuses on creating authentic cultural heritage presentation activities, challenging stereotypes, and improving understanding and appreciation of diversity in cultures and identities. Cultural sensitivity is essential in sustainable destination branding, reflecting local customs, traditions, beliefs, and practices through responsible tourism. Building respect for local customs, traditions, beliefs, and practices is crucial, and providing cultural education and training among stakeholders can enhance their awareness and sensitivity. Promoting cultural awareness can lead to more interaction with local communities and a more respectful and enriching tourist experience.

Figure 1. Framework for sustainable destination branding

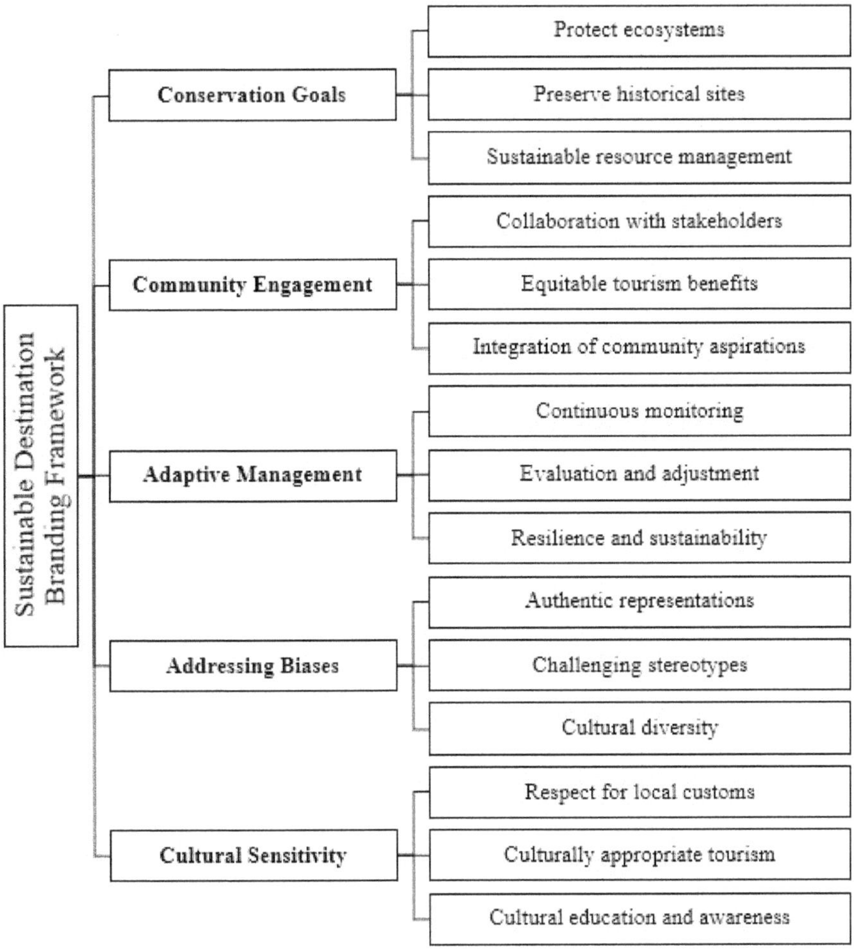

Heritage destinations can create a more inclusive tourism industry that is more sustainable for tourists and local communities by applying such principles within destination branding strategies. This benefits tourists and promotes the long-term protection and resilience of cultural and natural heritage sites and their surroundings. Some components of sustainable destination branding towards a more ethical and responsible tourist industry in support of protecting and appreciating cultural and natural heritage over time include long-term conservation objectives, involvement of local communities, adaptive management, consideration of bias, and cultural sensitivity.

5.4 Heritage Tourism Future Sustainability Trends

Since heritage tourism is rapidly evolving, addressing global issues to enhance tourist experiences requires sustainable practices. The future of HSM rests on the shoulders of innovations in ecotourism, AI, and strategic approaches towards bias mitigation, with critical innovations being regenerative tourism, community-based tourism (CBT), and environmental technologies like solar energy. Regenerative tourism aims to regenerate ecosystems and communities, while CBT ensures equitable distribution of benefits and fosters a sense of ownership. Similarly, AI in tourism applications can potentially improve the tourist experience. Table 10 outlines the branding, biases, management strategies, innovations, AI application, and worldwide challenges in heritage tourism to drive tourist attitudes and behaviours in a positive direction.

Table 10. Branding, biases, management strategies, innovations, AI applications, and global challenges in heritage tourism

Category	Aspect	Description	References
Branding Strategies	Historical Significance	Emphasising the site's importance as a cultural and historical landmark.	Akhtar and Anjum, 2022; Selcuk et al., 2023; Smith, 2020
	Cultural Heritage	Highlighting unique cultural narratives and traditions associated with the site.	Kainthola Tiwari and Chowdhary, 2021; Thompson, 2022
	Architectural Excellence	Showcasing intricate designs and craftsmanship that define the site's identity.	Majumder et al., 2021; Huamanchumo, Flores and Barrantes, 2020
	Natural Beauty	Promoting the surrounding landscapes and biodiversity that enhance the tourist experience.	Hameed and Khalid, 2018
	Adventure Tourism	Focusing on unique experiences such as safaris or guided tours that attract adventure seekers.	
	Romantic Symbolism	Leveraging stories that evoke emotional connections to enhance appeal (e.g., love stories).	Arunmozhi and Panneerselvam, 2013
Biases Identified	Cultural Biases	Differences in tourist expectations based on cultural backgrounds affect perceptions of significance.	Holder et al., 2024; Le Corre et al., 2024
	Social Biases	Perceptions of exclusivity and societal norms influence tourist behaviour and expectations.	Karayazi, Dane and Arentze, 2024
	Environmental Biases	Climate change and environmental conditions impact tourist experiences and satisfaction.	Cook, 2024
Management Implications	Promoting Community Involvement	Engaging local communities in tourism development fosters ownership and inclusivity.	Chhabra, Healy and Sills, 2003
	Sustainable Tourism Practices	Implementing measures to manage tourist numbers and reduce environmental impact is crucial.	Nag and Mishra, 2023a
	Cultural Sensitivity	Enhancing promotional materials with diverse narratives can improve tourist understanding.	Richards, 2007; Hvenegaard and Dearden, 1998
	Tourist Management	Strategies like timed entry tickets can help control crowds and minimise impacts on the site.	Ekinci and Hosany, 2006; Maxwell, 2012
	Pollution Control	Collaborating with local authorities to address pollution sources improves environmental conditions.	Ud Din, Nazneen and Jamil, 2024; Pedersen, 2002

continued on following page

Table 10. Continued

Category	Aspect	Description	References
Innovations in Ecotourism	Regenerative Tourism	Focuses on restoring ecosystems and communities rather than just minimising negative impacts.	Fennell, 2020
	Community-Based Tourism (CBT)	Empower local communities to lead tourism initiatives for equitable benefit distribution.	Chhabra, Healy and Sills, 2003
	Eco-Friendly Technologies	Integrates green technologies such as solar energy and waste recycling systems to reduce ecological footprints.	Nag and Mishra, 2023b
AI Applications in Tourism	Personalised Tourist Experiences	AI-driven analytics tailor recommendations based on individual preferences to improve satisfaction.	Fennell, Moorhouse and Macdonald, 2024
	Predictive Analytics	Analyses data trends to forecast tourist patterns and optimise resource allocation.	Plesa, 2024
	Sustainability Monitoring	Monitors environmental conditions using AI technologies for informed decision-making regarding conservation efforts.	Gade, Johnpaul and Miryala, 2024
Strategies to Address Global Challenges	Climate Action Initiatives	Develops climate action plans, including carbon footprint assessments and renewable energy usage.	Ryan and Silvanto, 2009, 2010
	Collaboration with Stakeholders	Engages local communities, government agencies, NGOs, and private sector partners in developing comprehensive strategies.	Ruggles and Silverman, 2009
	Ethical Tourism Practices	Promotes practices that respect local cultures and prioritise environmental stewardship for sustainable tourism development.	Baker and Cameron, 2008

In order to navigate the complexities of tourism development and activities with a focus on cultural heritage prosperity conservation, these aspects can be utilised, integrating innovations with technological advancements for a futuristic advancement of HSM. Heritage destinations can become more attractive and appealing whilst retaining their cultural integrity for decades to come through these strategies for enhanced sustainability and inclusiveness.

6 CONCLUSION

Exploring the way biases relate to the EDB of a destination and have solid implications for HSM through cases of heritage destinations such as the Taj Mahal in India, Machu Picchu in Peru, and Serengeti National Park in Tanzania show that they can have good branding and policy strategies advocating for sustainability besides enabling inclusivity and helping preserve cultural and natural integrity by promoting predictive analytics, cultural sensitivity, and responsible ethics. For instance, WHS Taj Mahal can benefit from predictive analytics and architectural value to optimise tourist management, helping avoid overcrowding during peak seasons while enhancing tourist experiences (refer to Figure 2). Similarly, Machu Picchu can adopt a multi-dimensional approach to destination branding, ensuring respect for local traditions and community involvement through cultural sensitivity, thus ensuring SDGs, greener waste management practices and preservation of the ecosystem and rich culture through sustainable tourism. Likewise, Serengeti National Park can optimise wildlife viewing without damaging the natural habitat by analysing tourist patterns and movements. This can lead to directed safari routes and community involvement in tourist programs, benefiting local communities and conserving their culture.

Figure 2. Checklist for ethical destination branding and ecotourism practices

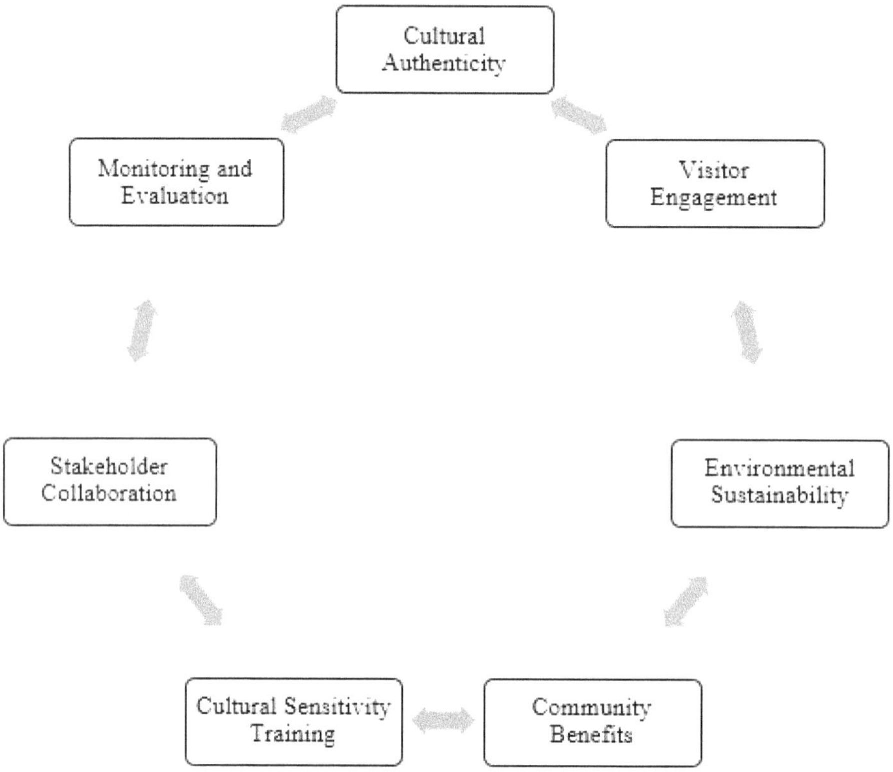

The study's implications extend beyond symbolic sites into informing practice on HSM worldwide, elaborating on ethical focus on destination branding to promote tourist satisfaction. At the same time, the movement of appreciation for cultural heritage is upscale, driving more STP. Modern tourism is continuously progressing with its embracement of predictive analytics with cultural sensitivity, leading the way for a worldwide inclusive and sustainable tourism industry. Its complexities have started to rub off on heritage sites, calling for an in-depth study into this dynamic with research that potentially discovers best practices and innovative approaches that may be used to manage heritage sites or shifting landscapes in tourism will help better develop our strategies, maintain better standards of ethics, improve cultural exchange, and protect world treasures for the sake of future generations.

7 PRACTICAL IMPLICATIONS

The study concludes with practical recommendations for sustainable tourism management, policy formulation, ecotourism stakeholders, and place branding, emphasising the importance of cultural sensitivity, authentic representation, community participation, and benefit sharing in tourism development and the need for STP that minimise the impact of tourists on the environment and promote environmental awareness. The study also underscores the need for effective monitoring and adaptive management to preserve cultural and natural resources while showing that education and awareness programs are essential to deepening cultural understanding, environmental stewardship, and responsible tourism practices in tourists. It also advocates for policy and regulation that legitimises the ethical destination brand and responsible tourism, involving government agencies, NGOs, and local authorities in developing culturally sensitive and environmentally sound regulations. Finally, it necessitates partnerships and collaborations with academia, the conservation sector, and the private sector to enhance the management of heritage sites and promote inclusive tourism development. These recommendations aim to improve authenticity, sustainability, and inclusiveness in ecotourism and destination branding, benefiting stakeholders and ensuring the best visit experience while conserving cultural heritage and promoting socio-economic well-being for future generations.

8 LIMITATIONS

In order to gain a holistic view of biases in EDB of destinations' influence on the management of heritage sites, it is required to highlight the limitations of the current study to pave the way for future research, including differences in cultural contexts, socio-economic conditions, and environments for lack of universal applicability of the finding and recommendations. Since data availability and quality are pertinent requirements for predictive analytics, it is not easy to apply the same in developing regions or far-flung places where deployment can be inhibited for data-driven strategies. The dynamic, ever-changing field of tourism and consumer behaviour constantly mandates updating and adjustments in branding strategies to ensure sustainability for more extended periods of applications. Although it is evident that ethical considerations in EDB are important, challenges persist in institutionalising cultural sensitivity and equitable benefit-sharing among various stakeholders, thus requiring ongoing research in broader governance structures, policy frameworks, and regulatory impacts on HSM.

9 FUTURE RESEARCH DIRECTIONS

The change in the efficiency and effectiveness of predictive analytics and branding strategies can be explored through longitudinal studies by exploring factors like time, tourist demographics, environmental conditions, and socio-economic factors. Future avenues for research, like cross-cultural comparisons in the existing biases towards EDB strategies to develop culturally adaptive approaches for various regions and heritage contexts, can be ventured by developing new and emerging technologies while considering tourism benefits and sustainability at heritage destinations. Inclusiveness and sustainability can be targeted by formulating and testing models on community participation in tourism planning to ensure development. Moreover, research and in-depth impact assessments are required on branding strategy for local communities, cultural heritage preservation, environmental sustainability support, and policy frameworks and structures for supporting ethical branding and sustainable tourism to provide insights towards evidence-based decisions.

REFERENCES

Aaker, D. (1991). Brand equity. *La gestione del valore della marca, 347*, 356.

Aas, C., Ladkin, A., & Fletcher, J. (2005). Stakeholder collaboration and heritage management. *Annals of Tourism Research*, 32(1), 28–48. DOI: 10.1016/j.annals.2004.04.005

Abebe, R., Aruleba, K., Birhane, A., Kingsley, S., Obaido, G., Remy, S. L., & Sadagopan, S. (2021). Narratives and counternarratives on data sharing in Africa. In *Proceedings of the 2021 ACM conference on fairness, accountability, and transparency* (pp. 329-341). DOI: 10.1145/3442188.3445897

Ahmad, Y. (2006). The scope and definitions of heritage: From tangible to intangible. *International Journal of Heritage Studies*, 12(3), 292–300. DOI: 10.1080/13527250600604639

Akhtar, M., & Anjum, U. (2022). Economic importance of tourism in India and prospects for sustainable development. *International Research Journal of Modernization in Engineering Technology and Science*, 4(6), 846.

Alagarsamy, S., Mehrolia, S., & Paul, J. (2024). Masstige scale: An alternative to measure brand equity. *International Journal of Consumer Studies*, 48(1), e12873. DOI: 10.1111/ijcs.12873

Alexandrou, E. (2020). *Digital Strategy in Museums: A case study of The Rijksmuseum.*

Anholt, S. (2006). The Anholt-GMI City Brands Index: How the World Sees the World's Cities. *Place Branding*, 2(1), 18–31. DOI: 10.1057/palgrave.pb.5990042

Arellano, A. (2011). Tourism in poor regions and social inclusion: The porters of the Inca Trail to Machu Picchu. *World Leisure Journal*, 53(2), 104–118. DOI: 10.1080/04419057.2011.580551

Arunmozhi, T., & Panneerselvam, A. (2013). Types of tourism in India. *International Journal of Current Research and Academic Review*, 1(1), 84–88.

Bakari, S. J. (2021). Challenges facing domestic tourism promotion-a case of Serengeti National Park-Tanzania. *Journal of Tourism and Hospitality S, 3.*

Baker, M. J., & Cameron, E. (2008). Critical success factors in destination marketing. *Tourism and Hospitality Research*, 8(2), 79–97. DOI: 10.1057/thr.2008.9

Balakrishnan, S. M. (2009). Strategic branding of destinations: A framework. *European Journal of Marketing*, 43(5/6), 611–629. DOI: 10.1108/03090560910946954

Butler, R. W. (1999). Sustainable tourism: A state-of-the-art review. *Tourism Geographies*, 1(1), 7–25. DOI: 10.1080/14616689908721291

Cajiao, D., Izurieta, J. C., Casafont, M., Reck, G., Castro, K., Santamaría, V., Cárdenas, S., & Leung, Y. F. (2020). Tourist use and impact monitoring in the Galapagos: An evolving programme with lessons learned. *Parks*, 26(2), 89–102. DOI: 10.2305/IUCN.CH.2020.PARKS-26-2DC.en

Campagnaro, F., Ghalkhani, M., Tumiati, R., Marin, F., Del Grande, M., Pozzebon, A., . . . Zorzi, M. (2024). Monitoring the Venice Lagoon: an IoT Cloud-Based Sensor Nerwork Approach. *arXiv preprint arXiv:2403.06915.*

. Carlson, B. (2012). Impacts of Infrastructure Related to Tourism on Machu Picchu.

Casado-Aranda, L. A., Sánchez-Fernández, J., & Ibáñez-Zapata, J. Á. (2023). Evaluating communication effectiveness through eye tracking: Benefits, state of the art, and unresolved questions. *International Journal of Business Communication*, 60(1), 24–61. DOI: 10.1177/2329488419893746

Chen, H., Chiang, R. H., & Storey, V. C. (2012). Business intelligence and analytics: From big data to big impact. *Management Information Systems Quarterly*, 36(4), 1165–1188. DOI: 10.2307/41703503

Chhabra, D., Healy, R., & Sills, E. (2003). Staged authenticity and heritage tourism. *Annals of Tourism Research*, 30(3), 702–719. DOI: 10.1016/S0160-7383(03)00044-6

Choi, A., Berridge, G., & Kim, C. (2020). The urban museum as a creative tourism attraction: London museum lates visitor motivation. *Sustainability (Basel)*, 12(22), 9382. DOI: 10.3390/su12229382

Cleere, G. S. (1989). *The House on Observatory Hill: Home of the Vice President of the United States*. Oceanographer of the Navy.

Coman, A., Grigore, A. M., Ardelean, A., & Maracine, R. (2020). The world of museums and web 2.0: Links between social media and the number of visitors in museums. In *Social Computing and Social Media. Design, Ethics, User Behavior, and Social Network Analysis: 12th International Conference, SCSM 2020, Held as Part of the 22nd HCI International Conference, HCII 2020, Copenhagen, Denmark, July 19–24, 2020* [Springer International Publishing.]. *Proceedings*, 22(Part I), 442–458.

Cook, G. (2024). *The Planning, Design, and Delivery of Environmental Education and Interpretation in Ecotourism: A Case Study of Tiritiri Matangi Island* (Doctoral dissertation, Auckland University of Technology).

Corona, L. (2021). Museums and communication: The case of the louvre museum at the COVID-19 age. *Humanities and Social Science Research*, 4(1), 15–p15. DOI: 10.30560/hssr.v4n1p15

. d'Hauteserre, A. M. (2004). Postcolonialism, colonialism, and tourism. *A companion to tourism, 235.*

Davenport, T. H., Harris, J. G., Jones, G. L., Lemon, K. N., Norton, D., & McCallister, M. B. (2007). The dark side of customer analytics. *Harvard Business Review*, 85(5), 37.

. Dimitrijevic, G. O., Silic, D., & Silic, I. (2022). CAN ECOTOURISM OFFER SUSTAINABLE DEVELOPMENT: WHY COSTA RICA SUCCEEDED. *Global journal of Business and Integral Security.*

Ekinci, Y., & Hosany, S. (2006). Destination personality: An application of brand personality to tourism destinations. *Journal of Travel Research*, 45(2), 127–139. DOI: 10.1177/0047287506291603

Fakeye, P. C., & Crompton, J. L. (1991). Image differences between prospective, first-time, and repeat visitors to the lower Rio Grande Valley. *Journal of Travel Research*, 30(2), 10–16. DOI: 10.1177/004728759103000202

Fennell, D. A. (2020). *Ecotourism*. Routledge. DOI: 10.4324/9780429346293

Fennell, D. A., Moorhouse, T. P., & Macdonald, D. W. (2024). Towards a model for the assessment of conservation, welfare, and governance in wildlife tourism attractions. *Journal of Ecotourism*, 23(2), 166–193. DOI: 10.1080/14724049.2022.2156523

Gade, J., Johnpaul, M., & Miryala, R. K. (2024). Tribal Tourism: A Literature-Based Study of Ethnographic Exploration of Culture and Sustainable Development. In *Managing Tourism and Hospitality Sectors for Sustainable Global Transformation* (pp. 169-183). IGI Global. DOI: 10.4018/979-8-3693-6260-0.ch012

Gardner, B. (2016). *Selling the Serengeti: The cultural politics of safari tourism.* University of Georgia Press. DOI: 10.1353/book44451

Garrod, B., & Fyall, A. (2000). Managing heritage tourism. *Annals of Tourism Research*, 27(3), 682–708. DOI: 10.1016/S0160-7383(99)00094-8

Gretzel, U., Fesenmaier, D. R., Formica, S., & O'Leary, J. T. (2006). Searching for the future: Challenges faced by destination marketing organizations. *Journal of Travel Research*, 45(2), 116–126. DOI: 10.1177/0047287506291598

Guo, H., Luo, Z., Li, M., Kong, S., & Jiang, H. (2022). A literature review of big data-based urban park research in visitor dimension. *Land (Basel)*, 11(6), 864. DOI: 10.3390/land11060864

Hall, C. M., & Piggin, R. (2002). Tourism business knowledge of World Heritage sites: A New Zealand case study. *International Journal of Tourism Research*, 4(5), 401–411. DOI: 10.1002/jtr.391

Hall, D. R., & Richards, G. (Eds.). (2000). *Tourism and sustainable community development* (p. 1). Routledge.

Hameed, B., & Khalid, A. (2018). Impact of ecotourism in ensuring the sustainable development of tourism industry in India. *International Journal of Recent Research Aspects*, 5(2), 46–50.

Hardy, A., Beeton, R. J., & Pearson, L. (2002). Sustainable tourism: An overview of the concept and its position in relation to conceptualisations of tourism. *Journal of Sustainable Tourism*, 10(6), 475–496. DOI: 10.1080/09669580208667183

Harrison, D., & Campus, N. (2004). Working with the tourism industry: A case study from Fiji. *Social Responsibility*, 1(1-2), 249–270.

Hatma Indra Jaya, P., Izudin, A., & Aditya, R. (2024). The role of ecotourism in developing local communities in Indonesia. *Journal of Ecotourism*, 23(1), 20–37. DOI: 10.1080/14724049.2022.2117368

Hede, A. M. (2008). World Heritage listing and the evolving issues related to tourism and heritage: Cases from Australia and New Zealand. *Journal of Heritage Tourism*, 2(3), 133–144. DOI: 10.2167/jht055.0

Holder, A., Walters, G., Ruhanen, L., & Mkono, M. (2024). Exploring tourist's socio-cultural aversions, self-congruity bias, attitudes and willingness to participate in indigenous tourism. *Journal of Vacation Marketing*, 30(2), 207–224. DOI: 10.1177/13567667221124343

Huamanchumo, R. M. E., Flores, C. E. G., & Barrantes, D. A. (2020). Ecotouristic activity of local entrepreneurs in the sustainability of the historical sanctuary forest of Pómac. *Journal of Tourism and Heritage Research: JTHR*, 3(3), 360–380.

Hudson, S., & Miller, G. (2005). Ethical orientation and awareness of tourism students. *Journal of Business Ethics*, 62(4), 383–396. DOI: 10.1007/s10551-005-0850-8

Hvenegaard, G., & Dearden, P. (1998). Ecotourism versus tourism in a Thai national park. *Annals of Tourism Research*, 25(3), 700–720. DOI: 10.1016/S0160-7383(98)00020-6

Johnston, A. (2000). Indigenous peoples and ecotourism: Bringing indigenous knowledge and rights into the sustainability equation. *Tourism Recreation Research*, 25(2), 89–96. DOI: 10.1080/02508281.2000.11014914

Jopp, R., Mair, J., DeLacy, T., & Fluker, M. (2015). Climate change adaptation: Destination management and the green tourist. *Tourism Planning & Development*, 12(3), 300–320. DOI: 10.1080/21568316.2014.988879

Kainthola Ms, S., Tiwari Ms, P., & Chowdhary Dr, N. R. (2021). Tourist Guides' perspectives of demarketing the Taj Mahal. *International Journal of Tour Guiding Research*, 2(1), 4.

Kaiza-Boshe, T. (2024). Towards Overcoming the Challenges to Adopting Ecosystem-Based Management Approach for Protected Areas: The Case of Serengeti Ecosystem. In *Land-Use Management-Recent Advances, New Perspectives, and Applications*. IntechOpen.

. Kamat, N. M. (2013). Sustainable Ecotourism Planning For Happier and Wealthier Goa. *Goa Today*, 1-10.

Karayazi, S. S., Dane, G., & Arentze, T. (2024). Visitors' heritage location choices in Amsterdam in times of mass tourism: A latent class analysis. *Journal of Heritage Tourism*, 19(4), 1–22. DOI: 10.1080/1743873X.2024.2331227

Kavaratzis, M., & Ashworth, G. J. (2005). City branding: An effective assertion of identity or a transitory marketing trick? *Tijdschrift voor Economische en Sociale Geografie*, 96(5), 506–514. DOI: 10.1111/j.1467-9663.2005.00482.x

Kefi, H., Besson, E., Zhao, Y., & Farran, S. (2024). Toward museum transformation: From mediation to social media-tion and fostering omni-visit experience. *Information & Management*, 61(1), 103890. DOI: 10.1016/j.im.2023.103890

Khaokhrueamuang, A. (2020). International exchange in tea tourism: reconceptualizing Japanese green tourism for sustainable farming communities. In *Tourism Development in Japan* (pp. 140–159). Routledge. DOI: 10.4324/9780429273513-8

Kim, H., & Fesenmaier, D. R. (2008). Persuasive design of destination web sites: An analysis of first impression. *Journal of Travel Research*, 47(1), 3–13. DOI: 10.1177/0047287507312405

King, E., Smith, M. P., Wilson, P. F., & Williams, M. A. (2021). Digital responses of UK museum exhibitions to the COVID-19 crisis, March–June 2020. *Curator (New York, N.Y.)*, 64(3), 487–504. DOI: 10.1111/cura.12413 PMID: 34230675

Kotler, P., & Gertner, D. (2007). Country as brand, product and beyond: A place marketing and brand management perspective. In *Destination branding* (pp. 55–71). Routledge.

Kumari, N. (2021). Impact of Eco-Tourism on the Indian Economy. *Gap Interdisciplinarities*, 12-16.

Larson, L. R., & Poudyal, N. C. (2012). Developing sustainable tourism through adaptive resource management: A case study of Machu Picchu, Peru. *Journal of Sustainable Tourism*, 20(7), 917–938. DOI: 10.1080/09669582.2012.667217

Le Corre, N., Saint-Pierre, A., Hughes, M., Peuziat, I., & Cosquer, A. (2024). Segmentation of visitor perceptions and attitudes as a tool for informing management and targeted communication strategies in Coastal and Marine Protected Areas. *Journal of Coastal Conservation*, 28(4), 57. DOI: 10.1007/s11852-024-01053-2

Leask, A., & Fyall, A. (2006). Researching the management of visitor attractions: International comparative study issues. *Tourism Recreation Research*, 31(2), 23–32. DOI: 10.1080/02508281.2006.11081259

Lee, T. H., & Jan, F. H. (2018). Ecotourism behavior of nature-based tourists: An integrative framework. *Journal of Travel Research*, 57(6), 792–810. DOI: 10.1177/0047287517717350

Li, T. T., Liu, F., & Soutar, G. N. (2021). Experiences, post-trip destination image, satisfaction and loyalty: A study in an ecotourism context. *Journal of Destination Marketing & Management*, 19, 100547. DOI: 10.1016/j.jdmm.2020.100547

Liang, Y., Yin, J., Pan, B., Lin, M. S., Miller, L., Taff, B. D., & Chi, G. (2022). Assessing the validity of mobile device data for estimating visitor demographics and visitation patterns in Yellowstone National Park. *Journal of Environmental Management*, 317, 115410. DOI: 10.1016/j.jenvman.2022.115410 PMID: 35751247

Majumder, S., Saha, S., Mukherjee, A., Das, J., Mukherjee, S., & Das, S. (2021). Sustainable Tourism and Ecotourism, The Future of Tourism Sector in India. *Global Management Journal*, 15(1/2), 332–345.

Mastika, I. K., & Nimran, U. (2020). Destination branding model of an ecological tourism village in Bali, Indonesia. *Geo Journal of Tourism and Geosites*, 31(3), 1068–1074. DOI: 10.30892/gtg.31319-542

Maxwell, K. (2009). *Making Machu Picchu: Embedding History and Embodying Nature in the Peruvian Andes*. Agrarian Studies Program, Yale, and Earth and Environment, Franklin and Marshall College.

Maxwell, K. (2012). Tourism, environment, and development on the inca trail. *The Hispanic American Historical Review*, 92(1), 143–171. DOI: 10.1215/00182168-1470995

McKercher, B., & Du Cros, H. (2002). *Cultural tourism: The partnership between tourism and cultural heritage management.* Routledge.

Miller-Rushing, A. J., Athearn, N., Blackford, T., Brigham, C., Cohen, L., Cole-Will, R., Edgar, T., Ellwood, E. R., Fisichelli, N., Pritz, C. F., Gallinat, A. S., Gibson, A., Hubbard, A., McLane, S., Nydick, K., Primack, R. B., Sachs, S., & Super, P. E. (2021). COVID-19 pandemic impacts on conservation research, management, and public engagement in US national parks. *Biological Conservation*, 257, 109038. DOI: 10.1016/j.biocon.2021.109038 PMID: 34580547

Morgan, N., Pritchard, A., & Pride, R. (2007). *Destination branding*. Routledge. DOI: 10.4324/9780080477206

Mowforth, M., & Munt, I. (2015). *Tourism and sustainability: Development, globalisation and new tourism in the third world.* Routledge. DOI: 10.4324/9781315795348

Mwaibofu, P. A. (2021). *Assessment of the Factors Affecting Tourists' Satisfaction at Ikona Wildlife Management Area in Serengeti, Tanzania* (Doctoral dissertation, The Open University of Tanzania).

Nabilah, A. F., & Safitri, R. (2024). Exploring Cultural-Based Ecotourism Destination Branding in the village of Ranu Pani. *AICCON*, 1, 553–564.

Nag, A. (2022). Industrial infrastructure development of cottage industries for inclusive economic growth in a sustainable manner: Case study of the urban growth centre in Bishnupur, West Bengal, India. *International Journal of Indian Culture and Business Management*, 26(2), 204–233. DOI: 10.1504/IJICBM.2022.123591

Nag, A. (2023). Industrial infrastructure and economic platform development for social and sustainable enterprise encouragement of cottage industries: Case study of Bishnupur West Bengal. *International Journal of Indian Culture and Business Management*, 28(4), 442–471. DOI: 10.1504/IJICBM.2023.130125

Nag, A., & Mishra, S. (2023a). Destination Competitiveness and Sustainability: Heritage Planning From the Perspective of the Tourism Industry Stakeholders. In *Cases on Traveler Preferences, Attitudes, and Behaviors: Impact in the Hospitality Industry* (pp. 1-32). IGI Global.

Nag, A., & Mishra, S. (2023b). Stakeholders' perception and competitiveness of heritage towns: A systematic literature review. *Tourism Management Perspectives*, 48, 101156. DOI: 10.1016/j.tmp.2023.101156

Nag, A., & Mishra, S. (2023c). Unlocking the Power of Stakeholder Perception: Enhancing Competitive Heritage Planning and Place-Making. In *Exploring Culture and Heritage Through Experience Tourism* (pp. 196-226). IGI Global.

Nag, A., & Mishra, S. (2024a). Mining Ghost Town Revitalization through Heritage Tourism Initiatives. *Journal of Mining and Environment*, 15(2), 439–461.

Nag, A., & Mishra, S. (2024b). Predictive Analytics for Heritage Site Visitor Patterns. In *Utilizing Smart Technology and AI in Hybrid Tourism and Hospitality* (pp. 140–185). IGI Global. DOI: 10.4018/979-8-3693-1978-9.ch007

Nag, A., & Mishra, S. (2024c). Revitalizing Mining Heritage Tourism: A Machine Learning Approach to Tourism Management. *Journal of Mining and Environment*.

Nag, A., & Mishra, S. (2024d). Tourism Management with AI Integration for Mining Heritage: A Literature Review Approach. *Journal of Mining and Environment*, 15(1), 115–149.

Nsemwa, R. (2020). *Assessment of Tourism Competitive Advantage of UNESCO World Heritage Sites in Tanzania: A case study of Serengeti National Park from 2000-2018* (Doctoral dissertation, The Open University of Tanzania).

Parwez, S. (2013). Case Study An Assessment of Delhi Tourism Sector: A Socio-Economic Developmental Perspective. *Globsyn Management Journal*, 94.

Pavelka, J. (2016). In the shadow of Machu Picchu: a case study of the Salkantay Trail. In *Mountain tourism: experiences, communities, environments and sustainable futures* (pp. 111–120). CABI. DOI: 10.1079/9781780644608.0111

Pedersen, D. (2002). Political violence, ethnic conflict, and contemporary wars: Broad implications for health and social well-being. *Social Science & Medicine*, 55(2), 175–190. DOI: 10.1016/S0277-9536(01)00261-1 PMID: 12144134

Pike, A., Béal, V., Cauchi-Duval, N., Franklin, R., Kinossian, N., Lang, T., Leibert, T., MacKinnon, D., Rousseau, M., Royer, J., Servillo, L., Tomaney, J., & Velthuis, S. (2024). 'Left behind places': A geographical etymology. *Regional Studies*, 58(6), 1167–1179. DOI: 10.1080/00343404.2023.2167972

Plesa, D. (2024). Enhancing culturally sensitive tourism in Finnish Lapland: exploring the role of the Sámi tourism guidelines.

Prough, J. S. (2022). *Kyoto revisited: heritage tourism in contemporary Japan*. University of Hawaii Press.

Qu, H., Kim, L. H., & Im, H. H. (2011). A model of destination branding: Integrating the concepts of the branding and destination image. *Tourism Management*, 32(3), 465–476. DOI: 10.1016/j.tourman.2010.03.014

Quoquab, F., Mohammad, J., & Mohd Sobri, A. M. (2021). Psychological engagement drives brand loyalty: Evidence from Malaysian ecotourism destinations. *Journal of Product and Brand Management*, 30(1), 132–147. DOI: 10.1108/JPBM-09-2019-2558

Richards, G. (2007). *Cultural tourism: Global and local perspectives*. Psychology Press.

Richter, U., & Tveteras, S. (2012). The case of Inkaterra: Pioneering ecotourism in Peru. In *Sustainable Hospitality and Tourism as Motors for Development* (pp. 24–36). Routledge.

Ritchie, J. B., & Crouch, G. I. (2003). *The competitive destination: A sustainable tourism perspective*. Cabi. DOI: 10.1079/9780851996646.0000

Ritchie, J. R., & Crouch, G. I. (2010). A model of destination competitiveness/sustainability: Brazilian perspectives. *Revista de Administração Pública*, 44(5), 1049–1066. DOI: 10.1590/S0034-76122010000500003

Ruggles, D. F., & Silverman, H. (2009). *Intangible heritage embodied*. Springer.

Ryan, J. (2015). Intangible cultural heritage: the new frontier of destination branding. In *Ideas in Marketing: Finding the New and Polishing the Old: Proceedings of the 2013 Academy of Marketing Science (AMS)Annual Conference* (pp. 388-390). Springer International Publishing. DOI: 10.1007/978-3-319-10951-0_147

Ryan, J., & Silvanto, S. (2009). The World Heritage List: The making and management of a brand. *Place Branding and Public Diplomacy*, 5(4), 290–300. DOI: 10.1057/pb.2009.21

Ryan, J., & Silvanto, S. (2010). World heritage sites: The purposes and politics of destination branding. *Journal of Travel & Tourism Marketing*, 27(5), 533–545. DOI: 10.1080/10548408.2010.499064

Salerno, G. M., & Russo, A. P. (2022). Venice as a short-term city. Between global trends and local lock-ins. In *Platform-Mediated Tourism* (pp. 90–109). Routledge. DOI: 10.4324/9781003230618-6

Santen, M. V. (2023). *Digital storytelling as a framework for a new narrative in museums* (Master's thesis).

Selcuk, O., Karakas, H., Cizel, B., & Ipekci Cetin, E. (2023). How does tourism affect protected areas?: A multi-criteria decision making application in UNESCO natural heritage sites. *Natural Hazards*, 117(2), 1923–1944. DOI: 10.1007/s11069-023-05934-x

Sharpley, R. (2009). *Tourism development and the environment: Beyond sustainability?* Routledge. DOI: 10.4324/9781849770255

Smith, L. (2020). Uses of heritage. In *Encyclopedia of global archaeology* (pp. 10969–10974). Springer International Publishing. DOI: 10.1007/978-3-030-30018-0_1937

Sotomayor, S., & Guillén, K. (2022). Tourism management competencies for visitor experience design among natural protected areas in Peru. *Journal of Ecotourism*, •••, 1–16. DOI: 10.1080/14724049.2022.2041647

Suklabaidya, P., & Aggarwal, M. (2020). Visitor Management at UNWHS: A Case study of Taj Mahal. *Atna Journal of Tourism Studies*, 15(2), 81–114. DOI: 10.12727/ajts.24.5

Thompson, J. (2022). *Edizioni WhiteStar.*

Throsby, D. (2012). Heritage economics: a conceptual framework. *The economics of uniqueness: Investing in historic city cores and cultural heritage assets for sustainable development*, 45-74.

Timothy, D. J., & Boyd, S. W. (2003). Heritage tourism.

Ud Din, N., Nazneen, S., & Jamil, B. (2024). Tourism crowding and resident approach/avoidance reactions through sustainable tourism: Moderating role of proenvironmental behavior. *Tourism Review*. Advance online publication. DOI: 10.1108/TR-10-2023-0678

UNESCO. (2012). Text of the Convention for the Safeguarding of Intangible Cultural Heritage. Retrieved from: https://www.unesco.org/culture/ich/index.php?lg=en&pg=00022 accessed on 25 June, 2024.

Wallace, R. (2019). Ecotourism in Asia: How strong branding creates opportunity for local economies and the environment. In *Positioning and branding tourism destinations for global competitiveness* (pp. 192-211). IGI Global.

Waller, M. A., & Fawcett, S. E. (2013). Data science, predictive analytics, and big data: A revolution that will transform supply chain design and management. *Journal of Business Logistics*, 34(2), 77–84. DOI: 10.1111/jbl.12010

Wang, Y., Cao, J., & Cai, X. (2024). The impact of environmental, social and governance performance on brand value: The role of the digitalisation level. *South African Journal of Business Management*, 55(1), 4448. DOI: 10.4102/sajbm.v55i1.4448

Weaver, D. B. (Ed.). (2001). *The encyclopedia of ecotourism*. Cabi Publishing. DOI: 10.1079/9780851993683.0000

Wheeler, F., Frost, W., & Weiler, B. (2011). Destination brand identity, values, and community: A case study from rural Victoria, Australia. *Journal of Travel & Tourism Marketing*, 28(1), 13–26. DOI: 10.1080/10548408.2011.535441

Wu, I. S. (2023). The Smithsonian's soft power: how foreigners engage the US national museum. In *Alternative Paths to Influence* (pp. 33–54). Routledge. DOI: 10.4324/9781003381037-3

Wu, J. (2013). Landscape sustainability science: Ecosystem services and human well-being in changing landscapes. *Landscape Ecology*, 28(6), 999–1023. DOI: 10.1007/s10980-013-9894-9

Ypeij, A. (2012). The intersection of gender and ethnic identities in the Cuzco–Machu Picchu tourism industry: Sácamefotos, tour guides, and women weavers. *Latin American Perspectives*, 39(6), 17–35. DOI: 10.1177/0094582X12454591

Zhang, Y., Li, X., Cárdenas, D. A., & Liu, Y. (2022). Calculating theme parks' tourism demand and attractiveness energy: A reverse gravity model and particle swarm optimization. *Journal of Travel Research*, 61(2), 314–330. DOI: 10.1177/0047287520977705

Chapter 10
Developing Destination Brand Identity Through Stakeholder Collaboration

Serkan Gün
https://orcid.org/0000-0002-2501-1078
Siirt Universty, Turkey

ABSTRACT

The brand helps make a significant difference in distinguishing goods and services and acts as an edge over the closest rivals (Aaker, 1991). Govers et al. (2007) claim that the consumption experience of travel "determines aspects of consumer behavior related to multiple emotional, sensory, and fantasy aspects of consumer behavior" (Hirschman and Holbrook, 1982). Morgan et al. (2004) state that location branding is a potent tool for marketing that can aid travellers in developing positive affective attachments and impressions. As they explain, the summation of perceived experiences that a tourist will encounter at a destination is the so-called "most important repertoire of beliefs that support the branding of a destination." (Barnes et al., 2014).

INTRODUCTION

The brand helps make a significant difference in distinguishing goods and services and acts as an edge over the closest rivals (Aaker, 1991). Govers et. al. (2007) found that the tourist consumption experience relates to diversified consumer behavioral aspects, it leads to the emotional, sensory and fantasy perspectives of the behavioral

DOI: 10.4018/979-8-3693-6700-1.ch010

aspects of tourist (Hirschman and Holbrook, 1982). Moreover, destination branding is key to achieveing the tourist positive attachment and memories of the destination (Morgan et. al. 2004). As they explain, the summation of perceived experiences that a tourist will encounter at a destination is the so-called set of the belives that leads to the destination branding (Barnes et. al. 2014).

As an industry the tourism perspective has maintained an upward and rapid growth rate over the last two decades, this makes it fast growing sector around the globe (UNWTO, 2016). Especially, recent researchers have started to explore the potential of branding concerning tourist destinations (Lin, 2015). Stepchenkova and Li (2014) assert that branding is a tool required for distinguishing and differentiating places with similar characteristics once the competition between destinations grows fierce (Luo et. al. 2020).

It can be result of destination branding that gained tourist attention due to its ability to influence the expectations that tourist develops about the particular location (Anholt, 2010; Martins, 2015). Destination branding is the strongest mode to ensure the recallability and reinforce the motivation along with positive memories connected with the prior experience (Ritchie and Ritchie, 1998). In strategic perspective, recent research shows that destination brand identity plays a povital role in comparions to the destination image (Piva and Prats, 2020). This means the destination branding should be based on positioning and communication strategies that depicts the orginial or real destination in order to deliver what is promised to the tourist ((Hankinson 2004).

Destination brand identity works as a mixture of nationality, history, cultural and economic relationship that develops the collaborative bond between the tourist and destinationc(Konecnik and Go, 2008). This leads to the invlovment of diverse set of stakeholders at both demand and supply stages (Tsaur et al., 2016). Social identity theory is best known for its ability to provide theoretical baseline to the destination branding (Tajfel, 1981), this is how stakeholders get associated with the destination in terms of emotions and cultural values (Rather, 2018). This perspective is vital to define the destination brand identity in term of the stakeholders. The process provides opportunity to the multiple stakeholders to get associated with the brand and develop their own meanings of brand identity (Suna and Alvarez, 2021).

It can be posited that in the absence of stakeholder involvement, the brand identity will remain static. Nevertheless, when some stakeholders attempt to adopt the brand, they can contribute to its construction. In such a situation, the role of the brand manager shifts from that of a brand guardian to that of a mediator between the various meanings contributed by stakeholders. This approach allows for the joint construction of the brand, although it is not a universal solution. It is not the case that every brand can attract stakeholders who can make the brand their own and create brand meaning together (Michel, 2017).

The tourism ecosystem encompasses a multitude of stakeholders who, collectively, facilitate the creation of a valuable experience for tourists (Hankinson, 2004). Although tourist organizations typically prioritize studies on the fundamental characteristics of a destination, they frequently neglect to consider the perspectives of destination stakeholders (Hankinson, 2004). The perceived value of destination is greatly infleunced by the stakeholders as they are having impact on tourist behavior (Day and Kour, 2021).

The further phase of the study will focus on the stakeholder role in developing brand identity and also dicusses the their contribution in enhances the brand identity.

Brand Identity

Brands have the role of differentiating and characterizing products and services produced for the market in line with the ideals of the enterprise (Kapferer, 1992). That is, businesses deploy their brand identities by defining and positioning their differences in ways that are consistent with their principles, therefore, appealing to their customers (Margulies, 1977). Brand identity is the desired internal image of a company and a promise to its clients, communicated through unique brand connections (Ghodeswar, 2008). In turn, a company's brand strategy is how a company decides to differentiate itself through its identity, and brand value to other stakeholders and customers on the outside like competitors, managers and employees that play their role in business success (Alvarado-Karste and Guzmán, 2020).

Under such a highly competitive climate, specific brand management measures should be taken. To develop brand identity it is of pivotal importance to understand the charateristics of the targeted brand. It was conceptualized in Europe in 1986 for the very first time by Kapferer. Due to the increasing recognition of the value of brand identity, the world has witnessed an increase in the wider recognition of the brand identity. Therefore, in this manner term is different from all other branding terms that provide the destination with a unique and identitcal personality (Janonis et al. 2007).

The term brand identity is often related to the pratices engaged by the businesses to gain competitive advantage and provide identity, facilitating branding that includes recognition to increase linkage and customer loyalty and level of brands. It causes a relationship to develop between the companies and the clients that have been possible by creating brand identity. Brand identity needs to be completed and promoted well by the brands as this can enable them to build fruitful relationships with their target customers. Such as, the attributes of the brand identity, like information about the brand image, reputation, and positioning provides surity of making best use of marketing strategies along with appropriate decision making in all other perspectives (Mao et. al. 2020).

According to the approaches practiced by brand specialists, brand identity can be defined (Ianenko et. al. 2020):

- The brand's external expression is the strategic concept, which is a set of complements.
- The question statement play crucial role in framing branding strategies that help to differentiate brand from alternatives offered in market.
- The brand's distinctive characteristics are reflected in the design, which serves to motivate potential purchasers.
- It enhances the overall brand image.

The basic purpose of brand identity is to highlight the unique charateristics of the brand. These differentiating perspectives lays foundation for strategic choices encompasing brand. There are two basic principal stages in developing brand identity. First, brand identity formation is concerned with the identification of significant differentiators between the brand and its competitors. This includes comparisons that allow consumers to distinguish the brand from others, as well as to position the brand and shape its concept. Second, the development of brand identity with the help of objectives defined by the brand developers (Ianenko et. al. 2020).

The term represents the distinctive features associated with the brand that represents the core identity in terms of the promises made to the consumer. The core idenity is the fundamental essense of the brand, which must remain unchanged even if brand expends into new markets or offer new products. The core identity is based on service, product characteristics, showroom enviornment, traveler profile and overall performance of the product. İn comparison to core identity, the extended identity represents the brand integrity and texture. This perspective is focused on the brand personality, logo's and symbols, and associations. To ensure the bonding between brand and consumer, brand identity should represent the business capacity tested over the time and unique selling proposition (Aaker and Joachimsthaler, 2000). Brand identity is the promise that is based on service, product, or organization superiority in technology to deliver what is promised (Ward et al., 1999). The organizations that have competitive advantage, consumer compatibility and purpose based brand identity will have distintive position in market with better price tags and value of merchandising (Ghodeswar, 2008).

Destination Branding

As world tourism continues to rise, the competition to develop stronger destination brands is intensifying (Quoquab et al., 2021). To be successful in competition, the concept of branding plays vital role in developing market. Consequently, it is considered imperative for all tourism destinations to establish brands (Ruiz-Real et al., 2020). The tourism destinations can differentiate themselves by creating stable and unique brands and developing strong behavioral and emotional bonds with tourists (Shi et. al. 2022).

Branding is of critical importance for the development of destinations and their differentiation it from competiting brands with similar offerings (Pike, 2005). Yesterday and even today, branding is the only way to position distinctively the offerings of one brand brand from others (Aaker 1991; Keller, 2003). The fundamental objective of destination branding is to create indelible service experiences for tourists, mitigate risks, and improve revisit perspective (Blain et. al. 2005). The tourist expectations of the destination plays critical role in improving the destination face value and creating memorable destination experience (Kashıf et. al. 2015).

This process that establishes the tourist destination is a long term process, contingent upon brand management practices and a multitude of factors (Apostolopoulou and Papadimitriou 2015). Given the complexity and qualitative richness of tourism destinations, the branding principles applied to goods and services must be adapted for destination branding (Pike et al., 2010). Destination branding, in conjunction with identification, enables a place to distinguish itself from its competitors due to its customer loyalty and unique value proposition, thereby creating brand value (Veríssimo, 2017).

To build a brand based on location that is often termed as destination brand. It is essential to consider how tourists will comprehend, perceive, and assess the brand. The conceptualization of naïve brands goes through different intervals in tourist psychological processing. A tourist's evaluation of a particular brand occurs indirectly or directly, and this affects the tourist's future purchasing decisions or non-purchasing behavior. New brands in the market undergo four fundamental stages. The first stage is to create awareness among the potential visiters and audiance (Radišić and Mihelić, 2006);

- Step one, create destination awareness in context of facilities and services offered at the destination.
- Step two, develop a brand with perspective to be recognized by second generation of visitors.
- Step three, the decision making stage, tourist makes choices to go for destination brand or its alternative.
- Step four, enhancing the concept of destination brand loyalty among the visitors.

The existing body of knowledge shows that there are four success factors in a destination brand (Baker and Cameron 2008). first, holistic orientation toward tourism planning. Second, the formation of destination image and identity. Third, encouraging stakeholder engagement and pariticipation. Fourth, measuring the brand growth (Kashıf et. al. 2015).

Baker (2007) conducted a comprehensive literature review and found important link between the brand and its competing offers. This is vital for those responsible for promoting a destination to comprehend and cultivate a distinctive and appealing destination brand identity in a highly competitive environment. He posits that the creation of an image, the development of an identity, and the communication of a vision to target tourists is vital to nuture a destination brand (Mishra, 2010).

Destination Brand Identity

Destination branding is regarded as a strategy for establishing and disseminating a distinctive identity that is meaningful to investors and tourists, thereby creating distinction between the competing brands (Qu et. al. 2011). Destination branding is often defined as a set of marketing efforts to nuture the growth brand elements such as the symbols, logo and signs, cartoons, slogans or other elements that provide a distintive representation to a certain brand (Blain, Levy, and Ritchie, 2005). Destination branding has emerged as a highly effective and widely utilized marketing instrument (Veríssimo et. al. 2017).

Buhalis (2000) defined the destination brand as blend of tourism based porducts offered to facilitate the tourist experiences. This lead to introduction of numerous offerings in terms of products and services to facilitate the tourist at destination. Given the duality of destinations, comprising both sections and the need to provide uninterrupted experiences to tourists, the participation and coordination of stakeholders in destinations are of great importance. This also affects the destination brand. Destinations that offer similar products and services must compete with one another. In this context, the brand represents a competitive advantage to the branding of destination. The concept of branding helps destinations to develop a distinctive image in comparison to the competing brands (Beerli and Martin 2004; García et. al. 2012), and this impacts the tourist decision making process (Bregoli, 2012).

Brand identity establishes the grounds how tourist perceives the destination brand. The branding is the blend of values orginating from different factors (Lemmetyinen and Go, 2010). Consequently, the brand identity is helpful in attaining and engaging the tourist with consistent set of values (Chernatony and Dall'Olmo Riley, 1999). To create a unwavering brand identity the destinations markting concept should be ultilized appropriately (Piva and Prats, 2020).

The concept of distinctiveness, competitive advantage and reliability leads to the development of brand identity (Gnoth, 2002; Ruzzier and Go, 2008). Moreover, a continous dialogue between the stakeholders and tourist creates space for further growth (Kavaratzis and Hatch, 2013; Saraniemi and Komppula, 2019). The collabrative interaction between the internal and external stakehoders further strengthens the concept of destination identity (Saraniemi and Komppula, 2019). In the end, we can conclude that destination identity is the outcome of collaborative engagement of different stakeholders. İts the identity that provides distintive postiion to the competiting brands (Kah et al., 2020; Yen et al., 2020). Moreoover, tourist experiences and memories plays a vital role in developing a healthy relationship between the tourist and industry (Hanna et al., 2021). Ruiz-Real et al. (2020) found that a set of well integrated offerings at the destination leads to the fullfilment of the pormises made to the tourist.

A brand identity that well coordinated and organized activities which leads to continuous and sustainable developmet of the destination. it's the brand identity that helps to heal the impact of negative experiences and their ability to hurt the brand identity (Augé, 2000). The public and private sector responsible for systematic implimentation of marketing strategies should ensure the focus on positioning and designing of destination brand identity. Later, its the brand-building efforts and these efforts should be continous which should add further value to the brand (Aaker and Joachimsthaler, 2000). Moreover, it is of pivotal importance to recognize the role of public figures who play positive role in development of brand identity. Further, brand identity is developed by the contirbution of multiple corners such as businesses, law enforcement agencies, public office holders, and the tourists. Similarly, the funding for brand developed is done by many stakeholders and it is crucial to create consensus among stakeholders to ensure the continous implementation of polices (Konecnik and Go, 2008).

Destination Stakeholder Collaboration

In addition to the two primary functions of a tourism destination, it also fulfills several crucial supporting roles. The core aim of the destination branding is to nurture the socioeconomic development of the local population. Moreover, infrastructural and businesses development should be well integrated that leads to the better living facilities and environmental conditions for both local residents and visiting tourists (Bornhorst et al., 2010). The stakeholder concept means that the destination is regarded as a part of the network of relationships with other stakeholders to ensure the continuous development of the destination branding. This may include the individuals, groups or subgroups that can influence the overall destination identity (Sheehan and Ritchie, 2005; Waligo et al., 2013; Gyrd-Jones and Kornum, 2013).

The concept of branding provides distinctive identity to the destinations. The active stakeholders are the primary contirbutors to enhance the destination identity (Joachimsthaler, 2002; Jones, 2005). This may destination branding a vital concept to be considered. Clarkson (1995) divides the destination stakeholders in two categories, the first one is the primary stakeholders, these are the people or organizations with active role and plays vital role in develop of destination. They are not directly part of the development of a destination or business, important entities that have an impact and are affected by it constitute the group of secondary stakeholders (Merrilees et. al. 2005). A destination can be considered to have a multitude of stakeholders. In general, stakeholders of destinations include hotels, tour operators, entrepreneurs, landowners, suppliers, banks, stateholders, insurance companies, local population, service providing companies and employee unions, the environmental stakeholders and many other relvent groups (Flagestad and Hope, 2001; Konecnik and Gartner, 2007). Whereas, the public and private sectors involved in the policy implementation plays vital role in development of destination brand as they are directly responsible for the outcome of these activities (Wagner and Peters, 2009).

Stakeholder Collaboration and Destination Brand Identity

The experiences of tourists at a destination are shaped by a multitude of actors (UNWTO 2007). The aforementioned actors are of considerable size and considerable diversity. So, it's the responsibility of the destination based business organizations to ensure the stakeholders relationships and continued efforts to enrich the tourist experience (Pike 2008; UNWTO 2007). There are multiple definations of stakeholders and are often described as the individuals, groups or organizations with ability to influence the business success. Pike (2008) defined the term as stakeholders are the people with influence over the business processes ensruing business success. Further, Morrison (2019) provided another definition that these are the individuals with direct or indirect interest in the success of the business.

The term destination branding is a collective pharse that has multiple outcomes for the tourism industry. İn this perspective, the development of destination brand is a collaborative and collective sum of the efforts made by the stakeholders (Morgan et. al. 2002). The concept of destination branding is reffered as the collective godo for all the stakeholders working together to improve the business perspective of the destination (Hardin, 1968). Whereas, stronger and greater destination brand is the positive outcome of collective collabaration among different players (Prideaux and Cooper, 2002). This concept is often known as the synergy effect due the collective and collaborative activities done in integrated manner by the stakeholders ensuring the stronger destinaiton brands (Laws et. al. 2002).

The collective and collaborative activities are one of the most prominent ways to establish the destination brands. This shared vision and mission leads to greater destination brand loyalty and endosrement from different social and economic corners that leads to the successful conceptualization of the destination branding (Bregoli, 2012).

What the concept of tourism as a multi-player industry underlines is collaboration among stakeholders regarding destination branding in the hsopitality and tourism industry. A tourism destination is a complex place where different players have quite dissimilar goals and objectives (Buhalis, 2000; Cooper et. al. 2005; Fyall and Garrod, 2005). Consequently, the chances of conflict gets higher from the divergent interests of various stakeholders represents a significant challenge that must be addressed within the collaborative process of destination branding (Marzano, 2006).

The process of ensuring and managing stakeholder participation encompasses the procedures by which stakeholders are identified, their interests are determined, and their interactions are managed. Stakeholder participation is of great significance in the destination branding process. While destination brand attributes are created and influenced not only by brand managers and their organizations, they are also the joint product of stakeholders and their partnerships (Parkerson and Saunders, 2005). In instances where the relationship between stakeholders is lacking in coordination, the reactions between the consumer and the brand are reflected in the relationships (Hankinson, 2004). Hankinson (2009) posits that collaboration with stakeholders provides a framework for understanding the destination's offerings to tourists, including their abilities, attitudes, and mindsets. This, in turn, facilitates the establishment of effective stakeholder partnerships and a cohesive structure. Consequently, brand performance is contingent upon the quality of stakeholder relationships (Hanna, 2011).

In its traditional sense, stakeholder engagement is defined as a set of organizational processes that facilitate stakeholders' involvement in activities that affect their lives and contributions (Greenwood and Kamoche, 2013). This definition emphasizes the perspective of the organization that manages the destination brand, which is responsible for managing stakeholders' interaction with the destination brand identity. For a destination brand identity to be effective, it must receive strong support from national stakeholders. Indeed, the most effective destination branding initiatives are those that bring together a variety of local stakeholders in support of the brand (Kavaratzis, 2012). They are therefore categorized about a region's brand identity due to the extent to which stakeholders participate, or not, in the region's brand identity initiatives. Merrilees et al. (2012) Primary Stakeholders: These are the stakeholders who are directly involved in a place brand operations. Secondary

Stakeholders: These are the individuals who are not directly engaged in the process of a place's brand identification, possibly but influenced or can influence (Casidy et. al. 2019).

The place branding has to have several stakeholders in the case that it is to be successful. Stakeholders' involvement is a critical component of any good branding strategy (Campelo et al., 2013; Konecnik and Go, 2008). In the destination brand identity, among others, the destination host community and enterprises' views are represented (Ma et al., 2022). A strong brand image establishment might be aided by the brand identity, which also determines the perception of the brand by the target market. Linked with this, the stakeholders' role in destination branding and message dissemination is a vital one that should be recognized (Nawaz et al., 2019). For this very reason, the participation of internal stakeholders in the process of branding is the key to the long-term survivability of a destination brand (Asim Nawaz et al., 2019). Other than this, a destination brand can only be developed by eyeing the interests of stakeholders and portraying the identity of that destination brand. It is the job of the local tourist community to communicate the promises of a brand and to determine the emotional and cognitive connections of the brand with a destination. Destination branding envelopes stakeholder involvement both in the process of creating this brand identity and in projecting this brand image to the visiting end (Yusof and Ismail, 2014).

Although collaboration has been theorized as a substantial aspect of destination branding, in practice, it can be quite hard to operate. The difficulties related to cooperation refer to insufficient communication, different political interests, imbalance in contributions of the stakeholders, and finally, structural failures of cooperative action (Mengkebayaer et al., 2022). Co-operation can be difficult when there is no concrete framework involved or no similar goals. This can result in no communication and understanding between stakeholders which may lead other partners to believe the partnership is ineffective. It is important to consider that when competitors cooperate, they may face risks. One such risk is that they may decrease the attractiveness of the destination if they enter into any cartel agreement to raise prices and limit competition (Ma et al., 2022).

REFERENCES

Aaker, D. (1991). *Managing brand equity*. Free Press Business.

Aaker, D. A., & Joachimsthaler, E. (2000). *Brand Leadership*. The Free Press.

Alvarado-Karste, D., & Guzmán, F. (2020). The effect of brand identity-cognitive style fit and social influence on consumer-based brand equity. *Journal of Product and Brand Management*, 29(7), 1–14. DOI: 10.1108/JPBM-06-2019-2419

Anholt, S. (2010). *Places: Identity, Image and Reputation*. Palgrave Macmillan.

Apostolopoulou, A., & Papadimitriou, D. (2015). The role of destination personality in predicting tourist behavior: Implications for branding mid-sized urban destinations. *Current Issues in Tourism*, 18(12), 1132–1151. DOI: 10.1080/13683500.2013.878319

Asim Nawaz, M., Asmi, F., & Nawaz, A. (2019). Willingness to consume Genetically Modified Food in Chinese perspective Public Understanding of Socio-Scientific Issue (SSIs) View project role of phobia's and allied influence on consumer novel food intentions. View project. Article in Pakistan Journal of Agricultural Sciences. DOI: 10.21162/PAKJAS/19.8837

Augé, M. (2000). *Non-Places: Introduction to an Anthropology of Supermodernity*. Verso.

Baker, B. (2007). *Destination Branding for Small Cities: The Essentials for Successful Place Branding*. Creative Leap Books.

Baker, M., & Cameron, E. (2008). Critical success factors in destination marketing. *Tourism and Hospitality Research*, 8(2), 79–95. DOI: 10.1057/thr.2008.9

Barnes, S. J., Mattsson, J., & Sørensen, F. (2014). Destination brand experience and visitor behavior: Testing a scale in the tourism context. *Annals of Tourism Research*, 48, 121–139. DOI: 10.1016/j.annals.2014.06.002

Beerli, A., & Martin, J. D. (2004). Tourists' Characteristics and the Perceived Image of Tourist Destinations: A Quantitative Analysis—A Case Study of Lanzarote, Spain. *Tourism Management*, 25(5), 623–636. DOI: 10.1016/j.tourman.2003.06.004

Blain, C., Levy, S., & Ritchie, J. R. (2005). Destination branding: Insights and practices from destination management organizations. *Journal of Travel Research*, 43(4), 328–338. DOI: 10.1177/0047287505274646

Bornhorst, T., Ritchie, J. R., & Sheehan, L. (2010). Determinants of tourism success for DMOs & destinations: An empirical examination of stakeholders' perspectives. *Tourism Management*, 31(5), 572–589. DOI: 10.1016/j.tourman.2009.06.008

Bregoli, I. (2012). Effects of DMO Coordination on Destination Brand Identity: A MixedMethod Study on the City of Edinburgh. *Journal of Travel Research*, 52(2), 212–224. DOI: 10.1177/0047287512461566

Buhalis, D. (2000). Marketing the competitive destination of the future. *Tourism Management*, 21(1), 97–116. DOI: 10.1016/S0261-5177(99)00095-3

Buhalis, D. (2000). Marketing the Competitive Destination of the Future. *Tourism Management*, 21(1), 97–116. DOI: 10.1016/S0261-5177(99)00095-3

Campelo, A., Aitken, R., Thyne, M., & Gnoth, J. (2013). Sense of Place: The Importance for Destination Branding. *Journal of Travel Research*, 53(2), 154–166. DOI: 10.1177/0047287513496474

Cassidy, R., Helmi, J., & Bridson, K. (2019). Drivers and inhibitors of national stakeholder engagement with place brand identity. *European Journal of Marketing*, 53(7), 1445–1465. DOI: 10.1108/EJM-04-2017-0275

Chernatony, L., & Dall'Olmo, R. F. (1999). Experts' Views about Defining Service Brands and the Principles of Service Branding. *Journal of Business Research*, 46(2), 181–192. DOI: 10.1016/S0148-2963(98)00021-6

Clarkson, M. B. (1995). A stakeholder framework for analyzing and evaluating. *Academy of Management Review*, 20(1), 92–117. DOI: 10.2307/258888

Cooper, C. P., Fletcher, J., Fyall, A., Gilbert, D., & Wanhill, S. (2005). Tourism: Principles and practice (3. b.). Harlow, England: Financial Times Prentice Hall.

Crockett, S., & Wood, L. (1999). Brand Western Australia: A Totally Integrated Approach to Destination Branding. *Journal of Vacation Marketing*, 5(3), 276–289. DOI: 10.1177/135676679900500307

Day, J., & Kaur, G. (2021). Destination Brand Equity and value creation for Internal stakeholders. Travel and Tourism Research Association: Advancing Tourism Research Globally.

Elisa, S., & Rimat, G. (2022). *Role of stakeholders in the branding process of a destination*. LAB University of Applied Sciences.

Escobar-Farfán, M., Cervera-Taulet, A., & Schlesinger, W. (2024). Destination brand identity: Challenges, opportunities, and future research agenda. *Cogent Social Sciences*, 10(1), 1–18. DOI: 10.1080/23311886.2024.2302803

Flagestad, A., & Hope, C. A. (2001). Strategic success in winter sports destinations – a sustainable value creation perspective. *Tourism Management*, 22(5), 445–561. DOI: 10.1016/S0261-5177(01)00010-3

Fyall, A., & Garrod, B. (2005). *Tourism marketing: A collaborative approach.* Channel View Publications.

García, J. A., Gómez, M., & Molina, A. (2012). A Destination-Branding Model: An Empirical Analysis Based on Stakeholders. *Tourism Management*, 33(3), 646–661. DOI: 10.1016/j.tourman.2011.07.006

Gehani, R. (2001). Enhancing brand equity and reputational capital with enterprise-wide complementary innovations. *Marketing Management Journal*, 11(1), 35–48.

Ghodeswar, B. M. (2008). Building brand identity in competitive markets: A conceptual model. *Journal of Product and Brand Management*, 17(1), 4–12. DOI: 10.1108/10610420810856468

Gnoth, J. (2002). Leveraging export brands through a tourism destination brand. *Journal of Brand Management*, 9(4), 262–280. DOI: 10.1057/palgrave.bm.2540077

Gonzalez-Mansilla, O., Berenguer-Contri, G., & Serra-Cantallops, A. (2019). The impact of value co-creation on hotel brand equity and customer satisfaction. *Tourism Management*, 75, 51–65. DOI: 10.1016/j.tourman.2019.04.024

Govers, R., Go, F. M., & Kumar, K. (2007). Virtual destination image - A new measurement approach. *Annals of Tourism Research*, 34(4), 977–997. DOI: 10.1016/j.annals.2007.06.001

Greenwood, M., & Kamoche, K. (2013). Social accounting as stakeholder knowledge appropriation. *The Journal of Management and Governance*, 17(3), 723–743. DOI: 10.1007/s10997-011-9208-z

Gyrd-Jones, R., & Kornum, N. (2013). Managing the co-created brand: Value and cultural complementarity in online and offline multistakeholder ecosystems. *Journal of Business Research*, 66(9), 1484–1493. DOI: 10.1016/j.jbusres.2012.02.045

Hankinson, G. (2001). Location Branding: A Study of the Branding Practices of 12 English Cities. *Journal of Brand Management*, 9(2), 127–142. DOI: 10.1057/palgrave.bm.2540060

Hankinson, G. (2004). Relational Network Brands: Towards a Conceptual Model of Place Brands. *Journal of Vacation Marketing*, 10(2), 109–121. DOI: 10.1177/135676670401000202

Hankinson, G. (2009). Managing destination brands: Establishing a theoretical foundation. *Journal of Marketing Management*, 25(1/2), 97–115. DOI: 10.1362/026725709X410052

Hanna, S., & Rowley, J. (2011). Towards a strategic place brand-management model. *Journal of Marketing Management*, 27(5-6), 458–476. DOI: 10.1080/02672571003683797

Hanna, S., Rowley, J., & Keegan, B. (2021). Place and destination branding: A review and conceptual mapping of the domain. *European Management Review*, 18(2), 105–117. DOI: 10.1111/emre.12433

Hardin, G. (1968). The tragedy of the commons. *Science*, 162(3859), 1243–1248. DOI: 10.1126/science.162.3859.1243 PMID: 5699198

Harris, F., & Chernatony, L. (2001). Corporate branding and corporate brand performance. *European Journal of Marketing*, 35(3/4), 441–456. DOI: 10.1108/03090560110382101

Hirschman, E. C., & Holbrook, M. B. (1982). Hedonic Consumption: Emerging Concepts, Methods, and Propositions. *Journal of Marketing*, 46(3), 92–101. DOI: 10.1177/002224298204600314

Ianenko, M., Stepanov, M., & Mironova, L. (2020). Brand identity development. E3S Web of Conferences(164), 1-7.

Im, H. H., Kim, S. S., Elliot, S., & Han, H. (2012). Conceptualizing destination brand equity dimensions from a consumer-based brand equity perspective. *Journal of Travel & Tourism Marketing*, 29(4), 385–403. DOI: 10.1080/10548408.2012.674884

Janonis, V., Dovalienė, A., & Virvilaitė, R. (2007). Relationship of Brand Identity and Image. *The Engineering Economist*, 1(51), 69–80.

Jochimsthaler, E. (2002). Commitment – Mitarbeiter – Die vergessene Zielgruppe für Markenerfolge. *Absatzwirtschaft*, 45(11), 28–34.

Jones, R. (2005). Finding sources of brand value - developing a stakeholder model of brand equity. *Journal of Brand Management*, 13(1), 10–32. DOI: 10.1057/palgrave.bm.2540243

Kah, J. A., Shin, H. J., & Lee, S. H. (2020). Traveler sensory-scape experiences and the formation of destination identity. *Tourism Geographies*, 24(2/3), 475–494.

Kapferer, N. J. (1992). *Strategic Brand Management*. Kogan Page.

Kashıf, M., Samsı, S. Z., & Sarıfuddın, S. (2015). Brand Equıty Of Lahore Fort As A Tourısm Destınatıon Brand. Revista de Administração de Empresas, 55(4).

Kavaratzis, M. (2012). From 'necessary evil' to necessity: Stakeholders' involvement in place branding. *Journal of Place Management and Development*, 5(1), 7–19. DOI: 10.1108/17538331211209013

Kavaratzis, M., & Hatch, M. J. (2013). The dynamics of place brands: An identity-based approach to place branding theory. *Marketing Theory*, 13(1), 69–86. DOI: 10.1177/1470593112467268

Keller, K. L. (2003). *Strategic brand management Upper Saddle River*. Prentice Hall.

Konecnik, M., & Gartner, W. C. (2007). Customer-based brand equity for a destination. *Annals of Tourism Research*, 34(2), 400–421. DOI: 10.1016/j.annals.2006.10.005

Konecnik, M., & Go, F. (2008). Tourism Destination Brand Identity: The Case of Slovenia. *Journal of Brand Management*, 15(3), 177–189. DOI: 10.1057/palgrave.bm.2550114

Laws, E., Scott, N., & Parfitt, N. (2002). Synergies in destination image management: A case study and conceptualization. *International Journal of Tourism Research*, 4(1), 39–55. DOI: 10.1002/jtr.353

Lemmetyinen, A., & Go, F. M. (2010). Building a Brand Identity in a Network of Cruise Baltic's Destinations: A Multi-Authoring Approach. *Journal of Brand Management*, 17(7), 519–531. DOI: 10.1057/bm.2010.5

Lin, Y. H. (2015). Innovative brand experience's influence on brand equity and brand satisfaction. *Journal of Business Research*, 68(11), 2254–2259. DOI: 10.1016/j.jbusres.2015.06.007

Luo, J., Dey, B. L., Yalkin, C., Sivarajah, U., Punjaisri, K., Huang, Y., & Yen, D. A. (2020). Millennial Chinese consumers' perceived destination brand value. *Journal of Business Research*, 116, 655–665. DOI: 10.1016/j.jbusres.2018.06.015

Ma, W., Tariq, A., Ali, M. W., Nawaz, M. A., & Wang, X. (2022). An Empirical Investigation of Virtual Networking Sites Discontinuance Intention: Stimuli Organism Response-Based Implication of User Negative Disconfirmation. *Frontiers in Psychology*, 13, 862568. DOI: 10.3389/fpsyg.2022.862568 PMID: 35602706

Mao, Y., Lai, Y., Luo, Y., Liu, S., Du, Y., Zhou, J., Ma, J., Bonaiuto, F., & Bonaiuto, M. (2020). Apple or Huawei: Understanding Flow, Brand Image, Brand Identity, Brand Personality and Purchase Intention of Smartphone. *Sustainability (Basel)*, 12(3391), 1–22. DOI: 10.3390/su12083391

Margulies, W. P. (1977). Make the most of your corporate identity. *Harvard Business Review*, 55(4), 66–74.

Martins, M. (2015). The Tourist Imagery, the Destination Image, and the Brand Image. *Journal of Tourism and Hospitality Management*, 3(2), 1–14. DOI: 10.15640/jthm.v3n2a1

Marzano, G. (2006). Relevance Of Power. In *The Collaborative Process Of Destination Branding*. The University of Queensland.

Marzano, G., & Scott, N. (2011). Stakeholder Power. In *Destination Branding: A Methodological Discussion*. Sustainable Tourism Cooperative Research Centre.

Mengkebayaer, M., Nawaz, M. A., & Sajid, M. U. (2022). Eco-destination loyalty: Role of perceived value and experience in framing destination attachment and equity with moderating role of destination memory. *Frontiers in Psychology*, 13, 908798. DOI: 10.3389/fpsyg.2022.908798 PMID: 36081735

Merrilees, B., Getz, D., & O'Brien, D. (2005). Marketing stakeholder analysis – branding the Brisbane Goodwill Games. *European Journal of Marketing*, 39(9/10), 1060–1077. DOI: 10.1108/03090560510610725

Merrilees, B., Miller, D., & Herrington, C. (2012). Multiple stakeholders and multiple city brand meanings. *European Journal of Marketing*, 46(7/8), 1032–1047. DOI: 10.1108/03090561211230188

Michel, G. (2017). From brand identity to polysemous brands: Commentary on "Performing identities: Processes of brand and stakeholder identity co-construction". *Journal of Business Research*, 70, 453–455. DOI: 10.1016/j.jbusres.2016.06.022

Miočić, B. K., Razović, M., & Klarin, T. (2016). Management Of Sustainable Tourism Destination Through Stakeholder Cooperation. *Management*, 21(2), 99–120.

Mishra, A. S. (2010). Destination Branding: A Case Study of Hong Kong. The IUP Journal of Brand Management, 7(3).

Morgan, N., Pritchard, A., & Piggott, R. (2002). New Zealand, is 100% pure. The creation of a powerful niche destination brand. *Journal of Brand Management*, 9(4/5), 335–354. DOI: 10.1057/palgrave.bm.2540082

Morgan, N., Pritchard, A., & Pride, R. (2004). *Destination branding (2. b.)*. Elsevier.

Morrison, A. (2019). *Marketing and Managing Tourism Destinations*. Routledge.

Nawaz, M. A., Asif, M., Asmi, F., & Nawaz, A. (2019). Willingess to consume genetically modified food in Chinese perspective. *Pakistan Journal of Agricultural Sciences*, 56(4), 799–808. Advance online publication. DOI: 10.21162/PAKJAS/19.8837

Parkerson, B., & Saunders, J. (2005). City branding: Can goods and services branding models be used to brand cities? *Place Branding and Public Diplomacy*, 1(3), 242–264. DOI: 10.1057/palgrave.pb.5990026

Perkins, R., Khoo-Lattimore, C., & Arcodia, C. (2020). Understanding the contribution of stakeholder collaboration towards regional destination branding: A systematic narrative literature review. *Journal of Hospitality and Tourism Management*, 43, 250–258. DOI: 10.1016/j.jhtm.2020.04.008

Pike, S. (2005). Tourism destination branding complexity. *Journal of Product and Brand Management*, 14(4), 258–259. DOI: 10.1108/10610420510609267

Pike, S. (2008). *Destination Marketing – An integrated marketing communication approach*. Butterworth-Heinemann.

Pike, S., Bianchi, C., Kerr, G., & Patti, C. (2010). Consumer-based brand equity for Australia as a long-haul tourism destination in an emerging market. *International Marketing Review*, 27(4), 434–449. DOI: 10.1108/02651331011058590

Piva, E., & Prats, L. ı. (2020). *Regional Destination and Brand Identity: The Case of Piedmont*. Scienze Regionali.

Prideaux, B., & Cooper, C. (2002). Marketing and destination growth: A symbiotic relationship or simple coincidence? *Journal of Vacation Marketing*, 9(1), 35–48. DOI: 10.1177/135676670200900103

Qu, H., Kim, L. H., & Im, H. H. (2011). A model of destination branding: Integrating the concepts of the branding and destination image. *Tourism Management*, 32(3), 465–476. DOI: 10.1016/j.tourman.2010.03.014

Quoquab, F., Mohammad, J., & Mohd Sobri, A. M. (2021). Psychological engagement drives brand loyalty: Evidence from Malaysian ecotourism destinations. *Journal of Product and Brand Management*, 30(1), 132–147. DOI: 10.1108/JPBM-09-2019-2558

Radišić, B. B., & Mihelić, B. (2006). The Tourıst Destınatıon Brand. *Tourism and Hospitality Management*, 12(2), 183–189. DOI: 10.20867/thm.12.2.16

Rather, R. A. (2018). Investigating the impact of customer brand identification on hospitality brand loyalty: A social identity perspective. *Journal of Hospitality Marketing & Management*, 27(5), 487–513. DOI: 10.1080/19368623.2018.1404539

Ritchie, J. B., & Ritchie, R. J. (1998). The Branding of Tourism Destinations: Past Achievements and Future Challenges. *Proceedings of the 1998 Annual Congress of the International Association of Scientific Experts in Tourism* (s. 89-116). Marrakech, Morocco: International Association of Scientific Experts in Tourism

Ruiz-Real, J. L., Uribe-Toril, J., & Gazquez-Abad, J. C. (2020). Destination branding: Opportunities and new challenges. *Journal of Destination Marketing & Management*, •••, 17.

Ruzzier, M., & Go, F. (2008). Tourism destination brand identity: The case of Slovenia. *Journal of Brand Management*, 15(3), 177–189. DOI: 10.1057/palgrave.bm.2550114

Saraniemi, S., & Komppula, R. (2019). The development of a destination brand identity: A story of stakeholder collaboration. *Current Issues in Tourism*, 22(9), 1116–1132. DOI: 10.1080/13683500.2017.1369496

Schmitt, B., & Simonson, A. (1997). *Marketing Aesthetics: The Strategic Management of Brands, Identity, and Image*. The Free Press.

Sheehan, L. R., & Ritchie, J. R. (2005). Destination stakeholders: Exploring Identity and Salience. *Annals of Tourism Research*, 32(3), 711–734. DOI: 10.1016/j.annals.2004.10.013

Shi, H., Liu, Y., Kumail, T., & Pan, L. (2022). Tourism destination brand equity, brand authenticity and revisit intention: The mediating role of tourist satisfaction and the moderating role of destination familiarity. *Tourism Review*, 77(3), 751–779. DOI: 10.1108/TR-08-2021-0371

Stepchenkova, S., & Li, X. (2014). Destination image: Do top-of-mind associations say it all? *Annals of Tourism Research*, 45, 46–62. DOI: 10.1016/j.annals.2013.12.004

Suna, B., & Alvarez, M. D. (2021). The role of gastronomy in shaping the destination's brand identity: An empirical analysis based on stakeholders' opinions. *Journal of Hospitality Marketing & Management*, 30(6), 738–758. DOI: 10.1080/19368623.2021.1877587

Tajfel, H. (1981). *Human groups and social categories: Studies in social psychology*. Cambridge University Press.

Tsaur, S. H., Yen, C. H., & Yan, Y. T. (2016). Destination brand identity: Scale development and validation. *Asia Pacific Journal of Tourism Research*, 21(12), 1310–1323. DOI: 10.1080/10941665.2016.1156003

UNWTO. (2007). *A Practical Guide to Tourism Destination Management.* World Tourism Organization.

UNWTO. (2016). UNWTO tourism highlights Retrieved from World Tourism Organization.

Veríssimo, J. M., Tiago, M. T., Tiago, F. G., & Jardim, J. S. (2017). Tourism destination brand dimensions: An exploratory approach. *Tourism & Management Studies*, 13(4), 1–8. DOI: 10.18089/tms.2017.13401

Wagner, O., & Peters, M. (2009). The Development And Communıcatıon Of Destınatıon Brand Identıty – The Case Of The Alps. Tourism Destination Development and Branding Eilat 2009 Conference Proceedings. Ben-Gurion University of the Negev.

Waligo, V. M., Clarke, J., & Hawkins, R. (2013). Implementing sustainable tourism: A multi-stakeholder involvement management framework. *Tourism Management*, 36, 342–353. DOI: 10.1016/j.tourman.2012.10.008

Ward, S., Larry, L., & Goldstine, J. (1999). What high-tech managers need to know about brands. *Harvard Business Review*, •••, 85–95.

Yen, C. H., Teng, H. Y., & Chang, S. T. (2020). Destination brand identity and emerging market tourists' perceptions. *Asia Pacific Journal of Tourism Research*, 25(12), 1311–1328. DOI: 10.1080/10941665.2020.1853578

Yusof, M. F., & Ismail, H. N. (2014). Destination Branding Identity from the Stakeholders' Perspectives. *Internatıonal Journal Of Buılt Envıronment And Sustaınabılıty*, 1(1), 71–75.

Chapter 11
Leveraging Market Research to Enhance Destination Branding in Chiang Mai

Olukemi Adedokun Fagbolu
National Open University of Nigeria, Nigeria

ABSTRACT

This chapter explores how a specific tourism destination can employ market research to develop a logo and slogan to gain a competitive advantage in the international and domestic tourism market through product differentiation, market segmentation, target marketing and branding strategies. It highlights possible strategies for destination brands to develop their marketing strategies and competitiveness. The study gathers historical data from existing literature about the selected destination for the study. Additionally, it observes the destination features and employs developed questions to interview the selected destination using a cluster sampling method to gather customer data. The study also makes recommendations for the destination for possible destination brand sustainability.

INTRODUCTION

Organizations utilize marketing strategies such as product differentiation, market segmentation, target marketing and branding for their products to understand and analyze the best market to serve (Kotler et al., 2017; Lewis & Chambers, 2000). Tourism destinations thrive to achieve brand development and improvement to gain a competitive advantage in the tourism market (Camilleri, 2024). Significantly,

DOI: 10.4018/979-8-3693-6700-1.ch011

logo and slogan showcases tourism destination brand in international and domestic tourism market.

Even though, Buhalis (2000) opines that tourism destination brand can be categorized for analysis by employing six (6) frameworks, comprising **a**ttractions, **a**ccessibility, **a**menities, **a**vailable packages, **a**ctivities and **a**ncillary services. People have been embarking on vacation or holiday for more than one million years ago and the activities during such trips have been identified with tourism. A destination is a product with many product lines of tangible and intangible socio-cultural entity (Seaton & Bennett, 1996). Tourism destinations are classified and identified by the destination authorities within a nation as a nation, region, province, state, local, city or location (Goeldner & Ritchie, 2009) etc according to related activities such as business, culture, recreation, history, ethnicity and so on (Smith, 1995).

Stakeholders in a tourism destination include host, governments, tourists, visitors, environmental groups, tourism industry sectors, destination management organization, institutions (Goeldner and Ritchie, 2009). However, many customers tend to be loyal to destination rather than brand while considering certain factors including reservation systems, new owners, failed tour operators and travel agents, investment status, and repositioning (Kotler et al, 2017; Pike, 2015).

Various attractions conduct market research on issues like travel, consumer behavior (Goeldner and Ritchie 2009; Lewis and Chambers, 2000; Schiffman and Kanuk, 2000) and so on by using suitable research design (Getz, 2008). Tourism destination brand has choice of different market strategies like local, regional, national and international market strategy through scope of market, geographical dimension of the market, point of entry to the market, what to achieve in the market etc. Strategy is a herald to marketing management while structure of the strategies is the same and based on framework of analysis of definition, objective, requirements and expected results.

Destination brand often face serious challenges both internally and externally while developing destination logo and slogan. Hence, to retain competitiveness in tourism market, situations might require redesigning or changing name for expansion of product lines, going into new geographical markets or even starting a completely new line leading to conducting market research to achieve competitive advantage. Thus, market research could be imperative to developing logo and slogan to increase brand competitiveness through product differentiation, market segmentation, target market and branding strategies in relation to its marketing strategies that will be a basis of reflecting new brand in the international and local tourism markets (Cooper, 2022; Foxall, 2017; Getz & Page, 2016; Goldsmith, 2016; Kotler et al., 2017).

The purpose of this chapter is to enlighten Destination Management Organization (DMO) on development of a logo and slogan that will be a basis of reflecting new brand in the tourism market through market research. Thus, of organization development provides foundation for this study. Organization development "is a system wide application and transfer of behavioral science knowledge to the planned development, improvement, and reinforcement of the strategies, structures, and processes that lead to organization effectiveness" (Cummings & Worley 2009, p. 2). The theory provides a valuable idea to understand and conceptualize organizations components. The approach fosters critical for innovation in planned change. In relation to strategic development, it is a useful tool in diagnosing and analyzing issues and for reasonable interventions in hospitality and tourism management industry (Fagbolu & Fallon, 2021; Fallon & Fagbolu, 2021).

CONCEPTUAL BACKGROUND

Research indicates its existence in various disciplines and practice through cultural, social, technological, environmental (G¨ossling, 2009), management and political phenomena. Social research agenda in tourism destination vary (Ritchie, Burns & Palmer, 2006; Brunt, 1997; Jennings 2010) according to situations and needs. Destination market research is a process and deals of people with different unpredictable behaviors (Veal, 2011). It is a very critical tool which helps destination management to know why people choose a destination or another, to discover customers' expectations and perceptions, to know the real competitor, rate of customer return business, acceptable of new concept, strategies in relation to competitive advantage, target market, extent of advertising, satisfaction and customer complaint and perception (Connolly & Mcging, 2007; Hallo & Manning, 2009).

Destination market research is a process with a distinct nature of human experience, advertising, forces, impacts and ethics (Chambers & Lewis 2000; Seaton & Bennett, 1996; Smith, 1995). However, research is based on what it will be used for and who will use it (Getz, 2008. Quantitative and qualitative paradigm (Schiffman & Kanuk, 2000) are useful approaches in carrying out market research in the context of destination branding. Goeldner and Ritchie (2009) argue that research does not make decision but rather helps the management to perform effective operation. Various organizations conduct research to determine best marketing strategies such as product differentiation, market segmentation and target marketing for their products in order to understand and analyze the best market to serve.

Strategic marketing is an embodiment of allocation of resources, setting of objective and identification of the market (Lewis and Chambers, 2000, Dimoska and Trimcev, 2012). Branding is one of the decisions involved in developing a tourism marketing strategy and an important part of product planning. Target market is to be considered when making other branding decisions after market segment has been determined. The brand symbols are made up of destination slogan, name, logo, and trade character but change frequently as a result of operation in dynamic environment. Situations might require redesigning or changing name for expansion of product lines, going into new geographical markets or even starting a complete new line. Hence, need to remain competitive in tourism market. This chapter, therefore, conceptualizes product differentiation, market segmentation, target marketing and branding.

PRODUCT DIFFERENTIATION

Product differentiation distinguishes a product but not better from that of the competitor to attract customers to the product that offers better price value, better problem solution and greater satisfaction. The bases for destination differentiation are both intangible and tangible which involve features that cannot be copied, appeal to a particular need/or want and create an image that can really surpass the specialized difference of the destination. In short, images, benefits, and differentiation are solely the perception of the consumer, not management.

Hence, a tourism destination feature denotes a tangible or intangible subset of the product the customer will buy while characteristics of the service being offered are often recognized to differentiate the product from the rest of competition (Cronjé & du Plessis, 2020; Guzman-Parra, Knollenberg et al., 2021; Vila-Oblitas & Maqueda-Lafuente, 2016). Whereby, customers only accept features that are translated into value before accepting the benefit. Lewis and Chambers (2000) disclose that a perceptual map tends to be useful while conducting internal analysis of consumer expectations and perceptionwhich indicates where the operation may be failing both internally relative to the

competition. Figure 1 below shows some of such attributes that can be measured based on customers expectation and perception of destination features.

Figure 1. A perceptual map of consumer expectation and perception

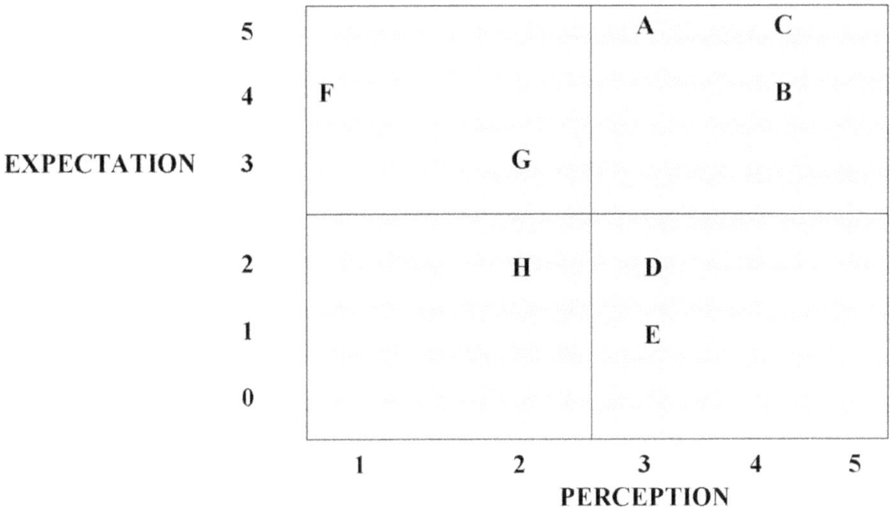

Features: A. Cleanliness B. Friendly Staff C. Price/Value
D. Bathroom E. Parking F. Quick Service
G. Room Furnishings H. Good Restaurants

The map tends to aid the best use of resources by indicating the expectation of the target

market and perception of performance based on the products' attributes (Gaki et al., 2016; Mussalam & Tajeddini, 2016; Smolčić & Soldić, 2017). These distinctive features should be especially emphasized if they are important to the customer while features that may not provide any benefits to the customer should be excluded from the presentation. The process is that each of the respondents will be asked to rate the importance of certain attributes in choosing a destination on a scale ranging from poor fair, good to excellent. However, once the needs of the customer have been established through a series of probes, the customer is introduced to the product benefits and features.

Thus, product differentiation is a significant marketing tool to familiarize and allow consumers within market segment and target market to try the product which can enable them to react favorably to the product. Meanwhile, differentiation can be regarded as a complementary strategy to market segmentation (Avraham & Ketter, 2016; Camilleri, 2024; Domínguez-Quintero, González-Rodríguez & Roldán, 2021; Kozak & Baloglu, 2011; Kunwar, 2015; Padlee, Thaw & Zulkiffli, 2019; Ramseook-Munhurrun, Seebaluck, & Naidoo, 2015).

Market Segmentation

According to Seaton (1996), "(market) segmentation is primarily an attempt to classify

populations into broad behavioral groupings, derived mainly from quantitative surveys" (p. 55). Lewis and Chambers (2000) opine that segmentation provides the destination authorities ability to stay close and understand tourists very well. Although, it is difficult to segment market in practice because of the heterogeneous nature of the tourism market. However, based on Figure 2 below, process of market segmentation comprises six major steps.

Figure 2. Process of market segmentation

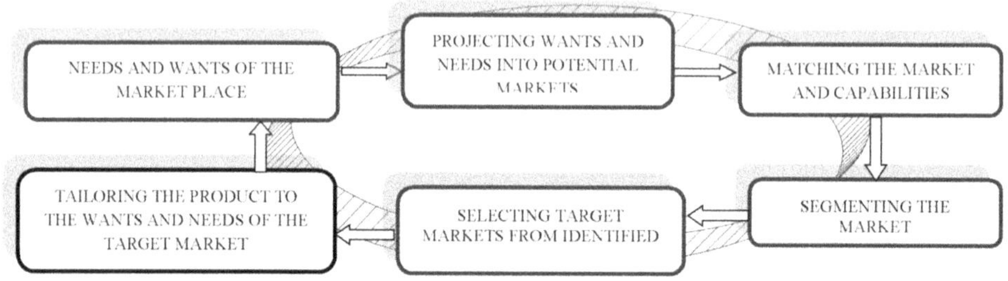

First, needs and wants of the marketplace. Second, projecting wants and needs into potential markets. Third, matching the market and capabilities. Fourth, segmenting the market. Fifth, selecting target from identified. Sixth, tailoring the product to the wants and needs of the target market. Thus, the basic segmentation strategy comprises geographic, demographic, and psychographic which is classified within continuum between psychocentrics, near psychocentrics, midcentrics, near allocentrics and allocentrics (Seaton, 1996). The other is usage strategy, very applicable more to tourism business than any other form of segmentation as it covers a wide range of categories. Market segmentation strategy is a unique tool that helps destinations management

organization to avoid a long and hectic approach in marketing the destination (Moutinho,

2011; Moutinho & Vargas-Sanchez, 2018). Segmentation, therefore, involves several statistical variables (Lewis and Chambers, 2000; Morrison, 2013). Smith (2013) indicates that groups of consumers could sometimes be regarded in such a way that their purchasing behavior would be homogenous relatively. After segmentation, the market potential is examined following selection of specific markets that destination can best serve by designing the product and services directly to them. Then, suitable media is identified and selected to reach to these markets (Smith, 2013).

Target Marketing

Target marketing is an approach by which destination choose which consumers it will direct its marketing program positioning and branding strategy to in a product-market segment. Although, the strategy overlap segmentation criteria but precisely involves undifferentiated targeting strategy, a concentrated targeting strategy and differentiated multi-target marketing destination as a product with different product lines (Lewis & Chambers, 2000; Moutinho, 2011; Moutinho & Vargas-Sanchez, 2018). As a result, various target markets are usually drawn from market segments like local, regional, domestic and international target market is appealing to attract young (adventure traveler), working class with high income (get away travelers) and retired people (social safety travelers). Target marketing is useful for many purposes such as destination branding based on the assumption is that the market is heterogeneous with different needs and wants (Özdemir & Yolal, 2017; Smith, 2013).

Branding

Branding is involved when developing marketing strategy for a tourism destination in presenting the image in domestic and international markets with common practice of either single name, multi-names or individual names. The success of the destination brand entails mobilization of marketing mix through the design of a homogenous product into product lines, correct and affordable price, distribution, and promotion to a defined market segment. Destination brand name is an asset, if it stands single mindedly for a specific package of value and benefits (Moutinho, 2011; Moutinho & Vargas-Sanchez, 2018; Seaton & Bennett, 1996).

The brand development process in tourism involves vision and mission, researching, to identify customer current perception and future expectation of the destination developing and implementing an organization's brand decisions brand. Implementation of branding decisions involves five steps. The process includes identifying a word or letter/number to identify the tourism service (brand name), selecting corporate symbol, design or attractive coloring or lettering and creating a branding philosophy. Others are choosing and personification of a brand name, deciding to seek legal protection that is trademark (brand mark or trade characters) (Camilleri, 2024; Woyo & Slabbert, 2021).

Relationship between Product Differentiation, Market Segmentation, Target Marketing and Destination Branding

This study illustrates the relationships between marketing strategies namely, product differentiation, market segmentation, target marketing and branding through Figure 3 below.

Figure 3. Relationship between product differentiation, market segmentation, target marketing and branding

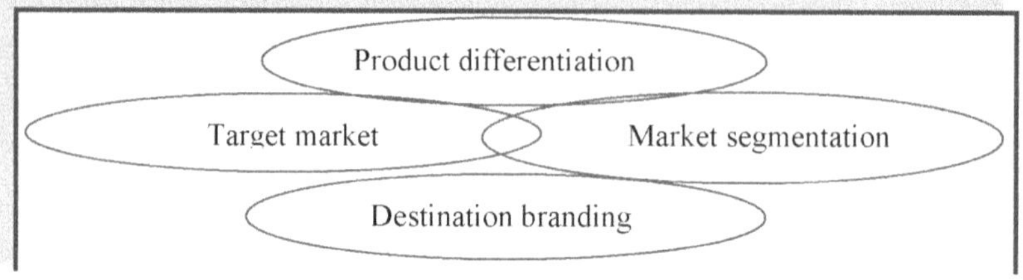

Product differentiation is an important marketing tool to familiarize and allow consumers within market segment and target market to try the product which can enable them to react favorably to the product. Hence, market segmentation is a complementary strategy to differentiation.

In tourism marketing strategy, product differentiation, market segmentation, target marketing and branding are applicable and useful tools used by marketers to achieve certain market and product objectives. Among such objectives are to outsmart the competition, seize marketing opportunity, satisfy customer needs and wants, maximize marketing efforts, increase sales, improve cost effectiveness of advertising, improve net profits, or to increase market share. Although, they are separate concepts and tools, they are highly interrelated towards achieving two main objectives. First, to marketing product lines and second, to maintaining competitive destination brand and (Bekjanov & Matyusupov, 2021; Ergashev & Jabborova, 2021; Olszewski-Strzyżowski, 2022; Streimikiene et al., 2021).

In the context of destination branding, the type of correlation that exists among the concepts, allows quantitative and/or qualitative approaches to gather data while conducting research to achieve best results during product differentiation, market segmentation, target market and destination branding (Cronjé & du Plessis, 2020; Foxall, 2017; Goldsmith, 2016). Although, Goeldner and Ritchie (2009) argue that research does not make decision but rather helps the management to perform effective operation. Significantly, market research is based on what it will be used for and who will use it (Getz & Page, 2016). Thus, the tools through market research are significant marketing strategies tools which are imperative to understanding and analyzing the best market to serve (Lewis & Chambers, 2000). However, this study further discloses other possible strategies for tourism destination brand in developing its marketing strategies and competitive advantage in the international and/or domestic tourism market.

Possible Strategies for Tourism Destination Brand in Developing its Marketing Strategies

The tourism destination has choice of different marketing strategies brand names that carry their own positioning status leading to brand switching process (Bideci & Albayrak, 2018; Muskat, Hörtnagl, Prayag & Wagner, 2019). Thus, the following possible strategies could be employed in developing marketing strategies. The strategies include:

- Matching product with needs.
- Optimally allocating and directing its resources.
- Using relevant market intelligence to sense change and to change strategies.
- Having greater ability to tailor behavior and logistics.
- Using effective mass media as the channels of distribution and marketing mix to the market along with the communications revolution.
- Being able to be unique in positioning and differentiating the destination from the competition.
- Determining strategies and enlarge the core market.
- Organizing frequent traveler programs.
- Maintaining consistent product lines and brand integrity.

Nonetheless, effectiveness of branding decisions should be ultimately always measured on insistence on the product for competitiveness.

Possible Strategies for the Destination Brand in Developing its Competitive Advantage

Destination brand can utilize under listed strategies while developing its competitive advantage by:

- Making brand name for customers fewer price comparisons.
- Willingness to stand behind service to always present a brand name with increasing social visibility and product prestige.
- Always presenting and maintaining less risk environment brand with favorable features to consumers.

Always reviewing marketing plan to identify and change potential target market within the market segment.
Increasing control of the distribution channel.
Promoting and selling entire destination product lines.
Entering new markets and to serving new customer groups.
Creating unique image in the minds of customers by looking outwards, destination may see gaps (opportunities), in the market that others have not covered, or gaps that are about to open due to regulatory changes, competitor action or social or economic movements (Moutinho, 2011; Moutinho & Vargas-Sanchez, 2018; Smith, 2013).

Thus, the destination can gauge the competitive advantage by itemizing issues such as relative market share, market growth potential, quality of the product, brand image, location of the destination, profitability, insight into the market, price competition, contact with the management, and effectiveness of the destination sales force. However, destination needs to search internal and external environment closely for opportunities that may exist (Moutinho, 2011).

Study Methodology

Due to the short nature of the study, exploratory research design is employed using qualitative method. It adopts purposive sampling method while interviewing the respondents entailing tourists and destination staff through extracted structured research instrument for customers and staff discovered from the literature using internet search engines (Lewis & Chambers, 2000; Goeldner & Ritchie, 2009). Meanwhile, the purpose of the research was discussed with each of the participants and allowed to opt out if so wish during the interview sections. A Thematic Analysis on Excel was employed to code and analyze the data.

A Thai lady translator was employed to translate the questions to Thai language before proceeding to the destination. This was done for two main reasons. First, to be able to interview any Thai tourists at the destination and, second, the researcher is not a Thai speaker. However, the researcher with the translator proceeded to the destination along with both English and Thai copies of the copies of the printed copies of the question to the destination.

Before travelling to the area, the researcher decided that all the possible tourists that researcher would come across at the destination will form the population for the study. Consequent to the duration of the stay at the destinations visited, she also decided to employ cluster sampling method to engage respondents and was able to interview twenty (20) only tourists comprising local and international tourists at the some of the destinations visited. The researcher with the assistance of the translator engaged in writing the responses of the interviewees to each of the questions asked during the interview sections since the questions are short in nature. They both also worked together to review the interview transcripts to code and develop the major discoveries and findings at the destination. The method encouraged equal opportunities to the respondents while conducting the interview (Bajpai, 2009; Egbulonu & Nwachukwu, 2001; Veal, 2011).

Choice of the tourism destination, Chiang Mai, for this study was uniquely influenced by researcher's three specific reasons. First, the destination is strategically located in Northern tourist region of Thailand. Second, the choice was inspired by quest to collect data for the study to compare and to really understand the data gathered from the literature review. Finally, to exploring Northern part of Thailand as a foreigner and to experience its uniqueness to the country tourism industry.

Chiang Mai Tourist Destination

Thailand is the premier travel destination for Southeast Asia and serves as a hub for reaching other sub-regions like Laos and so on. Chiang Mai has been in existence for seven hundred and seventeen years (717), founded by King Meg Rai the Great who was a very religious leader on Thursday, April 12, 1296, after conferment with his friends, King Ramkhamhaeng of Sukhothai and King Ngam Muang of Phayao. Chiang Mai today, is the capital and cultural core of the Lanna Kingdom and center of Bhudhism in northern Thailand and accessible by affordable road, rail and air. Chiang Mai destination is a base camp destination (Camilleri & Camilleri, 2018; Seaton and Bennett, 1996) regarded as a convenient starting point for other places in Thailand and Mekong.

The pictures below show some of the exciting moments and memorable experiences at the destination as shot by the researcher during the study (Chiang Mai Thailand Travel and Tourist Guide, n.d.; Thailand Regions, n.d.).

Figure 4. An elephant rider with the researcher and the translator at the Maesa elephant camp, Chiang Mai

Figure 5. Chiang Mai night bazaar shopping centre for tourists

Chiang Mai Tourist Destination: Discoveries

Tourism Authority of Thailand Chiang Mai Office is responsible for tourism in Chiang Mai. Chiang Mai Municipality Tourist Information Office is situated near Nawarat Bridge, The Pae Road, opposite Buddha Satan. The office consists of various officers who help tourists and of tourist police who act as security. Roles of the tourist office include increasing visitor figures and promoting destination bands, guardian of the image, conducting research into current demand factors and so on. The city is endowed with cultural, historic, man-made and natural attractions. The product lines include, jungle trekking and display, nightlife, hotels and restaurants, shopping, transportation, sight-seeing, day trips, adventure, elephant camps, snake camps, tiger camps, monkey training school, many cooking and massage schools, numerous outdoor activities, a variety of handicrafts workshops, various cultural performances, and breathtaking scenery etc, in fact, the list is inexhaustible. The pictures below show some of the exciting moments and memorable experiences at the destination as shot by the researcher during the study (Chiang Mai Thailand Travel and Tourist Guide, n.d.; Thailand Regions, n.d.).

Places visited include Maesa Elephant Camp founded in 1976 is the most popular tourist attractions in Thailand. It started with only five (5) elephants but now has seventy (70) elephants. At Chiang Mai King Cobra farm, the staff was proud to present the Snake Show as it is known for "Most exciting snake show in the world." The snake farm has variety of snake species both from Thailand and other countries. During display, snakes were caught by hands, mouth. Mae Rim Monkey School is where monkey is trained to perform certain functions like greeting, shopping, plucking of coconut from coconut tree, playing of basketball, identification and picking of numbers from 1 to 9, riding of bicycle and so. Tiger Kingdom Park and Restaurants was the next place visited during the study with sixty tigers. The first Tiger Kingdom branch was founded in Ubonrachatani in the year 2000 and was named Ubon Zoo. On 24th March, 2008. Tiger Kingdom Chiang Mai was founded I Chiang Mai as a 2nd branch of Ubon Zoo to earn more income for the extra space and enclosures that the tigers needed to be comfortable. Tigers were less active during the day, and this provides opportunity to go very close to them. At Siam Insect Zoo, discovery was at insect museum and live insect breeding farm at Maerim Chiang Mai. Other sites are Borsang Umbrella History, Shinawatra Silk Centre which was established in 1929 before produces longest finest quality hand woven silk. We also visited gem, silver and leather workshops.

The international competitors identified during the study include China, Myanmar, Laos, Cambodia and Vietnam while national competition are Phuket, Koh Samui, Krabi, Bangkok, Phi Phi Islands, Khao Lak, Locally, Chiang Rai, Mae Hong Son and Lampang, Phayao. The target markets for the destination include young, working class and retired prospective tourists. Since young ones like adventure tourism, working class ones have reasonable disposable income while the old one have the time and can to some extent afford the package. It is a common saying that "a day in Chiang Mai is enough to see things around town" but now, two weeks in Chiang Mai may not be long enough for travelers to experience all that Chiang Mai has to offer. The researcher hardly identified any Chiang Mai indigene or Thai tourists at the tourist attractions visited. Majority of the tourists present during the study visiting the destination are international tourists from Belgium, China, Denmark, France, Germany, Malaysia, Spain, and United States of America.

Chiang Mai Tourist Destination: Features

Chiang Mai, one of Asia's most attractive tourist destinations is unique with distinct features. The researcher observed that the destination features a variety of traditional and western style entertainment, accessibility by rail, road, bus and air, regular daily flights, rail service, overnight sleepers, centuries-old pagodas and temples next to modern convenience stores and boutique hotels. The attributes of the brand include terrific scenery, value for vacation money, parking lots, modern Thai culture, high level of hygiene, available and affordable trip, minimum communication barrier, pleasant weather, knowledge exchange, architecture, commerce, consistent and quick service, good hotel accommodation, restaurants and shopping centers at various destinations and specifically at Chiang Mai Night Bazaar, new food, encountering people with related interests, thrills, excitement and low cost excursions with spas and wellness opportunities, friendly and hospitable and polite staff. Others include politeness, and good reputation, and cold weather, diverse culture, levels of price, climate, accessibility, sport and recreational facilities, good infrastructure and superstructure, social and cultural features like language, art, attire, music, vocation, training, history, and leisure activities and so on.

Chiang Mai Tourist Destination: Challenges in Relation to its Marketing

Although, the destination has a strong picture of its prosperous potential trends and opportunities that can impact the city. It also possesses existing capabilities and vulnerable areas in the market when compared with the competition at Bangkok, Phuket, Laos, Malaysia and China. The internal situation is that some tourists have disturbing and rude behavior, cultural clashes, loudness, refusal to flush the toilet, public behavior like spitting, jumping queues, throwing litters all over sites and over balcony, too many people sleeping in hotel room otherwise called 'slept many to a room', self-laundry, bad driving habit like lack of respect for highway code and sudden stopping in the middle of busy roads and cross cultural issues (Shim, Oh & Jeong, 2017). Temples or Buddhism images erected in some public areas pose challenges to achievement of the expected results on increased growth, market share and profits and majorly competitive advantage because some tourists detest them (Olszewski-Strzyżowski, 2022; Streimikiene et al., 2021).

The destination is also faced with unfaithfulness or misinformation by tour operators (which I would have been a victim if not because of my knowledge in tourism destination), prices, attitude of residents and government in financing infrastructure capacity, a qualitative and quantitative inventory like top destination management organization (DMO) commitment, understanding of international markets and limited capital resources.

Externally, the challenge lies in positioning in a certain product class or to a certain market segment in a continuing search for greater market share. The trends of the environment, regulatory changes such as visa regulations, competitor action or social or economic movements in the market, changes in consumer behavior have impact on the destination attributes, power position of the customers' extent of competition, average profit margin, and threat of potential entrant and threat of substitute products (Girish, 2008).

CONCLUSION

A successful destination depends largely on market research. Tourism destination branding effort that is not directed by such research are wasted effort are bound to fail. Hence, conducting market research before developing destination brand in relation to product differentiation, market segmentation and target marketing can disclose certain destination characteristics. Extensive primary market research, therefore, is essential to explore considerable different views that would emerge because of perceived legitimacy of the various practices in the source and receiving markets.

Destination market research is a process with a distinct nature of human experience, forces and impacts (Camilleri & Camilleri, 2018; Lewis & Chambers, 2000; Seaton & Bennett, 1996; Smith, 2013). As a process it aids to deal with people of different unpredictable behaviors. As a very critical tool, is capable to assisting DMO to know why people choose a destination over another, to discover customers' expectations and perceptions, to know the real competitor, rate of customer return business, acceptable of new concept, strategies in relation to competitive advantage, target market, market segment, extent of advertising, satisfaction and customer complaint and perception of the destination (Connolly, 2007; Sharp, Sharp & Miller, 2015; Xiao et al., 2017).

Even though, insufficient support and coordination sector coupled with lack of understanding among public sector and private sector pose challenges and risks in destination branding development (Cronjé & du Plessis, 2020; Pike, 2017; Liang, Luo & Bao, 2021; Pham, Andereck & Vogt, 2019). Imperatively, gathering data based on market research on customer perception and not only management in developing a logo and slogan that can reflect a destination brand in international and domestic market could encourage a sustainable competitiveness achievement (Bichler & Lösch, 2019; Proyrungroj, 2022; Rungsuwannarat et al., 2015; Shone, Simmons & Dalziel, 2016;].

Figure 6 below shows an example of market research process for developing destination brand.

Figure 6. Market research process for developing a destination branding

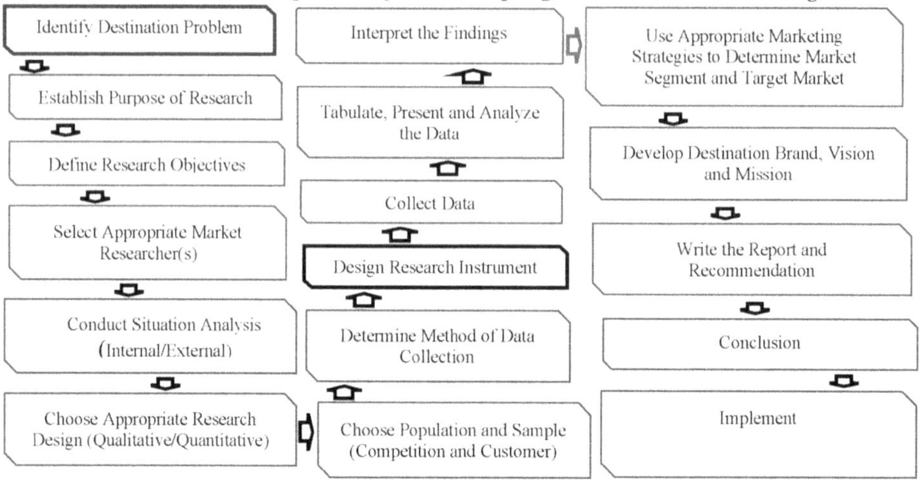

As a process it aids to deal with people of different unpredictable behaviors (Veal, 2011). A successful destination ought to depend largely on market research. This is a very significant tool imperative to assisting DMO to comprehend why tourists choose a particular destination over the other, to ascertain customers' expectations and perceptions, to discover the real competitor, rate of customer return business, acceptable of new concept, strategies in relation to competitive advantage, target market, extent of advertising, satisfaction and customer complaint and perception (Connolly, 2007; Sharp, Sharp & Miller, 2015; Xiao et al., 2017).

Recommendations for the Future of the Destination

Considering issues observed during the study, in a way, the brand is unique. As a result, in future, DMOs should:

1. Encourage local and regional market most importantly young and working-class people.

2. Maximize the amount of psychological experience for tourists to create brand loyalty and return visits.
3. Maximize profits for firms providing goods and services to tourists by collaborating with tour operators to package less visiting sites like Snake farm, Monkey training school etc. among their tour packages or itineraries.
4. Cooperate with other sectors to conserve the natural environment, ecosystems, biodiversity, reduce energy, waste, and pollutants through environmental management systems.
5. Organize enlightenment programs for the tour operators on respect and support local tradition cultures and cultural awareness through tourism marketing.
6. Encourage and support research on impacts of tourism to the city.
7. Provide a framework for raising the living standard of the people through the economic benefits of tourism and appropriate types of development within visitor centers and resorts.
8. Establishing a development program consistent with the cultural, social and economic philosophy of the government and the people of the in the city.
9. Aid in planning a publicity and sales campaign, selecting markets, selecting media and providing market research for development of destination brands.
10. As there are many target markets like the buffs, inners, venturers and so on, destination development management should consider discovering new markets, and overall conducting of sales and marketing program for the sites when evaluating the attractiveness of a potential brand.
11. It is important in future to rate how customers positioned an actual destination through perceptual mapping destination attributes that will be plotted on quadrants.
12. Continuously conducting market research.

REFERENCES

Ashworth, G. J., & Voogd, H. (2012). Marketing of tourism places: What are we doing? In *global tourist behavior* (pp. 5-19). Routledge.

Avraham, E., & Ketter, E. (2016). *Tourism marketing for developing countries: Battling stereotypes and crises in Asia, Africa and the Middle East*. Springer. DOI: 10.1057/9781137342157

Bajpai, N. (2009). *Business statistics*. Pearson Education India.

Bekjanov, D., & Matyusupov, B. (2021). Influence of innovative processes in the competitiveness of tourist destination. In *Innovation and entrepreneurial opportunities in community tourism* (pp. 243–263). IGI Global. DOI: 10.4018/978-1-7998-4855-4.ch014

Bichler, B. F., & Lösch, M. (2019). Collaborative governance in tourism: Empirical insights into a community-oriented destination. *Sustainability (Basel)*, 11(23), 6673. DOI: 10.3390/su11236673

Bideci, M., & Albayrak, T. (2018). An investigation of the domestic and foreign tourists' museum visit experiences. *International Journal of Culture, Tourism and Hospitality Research*, 12(3), 366–377. DOI: 10.1108/IJCTHR-02-2018-0029

Brunt, P. (1997). *Market research in travel and tourism* (1st ed.). Butterworth-Heinemann.

Buhalis, D. (2000). Marketing the competitive destination of the future. *Tourism Management*, 21(1), 97–116. DOI: 10.1016/S0261-5177(99)00095-3

Camilleri, M. A. (Ed.). (2024). *Tourism planning and destination marketing*. Emerald Publishing Limited. DOI: 10.1108/9781804558881

Camilleri, M. A., & Camilleri, M. A. (2018). *The tourism industry: An overview*. Springer International Publishing.

Chiang Mai Thailand Travel and Tourist Guide. (n.d.). *1 Stop Chiang Mai*. Retrieved from https://www.1stopchiangmai.com/

Connolly, P., & Mcging, G. (2007). High performance work practices and competitive advantage in the Irish hospitality sector. *International Journal of Contemporary Hospitality Management*, 19(3), 201–210. DOI: 10.1108/09596110710739903

Cooper, C. (2022). Essentials of tourism.

Cronjé, D. F., & du Plessis, E. (2020). A review on tourism destination competitiveness. *Journal of Hospitality and Tourism Management*, 45, 256–265. DOI: 10.1016/j.jhtm.2020.06.012

Cummings, T. G., & Worley, C. G. (2009). *Organization Development & Change* (9th ed.). Cengage Learning.

Domínguez-Quintero, A. M., González-Rodríguez, M. R., & Roldán, J. L. (2021). The role of authenticity, experience quality, emotions, and satisfaction in a cultural heritage destination. In *Authenticity and Authentication of Heritage* (pp. 103–117). Routledge. DOI: 10.4324/9781003130253-9

Ergashev, R. K., & Jabborova, Z. (2021). The importance of innovative activity in tourism. *European Scholar Journal*, 2(4), 467–472.

Fagbolu, O. A., & Fallon, J. (2021). Strategies exploration for academic achievement improvement through organization development intervention (ODI): A study of Kwara state university. *ABAC ODI Journal, Vision. Action. Outcome*, 8(1), 161–179.

Fallon, J., & Fagbolu, O. A. (2021). Developing possible strategies for academic achievement improvement of hospitality and tourism management students in Nigeria: A study of Kwara state university. *ABAC Journal*, 41(2), 177–203.

Foxall, G. R. (2017). Behavioral economics in consumer behavior analysis. *The Behavior Analyst*, 40(2), 309–313. DOI: 10.1007/s40614-017-0127-4

Gaki, E., Kostopoulou, S., Parisi, E., & Lagos, D. (2016). The evaluation of tourism satisfaction in island destinations: The case of the Ionian Islands of Greece.

Getz, D. (2008). Event Tourism: Definition, Evolution, and Research. *Tourism Management*, 29(3), 403–428. DOI: 10.1016/j.tourman.2007.07.017

Getz, D., & Page, S. J. (2016). Progress and prospects for event tourism research. *Tourism Management*, 52, 593–631. DOI: 10.1016/j.tourman.2015.03.007

Goeldner, C. R., & Ritchie, J. R. B. (2009). *Principles, Practices, Philosophies* (11th ed.). John Wiley & Sons, Inc.

Goldsmith, E. B. (2016). *Consumer economics: Issues and behaviors*. Routledge. DOI: 10.4324/9781315727363

Gössling, S.G¨Ossling. (2009). Carbon Neutral Destinations: A Conceptual Analysis. *Journal of Sustainable Tourism*, 17(1), 17–37. DOI: 10.1080/09669580802276018

Guzman-Parra, V. F., Vila-Oblitas, J. R., & Maqueda-Lafuente, J. (2016). Exploring the effects of destination image attributes on tourist satisfaction and destination loyalty: An application in Málaga, Spain. *Tourism & Management Studies*, 12(1), 67–73. DOI: 10.18089/tms.2016.12107

Hallo, J. C., & And Manning, R. E. (2009). Transportation and recreation: A case study of visitors driving for pleasure at Acadia National Park. *Journal of Transport Geography*, 17(6), 491–499. DOI: 10.1016/j.jtrangeo.2008.10.001

Jennings, G. (2010). *Tourism Research*. John Wiley & Sons.

Knollenberg, W., Duffy, L. N., Kline, C., & Kim, G. (2021). Creating competitive advantage for food tourism destinations through food and beverage experiences. *Tourism Planning & Development*, 18(4), 379–397. DOI: 10.1080/21568316.2020.1798687

Kotler, P., Bowen, J. T., Makens, J. C., & Baloglu, S. (2017). *Marketing for hospitality and tourism*. Pearson.

Kozak, M., & Baloglu, S. (2011). *Managing and marketing tourist destinations: Strategies to gain competitive edge* (1st ed.). Routledge.

Kunwar, R. R. (2015). Tourism crisis and disaster management. *The Gaze: Journal of Tourism and Hospitality*, 7, 1–36.

Lewis, R. C., & Chambers, R. E. (2000). *Marketing Leadership in Hospitality: Foundations and Practices* (3rd ed.). John Wiley & Sons, Inc.

Liang, Z., Luo, H., & Bao, J. (2021). A longitudinal study of residents' attitudes toward tourism development. *Current Issues in Tourism*, 24(23), 3309–3323. DOI: 10.1080/13683500.2021.1874314

Morrison, A. M. (2013). *Marketing and managing tourism destinations*. Routledge. DOI: 10.4324/9780203081976

Moutinho, L., & Vargas-Sanchez, A. (Eds.). (2018). *Strategic management in tourism. cabi tourism texts*. Cabi. DOI: 10.1079/9781786390240.0000

Muskat, B., Hörtnagl, T., Prayag, G., & Wagner, S. (2019). Perceived quality, authenticity, and price in tourists' dining experiences: Testing competing models of satisfaction and behavioral intentions. *Journal of Vacation Marketing*, 25(4), 480–498. DOI: 10.1177/1356766718822675

Mussalam, G. Q., & Tajeddini, K. (2016). Tourism in Switzerland: How perceptions of place attributes for short and long holiday can influence destination choice. *Journal of Hospitality and Tourism Management*, 26, 18–26. DOI: 10.1016/j.jhtm.2015.09.003

Olszewski-Strzyżowski, D. J. (2022). Promotional activities of selected National Tourism Organizations (NTOs) in the light of sustainable tourism (including sustainable transport). *Sustainability (Basel)*, 14(5), 2561. DOI: 10.3390/su14052561

Özdemir, C., & Yolal, M. (2017). Cross-cultural tourist behavior: An examination of tourists' behavior in guided tours. *Tourism and Hospitality Research*, 17(3), 314–324. DOI: 10.1177/1467358415589658

Padlee, S. F., Thaw, C. Y., & Zulkiffli, S. N. A. (2019). The relationship between service quality, customer satisfaction and behavioural intentions. *Tourism and Hospitality Management*, 25(1), 121–139. DOI: 10.20867/thm.25.1.9

Pham, K., Andereck, K., & Vogt, C. (2019). Local residents' perceptions about tourism development.

Pike, S. (2015). *Destination marketing: essentials*. Routledge. DOI: 10.4324/9781315691701

Pike, S. (2017). Destination positioning and temporality: Tracking relative strengths and weaknesses over time. *Journal of Hospitality and Tourism Management*, 31, 126–133. DOI: 10.1016/j.jhtm.2016.11.005

Proyrungroj, R. (2022). *Thailand's Image from the Perspectives of Chinese Non-Visitors and Visitors. Advances in Hospitality and Tourism Research*. AHTR.

Ramseook-Munhurrun, P., Seebaluck, V. N., & Naidoo, P. (2015). Examining the structural relationships of destination image, perceived value, tourist satisfaction and loyalty: Case of Mauritius. *Procedia: Social and Behavioral Sciences*, 175, 252–259. DOI: 10.1016/j.sbspro.2015.01.1198

Ritchie, B. W., Burns, P., & Palmer, C. (2008). *Tourism Research Methods: Integrating Theory with Practice*. CABI Publishing.

Rungsuwannarat, C., Michiels, N. N. T., Fujiwa, D., & Lin, F. (2015). A Comparative study of destination Image between Thailand and Indonesia. *APHEIT Journal*, 4(2), 5–26.

Schiffman, L. G., & Kanuk, L. L. (2000). *Consumer Behavior* (7th ed.). Prentice-Hall Inc.

Seaton, A. V., & Bennett, M. M. (Eds.). (1996). *Marketing tourism products: Concepts, issues, cases* (1st ed., pp. 28–54). International Thompson Business Press.

Sharp, R. L., Sharp, J. A., & Miller, C. A. (2015). An island in a sea of development: An examination of place attachment, activity type, and crowding in an urban national park. *Visitor Studies*, 18(2), 196–213. DOI: 10.1080/10645578.2015.1079101

Shim, C., Oh, E. J., & Jeong, C. (2017). A qualitative analysis of South Korean casino experiences: A perspective on the experience economy. *Tourism and Hospitality Research*, 17(4), 358–371. DOI: 10.1177/1467358415619673

Shone, M. C., Simmons, D. G., & Dalziel, P. (2016). Evolving roles for local government in tourism development: A political economy perspective. *Journal of Sustainable Tourism*, 24(12), 1674–1690. DOI: 10.1080/09669582.2016.1184672

Smith, S. L. J. (1995.). *Tourism analysis: a handbook* (2nd ed. ed.). Harlow Essex: Longman.

Smith, S. L. J. (2013). *Tourism analysis: A handbook* (2nd ed.). Routledge.

Smolčić, J. D., & Soldić, F. D. (2017). Satisfaction as a determinant of tourist expenditure. *Current Issues in Tourism*, 20(7), 691–704. DOI: 10.1080/13683500.2016.1175420

Streimikiene, D., Svagzdiene, B., Jasinskas, E., & Simanavicius, A. (2021). Sustainable tourism development and competitiveness: The systematic literature review. *Sustainable Development (Bradford)*, 29(1), 259–271. DOI: 10.1002/sd.2133

Thailand Regions. (n.d.). *Holiday Destinations in Thailand*. Retrieved from http:/ www.travelonline.com/Thailand/regions

Tourism Authority of Thailand. (n.d.). Thailand Travel Guide for Chiang Mai. Retrieved from https://www.tourismthailand.org/Where-to-

Veal, A. J. (2011). *Research methods for leisure and tourism: A practical guide* (4th ed.). Pearson Education Limited.

Woyo, E., & Slabbert, E. (2021). Tourism destination competitiveness: A view from suppliers operating in a country with political challenges. *Suid-Afrikaanse Tydskrif vir Ekonomiese en Bestuurswetenskappe*, 24(1), 3717. DOI: 10.4102/sajems.v24i1.3717

Xiao, X., Perry, E., Manning, R., Krymkowski, D., Valliere, W., & Reigner, N. (2017). Effects of transportation on racial/ethnic diversity of national park visitors. *Leisure Sciences*, 39(2), 126–143. DOI: 10.1080/01490400.2016.1151846

Chapter 12
Wine and Cultural Tourism as Niche Opportunities in Slovakia, Czechia, and Canada

Marica Mazurek
https://orcid.org/0000-0002-0564-3553
University of Zilina, Slovakia

ABSTRACT

This chapter will discuss recent advancements in the tourism industry, particularly in light of the COVID-19 time. Tourism destinations can profit from the sound effects of sustainable and niche tourism during economic downturns and unrest by enhancing their reputation, image, and level of service and utilizing their local cultural resources and legacy. The only travel locations that will be more successful and competitive are those that can investigate new product offerings and deal with the realities of the current environment. In tourist destinations, ecology and sustainability have begun to take centre stage. Niche tourism is a prime illustration of this kind of growth and provision. The study aims to explain the importance of wine tourism as a form of niche tourism and to add the importance of culinary and cultural tourism as additional niche tourism products. The Brand Niagara Region in Canada, Slovakia, and the Czech Republic will be the study's main subjects.

DOI: 10.4018/979-8-3693-6700-1.ch012

INTRODUCTION

The term competitiveness of the specific country or region is very complex consisting of different components as for instance geographical character, economy, demographic feature, clime, technology, politics, and environmental conditions. For this reason, it cannot be perceived only from the business and managerial point of view. Management and marketing are important tools improving the competitive advantage. Competitive advantage contains several crucial instruments boosting it. The existing environment of the destinations is a part of comparative advantage, but the tools how this environment is used belong to the competitive advantage approach. For instance, the environment protection and a sustainable approach are important factors of the sensitive environmental deployment or use.

The authors Crouch and Ritchie (2003) mentioned that the quality of human force, history, technology, culture, and the strong economy are dominant for the competitive advantage. Demand and supply, strategy, competition, and rivalry were all accepted as components of competitiveness by Porter (1990). The distribution of comparative advantage resources produces competitive advantage (Mengkebayaer et al., 2022). An issue of which elements have the most influence on competitiveness has been raised by the emergence of innovative approaches to competitiveness in various competitiveness models (e.g., Poon, Vanhove, Crouch & Ritchie, etc.).

Some activities or features, such as handicrafts, language, customs, gastronomy (food and drink), art and music, history, customary work practices, architecture, religion, the educational system, clothing, and leisure activities that reflect the local way of life, could enhance the competitive advantage, according to Ritchie and Zins (1978). Several of these components belong to the cultural heritage of the specific country or a region (Ma et al., 2022). They become an important part of the place identity creation and add to the authenticity and the forming of the projected place image which is perceived by visitors and create of their own image of a place.

"Tourism destination competitiveness is a general concept that encompasses price differentials coupled with exchange rate movements, productivity levels of various components of the tourist industry, and qualitative factors affecting the attractiveness or otherwise of a destination," according to the authors Dwyer, Forsyth & Rao, 2000; Matias, Nijkamp & Neto, 2007. Anholt (2007, p. 31) added that creating a competitive identity "isn't an advertising, design, or public relations exercise, although of course these techniques are essential for the promotion of the things that the country makes and does: its sport, its people, its investment and employment opportunities, its companies and their products and services, its music and art and other cultural products, its sport and tourist and heritage attractions." Also branding has a significant function as a tool of competitive advantage which enables to boost competitiveness.

A measurement of endowments, such as the resources that are already available and have the potential to be developed for tourism, is known as comparative advantage (Nawaz, Anwar, et al., 2019). Competitive advantage contains such components as the management, marketing, financing, security, partnerships, branding and marketing, governmental policy, etc. and the comparative advantage is built up by the natural resources, infrastructure (for instance transportation, tourism accommodation), historical monuments, climate, scenery, flora, fauna, climate, etc. These ideas were supported for instance by the authors as Kim and Dwyer (2003).

Sustainable approach has been also implemented into the concept of competitiveness. For instance Buhalis (2000, p. 106) who considers destination's competitiveness to be a result of combining sustainable, social, and economic ideas. The authors Crouch and Ritchie (2003) added to this idea with the statement that "A successful destination cannot spend their natural capital in order to be economically profitable," These ideas have influenced the concepts of competitiveness and have rooted the idea that in order to be competitive a country cannot totally deplete their precious natural resources for the success which could be only temporary, but the devastated character of the country could last for a very long time (Nawaz, Asif, et al., 2019).

This idea was highlighted by Crouch and Ritchie (2003), who underlined the above stated idea and expressed the opinion that the natural capital of destinations should be protected for the next generations and cannot be sacrificed for the growth of multiplication effect in the form for spending tourists and fulfilling their desires by the depletion of the life´s quality of the local people and their living environment. This paraphrased comment of the famous academic includes every facet of a competitive destination, as demonstrated by economic efficacy and efficiency, marketing strategy for consumer satisfaction, community building for community involvement, and sustainability for the preservation of natural resources (Nawaz et al., 2018).

When this term is applied to the competitiveness notion, it provides a clear explanation for the necessity of new tourist developments in substitution of the mass tourism (old tourism) streams. The sustainability method has gained popularity, particularly after it was realized that excessive tourism was destroying natural resources and endangering not just towns and communities but also the environment. The issues of sustainability were covered by a number of writers, including Cohen (2010), Han (2021), and Ioanides (2020). Novelli et al. (2024) provided support for the notion of sustainability and specialized tourism in their discussion, both of which are critical components of the sustainability concept. One type of specialty tourism is wine tourism (Rashid et al., 2019).

This is a potential approach to enhancing cultural tourism and creating a more specialized tourism offering within cultural tourism. As stated by Hall (1996), "wine tourism can be defined as visits to vineyards, wineries, wine festivals, and wine shows where visitors are primarily motivated by the opportunity to taste grape wines and/or experience the characteristics of a grape-wine region." The author (Hall, 2004) addressed the significance of culinary and wine tourism and backed the notion that visitor interest was expanding.

Porter argues that a company's ability to succeed depends not just on its positioning and strategy but also on how well-integrated it is into the environment (Vanhove, 2005, p. 114).

Wine and food are becoming important components of niche tourism especially among the seniors as well as families and young generation. As a part of niche tourism, they attract numerous visitors especially during this turbulent times of mass tourism development. Additional products which are in a focus of visitors is a culture and heritage of a destination. Generally speaking, local food, wine and culture are the magnets for tourists seeking positive experiences in a unique and more peaceful environment. According to Mottironi and Corrigliano (2013), this is crucial to understand in order to properly market the tourism product as food and develop a rural identity.

For this reason is wine tourism one of the expanding specialty tourism industries. It provides an alluring travel experience without exhausting the region's natural resources or drawing large numbers of visitors, it helps ensure the sustainability of the area. Because of this, wine tourism combined with culinary and cultural tourism may serve as an excellent model for sustainable territorial development.

RESEARCH METHODOLOGY

The case studies approach has been conducted in Niagara Region, Canada, Ontario, Slovakia, and the Czech Republic. This research was conducted over a period of four years, from 2006 to 2010, through interviews, winery visits, and discussions with the managerial representatives of wineries. Additionally, data were gathered through secondary sources.

Interviews with managers of several Niagara Region wineries (including Inniliskin and Jackson-Triggs winery) were used to arrange the vineyard tours during visits with University of Waterloo students and in-person conversations. Over the course of the four-year post-graduate education and job stay in Canada, multiple conversations were held.

Similar data were gathered in Slovakia through a number of trips to wineries and conversations with business owners in the wine production industry (e.g., at the Vinspacirka event held in the Slovak town of Banska Bystrica, in central Slovakia).

Many data have been gathered in the Czech Republic through in-person visits, interviews, and secondary data collecting.

Based on Yin's (2003) recommendations, the qualitative research approach makes use of the particular multi-case study structure. Multi-case studies and the synthesis of several perspectives have also been endorsed by Xiao and Smith (2006), Cresswell (2002), Patton (2002), and Vissak (2010). Multi-case studies provide researchers a better grasp of the issue under study and enable them to examine various approaches used by researchers from a wide range of cultural backgrounds.

The research goal of this study might raise a question if the wine, cultural, and culinary tourism are crucial for the competitiveness increase and for the promotion of the idea of sustainability through the concept of niche tourism support.

FINDINGS AND ANALYSIS

Brand Niagara - Wine Tourism and Cultural Tourism in Niagara Region

Niagara Region includes 12 municipalities: Niagara Falls, Niagara-on-the-Lake, Fort Erie, St. Catharines, Port Colborne, Thorold, Weinfleet, Welland, West Lincoln, Pelham, and Lincoln. Niagara Region located on the Niagara Peninsula. Visitors can enjoy wine, gastronomic, and cultural tourism on the Niagara Winery Route and Shaw Festival. This region is notable for the Welland Canal, Casino Niagara, and wedding tourism (called the "Honeymoon Capital of the World").

Despite of the fact that Canada has not such old history in comparison to some other parts of the world, Niagara Region contains also historical monuments. The United States and Great Britain engaged in a battle in this region, and a number of tourists are interested in visiting the battleground. The region's proximity to the United States of America is one of its advantages, as it is readily accessible to visitors from the United States. In the context of branding, Niagara Falls symbolizes the region, and it denotes the location or attributes that are most typical and authentic for the identification of the brand identity. Region identity is defined, as "abundant, authentic, beginnings, history, and inventive, one-of-a-kind, rare, surprising, unexpected, unique, vivid, and accessible."

Creating a brand image and brand identity in a proper way several years and requires using a serious marketing strategy. The authors Morgan, Pritchard, and Piggot (2003) claimed that it can "take many years to establish and brand image, establish name recognition, and develop strong awareness of a destination or product," In Niagara Region the stress has been given on the product innovation and the strategy formed in this region has been called Brand Niagara Original.

Based on the 2006 Travel Activity and Motivation Survey (TAMS) and a 2007 "return-to-sample" survey, the following secondary research result was produced on tourism product innovation in marketing techniques. This region's marketing strategy reinforced the need for tourism product innovation, which was included into Brand Niagara Original. The marketing products were segmented a priori and posteriori. This brand strategy was implemented for the entire destination, as well as for their products and events, such as the culinary and wine festivals. The Niagara Region is renowned for its 30 wineries in Niagara-on-the-Lake and 34 wineries in the Niagara Escarpment. Tourists frequently visit wineries, and they have become particularly popular among certain demographics, such as seniors, when combined with restaurants and culinary facilities. In 2025, North America will have a senior population exceeding 85 million, a trend that is also prevalent in other countries worldwide. This has the potential to improve the competitiveness of the tourist sector and generate a considerable opportunity for the growth of specialist tourism activities, such as wine tourism, when combined with culinary and cultural tourism.

Wine Tourism in Canada

Even though Canada has harsh weather, several regions are well-known for wine tourism and wine production. Canada has been a wine-loving country for more than 150 years, but in the 20th century, both locals and tourists began to recognize and enjoy wine more. Wine tourism in Canada is typical for British Columbia and Ontario. The origin of the Canadian wine brand could be closely connected with Germany, from where the wine types have been implemented. New technologies, increased wine production, and a variety of German wine varietals allowed Canada to cultivate and manufacture specific grapes.

This region's most well-known wine brand is ice wine, which is made from frozen grapes and has a higher alcohol percentage. Ontario is known for wine varieties like as Riesling, Chardonnay, Cabernet Franc, Gamay Noir, and Baco Noir, in addition to ice wine. Situated in the same latitude as Florence, Northern Italy, the Niagara Peninsula is the greatest wine area in Ontario, boasting growth conditions akin to those of Burgundy, France. Pelee Island, the North Shore of Lake Erie, and the Niagara Peninsula combine to form Ontario's wine country.

The most specialized wineries in the Niagara Region are, for example, Chateau des Charmes, Trius Winery, Inniskillin, and Peller Estates Winery in Niagara-on-the-Lake; and Cave Spring Cellars, Vineland Estates Winery, and Henry of Pelham Family Estate in Twenty Valley and St. Catharines. Even though some wineries are small, they are well-known for their limited-edition offerings. Examples of these include independent and artisanal wineries like Daniel Lenko, Hidden Bench, Tawse, and Ravine Vineyard, as well as Twenty Valley's Foreign Affair, which specializes in

Amarule-style wines. Other well-known wineries in the vicinity are Fielding Estates and Malivoire in the Twenty Valley, as well as Jackson-Triggs-Winery, Stratus, and Southbrook in Niagara-on-the-Lake.

The Niagara Region is familiar for the organizing of well-known cultural events like the Shaw festival, concerts, etc. G.B. Shaw is a major author of the regular performances at the Shaw Festival founded in 1962. Wine tasting, wine tours, and wine festivals are also typical for this region, for instance the Niagara Grape and Wine Festival,

Figure 1. Niagara region map (https://www.google.sk/search?q=wine+routes+in+Canada)

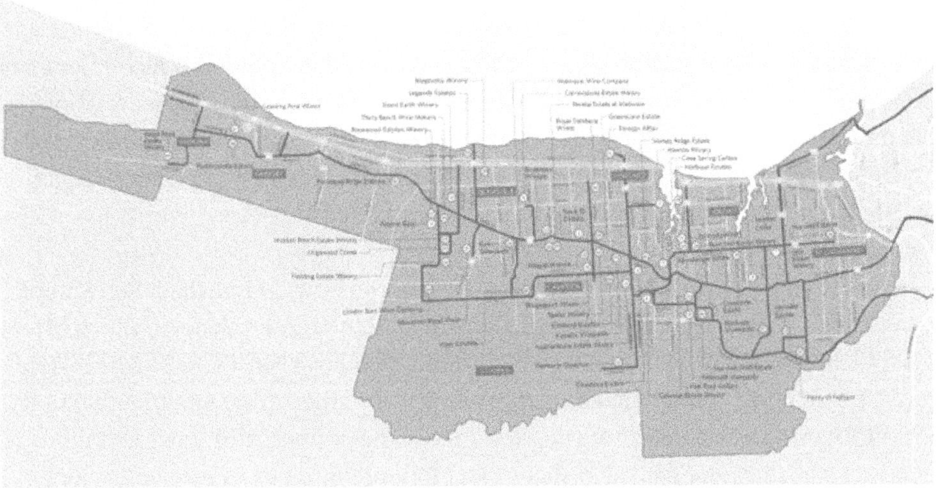

WINE TOURISM AND CULTURAL TOURISM IN SLOVAKIA

Slovakia occupies a diminutive 49,035 square kilometers in comparison to Canada's 985,003 square kilometers. Despite these factors, as well as the availability of land for wine production (terroir) and variations in climate, Slovakia is renowned for its high-quality wine. It is not among the most renowned wine-producing nations, such as Canada, France, Italy, Spain, Australia, and Portugal.

Slovakia comprises six wine-growing regions, which are further subdivided into forty subregions. Within these subregions, there are more than 603 municipalities, each of which possesses a distinctive natural environment, historical significance, and the capacity to hold wine tours and produce wine.

Slovakia has also seen a rise in popularity for niche tourism, which combines wine tours with historical sites and cultural activities. The Malokarpatska (Small Carpathian) wine region, the South Slovak wine region, the Tokaj wine region, the Central Slovak wine region, and the East Slovak wine region are the most well-known wine regions in Slovakia.

The Malokarpatska, or the Small Carpathian wine region, is the most renowned and historic region in Slovakia. It is located in the southwest, specifically in the vicinity of the cities of Modra and Pezinok. In the Small Carpathian region, it is quite common to organise celebrations that involve the sampling of a juvenile wine called "burciak," which is low in alcohol (6 percent). Slovakia is home to a number of well-known wine regions, including the Malokarpatska (Small Carpathian) wine region, the South Slovak wine region, the Tokaj wine region, the Central Slovak wine region, and the East Slovak wine region. One of the most well-known and historically significant wine regions in Slovakia is Malokarpatska, also known as the Small Carpathian wine region. This region is located in the southwest of the country, namely in the region that encompasses the cities of Modra and Pezinok.

In the region of the Small Carpathian Mountains, it is very popular to organise events that include the tasting of a young wine called "burciak," which has a low alcohol content of six percent.

Combining wine routes with cultural tourism can be accomplished, for example, by visiting Chateau Béla in southern Slovakia and the Elesko winery, which offers visitors the chance to view the Andy Warhol-themed Zoya Museum. Slovakian wine trails are genuine, well-planned, and promoted. In order to maintain authenticity, Slovak traditional costumes are worn by individuals in several wine and cultural goods establishments, who also share local folklore through songs and customs.

The old royal towns of Bratislava, Svätý Jur, Pezinok, Modra, Trnava, and the nearby Carpathian villages are all on the Small Carpathian wine trail. Wonderful churches, primarily dating from the 13th and 14th centuries, as well as chapels, cloisters, and other historic structures, are still standing in these towns.

The Nitra region is also known for producing high-quality wine, particularly Muller-Thurgau, Risling Vlasky, and Veltlinske Zelene (Veltlin Green). Situated in this location lies the magnificent Chateau Topolcianky, one of the most famous vineyards in Central Europe. Founded in 1933, the Chateau Topolcianky wine brand has gained recognition both domestically and internationally. The greatest Slovak and Moravian wine producers are invited to the well-known "Nitra Wine Festival," which is held in the fall in the Nitra region.

In addition to taking in diverse cultural and musical events, visitors can take a tour of the medieval wine cellars beneath Nitra Castle. Because it travels across four regions, the Nitra wine route is the longest in Slovakia. The Hontianska Wine

Route near the village of Hokovce (near the Hungarian border), the Zahorie Wine Route, and the unique Pozitavska Wine Route have all recently gained popularity.

Numerous cities began to host wine festivals and wine tastings. For example, in Banska Bystrica, Central Slovakia, it has become customary to host a wine festival called "Vinspacirka" (Wine Walking) every spring that is open to all wine producers and enthusiasts from both Slovakia and overseas.

The Tokaj wine region is one of the smallest in the world, but what makes this wine interesting is how good and well-liked it is. It needs a certain microclimate and subsurface (caused by igneous rocks). Wine routes have grown in popularity among tourists. The Tokaj region, for instance, is a popular destination for tourists who are interested in combining wine tourism, cultural tourism, and gastronomic tourism.

The exhibition on Toak Viticulture at the South Zemplin Museum in Trebisov, Eastern Slovakia, is a must-see. An additional attraction is the Tokaj Wine Road, which is renowned for its ability to integrate local customs, history, wine sampling, shopping, and discussions with winemakers. The South Zemplin Museum in Trebisov, Eastern Slovakia has an exhibition on Toak Viticulture, which is worth seeing. Another attraction is the Tokaj Wine Road, which is well-known for combining local customs, history, wine tasting, shopping, and a conversation with winemakers.

Figure 2. Map (https://winesurveyor.weebly.com/tour_slovakia.html)

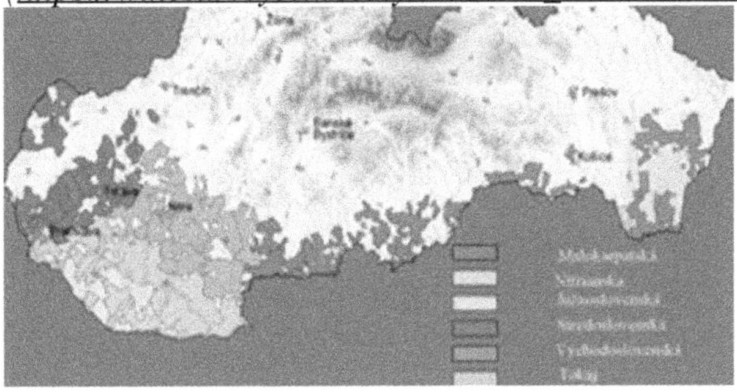

WINE TOURISM AND CULTURAL TOURISM IN CZECH REPUBLIC

The 78 866 km2 Czech Republic and the 22 349 km2 portion of Czech Republic Moravia are among the regions that are well-known for producing wine, particularly the southern portion of Moravia and certain regions of the Czech Republic. The Litomericka and Melnicka subregions are well-known in the Czech Republic, while the Znojemska, Mikulovska, Velkopavlovicka, and Slovacka subregions are well-known in Moravia. The wine-producing region of Moravia spans 17,241 hectares, and 96% of the region's vines are located there.

Although the Czech Republic is more known for its beer production, wine has gained popularity in the past, particularly during King Charles IV's reign. Nonetheless, the 20th century marked the beginning of the most significant phase in the evolution of wine production.

The wine from the southern area of Moravia, together with the sub-regions of Litomericka and Melnicka, is considered to be among the greatest in Europe due to its unique taste and acidity. The circumstances for producing wine in the Morava region are comparable to those in German wine regions. Some of the most well-liked wines are Welschriesling, Blaufrankish, Muller Thurgau, Chardonnay, and Riesling.

We concentrated on the regions that were shown from the available variety, particularly those that dealt with wine production and other cultural products that may strengthen the region's branding efforts. Slovacka Wine sub-region is one of them, located between the borders of Slovakia and Austria, two neighbouring countries. Traditional music, crafts, and national costumes are examples of typical cultural products from this region. This sub-region is known for its distinctive wine production, which is in high demand. Uherske Hradiste, a typical Slovak town, is also part of this sub-region.

When talking about wine and cultural tourism as a subset of niche tourism in the Czech Republic, it's important to note that interesting activities and the existence of cultural heritage are just as important to the nations and regions as wine production and winery visits. For example, it is noteworthy to discuss the establishment of Moravian Wine Trails in the Morava region, which strives to safeguard cultural assets and promote wine tourism in Moravia. As part of this initiative, bicycle paths were also constructed around the wineries. The residents of the Czech Republic as well as other nations, particularly Slovakia and other neighbouring countries, are growing to love these wine routes.

There are 1200 km of designated bike and e-bike paths in the network of bike trails. Wine, culture, and cycling are increasingly popular trends among modern citizens who want to recognize their country through its branding and a variety of well managed specialized and cultural products.

FINDINGS AND ANALYSIS

The survey's findings indicated that dining out, touring nearby culinary destinations, and planning activities with a culinary theme are all highly common and well-liked among tourists. The Niagara region has the potential to develop a product strategy comparable to that of the wine industry, orchards, natural beauty, food and wine festivals, France, Spain, Portugal, Austria, and Australia. This region is well-known for its numerous wineries (30 in Niagara-on-the-Lake and 34 in the Niagara Escarpment), golf courses and speciality foreign dining facilities. The study's findings indicated that sampling regional cuisine is the most preferred activity (55,7%). In order to assess the most promising items and determine whether the above-mentioned branding method was effective, patterns and attributes of visitor motivation and attractiveness were tracked in Niagara Region.

As a result of the province of Ontario's realization of the importance of culinary tourism products as a creative approach to tourism marketing strategy, the province developed the Wine and Culinary Tourism Action Plan. The plan's purpose was to give financial assistance for a new prospective product and to promote the development of the product itself. As one of the key goals, one of the primary aims was to recognize Ontario on a global scale as a destination for wine and culinary tourism marketing brands. Consequently, this development resulted in the establishment of Brand Niagara Original, as well as the requirement to build a branding strategy that is highly competitive and a regional brand. The branding strategies of the Niagara Region include the utilization of Brand Niagara Original, which is also included in the product range for wine tourism and in destination branding initiatives that emphasize the wine tourism business in the Niagara Region.

Despite the existence of wine routes and the growing popularity of wine tasting and wine tours among tourists from Slovakia and other nations, the situation in Slovakia was very different. Slovakia's branding strategy is still in its infancy, despite the existence of various effective regional agritourism and nation branding schemes. Like Canada, the nation did not completely understand the value of culinary tourism, and wineries occasionally had to employ their own financial resources and branding tactics to promote their products. Despite these circumstances, Slovakia has the potential to grow into a well-known wine tourist destination. It draws inspiration and best practices from a number of European nations, including Austria, France, Hungary, and the Czech Republic, but it also draws from Canada.

Similar to Slovakia and Canada, the Czech Republic has seen a rise in wine tourism, which is now a significant niche market and integral component of branding strategy. Even though the Czech Republic is better known for its beer production—Pilsner and other Czech brands are well-known worldwide—wine manufacturing started to gain popularity in the 14th century, during King Charles IV's reign. The 20th century saw the greatest increase in wine production. In addition to developing wine routes for cyclists interested in Czech wine brands, heritage, and a healthy lifestyle, the Czech Republic's wine tourism branding strategy is linked to the promotion of cultural goods in wine areas and sub-regions. This strategy has gained popularity not just in the Czech Republic but also in Slovakia and Canada, the two previously researched nations.

CONCLUSIONS

Regions or locales can benefit from alleged gentler and more sustainable principles so-called soft and more sustainable values during economic downturns and turmoil if they can improve their brand, image, and improving the quality of destination services while using their local cultural assets and heritage. It is critical to protect the scenery and ecosystem while also providing gastronomic, oenological, and cultural items. Control, preservation, protection and sustainable development measures will be used more extensively, especially during this period.

Niche tourism, like wine tourism and cultural tourism, exemplifies heightened competitiveness and effective tourism growth. The global downturn in mass tourism, as well as recent events created by the catastrophe produced by a new epidemic scenario such as COVID-19, have emphasised the need for more sustainable locations that offer less hectic places including niche products. Wine tourism and cultural tourism could be ideal examples of appropriate tourism offerings for such locations. It is critical to have a discussion about using speciality tourism, as demonstrated by wine tourism and cultural tourism. Moreover, academics, professionals, and governmental representatives can derive insights from these sustainable methodologies and acknowledge tourism as a symbiotic relationship between nature and tourism development.

Slovakia, the Czech Republic, and Canada were contrasted as three unique countries engaged with ecotourism and cultural tourism activities. Comparing their sizes and economic strength demonstrates that they are unique nations; nonetheless, despite their geographical and political differences, they are democratic states seeking to compete in the tourism business. In addition to delivering an engaging tourism experience, they hope to foster a positive image and reputation by supplying wine routes, culture, history, and legacy.

REFERENCES

Anholt, S. (2007). *Competitive Identity. The New Brand Management for Nations, Cities and Regions*. Palgrave Macmillan.

Buhalis, D. (2000). Marketing the competitive destination of the future. *Tourism Management*, 21(1), 97–116. DOI: 10.1016/S0261-5177(99)00095-3

Cohen, E. (2010). Authenticity, Equity and Sustainability in Tourism. *Journal of Sustainable Tourism*, 10(4), 267–276. DOI: 10.1080/09669580208667167

Creswell, J. W. (2002). *Educational research: Planning, conducting, and evaluating quantitative and qualitative research*. Merrill/Pearson.

Crouch, J., & Ritchie, B. (2003). *The competitive destination – a sustainable tourism perspective*. Cabi Publishing.

Dwyer, L.,Forsyth, P. & Rao, P. (2000). The price competitiveness of travel and tourism: A

Hall, C. M. (1996). Wine Tourism in New Zealand. In *Proceedings on Tourism Down under II: A Tourism Research Conference* (pp. 109–119). University of Otago.

Hall, C. M. (2004). *Wine, Food and Tourism Marketing*. Haworth Hospitality Press.

Han, H. (2021). *Sustainable Consumer Behaviour and the Environment*. Routledge. DOI: 10.4324/9781003256274

Ioannides, D., & Gyimothy, S. (2020). The COVID-19 crisis as an opportunity for escaping the unsustainable global tourism path. *Tourism Geographies*, 22(3), 624–632. DOI: 10.1080/14616688.2020.1763445

Kim, C., & Dwyer, L. (2003). Destination competitiveness and bilateral tourism flows between Australia and Korea. *Journal of Tourism Studies*, 14(2), 55–67. DOI: 10.21581/jts.2018.05.30.2.55

Ma, W., Tariq, A., Ali, M. W., Nawaz, M. A., & Wang, X. (2022). An Empirical Investigation of Virtual Networking Sites Discontinuance Intention: Stimuli Organism Response-Based Implication of User Negative Disconfirmation. *Frontiers in Psychology*, 13, 862568. DOI: 10.3389/fpsyg.2022.862568

Matias, A., Nijkamp, P., & Neto, P. (2007). *Advances in modern tourism research*. Physica Verlag. DOI: 10.1007/978-3-7908-1718-8

Mengkebayaer, M., Nawaz, M. A., & Sajid, M. U. (2022). Eco-destination loyalty: Role of perceived value and experience in framing destination attachment and equity with moderating role of destination memory. *Frontiers in Psychology*, 13, 908798. DOI: 10.3389/fpsyg.2022.908798

Morgan, N. J., Pritchard, A., & Piggot, R. (2003). Destination branding and the role of the stakeholders: The case of New Zealand. *Journal of Vacation Marketing*, 9(3), 285–289. DOI: 10.1177/135676670300900307

Nawaz, M. A., Anwar, A., Rongting, Z., & Nawaz, A. (2019). Factors influencing willingness to consume GMF in Chinese population: the moderating role of "Information Literacy" Immersive Media (IM): challenges and opportunities View project Strategic overview of belt and road initiative View project. *Article in Journal of Animal and Plant Sciences, 29*(4), 1088–1099. https://www.researchgate.net/publication/336825092

Nawaz, M. A., Asif, M., Asmi, F., & Nawaz, A. (2019).. . *WILLINGESS TO CONSUME GENETICALLY MODIFIED FOOD IN CHINESE PERSPECTIVE.*, 56(4), 799–808.

Nawaz, M. A., Shah, Z., Nawaz, A., Asmi, F., Hassan, Z., & Raza, J. (2018). Overload and exhaustion: Classifying SNS discontinuance intentions. *Cogent Psychology*, 5(1), 1515584. DOI: 10.1080/23311908.2018.1515584

Novelli, M., & Benson, A. (2004). *Niche Tourism. A Way forward to Sustainability?* Routledge.

Patton, Q. (2002). *Qualitative research and evaluation methods*. Sage Publications.

Porter, M. (1990). *The competitive Advantage of Nations*. The Maxmillan Press. DOI: 10.1007/978-1-349-11336-1

Rashid, R. M., Rashid, Q. U. A., Nawaz, M. A., & Akhtar, S. (2019). Young Chinese consumers' brand perception; the role of mianzi as moderator. *Journal of Public Affairs*, 19(4), e1930. DOI: 10.1002/pa.1930

Ritchie, J. R. B., & Zins, M. (1978). Culture as determinant of the attractiveness of a tourism region. *Annals of Tourism Research*, 5(2), 252–267. DOI: 10.1016/0160-7383(78)90223-2

Source: https://www.google.sk/search?q=wine+routes+in+Canada. Wine tasting routes to Canada. (Retrieved: May 10th, 2020).

Source: https://winesurveyor.weebly.com/tour_slovakia.html Wines of Slovakia. (Retrieved: May 12th, 2020).

Vanhove, N. (2005). *The Economics of Tourism Destinations.* Burlington: Elsevier. Corrigliano,M. A., Mottironi, C. (2013). Planning and Management of European Rural Peripheral Territories through Multifunctionality: The Case of Gastronomy Routes. In Costa, C., Panyik, E., & Buhalis, D. (Eds.), *Trends in European Tourism Planning and Organisation*. Channel View Publications.

Vissak, T. (2010). Recommendations for using the case study method in international business research. *The Qualitative Report*, 15(2), 370–388.

Xiao, H., & Smith, S. (2006). The making of tourism research: Insights from a social science journal. *Annals of Tourism Research*, 33(2), 490–507. DOI: 10.1016/j.annals.2006.01.004

Yin, R. K. (2003). *Case study research: Design and methods (3rded.). NewburyPark.* Sage Publications.

Chapter 13
Ecotourism and Sustainable Development in Chania

Panoraia Poulaki
https://orcid.org/0000-0002-2226-1557
University of the Aegean, Greece

Theodoros Rachiotis
https://orcid.org/0000-0002-2372-4883
National and Kapodistrian University of Athens, Greece

Nikolaos Vasilakis
https://orcid.org/0009-0002-3531-0968
Ionian University, Greece

ABSTRACT

This study investigates the potential of ecotourism in fostering sustainable development in Chania, Crete, focusing on environmental conservation, cultural preservation, and economic growth. A mixed-methods approach combines secondary research to establish a global and local theoretical framework with qualitative interviews with key stakeholders in Chania. The study assesses the current state of ecotourism, its impact on natural and cultural heritage, and barriers to sustainable tourism. Findings highlight ecotourism's role in raising environmental awareness and supporting local economies. However, challenges such as infrastructure, stakeholder cooperation, and ecological management persist. The study concludes that strategic planning and stakeholder collaboration are essential for ecotourism's success, balancing growth with resource preservation. Theoretical implications suggest ecotourism as a sustainable tourism model, while practical recommendations call for targeted

DOI: 10.4018/979-8-3693-6700-1.ch013

policies, employee training, and marketing strategies to position Chania as a top ecotourism destination.

1. INTRODUCTION

The local, regional, and national stakeholders have expressed concerns for many years about the interaction between travel and the environment. The global expansion of tourism has highlighted its impact on natural and cultural resources, necessitating coordinated policy responses, particularly within the European Union (Svoronou, 2003). Though it helps the local economy, tourism might severely tax ecosystems, infrastructure, and local businesses. Usually, this strain results in the loss or damage of natural and cultural assets (Tsitsoni, 2015). The flood of tourists in protected regions creates special difficulties that must be balanced with sustainable resource management against financial gains.

Ecotourism, as articulated by the International Ecotourism Society, is "responsible travel to natural areas that conserves the environment, supports the welfare of local communities, and incorporates interpretation and education." In contrast to mass tourism, ecotourism emphasizes the reduction of adverse effects while fostering biodiversity protection and advocating respect for indigenous cultures. It is seen as an alternative tourist model that favorably impacts environmental protection and local economic development (Tsartas, 2002). The development of ecotourism is facilitated by the diverse natural environment of Greece, which encompasses alpine regions, wetlands, and coastal areas. Many sites, especially those under protection by the Natura 2000 network, provide habitat for threatened species and the basis for visitor activities stressing cultural connection, hiking, and animal viewing. Previous studies have highlighted the environmental and financial possibilities of ecotourism in Greece; however, little is known about how it specifically affects local development, especially in areas like Chania, Crete.

This chapter seeks to fill this gap by analyzing the evolution of ecotourism in the Chania prefecture and its contribution to fostering sustainable local and regional development. Although several studies have examined the environmental dimensions of ecotourism, fewer have investigated its direct impact on local economies and populations, particularly in areas with fragile ecosystems. This chapter is important for its comprehensive analysis of how effectively executed ecotourism can serve as a driving force for sustainable development, safeguarding natural resources while fostering cultural preservation and economic advancement. This chapter enhances the existing research on sustainable tourism by examining Chania and elucidating the precise techniques required to reconcile environmental conservation with economic advancement. It enhances current ecotourism frameworks by providing novel insights on how places with distinctive natural and cultural resources might use ecotourism for sustainable development. Moreover, the results would be pertinent for policymakers, tourist stakeholders, and local communities aiming to establish or enhance ecotourism programs.

2. LITERATURE REVIEW

2.1 Ecotourism and Sustainable Development

Ecotourism is a kind of tourism that is driven by the desire for environmentally friendly experiences. Ecotourism, according to a more stringent definition, entails actively seeking out environmentally friendly experiences while also providing financial assistance for environmental management and education. Alexander von Humboldt is credited as the pioneer of the development of ecotourism (Bramwell, 2004). Ecotourism promotes nature as a primary attraction for tourists, regardless of whether their stay is casual or focused on specific activities like bird watching, rafting, climbing, or kayaking. These activities are carried out in a way that does not harm ecosystems. Ecotourism is primarily focused on the direct enjoyment of nature and the advantages it provides (Fennell, 2001; Mantas & Mylonaki, 2010).

Ecotourism is a viable remedy for revitalising rural and especially inland areas facing deterioration. Moreover, it is essential for maintaining social cohesion and fulfilling the modern tourist's need for involvement, action, and respite from urban life. It fosters a profound connection with environment and the indigenous culture. Ecotourism is an economic framework that functions in accordance with free market principles (Richards, 2018). Establishing quality standards for ecotourism is a multifaceted endeavour influenced by governmental policies and the anticipations of an informed and conscious customer base (Fletcher et al., 2018). Visitors have increasingly shown fatigue with traditional tourism, leading them to seek more authentic engagement with the destination's natural environment and its residents. Moreover, local residents and tourism industry professionals have acknowledged this emerging situation and are actively striving to promote innovative leisure activities that highlight both the enhancement and preservation of the distinctive characteristics of the region's natural environment (Ghete, 2015). Consequently, in the discourse on sustainable development, there is a discernible shift from intensive tourist modalities, such as mass tourism, to alternate alternatives. This kind of development, emphasising long-term environmental and social sustainability, is termed sustainable tourism, agrotourism, green development, or more broadly, ecotourism (Fennell, 2001; Andriotis, 2009; Poulaki et al., 2021).

2.1.1 Challenges of Ecotourism: Cultural Commodification and Economic Disparities

Even with the best of intentions, ecotourism may lead to cultural commodification—the selling and repackaging of local practices and ways of life for the advantage of visitors—often in an unauthentic manner. For example, while the ecotourism companies depending on their territory provide the Maasai people of Kenya little financial benefit, they are often represented in tourist marketing campaigns. This distortion and the lack of any clear advantages from tourism highlight how ecotourism might be utilized to profit from indigenous traditions rather than advance them (Columbia Climate School, 2021). In a similar vein, ecotourism has caused cultural disturbances as well as economic possibilities in Nepal. Research has shown that while the arrival of visitors helps the local economy, it may also change the customs and lives of the locals. Local traditions often get commercialized, resulting in a bare-bones portrayal of the culture to outsiders, which over time may weaken the feeling of identity inside the community (GeoJournal, 2021). By preventing indigenous populations from exerting control over the industry and prospering from it, the issue is further exacerbated by the involvement of foreign tour operators, as opposed to local communities.

In order to address these obstacles, it is imperative to establish a balance between environmental sustainability and cultural preservation. Cambodia and Bhutan are two examples of successful community-based tourism that have increased local influence in tourism operations and preserved local cultures. Within these models, local communities participate in decision-making processes, which promote sustainable economic development and protect cultural heritage (Environment, Development, and Sustainability, 2021).

Table 1. Household participation in ecotourism activities in Bousra, Cambodia

Ecotourism Participation	Number of Households (%)
Primary Income Source	30%
Secondary Income Source	57%
Non-Involvement	13%

(Kim et al., 2019)

2.1.2 Environmental and Socioeconomic Impacts

Regarding the environment, the observed impacts are as follows. a) The creation of big hotel complexes/resorts in response to strong demand leads to the modification of the natural features of the region. b) The overabundance of advertising for a place draws an exceedingly huge number of tourists, leading to catastrophic outcomes. c) Road construction and the development of unneeded structures have a detrimental impact on the natural environment. d) The presence of too many people in ecotourism places leads to negative consequences such as harm to archaeological sites, noise pollution, degradation of routes, littering, and increased danger of fire, ultimately disrupting the current equilibrium.

Researchers from around the world have looked at the social and economic problems that locals face because of ecotourism. These studies have found that there are similar problems with sharing income, getting people involved in the community, and making sure that tourist projects will last for a long time. The uneven sharing of financial benefits is one of the issues. In many ecotourism sites, particularly Botswana's Kalahari area, most tourism-related money goes to foreign businesses, therefore local residents gain quite little from the sector. A case study done in the Kalahari town of Khawa claims that ecotourism has helped the local economy, although much of the money made by the sector was under control of foreign businesses, thereby offering few financial advantages for the community. This mismatch has led to social disturbance and a deepening of economic disparity (Mbaiwa, 2005).

Ecotourism has given people in Nepal's Ghalegaun region new ways to make money, but most of the time, they don't have the tools or knowledge to fully take part in tourism-related activities. Due to this, international tour operators now dominate the market, with local communities receiving very little of the profits. Long-term sustainability is hampered by the lack of programs aimed at enhancing the capability of the local populace (K.C., 2016). South Africa's Hluhluwe-iMfolozi Park serves as a stark reminder of the socioeconomic problems related to ecotourism. Many locals who live close to the park have not reaped many financial rewards from their participation in tourism. Furthermore, conflicts emerge between conservation efforts and regional livelihoods, such as restrictions on land usage, which exacerbate socioeconomic inequality (Kumwenda, 2019).

Table 2. Community participation in ecotourism decision-making in Lar National Park, Iran

Level of Participation	Number of Participants (%)
Full Participation (Decision-Making)	25%
Partial Participation (Consultation)	45%
No Participation	30%

(Esmaeilzadeh et al., 2022)

2.2 Case Studies of Global Ecotourism Destinations

Ecotourism is becoming more popular worldwide, particularly at a time marked by heightened environmental awareness. Additionally, in this era, there is widespread and economical availability of several unique travel spots. Consequently, numerous countries are actively promoting their natural resources as a primary allure for visitors (Aref & Gill, 2009). Essentially, tourism plays a crucial role in showcasing a nation's natural assets while also accommodating large numbers of tourists. It is crucial to strike a delicate equilibrium between conservation and promotion in these destinations with vulnerable ecosystems. This will ensure the well-being of both the ecosystem and the tourism economy (Ammirato & Felicetti, 2013; Egresi, 2016; Poulaki et al., 2015).

There are several captivating ecotourism locations worldwide. The mention of ecotourism in Austria is noteworthy. German tourists constitute the highest proportion of visitors to Austria, accounting for 63% of all visitors, followed by 27% of visitors from Austria itself. There is a significant trend towards high-quality tourism, namely environmental tourism. A significant proportion of those travelling to and from Austria are driven by the desire to have a nature-oriented vacation in an ecologically pristine setting. The presence of the 'eco-tourism motivation' is apparent, with the primary interest of the ecotourist being the desire to immerse oneself in a distinct environment (Leuthold, 2001). Ecotourism is a crucial component of the Swiss tourism sector. Tourism that is closely connected to nature is highly valued, since tourists have a strong inclination towards pristine environment and uninterrupted scenery (Wood, 1997). Ecotourism comprises 40% of Switzerland's domestic tourism. Nature-oriented visitors tend to spend more than tourists with other preferences. Consumers are prepared to pay a premium of 10% to 20% for products or services that are of superior quality. These individuals are visitors who possess a profound fascination and heightened responsiveness towards the natural world. Ecotourism development also enhances the region's economy and fosters more collaboration and networking outside the region's limited confines.

Italy is seeing growth in ecotourism, with visitors showing a growing awareness of sustainable development, environmental preservation, and social improvement. Most tour companies in Italy include the phrase 'ecotourism' into their packages. The primary drivers of Italian ecotourism are the exploration of many cultures and the preservation of undisturbed natural environments, including their flora and wildlife (Buongiorno & Intini, 2021). The social and cultural dimensions (including other cultures, interactions with local people, and historical knowledge) are equally significant.

Furthermore, the Blue Mountains in South Wales, Australia, are renowned as one of the most prominent ecotourism destinations in mountainous regions. It has been officially recognized as a UNESCO historic site and is a popular destination for ecologists and hikers. The environment is unique and remarkable, showcasing exquisite waterfalls, a somewhat deep valley, and primaeval rainforest terrain. There are several ecotourism activities, with the most renowned ones being (Visit Blue Mountains, 2023). Visitors may explore the national parks and animals of the Blue Mountains on vehicle safaris. The skilled guides have expertise in geology, wildlife, flora, and local culture, so providing tourists with unique information and ensuring an amazing experience.

The globally renowned Amazon Forest, usually referred to as the Amazon, is a popular ecotourism site that attracts a significant influx of people each. This rainforest is situated in Brazil and is renowned for its abundant natural resources. It is sometimes referred to as the "oxygen lung" of the planet due to its contribution of 20% of the world's oxygen. The ecotourism in this area is mostly centered on its abundant and diverse wildlife, including many kinds of animals, plants, reptiles, amphibians, and mammals, as well as its extensive natural resources (Breiling, 2005). The Himalayas, located on the boundary between Nepal and Tibet, is the tallest mountain range in the world and includes the renowned Everest summit. Nepal has long been renowned as a premier ecotourism location, particularly favored by hikers. Enthusiasts of climbing, hiking, and other similar activities are drawn to Nepal to experience and immerse themselves in the majestic presence of the Himalayas (Global Voices, 2024). The extensive Himalayan complex has more than 140 mountain summits above an altitude of 7000 meters, along with several lakes. Nepal provides trekkers and mountaineers of all abilities and expertise with the chance to conquer Everest. There is a diverse range of gorges, woods, jungles, rivers, and other natural features. There are numerous ecotourism activities available, including ascending Mount Everest or other smaller peaks, hiking, mountaineering, exploring various mountains, taking helicopter flights for nature observation, engaging in kayak-rafting in the rivers found in the country's canyons, enjoying elephant rides in Chitwan National Park, and going on jeep safaris in the untamed jungle.

Furthermore, Alaska offers a remote wilderness that is irresistible to nature enthusiasts. It boasts a plethora of cycling routes with breathtaking scenery and an abundance of hiking trails for avid trekkers. Additionally, there are activities available such as rafting and kayaking (INSETE, 2022). Costa Rica is a highly sought-after nature destination, renowned for its abundant flora and fauna. Many ecologists and hikers consider it a natural paradise. It is a popular destination for tourists, drawing in thousands of visitors each year. There are various intriguing aspects that captivate the curiosity of those who come to explore. There are 26 natural parks, 8 biological reserves, 32 protected areas, and 11 forests in the area. There is a wide range of ecotourism activities available in the country that are highly popular among visitors (Tourism Today, 2024). These activities are widely recognized and popular, including wildlife tours, visits to the country's volcanoes, wildlife watching, hiking in the mountains and forests, river rafting, paragliding, and snorkeling.

Kenya is a popular destination for ecotourism in Africa. The country boasts a diverse array of approximately 50 national parks and wildlife sanctuaries, spanning from the renowned Maasai Mara National Park to the lesser-known Kaka Mega Nature Reserve. This country's development of ecotourism is backed by both public and private initiatives that are focused on the preservation of its abundant wildlife. Kenya is known for its unique wildlife, which includes a group of mammals referred to as the "big five" - elephants, rhinos, buffaloes, lions, and leopards (WWF, 2003). The country is home to a diverse range of landscapes, including savannahs, beaches, forests, snow-capped mountains, deserts, coral reefs, and rivers. These natural wonders draw in a significant number of tourists annually. Tourists can partake in a variety of activities during their visit to Kenya. These include thrilling 4x4 safaris on the vast savannahs, perfect for observing the diverse bird and wildlife species. For those seeking water adventures, kayaking and rafting are popular options along the country's eastern coast.

It is worth noting the Med Finohlu Villas eco-resort in Maldives, which comprises of 52 eco-villas situated along the island's coastline. The design of each villa adheres to ecological standards and operates on renewable energies. Water management, biodiversity, waste reduction, and recycling have all been given significant attention. Finohlu Villas offers a wide range of awareness activities, showcasing their strong commitment to ecotourism. There is a wide range of activities available, including diving, cultural events that showcase the local culture, history, and folklore, as well as informative lectures on marine life. The islands' breathtaking natural beauty lures in countless tourists from around the globe (INSETE, 2021). The enchanting allure of its pristine waters, captivating underwater world, picturesque snow-covered beaches, and the exquisite beauty of its tropical trees, including the graceful coconut palms, create a truly mesmerizing experience.

One of the most famous ecotourism destinations in the world is Fraser Island in Australia. Like many famous monuments (Machu Picchu), Fraser Island strictly accommodates a certain number of tourists so that ecotourism activities do not exceed the carrying capacity of the island. It has been designated as an ecotourist paradise and is primarily aimed at high-income travellers. It is under UNESCO protection and all tours/activities on the island are certified by Ecotourism Australia, whose principles are aligned with ecological beliefs. Eco-tours taking place on the island minimize the amount of luggage carried on each tour, strictly minimize and recycle all waste, use reusable food and beverage containers, source food from local suppliers thus enhancing the local economy, use seawater for washing dishes, regularly move their bases thus allowing the surrounding vegetation to regenerate and camping is allowed in designated areas within the National Park The locals of the island in conjunction with the guides try to pass on respect for their history and culture (INSETE, 2022). The main aim is for visitors to get away from everyday life and have unforgettable experiences and to end their tour of the island having gained knowledge and respect for this beautiful place and the people who have lived there. The strategic planning of the island and infrastructure has been done with attention to detail and aims to minimize energy and waste. Undoubtedly, it is considered one of the most ecologically successful examples in the world (UNWTO, 2024).

According to research conducted in Slovenia on community-based ecotourism in Pohorje, ecotourism accounted for 22% of family earnings, with additional income derived from local crafts and agriculture (Grošelj et al., 2016). These figures may show how important ecotourism is to the European rural economy. Traveler Willingness to Pay: In a 2021 poll conducted by the European Union, it was found that 55% of European travellers were prepared to pay more for ecotourism and other sustainable travel experiences. This demonstrates how ecotourism is becoming more and more popular across Europe and how higher-spending visitors may help local economies. Community Involvement: 45% of local communities directly engage in ecotourism operations in European protected regions, like the Slovak Tatra Mountains, by providing eco-friendly lodging options or guide services. By contrast, only 15% of respondents said they didn't engage in any tourism-related activities (Environment, Development, and Sustainability, 2021).

Table 3. Contribution of ecotourism to household income

Country	Contribution of Ecotourism to Household Income	Community Participation in Ecotourism (%)
Slovenia	22%	45%
Slovakia	18%	40%
Spain (Catalonia)	25%	50%

(Grošelj et al., 2016)

2.3 Ecotourism in Greece

Greece has always been a popular destination for tourists due to its abundant cultural, historical, and natural resources, making it a prime location for ecotourism. Recently, there has been a growing trend among travellers, both worldwide and in Greece, to feel tired and uninterested in the conventional kind of tourism. Specifically, the visitor is increasingly becoming more demanding in terms of the services offered. As a result, places that rely on the traditional tourist model of sea, sun, and sandy beaches are seeing a decline in demand. Tourists' increasing desire for revitalized and authentic experiences, free from consumerism and more sophisticated, is playing a crucial role in raising environmental consciousness. In addition, tourism is now experiencing a shift towards increased activity and reduced passivity (Sfakianakis, 2000; Stavrinoudis & Parthenis, 2009). Regarding the instance of Crete, there are several methods to explore the island via unconventional kinds of tourism. Several methods include engaging in ecotourism activities, such as seeing olive mills and traditional villages, participating in adventure tours, and going on nature excursions. Additionally, it should be mentioned that there are several hotels that are organic in nature, with bird sanctuaries and organic farms (Fountoulakis, 2019). Alternative tourism, particularly ecotourism, is well-suited for the region of Chania in Crete.

The correlation between tourism and the environment is a progressively significant matter, not only in connection to the advancement of tourism, but also in terms of safeguarding and endorsing the natural and cultural assets of a particular area. Often, tourism exerts tremendous strain on natural and cultural resources by exploiting them, leading to potential deterioration, substantial modification, or even complete extinction of these resources (Holden, 2008). The significant influx of visitors, particularly in protected regions, may sometimes give rise to substantial issues and hazards for ecosystems, both on a global scale and inside Greece.

The International Union for Conservation of Nature has provided a definition for a protected area: "A designated area on land and/or sea that is dedicated to the preservation and conservation of biological diversity and natural and associated cultural resources. It is managed through legal or other effective methods" (Dudley, 2008;

Holden, 2008). Protected regions include a distinct blend of biological, ecological, and cultural attributes, making them exceptionally distinctive. Additionally, they have significant scientific value since they cater to study requirements. Additionally, they serve as venues for environmental education. Protected areas are subject to legal protection to guarantee appropriate management (Holden, 2008; Fusteri, 2013). The focus is on safeguarding habitats, preserving genetic biodiversity, advancing scientific research, protecting the unique natural and cultural features, promoting education at local and broader levels, fostering sustainable tourism and compatible recreational activities, and managing natural resources in line with sustainability principles.

The Convention on Wetlands of International Importance, signed in 1971 in Ramsar, is an intergovernmental agreement that establishes the framework for international cooperation and national efforts to conserve, protect, and sustainably utilise wetlands as habitats for waterbirds (Fusteri, 2013). Over time, the Convention has expanded its coverage to include all elements of conserving and using wetlands in a sustainable manner. It acknowledges wetlands as distinct and significant ecosystems that play a crucial role in preserving biodiversity and benefiting human communities.

Undoubtedly, the immense worth of protected places is without question. It goes beyond only protecting biodiversity by also providing society with other vital ecosystem services, such as flood protection, tourism, and leisure activities. Presented below are examples of protected places in Greece that adhere to a set of commendable practices. The text mentions many instances of protected areas that showcase ecotourism practices, including the National Marine Park of Zakynthos, the Dadia-Lefkimi-Soufli forest, the Zagori region, and the Samaria National Park.

The National Marine Park of Zakynthos exemplifies a protected area that overlaps with a region of significant tourist growth, characterized by mass tourism. Approximately 70% of the yearly tourists to Zakynthos choose to stay inside this area (Konomos, 1989). The operation of the National Park aims to protect the nesting beaches of the sea turtle caretta caretta, the terrestrial coastal flora and fauna of the habitat and population of the Mediterranean monk seal monachus-monachus, the marine ecosystem, fish stocks and avifauna and especially migratory, while at the same time developing activities related to the sustainable economic development of the area and are harmonized with the protection of nature, landscape as well as cultural heritage.

Also worth mentioning is the Dadia-Lefkimi-Soufli Forest National Park, located in the center of the prefecture of Evros, occupying 428,000 acres, of which 72,900 are a special nature protection zone. The area has been protected since 1980 and has been included in the Natura 2000 network since 2006, since it is one of the most important biotopes at Greek and European level (Dadia National Park, 2022). At the same time, it is one of the most fully managed areas of the country, having a visitor management system and a formulated scientific monitoring plan, being a typical example of a Mediterranean ecosystem.

Dadia National Park is mostly characterized by forest vegetation, consisting primarily of pine forests, broadleaf forests, and mixed woods. Greece's distinctiveness stems from the presence of fully developed pine trees at low elevations. The delicate and appropriate use of natural resources plays a crucial role in preserving the biodiversity of the region, which is home to unique species of flora and wildlife. The center for the reception and information of visitors to Dadia National Park is of great significance, since it yearly welcomes a substantial number of tourists. The tourist presence does not pose any ecological issues or disrupt ecosystem functioning, since most tourists primarily visit the bird of prey observatory. Access to this observatory is carefully regulated by designated hiking routes. The Dadia forest is also linked to other advantages for the area (Dadia National Park, 2022). In addition to the natural advantages, there are also social and economic benefits associated with this location, since it is well recognized as one of Greece's top ecotourism attractions. The example of Dadia is very important and despite the impact that the fire in the summer of 2022 had on the area, residents, competent bodies and citizens from every part of Evros, but also of Greece, constantly organizing actions, send messages of optimism, always trying to highlight and promote the natural beauties of the area through their excellent cooperation.

An interesting example is the mountainous region of Zagori in the northwest of Greece. Nature in the area is of great interest due to the rich alternation of the landscape, being one of the most dynamic mountain tourism destinations in our country. The mountainous landscapes with the wild nature and the rare fauna and flora of the area have contributed to the fact that a large part of Zagori is a protection area and has been included in the National Park of Northern Pindos, the National Parks of Pindos and Vikos-Aoos, in the Natura network, while since 2010 it is also included in the European Geoparks Network. In addition to its exceptional natural beauty, the region has a strong cultural and architectural identity (Kousounis, 2022). By exploring the traditional towns and other landmarks, visitors get the opportunity to engage with the customs and culture of the region. The multitude of unique characteristics of Zagori has led to the attraction of a significant number of tourists each year (Kousounis, 2022; Tzimas, 2023). The stakeholders, including local actors and the local populace, acknowledged the area's advantages and tourist appeal, and played a vital role in developing several unique and alternative types of tourism in the region. Finally, according to the Hellenic Statistical Service, tourist traffic in Zagori seems to be on a very upward trend.

The Samaria National Park, located in the White Mountains of Crete, spans an area of 4,851 hectares and is widely acknowledged as one of our nation's most prominent protected regions. The region has distinctive biotopes and exceptional landscapes, distinguished by significant diversity and very uncommon flora and animals. The park serves as a sanctuary for the Cretan wild goat, a representative species of wild goat in the region. The European Council has bestowed the European certificate of the Council of Europe onto this Park. In 2004, the renewal of this award necessitated the creation of a Management Body and the division of the National Park into several zones. The island of Crete is renowned in Greece and Europe for its significant tourist appeal (Karterakis, 2020).

Furthermore, it should be noted that Lake Kerkini is a man-made reservoir situated in the northwestern region of Serres, about 40 kilometers away from Serres and 100 km away from Thessaloniki. The erection of the dam on the river Strymonas in 1932 had two main objectives: to control flood flows and to store water for summer agriculture. This wetland is classified as one of the ten Greek wetlands that have international importance according to the Ramsar Convention (Naziridis, 2012; Kerkini, 2021). It has considerable biological worth, which has been further boosted by its participation in the Natura 2000 Network. The area's rich biodiversity, including its diverse foliage, riverbank woods, many bird species, vast array of fish, and numerous animal species, represents a continuance of the pre-dam ecosystem (Koutsoumaraki, 1999; Naziridis, 2012). The Lake Kerkini in Greece serves as a seasonal breeding ground or habitat for 65% of all bird species found in the country. The lake has abundant flora due to the diverse array of plant species present (Kerkini, 2021; Tolis, 2010). According to the National Park's website, the region is home to reed plants, wet meadows, floating plants, and submerged vegetation.

Based on present studies, the impact of ecotourism on Greek local communities is the topic of many significant revelations. Ecotourism's earnings: Agrotourism, eco-lodges, and guiding services account for around twenty-three percent of family income in locations such as Prespa National Park in Northern Greece. Particularly in areas where traditional businesses like agriculture are less profitable, this shows the financial benefits ecotourism offers. Based on studies on community-based ecotourism (CBET) in protected areas like Mount Olympus, 35 percent of the local population is directly employed in the tourist business. More inclusive participation of stakeholders is needed as many individuals express concerns about being excluded from the decision-making procedures. Greek Ministry of Tourism polls show that ecotourists usually spend 25–30% more than other visitors. This is mostly due to their inclination for environmentally friendly activities and sustainable housing, which provide more value for the local communities they go to (INSETE, 2022).

Table 4. Income contribution of ecotourism to households in Prespa National Park, Greece

Income Source	Percentage of Total Household Income (%)
Ecotourism (Guiding, Eco-lodges)	23%
Agriculture	45%
Other Employment	32%

(INSETE, 2022)

Table 5. Community participation in ecotourism in Mount Olympus, Greece

Type of Involvement	Percentage of Local Population Involved (%)
Direct Participation (Tourism Services)	35%
Indirect Participation (Supply Chain)	20%
No Involvement	45%

(INSETE, 2022)

Table 6. Ecotourist spending compared to mass tourism in Greece

Tourist Type	Average Spending Per Day (EUR)
Ecotourist	€120
Mass Tourist	€90

(INSETE, 2022)

3. ECOTOURISM AND SUSTAINABLE DEVELOPMENT IN CHANIA, CRETE: LEVERAGING NATURAL AND CULTURAL RESOURCES FOR LONG-TERM GROWTH.

The Chania prefecture has been a highly sought-after tourist destination in recent years due to its favorable weather conditions, well-developed infrastructure, and high-quality services. The combination of these factors has led to a steady rise in tourist demand from the European market, which has had a significant impact in recent years. Factors including as tourism marketing, the economy, and geographical position have greatly contributed to the rise in visitor demand in the prefecture of Chania. The primary catalyst for the growth of tourism in this area is mass tourism, together with the emergence of alternative kinds of tourism, which in turn attracts a different segment of travellers (Visit Greece, 2022). Chania in Crete offers distinctive lodgings that prioritize the environment and ecotourism, impressing visitors with their green mindset. The establishment provides opportunities for individuals to connect with the natural world, dine on locally sourced goods in their restaurants, and engage in other activities within the stunning natural surroundings. The prefecture of Chania has unique characteristics that include an exceptional natural environment, abundant cultural legacy, and a history spanning from ancient times to the current day.

There is a significant desire to promote ecotourism by leveraging the unique natural resources of the region. The main objective is to attract a larger number of high-quality tourists and foster competition to support long-term sustainable development. Chania is a sought-after tourist destination seeking unconventional means of finding solace in a location that has exceptional natural, cultural, historical, and social attributes (Creta News, 2022). The preferred activities for visitors in the context of alternative tourism include leisurely walking, hiking, and exploring accessible coastal, hilly, semi-mountainous, or mountainous areas. These activities are enjoyed for their mild physical exertion, in a pristine natural setting, and with the opportunity to visit nearby attractions. Other popular activities include agrotourism, cultural tourism, and nature tourism. Tourists' engagement with food is notably remarkable. Various artefacts from past eras provide evidence of our predecessors' culinary expertise and cooking practices. It is noteworthy that cooking was mostly conducted outside, and some dishes were produced without the use of water, instead being steamed or grilled over charcoal. Their diet mostly consisted of legumes and vegetables, but they also consumed meat obtained via hunting and fishing (Visit Greece, 2022).

Food is a fundamental component of a place's culture, just as it has been in the past. Consuming food is a fundamental aspect of the tourist encounter, since travellers not only perceive visual and auditory stimuli, but also experience the flavors of local cuisine. Tourists choose places to get a more profound comprehension of the culture and way of life of the inhabitants (Visit Greece, 2022). Indeed, lifestyle encompasses not just food itself, but also the way it is prepared and the surrounding atmosphere in which it is consumed. Chania is renowned for its manufacturing of high-quality indigenous items, which are widely accessible in the tourist market and may be enjoyed as a standalone tourist attraction.

Milia village is in Chania and is an excellent case study of ecotourism and agrotourism. It was an abandoned village until the houses were converted into 13 excellent guesthouses made of stone and wood with a unique stay in Cretan nature without electricity. The houses have a farm that offers guests the opportunity to collect fresh fruits and vegetables and then cook in the kitchen or knead the bread of their choice. There are many activities that visitors enjoy and concern painting, music, yoga, stone constructions, etc. (Travel Crete, 2022). The gastronomic wealth plays a leading role and the participation of visitors in cooking is a pleasure, as is kneading and baking bread in the wood oven. Also, hiking trails in the beautiful Cretan land promise unique explorations.

4. CHALLENGES AND OPPORTUNITIES IN DEVELOPING SUSTAINABLE ECOTOURISM IN CHANIA, CRETE: A STRATEGIC APPROACH.

In recent years, the infrastructure and development framework of Chania prefecture have played a crucial role in promoting industrial activity (Trade and Services Institute, 2017b). In relation to the tourist demand in the prefecture being studied, there is continual monitoring of visitor influx and the specific motivations behind their travels, as well as an examination into the factors driving these trips. It is noteworthy that the recent increase in tourism has led to the emergence of several alternative forms of tourism (Fletcher et al., 2018; Zoumadaki, 2019; ITA, 2008; Kafouros, 2015; Rachiotis & Poulaki, 2024). The Chania prefecture strives to effectively meet the needs of tourists by simultaneously preserving and enhancing its offerings. Promoting alternative types of tourism may improve the quality of the visitor experience and contribute to the sustainable development of the prefecture in question. This can only be accomplished by implementing targeted measures, such as pursuing environmentally advantageous development practices that benefit both the current and future generations, while also ensuring that the development is equitable in terms of both economic and social aspects. Tourism in the prefecture of Chania should align with its cultural, natural, and human attributes to sustain its traditions and cultural legacy.

Nevertheless, collaboration between the public and commercial sectors is important to accomplish tourist growth. The implementation of necessary measures by local authorities to strategies, supervise, and execute interventions aimed at facilitating the development of the tourism sector is a vital undertaking. Ensuring the area's natural aesthetics are maintained while simultaneously improving the living conditions for the local population is an essential measure. Identifying suitable alternative tourist options, such as ecotourism, is an essential step. It is also important to embrace and implement an ecologically conscious corporate philosophy to raise awareness among those involved in the development initiative (UNEP & UNWTO, 2005; Rachiotis & Poulaki, 2024).

In Chania, a range of strategies are being used to promote ecotourism, including initiatives aimed at bolstering the local economy, conserving the environment, and fostering community engagement. Several projects and strategies have been periodically implemented with the aim of promoting the growth of ecotourism in the region, while encountering numerous challenges. The further growth plans of utmost importance are as follows (Koure, Hajjarian & Mosadeghi, 2022; Rachiotis & Poulaki, 2022; Guerrero-Moreno & Oliveira-Junior, 2024).

1. Conservation and safeguarding of natural resources.
2. Cooperation with the local community: Increasing public knowledge and providing education: Education programs targeting both locals and tourists aim to enhance understanding of environmental challenges and inspire active participation in conservation endeavours.
3. Promotion of Sustainable Tourism Practices: Certification and Quality Control: Ecotourism companies ensure the implementation of sustainable practices via the use of certifications and quality standards.

Several successful programs focusing on ecotourism activities have been implemented in the prefecture of Chania. One of the examples is the Samaria Gorge, where the management demonstrates successful preservation and use of tourism. The gorge's stringent regulations and preservation efforts draw several annual tourists, providing them with an opportunity to learn and appreciate Crete's natural legacy. Another initiative is focused on the Therisos region, particularly the hamlet of Therisos, renowned for its historical and natural splendor. Therisos has successfully integrated cultural tourism and ecotourism by implementing initiatives that enrich local cultural events and promote local goods. This combination provides tourists with exceptional and distinctive experiences. The many hiking trails are likewise a significant endeavor. To be more precise, the construction and upkeep of hiking routes in different regions of Chania, like the Selinos area, improve the accessibility to natural landscapes and encourage sustainable tourism. These paths provide tourists the chance to investigate local ecosystems and immerse themselves in the natural environment of Crete (Natura, 2000).

Notably, there have been ecotourism initiatives occurring in the prefecture of Chania in recent years. These activities are accessible to tourists via several websites that coordinate such endeavors. One of the activities available is the expedition of the Cretan mountains, starting from the coast and ascending to the summit. This is an exclusive excursion that occurs in Chania and provides the chance to thoroughly explore a significant portion of the White Mountains of Crete. During this exclusive trip, participants get the chance to engage with the local community and gain insight into the significance of the White Mountains and its towering peaks for hikers, climbers, and visitors. The journey starts at sea level, revealing the extensive regions that will be traversed throughout this expedition. Soon after beginning the journey, the visitor halts at a secluded organic farm to gather fresh produce, then proceeds into a gorge where they pause for photographs and to learn about the historical significance of the White Mountains, particularly during the war era. Additionally, a visit is scheduled at a military resistance museum, where the geological characteristics of Crete are elucidated to showcase the island's natural defence mechanisms. The itinerary included a visit to a restaurant where participants may have genuine Cretan cuisine (Proper Cretan Guide, n.d.).

Another noteworthy ecotourism activity that guests may conveniently access over the internet is the private transport service from Chania to Gramvousa and Balos. This adventure offers visitors the opportunity to see the mediaeval castle located on the island of Gramvousa, as well as the chance to swim in both Gramvousa and Balos. While transferring travellers from Chania to the port of Kissamos, they are provided with comprehensive information on the ship routes and the stunning natural scenery they will encounter on their journey to the island of Gramvousa. A significant ecotourism endeavor involves visiting the pristine villages of Chania to explore the genuine essence of Crete. During this excursion, guests can see the most remote and uninhabited villages of Chania, which are situated near the Apokorona region in Crete. Along the path, there is a designated stop where tourists may indulge in authentic organic yoghurt paired with honey from Crete, providing them with an opportunity to experience local goods. Additionally, it is noteworthy that just before to their arrival at the towns, a visit is paid to what is perhaps the most ancient olive tree on Earth (Proper Cretan Guide, n.d.).

Reference will also be made to another ecotourism activity that takes place in the prefecture of Chania and which has to do with an excursion to the lakes of Crete. Through this excursion visitors are given the opportunity to discover the lakes of Crete which are characterized by incredible flora and fauna, as well as by the Natura2000 environment that floods them. The journey starts from the lake of Agia and then leads to lake Kournas, one of the largest freshwater lakes in Crete. As part of the route, visitors can admire the habitat and taste all the organic fruits of Crete directly from the trees. Next stop is Lake Amari and the dam of Potami, from which there is magnificent nature and wonderful views. The tour guide is also a professional farmer, while this activity gives the opportunity to explore the authentic way of life and contact with the locals, creating in essence a complete ecotourism activity (Proper Cretan Guide, n.d.).

At this point, it is worth mentioning the coastal tourism program through which two tourist packages are proposed, one of which is ecotourism. This package concerns Balos and more specifically, as D. Mountakis, head of business consulting and responsible for the European programs of the Chamber of Chania, pointed out, the main issue of the program is *"reducing the time of stay of these visitors so that more visitors can visit it and does not burden the environment"* (Lyviakis, 2023). It is worth noting, however, that there are clearly significant challenges from these activities. More specifically, these challenges are the following (Guerrero-Moreno & Oliveira-Junior, 2024; Koure et al., 2022; Rachiotis & Poulaki, 2024):

1. Environmental Challenges: The management of tourist flows is critical to avoid overloading and degradation of natural resources. Continued efforts to monitor and control environmental impacts are therefore essential.
2. Social and Economic Challenges: Ensuring the participation and support of the local community remains a challenge, as continuous education and awareness is required. It is also important to preserve cultural identity and strengthen local businesses.
3. Necessity for Infrastructure Improvement: The development and improvement of infrastructure, such as roads and facilities, is necessary to support ecotourism activities. The balance between growth and conservation remains one of the biggest dilemmas (Rachiotis & Poulaki, 2024).

In summary, the development of ecotourism in Chania requires a concerted effort that includes the participation of the local community, the protection of natural resources and the promotion of sustainable tourism practices. The successes and challenges that have been faced in the region provide useful lessons for the future development of ecotourism in similar areas.

5. METHODOLOGY

Using a qualitative method, this research explained the role of ecotourism in Chania, Crete's local development. Throughout the study, judgement sampling was utilized to identify and include relevant interested people. Stakeholders in ecotourism efforts included representatives from travel firms and organizations, either directly or indirectly involved. Selecting people with particular knowledge or experience in ecotourism within the area was decided to be best using judgement sampling. Data were gathered via semi-structured interviews, allowing researchers the flexibility to investigate important ecotourism-related topics. Interviews were done in 2023 which people expressed their opinions on the socioeconomic, environmental, and financial effects of ecotourism in Chania. The interviews included subjects like job prospects, how ecotourism may be combined with local businesses like agriculture, and the difficulties in establishing environmentally friendly travel. Following a component of the data analysis process called theme analysis, the acquired qualitative data were transcribed. This methodology was chosen for its ability to identify themes and patterns in qualitative data. Four primary themes emerged from the interviews: employment, environmental consciousness, infrastructural advancement, and community participation in decision-making. The research meticulously analyzed the potential benefits and drawbacks of ecotourism in Chania. The accuracy of the study was not guaranteed using specialist software. Hand coding helped one to find recurrent patterns and ideas. This method guaranteed that the participants' opinions were faithfully portrayed in the study findings and allowed a better knowledge of their points of view.

5. RESULTS

Table 7. This table summarizes the key findings from the stakeholder interviews, showing the themes and descriptions

Theme	Description
Employment Opportunities	Encouraging the employment of residents in ecotourism sectors by creating new jobs
Connection with Primary Sector	Connecting ecotourism with the primary sector by incorporating various activities
Training for Local Businesses	Information and training for local tourist businesses on reducing environmental costs
Infrastructure for Environmental Awareness	Creating infrastructure for environmental information/ awareness and reducing visual nuisances
Management Plan for Ecotourism	Creation and implementation of a management plan for ecotourism activities
Cultural Identity Connection	Connecting ecotourism packages with the cultural identity of the area
Financial Benefits for Environmental Protection	Promotion of ecotourism with financially rewarding benefits in environmental protection
Walking Tourism and Local Products	Linking ecotourism with walking tourism and promoting local products
Improvement of Ecotourism Experience	Enhancing and improving the overall ecotourism experience
Synergies with Other Tourism Forms	Creating synergies between ecotourism and other mild forms of tourism
Promotion of Sustainable Development	Promoting sustainable tourist development to highlight the identity of the area
Education and Training	Providing ongoing education and training on current trends in the tourism market
Collaboration with Educational Institutions	Collaborating with educational institutions and research on ecotourism-related issues
Coupling of Mass Tourism and Volunteering	Successfully coupling mass tourism services with volunteering and ecotourism activities

continued on following page

Table 7. Continued

Theme	Description
Promotion of Natural, Historical, and Cultural Characteristics	Displaying and promoting the special natural, historical, and cultural aspects of the area
Promotion of Ecotourism Packages	Promoting ecotourism packages to both international and Greek businesses

(Rachiotis & Poulaki, 2024)

Chania in Crete has a unique opportunity for the advancement of ecotourism that fosters environmental conservation and local economic growth, owing to its rich cultural heritage, diverse landscapes, and commitment to sustainability. The island's breathtaking natural environment, characterized by its undulating terrain and pristine shoreline, offers several chances for ecotourism activities, including as agrotourism, hiking excursions, and wildlife observation. Chania has the potential to create reciprocal advantages that improve the quality of the visitor experience and support local producers by incorporating ecotourism with primary sector activities, such as regional agriculture and handicrafts. Additionally, ecotourism in Crete could significantly contribute to the preservation of the island's cultural identity by incorporating regional cultures, art, and traditions into tourist products. Crete can guarantee that ecotourism is both environmentally sustainable and economically beneficial by implementing effective governance, developing infrastructure, and providing ongoing training to local businesses. Chania has the potential to establish itself as a model location for sustainable development by adopting these concepts and collaborating with educational institutions and research institutes. This would allow the island to preserve its natural and cultural assets for future generations, while also offering visitors an authentic and rewarding experience.

7. DISCUSSION

Ecotourism plays a crucial role in the success of small businesses in rural areas that are vulnerable to environmental challenges, such as Chania, Crete. Alongside job creation, it fosters the growth of local economies by backing businesses such as restaurants, craft markets, and sustainable housing. Fletcher et al. (2018) indicate that ecotourism encourages tourists to invest more in locally produced goods, thereby benefiting local businesses, artists, and service providers directly. This holds particular significance in locations such as Chania, where ecotourism serves as a dependable source of income as traditional sectors like farming face decline (Poursanidis, 2015).

Environmental tourism can only last for a long time if it is carefully planned and managed. Too much reliance on tourism could leave locals vulnerable to changes in the number of tourists, which could cause economic unrest and damage to the environment (Komilis, 2007). To make sure that ecotourism, which is based on conservation, can last, economic activities must work with the protection of environmental and cultural resources. Community-based ecotourism projects help the local economy grow and protect the environment by letting people in the area keep an eye on and benefit from tourist activities (Mitchell & Murphy, 1991). This strategy not only protects the environment but also fosters a robust destination brand for locations such as Chania, Crete, where community-oriented tourism emphasizes ecological sustainability and cultural preservation. Consequently, it cultivates a genuine, equitable representation of the region, attracting travellers in pursuit of significant, sustainable travel experiences.

Some beneficial tourist initiatives in Chania, such as the Samaria Gorge management program, have the potential to both safeguard the environment and generate revenue. By restricting visitors and promoting conservation, these initiatives safeguard fragile ecosystems and generate substantial economic advantages for nearby communities (Karterakis, 2020). The tourism industry may also be able to extend its lifespan by incorporating training programs and initiatives into green activities (Rachiotis & Poulaki, 202?). In order to assist local communities, ecotourism should prioritize the preservation of a robust connection with the local economy and culture, the enhancement of infrastructure, and the promotion of long-term natural equilibrium.

Ecotourism has become an important part of the global effort to achieve sustainable development. Costa Rica, Kenya, and the Amazon are great examples of how economic growth and environmental protection can work together. Environmental tourism in Costa Rica has grown at a rate of 8% per year and now adds nearly $2.8 billion to the country's GDP (Honey, 2008). Focusing on protecting wildlife, getting people involved in the community, and giving people rewards paid for by the government are the main things that have made the country successful. Kenya's ecotourism business, on the other hand, makes over $1.2 billion a year by focusing on protecting animals and promoting travel that helps local communities. Nonetheless, issues such as overtourism and animal-human conflict occur, indicating the need for stricter regulations and more environmentally responsible acts (World Travel and Tourism Council, 2020). Uncontrolled tourism in the Amazon region harms the environment while generating $12 million per year for the local economy (Gössling, 1999).

When these patterns are compared to Chania, many potentials and challenges emerge. Chania possesses significant potential due to its rich cultural heritage and abundant natural resources. However, the region faces several obstacles, such as the conflict between ecotourism and conventional mass tourism, the strain caused by excessive visitor numbers, and the inadequacy of infrastructure to support sustainable tourism growth. To address these issues, Chania could benefit from adopting strategies similar to those used in Costa Rica, which emphasizes the preservation of nature in its tourism branding, and Kenya, which has successfully implemented community-based ecotourism projects that empower locals and integrate conservation efforts with economic activities. Additionally, utilizing concrete data—such as statistics on tourist numbers, the environmental impact of tourism activities, and the revenue generated by different forms of tourism—would help provide a clearer understanding of the benefits and drawbacks of ecotourism in Chania. This data-driven approach would support more effective planning and management, enabling Chania to strike a balance between attracting tourists and preserving its natural and cultural resources, thereby enhancing its destination brand as a sustainable and culturally rich ecotourism hub.

Ecotourism is a substantial economic force that contributes to the growth of both developed and impoverished nations. In 2019, the global ecotourism market was estimated to be worth $181.1 billion. This figure is projected to rise to $333.8 billion by 2027, with a 14.3% compound annual growth rate (CAGR) between 2021 and 2027 (Allied Market Research, 2021). Costa Rica is a prime example of a prospering ecotourism destination, with an annual industry revenue of $3.9 billion, or 6.5% of GDP. The nation's model, which draws more than 2.1 million ecotourists annually, is bolstered by robust environmental laws, conservation initiatives, and community involvement (Honey, 2008).Similarly, 39% of Kenya's land is set aside for wildlife conservancies, and the country's tourist industry brings in $1.6 billion a year. Kenya has imposed tourist restrictions to safeguard delicate ecosystems from issues like overtourism and animal-human conflicts (World Travel & Tourism Council, 2020).

In contrast, the ecotourism industry in Chania is still in its infancy, with the majority of travellers congregating in a limited number of popular locations, such as the Samaria Gorge. In 2019, Chania received more than 2 million visitors; however, only a small number of them engaged in ecotourism (Visit Greece, 2020). The local economy, which is heavily reliant on tourism, is at risk due to the threat posed by mass tourism to the vulnerable ecosystems in the area. By integrating knowledge from Kenya's community-based conservation strategies and Costa Rica's biodiversity-focused strategy, Chania's ecotourism framework may be enhanced. The financial benefits of transitioning from mass to ecotourism may be underscored by information regarding the purchasing patterns of visitors to Chania. For instance, the World Tourism Organization (2019) reports that ecotourists spend up to 60% more per day than bulk visitors. It is important to note that sustainable tourism strategies have the potential to stimulate local economies.

8. CONCLUSIONS-FUTURE RECOMMENDATIONS

As concluded in this study, ecotourism is an emerging kind of tourism that has gained significant momentum in recent years. It serves as a crucial catalyst for economic growth in many locations. This thesis examines the case of Chania, Crete, which presents numerous prospects for the advancement of ecotourism initiatives. These activities serve the dual purpose of safeguarding the environment, which is frequently at risk due to excessive tourism, and serving as a novel avenue for economic growth in the region. This is due to the organization of several packages offering alternative activities, which allow visitors to engage with the local community, experience local goods, and explore the historical and natural wonders of the area. This emerging kind of tourism offers the chance for economic growth while simultaneously safeguarding the environment and maintaining the long-term viability of the destination. By incorporating ecotourism into its tourism development initiatives, Chania can harmonize the advantages of heightened tourist activity with the conservation of its cultural and biological legacy, therefore reinforcing its status as a sustainable and appealing ecotourism destination.

In the future, several significant recommendations may be made to ensure that ecotourism in Chania continues to grow and flourish while protecting the city's natural and cultural heritage. Developing a comprehensive plan for sustainability management that considers the needs of the surrounding community and the environment comes first. This strategy should include ongoing observation of the effects of tourism on the surroundings to make sure that the activities of visitors do not beyond the capability of Chania's delicate ecosystems. Protected places, including those under the Natura 2000 network, which are especially sensitive to too much tourist activity, should get very special care. Second, growth of ecotourism depends mostly on community involvement. Local people should participate actively in tourism-related decision-making, and more work should be done to educate visitors as well as inhabitants on the need of sustainability. Workshops, alliances with nearby universities, and the inclusion of instructional programs in travel packages—where guests may learn about local cultures, traditions, and the need of environmental preservation—helps one to do this.

REFERENCES

Allied Market Research. (2021). *Ecotourism market by traveler type, age group, and sales channel: Global opportunity analysis and industry forecast, 2021–2027*. Allied Market Research. https://www.alliedmarketresearch.com/ecotourism-market-A06364

Ammirato, S., & Felicetti, A. (2013). The potential of agritourism in revitalizing rural communities: Some empirical results. In Camarinha-Matos, L. M., & Scherer, R. J. (Eds.), *Collaborative systems for reindustrialization. PRO-VE 2013. IFIP Advances in Information and Communication Technology* (Vol. 408). Springer., DOI: 10.1007/978-3-642-40543-3_52

Andriotis, K. (2009). *Sustainability and alternative tourism*. Stamoulis. (in Greek)

Anup, K. C. (2016). Ecotourism and its role in sustainable development of Nepal. INTECH Open Science, 31-59.

Aref, F., & Gill, S. S. (2009). Rural tourism development through rural cooperatives. *Nature and Science*, 7(10), 68–73.

Bramwell, B. (2004). Mass tourism, diversification and sustainability in southern Europe's coastal regions. In Bramwell, B. (Ed.), *Coastal mass tourism: Diversification and sustainable development in Southern Europe* (pp. 1–31). Channel View Publications., DOI: 10.21832/9781873150702-003

Breiling, M. (2005). Rural tourism: Experiences from Austria, opportunities for Japan. *Japanese Rural and Planning Society, Kinki Meeting, Awaji Landscape Panning and Horticultural Academy, Hokudan-cho, Hyogo.*

Briassoulis, H. (2000). Environmental impacts of tourism: A framework for analysis and evaluation. In Briassoulis, H., & Van der Straaten, J. (Eds.), *Tourism and the environment* (pp. 21–38). Springer., DOI: 10.1007/978-94-015-9584-1_2

Buongiorno, A., & Intini, M. (2021). Sustainable tourism and mobility in natural protected areas: Evidence from Apulia. *Sustainability*, 13(12), 6845. DOI: 10.3390/su13126845

Columbia Climate School. (2021, August 10). How ecotourism can harm indigenous communities. *State of the Planet*. https://news.climate.columbia.edu/2021/08/10/ecotourism-harm-indigenous-communities/

Cretanews. (2022). *Ecotourism in Rethymno and Chania centered on sea turtles*. https://www.cretanews.eu/kriti/oiko-tourismos-se-rethumno-kai-xania-me-epikentro-tis-thalassies-chelones/

Environment, Development, and Sustainability. (2021). Ecotourism development strategies and the importance of local community engagement. *SpringerLink*. https://link.springer.com/journal/10668

Esmaeilzadeh, H., Sadeghi, S. M. M., & Wolf, I. D. (2022). Local community participation in sustainable ecotourism development in protected areas, Iran. *Land (Basel)*, 11(10), 1871. DOI: 10.3390/land11101871

Fennell, D. A. (2001). *Ecotourism*. Ellin.

Fletcher, J., Fyall, A., Gilbert, D., & Wanhill, S. (2018). *Tourism: Principles and practice*. Pearson.

Fountoulakis, V. (2019). Partnership and joint plan for tourism in Chania. *Flashnews*. https://flashnews.gr/post/409030/sympraksh-kai-koino-plano-gia-ton-toyrismo-sta-xania-fwto-binteo

Fusteri, N. (2013). *Sustainable tourism development in protected areas* (No. GRI-2013-10318). Aristotle University of Thessaloniki. (In Greek).

GeoJournal. (2021). Ecotourism and its impact on indigenous people and their local environment. *SpringerLink*. https://link.springer.com/journal/10708

Ghete, A. M. (2015). The importance of youth tourism. *Annals of Faculty of Economics, University of Oradea. Faculty of Economics*, 1(2), 688–694.

Global Voices. (2024). https://el.globalvoices.org

Gossling, S. (2017). *Tourism, information technologies and sustainability: An exploratory view*. Taylor & Francis.

Greece, W. W. F. (2003). https://www.contentarchive.wwf.gr/images/pdfs/ecos.pdf

Greece, W. W. F. Hellenic Ornithological Society & Hellenic Society for Environment and Culture. (2009). *Hellenic Ramsar Wetlands: Protection and management assessment*. Athens. https://www.wwf.gr/images/pdfs/2012Jul_Epistoli_FD_NGOs.pdf

Grošelj, P., Hodges, D., & Stirn, L. Z. (2016). Participatory and multi-criteria analysis for forest (ecosystem) management: A case study of Pohorje Slovenia. *Forest Policy and Economics*, 71, 80–86. DOI: 10.1016/j.forpol.2015.05.006

Guerrero-Moreno, M. A., & Oliveira-Junior, J. M. B. (2024). Approaches, trends and gaps in community-based ecotourism research: A bibliometric analysis of publications between 2002 and 2022. *Sustainability (Basel)*, 16(1), 1–21. DOI: 10.3390/su16072639

Helmer, W., & Scholte, P. (1985). *Herpetological research in Evros, Greece: Proposal for a biogenetic reserve*. Research Institute for Nature Management and Catholic University.

Holden, A. (2008). *Environment and tourism*. Routledge.

Honey, M. (2008). *Ecotourism and sustainable development: Who owns paradise?* Island Press.

INSETE. (2021). *Destination Zakynthos*. https://insete.gr/wp-content/uploads/pdf/proorismoi/proorismos-zakunthos.pdf

INSETE. (2022). The average expenditure per journey of inbound tourists in Greece and Spain in 2019, 2021, and 2022. *INSETE*. https://insete.gr/studies/the-average-expenditure-per-journey-of-inbound-tourists-in-greece-and-spain-in-2019-2021-and-2022-2/?lang=en

INSETE. (2022). *Executive Summary 2030*. https://insete.gr/wp-content/uploads/2021/12/Executive-Summary_2030.pdf

INSETE. (2022). *Products and markets analysis*. https://insete.gr/wp-content/uploads/2021/12/21-12_Proionta-Agores.pdf

Institute of Trade and Services. (2017). *Mapping and analysis of business activity in Chania, Crete*. INEMY.

Kafouros, V. (2015). *Proposals for the development of cultural tourism in Greece*. KEPE.

Karterakis, N. (2020). *National Parks and their role in cultivating environmental awareness: The case of the Samaria Gorge* (In Greek).

KC, A., Rijal, K., & Sapkota, R. P. (2015). Role of ecotourism in environmental conservation and socioeconomic development in Annapurna conservation area, Nepal. *International Journal of Sustainable Development and World Ecology*, 22(3), 251–258.

Kim, M., Xie, Y., & Cirella, G. T. (2019). Sustainable transformative economy: Community-based ecotourism in Cambodia. *Sustainability (Basel)*, 11(18), 4977. DOI: 10.3390/su11184977

Komilis, P. (2007). *Ecotourism: The alternative perspective of sustainable tourism development*. Propombos. (In Greek)

Konomos, D. (1989). *Zakynthos. Five hundred years (1478-1978) Art Odyssey, Volume Five, Issue III. Secular art, Painting-Architecture*. Dinos Konomos. (In Greek)

Koure, F. K., Hajjarian, M., & Mosadeghi, R. (2022). Ecotourism development strategies and the importance of local community engagement. *Environment, Development and Sustainability*, 25(7), 6849–6877. DOI: 10.1007/s10668-022-02338-y

Kousounis, S. (2022). Zagori as a leading destination for alternative and thematic tourism. Approval of the nomination plan for its inscription on the list of World Heritage Sites (In Greek).

Koutsoumaraki, V. (1999). *Conceptual integration of agritourism in the context of sustainable tourism development: The case of the Kerkini lake region* (In Greek).

Kumwenda, B. (2019). Socio-economic impacts of community-based ecotourism in Hluhluwe-iMfolozi Park, South Africa. *African Journal of Hospitality, Tourism and Leisure*, 8(4), 1–15. https://www.ajhtl.com/uploads/7/1/6/3/7163688/article_41_vol_8_4__2019_unizul.pdf

Lake Kerkini National Park. (2021). Kerkini Lake Management Agency. http://kerkini.gr/

Leuthold, M. (2001). *The potentials of ecotourism in Austria*. Institute for Integrative Tourism and Leisure Research.

Livyiakis, G. (2023). Ecotourism is the solution for the protection of Balos. *Haniotika Nea*. https://www.haniotika-nea.gr/lysi-o-oikotoyrismos-gia-tin-prostasia-toy-mpaloy/

Lonn, P., Mizoue, N., Ota, T., Kajisa, T., & Yoshida, S. (2018). Evaluating the contribution of community-based ecotourism (CBET) to household income and livelihood changes: A case study of the Chambok CBET program in Cambodia. *Ecological Economics*, 151, 62–76. DOI: 10.1016/j.ecolecon.2018.04.036

Mantas, K., & Mylonaki, M. (2010). *The development of ecotourism in Crete* (Diploma thesis). TEI of Crete. (In Greek).

Mbaiwa, J. E. (2005). Wildlife resource utilization at Moremi Game Reserve and Khwai community area in the Okavango Delta, Botswana. *Journal of Environmental Management*, 77(2), 144–156. DOI: 10.1016/j.jenvman.2005.03.007 PMID: 16115724

Mbaiwa, J. E. (2015). Ecotourism in Botswana: 30 years later. *Journal of Ecotourism*, 14(2–3), 204–222. DOI: 10.1080/14724049.2015.1071378

Ministry of Environment and Energy. (2014). *National Biodiversity Strategy*. http://www.ypeka.gr/LinkClick.aspx?fileticket=2VfCIB5XfW4%3D&tabit=232&language=el-GR

Mitchell, L. S., & Murphy, P. E. (1991). Geography and tourism. *Annals of Tourism Research*, 22(2), 300–313.

Morand, S., Owers, K., & Borders, F. (2014). Biodiversity and emerging zoonoses. In *Confronting emerging zoonoses* (pp. 27–41). Springer., DOI: 10.1007/978-4-431-55120-1_3

Natura2000. (n.d.). *Guide to ecotourism in areas of the NATURA 2000 Network in Crete*. https://natura2000.crete.gov.gr/fileadmin/printmaterial/pdf_Gia%20Periferia_Ikotouristikos%20GR/04_ODIGOS%20GR%20A5_IKOTOURISTIKOS_Small_WEB.pdf

Naziridis, T. (2012). *Lake Kerkini National Park: Guide for the visitor and researcher*. Kerkini Lake Management Agency. (In Greek)

Paikou, A. (2005). *Investigation of the relationship between tourism and protected areas: Possibility of creating marine-diving parks in clusters of islands of Lesvos* (In Greek).

Poulaki, P., Lagos, D., & Balomenou, C. (2015). Religious tourism in Greece and regional development: The case of Samos Island. In *Proceedings of the 55th ERSA Congress, World Renaissance: Changing Roles for People and Places* (pp. 25-29). Lisbon, Portugal.

Poulaki, P., Stavrakakis, I., Tarazonas, D., Vasilakis, N., & Valeri, M. (2021). Sustainable development and cultural heritage in Greece. In Valeri, M., Scuttari, A., & Pechlaner, H. (Eds.), *Resilience and sustainability: Global dynamics and local actions*. Giappichelli.

Poursanidis, D. (2015). *Highlighting the marine areas of the Natura 2000 network in Crete* (technical guide). Region of Crete, Heraklion. (In Greek).

Rachiotis, T., & Poulaki, P. (2022). The contribution of cultural routes to the enhancement of urban cultural tourism. *Journal of Hospitality and Tourism*, 20(2), 31–46. DOI: 10.5281/zenodo.8322203

Rachiotis, T., & Poulaki, P. (2024). Cultural routes as a factor of sustainable management of cultural reserve and development of cultural tourism. *Sustainable Development, Culture, Traditions, 4*(A), 50-72. https://doi.org/DOI: 10.26341/issn.2241-4002-2024-4a-4-T02072

Rachiotis, T., & Poulaki, P. (2024). Innovating cultural tourism in Greece: The strategic role of tourist guides in heritage promotion. *Journal of Regional Socio-Economic Issues*, 14(2), 14–28.

Rachiotis, T., & Poulaki, P. (2024). Management of cultural routes as the new status quo in urban cultural tourism. In *Cultural tourism in urban areas* (pp. 165–181). Taylor & Francis-Routledge., DOI: 10.4324/9781032633374-14

Rachiotis, T., & Poulaki, P. (2024). Exploring the sustainability and management of overtourism in globally recognized destinations. *Journal of Regional & Socio-Economic Issues*, 14(2), 37–45. https://doi.org/10.26215/heal.3n9m-8v15

Richards, G. (2018). Cultural tourism: A review of recent research and trends. *Journal of Hospitality and Tourism Management*, 36, 12–21. DOI: 10.1016/j.jhtm.2018.03.005

Sfakianakis, M. (2000). *Alternative forms of tourism*. Ellin. (In Greek)

Stavrinoudis, Th., & Parthenis, S. (2009). The role and contribution of local, regional and national institutions and organizations in the development of alternative and special interest tourism. In Sotiriadis, M., & Farsari, I. (Eds.), *Alternative and special forms of tourism: planning, management and marketing*. Interbooks. (In Greek)

Svoronou, E. (2003). *Management methods of ecotourism and tourism in protected areas*. WWF Greece - Ministry of Environment, Spatial Planning and Public Works. (In Greek)

Tolis, K. N., (2010). *Assessment of the development potential of ecotourism in the Kerkini Lake National Park through the investigation of opinions and use of geographic information systems* (No. GRI 2010-5757). Aristotle University of Thessaloniki. (In Greek).

Tourism Today. (2024). https://www.tourismtoday.gr

Travel Crete. (2022). *Milia, a full organic village*. https://www.travel-crete.gr/el/tour/milia-a-full-organic-village

Tsitsoni, Th. (2015). Protected areas as a driver of sustainable development at the local and national level. Proceedings of the *17th Panhellenic Forestry Conference*. Kefalonia 4-8/10. (In Greek).

Tzimas, O. P., (2023). *Rural tourism in Zagori, Epirus and the evaluation of the tourist experience by visitors.* (In Greek).

UNEP & UNWTO. (2005). *Making tourism more sustainable - A guide for policy makers*. https://wedocs.unep.org/bitstream/handle/20.500.11822/8741/-Making%20Tourism%20More%20Sustainable_%20A%20Guide%20for%20Policy%20Makers-2005445.pdf?sequence=3&isAllowed=

UNEP-WCMC. (2017). *Protected Area Profile for Greece from the World Database of Protected Areas.* Available at: www.protectedplanet.net

UNWTO (United Nations World Tourism Organization). (2024). *Sustainable tourism for development: Statistical framework for measuring tourism sustainability*. UNWTO. https://www.unwto.org

Visit Blue Mountains. (2023). *Sustainable travel*. https://www.visitbluemountains.com.au/plan/sustainable-travel

Visit Greece. (2023). *Ecotourism*. https://www.visitgreece.gr/el/inspirations/ecotourism/

Wood, P. M. (1997). Biodiversity as the source of biological resources: A new look at biodiversity values. *Environmental Values*, 6(3), 251–268. DOI: 10.3197/096327197776679077

World Travel & Tourism Council. (2020). *Economic impact reports*.

Zakynthos National Marine Park. (2019). *Information report*. Zakynthos National Marine Park Management Stakeholder. (In Greek)

Zoumadaki, E. (2019). Chania: Tourism research: Airbnb, Elafonisi and... Monasteries in the first choices. https://flashnews.gr/post/383746/xania-ereyna-gia-ton-toyrismo-airbnb-elafonhsikai-monasthria-stis-prwtes-epiloges

Chapter 14
Fostering Ecotourism Brands Through Local Engagement in Peru and the Maldives

Gulen Hashmi
https://orcid.org/0000-0001-6949-6647
Glasgow Caledonian University, UK

Julie Roberts
https://orcid.org/0000-0001-6652-6994
Glasgow Caledonian University, UK

ABSTRACT

As a subset of sustainable tourism, ecotourism has increased in protected tourism sites and biodiversity hotspots as increasingly more tourists look for meaningful natural experiences. This necessitates understanding how to leverage tourist-local community engagement in ecotourism branding. The chapter focuses on two case studies from two contexts, which harness tourist-local community engagement in their ecotourism branding. While the first case study relates to the conservation of nature and cultural heritage within an Amazonian rainforest in Peru, the latter refers to preserving the ecosystems of the ocean in the Maldives. Although both cases leverage tourist-local community engagement to a certain extent, they heavily focus on uplifting local communities, guest education and scientific research in their ecotourism branding. The study lacks empirical evidence, yet it has managerial and policy implications. It advises managers and policymakers to foster a sustainable ecotourism brand with the tourist-local community interaction in mind.

DOI: 10.4018/979-8-3693-6700-1.ch014

INTRODUCTION

One emerging trend in the post-Covid-19 pandemic has been the growing interest in nature-based, open-air recreational tourism in sustainable and safe tourism destinations (UNWTO, 2021). Similarly, ecotourism market size having expanded quickly lately, it is further anticipated to grow from USD 219.53 billion in 2023 to USD 249.16 billion in 2024 at an annual growth rate of 13.5% (Ecotourism Global Market Report, 2024). The growth can be traced to the interest in authentic holiday experiences, the rise of responsible travel, government initiatives and polices, conservation of biodiversity and educational components. Ecotourism has been proliferating in protected tourism sites and biodiversity hotspots as increasingly more tourists prefer to have responsible and sustainable travel to natural areas to enjoy natural environments, learn about local cultures and acquire knowledge (Lee et al., 2023). At the same time, the growing demand in ecotourism among travelers of all ages presents branding opportunities and challenges for tourism and travel brands as well as destinations to generate additional revenue streams.

The International Ecotourism Society (TIES) defines ecotourism as '*responsible travel to natural areas that conserves the environment, improves the well-being of local people, and involves interpretation and education*' (TIES, 2015). As Fandeli (1999) in Giriwati et al. (2018) state, ecotourism involves travels and holiday experiences to natural environments mainly for leisure and recreation in addition to environmental preservation. An ecotourism approach encompasses conservation, community and sustainability (Boley & Green, 2016). As such, ecotourism has emerged not only for environmentally-friendly exploration of the natural habitats but also, as a means of enhancing local communities' well-being and educating guests with provision of awareness and sustainable practices.

With the increasing popularity of ecotourism, it has become imperative to businesses and destinations to create and maintain a stronger brand identity. Tajer & Demir (2022) highlight that where there is destination identity, there is tourism potential with both cultural and natural values. The location, historical and economic structure, as well as social and cultural structure of a place constitute important branding criteria, according to Demirkol & Taskiran (2019). Thus, development of ecotourism strategies in light of these criteria would enhance the image of destinations giving them a brand identity in ecotourism marketing efforts.

Peru and the Maldives have an important ecotourism potential with their unique habitats, protected areas, biosphere reserves and climatic features. However, both destinations' share in the global ecotourism market has started growing only recently. In Peru, for instance, ecotourism is reasonably well progressing. There is a clear need to highlight government policies considering that the country has fragile ecosystems, and the influence of environmental NGOs requires attention (Legrand et al., 2012). Remote areas of the country where there was poor tourism infrastructure have been developing recently; however, engagement of locals for efficient use of the Amazon River was found to be a win-win situation for the Amazon communities, the businesses and the government (McCarthy et al., 2013).

In the case of the Maldives, as part of the commitment to a Roadmap on Ecotourism pledge, the country's Ministry of Tourism launched the Ecotourism Framework and Roadmap in early 2024. This roadmap was developed in collaboration with the Climate Adaptation Project group under the Ministry of Climate Change, Environment and Energy as well as USAID. The pledge included protecting at least one reef, one mangrove and one uninhabited island from each atoll of the island. This visionary project has been crafted to promote responsible tourism initiatives across the archipelago and champion eco-friendly practices. In addition to various nationwide governmental initiatives in both Peru and the Maldives, many of the sustainability efforts are still led by the private sector, which harness business opportunities and win-win solutions in addressing societal challenges.

Branding is key to the success of any ecotourism business in the sense that it helps businesses and destinations in differentiating themselves from others in a crowded marketplace and attracting environmentally and socially conscious travelers. This, however, necessitates commitment to sustainability in terms of aligned mission, vision and core business values. Costa Rica is a good example of a leading destination in ecotourism, which has successfully formed a unique identity. The brand identity of the country centers on a concept named as 'pure life', which implies a symbiotic relationship between nature and humans.

Kotler & Keller (2015) emphasize the complex structure of creating a brand identity for ecotourism brands due to the intangibility it entails. The intangible elements include visitors' experience, their thoughts, beliefs and associations, which get them to visit a destination again (Trung & Khalifa, 2019). King et al. (2012) have identified three core ecotourism pillars to craft a mission-driven brand story, which are experiential learning, sustainable living and community-building. With these ecotourism pillars, they proposed three main ecotourism branding strategies: visitor education, brand awareness, and brand building.

Mai et al. (2020) argue that while the demand side of ecotourism necessitates responsible consumption among travellers, and have received reasonable amount of attention, the supply side concerning local community engagement has received limited focus. Although academic literature on ecotourism branding talks about tourists' involvement and community-led ecotourism as two emerging areas within sustainable tourism (Koure et al., 2022; Adom, 2019;), the interplay of these two has remained under-researched in the branding of ecotourism destinations.There is limited research on fostering tourist-local community engagement in ecotourism branding of rural and remote areas as well as vulnerable archipelagos, as demonstrated by the prevalence of exploratory studies in the literature (Mafi et al., 2020; Chen & Rahman, 2018; Harum et al., 2018). Furthermore, there is lack of case studies in Peru and the Maldives as thriving ecotourism destinations (Rosalina et al., 2021).

Therefore, this study aims at investigating how and to what extent, tourist-local community engagement is harnessed by ecotourism companies in their ecotourism branding. For this purpose, two complementary case studies from two different ecotourism contexts are introduced and analyzed using a case study strategy. Since ecotourism branding is a complex phenomenon, a case study as a research design helps portray different yet complementary contextual factors, shedding light upon potential differences and similarities. The chapter offers inspiration and value not only to tourism practitioners and Destination Management Organizations (DMOs), but also to academicians involved in ecological and marine research as well as other stakeholders such as local communities and visitors.

The chapter is structured to first illustrate the significance of tourist-local community engagement in ecotourism branding. The chapter then moves on to contextualise the case studies highlighting the methodological approach, and shedding light upon the different destination contexts, the challenges addressed, the ecotourism branding aspects deployed and the socio-economic and environmental benefits provided to the ecotourism destination. This is followed by Case Learnings where the findings from the two cases are outlined and learnings are discussed. Finally, the chapter concludes by highlighting the value each case brings to light as well as the recommendations for future studies in sustainable ecotourism branding.

Tourist Local Community Engagement in Ecotourism Branding

Ecotourism entails the management and governance of tourism activities in a way that preserves natural resources, striking a balance between the supply and demand side of tourism. In this regard, it addresses social challenges such as host community empowerment, income generation and capacity building of visitors in addition to employment opportunities it provides

(Samal & Dash, 2023). Ecotourism can be community-based or could entail an adventure component. Community-based ecotourism aims at cultural and economic diversity through engaging host communities in the governance of natural resources (Stone & Duffy, 2015). In other words, empowerment and engagement of host communities in ecotourism activities is the ultimate purpose. Furthermore, wildlife tourism, as a subset of ecotourism, revolves around the exploration of nature including ecological communities as well as animal and plant species

(Timothy & Boyd, 2014). Finally, another type of tourism associated with ecotourism is agritourism, which entails a trip to the villages and farmhouses in a countryside whereby tourists participate in festivals and traditional rural labor with the local residents (Fennell, 2014).

Ecotourism is also considered as a means to reduce environmental degradation such as biodiversity decline. However, in addition to minimizing negative impacts, it also contributes to enhancing the quality of various habitats such as wetlands, deserts, forests and marine habitats (Das & Chatterjee, 2015). It is an important contributor to the sustainable development of natural areas. As such, the local community is considered to have a significant role in ecotourism as they can affect sustainable tourism development to a great extent (Palmer & Chuamuangphan, 2018). In this regard, promoting ecotourism activities is necessary for achieving socio-economic development of a destination and environmental sustainability. Ecotourism is significant in the pursuit of adoption of sustainable practices, allocation of resources for environmental and biodiversity conservation, education of travellers through exchange between locals and tourists, local community empowerment, cultural heritage preservation, provision of alternative livelihoods and cultivation of global consciousness (Kumar et al., 2023).

Ecotourism was found to increase community resilience and boost cultural values (Musavengane & Kloppers, 2020). Since ecotourism sites are nature-based protected areas, it is of great significance to turn visitors into repeat tourists by providing memorable experiences through interactions with the local culture and environment. Sharma & Sarmah (2019) posit that engagement of travelers with host communities contributes to clean ecotourism destinations. Similarly, tourists' search for authentic experiences leads them to interact with local residents to learn about their indigenous heritage, resulting in overall visitors' satisfaction (Sharma & Sarmah, 2019; Rasoolimanesh et al., 2019).

Since the early days of ecotourism were more about awareness raising about environmental preservation, nature-based activities such as hiking and bird watching in remote areas were popular among nature and adventure lovers. However, as ecotourism evolved over the years, it became evident that visitors sought meaningful experiences with a human touch, which included learning about various cultures, traditions and cultural heritage.This shift in visitor interests and attitudes highlighted the importance of community engagement and cultural preservation as important pillars of ecotourism branding (Lee & Jan, 2018). This is noteworthy because as tourists seek authentic experiences for more meaning in their holidays (Guan et al., 2019), tourism businesses work harder to meet this demand by offering local experiences that involve engagement with local communities (Goodwin, 2013). As such, ecotourism branding promotes local community engagement in the preservation of ecosystems and biodiversity, which ultimately leads to economic incentives to the local community.

Although branding of tourist destinations became popular in the late 1990s, it is only in the last couple of decades that it started gaining attention of academia (Me & Buchalis, 2019). According to Mearns (2007), branding is about differentiating a business from its competitors, and it entails internal and external communication of organizational culture to various stakeholders. Branding helps a business to stay ahead of the game in the marketplace, creating business value. In this sense, integrating visitor experience into branding of tourism destinations helps differentiate a business, leading to business success (Berry, 1989). In the context of destination branding, a destination must be distinguished from others by means of various elements that differentiate it, creating a unique brand (Morgan et al., 2007). As such, destination branding may be defined as a process of getting acknowledgement and buy-in of various stakeholders through communication as well as advertising. Brand development centers on the personality of a destination, thus leans on cultural heritage, natural beauty and a unique identity to shape a campaign. This entails crafting a narrative that authentically represents the destination's uniqueness and attractiveness, focusing on brand identity, a connection with guests and visitors, and business goals.

In the context of ecotourism branding, The International Ecotourism Society (TIES) (2015) posits that those planning, implementing and marketing ecotourism need to: '*minimize physical, social, behavioral and psychological impacts; provide positive experiences for both visitors and hosts; build environmental and cultural awareness and respect; provide direct financial benefits for conservation, generate financial benefits for both locals and private sector; deliver memorable interpretative experiences to visitors; recognize the rights and spiritual beliefs of the indigenous people in a community and work in partnership with them to create empowerment; and design, construct and operate low-impact facilities*'. Bulbeck (2012) reduces these aspects to five, and posits that when planning ecotourism activities, the main aspects to consider are: '*the minimization of environmental impacts, the protection of nature, creating a possibility of educational potential, the participation of residents, and the sustainable development of the region*'. These dimensions also relate to ecotourism branding, the focus of which is to create customer experiences and satisfaction about a unique brand identity rather than profit (Zenker & Martin, 2011).

By integrating sustainable practices into their branding efforts, ecotourism businesses can enhance their brand equity. Brand equity is defined as the 'net present value' attributed to a brand (Shankar et al., 2008) as it builds trust, and drives positive change within the tourism industry. In this sense, branding activities of ecotourism businesses, in certain instances, can support a tourism destination's efforts towards sustainable development (Ushakov et al., 2018; Janjua et al., 2022).

This is reflected in the shared value proposition by Porter & Kramer (2011), which rests on the notion that when businesses act as businesses rather than charities, they become the most powerful force for good to offer win-win solutions in addressing today's sustainability challenges.

From the perspective of co-creation and collaboration in ecotourism branding, it is critical to understand tourism stakeholder groups and their influence on branding of ecotourism businesses (Yuliati et al., 2023). It is the critical role of destination stakeholders that determines the success or failure of branding efforts. Unlike product brands, destination brands are subject to more diverse stakeholder groups, and can be consumed for different purposes such as employment, economic development or building a brand identity (Balmer & Greyser, 2006). A tourism provider or a destination can use brand identity for positioning itself or its products. In this sense, the desired image of a destination is connected to its brand identity and lies largely in the control of its stakeholders. Thus, tourist and community engagement centered destination offerings, operations and governance models with a multi-stakeholder approach become important. Gong et al. (2019) assert that tourist-local community engagement is of paramount significance, and that it results in responsible behavior and tourists' appreciation and respect of local culture and heritage, resident safety, and adherence to regional tourism and pollution mitigation policies. Social engagement between local communities and tourists and the infrastructure development of the ecotourism sites eventually leads to sustainable tourism growth (Mai et al., 2020).

This highlights the importance of stakeholder theory, which is regarded as one of the relationship management theories which are essential to understanding ecotourism branding (Fyall, Garrod & Wang, 2012). According to Freeman (2010), a stakeholder is defined as any individual or group who has interest in an organization, and who can influence or be influenced by activities of that organization in question. The theory is relevant to ecotourism branding in order to identify stakeholders including guests and local communities. Stakeholder theory can be used to understand the extent of stakeholder power in the branding of destinations (Marzano and Scott, 2005). In the specific context of destinations, different stakeholder groups consisting of local residents, tourism authorities and local businesses can contribute to Collective brand building. Similarly, relationship-based approach is another concept which is instrumental in ecotourism branding as it emphasizes the importance of mutual benefits and win-win situations for stakeholders in a tourism destination (Ledingham, 2003; Choi & Cai, 2012).

From the Amazon Rainforest to the Maldives

This section introduces the two cases in detail. Both case studies leverage tourist-local community engagement to a different extent due to their unique context, yet they demonstrate complementary practices regarding the way they involve local communities in their ecotourism branding. The first case study presents an ecotourism company that places community engagement at the heart of its community-centered ecotourism business model and harnesses the indigenous community's knowledge as its unique brand identity. The second case study talks about a marine conservation project within a luxury resort hotel leading in sustainability and harnesses community engagement to initiate and lead transformation towards a destination's brand image.

Methodological Approach

The case studies in our study aimed to explore how and to what extent, tourist-local community engagement is leveraged in the ecotourism branding of two different ecotourism contexts from different regions. A case study is essential when there is a need to deeply understand the big picture of a certain case (O'Leary, 2004). Employing a case study strategy facilitated a holistic understanding of the ecotourism destination contexts. Furthermore, it provided useful insights that could be transferred to similar ecotourism contexts (Flyvbjerg, 2006). Finally, this strategy helped to broaden our perspectives through awareness of differences and similarities in the cases, leading us to delve deeper into the phenomenon (Merriam, 1998). According to Yin (2003), when 'why' and 'how' questions are the overarching drivers on a real-life context, then case studies should be the preferred strategy.

These grounds are also utilised within this chapter for understanding the extent of tourist-local community engagement in ecotourism branding. Exploring the main aspects of a case is scientifically fruitful, especially for the planning and execution of ecotourism branding, which is influenced by several factors such as participation of local communities or residents, educational potential of tourism activities, minimization of environmental impacts, protection of nature and the sustainable development of the destination. In our case, the two exploratory case studies are based on secondary data, which was obtained from online databases, from journal portals and online media. A comprehensive review of academic literature including journal articles and consultancy reports mainly published between 2021 and now, was undertaken, aiming to unveil the nature and extent of tourist-local community engagement for sustainable ecotourism branding.

Rainforest Expeditions, Peru

Context

Peru often comes under the list of ecotourism destinations due to its diverse natural resources and various ecological attractions that require preservation. The country's high biodiversity shapes its natural heritage. Wildlife watching and diverse vegetation characterize ecotourism in Peru. Travelers can learn a lot about the country's rich history, heritage and authentic traditions, coupled with relaxation opportunities in eco-lodges. For those interested in ancient sights and tropical forests, Peru has been developing as a new hotspot. The country possesses three different climatic zones, boasting local tropical rainforests where thousands of species live (Legrand, Simons-Kaufmann & Sloan, 2012). Visitors can walk along local natural reserves, visit the desert of Nazca and climb the Andes.

Although Peru has forests, of which seventy percent sit in the Amazon jungle, it suffers from deforestation due to wrong practices in agriculture, heavy extraction and cattle ranching. This poses a threat to its virgin rainforests and economic development that is fueled by income generation through tourism. Thus, Peru faces an ongoing challenge to strike a balance between sustainable tourism development and income generation. As Peru's popularity grows slowly, there are currently more eco-lodges than before, and many rainforest regions are more accessible in terms of infrastructure than previously (MINCETUR, 2020).

Overview of Rainforest Expeditions

Among Peruvian ecotourism businesses, *Rainforest Expeditions* stands out as a leading innovative ecotourism company. Founded in 1989 by a group of conservationists, the mission of *Rainforest Expeditions,* as stated on its corporate website, is: '*to create a harmonious relationship between tourism and nature, fostering a deep respect for the rainforest while supporting local communities*'. Specializing in the ecotourism expeditions with focus on wildlife observation, science and conservation, and authentic cultural immersion, *Rainforest Expeditions* ensures that majority of jobs and benefits in the country stay local. *Rainforest Expeditions* operates on an all-inclusive business model that covers land, river transportation, a wide array of excursions and activities, all meals and accommodation. The company owns and operates three ecolodges, which are named as *Posada Amazonas*, *Refugio Amazonas* and *Tambopata Research Center*, respectively. These ecolodges have been constructed to have minimal imprint on the surrounding fragile environment, featuring locally sourced materials and renewable energy sources.

Recycling efforts include prohibition of single-use plastics, responsible segregation of waste, with biodegradable materials processed in septic tanks. The ecolodges are the first carbon-neutral ones in the Tambopata National Reserve, and this covers daily operations, administrative offices and staff transportation. The company has carbon offsetting initiatives with a partner company that measures its carbon footprint. Furthermore, it collaborates with Nature Services Peru to provide guests with options to offset their travel emissions.

Posada Amazonas ecolodge is a 30-room jungle ecolodge situated in a 9,500-hectare communal reserve in the Tambopata River, which belongs to a community called *Ese Eja Native Community of Infierno*. The region boasts endangered species such as the giant river otter and the Amazonian turtle due to its rich biodiversity. The ecolodge has a business model in which this native community owns the lodge and *Rainforest Expeditions* takes care of its management and branding. Families with small children as well as cultural travelers and adventurers constitute the target market of this ecolodge due to wildlife observation opportunities in addition to ancient indigenous heritage. Guests are offered a large array of highly engaging experiences which include Jungle Night Walks, Giant River Otter Search, Parrot Clay Lick, Amazon Birdwatching, Jungle Mountain Biking, Night Lectures, Jungle Farm Visit, Children's Trail, Rainforest Tattoo and Sunset Cruise.

Refugio Amazonas ecolodge is a 32-room ecolodge situated on a 200-hectare private land consisting of Brazil nut forest, deep in the tropical jungle of the Tambopata National Reserve. It is the headquarters of the Wired Amazon Program thus guests can participate in scientific projects for the conservation of Tambopata when they visit this ecolodge. The ecolodge is ideal for adventure tourists seeking comfort and nature lovers short on time. The ecolodge offers a range of experiences unique to its location, which include Crested Eagle Nest Observation, Overlook Trail, Mammal Clay Lick, Parakeet Clay Lick, Tambopata Aerobotany, Brazil Nut Trail & Camp, Circle of Fire, AmazonCam Tambopata, Ethnobotanical Center of Nape, Canopy Tower and Oxbow Lake.

The *Tambopata Research Center* is an ecolodge with only 28 rooms located in the middle of the rainforest within the Tambopata National Reserve. It is one of the most remote ecolodges in South America, which boasts 300 meters (almost 1000 feet) of elevated walkways suitably located in between the floor and the canopy of the forest. This ecolodge is ideal for photographers and nature lovers due its secluded location. The ecolodge offers guest experiences, some of which are Rainforest Master Hike, Amazon Creek Trail Hike, Island Exploration & Pond, Bamboo Trail, Adventure to the Bowl, The World of Butterflies, Ceiba Walk, Monkey Search, Giants of the Amazon, Palm Swamp Trail, 8 Primates and Colorado Macaw Clay Lick.

Amazonian Conservation / Nature Protection

Rainforest Expeditions facilitates easy data collection for tropical field biologists, contributing to scientific discoveries. Therefore, the company collaborates with a community of citizen scientists for various tasks such as photographing monkeys for their catalog and tracking them via GPS or smartphones, contributing to wildlife research and conservation.

To remind guests of the importance of preservation after their visit and give them a transformative experience in the comfort of their home, Posada Amazonas offers virtual experiences through a pre-recorded video of 10-15 minutes. The video takes the audience through the most famous activities in Tambopata, whereby guests learn about the biodiversity of the Tambopata National Reserve, as well as stay emotionally connected to their Amazon experience for future visits to Posado Amazonas.

The Wired Amazon Program is an initiative by Rainforest Expeditions aimed at merging conservation efforts and scientific biodiversity research with the ecotourism experience in the Tambopata National Reserve and Bahuaja-Sonene National Park. The initiative was launched in 2016 and is actively engaging global citizen scientists to create a deeper connection with the Amazon rainforest. Some of the Wired Amazon Projects are the *AmazonCam* initiative which uses camera traps to monitor wildlife including the majestic jaguar; *8 Primates* which uses innovative bioacoustics monitoring and GPS tracking for the behavioral study and conservation of eight different primate species in the region; and *Aerobotany* which uses drones to monitor the health and phenology of rainforest canopy trees, supporting sustainable harvests and thousands of jobs in Madre de Dios. To maximize research impact and enhance research capabilities regarding the sustainability of conservation initiatives, *Rainforest Expeditions* collaborates with various academic institutions and organizations such as National University of San Marcos, San Diego Zoo Wildlife Alliance and Peruvian National Service of Natural Protected Areas (SERNANP).

Community Engagement

A fundamental aspect of *Rainforest Expeditions*' ethos is supporting local communities. Since its inception, *Rainforest Expeditions* has provided over 30 million Peruvian sols in income; fostered formal employment benefits and trained 200 individuals. In their Posada Amazonas

Lodge, 75% of profits directly benefit the community of Infierno as part of a strategic alliance-based business model. The formation of the community dates to 1974 when the Native Communities Law in Peru was passed, giving certain rights to indigenous Amazon communities. The law enabled communities to determine their territorial boundaries and obtain formal recognition of territorial rights. Claiming recognition as the first native official community in Madre de Dios, the community currently owns both banks of the Tambopata River. Twenty community members work as full-time employees, and annual incomes increase twenty-five percent annually resulting from the sharing of profits among the community members. As for visitors and guests, they experience the Ese Eja's life and provide support with conservation of their indigenous culture and lands.

This innovative win-win ecotourism business model operates in a way that the local community provides forest land, local culture and local ecological knowledge; and *Rainforest Expeditions* provides tourism management experience, marketing know-how and financial capital.

Guest Education & Engagement

Through the *Tambopapa Macaw Project*, which is one of the Wired Amazon projects, tourists and volunteers are engaged in hands-on conservation efforts, helping to protect these iconic birds. Initially focused on macaw ecology and conservation, the project has expanded to study parrots, clay licks and forest protection through tourism. Similarly, through the flagship project *Discovering New Species*, guests can participate in research activities where citizen scientists help discover new species of insects in the Amazon's hidden biodiversity. This contributes to bio-literacy through DNA sample submission to the International Barcode of Life (IBoL) which aims to achieve bio-literacy by instantly identifying living organisms using a DNA barcode library. As part of the *8 Primates project*, participation from individuals of all levels including guests staying at the Tambopata Research Center are encouraged to experience learning from researchers during mealtimes and spending unique moments with them and the monkeys. Through participating in the *AmazonCam Tambopata* initiative, Refugio Amazonas lodge guests can set camera traps during rainforest tours, providing valuable footage through motion-triggered cameras.

Tourist-local community Engagement

In addition to owning the ecolodge territory, the community of Infierno also takes care of daily operations and interactions with guests. Since members of the native community also work as community guides, local community and tourists can easily interact with and learn from each other on various tours and activities. One such tour is called the Ethnobotanical Walk close to the Posada Amazonas lodge. Guests can also visit an *Ethnobotanical Nape Center* where they meet the local community who share their traditions with guests and visitors to the area. Moreover, guests can meet farmers and taste local food at an organic form by taking a *Jungle Farm Visit* where guests can learn farming traditions and agricultural life of the communities in the Amazon.

The Maldives Underwater Initiative (MUI) by Six Senses Laamu, the Maldives

Context

The Maldives is an island nation that stands at an average height of just one meter above sea level. This makes unpredictable weather patterns and increased groundswell a threat to life on the coral atolls as the 2,500 coral reefs constitute a dominant ecosystem across the archipelago consisting of 1200 islands. As the seventh largest reef system in the world and the largest in the Indian Ocean, these atolls contain many coral species, and diverse megafauna. The Maldives is the world's lowest nation and considered as the most vulnerable country to climate change in the world.

In addition to rising sea levels, increases in ocean temperature are also impacting life on this island nation, which is protected from monsoon season swells by a natural barrier of coral reefs. Rise in ocean temperature leads to the symbiotic algae in the coral turn white – a process called bleaching – which in turn poses a threat to the vitality of the entire reef, sixty percent of which has already been bleached. While the very survival of the Maldives depends very much on limiting the impacts of climate change, most of the the nation's five hundred and forty thousand citizens that live on the 200 islands rely on tourism for their main income. In 2019 alone, tourism contributed to 56% of the nation's Gross Domestic Product (GDP), with 1.7 million tourists having visited the Maldivian archipelago (Worldbank, 2021).

Recognizing the importance of environmental protection and sustainability as well as the natural disposition of the country, the Maldives is embarking on a transformative journey towards ecotourism. With tourism and fishing as the two primary industries in the Maldives, the natural environment is significantly important to the Maldivian communities in terms of sustaining their livelihood, employment as well as food and water security. Leading the way in tuna fishing, the country depends on fishing for its primary income. Ecotourism has big business potential for the country's resorts, which have awareness of the unique ecosystems, natural beauty and tranquil atmosphere that attract visitors. Thus, Maldivian resorts, as private businesses, are leading the way in ensuring the development of ecotourism in the Maldives through sustainability initiatives aimed at raising ecotourism awareness, coral conservation and erosion prevention.

Overview of Initiative

One initiative that stands out among others in terms of its contribution to ecotourism branding of the Maldives is the Maldives Underwater Initiative (MUI). Based at Six Senses Laamu on the Olhuveli Island, the initiative aims at marine conservation. Located in a Mission Blue Hope Spot in the southern Laamu Atoll, boasting the Maldives' largest resort-based marine biology teams as well as the Marine Turtle Rescue Center led by veterinarians, the resort leads in the sustainability of the island. The initiative was formed in 2018, as a multi-stakeholder platform among the resort's marine biologists and three NGOs as partners. The marine research MUI undertakes fuels the sustainability and conservation measures at the Six Senses Laamu as it creates awareness and shares up-to-date research on marine resources.

MUI consists of staff from the resort, ten resort marine biologists, sustainability experts, community outreach specialists as well as its three partner NGOs, all of whom work together to contribute to guest education, marine research and community outreach goals. While the community outreach initiatives focus on local capacity-building through trainings and infrastructure to Laamu's residents, guest education includes activities such as junior marine biology program, guided snorkel outings, sunset dolphin cruises, nightly marine conservation presentations, weekly reef and beach clean-ups, local island experience, visiting seagrass meadows and reefs, and sustainability back-of-the-house tours. Some marine research focal topics include biodiversity surveys, megafauna monitoring and seagrass protection. Marine research is further shared with resort's stakeholders such as citizen science volunteers, guests and the community. A consequent outcome of this has been the Maldivian government's declaration of six new marine protection areas in Laamu Atoll.

Ocean Conservation / Nature Protection

On every dive and snorkel, the MUI and Deep Blue Divers (Six Senses Laamu's dive center) teams collect data on any megafauna sighted, which, in 2019 alone, summed up to over 1870 hours of survey time across 2256 surveys. Such information helps identify seasonal and tidal shifts in site preference for the animals in addition to abundance and hotspots which require greater protection, feeding into planning Laamu's protected areas which are managed by the residents. More specifically, the MUI team also collects data on the locations and timings of dolphin encounters by making estimates of pods sizes and compositions of calves and adults, which helps draw a picture of the movements, behavior and population of the dolphins. This, in turn, helps identify important areas for the conservation of whales and dolphins in Laamu.

Community Engagement

MUI also entails community-minded initiatives for the Raa Atoll locals to increase access to clean drinking water and medical care. MUI has an Education and Community Outreach Manager that oversees outreach programs centered on overfishing, overdevelopment and climate change. MUI collaborates with various stakeholders from schools and active local NGOs through quarterly meetings to foster environmental stewardship in young people to enact change. As such, MUI provides training and infrastructure to Laamu's residents so that they can tackle environmental issues better. An example of this community engagement is the *Eku Eku* program which brings together community leaders from all eleven inhibited islands to represent the atoll's 13,000 residents for a plastic-free atoll. The program supports local stakeholders and empowers them to lead sustainability projects in the atoll through the sustainability fund that offers financial support, and through provision of various courses such as grant writing or project management.

Since 2018, MUI has also been organizing a community festival in Laamu Atoll aimed at raising awareness for protection of sea turtles. The community festival has been growing over the years exponentially reaching about 1,500 participants before the Covid-19 outbreak. The festival hosted the country's first sport team medal winners and highlighted the important role of young people in making a difference to local communities. Having a balanced mix of fun and education for its participants, the community festival broadened its scope and adopted a theme called 'Our Ocean – Safe and Protected' for awareness raising.

During the pandemic years, in search of finding new ways of coming together for marine conservation as well as educating local stakeholders, MUI launched a virtual alternative to the festival through a community-driven social media campaign under the name 'Eku Eky Dhas Kerama', which translates to English as 'Learning from each other'. The *LaamafaruFestival2020* campaign, having reached over 38,000 people, over 11,000 views and eighty percent local audience, empowered the Laamu Atoll community to use digital communication for educating and inspiring one another. Furthermore, six local news websites published articles about the campaign and its success, scaling up the potential of Laamu Atoll's branding efforts to other atolls in the Maldives. The Year 2021 saw even better success with thousands of community members in seven different Laamafaru Festivals. This was essential due to the local travel restrictions during the pandemic. The educational activities taught by the resort team were about marine protected areas which included debates, speeches and performances of students, teachers, principles and local fishermen. The kids further participated in various competitions of plastic up-cycling, poster making and sand sculptures as well as engaging in beach clean-ups together with other community members.

Although MUI removes thousands of single-use plastic bottles and plastic bags through reef and beach clean-ups, it further tackles the issue of waste management at its roots, with education programs as well as making single-use plastic alternatives accessible and affordable to the local community. For instance, since 2019, Six Senses Laamu donated a total of 63 reverse osmosis water filters to all inhabited islands and all schools and helped to avoid around 1.6 million single-use plastic water bottles on a yearly basis.

Finally, since 2016, MUI has been running a six-month marine education program with Laamu Atoll's schools, which is called 'Hello Hallu'. The MUI team delivers this condensed education program by visiting all 13 schools in the atoll and facilitates the provision of marine ID books to schools through the Blue Marine Foundation (BLUE). The books help students with identifying and appreciating the marine life they see during their field trips. Furthermore, field trips are organized to coral reefs, seagrass meadows and mangrove forests as the three important habitats in the Maldives, whereby students learn about the interconnectivity of these habitats, inhabitants of each system, the threats they face and the functions they serve. MUI also teaches students snorkeling and enables the purchase of snorkeling equipment for schools in Laamu Atoll.

Guest Education & Engagement

MUI engages guests in educational activities such as immersive marine conservation experiences through a 217 square meter (2,336 square-foot) central exhibition space called the Sea Hub of Environmental Learning in Laamu (SHELL), where guests are invited to explore the vibrant local marine life. In addition to research and conservation activities, the MUI team conducts hands-on guest activities and presentations to contribute to sustainable resource management in Laamu.

Junior Marine Biology Program, with its thirteen different sessions on different skills and specialties, engages 7- to 12-year-old kids with science experiments, snorkeling adventures in the ocean, and teaching them to make their own conservation videos. Furthermore, the complimentary marine biologist-guided snorkels are run daily around the Olhuveli Island for spotting turtles, sharks and rays, and sharing stories about the colorful fish and invertebrate inhabitants of the house reef. Similarly, a guided seagrass snorkel lets guests explore diverse seagrass meadows. To explore reefs that offer different vistas, a snorkel boat tour is run four times a week further into Laamu Atoll in addition to private snorkel boats and private guided snorkels around the island. Through snorkel excursions, guests are educated about what makes up a coral reef, what bleaching is, how the organisms on a reef work together and what research MUI is undertaking to understand these processes. Through these excursions, guests add to their turtle ID database by collecting images of the facial scale patterns of the turtles they spot.

Daily dolphin sunset cruises for guests follow a *Dolphin Watching Code of Conduct* to minimize stress to the dolphins and was the first to be developed in collaboration with International Union for Conservation of Nature (IUCN) for the Maldives tourism industry. By answering questions related to dolphins, dolphin cruises give guests the opportunity to help the MUI team with their research. Furthermore, fun interactive marine life and sustainability presentations are delivered every night in the resort's ice cream parlor, whereby ideas are shared about how guests can help conserve the marine environment after their holiday, with topics such as 'Seagrass: Unsung Hero of the Sea' or 'Reefs in Recovery: Life After Bleaching'.

Tourist Local Community Engagement

MUI also offers guests the opportunity to engage with the local community in weekly reef and island clean-ups as an education on how waste should be managed for a plastic-free atoll. Furthermore, the complimentary sustainability back-of-the-house tour facilitates guests' interaction with the local communities through visits to the Earth Lab, Kukulhu Village chicken farm, onsite tailor, carpentry shop, host village and desalination plant. Finally, a tour of one of the 11 inhabited islands, L. Hithadhoo, gives guests the chance to experience the local culture while visiting the local school, the mosque and the homes of Hithadhoo's residents.

Contextualizing Case Learnings

By partnering with indigenous communities, *Rainforest Expeditions* ensures that their operations directly benefit the Amazon rainforest and its people. Through an innovative community-based ecotourism governance model that integrates the Ese Eja Native Community of Infierno, community members engage with guests in story-telling and showcasing of local traditions. Such tourist-local community interaction empowers the local community to take the lead in clearing any security or maintenance concerns. Finally, since the profits from this business model are shared among the community itself, this acts as a motivator for the community to take more interest and work more. This, in turn, leads to community cohesion and community participation. Promoting 'ownership' is crucial for community-based ecotourism (Stone, 2015), as lack of ownership of local people could result in less community participation (Chirenje, Giliba and Musamba, 2013). However, caution should be exercised regarding the grant of full ownership to community members and keeping them accountable, as this could, in fact, contribute to their vulnerability when something goes wrong (Thornham, 2013a). Also, it could further be rooted in the rationale of a broader '*field of power*' where dominant and managerial elites exert dominance (Skerratt et Steiner, 2013).

Committed to science, *Rainforest Expeditions* showcases how conservation can be made viable by finding a sustainable way in ecotourism. Utilizing the latest technology with active citizen participation and community participation in various Wired Amazon conservation projects such as Discovering New Species, AmazonCam or Tambopata Macaw Project, *Rainforest Expeditions* ensures that conservation efforts are both engaging and effective for the community as well as for guests. Indeed, as Pookhao et al. (2018) posit, Motivation, Opportunity, and Ability (MOA) constitute the pillars of good ecotourism. Similarly, interactive network platforms empower local communities to communicate with tourists, which in turn promotes the healthy growth of tourist-local community relationships (De Noni et al., 2019).

Furthermore, *Rainforest Expeditions* raises global awareness about the significance of Amazonian conservation through educational programs and direct participation of the host community. The company creates awareness about the importance of cultural diversity and promote respect for indigenous people and their rights. This awareness is further reinforced through the virtual videos the company provides to guests for a long-lasting awareness on rainforest conservation in the postvisit stage. In brand equity, awareness is essential and linked to the possibility that visitors remember the brand (Tasci, 2020). The indigenous community culture is further used as a unique brand identity to support tourism activities at the Tambopata National Reserve. This leads to a live community culture and a well-run and sustainable ecotourism business (Utama & Trimurti, 2019; Widari, Antara and Paturusi, 2019).

As for MUI, by tackling the sustainability challenge of ocean conservation and protecting the marine ecosystems within marine protected areas, MUI significantly contributes to sustainability of Maldivian tourism. Harnessing unique wildlife diversity, low tourism and strong local stakeholder relationships, MUI contributes to the branding of Laamu Atoll. MUI achieves this by developing and showcasing a well-managed, protected marine reserve with robust scientific input; harnessing strong community engagement; displaying public-private partnership as a sound management practice; and delivering measurable results under-and above water. Bringing science, marine conservation and education together, MUI serves as a regional role model and best practice in the branding of Maldives as an ecotourism destination. Indeed, businesses can be a force for good in leading social change by simultaneously creating business value and social value out of environmental and societal challenges (Porter and Kramer, 2011).

The marine research MUI has been undertaking over the years drives conservation measures not only at the Six Senses Laamu, but beyond, having led to the Maldivian government declaring protection for six marine areas. This aligns with Widari, Antara and Paturusi (2019)'s assertion that ecotourism attracts government interest to enable infrastructure, provide transportation routes, and establish information systems for visitor safety and security. To avoid negative impacts, collective processes to brand a place revolve around sustainability as the solution, thus as de Bruyn et al (2023) assert, holistic thinking sets the stage for understanding sustainability efforts and creating a collective brand identity in a destination.

The conservation efforts of both companies enable tourist engagement in various ecotourism activities and help them learn more about the local environment so that they can contribute to conservation efforts in collaboration with the local community. This leads to the intention to consume ecotourism products and forms the basis for pro-environmental branding efforts (Wang, 2022; Chi, 2021). Moreover, green and sustainable practices can fuel visitors' intention to revisit a destination (Kim & Thapa, 2017; Yu & Hwang, 2019). However, revisit intentions of tourists also depend on cultural intelligence, as people behave according to their cultural values where they grow in different countries and can adopt different cultural norms more effectively than others (Hofstede & Minkov, 2010). In fact, previous studies show that cultural intelligence has a significant and positive connection to branding of destinations (Frias-Jamilena et al., 2018; Ang et al., (2006).

CONCLUSIONS

In conclusion, sustainable ecotourism branding is rooted in a systems-thinking approach to marketing, which leads destinations to be economically healthy, and tourist experiences to be environmentally conscious and socially considerate. We could argue that for ecotourism to thrive, tourism businesses must be economically viable, natural ecosystems must be preserved, and host communities must be respected with ethical fairness. In the evolving context of tourism today, ecotourism branding is not only about the promotion of destinations but also about educating tourists and travellers on being socially responsible during their holidays and travels. In this respect, it has evolved to encompass community involvement, environmental conservation, responsible business practices and cultural preservation. This entails respecting local traditions, supporting local businesses, and minimizing the use of resources. It further requires facilitating education of tourists and local communities through exchange of learning in recreational, research-related and cultural activities that encourage responsibility for sustainable travel.

In terms of social benefits, our examination of the two case studies leads us to argue that tourist-local community engagement has a role in increasing the effectiveness of ecotourism branding by boosting the adaptive capacity and capabilities of communities such as collaboration, agility and visibility. Facilitating social interactions between tourists and local communities fosters learning, which further leads to the improvement of living standards for local communities, the revitalization of local artisanry and preservation of cultural traditions (Musavengane & Kloppers, 2020). In terms of environmental benefits, both case studies demonstrate that by facilitating responsible practices including preservation of various habitats, energy conservation and waste management in their branding, ecotourism businesses can help safeguard vulnerable natural habitats as well as biodiversity. This would help ecotourism businesses with increased revenues through attraction of environmentally-conscious travellers, who are happy to pay more for sustainable experiences. Furthermore, it would lead to prosperity of local tourism businesses, ultimately resulting in economic uplift through employment opportunities (Mansur et al., 2021). As such, benefits associated with ecotourism branding could be integrated into branding strategies of forward-thinking tourism businesses who strive for simultaneous creation of business value and societal value at large (Porter & Kramer, 2011).

The selected case studies offer a complementary view as to how tourist-local community engagement can aid in incentivising scientific ecosystems research as well as collaborative destination governance models, which are essential for sustainable ecotourism branding. An ecotourism business can promote the overall image of an ecotourism destination by creating a distinctive brand identity that involves the local community, a deep connection with tourists through provision of authentic experiences, and long-term goals such as sustainability. As such, the *Rainforest Expeditions* case study focuses on rainforest conservation by preserving the cultural heritage of the indigenous communities and empowering them to take ownership of the rainforest ecosystem as its guardians. *Rainforest Expeditions* is a good example of a community-led ecotourism model as it is a successful venture between a local community and an ecotourism company, highlighting the role of indigenous communities in contributing to tourists' education and co-creating a brand identity.

As for MUI, the resort-led multi-stakeholder initiative demonstrates how engaging tourists with local communities in educational activities helps preserve the ecosystems of a marine habitat in a fragile archipelago. Although previous literature shows that tourists participate in initiatives of ecotourism resorts mainly for leisure (Mansur et al., 2021), it would be interesting to explore how travellers' personal values enhance host communities' welfare in ecotourism branding efforts. MUI further demonstrates how a tourism business can become a role model and a force for good in shaping tourism policies towards a destination's ecotourism branding. The *MUI* case study focuses on ocean conservation by putting community at the heart of conservation in the Maldives.

The critical analysis of the case studies, although limited to academic articles, books and reports without empirical validation, sets the foundation for future case studies. These two cases were limited to two regions only, thus they may not stand as a representative of branding efforts in ecotourism concerning other regions of the world. Future research could focus on similar cases from other parts of the world to shed light upon differentiating contextual factors.

Furthermore, future studies could consider the branding of other types of tourism to compare and contrast differences and similarities in tourist-local community engagement.This study did not look into the economic aspect of branding, which could further be integrated into prospective studies. Future studies could also specifically address greater understanding of the pros and cons associated with ecotourism branding in different geographical settings where there may be different cultural norms that could affect the level and quality of tourist-local community interactions.

REFERENCES

Adom, D. (2019). The place and voice of local people, culture and traditions: A catalyst for ecotourism development in rural communities in Ghana. *Scientific African*, 6, e00184. DOI: 10.1016/j.sciaf.2019.e00184

Ang, S., Van Dyne, L., & Koh, C. (2006). Personality correlates of the four-factor model of cultural intelligence. *Group & Organization Management*, 31(1), 100–123. DOI: 10.1177/1059601105275267

Balmer, J., & Greyser, S. (2006). Corporate marketing: Integrating corporate identity, corporate branding, corporate communication, corporate image and corporate reputation. *European Journal of Marketing*, 40(7-8), 730–741. DOI: 10.1108/03090560610669964

Berry, N. C. (1989). Revitalizing brands. *Journal of Consumer Marketing*, 5(3), 15–20. DOI: 10.1108/eb008228

Boley, B. B., & Green, G. T. (2016). Ecotourism and natural resource conservation: The potential for a sustainable symbiotic relationship. *Journal of Ecotourism*, 15(1), 36–50. DOI: 10.1080/14724049.2015.1094080

Bulbeck, C. (2012). *Facing the wild*. Earthscan. DOI: 10.4324/9781849773850

Chen, H., & Rahman, I. (2018). Cultural tourism: An analysis of engagement, cultural contact, memorable tourism experience and destination loyalty. *Tourism Management Perspectives*, 26, 153–163. DOI: 10.1016/j.tmp.2017.10.006

Chi, N. T. K. (2021). Understanding the effects of eco-label, eco-brand, and social media on green consumption intention in ecotourism destinations. *Journal of Cleaner Production*, 321, 128995. DOI: 10.1016/j.jclepro.2021.128995

Chirenje, L. I., Giliba, R. A., & Musamba, E. B. (2013). Local communities' participation in decision-making processes through planning and budgeting in African countries. *Zhongguo Renkou Ziyuan Yu Huanjing*, 11(1), 10–16. DOI: 10.1080/10042857.2013.777198

Choi, S. H., & Cai, L. A. (2012). Destination loyalty and communication – a relationship-based tourist behavioural model. *International Journal of Strategic Communication*, 6(1), 45–58. DOI: 10.1080/1553118X.2011.634868

Das, M., & Chatterjee, B. (2015). Ecotourism: A panacea or a predicament? *Tourism Management Perspectives*, 14, 3–6. DOI: 10.1016/j.tmp.2015.01.002

de Bruyn, C., Said, F. B., Meyer, N., & Soliman, M. (2023). Research in tourism sustainability: A comprehensive bibliometric analysis from 1990 to 2022. *Heliyon*, 2023(9), e18874. DOI: 10.1016/j.heliyon.2023.e18874 PMID: 37636413

De Noni, I., Orsi, L., & Zanderighi, L. (2019). Stereotypical versus experiential destination branding: The case of Milan city. *City. Cultura e Scuola*, 17, 38–45. DOI: 10.1016/j.ccs.2018.10.001

Demirkol, S., & Taskiran, O. (2019). Destination branding process in tourism: A case study of Cittaslow Tarakli. *The Journal of Applied Social Sciences*, 3(2), 56–69.

Ecotourism Global Market Report (2024)._https://www.researchandmarkets.com/report/ecotourism (accessed 18.07.24)

Fennell, D. (2014). *Ecotourism*. Routledge. DOI: 10.4324/9780203382110

Ferguson, M. A. (1984). *Building theory in public relations: Interorganisational relationships*. Association for Education in Journalism and Mass Communication.

Flyvbjerg, B. (2006). Five misunderstandings about case-study research. *Qualitative Inquiry*, 12(2), 219–245. DOI: 10.1177/1077800405284363

Forrest, J. (2012). *Peru – culture smart!* Bravo Limited.

Freeman, R. E. (2010). *Strategic management: A stakeholder approach*. Cambridge University Press. DOI: 10.1017/CBO9781139192675

Frias-Jamilena, D. M., Sabioti-Ortiz, C. M., Martin-Santana, J. D., & Beerli-Palacio, A. (2018). The effect of cultural intelligence on consumer-based destination brand equity. *Annals of Tourism Research*, 72, 22–36. DOI: 10.1016/j.annals.2018.05.009

Fyall, A., Garrod, B., & Wang, Y. (2012). Destination collaboration: A critical review of theoretical approaches to a multi-dimensional phenomenon. *Journal of Destination Marketing & Management*, 1(1-2), 10–26. DOI: 10.1016/j.jdmm.2012.10.002

Gong, J., Detchkhajornjaroensri, P., & Knight, D. W. (2019). Responsible tourism in Bangkok, Thailand: Resident perceptions of Chinese tourist behaviour. *International Journal of Tourism Research*, 21(2), 221–233. DOI: 10.1002/jtr.2256

Goodwin H (2013). Community-based tourism in the developing world: delivering the goods? Progress in Responsible Tourism 3(1): Goodfellow: 31-56 31

Guan, J., Gao, J., & Zhang, C. (2019). Food heritagization and sustainable rural tourism destination: The case of China's yuanjia village. *Sustainability (Basel)*, 11(10), 2858. DOI: 10.3390/su11102858

Hofstede, G. H., & Minkov, M. (2010). *Cultures and organizations: Software of the mind.* McGraw-Hill.

Iqbal, A., Ramachandran, S., Siow, M. I., Subramaniam, T., & Afandi, S. H. M. (2022). Meaningful community participation for effective development of sustainable tourism: Bibliometric analysis towards a quintuple helix model. *Journal of Outdoor Recreation and Tourism*, 39, 100523. DOI: 10.1016/j.jort.2022.100523

Janjua, Z. U. A., Krishnapillai, G., & Rehman, M. (2022). Importance of the sustainability tourism marketing practices: An insight from rural community-based homestays in Malaysia. *Journal of Hospitality and Tourism Insights*, 6(2), 575–594. DOI: 10.1108/JHTI-10-2021-0274

Kim, M. S., Thapa, B., & Kim, H. (2017). International tourists' perceived sustainability of Jeju Island, South Korea. *Sustainability (Basel)*, 10(1), 73. DOI: 10.3390/su10010073

Kotler, P., & Keller, K. L. (2015). Marketing Management. Pearson Education. Available at: https://books.google.com.vn/books?id=PDUOrgEACAAJ

Kumar, R., Jebarajakirthy, C., Maseeh, H. I., Dhanda, K., Saha, R., & Dahiya, R. (2023). Two decades of brand hate research: A review and research agenda. *Marketing Intelligence & Planning*, 41(6), 763–789. DOI: 10.1108/MIP-01-2023-0030

Ledingham, J. A. (2003). Explicating relationship management as a general theory of public relations. *Journal of Public Relations Research*, 15(2), 1136–1146. DOI: 10.1207/S1532754XJPRR1502_4

Lee, S., Lee, N., Lee, T. J., & Hyun, S. S. (2023). The influence of social support from intermediary organizations on innovativeness and subjective happiness in community-based tourism. *Journal of Sustainable Tourism*, •••, 1–23. DOI: 10.1080/09669582.2023.2175836

Lee, T. H., & Jan, F. H. (2018). Development and validation of the ecotourism behaviour scale. *International Journal of Tourism Research*, 20(2), 191–203. DOI: 10.1002/jtr.2172

Legrand, W., Simons-Kaufmann, C., & Sloan, P. (2012). *Sustainable hospitality and tourism as motors for development.* Routledge. DOI: 10.4324/9780123851970

Mafi, M., Pratt, S., & Trupp, A. (2020). Determining ecotourism satisfaction attributes – a case study of an ecolodge in Fiji. *Journal of Ecotourism*, 19(4), 304–326. DOI: 10.1080/14724049.2019.1698585

Mai, A., Thi, K., Thi, T., & Le, T. (2020). Factors influencing on tourism sustainable development in Vietnam. *Management Science Letters*, 10(8), 1737–1742. DOI: 10.5267/j.msl.2020.1.006

Mansur, M., Brearley, F. Q., Esseen, P. J., Rode-Margono, E. J., & Tarigan, M. R. M. (2021). Ecology of Nepenthes clipeata on Gunung Kelam, Indonesian Borneo. *Plant Ecology & Diversity*, 14(3-4), 195–203. DOI: 10.1080/17550874.2021.1984602

Marzano, G., & Scott, N. (2005). Stakeholder power in destination branding: a methodological discussion. *Proceedings of the Destination Branding and Marketing for Regional Tourism Development Conference*, Macao, S.A.R. China 8-9 December, 203-212.

McCarthy, C., Miranda, C., Raub, K., Sainsbury, B., & Waterson, L. (2013). *Lonely planet Peru*. Lonely Planet.

McCarthy, C., Miranda, C., Raub, K., Sainsbury, B., & Waterson, L. (2013). *Lonely planet Peru*. Lonely Planet.

Me, K., & Buchalis, D. (2019). Cross-border tourism destination marketing: Prerequisites and critical success factors. *Journal of Destination Marketing & Management*, 14, 1–9.

Mearns, W. C. (2007). *The importance of being branded*. University of Auckland Business Review.

Merriam, S. B. (1998). *Qualitative research and case study applications in education*. Jossey-Bass Publishers.

MINAM. (2019). Apuntes del Bosque No 1: Cobertura y Deforestaci'on en Los Bosques Húmedos Amaz'onicos 2018. Programa Nacional de Conservaci'on de Bosque para la Mitigaci'on del Cambio Clim'atico. https://sinia.minam.gob. pe/ documentos/apuntes-bosque-no-1-cobertura-deforestacion-bosques-humedos\

Ministry of Foreign Trade and Tourism- Mincetur International tourist flow and foreign exchange income from inbound tourism. (2020). http://datosturismo.mincetur .gob.pe/appdatosTurismo/Content1.html July 15th.

Morgan, N., Pritchard, A., & Pride, R. (2007). *Destination branding: creating the unique destination proposition*. Routledge. DOI: 10.4324/9780080477206

Musavengane, R., & Kloppers, R. (2020). Social capital: An investment towards community resiliencein the collaborative natural resources management of community-based tourism schemes. *Tourism Management Perspectives*, 34, 100654. DOI: 10.1016/j.tmp.2020.100654

O'Leary, Z. (2004). *The essential guide to doing research* (1st ed.). Sage.

Palmer, N. J., & Chuamuangphan, N. (2018). Governance and local participation in ecotourism: community-level ecotourism stakeholders in Chiang Rai Province, Thailand. *J. Ecotourism 17* (3), 320-337. Available from Sheffield Hallam University Research Archive (SHURA) at: http://shura.shu.ac.uk/22231/

Pookhao, S. N., Bushell, R., & Hawkins, M. (2018). Community-based ecotourism: Beyond authenticity and the commodification of local people. *Journal of Ecotourism*, 17(3), 252–267. DOI: 10.1080/14724049.2018.1503502

Porter, M. E., & Kramer, M. R. (2011, January). Creating Shared Value: How to reinvent capitalism – and unleash a wave of innovation and growth. *Harvard Business Review*.

Rasoolimanesh, S. M., Md Noor, S., Schuberth, F., & Jaafar, M. (2019). Investigating the effects of tourist engagement on satisfaction and loyalty. *Service Industries Journal*, 39(7-8), 559–574. DOI: 10.1080/02642069.2019.1570152

Rosalina, P. D., Dupre, K., & Wang, Y. (2021). Rural tourism: A systematic literature review on definitions and challenges. *Journal of Hospitality and Tourism Management*, 47, 134–149. DOI: 10.1016/j.jhtm.2021.03.001

Samal, R., & Dash, M. (2023). Ecotourism, biodiversity conservation and livelihoods: Understanding the convergence and divergence. *Int.J Geoherit Parks*, 11(1), 1–20. DOI: 10.1016/j.ijgeop.2022.11.001

Shankar, V., Azar, P., & Fuller, M. (2008). Practice prize paper-BRAN*EQT: A multicategory brand equity model and its application at Allstate. *Marketing Science*, 27(4), 567–584. DOI: 10.1287/mksc.1070.0320

Sharma, N., & Sarmah, B. (2019). Consumer engagement in village ecotourism: A case of the cleanest village in asia-mawlynnong. *Journal of Global Scholars of Marketing Science*, 29(2), 248–265. DOI: 10.1080/21639159.2019.1577692

Sierra Praeli, Y. (2021). Peru alcanza cifra de deforestacion mas alta en los ultimos 20 anos._https://es.mongabay.com/2021/10/peru-aumenta-deforestacion-cifras-bosques/ (accessed 24.06.2024).

Skerratt, S., & Steiner, A. (2013). Working with communities-of-place: Complexities of empowerment. *Local Economy*, 28(3), 320–338. Advance online publication. DOI: 10.1177/0269094212474241

Stake, R. (1995). *The art of case study research. Thousand Oaks, London*. Sage Publications Ltd.

Stone, G. A., & Duffy, L. N. (2015). Transformative learning theory: A systematic review of travel and tourism scholarship. *Journal of Teaching in Travel & Tourism*, 15(3), 204–224. DOI: 10.1080/15313220.2015.1059305

Tajer, E., & Demir, S. (2022). Ecotourism strategy of UNESCO city in Iran: Applying a new quantitative method integrated with BMW. *Journal of Cleaner Production*, 376, 134284. DOI: 10.1016/j.jclepro.2022.134284

Tasci, A. D. (2020). Exploring the analytics for linking consumer-based brand equity (CBBE) and financial-based brand equity (FBBE) of destination or place brands. *Place Branding and Public Diplomacy*, 16(1), 36–59. DOI: 10.1057/s41254-019-00125-7

The International Ecotourism Society (TIES). (2015). What is ecotourism? https://www.ecotourism.org/what-is-ecotourism. (accessed 21.07.24).

Thornham, H. (2013a). Digital welfare only deepens the class divide. *The Conversation* 13-15. July.

Timothy, D., & Boyd, S. (2014). *Tourism and trails*. Channel View Publications. DOI: 10.21832/9781845414795

Trung, N. V. H., & Khalifa, G. S. A. (2019). Impact of destination image factors on revisit intentions of hotel's international tourists in Ba Ria-Vung Tau. [IJRTBT]. *International Journal on Recent Trends in Business and Tourism*, 3(2), 106–115.

Unesco World heritage sites in Peru. Paris, France. (2020). Available at: https://whc.unesco.org/en/statesparties/pe (accessed 24.06.2024).

UNWTO Impact assessment of the COVID-19 outbreak on international tourism. (2021). https://www.unwto.org/impact-assessment-of-the-Covid-19-outbreak-on-international-tourism July 17th.

Ushakov, D., Ermilova, M., & Andreeva, E. (2018). Destination branding as a tool for sustainable tourism development (the case of Bangkok, Thailand). *Advanced Science Letters*, 39(47), 6339–6342. Advance online publication. DOI: 10.1166/asl.2018.13048

Utama, I.G.B.R.; Trimurti, C.P. (2019). The ethical development of agritourism in protected territory Pelega Badung Bali, Indonesia. Jurnal Manajemen dan Kewirausahaan, 21(2): 114-119. DOI: https://doi.org/DOI: 10.9744/jmk.21.2.114-119

Wagner, O., & Peters, M. (2009). Can association methods reveal the effects of internal branding on tourism destination stakeholders. *Journal of Place Management and Development*, 2(1), 52–69. DOI: 10.1108/17538330910942807

Wang, K. Y. (2022). Sustainable tourism development based upon visitors' brand trust: A case of 100 religious attractions. *Sustainability (Basel)*, 14(4), 1977. DOI: 10.3390/su14041977

Widari, D. A. D. S., Antara, M., & Paturusi, S. A. (2019). Management strategy of Jatiluwih tourist attraction as part of world cultural heritage in Tabanan Regency, Bali Province. *International Journal of Social Science Research*, 7(1), 2327–5510. https://www.scilit.net/article/4e5d31f9124ec4c4bae932475f673af0. DOI: 10.5296/ijssr.v7i1.14248

Worldbank (2021). Available at: https://data.worldbank.org/indicator/SP.DYN.LE00.MA.IN?locations=MV (accessed 11.07.24)

Yin, R. (2003). *Case study research: design and methods*. Sage Publications Ltd.

Yu, C., & Hwang, Y. S. (2019). Do the social responsibility efforts of the destination affect the loyalty of tourists? *Sustainability (Basel)*, 11(7), 1998. DOI: 10.3390/su11071998

Yuliati, D., Susilowati, E., & Suliyati, T. (2023). Preservation of the old city of semarang, Central Java, Indonesia, and its development as a cultural tourism asset. *Cogent Social Sciences*, 9(1), 2170740. Advance online publication. DOI: 10.1080/23311886.2023.2170740

Zenker, S., & Martin, N. (2011). Measuring success in place marketing and branding. *Place Branding and Public Diplomacy*, 7(1), 32–41. DOI: 10.1057/pb.2011.5

Chapter 15
Awareness of Ecotourism and the Creation of Ecotouristic Destination Brands in Türkiye

Nil Sonuç
https://orcid.org/0000-0002-7572-9192
İzmir Katip Çelebi University, Turkey

ABSTRACT

This chapter aims to define and understand the current perception of ecotourism by analyzing the academic literature and identifying the perspectives of international and related national organizations. Following a global view of ecotourism, the Türkiye case is dealt with by examining the potential of ecotourism and the evolving phases of the ecotourism development path of Türkiye on the way to the creation of ecotouristic destination brands in this country. Compared to the classical mass tourism of sun-sea-sand, ecotourism has adopted an alternative tourism path, which is carried out to be more considerate of the protection of biodiversity and much more attentive in terms of human-environment interaction. Therefore, as international organizations emphasize, the sustainable management of ecotourism is advised, and ecotouristic destination branding is suggested to be developed for Türkiye.

DOI: 10.4018/979-8-3693-6700-1.ch015

INTRODUCTION: ECOTOURISM MARKET

After the COVID pandemic, the need and the movement for open air recreational and social events that let the people benefit from fresh air and green and blue beauties and treasures of the nature has increased in Türkiye and the World.

The nearly forgotten types of the ecotourism activities such as camping, trekking, festivals have become popular in Türkiye. These types of activities have reminded people of the crucial importance of breathing clean and fresh air in forests and green areas for their well-being with their relaxing and curative effects, and the adorability of natural lanscapes.

Some people sold whatever they had in the cities and they began to move to the rural areas. Some people have preferred more modest ways of living such as turning their old truck or bus into a caravan (TRT Haber 2024, Habertürk 2022, Chip 2020). And some became continuous voyagers travelling from one destination to other earning their livelihood selling little handicrafts they created. Some other turned into a minimalist way of life and preferred luxurious tiny houses or glamping. After the first shock, some of these people decided that they could no more survive with the drawbacks of the minimalist life and returned back to their old comfort areas. Some stayed still in the minimalist life. Investors to ecotourism also increased their income. For example, as pandemic arrived, changing sector to produce caravans, many businesses increased their income and even exported their products (Ekonomist, 2022).

These trends and tendencies moving ecotourism towards a higher popularity has affected all the stakeholders of tourism from governments to the investors, and from private tourism businesses to the voyagers. After the COVID pandemic, not a new but a recently disregarded horizon of tourism has revived thanks to the increasing demand for its well-being benefits. The ecotourism provides many well-being effects on people. That is why it is preferred by majority of community in Türkiye and the World.

Ecotourism represents the responsible tourism taking into account the environmental protection of natural areas and the well-being of residents according to the TIES[1] (TIES, 2015). Green and blue labeling systems are used for the branding of ecotouristic destinations. In addition, to discriminate and make it more clear, the ecotourism contains the strictest of the environmentally sustainable tourism praxis (Sonuç, 2020). However, one of the current problems of ecotourism management is its sustainability. Researches that try to develop more sustainable models of ecotourism management exist; for example, suggesting models or planification of ecotourism management comprising a flow of communication among all stakeholders and balancing the needs of ecosystem, people and economy (Saxena et al. 2024, Ashok et al. 2022, Aydın & Öztürk 2023, Du et al. 2024, Jayasekara et al. 2024).

The empowerment of women entrepereneurs in creation of ecotouristic products is another issue mentioned as well in researches (Karatas-Ozkan et al., 2024). On the other hand, the demand-side studies are made to determine the needs and motivations of the different type of ecotourists and to illuminate and increase their mindfulness levels about the preservation of nature during visitation (Li et al. 2024, Aktan et al. 2024, Thong et al. 2024).

In the first quarter of 2024, the levels of international tourism reached 97% of pre-pandemic levels. Europe welcomed 1% and Africa 5% more arrivals than pre-pandemic while Middle East exceeded by 36% pre-pandemic levels as the world's strongest growth area. Tourism GDP amounts to 3% of global GDP with an estimated USD 3.3 trillion. Türkiye is at top 5 countries according to UNWTO statistics in terms of tourist arrivals with 55.2 millions -which is 8% more than pre-pandemic levels of 2019-, in addition, at 7th rank with the tourism receipts of USD 49,5 billions in 2023 -that is meaning 44% more than pre-pandemic 2019 levels- (World Tourism Barometer, 2024). Despite the great earthquake called as the disaster of century, dated February 6, 2023 that impacted the economy negatively, Türkiye has reached far above the pre-pandemic levels of tourism which is a great success. Even if we can provide the general tourism statistics such as number of visitors and amount of receipts, it is not possible to reach ecotourism market specific statistics of Turkiye.

World ecotourism market size corresponds to USD 172,4 billion in 2022 and estimated to become USD 374, 2 billion in 2028 (STATISTA, 2024). According to another report, USD 219,53 billion in 2023 to USD 249,16 billion in 2024 at a CAGR [2]of 13.5% and will grow 428.97 billion in 2028-at CAGR of 14,5%- (Eco-tourism Global Market Report 2024). According to a compilation of various recent reports, 15% of tourists are estimated as eco-tourists, more than 35% of global travelers choose environmentally-friendly vacations, 45% of travelers are willing to pay 20% more for a sustainable tour operator, 71% have intention to plan more environmentally-friendly travel in the following 12 months and 80% cited reducing the environmental footprint is essential and for the supply side, Asian countries are the leader with a 25% global market share in 2019, and in addition local contribution of ecotourist areas is reported to provide 94% to employment (Lindner, 2024). STATISTA defines ecotourism, green and sustainable tourism as forms that do not give harm on social, economic, environmental aspects to destinations and locals and being responsible and ethical on the current debated issues such as overcrowding, rising greenhouse gas emissions and loss of socio-cultural authentcity. Furthermore, their 2022 market survey results confirm the willingness of travellers for adoption and preference of sustainable ways of travelling (STATISTA, 2024).

For the UNWTO since the year 1980, the celebration of World Tourism Day are acknowledged with a specific theme. The year 2002 was celebrated as World Ecotourism Day in Costa Rica and 2002 was declared by UNWTO as the World

Ecotourism Year and the World Ecotourism Summit was held in 2002, producing the Quebec Declaration on Ecotourism 2002. Additionally, many International Conferences were held by UNWTO and other NGOs for Ecotourism such as 3rd World Ecotourism Conference in 2011 in Cambodia by UNWTO, in 2021 in Tokat-Türkiye by TIES[3], GTSC[4] 2024 Sweden, GTSC 2023 Antalya, and so on.

When searched for the market shape and size of ecotourism an international standardization cannot be seen. According to Reportlinker (2024) where different ecotourism markets from the various regions of the World take place, the Global Ecotourism Market has three basic market segments as "young (aged 18-34), middle ages(35-54) and elderly(55-above) travelers". In Europe ecotourism market this segmentation by age groups varies as "young adults (aged 21-30), middle aged adults (31-50), senior adults (51-above)". Reportlinker (2024) cites the ecotourism product types in Türkiye as "wildlife tourism, adventure t.[5], cultural t., volunteer t." variations and In North America, the ecotourism types are called as "adventure t., wildlife t., cultural t., community t.", in East Asia "nature t., wildlife t., adventure t., cultural t.". In the same report list, Indonesia green tourism market is examined with terms "eco-tourism, sustainable travel, responsible tourism, nature-based tourism" and ecotourism in China is examined under simply three forms "nature t., culture t., adventure t." See Table 1 for a comparative analysis of ecotourism types in various locations of the World.

Table 1. Example forms of ecotourism in diverse parts of the world

<table>
<tr><th>COUNTRY/REGION</th><th colspan="4">TYPE/FORM OF ECOTOURISM</th></tr>
<tr><td>Indonesia (Green Tourism)</td><td>Nature-based t.[6]</td><td>Responsible tourism</td><td>Sustainable travel</td><td>Eco-tourism</td></tr>
<tr><td>North America</td><td>Community t.</td><td rowspan="3">Cultural t.</td><td rowspan="4">Adventure t.</td><td rowspan="3">Wildlife t.</td></tr>
<tr><td>Türkiye</td><td>Volunteer t.</td></tr>
<tr><td>East Asia</td><td rowspan="2">Nature t.</td></tr>
<tr><td>China</td><td>Culture t.</td><td></td></tr>
</table>

Compiled by Author according to information provided by Reportlinker (2024).

The reports and statistics of international organizations reflect that, today, the importance given to ecotourism increases worldwide with the volume of it's growth as well as the debated issues it has the ability or potential to hinder such as the loss of biodiversity and the rise in threatened species of flora and fauna and the loss of authenticity of the local cultures and environments, and the pollution of air, water and the problem of keeping the depletable resources.

Türkiye has a very high potential in ecotourism with a wide variety of flora and fauna surviving in its numerous national parks, ecotourism areas and other natural areas. Endemic plants of Türkiye are more than ten thousand species. More than three thousand of them are endemic to Türkiye only. The Anatolia is on the crossroads of Asia, Europe and Africa which means also an important area of stopover for the migratory birds thus ornitology. Needless to count the endemic fauna such as Van Cat, Anatolia Leopard, Caracal Caracal and many others. Ecotourism development areas such as Olive Corridor, Plateau Corridor, Black-Sea Coastal Corridor are planned by Ministry of Culture and Tourism (Tourism Strategy of Turkey-2023, 2007). Ministry of Agriculture and Forestry has also recently opened for visit certain areas as "Ecotourism Areas" for the service of tourism in Türkiye.

Examples of recent academic studies in Türkiye highlight the potential and rising popularity of ecoturism. A research showing the Çıldır Lake and its surrounding area located in the Eastern Türkiye exhibits its potential of ecotourism (Zariç et al, 2024). Another study suggests ecotourism guidance as a newly developed area of specialisation in tour guiding profession (Toksöz, 2024). A study discovers the problems of caravan tourists in Türkiye (Türkay et al., 2024). A research investigates the determination of trekking routes in Trabzon (A city in Black Sea Region of Türkiye) depending on the sustainability of a threatened (CR) endemic plant species (Scilla siberica) according to the IUCN[7] (Bektaş et al., 2024).

On the other hand, attempts to develop this niche area of tourism need to be more organized and coordinated. Also, professional marketing researches are required in order to understand the ecotourism demand profile and the different actors to create innovative and sustainable ecotouristic products and destination brands.

This chapter begins by describing important terminology related to ecotourism by giving examples for its increasing popularity examining the academic literature from Türkiye and around the World. Following the general evaluation, the study takes into consideration the Türkiye case and evaluates the development phases of ecotourism and the recent policies of ecotourism applied in Türkiye's tourism sector. The chapter conclude with suggestions of developing more sustainable ecotouristic destination brands in Türkiye.

Current Ecotourism Perspective: Philosophy, Concepts and Descriptions

The importance of the ecological balance is interpreted in an old Indian saying recited as when the trees, fish and potable water sources become extinct in the World, people will comprehend that money can not be eaten.

Ecotourism means tourism that is respectful to the lives of all the living creatures at the destination including the plants, animals and the local populations while travelling and practising the activities during the stay or trip. Ecotourism invites all tourists to be and behave consciously and responsibly while existing mindfully within the environment. Because each sides; both the visitee and the visitor live in the same World. That is just like it is told in the story of "Noah's Ark", all the creatures are on the same ship, and if one or more of the members go to extremes in their actions, the ship will sink inevitably. This means humans should comprehend that without learning or remembering to live harmoniously with the environment on the planet, humans themselves as well, are in danger of extinction. How ironic is the word harmonious: It keeps "harm" in it, just like the "yin-yang" is comprised of the balance of the opposites; and just like the "venom" and "anti-venom" are similarly the opposing ends. Still, if you succeed in living "harmoniously", you get rid of the "harm". The crux of the matter is to master the dosage. Equivalently, setting the boundaries correctly is a crucial matter. Clearly defined, to the end of one's boundaries the other's begin. Nevertheless, it is not always easy to define the boundaries of each of the living creatures strictly. Unfortunately, there begins the violation of the rights of one or another in case of failing to define the boundaries correctly. The balance among all living creatures to provide healthy and sustainable conditions of survival for all species is nearly impossible. However, trying to provide the balance to the maximum is humanistic, environmentalist and why not "*ecotourismable*". The current considerations of ecotourism thus should not prioritize only humans and the inheritance of humans but equally consider the sustainability of all species thus biological diversity is the key to this biocentric philosophy of environmentalism[8].

UNWTO's description of ecotourism puts the local ecological and environmental richnesses at the center together with the interests of the local communities' well-being with an emphasis on the visitor's responsible attitude towards those mentioned while experiencing and appreciating the local curiosities including both nature and culture (UNWTO Glossary of Tourism Terms).

IUCN has also emphasized the equal importance of human and biodiversity benefits in its meetings and publications such as The IUCN World Conservation Congress in 2016, IUCN Global Standard for NbS[9] in 2020 and the Resolution adopted to take action about the IUCN NbS in 2020 is published in 2022 (IUCN 2024, UNEP 2022).

Certification is aimed to be used for ascertaining the appropriate green or ecotouristic products and discriminating them from the illegitimate ones (Medina, 2005). Academic studies signalling the need for the development and revitalisation of green marketing certifications and ecolabeling also increase (Nistoreanu et al. 2020, Cretu et al. 2024, Ferretti et al. 2024, Bak&Bayram 2024, Motsaathebe & Hambira 2022, Rattan 2015, Maingi 2019). Regarding the certification of ecotourism and sustainable tourism destinations and products, various national and international labels exist for the standardisation of these products and services and exclusively for the conformity of sustainability and ecological and environmental issues. The green and blue labels such as "Green Globe[10], Green Key[11], Green Destinations[12],

Green Star[13], EU Ecolabel[14]" for the accomodation sector and destinations and "Blue Flag[15]" for the beaches, yachts and marinas can be exemplified.

Contrarily, "greenwashing" is used as an inculpative term in marketing. The businesses with "greenwashing" activities or the "greenwashing certification" of tourism businesses are seen as a threat to sustainable tourism or ecotourism practices (Muriithi&Ireri, 2024). Greenwashing is described as a false or partly false marketing information shared by the tourism companies that create an environmentallyconscious[16] perception in the eye of the consumer but the truth is unfortunately the opposite (Hernik, 2017). Greenwashing tourism businesses have experienced a drop in their sales (Papagiannakis et al, 2024).

In addition, the consumer side does not desire to have any doubt but desires to be ensured about the ecological activities of products or services supplied by tourism businesses (Rahman et al. 2015).

The reason why ecotourism is recognized as a predicament rather than a panacea in many cases in various parts of the World according to a study is that structural, operational and cultural problems have to be handled with more sustainable management and investigation methods (Das&Chatterjee, 2015).

When the ecotourism evolutionary phases are diagnosed, it is seen that the 1980s was the period for the educational aspect of environmental conservation. In the 1990s the socio-economic benefits were added with equity dimension to ecotourism. The 2000s increased the dimensions adding sustainability and ethics with the preservation of culture (Cobbinah, 2015). Thus among the main criteria of ecotourism are counted as; nature-based, preservation, conservation, education, awareness, ethics, responsibility, distribution of benefits and sustainability (Donohoe&Needham, 2006).

Ecotourism and Sustainable Tourism

Sustainable development as a concept was mentioned in the Brundtland Report (otherwise named Our Common Future) released by the WCED[17] (britannica.com). The environmental degradation was linked to the loss of the balance of the interconnection among the economic, social and environmental dimensions. If the social equity, economic growth, environmental problems are managed in an equally balanced manner, would form sustainability.

Ecotourism is an indispensable constituent of sustainable tourism (Kiper 2013, Mahmudova et al. 2024). The UNWTO describes sustainable tourism as a version taking account of the impacts of three basic pillars which are social, economic and environmental while reciprocatively addressing the benefits of other stakeholders such as visitors, hosts, the industry and the environment (unwto.org). This definition is the ideal and desired version of ecotourism. On the other hand, Weaver (2001a) discusses that ecotourism exists in varying forms even in mass tourism format. On the one hand nature-based, adventure, trekking and 3S tourism are suggested, and on the other sustainable, alternative, comsumptive or non-comsumptive tourism are mentioned (Weaver, 2001b).

More recently, the elaboration of the ecotourism and sustainable tourism relationship has been improved towards the more idealistic forms. The WTTC[18] together with the UN Tourism and the Sustainable Hospitality Alliance, has joined public and private authorities of the tourism sector and signed and shared a nature-positive vision for travel and tourism. The this formation aimed to stop biodiversity loss, reduce carbon emissions, reduce pollution, discourage unsustainable use of resources and protect nature and wildlife species.

Biodiversity and climate action are two issues emphasized by UNWTO lately in 2024. Ecotourism goes hand in hand with sustainable tourism. "Nature Positive Travel and Tourism Action" is the initiative of UNWTO and its reporting publication in 2024 with a content of sustainable ecotourism shares examples throughout the World. Nature positive travel and tourism signifies that the tourism sector is aware of the loss of biodiversity and takes action for the protection, conservation and restoration of the environment as well as the well-being of people, livelihoods and economies. Appreciation of nature and its close cultural environment by observation is the basic characteristic of nature-based tourism forms (unwto.org). Up-to-date academic studies emphasise-Voronkova et al. (2024), Sayfullayeva (2022), Saidmamatov et al. (2020), Alikhanova et al. 2024, Temirkulovich (2022)- the sustainable tourism and ecotourism reciprocatively supporting each other.

Ecotourism in the World: Main Ecotourism Destination Brands

The roots of ecotourism can be reached through the Alpinist French associations created for trekking tours in nature and in the mountains. "Club Alpin Français" was created in 1874 for example, and it was one of the earliest associations dedicated to mountaineering in all aspects (ffcam.fr).

It is difficult to design the ecotourism destination brands. The high or low potential and/or development possibilities of the different ecotourism areas may be defined and additionally, in order to determine the "ecotourism vision" and "realisation", research and decisions have to be made regarding the feasibility, managerial and marketing processes as suggested in Philippines case (Thompson, 2022).

The main characteristics of an eco-friendly destination brand can be counted as possessing rich biodiversity and an immense ecosystem (Wikipedia). Costa Rica is of the world's most renowned ecotouristic destination brands. Gleen Jampol has been subject to academic studies as an entrepreneur managing sustainable businesses and as an establisher and member of NGOs related to ecotourism such as TIES, Global Ecotourism Network and LACEN (Kaefer, 2022).[19] Costa Rica is an example destination where nature-based tourism is the main livelihood. However, if land use exposure to deforestation is not prevented, the area risks the loss of biodiversity and extinction of the species (Broadbent et al. 2012).

This is a common threat to all the ecotouristic destinations in the World. If the impact of ecotourism is positive, the awareness and consciousness of the people on importance of the environmental resources results in the protection of biodiversity. However, if there is an overuse or deforestation of the land area by the people, the result is the loss of the species and biodiversity and ends in economic loss as well as the ending of tourism activities and livelihoods.

Galapagos Islands is one of the world's most important genetic heritages of the World according to Darwin's trips. Costa Rica, Thailand, Nepal, Galapagos Islands, Kenya, Amazon Rainforest in Brazil are among the world's popular ecotouristic destinations. In Australia, green destinations are mentioned through destination certification(ecotourism.org.au). In Europe, businesses have created a web of entrepreneurs for a "booming" ecotourism market (rewildingeurope.com). Madagascar is an example for a UNWTO Project as a protected area for community-based ecotourism (unwto.org/project).

Ecotourism in Türkiye: Development and Creation of Ecotourism Destination Brands

Türkiye is one of the most tourist-attracting countries of the World. The World Tourism Statistics reflect in the last year 2023, that it was at top ten destinations attracting more than 55 millions of tourists. In terms of tourism revenues, the country is on the 7th rank among other destinations with 49,5 billion USD. The achievement of this success depends on the natural, cultural and geographical treasures that are kept alive since its long and uninterrupted settlement during history. As a land of multiple civilisations, Anatolia was inhabited by many states, kingdoms and empires throughout history. Its geo-strategically important situation located among three old world continents, Asia, Europe and Africa, makes it an important hub located on the commercial and economic routes of Silk, Spice and Royal Roads in history and still, it is on the heart of the commerce, economy and transportation as well communicating and joining together East and West. İstanbul, the commercial capital of the Republic of Türkiye has been the capital to the Byzantine and Ottoman Empires in the past and it is today not only an international hub for air transportation that carries importance for tourism but also a cultural tourism capital that attracted 17,4 million international tourists in 2023.

Tourism was boosted in the 1980s in Türkiye with mass tourism of sun-sea-sand, especially on the Mediterranean Riviera. The blue of this immense peninsula especially with the enormous beaches and luxurious accommodation facilities constructed in excessive numbers by the governmental incentives around the bays of Mediterranean shores has attracted many Europeans especially northern European tourists living with the lack of sunny days in their countries and desiring the warmness of the sun.

Following technological developments with increasing sharing culture using the internet and social media platforms, tourists also discovered that Türkiye is not all about sun-sea and sand. In Türkiye, there is also the adorable nature intertwined with both tangible and intangible cultural heritage. 21 properties of Türkiye are inscribed on the World Heritage list, 2 of which are mixed heritage which means having both cultural and natural heritage-Pamukkale-Hierapolis and Cappadocia- (whc.unecso.org, unesco.org.tr). However, the concept of "ecotourism" was mentioned as a term examined for tourism officially for the first time in the 8th Development Plan of the Turkish Government-that was planned for between the years 2000 and 2005 (Long Term Strategy and 8th Five Year Development Plan (2001-2005)). The diversification of tourism for a more sustainable tourism in Turkey with a more detailed strategy was elaborated on the Tourism Strategy of Turkey 2023(2007) document in 2007 with an Action Plan covering 2007 to 2013. In this strategy document, all tourism actors and tourism types such as cultural tourism, ecotourism, social tourism, main routes, areas and corridors for different tourism types have been scrutinized. Olive corridor, thermal and cultural tourism development areas, plateau tourism and winter tourism are some of the tourism types that are aimed to lead and manage a more sustainably developed tourism in Turkey. Every assignment of the action plan is not yet fully realised. In addition, Turkish tourism should take more steps to reach a scrutinely managed manner through sustainable development plans and policies. There are some regional efforts for the sustainability of tourism supported by various ecotourism routes and product suggestions such as the regional tourism development plans which attempt to develop more sustainable ecotourism destination brands such as by Fethiye (ftso.org.tr) and İzmir Peninsula Sustainable Development Strategy (izka.org.tr) by their local authorities of municipalities and/or other local actors such as NGOs, chambers of commerce, development agencies. However, taking action for certain sustainability issues such as activating all local actors together becomes an obstacle. To give an idea about the diversity of the potential ecotourism destinations and multiple potentialities of localities, some information regarding Türkiye may be presented here: Türkiye is located on a land surface of 783.562 km^2. This huge area is divided to seven geographical regions which are the Aegean, Mediterranean, Marmara, Black Sea, Central Anatolia, Eastern Anatolia and South Eastern Anatolia Regions. With 81 cities and a total population of 85 million 372 thousand 377 people, Türkiye constitutes the 1,1% of the World population. It is a large area with a huge population and as explained above with rich natural, cultural and historical heritage. The number of destinations and tourist products is so many that it is impossible for the tourists to visit all destinations in Türkiye at once. That is why, for the different periods of the year, diversification of forms of tourism is possible. The rising popularity of ecotourism makes it an advantageous option of diversification for the sustainability of tourism in Türkiye.

Ecotourism is a leading form of the tourism industry in Türkiye, especially following the cultural heritage tourism. As it is explained in previous titles about ecotourism above, current descriptions of ecotourism comprise cultural tourism as well. Türkiye has many natural protected areas -National Parks and Ecotourism Areas- that are adorned simultaneously with the ancient ruins of various civilizations and local people with authentic culture living beside the destinations that make the richness of the natural and cultural resources for ecotourism. Examples could be given such as the Lycian Region in Western Mediterranean Region, Termessos National Park in Antalya, Göreme National Park and Rock Sites of Cappadocia, Pamukkale-Hierapolis, Mount Kaçkar and Mount Ağrı (Ararat) National Parks all have their own natural and cultural beauties most of which are on UNESCO Heritage Lists as well (whc.unecso.org, unesco.org.tr). Hereby, an analysis of SWOT[20] is executed for the current situation of ecotourism in Türkiye to be more clearly identified.

Advantages of Türkiye Enabling Ecotourism Development (Strengths):

- ✓ Türkiye is located at the intersection point of three phytogeographical regions: Europe-Siberian, Mediterranean and İrano-Turanian (Davis et al., 1971) The variety of the number of endemic species of both flora and fauna forms the rich natural capital for the high ecotourism potential and different ecotourism destination brands.
- ✓ The potential of creating authentic ecotourism destination brands joining together the themes of nature, culture and sustainability. For example, the very precious saffron is collected in Safranbolu which is a slow city of Türkiye at the same time and very famous also for its authentic historical architecture of Ottoman Period.
- ✓ Historical and cultural heritage accompanying the natural capital. As an example, Termessos in Antalya is a National Park with an immense green forest area which hides in it a very important acropolis Termessos Antique City with its ruins dating back to the Roman period.
- ✓ Natural beauties with a possibility of interpretation, with mythological or other types of folk stories. For example, Ağrı, known as Mount Ararat in English by international tourists is the highest mountain in the country -5137m- for mountaineering. Noah's Ark is told to have landed there after the flood. Additionally, high mountains and mountain ranges for mountain sports such as skiing, paraliding, trekking and mountaineering.

- ✓ National Parks all around the Anatolia Peninsula from west to east, from north to south each region with its own characteristics (For example: Bolu Abant and Yedigöller National Parks in the Western Black Sea Region, Kaçkar Mountains National Park in the Eastern Black Sea Region, Kuşadası and Güzelçamlı National Parks in Aegean Region, Termessos National Park in Antalya in Mediterranean Region).
- ✓ Twelve Ecotourism Areas opened in 2019 for visitors for tourism purposes by the Ministry of Forestry and Agriculture, and the number of these areas continue to increase (ogm.gov.tr)
- ✓ Possession of a UNESCO Global Geopark in Kula in the Aegean Region and application of Zonguldak Coal Geopark to UNESCO Türkiye National Commission is realized by the Governorship of Zonguldak[21](2022).
- ✓ Rich water sources for adventure and sports tourism. 567 Blue Flag Beaches, 27 Blue Flag marinas, 9 Blue Flag yachts, 18 Blue Flag tourism boats(Blue Flag Turkey, 2024). Water skiing, parasailing, sailing and other sports related to the sea are practised on the Mediterranean shores. Also, river rafting is possible for the rafters who are exclusively experienced in the Çoruh River in Erzurum (in the Eastern Anatolia Region).
- ✓ Green Star labeling system exists and is applied for the hotels.
- ✓ Caves for speleology both on land and submarine.
- ✓ The first biological diversity Museum called "Biyosfer[22]" officially opened in 2023 Türkiye at Hacettepe University Center for Advanced Research of Biological Diversity.
- ✓ Institute for Research for Van Cats[23] at University Yüzüncü Yıl in Van (Van is the name of the city in the Eastern Anatolia Region).
- ✓ Monachus Monachus Special Protection Area[24] is around the shores of the Foça district in the Aegean Sea (Western Türkiye)
- ✓ Caretta Caretta satellite tracking project[25], and NGOs[26] for the protection of this species
- ✓ The hospitability of the Anatolian country people who share rural accommodation and gastronomy with the tourist without asking for anything in return (Collective work and sharing culture have always been villagers' customs and traditions in Anatolia. However, this tradition has shrinked because of rural-urban migration and as a result, rural depopulation).
- ✓ Established in 2009, the web of "Citta Slow Türkiye[27]" has reached to many different regions of Türkiye from North to South, east to West with 25 slow cities.
- ✓ goturkiye.com is the web site created by the Ministry of Culture and Tourism letting international tourists search for reliable information on the web in English and other several foreign languages.

- ✓ On the migration routes of birds, thus rich for ornithology. Example: Manyas Kuş Cenneti: Manyas Bird Paradise National Park.
- ✓ Richness of interpretation: Many folk stories and mythological stories related to the relationship of the pagan gods and other mythological characters and plants and animals. For example Apollon and Daphne the story of a girl who desired to stay eternally virgin escaping from Apollon, becomes a tree: Daphne(Laurus nobilis). Olive trees as the symbol of Goddess Athena and the tree is called eternal tree because of its benefits for health. Narcissus poeticus (planted in Karaburun in İzmir) is beautiful species of a flower also a term in psychology derives from this name narcissism, the person in love with himself.
- ✓ Attempts of Local Development Agencies to create local ecotourism destination brands. For example Çeşme in İzmir, Fethiye
- ✓ It is impossible to count all the potential destination examples in Türkiye if fictionalised, could become ecotouristic destination brands in case the sustainable tourism management plans are applied. Some examples are given here for creating support fort he realisation of ecotouristic destination brands.
- ✓ The advantage of media is used by the government to create an awareness about the rich ecotourism potential of Türkiye. For example, TRT documentary channel on TV, shows documentaries that informs the audiences about the variety of ecotouristic areas and the variety of plant and animal species in Türkiye and in the World. Documentaries such as "Ulak"(meaning "Messenger" in English) and "Yok Olmadan Keşfet"(Discover Before Exctinction) shown by TRT Belgesel channel on tv(possible to watch on the web, too).encourage and create the love of nature and awareness of the people &nature linkage.
- ✓ Prof. Dr. Çağan Şekercioğlu, the nature lover ecologist, academician, ornithologist, conservator of nature is the speaker of the documentary called "discover before extinction" published on TRT documentary channel and he contributes to the awareness of the biological diversity and its conservation. It is an advantage to have him as an active scientist of Türkiye working and creating international projects and publications related to nature conservation.

The Points to Consider for Improvement for Enhancing Ecotourism in Türkiye (Weaknesses):

- o Deficiency of central and local planning and policy and implications for ecotourism
- o Lack of technology integration for ecotourism marketing (including promotion, product creation, distribution, branding and so on)

- o Need for the development of a vision of participative and inclusive stakeholders
- o Need for improvement of the educative activities for increasing the awareness and consciousness of ecotourism in the society
- o Need for launching out educational and training programs for human resources specifically working in ecotourism business
- o Studies are needed to turn the potential of ecotouristic product or destination to ecotourism products and ecotouristic destination brands.
- o Lack of or insufficient waste management
- o Efforts are needed for zero waste
- o Lack of infrastructure
- o Over-construction and uncontrolled urbanism
- o Seasonal over-crowding

Promising Developments for Ecotourism Development in Türkiye (Opportunities):

- ✓ Memberships to international organizations such as UNESCO, UNWTO, Blue Flag.
- ✓ Increasing popularity of ecotourism and ecotourism destinations in Türkiye at the international online media (internet and social media)
- ✓ Growing web of national and international transportation.
- ✓ Increasing sharing culture of the individuals and travelers on their experiences, discoveries on the web
- ✓ Mentioning the ecotourism in the 8th Development Plan and 2023 Tourism Strategy documents
- ✓ The studies of some Local National Development Agencies, Local Municipalities and/or NGOs in an attempt to develop the ecotourism routes such as Fethiye and Çeşme.
- ✓ The announced Ecotourism Areas by the Ministry of Forestry and Agriculture of Türkiye
- ✓ Increasing pace of international publications by Turkish academicians emphasizing the requirement for the sustainability of ecotourism practices in Türkiye and reflecting the ecotourism's socio-economic beneficial aspects such as in (Yönet & Yirmibeşoğlu 2022, Aydın&Öztürk 2023).

The Subjects that Require Precautions for A More Sustainable Ecotourism Formation in Türkiye (Threats)

- o Climate change, natural disasters such as floods, fire, drought, earthquakes

- o Deterioration of the ecological balance
- o Endangered species of flora and fauna
- o The lack of or insufficieny of implication of the tourism plan and/or policies regarding ecotourism and/or sustainable tourism
- o The lack of cooperation, coordination and the missing relationships of the local and/or national stakeholders including the linkage between the sectoral and academic actors.

Examples of Türkiye's Natural Attractions and Potential Ecotourism Destination Brands:

If the roots of ecotourism in Türkiye are considered, the first eco-tourists in Türkiye could be suggested as the "Otacı[28]" or "Lokman Hekim" (in Anatolia the name given to healers or herb doctor with divine powers), who would go for a walk in the Taurus Mountains of Anatolia to collect the endemic plants for creating their own therapeutic applications and as treatment of many diseases. Or the doctors of Asclepieions to provide for their herbal treatments in Anatolia. Or the Dionysus[29] Festivals of Western Anatolia also could be in this list as the participants of the festival would adore the nature and all it provides for the well-being of all the participants.

For today, it is impossible to list and explain all the potential and actual ecotourism routes or the destinations with ecotourism content in Türkiye in such a chapter, books may not be enough. To remind, only the flora of Turkey is first published in 1965 by Peter Hadland Davis in an encyclopedic resource named "Flora of Turkey and The East Aegean Islands". Through the following years, the author's following team of students and academicians developed the publishment in 9 volumes, 11 and even 13 volumes. Today, the biologists continue to study and each day new species are added to the list. That is just an example to show the immensity and characteristics of the biological diversity in Türkiye that forms the resource for the basis of ecotourism destination branding. That is why, planning, management and marketing fort he creation of ecotourism destination brands in Türkiye requires great national and international effort. Even so, with the weaknesses and threats listed above, Türkiye still has a good ecotourism potential. Some examples for ecotourism activities never enough for representing the whole are given below:

Antalya Termessos National Park[30] with its unique natural beauty and Archeological Site as well as Skiing in the summer at the same destination on Taurus Mountain ranges.

Lykia Route: Lycian Cities (The 25 Cities of first fully executed Democracy in the World) and Trekking Route with uniquely beautiful nature. Some dispersed information is found through the web site of Ministry of Culture and

Tourism in Turkish language. Holistic, sustainable marketing and management efforts are needed for ecotourism destination branding.

The Route of Christianity in Anatolia exist in many different areas beginning from Hatay (Antakya), Psidia Antiochia (Isparta-Yalvaç), Demre(Myra), Cappadocia, Lycia, Seven Churches of Apocalypse (Aegean Region: İzmir(Smyrna, Ephesus, Pergamum), Manisa(Thyatira, Sardis, Philadelphia), Denizli(Laodikeia); İznik(Nikaia) and İzmit(Nikomedia)(The Great Councils of Christianity), İstanbul.

National Travel Agencies' tour programs with National Parks: Popular paths include Bolu Abant and Yedigöller National Parks tours (Black Sea Region)

Black Sea Kaçkar Mountains National Park: Potential for mountaineering and wild flora and fauna watching.

Ağrı Dağı National Park: For mountaineering. Potential of attracting mythological interpretations about the place where Noah's Ark landed for the salvation of the humanity and species.

Aladağlar National Park: Potential for various camping types including astronomical observations and wild flora and fauna watching.

Tunceli Munzur Vadisi: Motor Sports race during a moto fest took place in National Park route area(trthaber.com).

Bilecik ultra trail[31]: cherry run: Sports event organized in a natural setting aiming to gain people love of nature.

Cappadocia: UNESCO natural heritage (mixed heritage=both natural and cultural): Baloon tours are popular with beautiful unique scenery of fairy chimneys. Ihlara Valley, Kaymaklı and Derinkuyu underground cities, Göreme Open Air Museum

Pamukkale Travertins: UNESCO Natural+Cultural= Mixed Heritage: Formation of unique World-wide famous scenery of White travertins, Hierapolis Antique City and Natural Pool dating back to Roman period,.

According to the Reportlinker (2024): the ecotourism travel companies listed in the ecotourism report of Türkiye are: "Cappadocia Tours, Travel Atelier, Anatolian Sky, Exclusive Escapes, Argo Travel". Besides, many local and national travel agencies provide tours with ecotourism content.

CONCLUSION

Ecotourism is shortly described as a form of tourism comprised of activities that avoid harming the environment and local populations and that respect the socio-economic interests of the stakeholders while protecting the biological diversity. Practising ecotourism without respecting the issues in the defined perspective can create tensions among the different stakeholders including the biodiversity, local people, local natural and authenticity of cultural heritages. Creating ecotouristic destination brands is a hard business that should be managed under "*glocal*" considerations. "*Glocal*" is the combination of the words global and local creating a synergy when joined together. "Global", as that means adopting the sustainability approach and "local" meaning in terms of a convenient management for determining the extent of the usage of the local resources and succeding in the realisation of ecotourism programs with interrelationships of the stakeholders.

In the World succeeding ecotourism destinations exist such as Costa Rica, Kenya, Brazil Amazon Forests. However, the increasing popularity of ecotourism brings sustainability as an obligatory concern into strategy. The world's renowned destinations of ecotourism face the loss of biodiversity because of overtourism or the unsustainable ways of tourism management. The loss of corals is an alarming sign of the impacts of global warming and climate change as well as pollution (Economist, 2018). Türkiye as well has to research for developing and and applying sustainable actions in tourism sector for creating ecotouristic destination brands.

Türkiye is on its path to creating ecotourism destination brands. This country is geographically situated in a fortunate area rich in ecological resources that form a basis for ecotourism. Türkiye has the potential to develop many different ecotourism destination brands in its various locations. From Taurus Mountain ranges to the National Parks to newly created Ecotourism Areas, the country is highly varied in biodiversity both for flora and fauna including the diversity of its water resources for many sports and adventure tourism options, adding rich cultural and historical background accompanying local and rural cultural diversity and many additional countless available authentic resources. The country is also a popular international destination attracting 55,2 million tourists (Top 5 countries) with touristic revenue of USD 49,5 billion (7th rank in the World) in 2023 according to UNWTO (2024).

The advantage of possessing many resources requires a sustainable tourism management for ecotourism and to create ecotouristic destination brands in Türkiye. Efforts to promote the sustainability programs for enhancing the existence of Türkiye in the ecotourism market is still on a developing pace. Some examples of official websites and social media channels function but are not efficiently well-known enough yet[32]. Aditionally, Türkiye should turn its ecotouristic resources into the advantage of sustainable ecotourism products but with sustainable tourism policies and planning implications. Türkiye has maintained a dispersed structure of planning in its tourism management policies. Ministry of Culture and Tourism, Ministry of Agriculture and Forestry and additionally non-governmental organizations try to promote and produce plans and products for ecotourism. However, a coordination is needed among all the governmental and non-governmental bodies in order to protect the ecological resources and plan, manage, control the ecotourism processes.

Additionally, local perspectives of the ecotourism development plans have to be maintained in order to create unique and attractive ecotourism destination brands.

REFERENCES

Aktan, M., Zaman, U., Raza, S. H., & Koc, E. (2024). Demystifying tourists' intentional readiness for net zero transformation through environmental knowledge, conspicuous altruism, and greenwashing perceptions. *Asia Pacific Journal of Tourism Research*, 29(4), 495–514.

Alikhanova, S., Milner-Gulland, E. J., & Bull, J. W. (2024). Exploring the human-nature nexus towards effective nature-based solutions: The Aral Sea case. *Land Use Policy*, 139, 107073.

Ashok, S., Behera, M. D., Tewari, H. R., & Jana, C. (2022). Developing ecotourism sustainability maximization (ESM) model: A safe minimum standard for climate change mitigation in the Indian Himalayas. *Environmental Monitoring and Assessment*, 194(12), 914.

Aydin, I. Z., & Öztürk, A. (2023). Identifying, Monitoring, and Evaluating Sustainable Ecotourism Management Criteria and Indicators for Protected Areas in Türkiye: The Case of Camili Biosphere Reserve. *Sustainability (Basel)*, 15(4), 2933.

Bak, E., & Bayram, G. E. (2024). Redefining and Revitalized Community-Based Tourism: An Evaluation of Green Tourism Practises in Turkey. In Strategic Tourism Planning for Communities (pp. 197-209). Emerald Publishing Limited.

Bektaş, F., Özdemir Işık, B., Erbaş, Y. S., Bahar, E., & Kaya, S. (2024). Kullanıcı Potansiyeline Bağlı Koruma Statüsündeki Mavi Yıldız Çiçeğinin Sürdürülebilirliğine Yönelik Trabzon Kadıralak Yaylasında Yürüyüş Rotalarının Belirlenmesi. GSI Journals Serie A: Advancements in Tourism *Recreation and Sports Sciences*, 7(1), 48–66.

Blue Flag Turkey. (2024). https://www.mavibayrak.org.tr/en/

Broadbent, E. N., Zambrano, A. M. A., Dirzo, R., Durham, W. H., Driscoll, L., Gallagher, P., Salters, R., Schultz, J., Colmenares, A., & Randolph, S. G. (2012). The effect of land use change and ecotourism on biodiversity: A case study of Manuel Antonio, Costa Rica, from 1985 to 2008. *Landscape Ecology*, 27(5), 731–744.

Chip.com.tr. (2020) Web Site of CHIP Science and Tech Magazine. https://www.chip.com.tr/haber/eski-otobus-artik-bir-ev-eski-otobusu-karavan-yaptilar-sonuc-inanilmaz_88924.html

Cobbinah, P. B. (2015). Contextualising the meaning of ecotourism. *Tourism Management Perspectives*, 16, 179–189.

Cre u, R. C., Alecu, I. I., Răducan, D., & tefan, P. (2024). Research onto the implementation of the ecological label in agrotourism. *Scientific Papers. Series Management, Economic, Engineering in Agriculture and Rural Development*, 24(1).

Das, M., & Chatterjee, B. (2015). Ecotourism: A panacea or a predicament? *Tourism Management Perspectives*, 14, 3–16.

Davis, P. H., Harper, P. C., & Hedge, I. C. (1971). *Plant life of south-west Asia*. The Botanical Society of Edinburgh.

Donohoe, H. M., & Needham, R. D. (2006). Ecotourism: The Evolving Contemporary Definition. *Journal of Ecotourism*, 5(3), 192–210.

Du, Q., Guan, Q., Sun, Y., & Wang, Q. (2024). Assessment of Ecotourism Environmental Carrying Capacity in the Qilian Mountains, Northwest China. *Sustainability (Basel)*, 16(5), 1873.

Economist. (2018, Mar 21st). Why is so much of the world's coral dying? https://shorturl.at/fDVTp

Ecotourism Global Market Report. (2024). The Business Research Company https://www.researchandmarkets.com/report/ecotourism

Ekonomist. (2022) https://www.ekonomist.com.tr/ekonomist/pandemide-karavan-uretimine-gecti-sadece-4-ayda-14-ulkeye-ihracat-yapti-21910

Habertürk. (2022). Özel Halk Otobüsünden Akıllı Karavan yaptı (Turned the public bus into a smart caravan). https://www.haberturk.com/ozel-halk-otobusunden-akilli-karavan-yapti-3518024/4

Hernik, J. (2017). Greenwashing in Tourism, So How Companies Should Not Create An Image. *Challenges of Tourism and Business Logistics in the 21st Century, 1*(1), 13-17.

IUCN. (2024). https://www.iucn.org/blog/202404/human-rights-based-approach-iucns-global-standard-nature-based-solutions

Jayasekara, K. D. D. S., Rajapaksa, D., & Gunawardena, U. A. D. (2024). Impacts of Environmental Knowledge, Motives, and Behavior on Ecotourism. *Sustainability (Basel)*, 16(11), 4724.

Kaefer, F. (2022). Glenn Jampol on Tourism Business and Ecotourism in Costa Rica. In Sustainability Leadership in Tourism: Interviews, Insights, and Knowledge from Practice (pp. 267–271). Springer International Publishing. DOI: 10.1007/978-3-031-05314-6_41

Karatas-Ozkan, M., Tunalioglu, R., Ibrahim, S., Ozeren, E., Grinevich, V., & Kimaro, J. (2024). Actioning sustainability through tourism entrepreneurship: Women entrepreneurs as change agents navigating through the field of stakeholders. *Central European Management Journal*, 32(1), 31–56.

Kiper, T. (2013). *Role of ecotourism in sustainable development. InTech*. DOI: 10.5772/55749

Li, T., Liu, F., Soutar, G., & Webb, D. (2024). An application of the new visitation paradigm to ecotourism in China. *Journal of Ecotourism*, 23(1), 100–110.

Lindner, J. (2024, June 17). Ecotourism Industry Statistics. https://worldmetrics.org/ecotourism-industry-statistics/

Mahmudova, M., Kurbonbekova, M., & Mamadiyarov, Z. (2024, March). Exploring Eco-Tourism and Its Role in Sustainable Development: An example of Karakalpakstan. In *International Conference of Economics, Finance and Accounting Studies* (Vol. 3, pp. 64-67).

Maingi, S. W. (2019). Sustainable tourism certification, local governance and management in dealing with overtourism in East Africa. *Worldwide Hospitality and Tourism Themes*, 11(5), 532–551.

Medina, L. K. (2005). Ecotourism and certification: Confronting the principles and pragmatics of socially responsible tourism. *Journal of Sustainable Tourism*, 13(3), 281–295.

Motsaathebe, G. T., & Hambira, W. L. (2022). In pursuit of sustainable tourism in Botswana: Perceptions of Maun tourism accommodation operators on tourism certification and eco-labelling. In Southern African Perspectives on Sustainable Tourism Management: Tourism and Changing Localities (pp. 31–45). Springer International Publishing. DOI: 10.1007/978-3-030-99435-8_3

Muriithi, J. K., & Ireri, P. (2024). Ecotourism Principles, Responsible Travel, and Building a Sustainable Post-pandemic Destination Kenya. In Tourist Behaviour and the New Normal, Volume II: Implications for Sustainable Tourism Development (pp. 195-220). Cham: Springer Nature Switzerland.

Nistoreanu, P., Aluculesei, A. C., & Avram, D. (2020). Is Green Marketing a Label for Ecotourism? The Romanian Experience. *Information (Basel)*, 11(8), 389.

Papagiannakis, G. E., Vlachos, P. A., Koritos, C. D., & Kassinis, G. I. (2024). Are publicly traded tourism and hospitality providers greenwashing? *Tourism Management*, 103, 104893.

Rahman, I., Park, J., & Chi, C. G. Q. (2015). Consequences of "greenwashing": Consumers' reactions to hotels' green initiatives. *International Journal of Contemporary Hospitality Management*, 27(6), 1054–1081.

Rattan, J. K. (2015). Is certification the answer to creating a more sustainable volunteer tourism sector? *Worldwide Hospitality and Tourism Themes*, 7(2), 107–126.

Reportlinker. (2024). Ecotourism Market Reports 2024. https://shorturl.at/ZfShP

Saidmamatov, O., Matyakubov, U., Rudenko, I., Filimonau, V., Day, J., & Luthe, T. (2020). Employing ecotourism opportunities for sustainability in the Aral Sea Region: Prospects and challenges. *Sustainability (Basel)*, 12(21), 9249.

Saxena, A., Shanker, S., Sethi, D., Seth, M., & Saxena, A. (2024). *"Touchstones for the development of an inclusive approach for ecotourism as a service industry", Benchmarking: An International Journal*. DOI: 10.1108/BIJ-07-2023-0456

Sayfullayeva, M. S. (2022). Directions for the Practice of Sustainable Tourism for Ecotourism Destinations in Uzbekistan. *American Journal of Economics and Business Management*, 5(12), 98–109.

Sonuç, N. (2020). Environment, Tourism and Sustainability (Ecotourism Management, Environment and Sustainable Tourism). In Encyclopedia of Sustainable Management (pp. 1–6). Springer International Publishing. DOI: 10.1007/978-3-030-02006-4_456-1

Statista. (2024). Market size of the ecotourism sector worldwide in 2022, with a forecast for 2028 https://www.statista.com/statistics/1221034/ecotourism-market-size-global/

Temirkulovich, U. J. (2022). Development of Ecologization of Tourism: Experience of Foreign Countries. Indonesian Journal of Innovation Studies, 19.

Thompson, B. S. (2022). Ecotourism anywhere? The lure of ecotourism and the need to scrutinize the potential competitiveness of ecotourism developments. *Tourism Management*, 92, 104568.

Thong, J. Z., Lo, M. C., Ramayah, T., & Mohamad, A. A. (2024). Destination resources as precursors of ecotourism competitiveness: A study of totally protected areas in Sarawak, Malaysia during COVID-19 pandemic. *Journal of Ecotourism*, 23(2), 194–216.

TIES. (2015). Web site of The International Ecotourism Society. https://ecotourism.org/what-is-ecotourism/

Toksöz, D. (2024). Turist Rehberlerinin Alan Uzmanlığına Bakış Açıları Üzerine Görgül Bir Araştırma. *Güncel Turizm Araştırmaları Dergisi*, 8(1), 8–27.

Tourism Strategy of Turkey-2023. (2007). Action Plan2007-2013. Ministry of Culture and Tourism of Turkey. https://www.ktb.gov.tr/Eklenti/43537,turkeytourismstrat egy2023pdf.pdf?0&_tag1=796689BB12A540BE0672E65E48D10C07D6DAE291

Haber, T. R. T. (2024). Made own caravan and travelled: Kendi karavanını yapıp seyahate çıktı. https://www.trthaber.com/videolar/kendi-karavanini-yapip-seyahate -cikti-71827.html

Türkay, O., Dilmaç, E., & Taşarer, E. (2024). Turizmin "Özgürlük" ve "Yolda Olmak" Hâli: Türkiye'deki Karavan Turistlerini Anlamaya Yönelik Bir Araştırma. *Afyon Kocatepe Üniversitesi Sosyal Bilimler Dergisi*, 26(1), 385–408.

UNEP. (2022). Resolution adopted by the United Nations Environment Assembly on 2 March 2022, 5/5. Nature-based solutions for supporting sustainable development. https://wedocs.unep.org/bitstream/handle/20.500.11822/39864/NATURE -BASED%20SOLUTIONS%20FOR%20SUPPORTING%20SUSTAINABLE%20 DEVELOPMENT.%20English.pdf?sequence=1&isAllowed=y

Voronkova, V., Nikitenko, V., Oleksenko, R., Cherep, A., Cherep, O., & Harbar, H. (2024). The Creative Development of Green Ecotourism Concept as a Sustainable Development Factor. *Revista de la Universidad del Zulia*, 3/15(42), 370–388.

Weaver, D. B. (2001a). Ecotourism as mass tourism: Contradiction or reality? *The Cornell Hotel and Restaurant Administration Quarterly*, 42(2), 104–112.

Weaver, D. B. (2001b). Ecotourism in the context of other tourism types. In The encyclopedia of ecotourism (pp. 73–83). CABI Publishing. DOI: 10.1079/9780851993683.0073

World Tourism Barometer, U. N. (2024). https://www.unwto.org/un-tourism-world -tourism-barometer-data

Yönet, N. A., & Yirmibesoglu, F. (2022). Ecotourism as a Rural Development Model: As a Women Leaded Ecotourism Process of Piraziz Şeyhli Village (the Black Sea Region of Turkey). Planlama, 32(2).

Zariç, Ö. E., Çelekli, A., & Yaygır, S. (2024). Lakes of Turkey: Comprehensive review of Lake Çıldır. *Aquatic Sciences and Engineering*, 39(1), 54–63.

ENDNOTES

1 International Ecotourism Society

2 compound annual growth rate

3 The International Ecotourism Society (TIES)

4 Global Sustainable Tourism Conference

5 t.: used as an abbreviation for "tourism"

6 't.' used for 'tourism'.

7 International Union for Conservation of Nature

8 https://www.britannica.com/topic/environmentalism, https://www.britannica.com/topic/ethical-naturalism

9 Nature-based Solutions

10 Recognized by UNWTO: https://www.greenglobe.com/

11 Hotel, hostel, campsite, holiday parks, small accommodation, restaurants, conference centers, attractions are comprised: https://www.greenkey.global/

12 GTSC(Global Sustainable Tourism Council) recognized certification: https://www.greendestinations.org/

13 Equivalent of "Yeşil Yıldız" in Türkiye as a label for environmentally-conscious hotels.

14 Created by the European Commission for European Countries and for eco or sustainable certification of all products and services including accommodation (705 certified) and tourism businesses such as tour operators: https://www.ecolabels.fr/, https://environment.ec.europa.eu/

15 Global: https://www.blueflag.global/ and in Türkiye: https://www.mavibayrak.org.tr/en/

16 Being environmentally conscious means not only being mindful of the possible impact on the environment but also taking precautions for minimizing or eliminating the negative effects (https://drinkheartwater.com/).

17 World Commission on Environment and Development

18 World Travel and Tourism Council

[19] Latin America&Caribbean Ecotourism Network (LACEN)

[20] strengths, weaknesses, opportunities, threats

[21] Zonguldak is in the western Black Sea Region

[22] https://www.biyosfermuze.com/

[23] http://vankedisi.yyu.edu.tr/

[24] Ministry of Environment, Urbanis and Climate Change of Republic of Türkiye: https://ockb.csb.gov.tr/foca-ozel-cevre-koruma-bolgesi-i-2760

[25] Ministry of Environment, Urbanis and Climate Change of Republic of Türkiye: https://tvk.csb.gov.tr/ockb-deniz-kaplumbagalari-uydu-izleme-projesi-i-99640

[26] https://dekafok.org.tr/

[27] https://cittaslowturkiye.org/tr/

[28] "Ot" means herb in Turkish. "Otacı" is the person with healing knowledge.

[29] The Semi-God in mythology whose father is the God Zeus and mother Semele (the daughter of a king).

[30] https://antalya.ktb.gov.tr/TR-310935/termessos.html: Some pictures related to area can be seen

[31] https://itra.run/Races/RaceDetails/INTERNATIONAL.G%C3%96LPAZARI.ULTRA.TRAIL.K%C4%B0RAZ.KO%C5%9EUSU/2024/91737

[32] https://goturkiye.com/turkiyes-sustainable-tourism-program?pageIndex=0, https://sustainable.goturkiye.com/, https://www.instagram.com/goturkiye/, https://visitturkey.in/tourism/ecotourism-in-turkey/

Chapter 16
Village Tourism Balances Brand Identity and Sustainability in Montegridolfo

Manuela Presutti
University of Bologna, Italy

Francesco Maria Barbini
https://orcid.org/0000-0003-1495-0931
University of Bologna, Italy

Valeria lo Presti
University of Bologna, Italy

ABSTRACT

This paper explores the role of village tourism in promoting sustainable practices and enhancing destination branding, using the case study of Montegridolfo and Palazzo Viviani, a luxury hotel in Italy's Riviera Romagnola. Through ethnographic research, we investigate the motivations behind establishing a high-end hotel in a small, rich village far from mainstream tourist routes. The study examines how luxury tourism can foster sustainable development, support unique destination branding, and balance tourism growth with the preservation of cultural heritage and local identity. The case of Palazzo Viviani demonstrates the integration of eco-sustainable strategies within the luxury sector, highlighting the interplay between environmental responsibility, economic growth, and cultural revitalization. Our findings suggest that luxury tourism when properly managed, can provide ethical and economically sound development opportunities for rural destinations. The paper concludes by

DOI: 10.4018/979-8-3693-6700-1.ch016

offering strategic insights for developing sustainable luxury tourism models in similar small village settings

INTRODUCTION

Tourism processes encompass places and spaces that cannot be analyzed exclusively through their tangible aspects. From an anthropological and socio-cultural perspective, places and spaces result from social activity, functioning as procedural structures of meanings and values rather than mere physical entities. Territorial identity is relational, a social concept intertwined with cultural, political, ideological, and ethical processes in synergy with cultural heritage and local capital. Tourism destinations reflect the *genius loci* in the broadest sense of the concept by benefiting and systematizing not only tangible attractions but also (and especially) the history, cultural heritage, traditions, and social customs that represent unique, situated, and distinctive features. Every tourism destination has its own identity and brand, which are crucial to its tourism provision and consumption processes (Presutti, 2018). Thus, the tourist product can be seen as a blend of material and immaterial assets woven into the destination, with an intangible dimension not ancillary to the other.

Consequently, destination branding processes can leverage intangible distinctive features to provide tourists with more authentic and multidimensional experiences (Richards, 2018)

However, pursuing this opportunity requires a shift from interpreting a local context as mere territory to understanding it as a relational and social place with emotional characteristics. This aligns with the aim of this paper, which is to explore village tourism through a case study of establishing a luxury hotel in a small town on the hills of Riviera Romagnola in Italy. Montegridolfo is the name of this delightful village set in the countryside and characterized by rolling hills and olive groves; it has historical roots dating back to the Middle Ages. The walls of a castle enclose the ancient village that has recently been transformed into a 4-star hotel: the historic residence of Palazzo Viviani.

What is the rationale of an entrepreneurial investment in a luxury hotel in a small village far away from the traditional tourist routes? Can it foster sustainable development and support peculiar destination branding processes? How can the choice to redevelop a town into a luxury destination maintain the sustainability of its tourism while ensuring ethically and economically sound destination development?

Using ethnographic research, we discuss these research questions by illustrating how Palazzo Viviani exemplifies a brand destination creation, following an eco-sustainability approach.

The development of Palazzo Viviani, which now attracts luxury tourists, has stimulated the sustainable renovation of the Montegridolfo town. Once relatively unknown, Montegridolfo is becoming increasingly popular, welcoming Italian and international tourists attracted by traditional cuisine, history, and local culture. This paper provides several strategic and managerial implications for sustainable brand destination development in small villages.

THEORETICAL FRAMEWORK

New Trends in Tourism

Twenty years ago, the word "tourism" stood alone. Today, the term has been increasingly paired with adjectives to specify the type of tourism. The focus shifted to experiential, cultural, and sustainable tourism, reflecting the changes in tourists' tastes, choices, and desires. In recent years, the way of understanding tourism and the places it is carried out has also changed, especially considering the current pandemic era.

The term alternative tourism is usually used to describe an activity characterized by locally owned and controlled small-scale operations, offering experiences related to the environmental context and thus including educational tours and stays in rural locations (Oriade, Evans, 2011; Weaver, 2006, 2007/). Among the various forms of alternative tourism are community, slow, cultural, and sustainable. Several studies believe that alternative tourism has the potential to bring sustainable development to communities due to its participatory, localized, and environmentally sensitive nature.

The conflicting interests and objectives of the stakeholders involved inevitably affect the development of alternative forms of tourism (Rumagosa, 2020; Baggio et al., 2020). This mismatch is mainly associated with the lack of a clear definition of sustainability in academia and the overly complex and cumbersome approach of scholars towards the definition of sustainability (Ruhanen, 2008; Xiao, 2006). Lane (2009) believes this attitude is due to the stakeholders' lack of awareness of the factors driving the tourism market. Finally, the communities involved in alternative tourism must ensure they have a strategy to host and interact with tourists to benefit from their presence (Salazar, 2012).

Some experts argue that alternative tourism and its approaches and the encounters that result from it encourage valuable cultural exchanges between the guest and the host (Higgins-Desbiolles, 2008; Zahra, McGehee, 2013). Scholars praise these forms of tourism not only for their limited environmental impact but also because they offer small entrepreneurs, residents, and various local stakeholders significant opportunities to interact and participate with one another, thus spreading greater well-being within the relevant local context. In this regard, Prince and Ioannides (2017) write in their paper: "This participation is considered crucial to ensure the specific needs of community members are met through tourism." Environmentally sensitive, small-scale alternative tourism can thus be considered a form of sustainable tourism helpful in generating "local bottom-up development".

However, one of the main challenges associated with alternative tourism is the multidimensional concept of sustainability, whose operationality is often subjective, thus assuming a different connotation for each actor involved in the sector. Sustainable tourism can be defined as tourism development that meets the needs of the present without compromising the ability of future generations to meet their own needs (Weaver, 2006). This type of tourism uses resources wisely, minimizing negative impacts and maximizing positive ones.

The term cannot be understood unequivocally due to its future-oriented nature (Rist, 2002). Indeed, it is essential to remember that business owners and developers have relatively short-term perspectives and are therefore more inclined to emphasize immediate economic priorities to ensure their existence within the tourism market rather than control the environmental and social impact of the enterprise (Lane, 2009; Beckman et al., 2013).

In cases where an alternative form of tourism is promoted, there is always a latent risk that economic growth might divert local actors' interests from their original environmental sustainability goals (Coghlan & Noakes, 2012).

Local tourism entrepreneurs strive to offer their guests as many activities and experiences as possible, thus meeting market demands. The objectives of families, businesses, and organizations involved in alternative tourism often become contradictory as they seek to pursue their "idealistic" mission while recognizing the daily realities dictated by the global capitalist system. Supporting this thesis, Prince and Ioannides (2017) highlight: "Discussions over sustainability in alternative tourism should address the contexts of complexity, confusion, conflict, and reconciliation within which managerial decisions need to be applied effectively."

Prince and Ioannides (2017) demonstrated through an ethnographic study conducted within the Solheimar eco-village (Iceland) that to turn alternative tourism into a tool for community development, it is necessary to stimulate discussion forums between hosts and tourists. The goal is to gain greater awareness of the complexity of generating sustainable growth. This implies, as Lane (2009) suggests that tourism scholars should research more deeply the market dynamics driving tourism businesses and the synergies created with the community within which they are embedded. Salazar (2012) emphasizes: "Local communities must develop strategies for receiving and interacting with tourists as well as displaying themselves and their visible culture." Furthermore, as highlighted by Wheeler (2013, 2006), more significant interaction between the host and the host would help researchers understand how and to what extent human nature plays its role within the political and economic context. Therefore, according to authors Prince and Ioannides (2017), to contribute to the development of sustainable and alternative tourism theory, it is necessary to delve into ethnographic study methods that include on-site interviews and participant observation: "Immersing the researcher in the study context is ultimately proposed as the best way to bring forward these complex dynamics alternative tourism stakeholders face as these are part of the mundane activities that make up their reality."

In recent years, the emphasis on sustainable tourism has emphasized the role of the community. Community-Based Tourism (CBT) is: "A platform for local community to generate economic benefits through offering their products to tourists that range from the local communities, lifestyles, natural resources, and cultures. CBT is also characterized as a development program that enhances the social and cultural benefits of the local community through the social and cultural exchanges with tourists." The international organization, attentive to environmental needs, acknowledges that community tourism depends on local social and institutional structures. CBT should be viewed within the context of responsible tourism that satisfies tourists and enhances the destination's environment, providing benefits to residents. One of the fundamental principles of responsible tourism is the involvement of local communities and the direct benefits they receive.

The place of tourism is where the language allowing the community to expand is constructed, a space for introspective reflection for the community itself. It is no longer just about visiting or selling a territory but about living and knowing it. Community tourism should be understood as a space for sharing and spreading a new lexicon of hospitality consistent with the changes we are experiencing.

A community's product can become an actor in the tourism system, a topic of debate between locals and visitors about authenticity, quality, and origin (Barbini, Presutti, 2014). These discussions open a dialogue, for example, about a local product. When the tourist knows and consumes it, they come into contact with a peculiar experience that simultaneously enriches and changes both the product and the traveler. In transformational travel, the journey itself changes the tourist. Staying in a place must modify people and their attitude towards the host community, which in turn receives enrichment and awareness (Eugenio-Vela, Barniol-Carcasona, 2015).

The real protagonist now is the community: community-based tourism is indeed becoming the typical horizon to incorporate an increasing number of recovery experiences (Baker, Cameron, 2008).

In this context, slow tourism finds its place, representing a way of traveling designed to counter the hustle and bustle of our daily lives. Applied to the tourism sector, this idea promotes a slow travel experience with the opportunity to immerse oneself in the local culture while respecting nature. Slow Tourism's values urge travelers' involvement within the local community and the design of tourism as a development engine, even for lesser-known areas. It is a type of tourism that focuses on details and guides the visitor through discovering hidden places and local products, with full respect for the environment, to grasp every detail of the tourist experience.

Finally, rural tourism has the potential to stimulate local economic growth and social change thanks to its complementarity with other economic activities, its contribution to GDP and job creation, its ability to promote demand dispersion over time (combating seasonality), and through a broader territory. The UNWTO defines rural tourism as "a type of tourist activity in which the visitor's experience is related to a wide range of products generally associated with nature-based activities, agriculture, rural lifestyle/culture, fishing, and sightseeing.

The Village Tourism Model and Albergo Diffuso Phenomenon: the Importance Of Brand Territorial Identity

Village tourism involves tourists who seek a profoundly reflective and immersive recreational and cultural experience intertwined with encounters with local reality and communities, from which they emerge enriched. Typically located in rural or peripheral areas, a village is characterized by authenticity, uniqueness, beauty, social values, traditions, culture, landscape, and emotional connections between inhabitants and the territory, all defining its brand identity (Ezeuduji, 2015)

In recent years, Italian villages have been central to a complex economic and social debate. Indeed, while villages are distinctive markers of Italy, they are primarily located in inland and rural areas, subject to depopulation, demographic decline, aging populations, infrastructural neglect, and abandonment (Komppula, 2014).

Today, strategies and synergies are being implemented in small municipalities to revitalize the local economy, valorize heritage, and transform weaknesses into strengths for these territories. The valorization of rural areas necessitates a new form of territorialization where villages serve as the central axis to provide coherence and cohesion to the entire Italian local system. The gap between developed and underdeveloped areas can be related to geomorphological and infrastructural issues and the need to reform the communities that animate these "villages." Considering these unique territories from the perspective of those who live there is crucial. Therefore, working on developing and forming a village's identity and pride becomes fundamental, aiming to outline the -tangible and intangible - determinants of the territorial brand identity through which the town can generate value.

Behind the construction of a village's brand identity lies the idea of sustainable tourism as a process that meets the needs of present generations without compromising the ability of future generations to meet their own needs. Sustainable tourism can foster dialogue among individuals with diverse perspectives on village tourism and its economic, social, and environmental dimensions (Pan et al., 2017). The relationship between cultural heritage and territorial brand identity is closely intertwined. It invokes the theme of ecological sustainability, as cultural heritage and all its tangible and intangible assets positively influence local creativity through their existence and aesthetic values (Lalicic, 2020)

Entrepreneurial development of villages for tourism purposes can only be undertaken when it leverages a territorial identity capable of revitalizing an active and dynamic community, activating the sense of uniqueness of places in terms of narration and cultural heritage (Pan et al., 2017). Cultural and social revival must accompany economic feasibility evaluations of a village's development plan involving its various stakeholders. (Eshuis et al., 2018)

Various participants and inhabitants in a village can enrich the territorial context economically in different ways, from the simple capacity for narration and creation of local identity to creating value in the phases of tourism supply. The interaction of these participants and their specific contribution to value creation defines the reference tourism profile because various business segmentation layers can be identified even in a village. Tourism in these villages began relatively spontaneously (Casoli et al., 2023).

Due to its zero-impact approach, the Italian "alberghi diffusi" model may offer a functional solution for village tourism. The "albergo diffuso" is a hospitality model conceived by Giancarlo Dall'Ara, a professor of tourism marketing (Iseppi, 2021). This type of accommodation, which has recently spread across Europe and the world, originated in Italy from the idea of using renovated empty houses for tourism, financed by post-earthquake funds in Friuli (1976). The model has been applied in various Italian locations to enhance small historical centers, villages, ancient settlements, and rural or mountain areas without excluding the validity of solutions linked to significant single presences in differently urbanized contexts. In 2023, there were 130 "alberghi diffusi" in Italy, distributed as follows: 68 in historical centers, 27 in historical residences, and 35 in old farmhouses (Italian Association of Scattered Hotels, 2016). The highest concentration of scattered hotels is in Central Italy, with 48 units, followed by 25 units in Southern Italy, 23 units in Sicily and Sardinia, and 34 units in Northern Italy

The factors that distinguish the "albergo diffuso" from other hospitality models identified by several studies on this topic can be summarized as follows: the drivers that led to the enterprise's inception, the entrepreneur's characteristics, and the managerial system and governance style. The need to meet tourists' recent demands sustainably has led to the development and success of specific entrepreneurial formulas, including that of diffused hotels: "Tourists are becoming more sensitive to their leisure time experiences and are more interested in authenticity and having closer relations with the local population." When a tourism enterprise aspires to be sustainable, it should not remain isolated from its background. Still, it should create a broader network with other companies and stakeholders (Presutti et al., 2020), which is precisely what the diffused hospitality model is doing.

The effort of the National Association of Alberghi Diffusi, which has been working for years to export this Italian hospitality model, has been internationally recognized as a driver for promoting "Made in Italy" hospitality and Italian villages abroad (www.alberghidiffusi.it). It involves a careful and locally guided transformation that respects the relationship between the structure and its environment. The fundamental strategy is maintaining as many "local touches" as possible to convey visitors a greater sense of the place's uniqueness and identity.

On the website of the National Association of Alberghi Diffusi, the words of Simon Anholt, author of the Nation Brands Index (a ranking on the perception of the country brand based on six indicators including culture and heritage, investments, governance, and tourism), are reported: "Any place can become a tourist destination. The important thing is that it has its own story to tell." Indeed, the fundamental characteristic of villages is that they have one or more stories to pass on and for which they stand out (www.albergodiffuso.com).

The "albergo diffuso" aims to fulfill at least three main functions: animate village life by bringing tourism and creating initiatives, generate networks and supply chains of producers, i.e., allies in the process of enhancing the territory, and finally, help prevent depopulation of villages by creating job opportunities: "The basic idea is that, more than hotel guests, you become part of a real neighborhood for a few days, something that relates to the life of a temporary community. The hope is to create a new culture of hospitality and overturn the concept of tourist offerings: no longer a number of goods and services to be placed on the market at a certain price, but opportunities to improve the widespread quality of cultural, landscape, and environmental heritage, also for tourism enhancement."

The pandemic and resource crises necessitate reflection on the vision and implementation of tourism activities. Following this idea, a series of in-depth interviews were conducted with professionals and managers who have developed projects to recover and restore ancient villages and castles in Italy, turning them into high-quality structures, splendid jewels often located in lesser-known and remote areas away from the tourist destinations of major cities (Zavattaro et al.2015). The examples, results, and interview observations are based on personal analysis and interviews conducted by academics and print and digital media covering tourism (Tolkach, King, 2015).

These contributions can provide valuable insights to understand better the current tourism phenomenon (Zenker et al., 2017). Concepts such as proximity, familiarity, and authenticity must regain the importance they deserve within national tourism policies. They can also offer interesting alternative ideas for marketing and branding tourist destinations: "Tourism supply and demand are being deeply transformed, and territories need to improve their adaptability in order to respond properly to new tourist demands" (Zenker et al., 2020).

The definition of exciting new products combined with high-class service and a story to be narrated is an effective strategy to create memorable tourist experiences, which can be considered one of the most important aims of territorial branding policies. The concept of branding has expanded beyond products and services to include territories (Presutti et al., 2020). Territorial branding is crucial for regions without significant natural resources. Territorial branding is a relatively new marketing discipline that has gained recognition as a scientific field in the 21st century. The main objective of territorial branding is to create a positive image for countries, cities, and regions, attracting investments and tourists and improving economic and social conditions. By creating a favorable investment climate, these regions can attract financial inflows. Effective branding requires a team of specialists in brand management and regional marketing. In essence, the brand identity of a territory is a multifaceted concept that integrates tangible and intangible elements to create a cohesive and appealing image (Komppula et al., 2014). It involves understanding and leveraging the unique characteristics of the territory to differentiate it and position it effectively in the minds of its target audiences (Green et al., 2016). By effectively integrating albergo diffuso with brand identity, we can create a compelling narrative that resonates with guests seeking authentic, immersive experiences while maintaining a consistent and recognizable brand image. To achieve these goals, it is necessary to combine economic, sociological, and cultural dimensions, which focus on different aspects to increase the territorial brand identity. First, it is possible to focus on the economic benefits to create a favorable image among target groups such as residents, investors, and skilled professionals (Che-Ha et al., 2016). At the same time, it could be necessary to emphasize the role of brands in social differentiation, identification, and value formation (Beckman et al., 2013). A territorial brand exists in the minds of consumers and fosters geographical loyalty, which can sometimes be more significant than social identity. Along this direction, effective territorial branding requires inclusiveness, long-term partnerships, shared responsibility, trust, and engagement of all stakeholders (Campello et al., 2014). Finally, we propose that territorial branding should be culturally centered, protecting cultural values and guided by historical research and internal and external images of the territory. Overall, the process of building a territorial brand should be original and innovative, involving scientific research, stakeholder engagement, and a focus on cultural and historical aspects. This comprehensive approach aims to create a cohesive and attractive image that appeals to diverse audiences, including investors, tourists, and residents (Arnegger, Herz, 2016).

Luxury tourism and its Impact on the Local Community

Luxury tourism is a specialized sector of the tourism industry that caters to affluent travelers seeking high-end, exclusive experiences that offer comfort, personalized services, and access to unique or rare destinations. This segment is characterized by premium pricing and an emphasis on quality, with experiences often revolving around opulent accommodations, fine dining, private tours, and personalized attention. As global wealth increases, luxury tourism has expanded, with destinations increasingly offering bespoke experiences to meet the expectations of discerning clientele.

One key feature of luxury tourism is the demand for authenticity and exclusivity. Modern luxury travelers seek not only material comforts but also immersive experiences that connect them to a destination's culture, history, and environment. In rural locations like Montegridolfo, luxury tourism blends high-end services with the charm of heritage sites, local traditions, and pristine landscapes. This shift reflects a growing trend in which tourists value unique, localized, and culturally enriching experiences over standardized luxury offerings.

Sustainability has become an integral consideration within the luxury tourism market. As environmental and social awareness grows, many luxury tourists increasingly expect eco-friendly practices to be embedded in the experiences they consume. Luxury hotels and resorts now frequently integrate sustainable initiatives, such as energy-efficient systems, eco-friendly designs, locally sourced organic cuisine, and waste-reduction strategies. This alignment with sustainability adds value not only for tourists but also for host communities, which can benefit from environmentally responsible tourism that promotes local economic growth while minimizing its environmental footprint.

Luxury tourism can have a profound **positive** and **negative** impact on the local community, influencing socio-economic conditions, cultural identity, and environmental sustainability (Han et al., 2023; Lee et al., 2022; Gao et al., 2022; Sun et al., 2022). First of all, luxury tourism often brings significant financial investment to local communities. This can lead to the creation of direct and indirect jobs, such as employment in hotels, restaurants, transportation, and tourism-related services. Locals can also benefit from selling artisanal goods, providing guiding services, or catering to tourists' needs. Of course, luxury tourism development usually requires significant infrastructure improvements, including roads, communication systems, and public utilities. These developments not only cater to tourists but also improve residents' living standards. At the same time, luxury tourism often thrives on the uniqueness of local culture and heritage. To maintain appeal, there is typically a focus on preserving historical landmarks, local traditions, and cultural events, which might otherwise be at risk of neglect. The influx of affluent tourists interested in authentic experiences can incentivize the protection of local customs and architecture.

Indeed, hosting luxury tourism can raise the profile of a destination on the global stage, positioning the community as a prestigious, high-value location. This can open further investment and development opportunities, attracting more affluent visitors who contribute to the local economy. Finally, high-end tourists often expect environmental responsibility from luxury brands, which can lead to implementing sustainable practices. In some cases, luxury tourism operators introduce eco-friendly initiatives such as energy-efficient facilities, organic local sourcing, and conservation projects that benefit the broader community.

While luxury tourism brings wealth, it can also create significant income inequality. The wealth generated by high-end tourism often flows to external investors or the elite few who own the luxury establishments, leaving much of the local population excluded from the benefits. The local community may see increased living costs without proportional income increases, exacerbating economic divides. Moreover, the demand for "authentic" cultural experiences can lead to the commodification of local customs, rituals, and art. When culture is tailored to tourist preferences, it risks losing meaning and authenticity. Communities might commercialize their traditions to meet tourist expectations, diluting the integrity of their heritage. As luxury tourism developments expand, local communities may face displacement due to rising property values and the repurposing of traditional community spaces for tourism purposes. Locals may no longer be able to afford housing or rent, leading to the displacement of lower-income residents. It's very important to note that exposure to affluent tourists can lead to the adoption of external cultural norms and values, which may erode the traditional ways of life within the local community. Over time, residents may start to imitate the lifestyle and preferences of visitors, resulting in a dilution of their own cultural identity. Finally, despite potential sustainable initiatives, luxury tourism can also contribute to environmental stress. High-end resorts often consume significant natural resources, particularly water and energy. Overdevelopment to accommodate luxury standards can lead to habitat destruction, increased pollution, and the depletion of local ecosystems.

Challenges in Luxury Tourism: Overtourism, Technological Integration, and Post-Pandemic Travel

Luxury tourism, despite its focus on exclusivity and tailored experiences, is not immune to broader challenges affecting the global tourism industry. Key issues such as overtourism, technological integration, and post-pandemic travel trends reshape how destinations and businesses operate in this high-end market. These challenges require careful management to ensure luxury tourism can thrive while minimizing negative impacts on destinations and communities (Milano et al., 2022).

Overtourism, traditionally associated with mass tourism, is increasingly becoming a concern for luxury destinations. Even exclusive locations, which pride themselves on privacy and limited access, can suffer from overcrowding during peak seasons or as their popularity grows. In smaller, rural destinations like Montegridolfo, the strain of overtourism can be particularly severe due to limited infrastructure and resources.

The influx of luxury travelers can lead to the over-commercialization of cultural and historical assets, diluting the authentic experiences that originally attracted visitors. Additionally, increased tourist numbers can contribute to environmental degradation, stressing local ecosystems and threatening the area's sustainability. Managing overtourism in luxury destinations involves implementing strict visitor caps, promoting off-season travel, and encouraging more sustainable, low-impact tourism practices to preserve the exclusivity and environmental integrity of these areas (Wang et al., 2022).

Technological advancements are playing a critical role in transforming the luxury tourism experience. From personalized travel planning apps to AI-driven concierge services, luxury travelers increasingly expect seamless, tech-enabled services that enhance their experience. Smart rooms equipped with automated systems, digital personalization for in-room amenities, and virtual reality (VR) tours of destinations before travel are becoming common in luxury accommodations.

Moreover, the integration of technology is not just about enhancing the customer experience; it also offers tools for managing operational efficiency and sustainability. For instance, luxury hotels increasingly utilize IoT (Internet of Things) devices to monitor energy use, reduce waste, and optimize resource management. Additionally, mobile technologies allow travelers to engage with local culture through curated experiences without overwhelming local communities or ecosystems.

However, the challenge lies in striking a balance between offering high-tech experiences and preserving the human touch that defines luxury tourism. While technology can enhance convenience and personalization, over-reliance on it can erode the personalized, high-touch service that many luxury travelers expect (Kim, Park, 2022).

The COVID-19 pandemic has dramatically reshaped global tourism, with luxury tourism facing its own unique challenges in the post-pandemic landscape. During the pandemic, many travelers shifted towards more secluded, nature-based destinations, avoiding crowded urban areas. This has increased the demand for rural luxury tourism, with places like Montegridolfo gaining attention as ideal post-pandemic getaways that offer privacy, safety, and a connection to nature.

Health and safety have become top priorities for luxury travelers, and post-pandemic expectations include rigorous hygiene standards, flexibility in booking policies, and smaller, private group experiences. Furthermore, the concept of "revenge travel," where tourists make up for lost time by splurging on more elaborate vacations, has led to an increased demand for luxury services. This trend underscores the need for destinations to offer exclusive, safe, and bespoke experiences while also navigating ongoing travel restrictions and health protocols.

The pandemic has also accelerated the push towards sustainability in luxury tourism. Travelers are now more conscious of the environmental and social impact of their trips, seeking eco-friendly luxury options that align with their values. For destinations like Montegridolfo, post-pandemic tourism offers a unique opportunity to redefine luxury in a way that prioritizes sustainability, authenticity, and community well-being.

EMPIRICAL CASE STUDY

Methodology

This study employs a qualitative research approach, integrating both case study and ethnographic methods to explore the impact of a luxury hotel on the brand destination of the small local village where it is located, Montegridolfo, following an eco-sustainable approach. Our methodology is designed to capture this complex and multifaceted issue over a longitudinal historical period.

The case study method provides an in-depth examination of Palazzo Viviani and its renewal within Montegridolfo. It allows an understanding of the specific context and unique characteristics that have contributed to its influence on brand destination. This methodology aligns with the best practices in tourism research (Presutti, Lo Presti, 2022).

The interviews conducted for this study aimed to gather in-depth insights into the socio-cultural, economic, and environmental impacts of luxury tourism on Montegridolfo, focusing on both residents and key stakeholders, such as business owners and tourism professionals. A semi-structured interview format was employed, allowing consistency in questioning and flexibility to explore emergent topics of interest.

Respondents were selected through purposive sampling to ensure a diverse representation of voices from the community, including local business owners, hotel management, tourism authorities, and long-term residents. Participants were initially contacted via email or phone, following preliminary outreach efforts through local tourism associations and community networks. In-person interviews were conducted with individuals available in Montegridolfo, while remote interviews were arranged for those unavailable locally due to time constraints or travel restrictions.

The interview questions centered on key topics relevant to luxury tourism, including perceptions of its impact on the local community, involvement in sustainable practices, and the effects on cultural identity. Example questions included: "How do you perceive the influence of luxury tourism on the local economy?" and "To what extent do you think luxury tourism has affected community dynamics or cultural traditions?"

All interviews were audio-recorded with the participant's consent, ensuring accuracy in capturing their responses. Once completed, the recordings were transcribed verbatim using a combination of automated transcription software and manual verification. The research team reviewed the initial automated transcripts thoroughly to correct errors, capture nuances, and ensure that pauses, intonations, and non-verbal cues were appropriately noted. This hybrid transcription approach facilitated efficiency while maintaining a high level of accuracy. Transcripts were anonymized to protect the identities of participants, with personal identifiers removed during the transcription process. Thematic analysis was used to systematically identify, analyze, and report patterns or themes within the interview data. The analysis process followed Braun and Clarke's (2006) six-phase approach, which included familiarizing with the data, generating initial codes, searching for themes, reviewing themes, defining and naming themes, and writing up the results. This rigorous approach to interviewing and thematic analysis ensured that the data provided rich, reliable insights into the socio-cultural and environmental impacts of luxury tourism in Montegridolfo. The findings generated from this process offer a comprehensive understanding of how luxury tourism is perceived and its broader implications for the local community (Calero et al., 2019).

To achieve a rich and nuanced understanding of the phenomenon under investigation, we conducted an ethnographic study through long-term direct observation initiated during the renovation process of the structure (May 2021). We concluded with the reopening of Palazzo Viviani to tourists (April 2022). However, the observation has continued for the two years following the reopening until now. We also accessed and examined various archival documents, including municipal records, historical documents, marketing materials, and media articles. Finally, we interviewed several significant players, such as the resident manager, the owners, the mayor, some business entrepreneurs, and local community members.

The entire project was carried out through a detailed analysis of the elements that constitute the composite reality of the restoration, refurbishment, and tourism use of ancient villages in Italy (Unesco, 2020).

To draft a list of questions consistent with the project's goals, significant contributions came from consulting the book "L'Italia è bella dentro" by journalist Luca Martinelli, who was part of the National Strategy for Inner Areas (SNAI) working group from May 2017 to June 2019. This group aimed to develop the potential of Italy's inner areas (Martinelli, 2020). The book is a collection of best practices implemented in rural areas of Italy, showcasing stories of resilience and innovation where entrepreneurs and small associations aim to attribute economic value to inner areas, exploring the opportunities that marginal territories can offer. The exchange of ideas and observations contained in Martinelli's text provided a valuable framework for initiating a fruitful dialogue with the experts involved in the following research project.

An investigation was conducted among experts through email exchanges and phone calls. Founders and managers of several hospitality structures, which are considered the jewels of Italian rural tourism, were contacted. These experts were willing to share their passion, which was aligned with a vision of local tourism aimed at well-being. Thanks to their proactive attitude, a human relationship, as well as a professional one, was established. Their goal is to create a form of tourism based on mutual exchange between host and guest, where what is given is received and where the service provided is so well-crafted that it creates value. These experts have managed to create a market where their service is "recognized" and supported by a sense of belonging to the territory; their structures indeed incorporate identity and solidarity.

During the ethnographic research, the active collaboration and participation of Danilo Di Pasquale, hotel entrepreneur and former general manager of Palazzo Viviani, allowed the work to take a more practical and precise form, as it was corroborated by data analysis and their reworking. Following the initial qualitative approach, to simulate the start-up for the relaunch of Montegridolfo Castle in the tourism market, the USALI (Uniform System of Accounts for the Lodging Industry) model was used. This accounting standard for the hotel industry was developed in the United States in 1926 by some Chicago hoteliers who aimed to share experiences and develop agreements and guidelines for accounting. Since then, it has spread worldwide and is essential for profitable hotel management. It is mainly used as a reference by large international chains and serves as a tool for economic and financial planning. USALI is particularly valuable for establishing a dialogue with banks, investment companies, or, as in this case, the property owner.

By using this standard in managing the income statement, costs and revenues are associated with their respective areas of responsibility, allowing the calculation of the marginality of each hotel department. This breakdown is crucial for understanding management events and controlling management levers. Finally, USALI provides immediate and concise information on the hotel's performance, giving a clear view per department. In this sense, the contribution of expert Danilo Di Pasquale was fundamental, as he provided numbers and data from his previous hospitality management consulting experiences during the research phase and was willing to share his industry knowledge. Finally, to protect the identity and privacy of the hotels used as benchmarks, it was decided, in agreement with the property and Danilo Di Pasquale, to keep the sources anonymous.

Sustainable Tourism, Luxury, Destination Branding, and Rural Identity: From Theory to Montegridolfo Empirical Context

Luxury tourism is a growing trend in rural areas, where exclusivity and an immersive connection to nature and history offer an appeal that contrasts with more conventional urban luxury experiences. Montegridolfo, a village steeped in historical and cultural significance, exemplifies this trend. However, to fully understand its place within the broader luxury tourism market, it is essential to situate Montegridolfo in the context of critical theoretical frameworks related to rural tourism, destination branding, and sustainable tourism. A central theme in modern tourism development is sustainability, which is increasingly relevant in discussions of luxury tourism. Butler's (1980) work on the tourist area life cycle provides a useful lens to examine how Montegridolfo's luxury tourism offering might evolve and what steps should be taken to sustain its attractiveness over time. His model suggests that tourism destinations risk overexploitation and decline without careful management. For Montegridolfo, this raises questions about the balance between promoting luxury tourism and preserving the village's unique historical and environmental assets.

Sharpley (2009) critiques traditional sustainability models, arguing for a broader understanding of sustainable tourism, especially in the luxury sector, where eco-friendly practices can sometimes be at odds with luxury travelers' exclusive, resource-intensive demands. This tension is particularly relevant to Montegridolfo, where local businesses' approaches to sustainability, as reflected in their self-perceptions, could be further explored(Montegridolfo).

Font and McCabe's (2017) study highlights the importance of aligning marketing efforts with sustainability goals. This theme could be particularly pertinent to the branding of Montegridolfo as both a luxury and eco-conscious destination. By integrating sustainable practices into the branding and marketing of the village, Montegridolfo can appeal to a new class of luxury travelers who value exclusivity and environmental responsibility.

The branding of rural destinations like Montegridolfo requires careful consideration of how the village's unique historical and geographical assets are marketed to tourists. Morgan, Pritchard, and Pride (2011) explore how destination branding can manage place reputation and influence tourism success. Their framework could inform how Montegridolfo positions itself as a luxury destination, particularly by emphasizing its heritage and tranquil rural environment.

Similarly, Cai's (2002) model of cooperative branding for rural destinations emphasizes the importance of collaboration among stakeholders. In Montegridolfo, businesses, local authorities, and residents must work together to strengthen the village's brand as a luxury destination, ensuring that their collective efforts resonate with potential visitors.

The stakeholder approach explored by García, Gómez, and Molina (2012) further underscores this point. Their research highlights the role of community and business involvement in shaping a destination's brand. In the context of Montegridolfo, integrating local voices into the destination branding process would enhance the authenticity of the luxury experience and ensure that the brand reflects the village's unique identity.

Aeffe Group and Montegridolfo: A Company's Duty

To understand what the Aeffe Group has represented for Italian and international entrepreneurship, one can refer to Vogue Runway. This platform archives Vogue's content and offers a comprehensive view of the fashion world, stating that "it helped establish the Made in Italy movement" (www.vogue.com).

The key to understanding the group's values and mission lies in its founder's profile. Alberta Ferretti is described by the most prestigious and authoritative fashion magazines as a professional with brilliant entrepreneurial acumen. In interviews, the designer describes herself as an authentic and contemporary woman, emphasizing the importance of being true to oneself and always adhering to one's style (www.harpersbazaararabia.com).

A significant article in the Times of London in 2001 defines Ferretti as "a formidable industrialist." Journalist Liza Armstrong highlights the characteristics that distinguish the designer, proclaiming her "Italy's quiet achiever." The entrepreneur resides in Cattolica, where she was born and with which she has an indissoluble bond. The city is on the Adriatic coast, 327 km from Italy's fashion capital, Milan. In an article by Christopher Petkanas published in Travel Leisure (May 15, 2009), the city is described with adjectives like "pleasant" and "familiar," and thus far from the hustle and bustle. As stated in the interview, the designer "dares to live and work where the action isn't." In this atmosphere, the designer claims to find the concentration to create: "She cannot imagine life away from the local farmers who press small-batch oils from a single variety of olive, or from the fishermen who bring in the Adriatic's famously sweet baby sole." The designer's connection to Cattolica not only stimulated her artistic creativity. Her innate entrepreneurial spirit merged with the pursuit of an inspiring and carefree lifestyle inspired by "la dolce vita."

Thus, in 1988, along with a group of co-investors, she decided to bet on restoring a medieval palace in the village of Montegridolfo, a small center inland from Cattolica. Six years later, the Montegridolfo Castle's main structure would be renamed Palazzo Viviani. The distinctive feature of Montegridolfo is that it encompasses four different products and, therefore, four different markets to commercialize. The hotel rooms are located between the 13th-century Castle and other historical properties that have been acquired and restored. The rooms in Montegridolfo Castle (Palazzo Viviani) are enriched with unique elements, such as the original frescoes adorning the walls and ceilings of the most exclusive rooms.

Additionally, the entire furnishing was carefully selected to create a connection with the ancient structure. Moreover, the hotel complex includes some houses within the ancient village and apartments in the "new" town. While the accommodations within the ancient village maintain the historic and refined style of the Castle, the houses in the "new" village are of recent construction and thus characterized by contemporary architecture. Blooming climbing plants adorn the walls of the new village's residences. Finally, other rooms are located in the "Painter's House," near the pool with a sea view. Later, with their minimalist style, these rooms were transformed into a center called the "Wellness Workshop," a fitness area with access to a sauna and a massage cabin.

The palace offered various dining options, such as gourmet cuisine at the "Ristoro di Palazzo Viviani" and "L'Osteria dell'Accademia," where chef Maurizio Salvigni prepared typical recipes with local products. Outside the palace walls and within the village, there was the "Ritrovo del Vecchio Forno," a rustic pizzeria. Finally, there was also a brasserie and wine bar called "Grotta dei Gridolfi." The "Bottega delle Vivande" was the place to buy zero-kilometer food products like olive oil, cheeses such as Mondaino's fossa cheese, cured meats, honey, and jams. These specialties were available directly from local producers. Fresh products for immediate consumption, like sweets and fresh pasta, were made on-site in the workshop in the square of the "Vecchio Forno," where guests could watch the housewives rolling out the dough. The process was entirely visible so guests could observe their work, take photos, and learn from those expert gestures the dedication, care, and love for gastronomy—a unique and unrepeatable hospitality experience.

With the help of the municipality and especially without altering the village's atmosphere, Alberta Ferretti and her local partners undertook a complete restoration of the town, including the magnificent Clock Tower and the surrounding walls. The designer defines her mission as a "crusade": "Everyone said we were crazy, but being from here, we saw it as our duty." During the recovery and restoration project in Montegridolfo, designer Ferretti felt a deep nostalgia and was overwhelmed by her love for her region: "I was immediately struck by nostalgia, overwhelmed by how much this region means to me." Determined to restore the Palace, it seemed inevitable to her to proceed with the rehabilitation and enhancement of all the surrounding areas: "Restoring the Palace without restoring Montegridolfo would be selfish" (Travel Leisure, 2009).

Ideals and Market Positioning Choices: A Long Perspective

The former director of Palazzo Viviani (a 4-star establishment), Danilo Di Pasquale (1999-2003 / 2008-2012), recalls his experience within the structure as an outstanding professional opportunity, where: "The landscape and the structure coexisted in a kind of association and virtuous circle. If the population is educated to know the riches of the place where they reside, of their material and immaterial heritage, this definitely generates a positive effect for the hotel business."

In 1994, Palazzo Viviani opened its doors to the public, but the tourist destination started quietly, positioning itself in a new territorial market for this province of Romagna.

At this point, it is crucial to understand the competitive context of the tourism market in the 1990s. Most visitors to the area were families with medium-low spending power, mainly national tourists who preferred to spend the summer on the Romagna Riviera. Tourists of all ages crowded the beaches of Rimini, Riccione, and other coastal resorts in search of the "Movida." The Romagna hinterland and its food and wine heritage, resulting from a centuries-old tradition, were still an unknown and unexplored asset for most tourists (www.treccani.it).

At the end of the last century, the inland areas of the Romagna Riviera were neither known nor enjoyed by tourists. This is why the recovery plan for Montegridolfo marked a fundamental milestone in the political and urban history of the Emilia-Romagna region. With Montegridolfo's entry into the market and the conservative restoration of the Castle, the Ferretti family reversed the trend by educating the territory and the area's inhabitants to respect and value their roots. In this sense, Montegridolfo pioneered this part of the market. This initiative aimed to shift attention from the Riviera towards more forward-looking, cultured, and sustainable tourism.

For the first time, a territory in Romagna/North Marche offered a new tourist product to enhance its historical and cultural roots. "The recovery plan for Montegridolfo," continues Di Pasquale, "is an unprecedented operation for the Romagna territory that aims to welcome a selective, intercontinental, high-level market with a high propensity for spending, whose travel motivation lies in food and wine routes and cultural tourism. This type of tourist escapes the frenzy of the beaches and sees a unique potential in the Romagna hinterland. Coincidentally, a combination is generated that follows the travel motivations of those who frequent Tuscany with the Sienese hills, Umbria, Marche, and finally fits into this context Romagna with pioneering Montegridolfo."

It is precisely the famous article in Travel Leisure (2009) that seals the real market positioning of Montegridolfo. This event represents the official success of the project; the market had finally understood the need to differentiate the Romagna tourist product. Di Pasquale explains: "The magazine had grasped the unique selling proposition offered by Montegridolfo. Following the publication of the article, the first tour operators reluctantly agreed to contract the Castle."

In an area where the language of tourism professionals was that of full board, sea, and beach, evidently Montegridolfo offered a product inconsistent with the existing offer and was therefore greeted with distrust by tour operators and industry professionals.

As soon as the market recognized the potential of the structure and following the publication of articles in the most prestigious world travel magazines, the scenario changed dramatically. An example is the inclusion of the hotel in the renowned Karen Brown travel guide. Finally, further reinforcement of the positioning came from an article in HIP Hotels magazine, which is a benchmark within the Anglo-Saxon luxury tourism market. The Montegridolfo Castle had finally opened up to an international market. Before September 11, 2001, the market served was 80% American. Montegridolfo is no longer just another hotel in the area or the Castle restored "by the designer." The unique aspect is that it becomes an ambassador of a new tourism model. From here, the demand from the American, Japanese, and Russian markets spreads enormously. Montefiore Conca, Verucchio, San Leo, Torriana, and Gradara are discovered by this type of tourism, enchanted by the quality of food and wine and the beauty of the landscape.

"Our guests come from international origins: mainly German, Dutch, Belgian, French, British, and Irish, aged between 40 and 60 years. These travelers particularly enjoy road trips, love exploring the Italian hills, and are passionate about fine wines and traditional Italian cuisine. Their personalities are characterized by a lively curiosity, a sunny nature, and an extroverted attitude, always ready to make new discoveries and immerse themselves in the local beauties. Montegridolfo represents a fascinating stop on their journey where they can enjoy the tranquility of the medieval village and experience an authentic and memorable stay. These guests are attracted to the local food and wine culture, nature lovers, and constantly seeking a pleasant place where they feel welcomed. They are travelers who choose Slow Tourism, trying to live each moment with gratitude and appreciating the genuineness of the places they visit. Palazzo Viviani thus becomes an ideal reference point in their tours in Italy, offering a stay that combines modern comfort with historical charm" (Actual Director Manager of Palazzo Viviani)

Destination Analysis: History and Traditions of the Montegridolfo Fraction

To offer a careful and detailed analysis of the Montegridolfo hotel structure, it is important to analyze its historical and cultural context.

The origins of the village date back to the 13th century when the Gridolfi family from Rimini settled there. It was, in fact, in this phase of the Middle Ages that well-defended fortresses were built on the hills. These were able to oversee the landscape below, thus gaining a military advantage. The center was looted and burned in 1288 by the neighboring municipalities of Mondaino and Saludecio. With the settlement of Malatesta III, known as the "Guastafamiglia," lord of Rimini and Pesaro, in 1337, new walls were built with four imposing towers to defend the town. After a brief domination by the Montefeltros, the Castle returned to the hands of the Malatesta. In the following years, Montegridolfo was dominated by Cesare Borgia (1502), Venice (1504), and then became part of the Papal States in 1509 (montegridolfo.eu).

Despite the small size of the town, the area still has an original heritage of ancient churches and monuments. Outside the Castle walls are the Sanctuary of the Blessed Virgin of Graces and the Church of San Pietro, where typical architectural elements of the landscape are represented; these are undoubtedly historical sources and artistic-symbolic elements that stimulate visitors' curiosity. Additionally, near the Castle is the medieval church of San Rocco. The oratory dates back to 1427 and was an important reference center for the Montegridolfo community. Though small, its interior contains gems of popular art and devotion, including a painting from the Giotto school.

At the foot of the Castle walls is the Montegridolfo Gothic Line Museum, named after the line of fortifications set up by Hitler along the left bank of the Foglia, with which the Germans tried to hinder the Allies' advance. It was Romagna, and particularly the Rimini area, that witnessed one of the most dramatic moments of the Second World War. The battle involved 1,200,000 soldiers and the entire territory of the hills and hinterland. The museum, which from the outside looks like a bunker, displays war relics. On the museum walls are prints of propaganda contemporary to the historical period, both of Italian-German and Allied production. It is also possible to visit two of the eleven shelters dug by civilians in 1944 to take cover during the battle. Walking along the path leading to the Museum, the visitor can see the site of the Battle of Montegridolfo, where the German defenses were breached (August 31-September 1, 1944).

Near Montegridolfo, in the Romagna hinterland, there are a multitude of villages rich in stories and elements that make them unique. In modern times, passing on and preserving the stories within the social fabric remains inherent in the historical consciousness of this territory. The events related to the Second World War and their dramatic conclusion with the events linked to the Resistance and Liberation from Nazifascism are still alive in memory. Every year, on the occasion of the anniversary of the Liberation from German occupation, the population of Montegridolfo participates in the historical re-enactment "Montegridolfo Liberata," offering a plunge into the past. The event is meticulously set up, and its participants wear English and German uniforms, reenacting the Battle of Montegridolfo in which the commander of an English platoon, Gerard R. Norton, and the Allied army attacked and broke through the Gothic Line defenses.

A Potential Interpretative Framework

The extensive research effort leading to the realization of this paper aims to analyze in detail the case history of Montegridolfo. The development of a sustainable tourism system around the village has been achieved through the identification and awareness of economic and social mechanisms shaping the local identity and heritage. The ambitious project initiated by the owners of Palazzo Viviani to position this accommodation structure effectively in the luxury tourism sector has been connected with the interest to safeguard the village's history and identity and revitalize the destination brand.

Despite the village's small size, the area possesses an original historical and cultural heritage which, together with the view from the castle walls, has made it a flagship in the Italian tourism sector, particularly in the luxury segment. Palazzo Viviani Relais is the centerpiece of a new experiential luxury tourism model, unique in the area, based on knowledge and awareness of the characteristic traits of the Romagna hinterland and the desire to preserve its rural, slow character, combined with high standards of hospitality and hotel services. The recovery plan involved the entire village of Montegridolfo and represented almost a true "Renaissance" linked to the sensitivity and taste of its promoters.

The concept of sustainable tourism has indeed become a key discourse through which the entire tourism context is increasingly framing the dynamism and opportunities of the sector itself. Identity, sustainability, and territorial capital therefore constitute the ideal context for Montegridolfo to develop its competitive capacity as a territory, as they clarify both the uniqueness of each place and the continuous transformation towards profitable and stable business models.

The concept of albergo diffuso, or "scattered hotel," is pivotal in understanding the transformation of Montegridolfo. This model integrates accommodation into existing structures within a village, rather than constructing new buildings, thus preserving the architectural heritage and cultural landscape. In Montegridolfo, the hotel rooms are spread between the 13th-century Castle, known as Palazzo Viviani, and various restored historical properties within the village. This approach not only maintains the village's aesthetic and historical integrity but also fosters a sense of community among both residents and visitors

The restoration of Montegridolfo, spearheaded by designer Alberta Ferretti, involved meticulous attention to preserving the village's historical and cultural heritage. Ferretti, driven by her deep connection to the region, undertook a comprehensive restoration project that included not only Palazzo Viviani but also the entire village. This project was described as a "Renaissance" for Montegridolfo, blending sensitivity to the local heritage with high standards of hospitality. The village's medieval structures, such as the Clock Tower and surrounding walls, were restored without altering their historical atmosphere

Palazzo Viviani stands as the centerpiece of Montegridolfo's transformation into a luxury destination. The castle's rooms feature unique elements like original frescoes and carefully selected furnishings that connect with the ancient structure, offering guests an authentic historical experience. The hotel complex also includes accommodations in both the ancient and new villages, blending historical charm with contemporary comforts. The dining options at Palazzo Viviani further enhance this experience, with gourmet cuisine and local products creating a gastronomic journey that ties visitors to the region's traditions and flavors.

"The distribution of our rooms and apartments in various parts of the village allows us to offer an authentic and immersive experience where guests can live like locals, exploring the medieval village.We offer concierge services that are well acquainted with the area and can provide personalized recommendations on what to see and do in Montegridolfo and its surroundings. Even though the rooms are distributed, the central reception and welcome services offer a point of reference for guests, ensuring they have access to all the information and services they need during their stay"

The development of Montegridolfo as a luxury destination has had significant economic and social impacts on the local community. The influx of tourists has stimulated the local economy, created jobs and supported local businesses. The project has also fostered a sense of pride among residents, who participate in events like the historical re-enactment "Montegridolfo Liberata," which commemorates the village's role in World War II. These activities not only attract tourists but also reinforce the community's connection to its history and heritage.

Montegridolfo's approach to tourism is deeply rooted in sustainability. The village leverages its territorial capital—comprising its historical, cultural, and natural assets—to create a unique and sustainable tourism experience. This strategy involves a strong emphasis on social innovation, as seen in the community's involvement in preserving and promoting their heritage. Additionally, technological innovations, such as advanced hospitality services and eco-friendly practices, play a crucial role in maintaining the village's appeal as a sustainable destination.

The integration of Montegridolfo's historical and cultural heritage into its tourism offerings has been key to creating a strong local brand identity. This identity is built on the village's unique characteristics, such as its medieval architecture, historical significance, and traditional local products. By positioning itself as a luxury destination that offers an authentic and immersive experience, Montegridolfo attracts discerning tourists who value sustainability and cultural richness. The success of this branding strategy is evident in the village's growing popularity among both Italian and international visitors.

Luxury tourism in Montegridolfo, while capable of bringing substantial benefits to a local community through economic opportunities, cultural revitalization, and global recognition, also poses significant risks. These include potential cultural erosion, social inequalities, and environmental degradation. The ultimate impact depends on how well tourism is managed and whether the community is actively involved in the decision-making process. By balancing economic development with cultural preservation and sustainability, communities like Montegridolfo can ensure that luxury tourism contributes positively to both their short-term prosperity and long-term resilience.

In summary, Montegridolfo and Palazzo Viviani can be considered an excellent example of sustainable tourism through the albergo diffuso model for several reasons:

Preservation and Restoration of Historical Heritage

- Architectural Conservation: Montegridolfo's transformation into a tourist destination involved the meticulous restoration of its medieval structures. This not only preserved the historical integrity of buildings like the 13th-century Castle (Palazzo Viviani) but also maintained the village's aesthetic charm. This approach avoided the need for new construction, which can disrupt local landscapes and cultural heritage
- Cultural Revival: The restoration led by Alberta Ferretti brought a Renaissance to Montegridolfo. The careful restoration of frescoes, walls, and other historical features has turned the village into a living museum, where visitors can experience the authentic historical ambiance while enjoying modern comforts. This cultural preservation helps maintain the village's identity and provides a sense of continuity and authenticity. "At Palazzo Viviani, we warmly welcome guests, offering an environment where they can relax and appreciate the beautiful setting of Montegridolfo, feeling part of a centuries-old history. Upon the guest's arrival at the facility, it is our priority to introduce them to the magical and historical atmosphere of the place to engage them and make them aware of Montegridolfo's cultural richness. Our guests can discover all the information about the history of the facility also through our

official channels (website and social media), allowing them to start immersing themselves in the context of the village and Palazzo even during the pre-stay phase. Additionally, the guest directory in all rooms provides tips on the history of Hotel Palazzo Viviani"

Community Engagement and Economic Benefits

- Local Economic Boost: The development of Montegridolfo into a luxury destination has significantly boosted the local economy. It created jobs in hospitality, maintenance, and tourism services, supporting local businesses and artisans. This economic activity helps sustain the community and prevents depopulation, a common issue in rural areas. "We position ourselves as an ideal destination for slow tourism, inviting travelers to take their time exploring the village and surroundings without haste, enjoying the tranquility and natural beauty of the area. We collaborate with local producers of wine, olive oil, and artisans to offer our guests unique and authentic experiences, thus increasing the appeal of our offer. We organize and participate in local cultural events such as festivals and concerts, promoting the village as a center of cultural activities.
- Social benefits for local Community: The success of Montegridolfo's albergo diffuso model is heavily reliant on community involvement. The presence of Palazzo Viviani, a luxury hotel in Montegridolfo, has brought significant benefits to the local community, fostering both economic growth and social cohesion. Many residents of the village have experienced a direct economic boost, as the hotel provides employment opportunities ranging from hospitality roles to services such as local artisanal products and culinary offerings, creating a sustainable source of income for the village. Additionally, the hotel's focus on employing local workers has helped retain younger generations who might have otherwise left for employment opportunities in larger cities. he presence of Palazzo Viviani, a luxury hotel in Montegridolfo, has brought significant benefits to the local community, fostering both economic growth and social cohesion. Many residents of the village have experienced a direct economic boost, as the hotel provides employment opportunities ranging from hospitality roles to services such as local artisanal products and culinary offerings, creating a sustainable source of income for the village. Additionally, the hotel's focus on employing local workers has helped retain younger generations who might have otherwise left for employment opportunities in larger cities.
- Economic benefits for local community and network relationhsips: Beyond economic contributions, the hotel has become a catalyst for preserving and

promoting the cultural heritage of Montegridolfo. The restoration and maintenance of the medieval architecture within the Palazzo have enhanced the historical identity of the village, attracting visitors interested in its rich past. The local artisans, craftsmen, and artists have found a growing market for their work, as tourists seek authentic souvenirs and experiences, further integrating the community into the luxury tourism ecosystem. Furthermore, the increased visibility of Montegridolfo as a luxury destination has inspired a renewed sense of pride among residents. Community events, festivals, and cultural initiatives supported by the hotel have helped to strengthen social bonds and foster collaboration between the hotel management and the local populace. For example, festivals showcasing local traditions are co-hosted by the hotel, bringing both tourists and locals together in celebration, thereby reinforcing the community's cultural identity while enriching the tourist experience. Residents participate in historical reenactments and cultural events, such as "Montegridolfo Liberata," which not only attract tourists but also strengthen community bonds and pride. This active participation ensures that tourism development aligns with the interests and values of the local population. "For the reasons mentioned above, our accommodation facility has a synergistic relationship with the context in which it is located". Specifically, the local residents are the first to care about its reputation. Indeed, they spontaneously provide information to guests arriving at the facility, making them feel at home. It was the older residents of Montegridolfo who, when I took over as manager of the facility, provided me with the most important information for running the hotel. The dialogue with the local population was therefore crucial in both the knowledge of the context and the development of a tourism model that was consistent with the particularities of Montegridolfo". Local relationships involvement: For food and beverage procurement, Palazzo Viviani only turns to local suppliers to stimulate local activities and create a network of contacts with local businesses. Additionally, in the more prestigious rooms, it includes gift boxes with typical local products: honey, oil, and wine. With each of these local companies, Palazzo Viviani has established a relationship of trust and mutual respect, as to share the desire to enhance the territory's image and its riches. During the summer season, Palazzo Viviani has offered its large green spaces as a setting for the "Concerts at the Castle" evenings organized with the participation of the Municipality of Montegridolfo. Furthermore, thanks to this excellent relationship, historcal conferences were held where both guests of the facility and residents and outsiders could participate. "At the entrance to the village walls, a craft workshop has opened, and starting from the next season, we are developing workshops and experiential packages with this artisan to involve both adult and child guests of Palazzo Viviani in the faunal richness of Montegridolfo and respect for the environment". In recent years, the hotel has woven a bond with all the associations that are dedicated to preserving and enhancing the memory of the village. During World War II, the village of Montegridolfo was one of the strongholds of the eastern Gothic Line. For this reason, the Museum of the Gothic Line was established on the same battlefields. "One of the tasks of our front desk is to promote the village's history and its cultural centers; therefore, we provide daily information about the museum and its relics. In August, the park of Palazzo Viviani will host the event "Love and Art Move the World" promoted by local associations to promote local artists and musicians"

Sustainable Practices and Innovation

- Sustainable Tourism Practices: Montegridolfo emphasizes eco-friendly and sustainable tourism practices. By using existing buildings, the albergo diffuso model minimizes environmental impact compared to constructing new hotels. Additionally, the integration of local products and services reduces the carbon footprint associated with transportation and promotes local economies. "To raise guests' awareness about sustainability, we invite them not to waste resources and always use them wisely. Indeed, within the guest directory available in all rooms, we inform the guest to use water, air conditioning, and laundry products consciously. We also try to create awareness with our courtesy product lines, which have certifications attesting to the environmental commitment of the producing companies. To limit the use of vehicles within the village, we inform the guest before arrival via email to leave the car in the surrounding parking lots, and we handle luggage loading and unloading with our electric golf cart, thus reducing emissions and decreasing traffic in the village". In terms of environmental sustainability, the Palazzo has also implemented initiatives such as energy-efficient infrastructure and sustainable waste management, serving as a model for other local businesses. These initiatives not only minimize the environmental impact of the hotel but also inspire eco-friendly practices within the community, contributing to the long-term sustainability of the area.
- Technological sustainable Integration: Advanced hospitality services and eco-friendly technologies are incorporated to enhance visitor experiences while maintaining sustainability. For example, efficient energy use, waste management, and the use of local resources contribute to the village's sustainability goals. "I believe in the importance of environmental sustainability and will continue to implement initiatives to reduce our environmental im-

pact and raise awareness among guests about the importance of preserving our natural and cultural heritage. I foresee an increasingly close collaboration with local entities and associations to promote Montegridolfo as a destination for cultural tourism, involving guests in local events and activities to create a unique and memorable stay experience. Finally, I see a future where Palazzo Viviani becomes an international reference point for those seeking a stay that combines history, culture, and modern comfort in a unique and enchanting setting".

- Sustainable local events organization: Thanks to the "Giardini Aperti" initiative, on May 4, 2024, FAI members had the opportunity to be guided by our staff through the magnificent green spaces and learn about the prestigious history of Palazzo Viviani Castello di Montegridolfo. This collaboration represents a unique opportunity for us to promote the beauty and culture of the Montegridolfo village, consolidating the position as an "albergo diffuso" that offers an authentic and immersive experience in the heart of a medieval village. The event attracted numerous visitors, increased the visibility of the hotel, and strengthened several ties with the local community and supporters of the preservation of Italian heritage. "The event "Giardini Aperti" organized by FAI - Fondo per l'Ambiente Italiano had a significant impact on Palazzo Viviani, reinforcing our commitment to the conservation and enhancement of local heritage. We are excited to announce the beginning of our collaboration with FAI. Since its founding, FAI has been dedicated to preserving and enhancing Italy's rich historical, artistic, and landscape heritage".

Unique Branding and Authentic Experience

- Authentic Experience: The combination of historical charm with modern luxury offers a unique and authentic tourist experience. Guests stay in historically significant buildings with modern amenities, which creates a distinctive blend of old and new. This authenticity attracts discerning tourists who value cultural richness and sustainable practices. "We are very interested and strive to be active in associations representing the territory" (Owner of Palazzo Viviani).
- Strong Brand Identity: Montegridolfo has successfully created a strong local brand identity based on its unique characteristics. The village's medieval architecture, historical significance, and traditional local products are key elements of its brand. By promoting these aspects, Montegridolfo differentiates itself from other tourist destinations, appealing to a niche market of luxury and culture-focused tourists

- Widespread hotel: Palazzo Viviani Hotel is a perfect example of an albergo diffuso thanks to its structure that distributes rooms and apartments in various parts of the village, allowing guests to live an authentic and immersive experience. Guests can enjoy the local life, natural beauty, and rich history of Montegridolfo, creating a unique and unforgettable stay that meets the needs of modern travelers seeking authenticity, culture, and slow tourism. At the same time, it embodies the principles of "village tourism" as it emphasizes the experience of staying in a small village where visitors can immerse themselves in local life, explore the surrounding landscape, and participate in local activities and traditions. A stay at Palazzo Viviani celebrates the life, culture, and history of the village of Montegridolfo, guaranteeing guests a unique and unforgettable experience. "Being located in Montegridolfo deeply influences our sales strategy and service organization".

Economic and comprehensive Impact and Replicability

- Strategies: The occupancy rate varies depending on the period considered. During the months of June, July, and August, the average occupancy is around 80%. During private events held on weekends, the facility often reaches full occupancy (100%). The average room prices have increased from 2022 (year of opening) to 2024. Rates vary depending on the type of room, some of which are located within the ancient village while others are in the historical residences of the property. Competitive prices were initially proposed for the relaunch of the facility, and the rates have increased over these three years supported by strong demand and rising variable costs. "Palazzo Viviani is a seasonal facility: it opens its doors in April and ends its season in October. We target tourists and visitors interested in Italian culture, history, and gastronomy who want to experience staying in a medieval castle. We offer packages that include guided tours, local wine tastings, typical dinners, and cultural tours, allowing guests to fully immerse themselves in the life and culture of Montegridolfo".
- Holistic Development: The albergo diffuso model in Montegridolfo not only focuses on tourism but also on the overall development of the village. This includes improving infrastructure, preserving cultural sites, and promoting social cohesion. Such a comprehensive approach ensures that tourism benefits are broad-based and sustainable in the long term
- Model for Other Communities: Montegridolfo serves as an inspiring example for other rural communities seeking sustainable tourism development. Its success demonstrates how leveraging historical and cultural assets can create economic opportunities without compromising sustainability. This replicable

model can guide other villages in developing their unique, sustainable tourism strategies.

The importance of territorial connection with Montegridolfo

- The location in Montegridolfo influences and defines the sales strategy and services organization. "We use our unique location to offer an authentic stay experience that enhances the local culture and meets the needs of modern travelers seeking authenticity, culture, and relaxation." The real strength of the facility lies in the relationship between the structure and the surrounding environment. This means becoming a sort of place's ambassador: "As a manager of the facility, I have come into contact with residents who have transmitted to me the historical and cultural heritage of this jewel that is Montegridolfo. This exchange was followed by the actual involvement of local human resources within the facility. Indeed, all the staff live in the area and are proud to contribute to its success. Among the critical points, I would include a characteristic common to all widespread hotels, namely the issue related to logistics". The very fact that the facility is spread throughout the village leads to a substantial increase in operating costs. The dispersiveness linked to the vastness of the structure also generates logistical problems, leading to a waste of time and, consequently, costs that the facility must bear (e.g., the food and beverage supplier is required to not only transport but also provide a loading and unloading service for the goods).
- Palazzo Viviani Hotel and the village of Montegridolfo benefit reciprocally in a symbiosis that enhances the local history, culture, and economy. The hotel receives an authentic historical setting and community support while giving the village visibility, economic support, and cultural enhancement. This mutual exchange creates a prosperous and sustainable environment that enriches both guests and residents of Montegridolfo. "The training path followed up to now is certainly a fundamental basis for professional growth. In my training, I have gained valuable lessons in management and operations, and having the opportunity to apply them at Palazzo Viviani has allowed me to create a functional structure and develop a successful hospitality model. However, experience has taught me the importance of adaptation and constant updating. The tourism and hospitality industry is continuously evolving, influenced by changes in travelers' needs and preferences, technological innovations, and environmental sustainability challenges. For this reason, continuous training remains essential to stay competitive and offer high-quality services that meet market expectations."

CONCLUSIONS

Montegridolfo and Palazzo Viviani present a compelling case study on the success of sustainable albergo diffuso and the creation of a robust local brand identity. Located in the picturesque hills of the Riviera Romagnola, Montegridolfo combines historic charm with modern luxury, transforming itself into a unique destination that exemplifies the principles of sustainable tourism and community-based hospitality. Thus, Montegridolfo and Palazzo Viviani exemplify how the albergo diffuso model can successfully combine sustainable tourism with the creation of a solid local brand identity.

"The future I envision for Palazzo Viviani and Montegridolfo is bright and full of opportunities (Lidija, Solasotlga, 2019). I foresee growth based on a greater presence of international tourists interested in Italian culture and history and seeking an authentic and immersive stay. We will continue to develop unique and personalized experiences that allow guests to fully immerse themselves in the local culture, from culinary experiences to guided tours of the village and surroundings."

Through preserving historical structures, promoting local culture, and committing to sustainability, Montegridolfo has transformed itself into a premier destination for luxury tourism. This case study highlights the potential for small villages to leverage their unique assets to create sustainable economic opportunities and foster community pride, all while offering visitors an unparalleled and authentic experience (Papadimitriou et al., 2015).

The success of Montegridolfo serves as an inspiring example for other communities seeking to develop sustainable and culturally rich tourism models. The stronger the link between sustainable identity and territorial capital, the more it will be possible to generate processes that enhance local resources for tourist activities concerning village tourism. This will benefit local tourism and contribute to the growth of cultural heritage understood as a common good. Such a connection fosters relationships, a shared sense of belonging, and a propensity for innovation, creativity, knowledge, co-production, and cooperation.

In destinations like Montegridolfo, luxury tourism offers significant opportunities for economic development, cultural preservation, and sustainability. However, the challenge lies in balancing the exclusivity and demands of high-end tourism with the need to protect local traditions, ensure equitable economic benefits for residents, and maintain environmental integrity. The integration of luxury and sustainability is becoming increasingly critical as the industry evolves to meet the needs of both tourists and host communities.

A rational understanding of the decision-making process undertaken by luxury hospitality consumers before choosing a destination is increasingly important when the focus is concentrated on the albergo diffuso context. This future direction is challenging because the meanings of luxury and village hospitality are only sometimes simple and straightforward when associated with each other. Undoubtedly, the quality of the tangible combined with the intangible components could help delineate the overall experience to be offered in an economy dominated by experiential aspects. Therefore, it is necessary to focus on a series of intangible elements, whose presence is a prerequisite for enhancing, managing, and transforming possible external stimuli into opportunities for tourism development. However, this will be feasible only if other development mechanisms resulting from external policies are simultaneously activated (Barbini, Presutti, 2014; Presutti, Lo Presti, 2022).

In this regard, investing primarily in social innovation and, subsequently, in technological innovation is essential. Technological advancements can be crucial in transforming this village into an intelligent destination for sustainable tourism. This transformation can be achieved through technologically advanced solutions that meet the needs for higher tourism sustainability by enabling a higher focus on clean, green, ethical, and quality at all levels of the supply chain.

Finally, we conclude that Montegridolfo's positioning as a luxury rural destination can also be enriched by comparing it with similar rural areas that have successfully cultivated luxury tourism. Lane's (1994) seminal work on rural tourism highlights the unique appeal of the rural regions, such as their cultural heritage and natural landscapes, which are crucial in attracting tourists. Montegridolfo fits this model well with its medieval architecture and rural setting.

Cloke's (2007) theories on rurality and rural tourism deepen this perspective by exploring how rural areas use their unique identity to differentiate themselves in the tourism market. A comparative analysis with other Italian rural luxury destinations or European counterparts such as Provence or Tuscany could provide valuable insights into how Montegridolfo can develop its luxury tourism offer while maintaining its rural charm.

Carvalho, Kastenholz, and Marques (2014) conducted a comparative analysis of rural tourism destinations in Portugal to explore how marketing strategies can shape perceptions and attract luxury tourists. Their findings suggest that Montegridolfo could benefit from adopting similar strategies, focusing on authenticity, exclusivity, and personalized experiences to appeal to high-end travelers.

Understanding the broader trends in luxury tourism is essential to place Montegridolfo in a global context. Danziger (2005) and Kapferer & Bastien (2012) provide insights into the psychology of luxury consumers, highlighting the importance of exclusivity and differentiation in luxury branding. These studies can help inform how Montegridolfo's luxury tourism product is marketed to affluent tourists seeking unique, high-end experiences that cannot be found elsewhere.

In addition, recent reports such as the UNWTO (2022) Global Report on Luxury Tourism indicate that luxury tourism is shifting towards more sustainable and experiential models. These studies can help inform how Montegridolfo's luxury tourism product is marketed to affluent tourists seeking unique, high-end experiences that cannot be found elsewhere (Sasana et al., 2020).

In addition, recent reports such as the UNWTO (2022) Global Report on Luxury Tourism indicate that luxury tourism is shifting towards more sustainable and experiential models. In this context, Montegridolfo's businesses could explore incorporating more immersive, culturally rich experiences into their offerings, catering to tourists who seek luxury and meaningful engagement with local heritage and communities. At the same time, Richards and Wilson's (2006) discussion of creative tourism provides another level of understanding, particularly in how cultural heritage can offer unique and differentiated tourist experiences. Montegridolfo's medieval charm and history should be preserved and creatively marketed as part of the luxury experience, enhancing the village's appeal to discerning tourists seeking more than just physical luxury.

ACKNOWLEDGMENTS

We would like to express our sincere gratitude to Mr. Simone Badioli, the founder of Palazzo Viviani Hotel, for his invaluable cooperation and for allowing us to conduct our study within his organization. Our work has greatly benefited from his contributions and the support provided by his team.

REFERENCES

Aberg, K. G. (2014). The importance of being local: Prioritizing knowledge in recruitment for destination development. *Tourism Review*, 69(3), 229–243. DOI: 10.1108/TR-06-2013-0026

Arnegger, J., & Herz, M. (2016). Economic and destination image impacts of mega-events in emerging tourist destinations. *Journal of Destination Marketing & Management*, 5(2), 76–85. DOI: 10.1016/j.jdmm.2015.11.007

Baggio, R., Scott, N., & Cooper, C. (2010). Improving tourism destination governance: A complexity science approach. *Tourism Review*, 65(4), 51–60. DOI: 10.1108/16605371011093863

Baker, M. J., & Cameron, E. (2000). Critical success factors in destination marketing. *Tourism and Hospitality Research*, 8(2), 79–97. DOI: 10.1057/thr.2008.9

Barbini, F. M., & Presutti, M. (2014). Transforming a peripheral area in an emerging tourism destination. *Tourism Geographies*, 16(2), 190–206. DOI: 10.1080/14616688.2014.888589

Beckman, E., Kumar, A., & Kim, Y. (2013). The impact of brand experience on downtown success. *Journal of Travel Research*, 52(5), 646–658. DOI: 10.1177/0047287513478502

Butler, R. W. (1980). The concept of a tourist area cycle of evolution: Implications for management of resources. *The Canadian Geographer. Geographe Canadien*, 24(1), 5–12. DOI: 10.1111/j.1541-0064.1980.tb00970.x

Cai, L. A. (2002). Cooperative branding for rural destinations. *Annals of Tourism Research*, 29(3), 720–742. DOI: 10.1016/S0160-7383(01)00080-9

Calero, C., & Turner, L. W. (2019). Regional economic development and tourism: A literature review to highlight future directions for regional tourism research. *Tourism Economics*, •••, 1–24.

Campelo, A., Aitken, R., & Thyns, M. (2014). Sense of place: The importance for destination branding. *Journal of Travel Research*, 53(2), 154–166. DOI: 10.1177/0047287513496474

Casoli, D., Corsini, N., Presutti, M., & Magnini, V. (2023). Why (not) participating in an adventure motorcycle tourism event? *Tourism Analysis*, 28(4), 587–602. DOI: 10.3727/108354223X16833130470150

Coghlan, A., & Noakes, S. (2012). Towards an understanding of the drivers of commercialization in the volunteer tourism sector. *Tourism Recreation Research*, 37(2), 123–131. DOI: 10.1080/02508281.2012.11081697

Eshuis, J., Braun, E., Klijn, E. H., & Zenker, S. (2018). The differential effect of different stakeholder groups in place marketing. *Environmental and Planning C. Politics and Space*, 36, 916–936.

Eugenio-Vela, J., & Barniol-Carcasona, M. (2015). The relationship between rural branding and local development. A case-study in Catalonia's countryside: Territoris Serens (El Llucanes). *Journal of Rural Studies*, 37, 108–119. DOI: 10.1016/j.jrurstud.2015.01.001

Ezeuduji, I. O. (2015). Strategic event-based rural tourism development for sub-Saharan Africa. *Current Issues in Tourism*, 18(3), 212–228. DOI: 10.1080/13683500.2013.787049

Font, X., & McCabe, S. (2017). Sustainability and marketing in tourism: Its contexts, paradoxes, approaches, challenges and potential. *Journal of Sustainable Tourism*, 25(7), 869–883. DOI: 10.1080/09669582.2017.1301721

Gao, L., Huang, S., Zhang, Y., & Xu, H. (2022). The role of sustainable tourism practices in enhancing tourists' experience in luxury resorts: A case study of the Maldives. *Sustainability*, 14(12), 7382.

García, J. A., Gómez, M., & Molina, A. (2012). A destination-branding model: An empirical analysis based on stakeholders. *Tourism Management*, 33(3), 646–661. DOI: 10.1016/j.tourman.2011.07.006

Green, A., Grace, D., & Perkins, H. (2016). City branding research and practice: An integrative review. *Journal of Brand Management*, 23(3), 252–272. DOI: 10.1057/bm.2016.8

Han, H., Al-Ansi, A., & Chua, B.-L. (2023). Tourist Perceptions of Luxury Hotel Attributes and Their Impacts on Behavioral Intentions: The Role of Sustainability Practices. *Journal of Destination Marketing & Management*, 29, 100795.

Hanna, S., & Rowley, J. (2015). Towards a model of the place brand web. *Tourism Management*, 48, 100–112. DOI: 10.1016/j.tourman.2014.10.012

Higgins-Desbiolles, F. (2008). Justice tourism and alternative globalisation. *Journal of Sustainable Tourism*, 16(3), 345–364. DOI: 10.1080/09669580802154132

Iseppi, F. (2021). Modello Italia: Il turismo di prossimità da solo non basta. *Vita*, 5, 34–36.

Kim, J., & Park, E. (2022). The impact of virtual reality (VR) in tourism marketing: A meta-analysis. *Journal of Travel Research*, 61(4), 860–878.

Komppula, R. (2014). The role of individual entrepreneurs in the development of competitiveness for a rural tourism destination – A case study. *Tourism Management*, 40, 361–371. DOI: 10.1016/j.tourman.2013.07.007

Lalicic, L. (2020). Solastalgia: An application in the overtourism context. *Annals of Tourism Research*, 82, 102766. DOI: 10.1016/j.annals.2019.102766

Lane, B. (2009). Thirty years of sustainable tourism: Drivers, progress, problems and the future. In Gössling, S., Hall, C. M., & Weaver, D. (Eds.), *Sustainable Tourism Futures* (pp. 19–32). Routledge. DOI: 10.4324/9780203884256-10

Lee, S., Hwang, J., & Jang, J. (2022). Luxury hotel guests' perceptions of sustainability practices: The impact on brand loyalty and willingness to pay. *Journal of Hospitality & Tourism Research (Washington, D.C.)*, 46(5), 859–881.

Milano, C., Cheer, J. M., & Novelli, M. (2022). Overtourism, Digital Media, and the Promotion of 'Sustainable Tourism' in Crisis: Exploring the Role of Social Media Influencers in a Post-COVID-19 World. *Journal of Sustainable Tourism*, 30(8), 1711–1732.

Morgan, N., Pritchard, A., & Pride, R. (2011). *Destination brands: Managing place reputation* (3rd ed.). Butterworth-Heinemann.

Oriade, A., & Evans, M. (2011). Sustainable and alternative tourism. In Robinson, P., Heitmann, S., & Dieke, P. (Eds.), *Research Themes for Tourism* (pp. 69–86). Cabi. DOI: 10.1079/9781845936846.0069

Pan, L., Zhang, M., Gursoy, D., & Lu, L. (2017). Development and validation of a destination personality scale for mainland Chinese travelers. *Tourism Management*, 59, 302–315. DOI: 10.1016/j.tourman.2016.08.005

Papadimitriou, D., Apostolopoulou, A., & Kaplanidou, K. (2015). Destination personality, effective image, and behavioural intentions in domestic urban tourism. *Journal of Travel Research*, 54(3), 302–315. DOI: 10.1177/0047287513516389

Presutti, M. (2018). *Analisi imprenditoriale ed economica del festival del cinema. Un modello interpretativo ed economico del festival del cinema.* Aracne.

Presutti, M., & Lo Presti, V. (2022). *Il turismo esperienziale di nicchia: analisi strategica e prospettive future nella realtà dei borghi. Il Caso di Palazzo Viviani.* Maggioli.

Presutti, M., Savioli, M., & Odorici, V. (2020). Strategic orientation of hotels: Evidence from a contingent approach. *Tourism Economics*, 26(7), 1212–1230. DOI: 10.1177/1354816619868886

Prince, S., & Ioannides, D. (2017). Contextualizing the complexities of managing alternative tourism at the community-level: A case study of a Nordic eco-village. *Tourism Management*, 60, 348–356. DOI: 10.1016/j.tourman.2016.12.015

Richards, G. (2018). Cultural tourism: A review of recent research and trends. *Journal of Hospitality and Tourism Management*, 36, 12–21. DOI: 10.1016/j.jhtm.2018.03.005

Romagosa, F. (2020). The Covid-19 crisis: Opportunities for sustainable and proximity tourism. *Tourism Geographies*, 22(3), 690–694. DOI: 10.1080/14616688.2020.1763447

Ruhanen, L. (2008). Progressing the sustainability debate: A knowledge management approach to sustainable tourism planning. *Current Issues in Tourism*, 11(5), 429–455. DOI: 10.1080/13683500802316030

Salazar, N. B. (2012). Community-based cultural tourism: Issues, threats and opportunities. *Journal of Sustainable Tourism*, 20(1), 9–22. DOI: 10.1080/09669582.2011.596279

Sasana, H., Atmanti, H. D., & Muid, D. (2017). The strategy development of the region in support Borobudur tourism cluster competitiveness regions in Indonesia. *Journal of Environtmental Management and Tourism*, 8(24), 1517–1528. DOI: 10.14505/jemt.v8.8(24).07

Sharpley, R. (2009). *Tourism development and the environment: Beyond sustainability?* Earthscan. DOI: 10.4324/9781849770255

Sun, M., Ye, B. H., & Law, R. (2022). Sustainability and luxury tourism: The influence of hotel sustainability practices on tourist satisfaction in luxury hotels. *Journal of Travel & Tourism Marketing*, 39(2), 166–179.

Tolkach, D., & King, B. (2015). Strengthening community-based tourism in a new resource-based island nation: Why and how? *Tourism Management*, 48, 386–398. DOI: 10.1016/j.tourman.2014.12.013

Wang, D., Xiang, Z., & Fesenmaier, D. R. (2022). Big data and travel marketing: Prospects and challenges. *Tourism Management*, 91, 104473.

Weaver, D. (2006). *Sustainable Tourism: Theory and Practice*. Elsevier.

Weaver, D. (2007). Towards sustainable mass tourism: Paradigm shift or paradigm nudge? *Tourism Recreation Research*, 32(3), 65–69. DOI: 10.1080/02508281.2007.11081541

Xiao, H. (2006). Towards a research agenda for knowledge management in tourism. *Tourism and Hospitality Planning & Development*, 3(2), 143–157. DOI: 10.1080/14790530600938436

Zahra, A., & McGehee, N. G. (2013). Volunteer tourism: A host-community capital perspective. *Annals of Tourism Research*, 42, 22–45. DOI: 10.1016/j.annals.2013.01.008

Zavattaro, S., Daspit, J., & Adams, F. (2015). Assessing managerial methods for evaluative place brand equity: A qualitative investigation. *Tourism Management*, 47, 11–21. DOI: 10.1016/j.tourman.2014.08.018

Zenker, S., Braun, E., & Peterson, S. (2017). Branding the destination versus the place: The effects of brand complexity and identification for residents and visitors. *Tourism Management*, 58, 15–27. DOI: 10.1016/j.tourman.2016.10.008

Compilation of References

Aaker, D. (1991). Brand equity. *La gestione del valore della marca, 347*, 356.

Aaker, D. (1991). *Managing brand equity*. Free Press Business.

Aaker, D. A., & Joachimsthaler, E. (2000). *Brand Leadership*. The Free Press.

Aas, C., Ladkin, A., & Fletcher, J. (2005). Stakeholder collaboration and heritage management. *Annals of Tourism Research*, 32(1), 28–48. DOI: 10.1016/j.annals.2004.04.005

Abebe, R., Aruleba, K., Birhane, A., Kingsley, S., Obaido, G., Remy, S. L., & Sadagopan, S. (2021). Narratives and counternarratives on data sharing in Africa. In *Proceedings of the 2021 ACM conference on fairness, accountability, and transparency* (pp. 329-341). DOI: 10.1145/3442188.3445897

Aberg, K. G. (2014). The importance of being local: Prioritizing knowledge in recruitment for destination development. *Tourism Review*, 69(3), 229–243. DOI: 10.1108/TR-06-2013-0026

Abkenar, S. B., Kashani, M. H., Mahdipour, E., & Jameii, S. M. (2021). Big data analytics meets social media: A systematic review of techniques, open issues, and future directions. *Telematics and Informatics*, 57, 101517. DOI: 10.1016/j.tele.2020.101517 PMID: 34887614

Abukari, H., & Mwalyosi, R. B. (2020). Local communities' perceptions about the impact of protected areas on livelihoods and community development. *Global Ecology and Conservation*, 22, e00909. DOI: 10.1016/j.gecco.2020.e00909

Adikaram, K. K. N. B., & Surangi, H. A. K. N. S. (2024). Creating opportunities in a challenging environment: Experiential crisis learning behaviour of tourism SMEs in Sri Lanka. *Cogent Business & Management*, 11(1), 2314803. Advance online publication. DOI: 10.1080/23311975.2024.2314803

Adom, D. (2019). The place and voice of local people, culture and traditions: A catalyst for ecotourism development in rural communities in Ghana. *Scientific African*, 6, e00184. DOI: 10.1016/j.sciaf.2019.e00184

Ahmad, Y. (2006). The scope and definitions of heritage: From tangible to intangible. *International Journal of Heritage Studies*, 12(3), 292–300. DOI: 10.1080/13527250600604639

Ajzen, I. (1985). From intentions to actions: A theory of planned behavior. In *Action control: From cognition to behavior* (pp. 11–39). Springer. DOI: 10.1007/978-3-642-69746-3_2

Akhtar, M., & Anjum, U. (2022). Economic importance of tourism in India and prospects for sustainable development. *International Research Journal of Modernization in Engineering Technology and Science*, 4(6), 846.

Akhtar, N., Sun, J., Akhtar, M. N., & Chen, J. (2019). How attitude ambivalence from conflicting online hotel reviews affects consumers' behavioural responses: The moderating role of dialecticism☆. *Journal of Hospitality and Tourism Management*, 41, 28–40. DOI: 10.1016/j.jhtm.2019.09.003

Akkaya, Ö., Arslan, Ö., & Zerenler, M. (2024). Revisiting the host city: Examining event quality, host city evaluation, place attachment and destination brand equity from the spectators at the Konya Islamic Games 2022. *Journal of Convention & Event Tourism*, •••, 1–29. DOI: 10.1080/15470148.2024.2382145

Aktan, M., Zaman, U., & Nawaz, S. (2021). Examining destinations' personality and brand equity through the lens of expats: Moderating role of expat's cultural intelligence. *Asia Pacific Journal of Tourism Research*, 26(8), 849–865. DOI: 10.1080/10941665.2021.1925314

Aktan, M., Zaman, U., Raza, S. H., & Koc, E. (2024). Demystifying tourists' intentional readiness for net zero transformation through environmental knowledge, conspicuous altruism, and greenwashing perceptions. *Asia Pacific Journal of Tourism Research*, 29(4), 495–514.

Al Balushi, M. K., Hussain, K., & Al Mahrouqi, A. N. (2024). Strategic University Positioning: Fostering Student Satisfaction and Well-being. *Current Psychology (New Brunswick, N.J.)*, 43(29), 1–13. DOI: 10.1007/s12144-024-06104-3

Al Balushi, M. K., Soliman, M., Kennedy, R. E., & Palla, A. H. (2024). Shifts in tourism knowledge: HEI contributions to destination branding and economic development. In *Shifts in Knowledge Sharing and Creativity for Business Tourism* (pp. 145–162). IGI Global.

Al Balushi, M., Butt, I., & Al Siyabi, K. (2013). Review of awareness and views on branding Oman as a nation. *International Journal of Business and Economics*, 5(1), 7–19.

Alagarsamy, S., Mehrolia, S., & Paul, J. (2024). Masstige scale: An alternative to measure brand equity. *International Journal of Consumer Studies*, 48(1), e12873. DOI: 10.1111/ijcs.12873

Aldboush, H. H., & Ferdous, M. (2023). Building trust in fintech: An analysis of ethical and privacy considerations in the intersection of big data, AI, and customer trust. *International Journal of Financial Studies*, 11(3), 90. DOI: 10.3390/ijfs11030090

Alexandrou, E. (2020). *Digital Strategy in Museums: A case study of The Rijksmuseum.*

Ali, D., & Xiaoying, L. (2021). The influence of content and non-content cues of tourism information quality on the creation of destination image in social media: A study of Khyber Pakhtunkhwa, Pakistan. [LASSIJ]. *Liberal Arts and Social Sciences International Journal*, 5(1), 245–265. DOI: 10.47264/idea.lassij/5.1.17

Alikhanova, S., Milner-Gulland, E. J., & Bull, J. W. (2024). Exploring the human-nature nexus towards effective nature-based solutions: The Aral Sea case. *Land Use Policy*, 139, 107073.

Allied Market Research. (2021). *Ecotourism market by traveler type, age group, and sales channel: Global opportunity analysis and industry forecast, 2021–2027.* Allied Market Research. https://www.alliedmarketresearch.com/ecotourism-market-A06364

Altassan, A. (2023). Sustainability of Heritage Villages through Eco-Tourism Investment (Case Study: Al-Khabra Village, Saudi Arabia). *Sustainability (Basel)*, 15(9), 7172. DOI: 10.3390/su15097172

Alvarado-Karste, D., & Guzmán, F. (2020). The effect of brand identity-cognitive style fit and social influence on consumer-based brand equity. *Journal of Product and Brand Management*, 29(7), 971–984. DOI: 10.1108/JPBM-06-2019-2419

Ameen, N., Cheah, J.-H., Ali, F., El-Manstrly, D., & Kulyciute, R. (2023). Risk, Trust, and the Roles of Human Versus Virtual Influencers. *Journal of Travel Research*, 63(6), 1370–1394. DOI: 10.1177/00472875231190601

Ammirato, S., & Felicetti, A. (2013). The potential of agritourism in revitalizing rural communities: Some empirical results. In Camarinha-Matos, L. M., & Scherer, R. J. (Eds.), *Collaborative systems for reindustrialization. PRO-VE 2013. IFIP Advances in Information and Communication Technology* (Vol. 408). Springer., DOI: 10.1007/978-3-642-40543-3_52

Ammirato, S., Felicetti, A. M., Della Gala, M., Raso, C., & Cozza, M. (2018). Smart tourism destinations: can the destination management organizations exploit benefits of the ICTs? Evidences from a multiple case study. Collaborative Networks of Cognitive Systems: 19th IFIP WG 5.5 Working Conference on Virtual Enterprises, PRO-VE 2018, Cardiff, UK, September 17-19, 2018, Proceedings 19, Arman, M., & Lamiyar, U. R. (2023). Exploring the implication of ChatGPT AI for business: Efficiency and challenges. *International Journal of Marketing and Digital Creative*, 1(2), 64–84. DOI: 10.31098/ijmadic.v1i2.1872

Andrade, G. S. M., & Rhodes, J. R. (2012). Protected Areas and Local Communities: An Inevitable Partnership toward Successful Conservation Strategies? *Ecology and Society*, 17(4), art14. Advance online publication. DOI: 10.5751/ES-05216-170414

Andriotis, K. (2009). *Sustainability and alternative tourism.* Stamoulis. (in Greek)

Ang, S., Van Dyne, L., & Koh, C. (2006). Personality correlates of the four-factor model of cultural intelligence. *Group & Organization Management*, 31(1), 100–123. DOI: 10.1177/1059601105275267

Anholt, S. (2006). The Anholt-GMI City Brands Index: How the World Sees the World's Cities. *Place Branding*, 2(1), 18–31. DOI: 10.1057/palgrave.pb.5990042

Anholt, S. (2007). *Competitive Identity. The New Brand Management for Nations, Cities and Regions.* Palgrave Macmillan.

Anholt, S. (2010). *Places: Identity, Image and Reputation.* Palgrave Macmillan.

An, S., & Park, H. (2023). Factors driving community engagement through social capital formation - focusing on community-based eco-tourism in Dongbaek Village, Jeju, Korea. *International Journal of Global Environmental Issues*, 22(4), 355–374. DOI: 10.1504/IJGENVI.2023.136294

Anup, K. C. (2016). Ecotourism and its role in sustainable development of Nepal. INTECH Open Science, 31-59.

Anwar, R. K., Saepudin, E., & Rukmana, E. N. (2023a). Eco-tourism and economic striving of the locals: From participation to empowerment. *Journal of Infrastructure Policy and Development*, 8(2). Advance online publication. DOI: 10.24294/jipd.v8i2.3038

Apostolopoulou, A., & Papadimitriou, D. (2015). The role of destination personality in predicting tourist behavior: Implications for branding mid-sized urban destinations. *Current Issues in Tourism*, 18(12), 1132–1151. DOI: 10.1080/13683500.2013.878319

Aref, F., & Gill, S. S. (2009). Rural tourism development through rural cooperatives. *Nature and Science*, 7(10), 68–73.

Arellano, A. (2011). Tourism in poor regions and social inclusion: The porters of the Inca Trail to Machu Picchu. *World Leisure Journal*, 53(2), 104–118. DOI: 10.1080/04419057.2011.580551

Aria, M., & Cuccurullo, C. (2017). Bibliometrix: An R-tool for comprehensive science mapping analysis. *Journal of Informetrics*, 11(4), 959–975. DOI: 10.1016/j.joi.2017.08.007

Arici, H. E., Arasli, H., Koseoglu, M. A., Saydam, M. B., & Olorunsola, V. O. (2024). Financial determinants of governance scores in hospitality and tourism enterprises. *Quality & Quantity*. Advance online publication. DOI: 10.1007/s11135-023-01820-7

Arnegger, J., & Herz, M. (2016). Economic and destination image impacts of mega-events in emerging tourist destinations. *Journal of Destination Marketing & Management*, 5(2), 76–85. DOI: 10.1016/j.jdmm.2015.11.007

Aro, K., Suomi, K., & Saraniemi, S. (2018). Antecedents and consequences of destination brand love—A case study from Finnish Lapland. *Tourism Management*, 67, 71–81. DOI: 10.1016/j.tourman.2018.01.003

Arora, M., & Chandel, M. (2024). Role of Artificial Intelligence in Promoting Green Destinations for Sustainable Tourism Development. In *The Role of Artificial Intelligence in Regenerative Tourism and Green Destinations* (pp. 247–260). Emerald Publishing Limited., DOI: 10.1108/978-1-83753-746-420241016

Arriaga Navarrete, R., & González Pérez, C. R. (2019). The tourism sector and its productive linkages: An input-output analysis and endogenous consumption. *Revista de economía*, 36(92), 94–128.

Arunmozhi, T., & Panneerselvam, A. (2013). Types of tourism in India. *International Journal of Current Research and Academic Review*, 1(1), 84–88.

Ashley, C., & Tuten, T. (2015). Creative strategies in social media marketing: An exploratory study of branded social content and consumer engagement. *Psychology and Marketing*, 32(1), 15–27. DOI: 10.1002/mar.20761

Ashok, S., Behera, M. D., Tewari, H. R., & Jana, C. (2022). Developing ecotourism sustainability maximization (ESM) model: A safe minimum standard for climate change mitigation in the Indian Himalayas. *Environmental Monitoring and Assessment*, 194(12), 914.

Ashton, A. S. (2015). Developing a Tourist Destination Brand Value: The Stakeholders' Perspective. *Tourism Planning & Development*, 12(4), 398–411. DOI: 10.1080/21568316.2015.1013565

Ashworth, G. J., & Voogd, H. (2012). Marketing of tourism places: What are we doing? In *global tourist behavior* (pp. 5-19). Routledge.

Asim Nawaz, M., Asmi, F., & Nawaz, A. (2019). Willingness to consume Genetically Modified Food in Chinese perspective Public Understanding of Socio-Scientific Issue (SSIs) View project role of phobia's and allied influence on consumer novel food intentions. View project. Article in Pakistan Journal of Agricultural Sciences. DOI: 10.21162/PAKJAS/19.8837

Augé, M. (2000). *Non-Places: Introduction to an Anthropology of Supermodernity*. Verso.

Au-Yong-Oliveira, M., Pesqueira, A., Sousa, M. J., Dal Mas, F., & Soliman, M. (2021). The potential of big data research in healthcare for medical doctors' learning. *Journal of Medical Systems*, 45(1), 13. DOI: 10.1007/s10916-020-01691-7 PMID: 33409620

Avraham, E., & Ketter, E. (2016). *Tourism marketing for developing countries: Battling stereotypes and crises in Asia, Africa and the Middle East*. Springer. DOI: 10.1057/9781137342157

Aydin, I. Z., & Öztürk, A. (2023). Identifying, Monitoring, and Evaluating Sustainable Ecotourism Management Criteria and Indicators for Protected Areas in Türkiye: The Case of Camili Biosphere Reserve. *Sustainability (Basel)*, 15(4), 2933.

Azinuddin, M., Mohammad Nasir, M. B., Hanafiah, M. H., Mior Shariffuddin, N. S., & Kamarudin, M. K. A. (2022). Interlinkage of Perceived Ecotourism Design Affordance, Perceived Value of Destination Experiences, Destination Reputation, and Loyalty. *Sustainability (Basel)*, 14(18), 11371. DOI: 10.3390/su141811371

Azis, S. S. A., Sipan, I., Sapri, M., & Zafirah, A. M. (2018). Creating an innocuous mangrove ecosystem: Understanding the influence of ecotourism products from Malaysian and international perspectives. *Ocean and Coastal Management*, 165, 416–427. DOI: 10.1016/j.ocecoaman.2018.09.014

Baber, R., & Baber, P. (2023). Influence of social media marketing efforts, e-reputation, and destination image on intention to visit among tourists: Application of SOR model. *Journal of Hospitality and Tourism Insights*, 6(5), 2298–2316. DOI: 10.1108/JHTI-06-2022-0270

Baggio, R., Scott, N., & Cooper, C. (2010). Improving tourism destination governance: A complexity science approach. *Tourism Review*, 65(4), 51–60. DOI: 10.1108/16605371011093863

Bajpai, N. (2009). *Business statistics*. Pearson Education India.

Bak, E., & Bayram, G. E. (2024). Redefining and Revitalized Community-Based Tourism: An Evaluation of Green Tourism Practises in Turkey. In Strategic Tourism Planning for Communities (pp. 197-209). Emerald Publishing Limited.

Baker, B. (2007). *Destination Branding for Small Cities: The Essentials for Successful Place Branding*. Creative Leap Books.

Baker, M. J., & Cameron, E. (2008). Critical success factors in destination marketing. *Tourism and Hospitality Research*, 8(2), 79–97. DOI: 10.1057/thr.2008.9

Bakri, M., Krisjanous, J., & Richard, J. E. (2022). Examining Sojourners as Visual Influencers in VFR (Visiting Friends and Relatives) Tourism: A Rhetorical Analysis of User-Generated Images. *Journal of Travel Research*, 62(8), 1685–1706. DOI: 10.1177/00472875221138975

Balagué, C., Martin-Fuentes, E., & Jesús Gómez, M. (2016a). Reliability of authenticated versus non-authenticated hotel reviews: TripAdvisor and Booking.com case. *Cuadernos de Turismo*, 38, 63–82. DOI: 10.6018/turismo.38.271351

Balakrishnan, S. M. (2009). Strategic branding of destinations: A framework. *European Journal of Marketing*, 43(5/6), 611–629. DOI: 10.1108/03090560910946954

Balasubramaniam, N., Kauppinen, M., Hiekkanen, K., & Kujala, S. (2022). Transparency and explainability of AI systems: Ethical guidelines in practice. *Information and Software Technology*, 159, 3–18. DOI: 10.1016/j.infsof.2023.107197

Balmer, J., & Greyser, S. (2006). Corporate marketing: Integrating corporate identity, corporate branding, corporate communication, corporate image and corporate reputation. *European Journal of Marketing*, 40(7-8), 730–741. DOI: 10.1108/03090560610669964

Baloch, Q. B., Shah, S. N., Iqbal, N., Sheeraz, M., Asadullah, M., Mahar, S., & Khan, A. U. (2023). Impact of tourism development upon environmental sustainability: A suggested framework for sustainable ecotourism. *Environmental Science and Pollution Research International*, 30(3), 5917–5930. DOI: 10.1007/s11356-022-22496-w PMID: 35984561

Bandinelli, C. (2020). The effect of User-Generated Content to promote tourism destinations: the importance of perceived authenticity and trust (Doctoral dissertation).

Barabási, A.-L. (2003). *Linked: How Everything is Connected to Everything Else and What It Means for Business, Science, and Everyday Life*. Plume.

Barbini, F. M., & Presutti, M. (2014). Transforming a peripheral area in an emerging tourism destination. *Tourism Geographies*, 16(2), 190–206. DOI: 10.1080/14616688.2014.888589

Barnes, S. J., Mattsson, J., & Sørensen, F. (2014). Destination brand experience and visitor behavior: Testing a scale in the tourism context. *Annals of Tourism Research*, 48, 121–139. DOI: 10.1016/j.annals.2014.06.002

Bastrygina, T., Lim, W. M., Jopp, R., & Weissmann, M. A. (2024). Unraveling the power of social media influencers: Qualitative insights into the role of Instagram influencers in the hospitality and tourism industry. *Journal of Hospitality and Tourism Management*, 58, 214–243. DOI: 10.1016/j.jhtm.2024.01.007

Batool, N., Wani, M. D., Shah, S. A., & Dada, Z. A. (2024). Tourists' attitude and willingness to pay on conservation efforts: Evidence from the west Himalayan eco-tourism sites. *Environment, Development and Sustainability*. Advance online publication. DOI: 10.1007/s10668-024-04679-2

Beckman, E., Kumar, A., & Kim, Y. (2013). The impact of brand experience on downtown success. *Journal of Travel Research*, 52(5), 646–658. DOI: 10.1177/0047287513478502

Beerli, A., & Martin, J. D. (2004). Tourists' Characteristics and the Perceived Image of Tourist Destinations: A Quantitative Analysis—A Case Study of Lanzarote, Spain. *Tourism Management*, 25(5), 623–636. DOI: 10.1016/j.tourman.2003.06.004

Bekjanov, D., & Matyusupov, B. (2021). Influence of innovative processes in the competitiveness of tourist destination. In *Innovation and entrepreneurial opportunities in community tourism* (pp. 243–263). IGI Global. DOI: 10.4018/978-1-7998-4855-4.ch014

Bektaş, F., Özdemir Işık, B., Erbaş, Y. S., Bahar, E., & Kaya, S. (2024). Kullanıcı Potansiyeline Bağlı Koruma Statüsündeki Mavi Yıldız Çiçeğinin Sürdürülebilirliğine Yönelik Trabzon Kadıralak Yaylasında Yürüyüş Rotalarının Belirlenmesi. GSI Journals Serie A: Advancements in Tourism *Recreation and Sports Sciences*, 7(1), 48–66.

Belanche, D., Belk, R. W., Casaló, L. V., & Flavián, C. (2024). The dark side of artificial intelligence in services. *Service Industries Journal*, 44(3-4), 149–172. DOI: 10.1080/02642069.2024.2305451

Berry, N. C. (1989). Revitalizing brands. *Journal of Consumer Marketing*, 5(3), 15–20. DOI: 10.1108/eb008228

Bichler, B. F., & Lösch, M. (2019). Collaborative governance in tourism: Empirical insights into a community-oriented destination. *Sustainability (Basel)*, 11(23), 6673. DOI: 10.3390/su11236673

Bideci, M., & Albayrak, T. (2018). An investigation of the domestic and foreign tourists' museum visit experiences. *International Journal of Culture, Tourism and Hospitality Research*, 12(3), 366–377. DOI: 10.1108/IJCTHR-02-2018-0029

Binangun, J., & Dutha, I. (2020). Sustainability Concept in Ecotourism on Domestic Tourists of Generation Z. 2nd IConBMT (International Conference on Business, Management, Management, Technology) 2020.

Björk, P. (2000). Ecotourism from a conceptual perspective, an extended definition of a unique tourism form. *International Journal of Tourism Research*, 2(3), 189–202. DOI: 10.1002/(SICI)1522-1970(200005/06)2:3<189::AID-JTR195>3.0.CO;2-T

Blain, C., Levy, S., & Ritchie, J. R. (2005). Destination branding: Insights and practices from destination management organizations. *Journal of Travel Research*, 43(4), 328–338. DOI: 10.1177/0047287505274646

Blue Flag Turkey. (2024). https://www.mavibayrak.org.tr/en/

Boley, B. B., & Green, G. T. (2015). Ecotourism and natural resource conservation: The 'potential' for a sustainable symbiotic relationship. *Journal of Ecotourism*, 15(1), 36–50. DOI: 10.1080/14724049.2015.1094080

Bontempi, A., Venturi, P., Del Bene, D., Scheidel, A., Zaldo-Aubanell, Q., & Zaragoza, R. M. (2023). Conflict and conservation: On the role of protected areas for environmental justice. *Global Environmental Change*, 82, 102740. DOI: 10.1016/j.gloenvcha.2023.102740

Bonye, S. Z., Yiridomoh, G. Y., & Nsiah, V. (2023). Our forest, our livelihood: Natural resources' use controversies and community livelihood sustainability in the Mole National Park, Ghana. *Land Use Policy*, 127, 106589. DOI: 10.1016/j.landusepol.2023.106589

Borgatti, S. P., Everett, M. G., & Johnson, J. C. (2018). *Analyzing Social Networks* (2nd ed.). SAGE Publications.

Bornhorst, T., Ritchie, J. R., & Sheehan, L. (2010). Determinants of tourism success for DMOs & destinations: An empirical examination of stakeholders' perspectives. *Tourism Management*, 31(5), 572–589. DOI: 10.1016/j.tourman.2009.06.008

Bramwell, B. (2004). Mass tourism, diversification and sustainability in southern Europe's coastal regions. In Bramwell, B. (Ed.), *Coastal mass tourism: Diversification and sustainable development in Southern Europe* (pp. 1–31). Channel View Publications., DOI: 10.21832/9781873150702-003

Bregoli, I. (2012). Effects of DMO Coordination on Destination Brand Identity: A MixedMethod Study on the City of Edinburgh. *Journal of Travel Research*, 52(2), 212–224. DOI: 10.1177/0047287512461566

Breiling, M. (2005). Rural tourism: Experiences from Austria, opportunities for Japan. *Japanese Rural and Planning Society, Kinki Meeting, Awaji Landscape Panning and Horticultural Academy, Hokudan-cho, Hyogo.*

Briassoulis, H. (2000). Environmental impacts of tourism: A framework for analysis and evaluation. In Briassoulis, H., & Van der Straaten, J. (Eds.), *Tourism and the environment* (pp. 21–38). Springer., DOI: 10.1007/978-94-015-9584-1_2

Broadbent, E. N., Zambrano, A. M. A., Dirzo, R., Durham, W. H., Driscoll, L., Gallagher, P., Salters, R., Schultz, J., Colmenares, A., & Randolph, S. G. (2012). The effect of land use change and ecotourism on biodiversity: A case study of Manuel Antonio, Costa Rica, from 1985 to 2008. *Landscape Ecology*, 27(5), 731–744.

Brunt, P. (1997). *Market research in travel and tourism* (1st ed.). Butterworth-Heinemann.

Buckley, R. (2009). *Ecotourism: Principles and practices*. CABI.

Buckley, R. (2009). Evaluating the net effects of ecotourism on the environment: A framework, first assessment and future research. *Journal of Sustainable Tourism*, 17(6), 643–672. DOI: 10.1080/09669580902999188

Buhalis, D. (2000). Marketing the competitive destination of the future. *Tourism Management*, 21(1), 97–116. DOI: 10.1016/S0261-5177(99)00095-3

Buhalis, D., & Main, H. (1998). Information technology in peripheral small and medium hospitality enterprises: Strategic analysis and critical factors. *International Journal of Contemporary Hospitality Management*, 10(5), 198–202. DOI: 10.1108/09596119810227811

Bulbeck, C. (2012). *Facing the wild*. Earthscan. DOI: 10.4324/9781849773850

Bulchand-Gidumal, J., William Secin, E., O'Connor, P., & Buhalis, D. (2024). Artificial intelligence's impact on hospitality and tourism marketing: Exploring key themes and addressing challenges. *Current Issues in Tourism*, 27(14), 2345–2362. DOI: 10.1080/13683500.2023.2229480

Buongiorno, A., & Intini, M. (2021). Sustainable tourism and mobility in natural protected areas: Evidence from Apulia. *Sustainability*, 13(12), 6845. DOI: 10.3390/su13126845

Butler, R. W. (1980). The concept of a tourist area cycle of evolution: Implications for management of resources. *The Canadian Geographer. Geographe Canadien*, 24(1), 5–12. DOI: 10.1111/j.1541-0064.1980.tb00970.x

Butler, R. W. (1999). Sustainable tourism: A state-of-the-art review. *Tourism Geographies*, 1(1), 7–25. DOI: 10.1080/14616689908721291

Cai, L. A. (2002). Cooperative branding for rural destinations. *Annals of Tourism Research*, 29(3), 720–742. DOI: 10.1016/S0160-7383(01)00080-9

Cajiao, D., Izurieta, J. C., Casafont, M., Reck, G., Castro, K., Santamaría, V., Cárdenas, S., & Leung, Y. F. (2020). Tourist use and impact monitoring in the Galapagos: An evolving programme with lessons learned. *Parks*, 26(2), 89–102. DOI: 10.2305/IUCN.CH.2020.PARKS-26-2DC.en

Calderón-Fajardo, V., Anaya-Sánchez, R., & Molinillo, S. (2024). Understanding destination brand experience through data mining and machine learning. *Journal of Destination Marketing & Management*, 31, 100862. DOI: 10.1016/j.jdmm.2024.100862

Calero, C., & Turner, L. W. (2019). Regional economic development and tourism: A literature review to highlight future directions for regional tourism research. *Tourism Economics*, •••, 1–24.

Camacho-Ruiz, M., Carrasco, R. A., Fernández-Avilés, G., & LaTorre, A. (2023). Tourism destination events classifier based on artificial intelligence techniques. *Applied Soft Computing*, 148, 110914. DOI: 10.1016/j.asoc.2023.110914

Camilleri, M. A. (Ed.). (2024). *Tourism planning and destination marketing*. Emerald Publishing Limited. DOI: 10.1108/9781804558881

Camilleri, M. A., & Camilleri, M. A. (2018). *The tourism industry: An overview*. Springer International Publishing.

Campagnaro, F., Ghalkhani, M., Tumiati, R., Marin, F., Del Grande, M., Pozzebon, A., . . . Zorzi, M. (2024). Monitoring the Venice Lagoon: an IoT Cloud-Based Sensor Nerwork Approach. *arXiv preprint arXiv:2403.06915*.

Campelo, A., Aitken, R., Thyne, M., & Gnoth, J. (2013). Sense of Place: The Importance for Destination Branding. *Journal of Travel Research*, 53(2), 154–166. DOI: 10.1177/0047287513496474

Cao, J., Zhang, J., Wang, C., Hu, H., & Yu, P. (2020). How far is the ideal destination? Distance desire, ways to explore the antinomy of distance effects in tourist destination choice. *Journal of Travel Research*, 59(4), 614–630. DOI: 10.1177/0047287519844832

Cario, J. E. (2012). *Pinterest marketing: An hour a day*. John Wiley & Sons.

Carvalho, I., & Ivanov, S. (2024). ChatGPT for tourism: Applications, benefits and risks. *Tourism Review*, 79(2), 290–303. DOI: 10.1108/TR-02-2023-0088

Casado-Aranda, L. A., Sánchez-Fernández, J., & Ibáñez-Zapata, J. Á. (2023). Evaluating communication effectiveness through eye tracking: Benefits, state of the art, and unresolved questions. *International Journal of Business Communication*, 60(1), 24–61. DOI: 10.1177/2329488419893746

Casoli, D., Corsini, N., Presutti, M., & Magnini, V. (2023). Why (not) participating in an adventure motorcycle tourism event? *Tourism Analysis*, 28(4), 587–602. DOI: 10.3727/108354223X16833130470150

Cassidy, R., Helmi, J., & Bridson, K. (2019). Drivers and inhibitors of national stakeholder engagement with place brand identity. *European Journal of Marketing*, 53(7), 1445–1465. DOI: 10.1108/EJM-04-2017-0275

Ceballos-LascuráIn, H. (1996). *Tourism, Ecotourism, and Protected Areas: The State of Nature-Based Tourism Around the World and Guidelines for Its Development*. http://ci.nii.ac.jp/ncid/BA32002622

Cernea, M. M., & Schmidt-Soltau, K. (2006). Poverty Risks and National Parks: Policy Issues in Conservation and Resettlement. *World Development*, 34(10), 1808–1830. DOI: 10.1016/j.worlddev.2006.02.008

Cetin, M. (2015). Evaluation of the sustainable tourism potential of a protected area for landscape planning: A case study of the ancient city of Pompeipolis in Kastamonu. *International Journal of Sustainable Development and World Ecology*, 22(6), 490–495. DOI: 10.1080/13504509.2015.1081651

Chakraborty, P., & Ghosal, S. (2024). An eco-social exploration of tourism area evolution in mountains through stakeholders' perspective. *Environmental Development*, 49, 100963. Advance online publication. DOI: 10.1016/j.envdev.2024.100963

Chaplin-Kramer, R., Neugarten, R. A., Gonzalez-Jimenez, D., Ahmadia, G., Baird, T. D., Crane, N., Delgoulet, E., Eyster, H. N., Kurashima, N., Llopis, J. C., Millington, A., Pawlowska-Mainville, A., Rulmal, J., Saunders, F., Shrestha, S., Vaughan, M. B., Winter, K. B., Wongbusarakum, S., & Pascual, U. (2023). Transformation for inclusive conservation: Evidence on values, decisions, and impacts in protected areas. *Current Opinion in Environmental Sustainability*, 64, 101347. DOI: 10.1016/j.cosust.2023.101347

Cheng, X., Xue, T., Yang, B. and Ma, B. (2023), "A digital transformation approach in hospitality and tourism research", International Journal of Contemporary Hospitality Management, Vol. ahead-of-print No. ahead-of-print, .DOI: 10.1108/IJCHM-06-2022-0679

Chen, H., Chiang, R. H., & Storey, V. C. (2012). Business intelligence and analytics: From big data to big impact. *Management Information Systems Quarterly*, 36(4), 1165–1188. DOI: 10.2307/41703503

Chen, H., & Rahman, I. (2018). Cultural tourism: An analysis of engagement, cultural contact, memorable tourism experience and destination loyalty. *Tourism Management Perspectives*, 26, 153–163. DOI: 10.1016/j.tmp.2017.10.006

Chen, R., Zhou, Z., Zhan, G., & Zhou, N. (2020). The impact of destination brand authenticity and destination brand self-congruence on tourist loyalty: The mediating role of destination brand engagement. *Journal of Destination Marketing & Management*, 15, 100402. DOI: 10.1016/j.jdmm.2019.100402

Chernatony, L., & Dall'Olmo, R. F. (1999). Experts' Views about Defining Service Brands and the Principles of Service Branding. *Journal of Business Research*, 46(2), 181–192. DOI: 10.1016/S0148-2963(98)00021-6

Chhabra, D., Healy, R., & Sills, E. (2003). Staged authenticity and heritage tourism. *Annals of Tourism Research*, 30(3), 702–719. DOI: 10.1016/S0160-7383(03)00044-6

Chiang Mai Thailand Travel and Tourist Guide. (n.d.). *1 Stop Chiang Mai*. Retrieved from https://www.1stopchiangmai.com/

Chiariotti, F. (2021). A survey on 360-degree video: Coding, quality of experience and streaming. *Computer Communications*, 177, 133–155. DOI: 10.1016/j.comcom.2021.06.029

Chigora, F., Ndlovu, J., & Nyagadza, B. (2024). Building positive Zimbabwean tourism festival, event and destination brand image and equity: A systematic literature review. *Cogent Social Sciences*, 10(1), 2318867. DOI: 10.1080/23311886.2024.2318867

Chi, N. T. K. (2021). Understanding the effects of eco-label, eco-brand, and social media on green consumption intention in ecotourism destinations. *Journal of Cleaner Production*, 321, 128995. DOI: 10.1016/j.jclepro.2021.128995

Chi, O. H., Gursoy, D., & Chi, C. G. (2022). Tourists' attitudes toward the use of artificially intelligent (AI) devices in tourism service delivery: Moderating role of service value seeking. *Journal of Travel Research*, 61(1), 170–185. DOI: 10.1177/0047287520971054

Chip.com.tr. (2020) Web Site of CHIP Science and Tech Magazine. https://www.chip.com.tr/haber/eski-otobus-artik-bir-ev-eski-otobusu-karavan-yaptilar-sonuc-inanilmaz_88924.html

Chirenje, L. I., Giliba, R. A., & Musamba, E. B. (2013). Local communities' participation in decision-making processes through planning and budgeting in African countries. *Zhongguo Renkou Ziyuan Yu Huanjing*, 11(1), 10–16. DOI: 10.1080/10042857.2013.777198

Choi, A., Berridge, G., & Kim, C. (2020). The urban museum as a creative tourism attraction: London museum lates visitor motivation. *Sustainability (Basel)*, 12(22), 9382. DOI: 10.3390/su12229382

Choi, S. H., & Cai, L. A. (2012). Destination loyalty and communication – a relationship-based tourist behavioural model. *International Journal of Strategic Communication*, 6(1), 45–58. DOI: 10.1080/1553118X.2011.634868

Chu, J. (2020). Sustainable Travel on YouTube: Discussion and Perception: How do YouTube travel vlogs discuss sustainable travel? How are they perceived?.

Cimbaljević, M., Stankov, U., & Pavluković, V. (2019). Going beyond the traditional destination competitiveness–reflections on a smart destination in the current research. *Current Issues in Tourism*, 22(20), 2472–2477. DOI: 10.1080/13683500.2018.1529149

Clarkson, M. B. (1995). A stakeholder framework for analyzing and evaluating. *Academy of Management Review*, 20(1), 92–117. DOI: 10.2307/258888

Cleere, G. S. (1989). *The House on Observatory Hill: Home of the Vice President of the United States*. Oceanographer of the Navy.

Cobbinah, P. B. (2015). Contextualising the meaning of ecotourism. *Tourism Management Perspectives*, 16, 179–189.

Coghlan, A., & Noakes, S. (2012). Towards an understanding of the drivers of commercialization in the volunteer tourism sector. *Tourism Recreation Research*, 37(2), 123–131. DOI: 10.1080/02508281.2012.11081697

Cohen, E. (2010). Authenticity, Equity and Sustainability in Tourism. *Journal of Sustainable Tourism*, 10(4), 267–276. DOI: 10.1080/09669580208667167

Columbia Climate School. (2021, August 10). How ecotourism can harm indigenous communities. *State of the Planet*. https://news.climate.columbia.edu/2021/08/10/ecotourism-harm-indigenous-communities/

Coman, A., Grigore, A. M., Ardelean, A., & Maracine, R. (2020). The world of museums and web 2.0: Links between social media and the number of visitors in museums. In *Social Computing and Social Media. Design, Ethics, User Behavior, and Social Network Analysis: 12th International Conference, SCSM 2020, Held as Part of the 22nd HCI International Conference, HCII 2020, Copenhagen, Denmark, July 19–24, 2020* [Springer International Publishing.]. *Proceedings*, 22(Part I), 442–458.

Confetto, M. G., Conte, F., Palazzo, M., & Siano, A. (2023). Digital destination branding: A framework to define and assess European DMOs practices. *Journal of Destination Marketing & Management*, 30, 100804. DOI: 10.1016/j.jdmm.2023.100804

Connolly, P., & Mcging, G. (2007). High performance work practices and competitive advantage in the Irish hospitality sector. *International Journal of Contemporary Hospitality Management*, 19(3), 201–210. DOI: 10.1108/09596110710739903

Cook, G. (2024). *The Planning, Design, and Delivery of Environmental Education and Interpretation in Ecotourism: A Case Study of Tiritiri Matangi Island* (Doctoral dissertation, Auckland University of Technology).

Cooper, C. (2022). Essentials of tourism.

Cooper, C. P., Fletcher, J., Fyall, A., Gilbert, D., & Wanhill, S. (2005). Tourism: Principles and practice (3. b.). Harlow, England: Financial Times Prentice Hall.

Corona, L. (2021). Museums and communication: The case of the louvre museum at the COVID-19 age. *Humanities and Social Science Research*, 4(1), 15–p15. DOI: 10.30560/hssr.v4n1p15

Cotter, K., Medeiros, M., Pak, C., & Thorson, K. (2021). "Reach the right people": The politics of "interests" in Facebook's classification system for ad targeting. *Big Data & Society*, 8(1), 2053951721996046. DOI: 10.1177/2053951721996046

Cox, C., & Wray, M. (2011). Best Practice Marketing for Regional Tourism Destinations. *Journal of Travel & Tourism Marketing*, 28(5), 524–540. DOI: 10.1080/10548408.2011.588112

Creswell, J. W. (2002). *Educational research: Planning, conducting, and evaluating quantitative and qualitative research*. Merrill/Pearson.

Cretanews. (2022). *Ecotourism in Rethymno and Chania centered on sea turtles*. https://www.cretanews.eu/kriti/oiko-tourismos-se-rethumno-kai-xania-me-epikentro-tis-thalassies-chelones/

Cre u, R. C., Alecu, I. I., Răducan, D., & tefan, P. (2024). Research onto the implementation of the ecological label in agrotourism. *Scientific Papers. Series Management, Economic, Engineering in Agriculture and Rural Development*, 24(1).

Crockett, S., & Wood, L. (1999). Brand Western Australia: A Totally Integrated Approach to Destination Branding. *Journal of Vacation Marketing*, 5(3), 276–289. DOI: 10.1177/135676679900500307

Cronjé, D. F., & du Plessis, E. (2020). A review on tourism destination competitiveness. *Journal of Hospitality and Tourism Management*, 45, 256–265. DOI: 10.1016/j.jhtm.2020.06.012

Crouch, J., & Ritchie, B. (2003). *The competitive destination – a sustainable tourism perspective*. Cabi Publishing.

Cummings, T. G., & Worley, C. G. (2009). *Organization Development & Change* (9th ed.). Cengage Learning.

Cuomo, M. T., Tortora, D., Foroudi, P., Giordano, A., Festa, G., & Metallo, G. (2021). Digital transformation and tourist experience co-design: Big social data for planning cultural tourism. *Technological Forecasting and Social Change*, 162, 120345. DOI: 10.1016/j.techfore.2020.120345

Curlin, T., Jaković, B., & Miloloža, I. (2019). Twitter usage in Tourism: Literature Review. In Business Systems Research (Vol. 10, Issue 1, pp. 102–119). Sciendo. DOI: 10.2478/bsrj-2019-0008

da Silva, M. B. D. O., Moreira, M. C. D. S., de Souza, Á. G. R., Arruda, D. D. O., & Mariani, M. A. P. (2019). Gastronomy on TripAdvisor: what tourists comment about restaurants in Bonito-MS-Brazil?.

Das, M., & Chatterjee, B. (2015). Ecotourism: A panacea or a predicament? *Tourism Management Perspectives*, 14, 3–6. DOI: 10.1016/j.tmp.2015.01.002

Davenport, T. H., Harris, J. G., Jones, G. L., Lemon, K. N., Norton, D., & McCallister, M. B. (2007). The dark side of customer analytics. *Harvard Business Review*, 85(5), 37.

Davis, P. H., Harper, P. C., & Hedge, I. C. (1971). *Plant life of south-west Asia*. The Botanical Society of Edinburgh.

Day, J., & Kaur, G. (2021). Destination Brand Equity and value creation for Internal stakeholders. Travel and Tourism Research Association: Advancing Tourism Research Globally.

De Bruyn, L. L., Duong, T. M. P., Kristiansen, P., Marshall, G. R., & Wilkes, J. (2022). The Role of Livelihood Initiatives in Reducing Non-wood Forest Product Reliance in Protected Areas of Southern Vietnam: Opportunities and Challenges. In *Sitra* (pp. 221–251). DOI: 10.1007/978-3-030-99313-9_10

de Bruyn, C., Said, F. B., Meyer, N., & Soliman, M. (2023). Research in tourism sustainability: A comprehensive bibliometric analysis from 1990 to 2022. *Heliyon*, 9(8), e18874. Advance online publication. DOI: 10.1016/j.heliyon.2023.e18874 PMID: 37636413

De Noni, I., Orsi, L., & Zanderighi, L. (2019). Stereotypical versus experiential destination branding: The case of Milan city. *City. Cultura e Scuola*, 17, 38–45. DOI: 10.1016/j.ccs.2018.10.001

Dedeoğlu, B. B., Van Niekerk, M., Küçükergin, K. G., De Martino, M., & Okumuş, F. (2020). Effect of social media sharing on destination brand awareness and destination quality. *Journal of Vacation Marketing*, 26(1), 33–56. DOI: 10.1177/1356766719858644

Dekimpe, M. G., Steenkamp, J.-B. E. M., Mellens, M., & Vanden Abeele, P. (1997). Decline and variability in brand loyalty. *International Journal of Research in Marketing*, 14(5), 405–420. DOI: 10.1016/S0167-8116(97)00020-7

Demirkol, S., & Taskiran, O. (2019). Destination branding process in tourism: A case study of Cittaslow Tarakli. *The Journal of Applied Social Sciences*, 3(2), 56–69.

Doborjeh, Z., Hemmington, N., Doborjeh, M., & Kasabov, N. (2022). Artificial intelligence: A systematic review of methods and applications in hospitality and tourism. *International Journal of Contemporary Hospitality Management*, 34(3), 1154–1176. DOI: 10.1108/IJCHM-06-2021-0767

Domínguez-Quintero, A. M., González-Rodríguez, M. R., & Roldán, J. L. (2021). The role of authenticity, experience quality, emotions, and satisfaction in a cultural heritage destination. In *Authenticity and Authentication of Heritage* (pp. 103–117). Routledge. DOI: 10.4324/9781003130253-9

Donohoe, H. M., & Needham, R. D. (2006). Ecotourism: The Evolving Contemporary Definition. *Journal of Ecotourism*, 5(3), 192–210.

Drivas, I. C., Kouis, D., Kyriaki-Manessi, D., & Giannakopoulou, F. (2022). Social media analytics and metrics for improving users engagement. *Knowledge (Beverly Hills, Calif.)*, 2(2), 225–242.

Du, Q., Guan, Q., Sun, Y., & Wang, Q. (2024). Assessment of Ecotourism Environmental Carrying Capacity in the Qilian Mountains, Northwest China. *Sustainability (Basel)*, 16(5), 1873.

Dwivedi, Y. K., Pandey, N., Currie, W., & Micu, A. (2024). Leveraging ChatGPT and other generative artificial intelligence (AI)-based applications in the hospitality and tourism industry: Practices, challenges and research agenda. *International Journal of Contemporary Hospitality Management*, 36(1), 1–12. DOI: 10.1108/IJCHM-05-2023-0686

Dwyer, L.,Forsyth, P. & Rao, P. (2000). The price competitiveness of travel and tourism: A

Economist. (2018, Mar 21st). Why is so much of the world's coral dying? https://shorturl.at/fDVTp

Ecotourism Global Market Report (2024)._https://www.researchandmarkets.com/report/ecotourism (accessed 18.07.24)

Ecotourism Global Market Report. (2024). The Business Research Company https://www.researchandmarkets.com/report/ecotourism

Ekinci, Y., & Hosany, S. (2006). Destination personality: An application of brand personality to tourism destinations. *Journal of Travel Research*, 45(2), 127–139. DOI: 10.1177/0047287506291603

Ekonomist. (2022) https://www.ekonomist.com.tr/ekonomist/pandemide-karavan-uretimine-gecti-sadece-4-ayda-14-ulkeye-ihracat-yapti-21910

Elayouty, A. M. A., Yacout, O. M., & Elgharbawy, A. H. (2023). A Proposed Conceptual Framework for the Mediating Role of Experiential Value between Ecotourism Brand Experience and Tourist Satisfaction. *Journal of Business and Management Review*, 4(12), 952–963.

Elisa, S., & Rimat, G. (2022). *Role of stakeholders in the branding process of a destination*. LAB University of Applied Sciences.

Environment, Development, and Sustainability. (2021). Ecotourism development strategies and the importance of local community engagement. *SpringerLink*. https://link.springer.com/journal/10668

Ergashev, R. K., & Jabborova, Z. (2021). The importance of innovative activity in tourism. *European Scholar Journal*, 2(4), 467–472.

Escobar-Farfán, M., Cervera-Taulet, A., & Schlesinger, W. (2024). Destination brand identity: Challenges, opportunities, and future research agenda. *Cogent Social Sciences*, 10(1), 2302803. DOI: 10.1080/23311886.2024.2302803

Eshuis, J., Braun, E., Klijn, E. H., & Zenker, S. (2018). The differential effect of different stakeholder groups in place marketing. *Environmental and Planning C. Politics and Space*, 36, 916–936.

Esmaeilzadeh, H., Sadeghi, S. M. M., & Wolf, I. D. (2022). Local community participation in sustainable ecotourism development in protected areas, Iran. *Land (Basel)*, 11(10), 1871. DOI: 10.3390/land11101871

Eugenio-Vela, J., & Barniol-Carcasona, M. (2015). The relationship between rural branding and local development. A case-study in Catalonia's countryside: Territoris Serens (El Llucanes). *Journal of Rural Studies*, 37, 108–119. DOI: 10.1016/j.jrurstud.2015.01.001

Evans, D., Bratton, S., & McKee, J. (2021). *Social media marketing*. AG Printing & Publishing.

Ewart, M., Scherrer, P., & Dimmock, K. (2024). Managing commercial tourism for conservation and sustainable use: Policy instrument interactions in Cape Byron Marine Park, Australia. *Marine Policy*, 166, 106233. DOI: 10.1016/j.marpol.2024.106233

Ezeuduji, I. O. (2015). Strategic event-based rural tourism development for sub-Saharan Africa. *Current Issues in Tourism*, 18(3), 212–228. DOI: 10.1080/13683500.2013.787049

Fagbolu, O. A., & Fallon, J. (2021). Strategies exploration for academic achievement improvement through organization development intervention (ODI): A study of Kwara state university. *ABAC ODI Journal, Vision. Action. Outcome*, 8(1), 161–179.

Fakeye, P. C., & Crompton, J. L. (1991). Image differences between prospective, first-time, and repeat visitors to the lower Rio Grande Valley. *Journal of Travel Research*, 30(2), 10–16. DOI: 10.1177/004728759103000202

Fallon, J., & Fagbolu, O. A. (2021). Developing possible strategies for academic achievement improvement of hospitality and tourism management students in Nigeria: A study of Kwara state university. *ABAC Journal*, 41(2), 177–203.

Farjoun, M., & Fiss, P. C. (2022). Thriving on contradiction: Toward a dialectical alternative to fit-based models in strategy (and beyond). *Strategic Management Journal*, 43(2), 340–369. DOI: 10.1002/smj.3342

FasterCapital. (n.d.). *Centrality measures in social network analysis*. Retrieved October 17, 2024, from https://fastercapital.com/topics/centrality-measures-in-social-network-analysis.html

Femenia-Serra, F., Perles-Ribes, J. F., & Ivars-Baidal, J. A. (2019). Smart destinations and tech-savvy millennial tourists: Hype versus reality. *Tourism Review*, 74(1), 63–81. DOI: 10.1108/TR-02-2018-0018

Fennell, D. A. (1999). *Ecotourism: An Introduction*. http://ci.nii.ac.jp/ncid/BA4004316X

Fennell, D. A. (2020). *Ecotourism*. Routledge. DOI: 10.4324/9780429346293

Fennell, D. A., Moorhouse, T. P., & Macdonald, D. W. (2024). Towards a model for the assessment of conservation, welfare, and governance in wildlife tourism attractions. *Journal of Ecotourism*, 23(2), 166–193. DOI: 10.1080/14724049.2022.2156523

Ferguson, M. A. (1984). *Building theory in public relations: Interorganisational relationships*. Association for Education in Journalism and Mass Communication.

Filieri, R., Acikgoz, F., Ndou, V., & Dwivedi, Y. (2021). Is TripAdvisor still relevant? The influence of review credibility, review usefulness, and ease of use on consumers' continuance intention. *International Journal of Contemporary Hospitality Management*, 33(1), 199–223. DOI: 10.1108/IJCHM-05-2020-0402

Filieri, R., D'Amico, E., Destefanis, A., Paolucci, E., & Raguseo, E. (2021). Artificial intelligence (AI) for tourism: An European-based study on successful AI tourism start-ups. *International Journal of Contemporary Hospitality Management*, 33(11), 4099–4125. DOI: 10.1108/IJCHM-02-2021-0220

Flagestad, A., & Hope, C. A. (2001). Strategic success in winter sports destinations – a sustainable value creation perspective. *Tourism Management*, 22(5), 445–561. DOI: 10.1016/S0261-5177(01)00010-3

Fletcher, J., Fyall, A., Gilbert, D., & Wanhill, S. (2018). *Tourism: Principles and practice*. Pearson.

Flyvbjerg, B. (2006). Five misunderstandings about case-study research. *Qualitative Inquiry*, 12(2), 219–245. DOI: 10.1177/1077800405284363

Font, X., & McCabe, S. (2017). Sustainability and marketing in tourism: Its contexts, paradoxes, approaches, challenges and potential. *Journal of Sustainable Tourism*, 25(7), 869–883. DOI: 10.1080/09669582.2017.1301721

Forrest, J. (2012). *Peru – culture smart!* Bravo Limited.

Fountoulakis, V. (2019). Partnership and joint plan for tourism in Chania. *Flashnews*. https://flashnews.gr/post/409030/sympraksh-kai-koino-plano-gia-ton-toyrismo-sta-xania-fwto-binteo

Foxall, G. R. (2017). Behavioral economics in consumer behavior analysis. *The Behavior Analyst*, 40(2), 309–313. DOI: 10.1007/s40614-017-0127-4

Freeman, L. C. (1977). A set of measures of centrality based on betweenness. *Sociometry*, 40(1), 35. DOI: 10.2307/3033543

Freeman, L. C. (1978). Centrality in social networks conceptual clarification. *Social Networks*, 1(3), 215–239. DOI: 10.1016/0378-8733(78)90021-7

Freeman, R. E. (2010). *Strategic management: A stakeholder approach*. Cambridge University Press. DOI: 10.1017/CBO9781139192675

Frias-Jamilena, D. M., Sabioti-Ortiz, C. M., Martin-Santana, J. D., & Beerli-Palacio, A. (2018). The effect of cultural intelligence on consumer-based destination brand equity. *Annals of Tourism Research*, 72, 22–36. DOI: 10.1016/j.annals.2018.05.009

Fusté-Forné, F., & Orea-Giner, A. (2023). Gastronomy in tourism management and marketing: an interview with ChatGPT. *ROBONOMICS: The Journal of the Automated Economy, 4*, 42-42. https://www.journal.robonomics.science/index.php/rj/article/view/42

Fusteri, N. (2013). *Sustainable tourism development in protected areas* (No. GRI-2013-10318). Aristotle University of Thessaloniki. (In Greek).

Fyall, A., & Garrod, B. (2005). *Tourism marketing: A collaborative approach*. Channel View Publications.

Fyall, A., Garrod, B., & Wang, Y. (2012). Destination collaboration: A critical review of theoretical approaches to a multi-dimensional phenomenon. *Journal of Destination Marketing & Management*, 1(1-2), 10–26. DOI: 10.1016/j.jdmm.2012.10.002

Gade, J., Johnpaul, M., & Miryala, R. K. (2024). Tribal Tourism: A Literature-Based Study of Ethnographic Exploration of Culture and Sustainable Development. In *Managing Tourism and Hospitality Sectors for Sustainable Global Transformation* (pp. 169-183). IGI Global. DOI: 10.4018/979-8-3693-6260-0.ch012

Gaki, E., Kostopoulou, S., Parisi, E., & Lagos, D. (2016). The evaluation of tourism satisfaction in island destinations: The case of the Ionian Islands of Greece.

Gao, L., Huang, S., Zhang, Y., & Xu, H. (2022). The role of sustainable tourism practices in enhancing tourists' experience in luxury resorts: A case study of the Maldives. *Sustainability*, 14(12), 7382.

García, J. A., Gómez, M., & Molina, A. (2012). A Destination-Branding Model: An Empirical Analysis Based on Stakeholders. *Tourism Management*, 33(3), 646–661. DOI: 10.1016/j.tourman.2011.07.006

García-Madurga, M. Á., & Grilló-Méndez, A. J. (2023). Artificial Intelligence in the Tourism Industry: An Overview of Reviews. In Administrative Sciences (Vol. 13, Issue 8). Multidisciplinary Digital Publishing Institute (MDPI). https://doi.org/ DOI: 10.3390/admsci13080172

Gardner, B. (2016). *Selling the Serengeti: The cultural politics of safari tourism*. University of Georgia Press. DOI: 10.1353/book44451

Garrod, B., & Fyall, A. (2000). Managing heritage tourism. *Annals of Tourism Research*, 27(3), 682–708. DOI: 10.1016/S0160-7383(99)00094-8

Gehani, R. (2001). Enhancing brand equity and reputational capital with enterprise-wide complementary innovations. *Marketing Management Journal*, 11(1), 35–48.

GeoJournal. (2021). Ecotourism and its impact on indigenous people and their local environment. *SpringerLink*. https://link.springer.com/journal/10708

Getz, D. (2008). Event Tourism: Definition, Evolution, and Research. *Tourism Management*, 29(3), 403–428. DOI: 10.1016/j.tourman.2007.07.017

Getz, D., & Page, S. J. (2016). Progress and prospects for event tourism research. *Tourism Management*, 52, 593–631. DOI: 10.1016/j.tourman.2015.03.007

Ghaderi, Z., Esfehani, M. H., Fennell, D., & Shahabi, E. (2021). Community participation towards conservation of Touran National Park (TNP): An application of reciprocal altruism theory. *Journal of Ecotourism*, 22(2), 281–295. DOI: 10.1080/14724049.2021.1991934

Ghandour, A., Kintonova, A., Demidchik, N., & Sverdlikova, E. (2021). Solving tourism management challenges by means of mobile augmented reality applications. [IJWLTT]. *International Journal of Web-Based Learning and Teaching Technologies*, 16(6), 1–16. DOI: 10.4018/IJWLTT.293280

Ghete, A. M. (2015). The importance of youth tourism. *Annals of Faculty of Economics, University of Oradea. Faculty of Economics*, 1(2), 688–694.

Ghodeswar, B. M. (2008). Building brand identity in competitive markets: A conceptual model. *Journal of Product and Brand Management*, 17(1), 4–12. DOI: 10.1108/10610420810856468

Giertz, J. N., Weiger, W. H., Törhönen, M., & Hamari, J. (2022). Content versus community focus in live streaming services: How to drive engagement in synchronous social media. *Journal of Service Management*, 33(1), 33–58. DOI: 10.1108/JOSM-12-2020-0439

Giuffredi-Kähr, A., Petrova, A., & Malär, L. (2022). Sponsorship Disclosure of Influencers–A Curse or a Blessing? *Journal of Interactive Marketing*, 57(1), 18–34. DOI: 10.1177/10949968221075686

Global Voices. (2024). https://el.globalvoices.org

Gnoth, J. (2002). Leveraging export brands through a tourism destination brand. *Journal of Brand Management*, 9(4), 262–280. DOI: 10.1057/palgrave.bm.2540077

Goeldner, C. R., & Ritchie, J. R. B. (2009). *Principles, Practices, Philosophies* (11th ed.). John Wiley & Sons, Inc.

Goldsmith, E. B. (2016). *Consumer economics: Issues and behaviors*. Routledge. DOI: 10.4324/9781315727363

Gong, J., Detchkhajornjaroensri, P., & Knight, D. W. (2019). Responsible tourism in Bangkok, Thailand: Resident perceptions of Chinese tourist behaviour. *International Journal of Tourism Research*, 21(2), 221–233. DOI: 10.1002/jtr.2256

Gonzalez-Mansilla, O., Berenguer-Contri, G., & Serra-Cantallops, A. (2019). The impact of value co-creation on hotel brand equity and customer satisfaction. *Tourism Management*, 75, 51–65. DOI: 10.1016/j.tourman.2019.04.024

Goodwin H (2013). Community-based tourism in the developing world: delivering the goods? Progress in Responsible Tourism 3(1): Goodfellow: 31-56 31

Gossling, S. (2017). *Tourism, information technologies and sustainability: An exploratory view*. Taylor & Francis.

Gössling, S.G¨Ossling. (2009). Carbon Neutral Destinations: A Conceptual Analysis. *Journal of Sustainable Tourism*, 17(1), 17–37. DOI: 10.1080/09669580802276018

Govers, R., Go, F. M., & Kumar, K. (2007). Virtual destination image - A new measurement approach. *Annals of Tourism Research*, 34(4), 977–997. DOI: 10.1016/j.annals.2007.06.001

Granovetter, M. S. (1973). The Strength of Weak Ties. *American Journal of Sociology*, 78(6), 1360–1380. DOI: 10.1086/225469

Greece, W. W. F. Hellenic Ornithological Society & Hellenic Society for Environment and Culture. (2009). *Hellenic Ramsar Wetlands: Protection and management assessment*. Athens. https://www.wwf.gr/images/pdfs/2012Jul_Epistoli_FD_NGOs.pdf

Greece, W. W. F. (2003). https://www.contentarchive.wwf.gr/images/pdfs/ecos.pdf

Green, A., Grace, D., & Perkins, H. (2016). City branding research and practice: An integrative review. *Journal of Brand Management*, 23(3), 252–272. DOI: 10.1057/bm.2016.8

Greenwood, M., & Kamoche, K. (2013). Social accounting as stakeholder knowledge appropriation. *The Journal of Management and Governance*, 17(3), 723–743. DOI: 10.1007/s10997-011-9208-z

Gretzel, U., Fesenmaier, D. R., Formica, S., & O'Leary, J. T. (2006). Searching for the future: Challenges faced by destination marketing organizations. *Journal of Travel Research*, 45(2), 116–126. DOI: 10.1177/0047287506291598

Gretzel, U., & Yoo, K. H. (2008). Use and Impact of Online travel Reviews. *Information and Communication Technologies in Tourism*, 1(1), 35–46. DOI: 10.1007/978-3-211-77280-5_4

Grošelj, P., Hodges, D., & Stirn, L. Z. (2016). Participatory and multi-criteria analysis for forest (ecosystem) management: A case study of Pohorje Slovenia. *Forest Policy and Economics*, 71, 80–86. DOI: 10.1016/j.forpol.2015.05.006

Grundner, L., & Neuhofer, B. (2021). The bright and dark sides of artificial intelligence: A futures perspective on tourist destination experiences. *Journal of Destination Marketing & Management*, 19, 100511. DOI: 10.1016/j.jdmm.2020.100511

Guan, J., Gao, J., & Zhang, C. (2019). Food heritagization and sustainable rural tourism destination: The case of China's yuanjia village. *Sustainability (Basel)*, 11(10), 2858. DOI: 10.3390/su11102858

Guerrero-Moreno, M. A., & Oliveira-Junior, J. M. B. (2024). Approaches, trends and gaps in community-based ecotourism research: A bibliometric analysis of publications between 2002 and 2022. *Sustainability (Basel)*, 16(1), 1–21. DOI: 10.3390/su16072639

Gumede, T. K., & Nzama, A. T. (2022). Approaches toward Community Participation Enhancement in Ecotourism. In *IntechOpen eBooks*. DOI: 10.5772/intechopen.100295

Güngör, G., & Akar, T. (2022). Kentin Simgesini Görünür Kılmak: Kızkulesi'nden Kızkalesi'ne Bir Aydınlatma Diyaloğu. *The Turkish Online Journal of Design Art and Communication*, 12(2), 300–315.

Guo, H., Luo, Z., Li, M., Kong, S., & Jiang, H. (2022). A literature review of big data-based urban park research in visitor dimension. *Land (Basel)*, 11(6), 864. DOI: 10.3390/land11060864

Guri, E. A., Osumanu, I. K., & Bonye, S. Z. (2020). Eco-cultural tourism development in Ghana: Potentials and expected benefits in the Lawra Municipality. *Journal of Tourism and Cultural Change*, 19(4), 458–476. DOI: 10.1080/14766825.2020.1737095

Guzman-Parra, V. F., Vila-Oblitas, J. R., & Maqueda-Lafuente, J. (2016). Exploring the effects of destination image attributes on tourist satisfaction and destination loyalty: An application in Málaga, Spain. *Tourism & Management Studies*, 12(1), 67–73. DOI: 10.18089/tms.2016.12107

Gyrd-Jones, R., & Kornum, N. (2013). Managing the co-created brand: Value and cultural complementarity in online and offline multistakeholder ecosystems. *Journal of Business Research*, 66(9), 1484–1493. DOI: 10.1016/j.jbusres.2012.02.045

Haber, T. R. T. (2024). Made own caravan and travelled: Kendi karavanını yapıp seyahate çıktı. https://www.trthaber.com/videolar/kendi-karavanini-yapip-seyahate-cikti-71827.html

Habertürk. (2022). Özel Halk Otobüsünden Akıllı Karavan yaptı (Turned the public bus into a smart caravan). https://www.haberturk.com/ozel-halk-otobusunden-akilli-karavan-yapti-3518024/4

Haenlein, M., Anadol, E., Farnsworth, T., Hugo, H., Hunichen, J., & Welte, D. (2020). Navigating the new era of influencer marketing: How to be successful on Instagram, TikTok, & Co. *California Management Review*, 63(1), 5–25. DOI: 10.1177/0008125620958166

Haleem, A., Javaid, M., Qadri, M. A., Singh, R. P., & Suman, R. (2022). Artificial intelligence (AI) applications for marketing: A literature-based study. *International Journal of Intelligent Networks*, 3, 119–132. DOI: 10.1016/j.ijin.2022.08.005

Hall, C. M. (1996). Wine Tourism in New Zealand. In *Proceedings on Tourism Down under II: A Tourism Research Conference* (pp. 109–119). University of Otago.

Hall, C. M. (2004). *Wine, Food and Tourism Marketing*. Haworth Hospitality Press.

Hall, C. M., & Piggin, R. (2002). Tourism business knowledge of World Heritage sites: A New Zealand case study. *International Journal of Tourism Research*, 4(5), 401–411. DOI: 10.1002/jtr.391

Hall, D. R., & Richards, G. (Eds.). (2000). *Tourism and sustainable community development* (p. 1). Routledge.

Hallo, J. C., & And Manning, R. E. (2009). Transportation and recreation: A case study of visitors driving for pleasure at Acadia National Park. *Journal of Transport Geography*, 17(6), 491–499. DOI: 10.1016/j.jtrangeo.2008.10.001

Hamdy, A., Zhang, J., & Eid, R. (2024). Does destination gender matter for destination brand attachment and brand love? The moderating role of destination involvement. *Marketing Intelligence & Planning*, 42(1), 120–148. DOI: 10.1108/MIP-05-2023-0211

Hameed, B., & Khalid, A. (2018). Impact of ecotourism in ensuring the sustainable development of tourism industry in India. *International Journal of Recent Research Aspects*, 5(2), 46–50.

Han, H. (2021). *Sustainable Consumer Behaviour and the Environment*. Routledge. DOI: 10.4324/9781003256274

Han, H., Al-Ansi, A., & Chua, B.-L. (2023). Tourist Perceptions of Luxury Hotel Attributes and Their Impacts on Behavioral Intentions: The Role of Sustainability Practices. *Journal of Destination Marketing & Management*, 29, 100795.

Hankinson, G. (2001). Location Branding: A Study of the Branding Practices of 12 English Cities. *Journal of Brand Management*, 9(2), 127–142. DOI: 10.1057/palgrave.bm.2540060

Hankinson, G. (2004). Relational Network Brands: Towards a Conceptual Model of Place Brands. *Journal of Vacation Marketing*, 10(2), 109–121. DOI: 10.1177/135676670401000202

Hankinson, G. (2009). Managing destination brands: Establishing a theoretical foundation. *Journal of Marketing Management*, 25(1/2), 97–115. DOI: 10.1362/026725709X410052

Hanna, S., & Rowley, J. (2011). Towards a strategic place brand-management model. *Journal of Marketing Management*, 27(5-6), 458–476. DOI: 10.1080/02672571003683797

Hanna, S., & Rowley, J. (2015). Towards a model of the place brand web. *Tourism Management*, 48, 100–112. DOI: 10.1016/j.tourman.2014.10.012

Hanna, S., Rowley, J., & Keegan, B. (2021). Place and destination branding: A review and conceptual mapping of the domain. *European Management Review*, 18(2), 105–117. DOI: 10.1111/emre.12433

Haq, M. D., Tseng, T. H., Cheng, H. L., Chiu, C. M., & Kuo, Y. H. (2024). This country is Loveable: A model of destination brand love considering consumption authenticity and social experience. *Journal of Destination Marketing & Management*, 32, 100878. DOI: 10.1016/j.jdmm.2024.100878

Hardin, G. (1968). The tragedy of the commons. *Science*, 162(3859), 1243–1248. DOI: 10.1126/science.162.3859.1243 PMID: 5699198

Hardy, A., Beeton, R. J., & Pearson, L. (2002). Sustainable tourism: An overview of the concept and its position in relation to conceptualisations of tourism. *Journal of Sustainable Tourism*, 10(6), 475–496. DOI: 10.1080/09669580208667183

Harrigan, P., Daly, T. M., Coussement, K., Lee, J. A., Soutar, G. N., & Evers, U. (2021). Identifying influencers on social media. *International Journal of Information Management*, 56, 102246. Advance online publication. DOI: 10.1016/j.ijinfomgt.2020.102246

Harris, F., & Chernatony, L. (2001). Corporate branding and corporate brand performance. *European Journal of Marketing*, 35(3/4), 441–456. DOI: 10.1108/03090560110382101

Harrison, D., & Campus, N. (2004). Working with the tourism industry: A case study from Fiji. *Social Responsibility*, 1(1-2), 249–270.

Hassan, . (2010). Perception of destination branding measures: A case study of Alexandria destination marketing organizations. *International Journal of Euro-Mediterranean Studies*, 3(2), 269–288.

Hatma Indra Jaya, P., Izudin, A., & Aditya, R. (2024). The role of ecotourism in developing local communities in Indonesia. *Journal of Ecotourism*, 23(1), 20–37. DOI: 10.1080/14724049.2022.2117368

Hede, A. M. (2008). World Heritage listing and the evolving issues related to tourism and heritage: Cases from Australia and New Zealand. *Journal of Heritage Tourism*, 2(3), 133–144. DOI: 10.2167/jht055.0

Helmer, W., & Scholte, P. (1985). *Herpetological research in Evros, Greece: Proposal for a biogenetic reserve*. Research Institute for Nature Management and Catholic University.

Herath, G. (2002). Research methodologies for planning ecotourism and nature conservation. *Tourism Economics*, 8(1), 77–101. DOI: 10.5367/000000002101298007

Hernik, J. (2017). Greenwashing in Tourism, So How Companies Should Not Create An Image. *Challenges of Tourism and Business Logistics in the 21st Century, 1*(1), 13-17.

Herrero Amo, M. D., & De Stefano, M. C. (2019). Public–private partnership as an innovative approach for sustainable tourism in Guanacaste, Costa Rica. *Worldwide Hospitality and Tourism Themes*, 11(2), 130–139. DOI: 10.1108/WHATT-11-2018-0078

Higgins-Desbiolles, F. (2008). Justice tourism and alternative globalisation. *Journal of Sustainable Tourism*, 16(3), 345–364. DOI: 10.1080/09669580802154132

Hirschman, E. C., & Holbrook, M. B. (1982). Hedonic Consumption: Emerging Concepts, Methods, and Propositions. *Journal of Marketing*, 46(3), 92–101. DOI: 10.1177/002224298204600314

Hofstede, G. H., & Minkov, M. (2010). *Cultures and organizations: Software of the mind*. McGraw-Hill.

Holden, A. (2008). *Environment and tourism*. Routledge.

Holder, A., Walters, G., Ruhanen, L., & Mkono, M. (2024). Exploring tourist's socio-cultural aversions, self-congruity bias, attitudes and willingness to participate in indigenous tourism. *Journal of Vacation Marketing*, 30(2), 207–224. DOI: 10.1177/13567667221124343

Honey, M. (2008). *Ecotourism and sustainable development: Who owns paradise?* Island Press.

Honey, M. (2009). Ecotourism and sustainable development: Who owns paradise? *Choice (Chicago, Ill.)*, 46(06), 46–3341. DOI: 10.5860/CHOICE.46-3341

Hosany, S., Ekinci, Y., & Uysal, M. (2006). Destination image and destination personality: An application of branding theories to tourism places. *Journal of Business Research*, 59(5), 638–642. DOI: 10.1016/j.jbusres.2006.01.001

Hosany, S., & Gilbert, D. (2010). Measuring tourists' emotional experiences toward hedonic holiday destinations. *Journal of Travel Research*, 49(4), 513–526. DOI: 10.1177/0047287509349267

Huamanchumo, R. M. E., Flores, C. E. G., & Barrantes, D. A. (2020). Ecotouristic activity of local entrepreneurs in the sustainability of the historical sanctuary forest of Pómac. *Journal of Tourism and Heritage Research: JTHR*, 3(3), 360–380.

Huang, A., Ozturk, A. B., Zhang, T., de la Mora Velasco, E., & Haney, A. (2024). Unpacking AI for hospitality and tourism services: Exploring the role of perceived enjoyment on future use intentions. *International Journal of Hospitality Management*, 119, 103693. DOI: 10.1016/j.ijhm.2024.103693

Hudson, S., & Miller, G. (2005). Ethical orientation and awareness of tourism students. *Journal of Business Ethics*, 62(4), 383–396. DOI: 10.1007/s10551-005-0850-8

Hudson, S., & Ritchie, J. B. (2009). Branding a memorable destination experience. The case of 'Brand Canada'. *International Journal of Tourism Research*, 11(2), 217–228. DOI: 10.1002/jtr.720

Hu, H., Zhang, Y., Wang, C., & Yu, P. (2024). Factors Influencing Tourists' Intention and Behavior toward Tourism Waste Classification: A Case Study of the West Lake Scenic Spot in Hangzhou, China. *Sustainability (Basel)*, 16(3), 1231. Advance online publication. DOI: 10.3390/su16031231

Hvenegaard, G., & Dearden, P. (1998). Ecotourism versus tourism in a Thai national park. *Annals of Tourism Research*, 25(3), 700–720. DOI: 10.1016/S0160-7383(98)00020-6

Ianenko, M., Stepanov, M., & Mironova, L. (2020). Brand identity development. E3S Web of Conferences(164), 1-7.

İbret, Ü., Aydınözü, D., & Uğurlu, M. (2015). KASTAMONU ŞEHRİNDE KÜLTÜR VE İNANÇ TURİZMİ. *Marmara Coğrafya Dergisi*, 0(32), 239–269. DOI: 10.14781/mcd.00582

Im, H. H., Kim, S. S., Elliot, S., & Han, H. (2012). Conceptualizing destination brand equity dimensions from a consumer-based brand equity perspective. *Journal of Travel & Tourism Marketing*, 29(4), 385–403. DOI: 10.1080/10548408.2012.674884

INSETE. (2021). *Destination Zakynthos*. https://insete.gr/wp-content/uploads/pdf/proorismoi/proorismos-zakunthos.pdf

INSETE. (2022). *Executive Summary 2030*. https://insete.gr/wp-content/uploads/2021/12/Executive-Summary_2030.pdf

INSETE. (2022). *Products and markets analysis*. https://insete.gr/wp-content/uploads/2021/12/21-12_Proionta-Agores.pdf

INSETE. (2022). The average expenditure per journey of inbound tourists in Greece and Spain in 2019, 2021, and 2022. *INSETE*. https://insete.gr/studies/the-average-expenditure-per-journey-of-inbound-tourists-in-greece-and-spain-in-2019-2021-and-2022-2/?lang=en

Institute of Trade and Services. (2017). *Mapping and analysis of business activity in Chania, Crete*. INEMY.

Ioannides, D., & Gyimothy, S. (2020). The COVID-19 crisis as an opportunity for escaping the unsustainable global tourism path. *Tourism Geographies*, 22(3), 624–632. DOI: 10.1080/14616688.2020.1763445

Ioppolo, G., Saija, G., & Salomone, R. (2012). From coastal management to environmental management: The sustainable eco-tourism program for the mid-western coast of Sardinia (Italy). *Land Use Policy*, 31, 460–471. DOI: 10.1016/j.landusepol.2012.08.010

Ip-Soo-Ching, J. M., Zyngier, S., & Nayeem, T. (2019). Ecotourism and environmental sustainability knowledge: An open knowledge sharing approach among stakeholders. *Australian Journal of Environmental Education*, 35(1), 62–82. DOI: 10.1017/aee.2018.45

Iqbal, A., Ramachandran, S., Siow, M. I., Subramaniam, T., & Afandi, S. H. M. (2022). Meaningful community participation for effective development of sustainable tourism: Bibliometric analysis towards a quintuple helix model. *Journal of Outdoor Recreation and Tourism*, 39, 100523. DOI: 10.1016/j.jort.2022.100523

Iseppi, F. (2021). Modello Italia: Il turismo di prossimità da solo non basta. *Vita*, 5, 34–36.

Islam, M. A., Aldaihani, F. M. F., & Saatchi, S. G. (2023). Artificial intelligence adoption among human resource professionals: Does market turbulence play a role? *Global Business and Organizational Excellence*, 42(6), 59–74. DOI: 10.1002/joe.22226

Iswanto, D., Handriana, T., Rony, A. H. N., & Sangadji, S. S. (2024). Influencers in Tourism Digital Marketing: A Comprehensive Literature Review. *International Journal of Sustainable Development and Planning*, 19(2), 739–749. DOI: 10.18280/ijsdp.190231

IUCN. (2024). https://www.iucn.org/blog/202404/human-rights-based-approach-iucns-global-standard-nature-based-solutions

Ivanov, S., & Soliman, M. (2023). Game of algorithms: ChatGPT implications for the future of tourism education and research. *Journal of Tourism Futures*, 9(2), 214–221. DOI: 10.1108/JTF-02-2023-0038

Ivanov, S., Soliman, M., Tuomi, A., Alkathiri, N. A., & Al-Alawi, A. N. (2024). Drivers of generative AI adoption in higher education through the lens of the Theory of Planned Behaviour. *Technology in Society*, 77, 102521. DOI: 10.1016/j.techsoc.2024.102521

Jaboob, . (2023). Digital Technologies as a Key Driver of Sustainable Global Higher Education. In *Technologies for Sustainable Global Higher Education* (pp. 77–94). Auerbach Publications. DOI: 10.1201/9781003424543-5

Jamil, K., Dunnan, L., Gul, R. F., Shehzad, M. U., Gillani, S. H. M., & Awan, F. H. (2022a). Role of social media marketing activities in influencing customer intentions: A perspective of a new emerging era. *Frontiers in Psychology*, 12, 808525. DOI: 10.3389/fpsyg.2021.808525 PMID: 35111111

Jamil, K., Hussain, Z., Gul, R. F., Shahzad, M. A., & Zubair, A. (2022b). The effect of consumer self-confidence on information search and share intention. *Information Discovery and Delivery*, 50(3), 260–274. DOI: 10.1108/IDD-12-2020-0155

Janjua, Z. U. A., Krishnapillai, G., & Rehman, M. (2022). Importance of the sustainability tourism marketing practices: An insight from rural community-based homestays in Malaysia. *Journal of Hospitality and Tourism Insights*, 6(2), 575–594. DOI: 10.1108/JHTI-10-2021-0274

Janonis, V., Dovalienė, A., & Virvilaitė, R. (2007). Relationship of Brand Identity and Image. *The Engineering Economist*, 1(51), 69–80.

Jayasekara, K. D. D. S., Rajapaksa, D., & Gunawardena, U. A. D. (2024). Impacts of Environmental Knowledge, Motives, and Behavior on Ecotourism. *Sustainability (Basel)*, 16(11), 4724.

Jebbouri, A., Zhang, H., Imran, Z., Iqbal, J., & Bouchiba, N. (2022). Impact of destination image formation on tourist trust: Mediating role of tourist satisfaction. *Frontiers in Psychology*, 13, 845538. DOI: 10.3389/fpsyg.2022.845538 PMID: 35432069

Jennings, G. (2010). *Tourism Research.* John Wiley & Sons.

Jiménez-Barreto, J., Rubio, N., & Campo, S. (2020). Destination brand authenticity: What an experiential simulacrum! A multigroup analysis of its antecedents and outcomes through official online platforms. *Tourism Management*, 77, 104022. DOI: 10.1016/j.tourman.2019.104022

Jochimsthaler, E. (2002). Commitment – Mitarbeiter – Die vergessene Zielgruppe für Markenerfolge. *Absatzwirtschaft*, 45(11), 28–34.

Johnston, A. (2000). Indigenous peoples and ecotourism: Bringing indigenous knowledge and rights into the sustainability equation. *Tourism Recreation Research*, 25(2), 89–96. DOI: 10.1080/02508281.2000.11014914

Jones, R. (2005). Finding sources of brand value - developing a stakeholder model of brand equity. *Journal of Brand Management*, 13(1), 10–32. DOI: 10.1057/palgrave.bm.2540243

Jopp, R., Mair, J., DeLacy, T., & Fluker, M. (2015). Climate change adaptation: Destination management and the green tourist. *Tourism Planning & Development*, 12(3), 300–320. DOI: 10.1080/21568316.2014.988879

Juliana, J., Syiva, A. N., Rosida, R., Permana, E., Zulfikar, R. M., Abduh, M., & Inomjon, Q. (2024). Revisit Intention Muslim Tourists to Halal Tourism in Yogyakarta: Analysis of Facilities, Promotion, Electronic Word of Mouth, and Religiosity. *Review of Islamic Economics and Finance*, 7(1), 1–22.

Junus, S. Z., Hambali, K. A., Iman, A. H. M., Abas, M. A., & Hassin, N. H. (2020). Visitor's perception and attitude toward the ecotourism resources at Taman Negara Kuala Koh, Kelantan. *IOP Conference Series. Earth and Environmental Science*, 549(1), 12088. DOI: 10.1088/1755-1315/549/1/012088

Kaefer, F. (2022). Glenn Jampol on Tourism Business and Ecotourism in Costa Rica. In Sustainability Leadership in Tourism: Interviews, Insights, and Knowledge from Practice (pp. 267–271). Springer International Publishing. DOI: 10.1007/978-3-031-05314-6_41

Kafouros, V. (2015). *Proposals for the development of cultural tourism in Greece.* KEPE.

Kah, J. A., Shin, H. J., & Lee, S. H. (2020). Traveler sensory-scape experiences and the formation of destination identity. *Tourism Geographies*, 24(2/3), 475–494.

Kainthola Ms, S., Tiwari Ms, P., & Chowdhary Dr, N. R. (2021). Tourist Guides' perspectives of demarketing the Taj Mahal. *International Journal of Tour Guiding Research*, 2(1), 4.

Kaiza-Boshe, T. (2024). Towards Overcoming the Challenges to Adopting Ecosystem-Based Management Approach for Protected Areas: The Case of Serengeti Ecosystem. In *Land-Use Management-Recent Advances, New Perspectives, and Applications*. IntechOpen.

Kamila, M. K., & Jasrotia, S. S. (2023). Ethical issues in the development of artificial intelligence: recognizing the risks. *International Journal of Ethics and Systems*(ahead-of-print). https://doi.org/DOI: 10.1108/IJOES-05-2023-0107

Kamruzzaman, L. (2024). Subjective vs. objective assessment of the economic impacts of light rail transit: The case of G:Link in Gold Coast, Australia. *Journal of Transport Geography*, 117, 103883. Advance online publication. DOI: 10.1016/j.jtrangeo.2024.103883

Kapferer, N. J. (1992). *Strategic Brand Management*. Kogan Page.

Karagöz, H. A., Demirçiftçi, T., & Erkmen, E. (2022). Local Restaurants' Effect on Tourist Experience: A Case from Istanbul. *Journal of Economy Culture and Society*, 0(65), 313–327. DOI: 10.26650/JECS2021-1007826

Karatas-Ozkan, M., Tunalioglu, R., Ibrahim, S., Ozeren, E., Grinevich, V., & Kimaro, J. (2024). Actioning sustainability through tourism entrepreneurship: Women entrepreneurs as change agents navigating through the field of stakeholders. *Central European Management Journal*, 32(1), 31–56.

Karayazi, S. S., Dane, G., & Arentze, T. (2024). Visitors' heritage location choices in Amsterdam in times of mass tourism: A latent class analysis. *Journal of Heritage Tourism*, 19(4), 1–22. DOI: 10.1080/1743873X.2024.2331227

Karterakis, N. (2020). *National Parks and their role in cultivating environmental awareness: The case of the Samaria Gorge* (In Greek).

Kasapoğlu, C., Aksoy, R., & Başkol, M. (2023). Assessing Destination Brand Associations on Twitter: The case of Istanbul. [AHTR]. *Advances in Hospitality and Tourism Research*, 11(4), 443–475. DOI: 10.30519/ahtr.1116172

Kashıf, M., Samsı, S. Z., & Sarıfuddın, S. (2015). Brand Equıty Of Lahore Fort As A Tourısm Destınatıon Brand. Revista de Administração de Empresas, 55(4).

Kaushik, K., Khan, A., Kumari, A., Sharma, I., & Dubey, R. (2024). Ethical Considerations in AI-Based Cybersecurity. In *Next-Generation Cybersecurity: AI, ML, and Blockchain* (pp. 437-470). Springer. https://doi.org/DOI: 10.1007/978-981-97-1249-6_19

Kavaratzis, M. (2012). From 'necessary evil' to necessity: Stakeholders' involvement in place branding. *Journal of Place Management and Development*, 5(1), 7–19. DOI: 10.1108/17538331211209013

Kavaratzis, M., & Ashworth, G. J. (2005). City branding: An effective assertion of identity or a transitory marketing trick? *Tijdschrift voor Economische en Sociale Geografie*, 96(5), 506–514. DOI: 10.1111/j.1467-9663.2005.00482.x

Kavaratzis, M., & Hatch, M. J. (2013). The dynamics of place brands: An identity-based approach to place branding theory. *Marketing Theory*, 13(1), 69–86. DOI: 10.1177/1470593112467268

KC, A., Rijal, K., & Sapkota, R. P. (2015). Role of ecotourism in environmental conservation and socioeconomic development in Annapurna conservation area, Nepal. *International Journal of Sustainable Development and World Ecology*, 22(3), 251–258.

Keegan, B. J., & Rowley, J. (2017). Evaluation and decision making in social media marketing. *Management Decision*, 55(1), 15–31. DOI: 10.1108/MD-10-2015-0450

Kefi, H., Besson, E., Zhao, Y., & Farran, S. (2024). Toward museum transformation: From mediation to social media-tion and fostering omni-visit experience. *Information & Management*, 61(1), 103890. DOI: 10.1016/j.im.2023.103890

Keitumetse, S. O. (2009). The Eco-tourism of Cultural Heritage Management (ECT-CHM): Linking Heritage and 'Environment' in the Okavango Delta Regions of Botswana. *International Journal of Heritage Studies*, 15(2–3), 223–244. DOI: 10.1080/13527250902890811

Keller, K. L. (2003). *Strategic brand management Upper Saddle River*. Prentice Hall.

Khanh, C. N. T., & Phong, L. T. (2020). Impact of environmental belief and nature-based destination image on ecotourism attitude. *Journal of Hospitality and Tourism Insights*. DOI: 10.1108/JHTI-03-2020-0027

Khan, I., & Fatma, M. (2021). Online destination brand experience and authenticity: Does individualism-collectivism orientation matter? *Journal of Destination Marketing & Management*, 20, 100597. DOI: 10.1016/j.jdmm.2021.100597

Khaokhrueamuang, A. (2020). International exchange in tea tourism: reconceptualizing Japanese green tourism for sustainable farming communities. In *Tourism Development in Japan* (pp. 140–159). Routledge. DOI: 10.4324/9780429273513-8

Khumtaveeporn, I., & Wattanasuwan, K. (2023). AI Sentiment Analysis for Destination Branding: A Case Study of Buriram, Thailand. *Journal of Business Administration*, 46(180), 50–74.

Kilipiri, E., Papaioannou, E., & Kotzaivazoglou, I. (2023). Social media and influencer marketing for promoting sustainable tourism destinations: The instagram case. *Sustainability (Basel)*, 15(8), 6374. DOI: 10.3390/su15086374

Kim, C., & Dwyer, L. (2003). Destination competitiveness and bilateral tourism flows between Australia and Korea. *Journal of Tourism Studies*, 14(2), 55–67. DOI: 10.21581/jts.2018.05.30.2.55

Kim, H., & Fesenmaier, D. R. (2008). Persuasive design of destination web sites: An analysis of first impression. *Journal of Travel Research*, 47(1), 3–13. DOI: 10.1177/0047287507312405

Kim, H., So, K. K. F., Shin, S., & Li, J. (2024). Artificial intelligence in hospitality and tourism: Insights from industry practices, research literature, and expert opinions. *Journal of Hospitality & Tourism Research (Washington, D.C.)*, 10963480241229235, 10963480241229235. Advance online publication. DOI: 10.1177/10963480241229235

Kim, J., & Park, E. (2022). The impact of virtual reality (VR) in tourism marketing: A meta-analysis. *Journal of Travel Research*, 61(4), 860–878.

Kim, M. S., Thapa, B., & Kim, H. (2017). International tourists' perceived sustainability of Jeju Island, South Korea. *Sustainability (Basel)*, 10(1), 73. DOI: 10.3390/su10010073

Kim, M., Xie, Y., & Cirella, G. T. (2019). Sustainable transformative economy: Community-based ecotourism in Cambodia. *Sustainability (Basel)*, 11(18), 4977. DOI: 10.3390/su11184977

Kim, S. I., Al-Ansi, A., Lee, J. S., Chua, B. L., Phucharoen, C., & Han, H. (2024). Wellness tourism experience and destination brand love. *Journal of Travel & Tourism Marketing*, 41(7), 988–1004. DOI: 10.1080/10548408.2024.2369752

King, E., Smith, M. P., Wilson, P. F., & Williams, M. A. (2021). Digital responses of UK museum exhibitions to the COVID-19 crisis, March–June 2020. *Curator (New York, N.Y.)*, 64(3), 487–504. DOI: 10.1111/cura.12413 PMID: 34230675

Kiper, T. (2013). *Role of ecotourism in sustainable development. InTech*. DOI: 10.5772/55749

Kirilenko, A., Emin, K., & Tavares, K. C. N. (2023). Instagram travel influencers coping with COVID-19 travel disruption. *Information Technology & Tourism*, 26(1), 119–146. DOI: 10.1007/s40558-023-00276-7

Kirkby, C. A., Giudice, R., Day, B., Turner, K., Soares-Filho, B. S., Oliveira-Rodrigues, H., & Yu, D. W. (2011). Closing the ecotourism-conservation loop in the Peruvian Amazon. *Environmental Conservation*, 38(1), 6–17. DOI: 10.1017/S0376892911000099

Kishan, K., Mishra, A., Tiwari, V., & Vemuri, V. P. (2024). Artificial Intelligence: The Next Frontier for Marketing in the Tourism Industry. *Academy of Marketing Studies Journal*, 28(1).

Kladou, S., Giannopoulos, A. A., & Mavragani, E. (2015). Destination brand equity research from 2001 to 2012. *Tourism Analysis*, 20(2), 189–200. DOI: 10.3727/108354215X14265319207399

Kladou, S., & Mavragani, E. (2015). Assessing destination image: An online marketing approach and the case of TripAdvisor. *Journal of Destination Marketing & Management*, 4(3), 187–193.

Knani, M., Echchakoui, S., & Ladhari, R. (2022). Artificial intelligence in tourism and hospitality: Bibliometric analysis and research agenda. *International Journal of Hospitality Management*, 107, 103317. DOI: 10.1016/j.ijhm.2022.103317

Knollenberg, W., Duffy, L. N., Kline, C., & Kim, G. (2021). Creating competitive advantage for food tourism destinations through food and beverage experiences. *Tourism Planning & Development*, 18(4), 379–397. DOI: 10.1080/21568316.2020.1798687

Komilis, P. (2007). *Ecotourism: The alternative perspective of sustainable tourism development*. Propombos. (In Greek)

Komppula, R. (2014). The role of individual entrepreneurs in the development of competitiveness for a rural tourism destination – A case study. *Tourism Management*, 40, 361–371. DOI: 10.1016/j.tourman.2013.07.007

Koncul, N. (2012). Wellness: A new mode of tourism. In Ekonomska Istrazivanja (Vol. 25, Issue 2, pp. 525–534). Faculty of Economics and Tourism "Dr. Mijo Mirkovic." https://doi.org/DOI: 10.1080/1331677X.2012.11517521

Konecnik, M., & Gartner, W. C. (2007). Customer-based brand equity for a destination. *Annals of Tourism Research*, 34(2), 400–421. DOI: 10.1016/j.annals.2006.10.005

Konecnik, M., & Go, F. (2008). Tourism Destination Brand Identity: The Case of Slovenia. *Journal of Brand Management*, 15(3), 177–189. DOI: 10.1057/palgrave.bm.2550114

Kong, H., Wang, K., Qiu, X., Cheung, C., & Bu, N. (2023). 30 years of artificial intelligence (AI) research relating to the hospitality and tourism industry. *International Journal of Contemporary Hospitality Management*, 35(6), 2157–2177. DOI: 10.1108/IJCHM-03-2022-0354

Konomos, D. (1989). *Zakynthos. Five hundred years (1478-1978) Art Odyssey, Volume Five, Issue III. Secular art, Painting-Architecture.* Dinos Konomos. (In Greek)

Korteling, J., van de Boer-Visschedijk, G. C., Blankendaal, R. A., Boonekamp, R. C., & Eikelboom, A. R. (2021). Human-versus artificial intelligence. *Frontiers in Artificial Intelligence*, 4, 622364. DOI: 10.3389/frai.2021.622364 PMID: 33981990

Koruyan, K., & Akatas, E. (2022). Destination Image Analysis with User-Generated Content: A Computer Vision and Machine Learning Approach. *Journal of Tourism & Gastronomy Studies*, 10(3), 2126–2143. DOI: 10.21325/jotags.2022.1085

Kotler, P., & Keller, K. L. (2015). Marketing Management. Pearson Education. Available at: https://books.google.com.vn/books?id=PDUOrgEACAAJ

Kotler, P., Bowen, J. T., Makens, J. C., & Baloglu, S. (2017). *Marketing for hospitality and tourism.* Pearson.

Kotler, P., & Gertner, D. (2007). Country as brand, product and beyond: A place marketing and brand management perspective. In *Destination branding* (pp. 55–71). Routledge.

Koure, F. K., Hajjarian, M., & Mosadeghi, R. (2022). Ecotourism development strategies and the importance of local community engagement. *Environment, Development and Sustainability*, 25(7), 6849–6877. DOI: 10.1007/s10668-022-02338-y

Kousounis, S. (2022). Zagori as a leading destination for alternative and thematic tourism. Approval of the nomination plan for its inscription on the list of World Heritage Sites (In Greek).

Koutsoumaraki, V. (1999). *Conceptual integration of agritourism in the context of sustainable tourism development: The case of the Kerkini lake region* (In Greek).

Kozak, M., & Baloglu, S. (2011). *Managing and marketing tourist destinations: Strategies to gain competitive edge* (1st ed.). Routledge.

Kreiss, D., Lawrence, R. G., & McGregor, S. C. (2020). In their own words: Political practitioner accounts of candidates, audiences, affordances, genres, and timing in strategic social media use. In *Studying Politics Across Media* (pp. 8–31). Routledge. DOI: 10.4324/9780429202483-2

Krishnapillai, G., & Rehman, M. (2023). Enhancing Brand Equity Through Sustainable Tourism Marketing: A Study on Home-Stays in Malaysia. *Asian Academy of Management Journal*, 28(1), 237–263. DOI: 10.21315/aamj2023.28.1.10

Ku, E. C., & Chen, C.-D. (2024). Artificial intelligence innovation of tourism businesses: From satisfied tourists to continued service usage intention. *International Journal of Information Management*, 76, 102757. DOI: 10.1016/j.ijinfomgt.2024.102757

Kumail, T., Qeed, M. A. A., Aburumman, A., Abbas, S. M., & Sadiq, F. (2022). How destination brand equity and destination brand authenticity influence destination visit intention: Evidence from the United Arab Emirates. *Journal of Promotion Management*, 28(3), 332–358. DOI: 10.1080/10496491.2021.1989540

Kumari, N. (2021). Impact of Eco-Tourism on the Indian Economy. *Gap Interdisciplinarities*, 12-16.

Kumar, R., Jebarajakirthy, C., Maseeh, H. I., Dhanda, K., Saha, R., & Dahiya, R. (2023). Two decades of brand hate research: A review and research agenda. *Marketing Intelligence & Planning*, 41(6), 763–789. DOI: 10.1108/MIP-01-2023-0030

Kumar, V., Ashraf, A. R., & Nadeem, W. (2024). AI-powered marketing: What, where, and how? *International Journal of Information Management*, 77, 102783. DOI: 10.1016/j.ijinfomgt.2024.102783

Kummitha, H. R. (2020). Eco-entrepreneurs organizational attitude towards sustainable community ecotourism development. *The Central European Journal of Regional Development and Tourism*, 12(1), 85–101. DOI: 10.32725/det.2020.005

Kumwenda, B. (2019). Socio-economic impacts of community-based ecotourism in Hluhluwe-iMfolozi Park, South Africa. *African Journal of Hospitality, Tourism and Leisure*, 8(4), 1–15. https://www.ajhtl.com/uploads/7/1/6/3/7163688/article_41_vol_8_4__2019_unizul.pdf

Kunwar, R. R. (2015). Tourism crisis and disaster management. *The Gaze: Journal of Tourism and Hospitality*, 7, 1–36.

Kusumaningrum, S. D. (2023). Sustainability and destination branding: A review of research trends. *Turisztikai És Vidékfejlesztési Tanulmányok*, 7(4), 110–127. DOI: 10.15170/TVT.2022.07.04.08

Lake Kerkini National Park. (2021). Kerkini Lake Management Agency. http://kerkini.gr/

Lalicic, L. (2020). Solastalgia: An application in the overtourism context. *Annals of Tourism Research*, 82, 102766. DOI: 10.1016/j.annals.2019.102766

Lane, B. (2009). Thirty years of sustainable tourism: Drivers, progress, problems and the future. In Gössling, S., Hall, C. M., & Weaver, D. (Eds.), *Sustainable Tourism Futures* (pp. 19–32). Routledge. DOI: 10.4324/9780203884256-10

Larson, L. R., & Poudyal, N. C. (2012). Developing sustainable tourism through adaptive resource management: A case study of Machu Picchu, Peru. *Journal of Sustainable Tourism*, 20(7), 917–938. DOI: 10.1080/09669582.2012.667217

Lasgorceix, A., & Kothari, A. (2009). Displacement and relocation of protected areas: a synthesis and analysis of case studies. *Economic and Political Weekly/ Economic & Political Weekly, 44*(49), 37–47. https://kalpavriksh.org/images/CLN/Media_Displacement%20from%20PAs_EPW_5Nov.pdf

Law, R., Lin, K. J., Ye, H., & Fong, D. K. C. (2024). Artificial intelligence research in hospitality: A state-of-the-art review and future directions. *International Journal of Contemporary Hospitality Management*, 36(6), 2049–2068. DOI: 10.1108/IJCHM-02-2023-0189

Laws, E., Scott, N., & Parfitt, N. (2002). Synergies in destination image management: A case study and conceptualization. *International Journal of Tourism Research*, 4(1), 39–55. DOI: 10.1002/jtr.353

Le Corre, N., Saint-Pierre, A., Hughes, M., Peuziat, I., & Cosquer, A. (2024). Segmentation of visitor perceptions and attitudes as a tool for informing management and targeted communication strategies in Coastal and Marine Protected Areas. *Journal of Coastal Conservation*, 28(4), 57. DOI: 10.1007/s11852-024-01053-2

Leask, A., & Fyall, A. (2006). Researching the management of visitor attractions: International comparative study issues. *Tourism Recreation Research*, 31(2), 23–32. DOI: 10.1080/02508281.2006.11081259

Ledingham, J. A. (2003). Explicating relationship management as a general theory of public relations. *Journal of Public Relations Research*, 15(2), 1136–1146. DOI: 10.1207/S1532754XJPRR1502_4

Lee, S., Hwang, J., & Jang, J. (2022). Luxury hotel guests' perceptions of sustainability practices: The impact on brand loyalty and willingness to pay. *Journal of Hospitality & Tourism Research (Washington, D.C.)*, 46(5), 859–881.

Lee, S., Lee, N., Lee, T. J., & Hyun, S. S. (2023). The influence of social support from intermediary organizations on innovativeness and subjective happiness in community-based tourism. *Journal of Sustainable Tourism*, •••, 1–23. DOI: 10.1080/09669582.2023.2175836

Lee, T. H., & Jan, F. H. (2018). Development and validation of the ecotourism behaviour scale. *International Journal of Tourism Research*, 20(2), 191–203. DOI: 10.1002/jtr.2172

Lee, T. H., & Jan, F. H. (2018). Ecotourism behavior of nature-based tourists: An integrative framework. *Journal of Travel Research*, 57(6), 792–810. DOI: 10.1177/0047287517717350

Legrand, W., Simons-Kaufmann, C., & Sloan, P. (2012). *Sustainable hospitality and tourism as motors for development*. Routledge. DOI: 10.4324/9780123851970

Lemmetyinen, A., & Go, F. M. (2010). Building a Brand Identity in a Network of Cruise Baltic's Destinations: A Multi-Authoring Approach. *Journal of Brand Management*, 17(7), 519–531. DOI: 10.1057/bm.2010.5

Leroi-Werelds, S., Streukens, S., Brady, M. K., & Swinnen, G. (2014). Assessing the value of commonly used methods for measuring customer value: A multi-setting empirical study. *Journal of the Academy of Marketing Science*, 42(4), 430–451. DOI: 10.1007/s11747-013-0363-4

Le, T. H., Novais, M. A., Arcodia, C., Berchtenbreiter, R., Humpe, A., & Nguyen, N. (2024). How authenticity in events fosters social sustainability: Towards an authenticity ecosystem and implications for destination management. *Tourism Management Perspectives*, 51, 101222. DOI: 10.1016/j.tmp.2024.101222

Leung, X. Y., Zhong, Y. S., & Sun, J. (2025). The impact of social media influencer's age cue on older adults' travel intention: The moderating roles of travel cues and travel constraints. *Tourism Management*, 106, 104979. Advance online publication. DOI: 10.1016/j.tourman.2024.104979

Leuthold, M. (2001). *The potentials of ecotourism in Austria*. Institute for Integrative Tourism and Leisure Research.

Lewin, K. (1947). *Field Theory in Social Science: Selected Theoretical Papers*. Harper & Row.

Lewis, R. C., & Chambers, R. E. (2000). *Marketing Leadership in Hospitality: Foundations and Practices* (3rd ed.). John Wiley & Sons, Inc.

Liang, Y., Yin, J., Pan, B., Lin, M. S., Miller, L., Taff, B. D., & Chi, G. (2022). Assessing the validity of mobile device data for estimating visitor demographics and visitation patterns in Yellowstone National Park. *Journal of Environmental Management*, 317, 115410. DOI: 10.1016/j.jenvman.2022.115410 PMID: 35751247

Liang, Z., Luo, H., & Bao, J. (2021). A longitudinal study of residents' attitudes toward tourism development. *Current Issues in Tourism*, 24(23), 3309–3323. DOI: 10.1080/13683500.2021.1874314

Lindner, J. (2024, June 17). Ecotourism Industry Statistics. https://worldmetrics.org/ecotourism-industry-statistics/

Lin, S., Xu, S., Liu, Y., & Zhang, L. (2024). Destination brand experience, brand positioning, and intention to visit: A multi-destination comparison study. *Journal of Vacation Marketing*, 30(3), 599–614. DOI: 10.1177/13567667231155646

Lin, Y. H. (2015). Innovative brand experience's influence on brand equity and brand satisfaction. *Journal of Business Research*, 68(11), 2254–2259. DOI: 10.1016/j.jbusres.2015.06.007

Li, T., Liu, F., & Soutar, G. N. (2020, December). (Tina), Liu, F., & Soutar, G. N. (2021). Experiences, post-trip destination image, satisfaction and loyalty: A study in an ecotourism context. *Journal of Destination Marketing & Management*, 19, 100547. DOI: 10.1016/j.jdmm.2020.100547

Li, T., Liu, F., Soutar, G., & Webb, D. (2024). An application of the new visitation paradigm to ecotourism in China. *Journal of Ecotourism*, 23(1), 100–110.

Liu, Z., & Park, S. (2015). What makes a useful online review? Implication for travel product websites. *Tourism Management*, 47(1), 140–151. DOI: 10.1016/j.tourman.2014.09.020

Livyiakis, G. (2023). Ecotourism is the solution for the protection of Balos. *Haniotika Nea*. https://www.haniotika-nea.gr/lysi-o-oikotoyrismos-gia-tin-prostasia-toy-mpaloy/

Lonardi, S., Scholl-Grissemann, U., Peters, M., & Messner, N. (2024). Leveraging minority language in destination online marketing: Evidence from Alta Badia, Italy. *Journal of Destination Marketing & Management*, 31, 100857. DOI: 10.1016/j.jdmm.2024.100857

Londoño, M. P. L., & Hernandez-Maskivker, G. (2016). Green practices in hotels: The case of the GreenLeaders Program from TripAdvisor. *Sustainable Tourisim VII*, 1, 1–13. DOI: 10.2495/ST160011

Long, P. H., Woyo, E., Pham, T. H., & Dao, T. X. T. (2022). Value co-creation and destination brand equity: Understanding the role of social commerce information sharing. *Journal of Hospitality and Tourism Insights*, 6(5), 1796–1817. DOI: 10.1108/JHTI-04-2022-0123

Lonn, P., Mizoue, N., Ota, T., Kajisa, T., & Yoshida, S. (2018). Evaluating the contribution of community-based ecotourism (CBET) to household income and livelihood changes: A case study of the Chambok CBET program in Cambodia. *Ecological Economics*, 151, 62–76. DOI: 10.1016/j.ecolecon.2018.04.036

Loureiro, S. M. C. (2020). How does the experience and destination authenticity influence "affect"? *Anatolia*, 31(3), 449–465. DOI: 10.1080/13032917.2020.1760903

Lucrezi, S., & Cilliers, C. D. (2022). Factors Influencing marine wildlife voluntourists' satisfaction and post-experience attitudes: Evidence from Southern Africa. *Journal of Ecotourism*, 23(1), 56–80. DOI: 10.1080/14724049.2022.2122983

Lund, N. F., Cohen, S. A., & Scarles, C. (2018). The power of social media storytelling in destination branding. *Journal of Destination Marketing & Management*, 8, 271–280. DOI: 10.1016/j.jdmm.2017.05.003

Luo, J., Dey, B. L., Yalkin, C., Sivarajah, U., Punjaisri, K., Huang, Y., & Yen, D. A. (2020). Millennial Chinese consumers' perceived destination brand value. *Journal of Business Research*, 116, 655–665. DOI: 10.1016/j.jbusres.2018.06.015

Luz, A. C., & Ruiz-Mallén, I. (2020). Community-Based Management and Research to Forest Conservation. In *Encyclopedia of the UN sustainable development goals* (pp. 148–161). DOI: 10.1007/978-3-319-71065-5_133-1

Lv, X., Yang, Y., Qin, D., Cao, X., & Xu, H. (2022). Artificial intelligence service recovery: The role of empathic response in hospitality customers' continuous usage intention. *Computers in Human Behavior*, 126, 106993. DOI: 10.1016/j.chb.2021.106993

MacCannell, D. (1973). Staged authenticity: Arrangements of social space in tourist settings. *American Journal of Sociology*, 79(3), 589–603. DOI: 10.1086/225585

Machado Carvalho, M. A. (2024). Influencing the follower behavior: The role of homophily and perceived usefulness, credibility and enjoyability of travel content. *Journal of Hospitality and Tourism Insights*, 7(2), 1091–1110. DOI: 10.1108/JHTI-09-2023-0648

Madrigal-moreno, S., Madrigal-moreno, F., & Juárez-lópez, B. (2020). Internet y redes sociales en la construcción de la reputación digital de la organización del sector turístico. Revista Espacios, 41(14).

Mafi, M., Pratt, S., & Trupp, A. (2020). Determining ecotourism satisfaction attributes – a case study of an ecolodge in Fiji. *Journal of Ecotourism*, 19(4), 304–326. DOI: 10.1080/14724049.2019.1698585

Mahmudova, M., Kurbonbekova, M., & Mamadiyarov, Z. (2024, March). Exploring Eco-Tourism and Its Role in Sustainable Development: An example of Karakalpakstan. In *International Conference of Economics, Finance and Accounting Studies* (Vol. 3, pp. 64-67).

Mai, A., Thi, K., Thi, T., & Le, T. (2020). Factors influencing on tourism sustainable development in Vietnam. *Management Science Letters*, 10(8), 1737–1742. DOI: 10.5267/j.msl.2020.1.006

Maingi, S. W. (2019). Sustainable tourism certification, local governance and management in dealing with overtourism in East Africa. *Worldwide Hospitality and Tourism Themes*, 11(5), 532–551.

Majeed, S., Zhou, Z., & Kim, W. G. (2024). Destination brand image and destination brand choice in the context of health crisis: Scale development. *Tourism and Hospitality Research*, 24(1), 134–151. DOI: 10.1177/14673584221126798

Majumder, S., Saha, S., Mukherjee, A., Das, J., Mukherjee, S., & Das, S. (2021). Sustainable Tourism and Ecotourism, The Future of Tourism Sector in India. *Global Management Journal*, 15(1/2), 332–345.

Maksanova, L., Bardakhanova, T., Budaeva, D., Mikheeva, A., Lubsanova, N., Sharaldaeva, V., Eremko, Z., Andreeva, A., Ayusheeva, S., & Khrebtova, T. (2023). Ecotourism Development in the Russian Areas under Nature Protection. *Sustainability (Basel)*, 15(18), 13661. DOI: 10.3390/su151813661

Mameli, M., Paolanti, M., Morbidoni, C., Frontoni, E., & Teti, A. (2022). Social media analytics system for action inspection on social networks. *Social Network Analysis and Mining*, 12(1), 33. DOI: 10.1007/s13278-021-00853-w PMID: 35154503

Mansur, M., Brearley, F. Q., Esseen, P. J., Rode-Margono, E. J., & Tarigan, M. R. M. (2021). Ecology of Nepenthes clipeata on Gunung Kelam, Indonesian Borneo. *Plant Ecology & Diversity*, 14(3-4), 195–203. DOI: 10.1080/17550874.2021.1984602

Mantas, K., & Mylonaki, M. (2010). *The development of ecotourism in Crete* (Diploma thesis). TEI of Crete. (In Greek).

Mao, Y., Lai, Y., Luo, Y., Liu, S., Du, Y., Zhou, J., Ma, J., Bonaiuto, F., & Bonaiuto, M. (2020). Apple or Huawei: Understanding Flow, Brand Image, Brand Identity, Brand Personality and Purchase Intention of Smartphone. *Sustainability (Basel)*, 12(3391), 1–22. DOI: 10.3390/su12083391

Margulies, W. P. (1977). Make the most of your corporate identity. *Harvard Business Review*, 55(4), 66–74.

Martin-Fuentes, E., Mateu, C., & Fernandez, C. (2020). The more the merrier? Number of reviews versus score on TripAdvisor and Booking.com. *International Journal of Hospitality & Tourism Administration*, 21(1), 1–14. DOI: 10.1080/15256480.2018.1429337

Martins, M. (2015). The Tourist Imagery, the Destination Image, and the Brand Image. *Journal of Tourism and Hospitality Management*, 3(2), 1–14. DOI: 10.15640/jthm.v3n2a1

Marzano, G., & Scott, N. (2005). Stakeholder power in destination branding: a methodological discussion. *Proceedings of the Destination Branding and Marketing for Regional Tourism Development Conference*, Macao, S.A.R. China 8-9 December, 203-212.

Marzano, G. (2006). Relevance Of Power. In *The Collaborative Process Of Destination Branding*. The University of Queensland.

Marzano, G., & Scott, N. (2011). Stakeholder Power. In *Destination Branding: A Methodological Discussion*. Sustainable Tourism Cooperative Research Centre.

Masciantonio, A., Bourguignon, D., Bouchat, P., Balty, M., & Rimé, B. (2021). Don't put all social network sites in one basket: Facebook, Instagram, Twitter, TikTok, and their relations with well-being during the COVID-19 pandemic. *PLoS One*, 16(3), e0248384. DOI: 10.1371/journal.pone.0248384 PMID: 33705462

Maslej, N., Fattorini, L., Brynjolfsson, E., Etchemendy, J., Ligett, K., Lyons, T., Manyika, J., Ngo, H., Niebles, J. C., & Parli, V. (2023). Artificial intelligence index report 2023. *arXiv preprint arXiv:2310.03715*. https://doi.org//arXiv.2310.03715DOI: 10.48550

Mastika, I. K., & Nimran, U. (2020). Destination branding model of an ecological tourism village in Bali, Indonesia. *Geo Journal of Tourism and Geosites*, 31(3), 1068–1074. DOI: 10.30892/gtg.31319-542

Matias, A., Nijkamp, P., & Neto, P. (2007). *Advances in modern tourism research*. Physica Verlag. DOI: 10.1007/978-3-7908-1718-8

Matiza, T., & Slabbert, E. (2024). The Celebrity Influencer: Delineating the Effect of Tourism-Oriented Short Video Marketing on International Tourist Conation. *Journal of Global Marketing*, 37(4), 331–349. DOI: 10.1080/08911762.2024.2377741

Matthiopoulos, J., Fieberg, J., Aarts, G., Beyer, H. L., Morales, J. M., & Haydon, D. T. (2015). Establishing the link between habitat selection and animal population dynamics. *Ecological Monographs*, 85(3), 413–436. DOI: 10.1890/14-2244.1

Ma, W., Tariq, A., Ali, M. W., Nawaz, M. A., & Wang, X. (2022). An Empirical Investigation of Virtual Networking Sites Discontinuance Intention: Stimuli Organism Response-Based Implication of User Negative Disconfirmation. *Frontiers in Psychology*, 13, 862568. DOI: 10.3389/fpsyg.2022.862568 PMID: 35602706

Maxwell, K. (2009). *Making Machu Picchu: Embedding History and Embodying Nature in the Peruvian Andes*. Agrarian Studies Program, Yale, and Earth and Environment, Franklin and Marshall College.

Maxwell, K. (2012). Tourism, environment, and development on the inca trail. *The Hispanic American Historical Review*, 92(1), 143–171. DOI: 10.1215/00182168-1470995

Mazzarol, T., Sweeney, J., & Soutar, G. (2007). Conceptualizing word-of-mouth activity, triggers and conditions: an exploratory study.

Mbaiwa, J. E. (2005). Wildlife resource utilization at Moremi Game Reserve and Khwai community area in the Okavango Delta, Botswana. *Journal of Environmental Management*, 77(2), 144–156. DOI: 10.1016/j.jenvman.2005.03.007 PMID: 16115724

Mbaiwa, J. E. (2015). Ecotourism in Botswana: 30 years later. *Journal of Ecotourism*, 14(2–3), 204–222. DOI: 10.1080/14724049.2015.1071378

McCarthy, C., Miranda, C., Raub, K., Sainsbury, B., & Waterson, L. (2013). *Lonely planet Peru*. Lonely Planet.

McKercher, B., & Du Cros, H. (2002). *Cultural tourism: The partnership between tourism and cultural heritage management*. Routledge.

McLane, A. J., Semeniuk, C., McDermid, G. J., & Marceau, D. J. (2011). The role of agent-based models in wildlife ecology and management. *Ecological Modelling*, 222(8), 1544–1556. DOI: 10.1016/j.ecolmodel.2011.01.020

Mearns, W. C. (2007). *The importance of being branded*. University of Auckland Business Review.

Medina, L. K. (2005). Ecotourism and certification: Confronting the principles and pragmatics of socially responsible tourism. *Journal of Sustainable Tourism*, 13(3), 281–295.

Megahed, F. M., Chen, Y.-J., Ferris, J. A., Knoth, S., & Jones-Farmer, L. A. (2024). How generative AI models such as ChatGPT can be (mis) used in SPC practice, education, and research? An exploratory study. *Quality Engineering*, 36(2), 287–315. DOI: 10.1080/08982112.2023.2206479

Me, K., & Buchalis, D. (2019). Cross-border tourism destination marketing: Prerequisites and critical success factors. *Journal of Destination Marketing & Management*, 14, 1–9.

MENA Report. (2017). Canada: Toronto designated a UNESCO Creative City of Media Arts. *MENA Report*

Meng, B., Chi, X., Kim, J. J., Kim, G., Quan, W., & Han, H. (2024). Traveling with pets and staying at a pet-friendly hotel: A combination effect of the BRT, TPB, and NAM on consumer behaviors. *International Journal of Hospitality Management*, 120, 103771. Advance online publication. DOI: 10.1016/j.ijhm.2024.103771

Meng, B., Zhang, J., & Choi, K. (2024). The formation of parasocial relationships in tourism social media: A rational and emotional trust-building process. *International Journal of Tourism Research*, 26(3), e2650. Advance online publication. DOI: 10.1002/jtr.2650

Mengkebayaer, M., Nawaz, M. A., & Sajid, M. U. (2022). Eco-destination loyalty: Role of perceived value and experience in framing destination attachment and equity with moderating role of destination memory. *Frontiers in Psychology*, 13, 908798. DOI: 10.3389/fpsyg.2022.908798 PMID: 36081735

Merriam, S. B. (1998). *Qualitative research and case study applications in education*. Jossey-Bass Publishers.

Merrilees, B., Getz, D., & O'Brien, D. (2005). Marketing stakeholder analysis – branding the Brisbane Goodwill Games. *European Journal of Marketing*, 39(9/10), 1060–1077. DOI: 10.1108/03090560510610725

Merrilees, B., Miller, D., & Herrington, C. (2012). Multiple stakeholders and multiple city brand meanings. *European Journal of Marketing*, 46(7/8), 1032–1047. DOI: 10.1108/03090561211230188

Meyer, N., Ben Said, F., Alkathiri, N. A., & Soliman, M. (2023). A scientometric analysis of entrepreneurial and the digital economy scholarship: State of the art and an agenda for future research. *Journal of Innovation and Entrepreneurship*, 12(1), 70. DOI: 10.1186/s13731-023-00340-w

Michel, G. (2017). From brand identity to polysemous brands: Commentary on "Performing identities: Processes of brand and stakeholder identity co-construction". *Journal of Business Research*, 70, 453–455. DOI: 10.1016/j.jbusres.2016.06.022

Milano, C., Cheer, J. M., & Novelli, M. (2022). Overtourism, Digital Media, and the Promotion of 'Sustainable Tourism' in Crisis: Exploring the Role of Social Media Influencers in a Post-COVID-19 World. *Journal of Sustainable Tourism*, 30(8), 1711–1732.

Milgram, S. (1967). The small world problem. *Psychology Today*, 1(1), 61–67.

Miličević, K., Mihalič, T., & Sever, I. (2017). An investigation of the relationship between destination branding and destination competitiveness. *Journal of Travel & Tourism Marketing*, 34(2), 209–221. DOI: 10.1080/10548408.2016.1156611

Miller, A. B., Cox, C., & Morse, W. C. (2023). Ecotourism, wildlife conservation, and agriculture in Costa Rica through a social-ecological systems lens. *Frontiers in Sustainable Tourism*, 2, 1179887. Advance online publication. DOI: 10.3389/frsut.2023.1179887

Miller, F., Ha, T. T. P., Van Da, H., Thuy, N. T. T., & Ngo, B. H. (2022). Double displacement – Interactions between resettlement, environmental change and migration. *Geoforum*, 129, 13–27. DOI: 10.1016/j.geoforum.2021.12.016

Miller-Rushing, A. J., Athearn, N., Blackford, T., Brigham, C., Cohen, L., Cole-Will, R., Edgar, T., Ellwood, E. R., Fisichelli, N., Pritz, C. F., Gallinat, A. S., Gibson, A., Hubbard, A., McLane, S., Nydick, K., Primack, R. B., Sachs, S., & Super, P. E. (2021). COVID-19 pandemic impacts on conservation research, management, and public engagement in US national parks. *Biological Conservation*, 257, 109038. DOI: 10.1016/j.biocon.2021.109038 PMID: 34580547

MINAM. (2019). Apuntes del Bosque No 1: Cobertura y Deforestaci'on en Los Bosques Húmedos Amaz'onicos 2018. Programa Nacional de Conservaci'on de Bosque para la Mitigaci'on del Cambio Clim'atico. https://sinia.minam.gob. pe/documentos/apuntes-bosque-no-1-cobertura-deforestacion-bosques-humedos\

Ministry of Environment and Energy. (2014). *National Biodiversity Strategy*. http://www.ypeka.gr/LinkClick.aspx?fileticket=2VfCIB5XfW4%3D&tabit=232&language=el-GR

Ministry of Foreign Trade and Tourism- Mincetur International tourist flow and foreign exchange income from inbound tourism. (2020). http://datosturismo.mincetur.gob.pe/appdatosTurismo/Content1.html July 15th.

Miočić, B. K., Razović, M., & Klarin, T. (2016). Management Of Sustaınable Tourısm Destınatıon Through Stakeholder Cooperatıon. *Management*, 21(2), 99–120.

Mishra, A. S. (2010). Destination Branding: A Case Study of Hong Kong. The IUP Journal of Brand Management, 7(3).

Mitchell, L. S., & Murphy, P. E. (1991). Geography and tourism. *Annals of Tourism Research*, 22(2), 300–313.

Montenegro-Pazmiño, E., & Muñoz, G. (2024). Unveiling Social Dynamics in People's Perception of Raptors to Guide Effective Conservation Strategies. *Journal of Ethnobiology*, 44(2), 112–128. DOI: 10.1177/02780771241250117

Morando, M., & Platania, S. (2022). Luxury Tourism Consumption in the Accommodation Sector: The Mediation Role of Destination Brand Love for Potential Tourists. *Sustainability (Basel)*, 14(7), 4007. Advance online publication. DOI: 10.3390/su14074007

Morand, S., Owers, K., & Borders, F. (2014). Biodiversity and emerging zoonoses. In *Confronting emerging zoonoses* (pp. 27–41). Springer., DOI: 10.1007/978-4-431-55120-1_3

Moreno, A., Jabreel, M., & Huertas, A. (2015). Automatic analysis of the communication of tourist destination brands through social networks. In *10th International Conference on Intelligent Systems and Knowledge Engineering (ISKE)* (pp. 546-553). IEEE. https://doi.org/DOI: 10.1109/ISKE.2015.22

Moreno, J. L. (1934). *Who Shall Survive?* Beacon House.

Moreno, J. L., & Jennings, H. H. (1938). Statistics of social constellations. *Sociometry*, 1(3), 342–374. DOI: 10.2307/2785588

Morgan, N. J., Pritchard, A., & Piggott, R. (2003). Destination branding and the role of the stakeholders: The case of New Zealand. *Journal of Vacation Marketing*, 9(3), 285–299. Advance online publication. DOI: 10.1177/135676670300900307

Morgan, N., Pritchard, A., & Piggott, R. (2002). New Zealand, is 100% pure. The creation of a powerful niche destination brand. *Journal of Brand Management*, 9(4/5), 335–354. DOI: 10.1057/palgrave.bm.2540082

Morgan, N., Pritchard, A., & Pride, R. (2004). *Destination branding (2. b.)*. Elsevier.

Morgan, N., Pritchard, A., & Pride, R. (2007). *Destination branding: creating the unique destination proposition*. Routledge. DOI: 10.4324/9780080477206

Morgan, N., Pritchard, A., & Pride, R. (2011). *Destination brands: Managing place reputation* (3rd ed.). Butterworth-Heinemann.

Morrison, A. (2019). *Marketing and Managing Tourism Destinations.* Routledge.

Morrison, A. M. (2013). *Marketing and managing tourism destinations.* Routledge. DOI: 10.4324/9780203081976

Motoki, K., Park, J., Pathak, A., & Spence, C. (2023). Creating luxury brand names in the hospitality and tourism sector: The role of sound symbolism in destination branding. *Journal of Destination Marketing & Management*, 30, 100815. Advance online publication. DOI: 10.1016/j.jdmm.2023.100815

Motsaathebe, G. T., & Hambira, W. L. (2022). In pursuit of sustainable tourism in Botswana: Perceptions of Maun tourism accommodation operators on tourism certification and eco-labelling. In Southern African Perspectives on Sustainable Tourism Management: Tourism and Changing Localities (pp. 31–45). Springer International Publishing. DOI: 10.1007/978-3-030-99435-8_3

Moutinho, L., & Vargas-Sanchez, A. (Eds.). (2018). *Strategic management in tourism. cabi tourism texts.* Cabi. DOI: 10.1079/9781786390240.0000

Mowforth, M., & Munt, I. (2015). *Tourism and sustainability: Development, globalisation and new tourism in the third world.* Routledge. DOI: 10.4324/9781315795348

Munawir, K., Koerniawan, M. D., & Dewancker, B. J. (2019). Visitor Perceptions and effectiveness of place branding strategies in thematic parks in Bandung City using text mining based on Google Maps user reviews. *Sustainability (Basel)*, 11(7), 2123. DOI: 10.3390/su11072123

Muriithi, J. K., & Ireri, P. (2024). Ecotourism Principles, Responsible Travel, and Building a Sustainable Post-pandemic Destination Kenya. In Tourist Behaviour and the New Normal, Volume II: Implications for Sustainable Tourism Development (pp. 195-220). Cham: Springer Nature Switzerland.

Musavengane, R., & Kloppers, R. (2020). Social capital: An investment towards community resiliencein the collaborative natural resources management of community-based tourism schemes. *Tourism Management Perspectives*, 34, 100654. DOI: 10.1016/j.tmp.2020.100654

Muskat, B., Hörtnagl, T., Prayag, G., & Wagner, S. (2019). Perceived quality, authenticity, and price in tourists' dining experiences: Testing competing models of satisfaction and behavioral intentions. *Journal of Vacation Marketing*, 25(4), 480–498. DOI: 10.1177/1356766718822675

Mussalam, G. Q., & Tajeddini, K. (2016). Tourism in Switzerland: How perceptions of place attributes for short and long holiday can influence destination choice. *Journal of Hospitality and Tourism Management*, 26, 18–26. DOI: 10.1016/j.jhtm.2015.09.003

Mwaibofu, P. A. (2021). *Assessment of the Factors Affecting Tourists' Satisfaction at Ikona Wildlife Management Area in Serengeti, Tanzania* (Doctoral dissertation, The Open University of Tanzania).

Nabilah, A. F., & Safitri, R. (2024). Exploring Cultural-Based Ecotourism Destination Branding in the village of Ranu Pani. *AICCON*, 1, 553–564.

Nag, A., & Mishra, S. (2023a). Destination Competitiveness and Sustainability: Heritage Planning From the Perspective of the Tourism Industry Stakeholders. In *Cases on Traveler Preferences, Attitudes, and Behaviors: Impact in the Hospitality Industry* (pp. 1-32). IGI Global.

Nag, A., & Mishra, S. (2023c). Unlocking the Power of Stakeholder Perception: Enhancing Competitive Heritage Planning and Place-Making. In *Exploring Culture and Heritage Through Experience Tourism* (pp. 196-226). IGI Global.

Nag, A. (2022). Industrial infrastructure development of cottage industries for inclusive economic growth in a sustainable manner: Case study of the urban growth centre in Bishnupur, West Bengal, India. *International Journal of Indian Culture and Business Management*, 26(2), 204–233. DOI: 10.1504/IJICBM.2022.123591

Nag, A. (2023). Industrial infrastructure and economic platform development for social and sustainable enterprise encouragement of cottage industries: Case study of Bishnupur West Bengal. *International Journal of Indian Culture and Business Management*, 28(4), 442–471. DOI: 10.1504/IJICBM.2023.130125

Nag, A., & Mishra, S. (2023b). Stakeholders' perception and competitiveness of heritage towns: A systematic literature review. *Tourism Management Perspectives*, 48, 101156. DOI: 10.1016/j.tmp.2023.101156

Nag, A., & Mishra, S. (2024a). Mining Ghost Town Revitalization through Heritage Tourism Initiatives. *Journal of Mining and Environment*, 15(2), 439–461.

Nag, A., & Mishra, S. (2024b). Predictive Analytics for Heritage Site Visitor Patterns. In *Utilizing Smart Technology and AI in Hybrid Tourism and Hospitality* (pp. 140–185). IGI Global. DOI: 10.4018/979-8-3693-1978-9.ch007

Nag, A., & Mishra, S. (2024c). Revitalizing Mining Heritage Tourism: A Machine Learning Approach to Tourism Management. *Journal of Mining and Environment*.

Nag, A., & Mishra, S. (2024d). Tourism Management with AI Integration for Mining Heritage: A Literature Review Approach. *Journal of Mining and Environment*, 15(1), 115–149.

Nahuelhual, L., Carmona, A., Aguayo, M., & Echeverria, C. (2013). Land use change and ecosystem services provision: A case study of recreation and ecotourism opportunities in southern Chile. *Landscape Ecology*, 29(2), 329–344. DOI: 10.1007/s10980-013-9958-x

Nardi, B. A., Schiano, D. J., Gumbrecht, M., & Swartz, L. (2007). Why we blog. *Communications of the ACM*, 47(12), 41–46. DOI: 10.1145/1035134.1035163

Natura2000. (n.d.). *Guide to ecotourism in areas of the NATURA 2000 Network in Crete*. https://natura2000.crete.gov.gr/fileadmin/printmaterial/pdf_Gia%20Periferia_Ikotouristikos%20GR/04_ODIGOS%20GR%20A5_IKOTOURISTIKOS_Small_WEB.pdf

Nawaz, M. A., Anwar, A., Rongting, Z., & Nawaz, A. (2019). Factors influencing willingness to consume GMF in Chinese population: the moderating role of "Information Literacy" Immersive Media (IM): challenges and opportunities View project Strategic overview of belt and road initiative View project. *Article in Journal of Animal and Plant Sciences, 29*(4), 1088–1099. https://www.researchgate.net/publication/336825092

Nawaz, M. A., Asif, M., Asmi, F., & Nawaz, A. (2019).. . *WILLINGESS TO CONSUME GENETICALLY MODIFIED FOOD IN CHINESE PERSPECTIVE.*, 56(4), 799–808.

Nawaz, M. A., Shah, Z., Nawaz, A., Asmi, F., Hassan, Z., & Raza, J. (2018). Overload and exhaustion: Classifying SNS discontinuance intentions. *Cogent Psychology*, 5(1), 1515584. DOI: 10.1080/23311908.2018.1515584

Naziridis, T. (2012). *Lake Kerkini National Park: Guide for the visitor and researcher*. Kerkini Lake Management Agency. (In Greek)

Nematollahi, S., Afghari, S., Kienast, F., & Fakheran, S. (2022). Spatial prioritization for Ecotourism through applying the Landscape Resilience Model. *Land (Basel)*, 11(10), 1682. DOI: 10.3390/land11101682

Neto, F. (2003). A new approach to sustainable tourism development: Moving beyond environmental protection. *Natural Resources Forum*, 27(3), 212–222. DOI: 10.1111/1477-8947.00056

Nistoreanu, P., Aluculesei, A. C., & Avram, D. (2020). Is Green Marketing a Label for Ecotourism? The Romanian Experience. *Information (Basel)*, 11(8), 389.

Nogueira, S., & Carvalho, J. M. S. (2024). Unlocking the dichotomy of place identity/ place image and its impact on place satisfaction for ecotourism destinations. *Journal of Ecotourism*, 23(1), 1–19. DOI: 10.1080/14724049.2022.2106236

Novelli, M., & Benson, A. (2004). *Niche Tourism. A Way forward to Sustainability?* Routledge.

Nsemwa, R. (2020). *Assessment of Tourism Competitive Advantage of UNESCO World Heritage Sites in Tanzania: A case study of Serengeti National Park from 2000-2018* (Doctoral dissertation, The Open University of Tanzania).

O'Leary, Z. (2004). *The essential guide to doing research* (1st ed.). Sage.

Oğuztimur, S. (2017). *Modeling a City's Branding Tools: The Case of Istanbul.* InTech., DOI: 10.5772/intechopen.69269

Oladeji, S. O., Awolala, D. O., & Alabi, O. I. (2021). Evaluation of sustainable ecotourism practices in Oke-Idanre Hills, Ondo-State, Nigeria. *Environment, Development and Sustainability*, 24(2), 2656–2684. DOI: 10.1007/s10668-021-01550-6

Olszewski-Strzyżowski, D. J. (2022). Promotional activities of selected National Tourism Organizations (NTOs) in the light of sustainable tourism (including sustainable transport). *Sustainability (Basel)*, 14(5), 2561. DOI: 10.3390/su14052561

Orea-Giner, A., De-Pablos-Heredero, C., & Vacas Guerrero, T. (2019). Sustainability, economic value and socio-cultural impacts of museums: A theoretical proposition of a research method. *Museum Management and Curatorship*, 36(1), 48–61. DOI: 10.1080/09647775.2019.1700468

Oriade, A., & Evans, M. (2011). Sustainable and alternative tourism. In Robinson, P., Heitmann, S., & Dieke, P. (Eds.), *Research Themes for Tourism* (pp. 69–86). Cabi. DOI: 10.1079/9781845936846.0069

Ouboter, D. A., Kadosoe, V. S., & Ouboter, P. E. (2021). Impact of ecotourism on abundance, diversity and activity patterns of medium-large terrestrial mammals at Brownsberg Nature Park, Suriname. *PLoS One*, 16(6), e0250390. DOI: 10.1371/ journal.pone.0250390 PMID: 34077471

Ouvrein, G., Pabian, S., Giles, D., Hudders, L., & De Backer, C. (2021). The web of influencers. A marketing-audience classification of (potential) social media influencers. *Journal of Marketing Management*, 37(13-14), 1313–1342. DOI: 10.1080/0267257X.2021.1912142

Özdemir, C., & Yolal, M. (2017). Cross-cultural tourist behavior: An examination of tourists' behavior in guided tours. *Tourism and Hospitality Research*, 17(3), 314–324. DOI: 10.1177/1467358415589658

Padlee, S. F., Thaw, C. Y., & Zulkiffli, S. N. A. (2019). The relationship between service quality, customer satisfaction and behavioural intentions. *Tourism and Hospitality Management*, 25(1), 121–139. DOI: 10.20867/thm.25.1.9

Paikou, A. (2005). *Investigation of the relationship between tourism and protected areas: Possibility of creating marine-diving parks in clusters of islands of Lesvos* (In Greek).

Palmer, N. J., & Chuamuangphan, N. (2018). Governance and local participation in ecotourism: community-level ecotourism stakeholders in Chiang Rai Province, Thailand. *J. Ecotourism 17* (3), 320-337. Available from Sheffield Hallam University Research Archive (SHURA) at: http://shura.shu.ac.uk/22231/

Pan, L., Zhang, M., Gursoy, D., & Lu, L. (2017). Development and validation of a destination personality scale for mainland Chinese travelers. *Tourism Management*, 59, 302–315. DOI: 10.1016/j.tourman.2016.08.005

Paolanti, M., Mancini, A., Frontoni, E., Felicetti, A., Marinelli, L., Marcheggiani, E., & Pierdicca, R. (2021). Tourism destination management using sentiment analysis and geo-location information: A deep learning approach. *Information Technology & Tourism*, 23(2), 241–264. DOI: 10.1007/s40558-021-00196-4

Papadimitriou, D., Apostolopoulou, A., & Kaplanidou, K. (2015). Destination personality, effective image, and behavioural intentions in domestic urban tourism. *Journal of Travel Research*, 54(3), 302–315. DOI: 10.1177/0047287513516389

Papagiannakis, G. E., Vlachos, P. A., Koritos, C. D., & Kassinis, G. I. (2024). Are publicly traded tourism and hospitality providers greenwashing? *Tourism Management*, 103, 104893.

Parkerson, B., & Saunders, J. (2005). City branding: Can goods and services branding models be used to brand cities? *Place Branding and Public Diplomacy*, 1(3), 242–264. DOI: 10.1057/palgrave.pb.5990026

Patton, Q. (2002). *Qualitative research and evaluation methods*. Sage Publications.

Paul, H., & Brad, O. (1997). Ecotourism: A guide for marketers. *European Business Review*, 97(5), 231–236. DOI: 10.1108/09555349710179843

Paul, I., & Roy, G. (2023). Tourist's engagement in eco-tourism: A review and research agenda. *Journal of Hospitality and Tourism Management*, 54, 316–328. DOI: 10.1016/j.jhtm.2023.01.002

Pavelka, J. (2016). In the shadow of Machu Picchu: a case study of the Salkantay Trail. In *Mountain tourism: experiences, communities, environments and sustainable futures* (pp. 111–120). CABI. DOI: 10.1079/9781780644608.0111

Pedersen, D. (2002). Political violence, ethnic conflict, and contemporary wars: Broad implications for health and social well-being. *Social Science & Medicine*, 55(2), 175–190. DOI: 10.1016/S0277-9536(01)00261-1 PMID: 12144134

Penpece Demirer, D., & Büyükeke, A. (2024). Unravelling tourism destination's competitiveness using big data analytics: A comparative analysis. *Kybernetes*. Advance online publication. DOI: 10.1108/K-12-2023-2580

Perkins, R., Khoo-Lattimore, C., & Arcodia, C. (2020). Understanding the contribution of stakeholder collaboration towards regional destination branding: A systematic narrative literature review. *Journal of Hospitality and Tourism Management*, 43, 250–258. DOI: 10.1016/j.jhtm.2020.04.008

Pham, K., Andereck, K., & Vogt, C. (2019). Local residents' perceptions about tourism development.

Pham, H. S. T., & Khanh, C. N. T. (2020). Ecotourism intention: The roles of environmental concern, time perspective and destination image. *Tourism Review*, 76(5), 1141–1153. DOI: 10.1108/TR-09-2019-0363

Phon, S., Phon, S., & Touch, V. (2024). Factors Influencing the Community-Based Ecotourism Development in Cambodia: Structural Equation Model Analysis. *Utsaha: Journal of Entrepreneurship*, 87–107.

Phu, T. N. (2024). Factors Affecting Regional Linkages in Tourism Development, Case Study of A Giang Province and its Surrounding Area in Mekong Delta. *Journal of Sustainability Science and Management*, 19(2), 214–239. DOI: 10.46754/jssm.2024.02.011

Pike, A., Béal, V., Cauchi-Duval, N., Franklin, R., Kinossian, N., Lang, T., Leibert, T., MacKinnon, D., Rousseau, M., Royer, J., Servillo, L., Tomaney, J., & Velthuis, S. (2024). 'Left behind places': A geographical etymology. *Regional Studies*, 58(6), 1167–1179. DOI: 10.1080/00343404.2023.2167972

Pike, S. (2005). Tourism destination branding complexity. *Journal of Product &Amp. Journal of Product and Brand Management*, 14(4), 258–259. DOI: 10.1108/10610420510609267

Pike, S. (2008). *Destination Marketing – An integrated marketing communication approach*. Butterworth-Heinemann.

Pike, S. (2015). *Destination marketing: essentials*. Routledge. DOI: 10.4324/9781315691701

Pike, S. (2017). Destination positioning and temporality: Tracking relative strengths and weaknesses over time. *Journal of Hospitality and Tourism Management*, 31, 126–133. DOI: 10.1016/j.jhtm.2016.11.005

Pike, S., Bianchi, C., Kerr, G., & Patti, C. (2010). Consumer-based brand equity for Australia as a long-haul tourism destination in an emerging market. *International Marketing Review*, 27(4), 434–449. DOI: 10.1108/02651331011058590

Piva, E., & Prats, L. ı. (2020). *Regional Destination and Brand Identity: The Case of Piedmont*. Scienze Regionali.

Polat, E., Çelik, F., Ibrahim, B., & Gursoy, D. (2024). Past, present, and future scene of influencer marketing in hospitality and tourism management. *Journal of Travel & Tourism Marketing*, 41(3), 322–343. DOI: 10.1080/10548408.2024.2317741

Pookhao, S. N., Bushell, R., & Hawkins, M. (2018). Community-based ecotourism: Beyond authenticity and the commodification of local people. *Journal ofEcotourism*, 17(3), 252–267. DOI: 10.1080/14724049.2018.1503502

Pop, R.-A., Săplăcan, Z., Dabija, D.-C., & Alt, M.-A. (2022). The impact of social media influencers on travel decisions: The role of trust in consumer decision journey. *Current Issues in Tourism*, 25(5), 823–843. DOI: 10.1080/13683500.2021.1895729

Porter, M. (1990). *The competitive Advantage of Nations*. The Maxmillan Press. DOI: 10.1007/978-1-349-11336-1

Porter, M. E., & Kramer, M. R. (2011, January). Creating Shared Value: How to reinvent capitalism – and unleash a wave of innovation and growth. *Harvard Business Review*.

Poulaki, P., Lagos, D., & Balomenou, C. (2015). Religious tourism in Greece and regional development: The case of Samos Island. In *Proceedings of the 55th ERSA Congress, World Renaissance: Changing Roles for People and Places* (pp. 25-29). Lisbon, Portugal.

Poulaki, P., Stavrakakis, I., Tarazonas, D., Vasilakis, N., & Valeri, M. (2021). Sustainable development and cultural heritage in Greece. In Valeri, M., Scuttari, A., & Pechlaner, H. (Eds.), *Resilience and sustainability: Global dynamics and local actions*. Giappichelli.

Poursanidis, D. (2015). *Highlighting the marine areas of the Natura 2000 network in Crete* (technical guide). Region of Crete, Heraklion. (In Greek).

Prakhar, P., Jaiswal, R., & Khan, M. I. A. (2024). Bibliometric Perspectives on Sustainable Tourism and Future Research Agenda. In *Managing Tourism and Hospitality Sectors for Sustainable Global Transformation* (pp. 1–16). IGI Global. DOI: 10.4018/979-8-3693-6260-0.ch001

Prasiasa, D. P. O., Widari, D. A. D. S., & Susanti, P. H. (2023). Authenticity and Commodification of Creative Industry Products in The Tourism Sector, Bali. Mudra Jurnal Seni Budaya, 38(3).

Praswati, A. N., Wardani, N. M., & Rohim, M. (2021). The Impact of Online Destination Brand Experience, Destination Brand Authenticity and Tourist Destination Image on Behavioral Intentions. *Journal of Indonesian Tourism and Development Studies*, 9(3), 145–152. DOI: 10.21776/ub.jitode.2021.009.03.01

Presutti, M. (2018). *Analisi imprenditoriale ed economica del festival del cinema. Un modello interpretativo ed economico del festival del cinema*. Aracne.

Presutti, M., & Lo Presti, V. (2022). *Il turismo esperienziale di nicchia: analisi strategica e prospettive future nella realtà dei borghi. Il Caso di Palazzo Viviani*. Maggioli.

Presutti, M., Savioli, M., & Odorici, V. (2020). Strategic orientation of hotels: Evidence from a contingent approach. *Tourism Economics*, 26(7), 1212–1230. DOI: 10.1177/1354816619868886

Prideaux, B., & Cooper, C. (2002). Marketing and destination growth: A symbiotic relationship or simple coincidence? *Journal of Vacation Marketing*, 9(1), 35–48. DOI: 10.1177/135676670200900103

Prince, S., & Ioannides, D. (2017). Contextualizing the complexities of managing alternative tourism at the community-level: A case study of a Nordic eco-village. *Tourism Management*, 60, 348–356. DOI: 10.1016/j.tourman.2016.12.015

Prough, J. S. (2022). *Kyoto revisited: heritage tourism in contemporary Japan*. University of Hawaii Press.

Proyrungroj, R. (2022). *Thailand's Image from the Perspectives of Chinese Non-Visitors and Visitors. Advances in Hospitality and Tourism Research*. AHTR.

Qing, W., Safeer, A. A., & Khan, M. S. (2024). Influence of social media communication on consumer purchase decisions: Do luxury hotels value perceived brand authenticity, prestige, and familiarity? *Journal of Hospitality and Tourism Technology*, 15(3), 465–478. DOI: 10.1108/JHTT-09-2023-0282

Qiu, L., Li, X., & Choi, S. (2024). Exploring the influence of short video platforms on tourist attitudes and travel intention: A social–technical perspective. *Journal of Destination Marketing & Management*, 31, 100826. Advance online publication. DOI: 10.1016/j.jdmm.2023.100826

Qu, H., Kim, L. H., & Im, H. H. (2011). A model of destination branding: Integrating the concepts of the branding and destination image. *Tourism Management*, 32(3), 465–476. DOI: 10.1016/j.tourman.2010.03.014

Quoquab, F., Mohammad, J., & Mohd Sobri, A. M. (2021). Psychological engagement drives brand loyalty: Evidence from Malaysian ecotourism destinations. *Journal of Product and Brand Management*, 30(1), 132–147. DOI: 10.1108/JPBM-09-2019-2558

Quynh, N. H., Hoai, N. T., & Loi, N. Van. (2021). The role of emotional experience and destination image on ecotourism satisfaction. *Spanish Journal of Marketing - ESIC, 25*(2), 312–332. DOI: 10.1108/SJME-04-2020-0055

Rabadán-Martín, I., Aguado-Correa, F., & Padilla-Garrido, N. (2019). Facing new challenges in rural tourism: Signaling quality via website. *Information Technology & Tourism*, 21(4), 559–576. DOI: 10.1007/s40558-019-00157-y

Rachiotis, T., & Poulaki, P. (2024). Cultural routes as a factor of sustainable management of cultural reserve and development of cultural tourism. *Sustainable Development, Culture, Traditions, 4*(A), 50-72. https://doi.org/DOI: 10.26341/issn.2241-4002-2024-4a-4-T02072

Rachiotis, T., & Poulaki, P. (2022). The contribution of cultural routes to the enhancement of urban cultural tourism. *Journal of Hospitality and Tourism*, 20(2), 31–46. DOI: 10.5281/zenodo.8322203

Rachiotis, T., & Poulaki, P. (2024). Exploring the sustainability and management of overtourism in globally recognized destinations. *Journal of Regional & Socio-Economic Issues*, 14(2), 37–45. https://doi.org/10.26215/heal.3n9m-8v15

Rachiotis, T., & Poulaki, P. (2024). Innovating cultural tourism in Greece: The strategic role of tourist guides in heritage promotion. *Journal of Regional Socio-Economic Issues*, 14(2), 14–28.

Rachiotis, T., & Poulaki, P. (2024). Management of cultural routes as the new status quo in urban cultural tourism. In *Cultural tourism in urban areas* (pp. 165–181). Taylor & Francis-Routledge., DOI: 10.4324/9781032633374-14

Radišić, B. B., & Mihelić, B. (2006). The Tourıst Destınatıon Brand. *Tourism and Hospitality Management*, 12(2), 183–189. DOI: 10.20867/thm.12.2.16

Rahmafitria, F., & Kaswanto, R. L. (2024). The role of eco-attraction in the intention to conduct low-carbon actions: A study of visitor behavior in urban forests. *International Journal of Tourism Cities*, 10(3), 881–904. DOI: 10.1108/IJTC-07-2023-0138

Rahman, I., Park, J., & Chi, C. G. Q. (2015). Consequences of "greenwashing": Consumers' reactions to hotels' green initiatives. *International Journal of Contemporary Hospitality Management*, 27(6), 1054–1081.

Ramseook-Munhurrun, P., Seebaluck, V. N., & Naidoo, P. (2015). Examining the structural relationships of destination image, perceived value, tourist satisfaction and loyalty: Case of Mauritius. *Procedia: Social and Behavioral Sciences*, 175, 252–259. DOI: 10.1016/j.sbspro.2015.01.1198

Rashid, R. M., Rashid, Q. U. A., Nawaz, M. A., & Akhtar, S. (2019). Young Chinese consumers' brand perception; the role of mianzi as moderator. *Journal of Public Affairs*, 19(4), e1930. DOI: 10.1002/pa.1930

Rasoolimanesh, S. M., Md Noor, S., Schuberth, F., & Jaafar, M. (2019). Investigating the effects of tourist engagement on satisfaction and loyalty. *Service Industries Journal*, 39(7-8), 559–574. DOI: 10.1080/02642069.2019.1570152

Rather, R. A. (2018). Investigating the impact of customer brand identification on hospitality brand loyalty: A social identity perspective. *Journal of Hospitality Marketing & Management*, 27(5), 487–513. DOI: 10.1080/19368623.2018.1404539

Rattan, J. K. (2015). Is certification the answer to creating a more sustainable volunteer tourism sector? *Worldwide Hospitality and Tourism Themes*, 7(2), 107–126.

Rawat, G. S., & Adhikari, B. S. (2015). Ecology and management of grassland habitats in India. In *ENVIS Bulletin: Wildlife & Protected Areas*. ENVIS Bulletin: Wildlife & Protected Areas.

Razak, R. A., & Mansor, N. A. (2021). Instagram influencers in social media-induced tourism: Rethinking tourist trust towards tourism destination. In *Impact of new media in tourism* (pp. 135–144). IGI Global. DOI: 10.4018/978-1-7998-7095-1.ch009

Rehman, S., Arshad, N., & Nasir, A. (2024). Destination Revisit Intention, Continuity, Survival, Success. In *Supporting Environmental Stability Through Ecotourism* (pp. 198-218). https://doi.org/DOI: 10.4018/979-8-3693-1030-4.ch011

Reportlinker. (2024). Ecotourism Market Reports 2024. https://shorturl.at/ZfShP

Rezaeinejad, I., & Khaniwadekar, A. (2021). The role of Eco-tourism in sustainable development: case study eco-tourism challenges in Iran. *E3S Web of Conferences, 311*, 2004.

Richards, G. (2007). *Cultural tourism: Global and local perspectives*. Psychology Press.

Richards, G. (2018). Cultural tourism: A review of recent research and trends. *Journal of Hospitality and Tourism Management*, 36, 12–21. DOI: 10.1016/j.jhtm.2018.03.005

Richter, U., & Tveteras, S. (2012). The case of Inkaterra: Pioneering ecotourism in Peru. In *Sustainable Hospitality and Tourism as Motors for Development* (pp. 24–36). Routledge.

Rini, E. S., Rombe, E., & Tarigan, M. I. (2024). Brand destination loyalty: The antecedents of destination brand experience. *Cogent Business & Management*, 11(1), 2320992. DOI: 10.1080/23311975.2024.2320992

Ritchie, B. W., Burns, P., & Palmer, C. (2008). *Tourism Research Methods: Integrating Theory with Practice*. CABI Publishing.

Ritchie, J. B., & Crouch, G. I. (2003). *The competitive destination: A sustainable tourism perspective*. Cabi. DOI: 10.1079/9780851996646.0000

Ritchie, J. B., & Ritchie, R. J. (1998). The Branding of Tourism Destinations: Past Achievements and Future Challenges. *Proceedings of the 1998 Annual Congress of the International Association of Scientific Experts in Tourism* (s. 89-116). Marrakech, Morocco: International Association of Scientific Experts in Tourism

Ritchie, J. R. B., & Zins, M. (1978). Culture as determinant of the attractiveness of a tourism region. *Annals of Tourism Research*, 5(2), 252–267. DOI: 10.1016/0160-7383(78)90223-2

Ritchie, J. R., & Crouch, G. I. (2010). A model of destination competitiveness/sustainability: Brazilian perspectives. *Revista de Administração Pública*, 44(5), 1049–1066. DOI: 10.1590/S0034-76122010000500003

Rivera, M. A., & Croes, R. (2010). Ecotourists' loyalty: Will they tell about the destination or will they return? *Journal of Ecotourism*, 9(2), 85–103. DOI: 10.1080/14724040902795964

Roethlisberger, F. J., & Dickson, W. J. (1939). *Management and the Worker*. Harvard University Press.

Romagosa, F. (2020). The Covid-19 crisis: Opportunities for sustainable and proximity tourism. *Tourism Geographies*, 22(3), 690–694. DOI: 10.1080/14616688.2020.1763447

Rosalina, P. D., Dupre, K., & Wang, Y. (2021). Rural tourism: A systematic literature review on definitions and challenges. *Journal of Hospitality and Tourism Management*, 47, 134–149. DOI: 10.1016/j.jhtm.2021.03.001

Roseta, P., Sousa, B. B., & Roseta, L. (2020). Determiners in the consumer's purchase decision process in ecotourism contexts: a Portuguese case study. *Geosciences*. https://www.mdpi.com/2076-3263/10/6/224

Roxas, F. M. Y., Rivera, J. P. R., & Gutierrez, E. L. M. (2020). Mapping stakeholders' roles in governing sustainable tourism destinations. *Journal of Hospitality and Tourism Management*, 45, 387–398. DOI: 10.1016/j.jhtm.2020.09.005

Roy, M., & Sharmin, Z. (2021). Consumer Demand for Ecotourism Products and Services in Sajek Valley of Bangladesh. In (pp. 217-244). Tourism Products and Services in Bangladesh: Concept Analysis and Development Suggestions. DOI: 10.1007/978-981-33-4279-8_10

Ruggeri, G., Corsi, S., & Mazzocchi, C. (2023). A bibliometric analysis of wine economics and business research: Insights, trends, and future directions. *International Journal of Wine Business Research*, 36(1), 14–39. DOI: 10.1108/IJWBR-06-2023-0032

Ruggles, D. F., & Silverman, H. (2009). *Intangible heritage embodied*. Springer.

Ruhanen, L. (2008). Progressing the sustainability debate: A knowledge management approach to sustainable tourism planning. *Current Issues in Tourism*, 11(5), 429–455. DOI: 10.1080/13683500802316030

Ruiz-Real, J. L., Uribe-Toril, J., & Gazquez-Abad, J. C. (2020). Destination branding: Opportunities and new challenges. *Journal of Destination Marketing & Management*, •••, 17.

Rungsuwannarat, C., Michiels, N. N. T., Fujiwa, D., & Lin, F. (2015). A Comparative study of destination Image between Thailand and Indonesia. *APHEIT Journal*, 4(2), 5–26.

Ryan, J. (2015). Intangible cultural heritage: the new frontier of destination branding. In *Ideas in Marketing: Finding the New and Polishing the Old: Proceedings of the 2013 Academy of Marketing Science (AMS)Annual Conference* (pp. 388-390). Springer International Publishing. DOI: 10.1007/978-3-319-10951-0_147

Ryan, J., & Silvanto, S. (2009). The World Heritage List: The making and management of a brand. *Place Branding and Public Diplomacy*, 5(4), 290–300. DOI: 10.1057/pb.2009.21

Ryan, J., & Silvanto, S. (2010). World heritage sites: The purposes and politics of destination branding. *Journal of Travel & Tourism Marketing*, 27(5), 533–545. DOI: 10.1080/10548408.2010.499064

Saidmamatov, O., Matyakubov, U., Rudenko, I., Filimonau, V., Day, J., & Luthe, T. (2020). Employing ecotourism opportunities for sustainability in the Aral Sea Region: Prospects and challenges. *Sustainability (Basel)*, 12(21), 9249.

Sakar, A. S. (2022). The Brand Personality of Konya City As a Touristic Destination. *Selçuk Turizm Ve Bilişim Araştırmaları Dergisi*, 1(2), 25–31.

Salazar, N. B. (2012). Community-based cultural tourism: Issues, threats and opportunities. *Journal of Sustainable Tourism*, 20(1), 9–22. DOI: 10.1080/09669582.2011.596279

Salerno, G. M., & Russo, A. P. (2022). Venice as a short-term city. Between global trends and local lock-ins. In *Platform-Mediated Tourism* (pp. 90–109). Routledge. DOI: 10.4324/9781003230618-6

Salouw, E., Setiawan, B., Roychansyah, M. S., & Sarwadi, A. (2024). Bibliometric Analysis of Tourism and Community Participation Research: A Comparison of Scopus and Web of Science Databases. *International Journal of Sustainable Development and Planning*, 19(4), 1415–1422. DOI: 10.18280/ijsdp.190419

Samaddar, K., & Mondal, S. (2024). Priming tourists with traditional gastronomic delicacies: Embracing a responsible approach towards sustainable consumption practice. *Consumer Behavior in Tourism and Hospitality*, 19(3), 383–403. DOI: 10.1108/CBTH-03-2023-0026

Samal, R., & Dash, M. (2022a). Ecotourism, biodiversity conservation and livelihoods: Understanding the convergence and divergence. *International Journal of Geoheritage and Parks*, 11(1), 1–20. DOI: 10.1016/j.ijgeop.2022.11.001

Sana, C., Chakraborty, S., Adil, M., & Sadiq, M. (2023). Ecotourism experience: A systematic review and future research agenda. *International Journal of Consumer Studies*, 47(6), 2131–2156. DOI: 10.1111/ijcs.12902

Sánchez-Amboage, E., Castellanos-García, P., & Crespo-Pereira, V. (2024). Traveler segmentation through Instagram Fashion Influencers. Mirror Tourist as a new segment consumer group. *Journal of Retailing and Consumer Services*, 78, 103735. Advance online publication. DOI: 10.1016/j.jretconser.2024.103735

Santen, M. V. (2023). *Digital storytelling as a framework for a new narrative in museums* (Master's thesis).

Saout, S. L., Hoffmann, M., Shi, Y., Hughes, A., Bernard, C., Brooks, T. M., Bertzky, B., Butchart, S. H. M., Stuart, S. N., Badman, T., & Rodrigues, A. S. L. (2013). Protected Areas and Effective Biodiversity Conservation. *Science*, 342(6160), 803–805. DOI: 10.1126/science.1239268 PMID: 24233709

Saraniemi, S. (2011). From destination image building to identity-based branding. *International Journal of Culture, Tourism and Hospitality Research*, 5(3), 247–254. DOI: 10.1108/17506181111156943

Saraniemi, S., & Komppula, R. (2019). The development of a destination brand identity: A story of stakeholder collaboration. *Current Issues in Tourism*, 22(9), 1116–1132. DOI: 10.1080/13683500.2017.1369496

Sarma, U. K., & Barpujari, I. (2022). Realizing a rights-based approach to resettlement from protected areas: Lessons from Satpura Tiger Reserve, Madhya Pradesh (India). *Land Use Policy*, 125, 106494. DOI: 10.1016/j.landusepol.2022.106494

Sasana, H., Atmanti, H. D., & Muid, D. (2017). The strategy development of the region in support Borobudur tourism cluster competitiveness regions in Indonesia. *Journal of Environtmental Management and Tourism*, 8(24), 1517–1528. DOI: 10.14505/jemt.v8.8(24).07

Saxena, A., Shanker, S., Sethi, D., Seth, M., & Saxena, A. (2024). *"Touchstones for the development of an inclusive approach for ecotourism as a service industry", Benchmarking: An International Journal*. DOI: 10.1108/BIJ-07-2023-0456

Sayfullayeva, M. S. (2022). Directions for the Practice of Sustainable Tourism for Ecotourism Destinations in Uzbekistan. *American Journal of Economics and Business Management*, 5(12), 98–109.

Schiffman, L. G., & Kanuk, L. L. (2000). *Consumer Behavior* (7th ed.). Prentice-Hall Inc.

Schmitt, B., & Simonson, A. (1997). *Marketing Aesthetics: The Strategic Management of Brands, Identity, and Image*. The Free Press.

Scott, J. (2017). *Social Network Analysis: A Handbook* (4th ed.). SAGE Publications. DOI: 10.4135/9781529716597

Seaton, A. V., & Bennett, M. M. (Eds.). (1996). *Marketing tourism products: Concepts, issues, cases* (1st ed., pp. 28–54). International Thompson Business Press.

Selcuk, O., Karakas, H., Cizel, B., & Ipekci Cetin, E. (2023). How does tourism affect protected areas?: A multi-criteria decision making application in UNESCO natural heritage sites. *Natural Hazards*, 117(2), 1923–1944. DOI: 10.1007/s11069-023-05934-x

Seyyedamiri, N., Pour, A. H., Zaeri, E., & Nazarian, A. (2022). Understanding destination brand love using machine learning and content analysis method. *Current Issues in Tourism*, 25(9), 1451–1466. DOI: 10.1080/13683500.2021.1924634

Sfakianakis, M. (2000). *Alternative forms of tourism*. Ellin. (In Greek)

Shang, W., Yuan, Q., & Chen, N. (2020). Examining structural relationships among brand experience, existential authenticity, and place attachment in slow tourism destinations. *Sustainability (Basel)*, 12(7), 2784. DOI: 10.3390/su12072784

Shankar, V., Azar, P., & Fuller, M. (2008). Practice prize paper-BRAN*EQT: A multicategory brand equity model and its application at Allstate. *Marketing Science*, 27(4), 567–584. DOI: 10.1287/mksc.1070.0320

Sharma, N., & Sarmah, B. (2019). Consumer engagement in village ecotourism: A case of the cleanest village in asia-mawlynnong. *Journal of Global Scholars of Marketing Science*, 29(2), 248–265. DOI: 10.1080/21639159.2019.1577692

Sharma, P. (2022). Understanding destination evangelism: A social media viewpoint. *Marketing Intelligence & Planning*, 40(1), 72–88. DOI: 10.1108/MIP-04-2021-0128

Sharma, P., & Nayak, J. K. (2020). Examining experience quality as the determinant of tourist behavior in niche tourism: An analytical approach. *Journal of Heritage Tourism*, 15(1), 76–92. DOI: 10.1080/1743873X.2019.1608212

Sharma, R. A. (2011). Co-Management of Protected Areas in South Asia with Special Reference to Bangladesh. *Asia-Pacific Journal of Rural Development*, 21(1), 1–28. DOI: 10.1177/1018529120110101

Sharmin, F., Sultan, M. T., Badulescu, D., Badulescu, A., Borma, A., & Li, B. (2021). Sustainable destination marketing ecosystem through smartphone-based social media: The consumers' acceptance perspective. *Sustainability (Basel)*, 13(4), 2308. DOI: 10.3390/su13042308

Sharpley, R. (2006). Ecotourism: A consumption perspective. *Journal of Ecotourism*, 5(1–2), 7–22. DOI: 10.1080/14724040608668444

Sharpley, R. (2009). *Tourism development and the environment: Beyond sustainability?* Routledge. DOI: 10.4324/9781849770255

Sharp, R. L., Sharp, J. A., & Miller, C. A. (2015). An island in a sea of development: An examination of place attachment, activity type, and crowding in an urban national park. *Visitor Studies*, 18(2), 196–213. DOI: 10.1080/10645578.2015.1079101

Shasha, Z. T., Geng, Y., Sun, H., Musakwa, W., & Sun, L. (2020). Past, current, and future perspectives on eco-tourism: A bibliometric review between 2001 and 2018. *Environmental Science and Pollution Research International*, 27(19), 23514–23528. DOI: 10.1007/s11356-020-08584-9 PMID: 32307679

Sheehan, L. R., & Ritchie, J. R. (2005). Destination stakeholders: Exploring Identity and Salience. *Annals of Tourism Research*, 32(3), 711–734. DOI: 10.1016/j.annals.2004.10.013

Shi, H., Liu, Y., Kumail, T., & Pan, L. (2022). Tourism destination brand equity, brand authenticity and revisit intention: The mediating role of tourist satisfaction and the moderating role of destination familiarity. *Tourism Review*, 77(3), 751–779. DOI: 10.1108/TR-08-2021-0371

Shim, C., Oh, E. J., & Jeong, C. (2017). A qualitative analysis of South Korean casino experiences: A perspective on the experience economy. *Tourism and Hospitality Research*, 17(4), 358–371. DOI: 10.1177/1467358415619673

Shin, H. H., & Jeong, M. (2022). Redefining luxury service with technology implementation: The impact of technology on guest satisfaction and loyalty in a luxury hotel. *International Journal of Contemporary Hospitality Management*, 34(4), 1491–1514. DOI: 10.1108/IJCHM-06-2021-0798

Shone, M. C., Simmons, D. G., & Dalziel, P. (2016). Evolving roles for local government in tourism development: A political economy perspective. *Journal of Sustainable Tourism*, 24(12), 1674–1690. DOI: 10.1080/09669582.2016.1184672

Shoo, R. A., & Songorwa, A. N. (2013). Contribution of eco-tourism to nature conservation and improvement of livelihoods around Amani nature reserve, Tanzania. *Journal of Ecotourism*, 12(2), 75–89. DOI: 10.1080/14724049.2013.818679

Shuqair, S., Viglia, G., Costa Pinto, D., & Mattila, A. S. (2024). Reducing resistance to sponsorship disclosure: The role of experiential versus material posts. *Journal of Travel Research*, 63(4), 959–973. DOI: 10.1177/00472875231171668

Sierra Praeli, Y. (2021). Peru alcanza cifra de deforestacion mas alta en los ultimos 20 anos._https://es.mongabay.com/2021/10/peru-aumenta-deforestacion-cifras-bosques/ (accessed 24.06.2024).

Singh, R., Sibi, P. S., Sharma, P., Tamang, M., & Singh, A. K. (2021). Twenty years of journal of quality assurance in hospitality & tourism: A bibliometric assessment. *Journal of Quality Assurance in Hospitality &Amp. Tourism (Zagreb)*, 23(2), 482–507. DOI: 10.1080/1528008X.2021.1884931

Sisriany, S., & Furuya, K. (2024). Understanding the Spatial Distribution of Ecotourism in Indonesia and Its Relevance to the Protected Landscape. *Land (Basel)*, 13(3), 370. Advance online publication. DOI: 10.3390/land13030370

Skerratt, S., & Steiner, A. (2013). Working with communities-of-place: Complexities of empowerment. *Local Economy*, 28(3), 320–338. Advance online publication. DOI: 10.1177/0269094212474241

Smith, S. L. J. (1995.). *Tourism analysis: a handbook* (2nd ed. ed.). Harlow Essex: Longman.

Smith, L. (2020). Uses of heritage. In *Encyclopedia of global archaeology* (pp. 10969–10974). Springer International Publishing. DOI: 10.1007/978-3-030-30018-0_1937

Smith, S. L. J. (2013). *Tourism analysis: A handbook* (2nd ed.). Routledge.

Smolčić, J. D., & Soldić, F. D. (2017). Satisfaction as a determinant of tourist expenditure. *Current Issues in Tourism*, 20(7), 691–704. DOI: 10.1080/13683500.2016.1175420

Smuha, N. A. (2021). From a 'race to AI'to a 'race to AI regulation': Regulatory competition for artificial intelligence. *Law, Innovation and Technology*, 13(1), 57–84. DOI: 10.1080/17579961.2021.1898300

Snyman, S. (2020). The role of private sector ecotourism in local socio-economic development in southern Africa. In *Routledge eBooks* (pp. 47–68). DOI: 10.4324/9780429423437-4

Snyman, S. (2016). The role of private sector ecotourism in local socio-economic development in southern Africa. *Journal of Ecotourism*, 16(3), 247–268. DOI: 10.1080/14724049.2016.1226318

Sobhani, P., Esmaeilzadeh, H., Wolf, I. D., Deljouei, A., Marcu, M. V., & Sadeghi, S. M. M. (2023). Evaluating the ecological security of ecotourism in protected area based on the DPSIR model. *Ecological Indicators*, 155, 110957. Advance online publication. DOI: 10.1016/j.ecolind.2023.110957

Soliman, M., & Al Balushi, M. (2023). Unveiling destination evangelism through generative AI tools. *ROBONOMICS: The Journal of the Automated Economy, 4*(54), 1. https://journal.robonomics.science/index.php/rj/article/view/54

Soliman, M., Al Balushi, M. K., & Kennedy, R. (2024). Digital marketing for cruise tourism in Oman: Opportunities and challenges. *Social Media Strategies for Tourism Interactivity*, 106-131. https://doi.org/DOI: 10.4018/979-8-3693-0960-5.ch005

Soliman, M., Al-Shanfari, L. S., & Gulvady, S. (2023). Sensory marketing and accessible tourism: An AI-generated article. *ROBONOMICS: The Journal of the Automated Economy, 4*, 53. https://journal.robonomics.science/index.php/rj/article/view/53

Soliman, M., Fatnassi, T., Elgammal, I., & Figueiredo, R. (2023). Exploring the major trends and emerging themes of artificial intelligence in the scientific leading journals amidst the COVID-19 era. *Big Data and Cognitive Computing*, 7(1), 12. DOI: 10.3390/bdcc7010012

Soliman, M., Gulvady, S., Lyulyov, O., & Pimonenko, T. (2023). Research trends and themes in the top-tier tourism, leisure and hospitality journals: A bibliometric and network analysis before and during the COVID-19 era. *International Journal of Hospitality and Tourism Systems*, 16(1). http://www.publishingindia.com/ijhts/24/research-trends-and-themes-in-the-top-tier-tourism-leisure-and-hospitality-journals-a-bibliometric-and-network-analysis-before-and-during-the-covid-19-era/32022/76862/

Song, M., Chen, H., Wang, Y., & Duan, Y. (2024). Can AI fully replace human designers? Matching effects between declared creator types and advertising appeals on tourists' visit intentions. *Journal of Destination Marketing & Management*, 32, 100892. DOI: 10.1016/j.jdmm.2024.100892

Sonuç, N. (2020). Environment, Tourism and Sustainability (Ecotourism Management, Environment and Sustainable Tourism). In Encyclopedia of Sustainable Management (pp. 1–6). Springer International Publishing. DOI: 10.1007/978-3-030-02006-4_456-1

Sotomayor, S., & Guillén, K. (2022). Tourism management competencies for visitor experience design among natural protected areas in Peru. *Journal of Ecotourism*, •••, 1–16. DOI: 10.1080/14724049.2022.2041647

Source: https://winesurveyor.weebly.com/tour_slovakia.html Wines of Slovakia. (Retrieved: May 12th, 2020).

Source: https://www.google.sk/search?q=wine+routes+in+Canada. Wine tasting routes to Canada. (Retrieved: May 10th, 2020).

Stake, R. (1995). *The art of case study research. Thousand Oaks, London*. Sage Publications Ltd.

Stamboulis, Y., & Skayannis, P. (2003). Innovation strategies and technology for experience-based tourism. *Tourism Management*, 24(1), 35–43. DOI: 10.1016/S0261-5177(02)00047-X

Statista. (2024). Market size of the ecotourism sector worldwide in 2022, with a forecast for 2028 https://www.statista.com/statistics/1221034/ecotourism-market-size-global/

Stavrinoudis, Th., & Parthenis, S. (2009). The role and contribution of local, regional and national institutions and organizations in the development of alternative and special interest tourism. In Sotiriadis, M., & Farsari, I. (Eds.), *Alternative and special forms of tourism: planning, management and marketing*. Interbooks. (In Greek)

Stepchenkova, S., & Li, X. (2014). Destination image: Do top-of-mind associations say it all? *Annals of Tourism Research*, 45, 46–62. DOI: 10.1016/j.annals.2013.12.004

Sterling, E. J., Betley, E., Sigouin, A., Gomez, A., Toomey, A., Cullman, G., Malone, C., Pekor, A., Arengo, F., Blair, M., Filardi, C., Landrigan, K., & Porzecanski, A. L. (2017). Assessing the evidence for stakeholder engagement in biodiversity conservation. *Biological Conservation*, 209, 159–171. DOI: 10.1016/j.biocon.2017.02.008

Stone, G. A., & Duffy, L. N. (2015). Transformative learning theory: A systematic review of travel and tourism scholarship. *Journal of Teaching in Travel & Tourism*, 15(3), 204–224. DOI: 10.1080/15313220.2015.1059305

Streimikiene, D., Svagzdiene, B., Jasinskas, E., & Simanavicius, A. (2021). Sustainable tourism development and competitiveness: The systematic literature review. *Sustainable Development (Bradford)*, 29(1), 259–271. DOI: 10.1002/sd.2133

Stronza, A. (2007). The Economic Promise of Ecotourism for Conservation. *Journal of Ecotourism*, 6(3), 210–230. DOI: 10.2167/joe177.0

Stronza, A., & Gordillo, J. (2008). Community views of ecotourism. *Annals of Tourism Research*, 35(2), 448–468. DOI: 10.1016/j.annals.2008.01.002

Stsiampkouskaya, K., Joinson, A., Piwek, L., & Stevens, L. (2021). Imagined audiences, emotions, and feedback expectations in social media photo sharing. *Social Media + Society*, 7(3), 20563051211035692. DOI: 10.1177/20563051211035692

Suklabaidya, P., & Aggarwal, M. (2020). Visitor Management at UNWHS: A Case study of Taj Mahal. *Atna Journal of Tourism Studies*, 15(2), 81–114. DOI: 10.12727/ajts.24.5

Suna, B., & Alvarez, M. D. (2021). The role of gastronomy in shaping the destination's brand identity: An empirical analysis based on stakeholders' opinions. *Journal of Hospitality Marketing & Management*, 30(6), 738–758. DOI: 10.1080/19368623.2021.1877587

Sun, M., Ye, B. H., & Law, R. (2022). Sustainability and luxury tourism: The influence of hotel sustainability practices on tourist satisfaction in luxury hotels. *Journal of Travel & Tourism Marketing*, 39(2), 166–179.

Svoronou, E. (2003). *Management methods of ecotourism and tourism in protected areas*. WWF Greece - Ministry of Environment, Spatial Planning and Public Works. (In Greek)

Tafesse, W., & Wood, B. P. (2021). Followers' engagement with instagram influencers: The role of influencers' content and engagement strategy. *Journal of Retailing and Consumer Services*, 58, 102303. Advance online publication. DOI: 10.1016/j.jretconser.2020.102303

Tajer, E., & Demir, S. (2022). Ecotourism strategy of UNESCO city in Iran: Applying a new quantitative method integrated with BMW. *Journal of Cleaner Production*, 376, 134284. DOI: 10.1016/j.jclepro.2022.134284

Tajfel, H. (1981). *Human groups and social categories: Studies in social psychology*. Cambridge University Press.

Tanaka, S., Kim, C., Takahashi, H., & Nishihara, A. (2024). Impact of brand authenticity on word-of-mouth for tourism souvenirs. *Cogent Business & Management*, 11(1), 2290222. DOI: 10.1080/23311975.2023.2290222

Tarigan, M. I., Lubis, A. N., Rini, E. S., & Sembiring, B. K. F. (2023). Antecedents of destination brand experience. *Journal Of Sustainable Tourism And Entrepreneurship*, 4(2), 131–141. DOI: 10.35912/joste.v4i2.428

Tasci, A. D. (2020). Exploring the analytics for linking consumer-based brand equity (CBBE) and financial-based brand equity (FBBE) of destination or place brands. *Place Branding and Public Diplomacy*, 16(1), 36–59. DOI: 10.1057/s41254-019-00125-7

Temirkulovich, U. J. (2022). Development of Ecologization of Tourism: Experience of Foreign Countries. Indonesian Journal of Innovation Studies, 19.

Teng, H. Y., & Chen, C. Y. (2020). Enhancing celebrity fan-destination relationship in film-induced tourism: The effect of authenticity. *Tourism Management Perspectives*, 33, 100605. DOI: 10.1016/j.tmp.2019.100605

Thailand Regions. (n.d.). *Holiday Destinations in Thailand.* Retrieved from http:/ www.travelonline.com/Thailand/regions

The International Ecotourism Society (TIES). (2015). What is ecotourism? https:// www.ecotourism.org/what-is-ecotourism. (accessed 21.07.24).

The International Ecotourism Society. (2015). *What Is Ecotourism?* ecotourism. org. Retrieved September 28, 2024, from https://ecotourism.org/what-is-ecotourism/

Thompson, B. S. (2022). Ecotourism anywhere? The lure of ecotourism and the need to scrutinize the potential competitiveness of ecotourism developments. *Tourism Management*, 92, 104568.

Thompson, J. (2022). *Edizioni WhiteStar.*

Thong, J. Z., Lo, M. C., Ramayah, T., & Mohamad, A. A. (2024). Destination resources as precursors of ecotourism competitiveness: A study of totally protected areas in Sarawak, Malaysia during COVID-19 pandemic. *Journal of Ecotourism*, 23(2), 194–216.

Thornham, H. (2013a). Digital welfare only deepens the class divide. *The Conversation* 13-15. July.

TIES. (2015). Web site of The International Ecotourism Society. https://ecotourism .org/what-is-ecotourism/

Tiger Conservation Plan for the Buffer Zone of the Kanha Tiger Reserve. (n.d.). In www.mpforest.gov.in. Retrieved September 28, 2024, from https://www.mpforest .gov.in/img/files/Kanha_TCP_Buffer.pdf

Timothy, D., & Boyd, S. (2014). *Tourism and trails.* Channel View Publications. DOI: 10.21832/9781845414795

Toksöz, D. (2024). Turist Rehberlerinin Alan Uzmanlığına Bakış Açıları Üzerine Görgül Bir Araştırma. *Güncel Turizm Araştırmaları Dergisi*, 8(1), 8–27.

Tolis, K. N., (2010). *Assessment of the development potential of ecotourism in the Kerkini Lake National Park through the investigation of opinions and use of geographic information systems* (No. GRI 2010-5757). Aristotle University of Thessaloniki. (In Greek).

Tolkach, D., & King, B. (2015). Strengthening community-based tourism in a new resource-based island nation: Why and how? *Tourism Management*, 48, 386–398. DOI: 10.1016/j.tourman.2014.12.013

Torres-Moraga, E., & Barra, C. (2023). Does destination brand experience help build trust? Disentangling the effects on trust and trustworthiness. *Journal of Destination Marketing & Management*, 27, 100767. DOI: 10.1016/j.jdmm.2023.100767

Tourism Authority of Thailand. (n.d.). Thailand Travel Guide for Chiang Mai. Retrieved from https://www.tourismthailand.org/Where-to-

Tourism Strategy of Turkey-2023. (2007). Action Plan2007-2013. Ministry of Culture and Tourism of Turkey. https://www.ktb.gov.tr/Eklenti/43537,turkeytourismstrat egy2023pdf.pdf?0&_tag1=796689BB12A540BE0672E65E48D10C07D6DAE291

Tourism Today. (2024). https://www.tourismtoday.gr

Travel Crete. (2022). *Milia, a full organic village*. https://www.travel-crete.gr/el/tour/milia-a-full-organic-village

Trung, N. V. H., & Khalifa, G. S. A. (2019). Impact of destination image factors on revisit intentions of hotel's international tourists in Ba Ria-Vung Tau. [IJRTBT]. *International Journal on Recent Trends in Business and Tourism*, 3(2), 106–115.

Tsaur, S. H., Yen, C. H., & Yan, Y. T. (2016). Destination brand identity: Scale development and validation. *Asia Pacific Journal of Tourism Research*, 21(12), 1310–1323. DOI: 10.1080/10941665.2016.1156003

Tsitsoni, Th. (2015). Protected areas as a driver of sustainable development at the local and national level. Proceedings of the *17th Panhellenic Forestry Conference*. Kefalonia 4-8/10. (In Greek).

Tubey, W. C., Kyalo, D. N., & Mulwa, A. S. (2020). Environmental conservation strategies and sustainability of community-based tourism in Kenya: A case of Maasai Mara conservancies. *International Journal of Tourism Policy*, 10(2), 123. DOI: 10.1504/IJTP.2020.110864

Tulasi, E. E., Ashiaby, O. E., Kodua, P., Ahlijah, B., & Agyeman-Duah, M. O. (2024). The role of aesthetics in tourist satisfaction in the Ghanaian hospitality industry. *Heliyon*, 10(1), e32944. DOI: 10.1016/j.heliyon.2024.e32944 PMID: 38994054

Tuominen, P. (2011). The influence of TripAdvisor consumer-generated travel reviews on hotel performance.

Türkay, O., Dilmaç, E., & Taşarer, E. (2024). Turizmin "Özgürlük" ve "Yolda Olmak" Hâli: Türkiye'deki Karavan Turistlerini Anlamaya Yönelik Bir Araştırma. *Afyon Kocatepe Üniversitesi Sosyal Bilimler Dergisi*, 26(1), 385–408.

Turner, R. L. (2004). COMMUNITIES, WILDLIFE CONSERVATION, AND TOURISM-BASED DEVELOPMENT: CAN COMMUNITY-BASED NATURE TOURISM LIVE UP TO ITS PROMISE? *Journal of International Wildlife Law and Policy*, 7(3–4), 161–182. DOI: 10.1080/13880290490883232

Tuten, T. L. (2023). Social media marketing. Sage publications limited.

Tzimas, O. P., (2023). *Rural tourism in Zagori, Epirus and the evaluation of the tourist experience by visitors.* (In Greek).

Ud Din, N., Nazneen, S., & Jamil, B. (2024). Tourism crowding and resident approach/avoidance reactions through sustainable tourism: Moderating role of proenvironmental behavior. *Tourism Review*. Advance online publication. DOI: 10.1108/TR-10-2023-0678

Ulker-Demirel, E., & Ciftci, G. (2020). A systematic literature review of the theory of planned behavior in tourism, leisure and hospitality management research. *Journal of Hospitality and Tourism Management*, 43, 209–219. DOI: 10.1016/j.jhtm.2020.04.003

Ülker, P., Ülker, M., & Karamustafa, K. (2022). Bibliometric analysis of bibliometric studies in the field of tourism and hospitality. *Journal of Hospitality and Tourism Insights*, 6(2), 797–818. DOI: 10.1108/JHTI-10-2021-0291

UN Tourism | Bringing the world closer. (2024). Retrieved October 17, 2024, from https://www.unwto.org/

UNEP & UNWTO. (2005). *Making tourism more sustainable - A guide for policy makers.* https://wedocs.unep.org/bitstream/handle/20.500.11822/8741/-Making%20Tourism%20More%20Sustainable_%20A%20Guide%20for%20Policy%20Makers-2005445.pdf?sequence=3&isAllowed=

UNEP. (2022). Resolution adopted by the United Nations Environment Assembly on 2 March 2022, 5/5. Nature-based solutions for supporting sustainable development. https://wedocs.unep.org/bitstream/handle/20.500.11822/39864/NATURE-BASED%20SOLUTIONS%20FOR%20SUPPORTING%20SUSTAINABLE%20DEVELOPMENT.%20English.pdf?sequence=1&isAllowed=y

UNEP-WCMC. (2017). *Protected Area Profile for Greece from the World Database of Protected Areas.* Available at: www.protectedplanet.net

Unesco World heritage sites in Peru. Paris, France. (2020). Available at: https://whc.unesco.org/en/statesparties/pe (accessed 24.06.2024).

UNESCO. (2012). Text of the Convention for the Safeguarding of Intangible Cultural Heritage. Retrieved from: https://www.unesco.org/culture/ich/index.php?lg=en&pg=00022 accessed on 25 June, 2024.

UNWTO (United Nations World Tourism Organization). (2024). *Sustainable tourism for development: Statistical framework for measuring tourism sustainability.* UNWTO. https://www.unwto.org

UNWTO Impact assessment of the COVID-19 outbreak on international tourism. (2021). https://www.unwto.org/impact-assessment-of-the-Covid-19-outbreak-on-international-tourism July 17th.

UNWTO. (2007). *A Practical Guide to Tourism Destination Management.* World Tourism Organization.

UNWTO. (2016). UNWTO tourism highlights Retrieved from World Tourism Organization.

Ushakov, D., Ermilova, M., & Andreeva, E. (2018). Destination branding as a tool for sustainable tourism development (the case of Bangkok, Thailand). *Advanced Science Letters*, 39(47), 6339–6342. Advance online publication. DOI: 10.1166/asl.2018.13048

Utama, I.G.B.R.; Trimurti, C.P. (2019). The ethical development of agritourism in protected territory Pelega Badung Bali, Indonesia. Jurnal Manajemen dan Kewirausahaan, 21(2): 114-119. DOI: https://doi.org/DOI: 10.9744/jmk.21.2.114-119

Uysal, Ü. (2017). A brief history of city branding in istanbul., 117-131. https://doi.org/DOI: 10.4018/978-1-5225-0576-1.ch006

Uysal, Ü., & Özden, P. (2011). *Cultural tourism as a tool for urban regeneration in İstanbul.* WIT Press., DOI: 10.2495/ST110351

Vallejo, G., Gonzalo, F., Rafael, M., Genaro, O., Nuria, M., & Fernando, C. (2017). *Usos, actitudes y tendencias del consumidor digital en la compra y consumo de viajes.* Observatorio Digital IAB Spain.

Van Dijck, J., & Poell, T. (2013). Understanding social media logic. *Media and Communication*, 1(1), 2–14. DOI: 10.17645/mac.v1i1.70

Van Laer, T., Edson Escalas, J., Ludwig, S., & Van Den Hende, E. A. (2019). What happens in Vegas stays on TripAdvisor? A theory and technique to understand narrativity in consumer reviews. *The Journal of Consumer Research*, 46(2), 267–285.

Vanhove, N. (2005). *The Economics of Tourism Destinations.* Burlington: Elsevier. Corrigliano,M. A., Mottironi, C. (2013). Planning and Management of European Rural Peripheral Territories through Multifunctionality: The Case of Gastronomy Routes. In Costa, C., Panyik, E., & Buhalis, D. (Eds.), *Trends in European Tourism Planning and Organisation*. Channel View Publications.

Vargo, S. L., Koskela-Huotari, K., & Vink, J. (2020). Service-dominant logic: foundations and applications. In *The Routledge handbook of service research insights and ideas* (pp. 3–23). Routledge. DOI: 10.4324/9781351245234-1

Varsha, P. (2023). How can we manage biases in artificial intelligence systems–A systematic literature review. *International Journal of Information Management Data Insights*, 3(1), 100165. DOI: 10.1016/j.jjimei.2023.100165

Veal, A. J. (2011). *Research methods for leisure and tourism: A practical guide* (4th ed.). Pearson Education Limited.

Veríssimo, J. M., Tiago, M. T., Tiago, F. G., & Jardim, J. S. (2017). Tourism destination brand dimensions: An exploratory approach. *Tourism & Management Studies*, 13(4), 1–8. DOI: 10.18089/tms.2017.13401

Vila-López, N., Kuster-Boluda, I., Mora-Pérez, E., & Sarabia Sanchez, F. (2024). The role of sports on destination branding: A bibliometric study. *Journal of Vacation Marketing*, 13567667241272811. Advance online publication. DOI: 10.1177/13567667241272811

Virutamasen, P., Ahadi, N., Wang, J., Zanjanab, A. G., Wongpreedee, K., & Sohaee, N. (2024). Contextual Based E-Tourism Application: A Personalized Attraction Recommendation System for Destination Branding and Cultivating Tourism Experiences. 2024 5th Technology Innovation Management and Engineering Science International Conference (TIMES-iCON), Wang, R., Luo, J., & Huang, S. S. (2020). Developing an artificial intelligence framework for online destination image photos identification. *Journal of Destination Marketing & Management*, 18, 100512. DOI: 10.1016/j.jdmm.2020.100512

Visit Blue Mountains. (2023). *Sustainable travel.* https://www.visitbluemountains.com.au/plan/sustainable-travel

Visit Greece. (2023). *Ecotourism.* https://www.visitgreece.gr/el/inspirations/ecotourism/

Vissak, T. (2010). Recommendations for using the case study method in international business research. *The Qualitative Report*, 15(2), 370–388.

Voronkova, V., Nikitenko, V., Oleksenko, R., Cherep, A., Cherep, O., & Harbar, H. (2024). The Creative Development of Green Ecotourism Concept as a Sustainable Development Factor. *Revista de la Universidad del Zulia*, 3/15(42), 370–388.

Wagner, O., & Peters, M. (2009). The Development And Communıcatıon Of Destınatıon Brand Identıty – The Case Of The Alps. Tourism Destination Development and Branding Eilat 2009 Conference Proceedings. Ben-Gurion University of the Negev.

Wagner, O., & Peters, M. (2009). Can association methods reveal the effects of internal branding on tourism destination stakeholders. *Journal of Place Management and Development*, 2(1), 52–69. DOI: 10.1108/17538330910942807

Wakefield, C. (2023). Exploring Social Media as Engagement in UK Development-led Archaeology (Doctoral dissertation, University of York).

Waligo, V. M., Clarke, J., & Hawkins, R. (2013). Implementing sustainable tourism: A multi-stakeholder involvement management framework. *Tourism Management*, 36, 342–353. DOI: 10.1016/j.tourman.2012.10.008

Wallace, R. (2019). Ecotourism in Asia. In *Advances in hospitality, tourism and the services industry (AHTSI) book series* (pp. 192–211). DOI: 10.4018/978-1-5225-7253-4.ch009

Wallace, R. (2019). Ecotourism in Asia: How strong branding creates opportunity for local economies and the environment. In *Positioning and branding tourism destinations for global competitiveness* (pp. 192-211). IGI Global.

Waller, M. A., & Fawcett, S. E. (2013). Data science, predictive analytics, and big data: A revolution that will transform supply chain design and management. *Journal of Business Logistics*, 34(2), 77–84. DOI: 10.1111/jbl.12010

Wang, C. N., Tran, K. M., Huang, C. C., Wang, Y. H., & Dang, T. T. (2022). Supporting Luxury Hotel Recovered in Times of COVID-19 by Applying TRIZ Method: A Case Study in Taiwan. *Systems*, 10(2), 33. Advance online publication. DOI: 10.3390/systems10020033

Wang, D., Shen, C. C., Tseng, T. A., & Lai, C. Y. (2024). What is the most influential authenticity of beliefs, places, or actions on the pilgrimage tourism destination attachment? *Sustainability (Basel)*, 16(1), 431. DOI: 10.3390/su16010431

Wang, D., Xiang, Z., & Fesenmaier, D. R. (2022). Big data and travel marketing: Prospects and challenges. *Tourism Management*, 91, 104473.

Wang, H., Xiong, L., & Gage, R. (2021). Cultivating destination brand ambassadors in rural China: Examining the role of residents' welcoming nature. *International Journal of Tourism Research*, 23(6), 1027–1041. DOI: 10.1002/jtr.2460

Wang, K. Y. (2022). Sustainable tourism development based upon visitors' brand trust: A case of 100 religious attractions. *Sustainability (Basel)*, 14(4), 1977. DOI: 10.3390/su14041977

Wang, X., Mou, N., Zhu, S., Yang, T., Zhang, X., & Zhang, Y. (2024). How to perceive tourism destination image? A visual content analysis based on inbound tourists' photos. *Journal of Destination Marketing & Management*, 33, 100923. DOI: 10.1016/j.jdmm.2024.100923

Wang, Y., Cao, J., & Cai, X. (2024). The impact of environmental, social and governance performance on brand value: The role of the digitalisation level. *South African Journal of Business Management*, 55(1), 4448. DOI: 10.4102/sajbm.v55i1.4448

Ward, S., Larry, L., & Goldstine, J. (1999). What high-tech managers need to know about brands. *Harvard Business Review*, •••, 85–95.

Wasserman, S., & Faust, K. (1994). *Social Network Analysis: Methods and Applications*. Cambridge University Press. DOI: 10.1017/CBO9780511815478

Watts, D. (2003). *Six Degrees: The Science of a Connected Age*. W. W. Norton & Company.

Watts, D. J., & Strogatz, S. H. (1998). Collective dynamics of 'small-world' networks. *Nature*, 393(6684), 440–442. DOI: 10.1038/30918 PMID: 9623998

Weaver, D. B. (2001b). Ecotourism in the context of other tourism types. In The encyclopedia of ecotourism (pp. 73–83). CABI Publishing. DOI: 10.1079/9780851993683.0073

Weaver, D. (2006). *Sustainable Tourism: Theory and Practice*. Elsevier.

Weaver, D. (2007). Towards sustainable mass tourism: Paradigm shift or paradigm nudge? *Tourism Recreation Research*, 32(3), 65–69. DOI: 10.1080/02508281.2007.11081541

Weaver, D. B. (2001a). Ecotourism as mass tourism: Contradiction or reality? *The Cornell Hotel and Restaurant Administration Quarterly*, 42(2), 104–112.

Weaver, D. B. (Ed.). (2001). *The encyclopedia of ecotourism*. Cabi Publishing. DOI: 10.1079/9780851993683.0000

Wheeler, F., Frost, W., & Weiler, B. (2011). Destination brand identity, values, and community: A case study from rural Victoria, Australia. *Journal of Travel & Tourism Marketing*, 28(1), 13–26. DOI: 10.1080/10548408.2011.535441

Wichels, S. (2014). Nuevos desafíos en Relaciones Públicas 2.0: La creciente influencia de las plataformas de online review en Turismo / New Challenges in Public Relations 2.0: The growing influence of online review platforms in Tourism. DOI: 10.5783/RIRP-7-2014-12-197-216

Widari, D. A. D. S., Antara, M., & Paturusi, S. A. (2019). Management strategy of Jatiluwih tourist attraction as part of world cultural heritage in Tabanan Regency, Bali Province. *International Journal of Social Science Research*, 7(1), 2327–5510. https://www.scilit.net/article/4e5d31f9124ec4c4bae932475f673af0. DOI: 10.5296/ijssr.v7i1.14248

Wirtz, J., & Pitardi, V. (2023). How intelligent automation, service robots, and AI will reshape service products and their delivery. *Italian Journal of Marketing*, 2023(3), 289–300. DOI: 10.1007/s43039-023-00076-1

Wood, P. M. (1997). Biodiversity as the source of biological resources: A new look at biodiversity values. *Environmental Values*, 6(3), 251–268. DOI: 10.3197/096327197776679077

World Tourism Barometer, U. N. (2024). https://www.unwto.org/un-tourism-world-tourism-barometer-data

World Travel & Tourism Council. (2020). *Economic impact reports*.

Worldbank (2021). Available at: https://data.worldbank.org/indicator/SP.DYN.LE00.MA.IN?locations=MV (accessed 11.07.24)

Woyo, E., & Slabbert, E. (2021). Tourism destination competitiveness: A view from suppliers operating in a country with political challenges. *Suid-Afrikaanse Tydskrif vir Ekonomiese en Bestuurswetenskappe*, 24(1), 3717. DOI: 10.4102/sajems.v24i1.3717

Wu, I. S. (2023). The Smithsonian's soft power: how foreigners engage the US national museum. In *Alternative Paths to Influence* (pp. 33–54). Routledge. DOI: 10.4324/9781003381037-3

Wu, J. (2013). Landscape sustainability science: Ecosystem services and human well-being in changing landscapes. *Landscape Ecology*, 28(6), 999–1023. DOI: 10.1007/s10980-013-9894-9

www.kanhatigerreserve.org. (n.d.). kanhatigerreserve.org. Retrieved September 28, 2024, from https://www.kanhatigerreserve.org/flora-and-fauna

Xiang, Z., Wöber, K., & Fesenmaier, D. R. (2008). Representation of the online tourism domain in search engines. *Journal of Travel Research*, 47(2), 137–150. DOI: 10.1177/0047287508321193

Xiao, H. (2006). Towards a research agenda for knowledge management in tourism. *Tourism and Hospitality Planning & Development*, 3(2), 143–157. DOI: 10.1080/14790530600938436

Xiao, H., & Smith, S. (2006). The making of tourism research: Insights from a social science journal. *Annals of Tourism Research*, 33(2), 490–507. DOI: 10.1016/j.annals.2006.01.004

Xiao, X., Perry, E., Manning, R., Krymkowski, D., Valliere, W., & Reigner, N. (2017). Effects of transportation on racial/ethnic diversity of national park visitors. *Leisure Sciences*, 39(2), 126–143. DOI: 10.1080/01490400.2016.1151846

Xie-Carson, L., & Benckendorff, P. (2024). Insta-fame or insta-flop? The pitfalls of using virtual influencers in tourism marketing. *Journal of Hospitality and Tourism Management*, 60, 116–126. DOI: 10.1016/j.jhtm.2024.06.014

Xie-Carson, L., Magor, T., Benckendorff, P., & Hughes, K. (2023). All hype or the real deal? Investigating user engagement with virtual influencers in tourism. *Tourism Management*, 99, 104779. Advance online publication. DOI: 10.1016/j.tourman.2023.104779

Xu, J., & Au, T. (2023). Destination competitiveness since 2010: Research themes, approaches, and agenda. *Tourism Review*, 78(3), 665–696. DOI: 10.1108/TR-10-2022-0494

Yang, L., Hu, X., Lee, H. M., & Zhang, Y. (2023). The impacts of ecotourists' perceived authenticity and perceived values on their behaviors: Evidence from Huangshan World Natural and Cultural Heritage Site. *Sustainability (Basel)*, 15(2), 1551. DOI: 10.3390/su15021551

Yasin, A., Raza, S. H., Pembecioglu, N., Zaman, U., Ogadimma, E. C., Khan, A. M., & Khan, S. W. (2023). Modeling the impact of social media influencers on intention to visit ecotourism destinations in the global south. In *Handbook of Research on Deconstructing Culture and Communication in the Global South*. IGI Global. DOI: 10.4018/978-1-6684-8093-9.ch021

Yen, C.-H., Teng, H.-Y., & Chang, S.-T. (2020). Destination brand identity and emerging market tourists' perceptions. *Asia Pacific Journal of Tourism Research*, 25(12), 1311–1328. DOI: 10.1080/10941665.2020.1853578

Yilmaz, G., Kilicarslan, D., & Caber, M. (2020). How does a destination's food image serve the common targets of the UNESCO creative cities network? *International Journal of Tourism Cities*, 6(4), 785–812. DOI: 10.1108/IJTC-07-2019-0115

Yin, R. (2003). *Case study research: design and methods*. Sage Publications Ltd.

Yin, R. K. (2003). *Case study research: Design and methods (3rded.). NewburyPark*. Sage Publications.

Yönet, N. A., & Yirmibesoglu, F. (2022). Ecotourism as a Rural Development Model: As a Women Leaded Ecotourism Process of Piraziz Şeyhli Village (the Black Sea Region of Turkey). Planlama, 32(2).

Ypeij, A. (2012). The intersection of gender and ethnic identities in the Cuzco–Machu Picchu tourism industry: Sácamefotos, tour guides, and women weavers. *Latin American Perspectives*, 39(6), 17–35. DOI: 10.1177/0094582X12454591

Yu, C., & Hwang, Y. S. (2019). Do the social responsibility efforts of the destination affect the loyalty of tourists? *Sustainability (Basel)*, 11(7), 1998. DOI: 10.3390/su11071998

Yuliana, Y., Rini, E. S., Situmorang, S. H., & Silalahi, A. S. (2023). Mediating role of authenticity in the relationship between destination image and destination loyalty. *Innovative Marketing*, 19(4), 14–25. DOI: 10.21511/im.19(4).2023.02

Yuliati, D., Susilowati, E., & Suliyati, T. (2023). Preservation of the old city of semarang, Central Java, Indonesia, and its development as a cultural tourism asset. *Cogent Social Sciences*, 9(1), 2170740. Advance online publication. DOI: 10.1080/23311886.2023.2170740

Yusof, M. F., & Ismail, H. N. (2014). Destination Branding Identity from the Stakeholders' Perspectives. *Internatıonal Journal Of Buılt Envıronment And Sustaınabılıty*, 1(1), 71–75.

Zahra, A., & McGehee, N. G. (2013). Volunteer tourism: A host-community capital perspective. *Annals of Tourism Research*, 42, 22–45. DOI: 10.1016/j.annals.2013.01.008

Zakynthos National Marine Park. (2019). *Information report*. Zakynthos National Marine Park Management Stakeholder. (In Greek)

Zariç, Ö. E., Çelekli, A., & Yaygır, S. (2024). Lakes of Turkey: Comprehensive review of Lake Çıldır. *Aquatic Sciences and Engineering*, 39(1), 54–63.

Zavattaro, S., Daspit, J., & Adams, F. (2015). Assessing managerial methods for evaluative place brand equity: A qualitative investigation. *Tourism Management*, 47, 11–21. DOI: 10.1016/j.tourman.2014.08.018

Zenker, S., Braun, E., & Peterson, S. (2017). Branding the destination versus the place: The effects of brand complexity and identification for residents and visitors. *Tourism Management*, 58, 15–27. DOI: 10.1016/j.tourman.2016.10.008

Zenker, S., & Martin, N. (2011). Measuring success in place marketing and branding. *Place Branding and Public Diplomacy*, 7(1), 32–41. DOI: 10.1057/pb.2011.5

Zhang, H., Liang, Q., Li, Y., & Gao, P. (2023). Promoting eco-tourism for the green economic recovery in ASEAN. *Economic Change and Restructuring*, 56(3), 2021–2036. DOI: 10.1007/s10644-023-09492-x

Zhang, H., Zang, Z., Zhu, H., Uddin, M. I., & Amin, M. A. (2022). Big data-assisted social media analytics for business model for business decision making system competitive analysis. *Information Processing & Management*, 59(1), 102762. DOI: 10.1016/j.ipm.2021.102762

Zhang, K., Chen, Y., & Li, C. (2019). Discovering the tourists' behaviors and perceptions in a tourism destination by analyzing photos' visual content with a computer deep learning model: The case of Beijing. *Tourism Management*, 75, 595–608. DOI: 10.1016/j.tourman.2019.07.002

Zhang, M., Liu, Y., Wang, Y., & Zhao, L. (2022). How to retain customers: Understanding the role of trust in live streaming commerce with a socio-technical perspective. *Computers in Human Behavior*, 127, 107052. DOI: 10.1016/j.chb.2021.107052

Zhang, Y., Li, X., Cárdenas, D. A., & Liu, Y. (2022). Calculating theme parks' tourism demand and attractiveness energy: A reverse gravity model and particle swarm optimization. *Journal of Travel Research*, 61(2), 314–330. DOI: 10.1177/0047287520977705

Zhao, C., & Shen, H. (2024). The Moderating Effect of Ski Influencer on Ski Tourism Intention. *SAGE Open*, 14(2), 21582440241242318. Advance online publication. DOI: 10.1177/21582440241242318

Zhou, W., Zheng, B., Zhang, Z., Song, Z., & Duan, W. (2021). The role of eco-tourism in ecological conservation in giant panda nature reserve. *Journal of Environmental Management*, 295, 113077. DOI: 10.1016/j.jenvman.2021.113077 PMID: 34146778

Zhou, Z., Wang, Y., & Zhou, N. (2023). Effects of multidimensional destination brand authenticity on destination brand well-being: The mediating role of self-congruence. *Current Issues in Tourism*, 26(21), 3532–3546. DOI: 10.1080/13683500.2022.2134985

Zoumadaki, E. (2019). Chania: Tourism research: Airbnb, Elafonisi and... Monasteries in the first choices. https://flashnews.gr/post/383746/xania-ereyna-gia-ton-toyrismo-airbnb-elafonhsikai-monasthria-stis-prwtes-epiloges

About the Contributors

Muhammad Abrar is a professor of management sciences (marketing) and currently serving as a professor/director at Lyallpur Business School, Government College University, Faisalabad, Pakistan. He received his PhD in business administration (marketing) from the Huazhong University of Science and Technology, Wuhan, China. He holds an MBA from Bahauddin Zakariya University, Multan, Pakistan and an M.Sc. (Hons.) Agronomy degree from the University of Agriculture, Faisalabad, Pakistan. He is a well-known scholar in his research areas (Brand Management, Supply Chain Management, Digital Marketing, Services Marketing, Management, and Business Education). He edited the five books published by IGI-Global & Springer Nature. His scholarly peer-reviewed research articles have been published in the top journals, e.g., International Journal of Contemporary Hospitality Management, Journal of Enterprise Information Management, Management Decision, Journal of Competitiveness, Asia Pacific Journal of Marketing and Logistics, Total Quality Management & Business Excellence, Marketing Intelligence & Planning, Economic and Industrial Democracy, International Journal of Emerging Markets, Chinese Management Studies, Autex Research Journal, SAGE Open, Quality & Quantity, Industria Textila, Journal of Islamic Marketing. He can be contacted at: abrarphd@gmail.com, abrarphd@gcuf.edu.pk

Muhammad Asim Nawaz is an assistant professor of marketing and currently serving at Lyallpur Business School, Government College University Faisalabad, Pakistan. He received his PhD from the School of Management, University of Science and Technology of China, in 2019. He holds an MBA and BBA in Marketing from the University of Central Punjab, Lahore, Pakistan. His research interests include destination brand management, destination loyalty, revisit intention, and consumer behaviour. He has supervised many master's and PhD candidates at the business school. He has published research articles in numerous national and international generals. He serves as an article editor with Sage Open and a reviewer with many well-known international journals. He is enthusiastic about working in challenging situations and completing new projects and assignments.

Faiqa Kiran is an assistant professor of Marketing at Lyallpur Business School, Faculty of Economics and Management Sciences, Government College University, Faisalabad. Her research interests include: consumer behavior, social media marketing, and branding. She has supervised many master's and PhD candidates at the business school. She has published research articles in numerous national and international generals. She is enthusiastic to work in challenging and take up new projects and assignments.

***

Muhammad Abrar is a professor of management sciences (marketing) and currently serving as a professor/director at Lyallpur Business School, Government College University, Faisalabad, Pakistan. He received his PhD in business administration (marketing) from the Huazhong University of Science and Technology, Wuhan, China. He holds an MBA from Bahauddin Zakariya University, Multan, Pakistan and an M.Sc. (Hons.) Agronomy degree from the University of Agriculture, Faisalabad, Pakistan. He is a well-known scholar in his research areas (Brand Management, Supply Chain Management, Digital Marketing, Services Marketing, Management, and Business Education). He edited the five books published by IGI-Global & Springer Nature. His scholarly peer-reviewed research articles have been published in the top journals, e.g., International Journal of Contemporary Hospitality Management, Journal of Enterprise Information Management, Management Decision, Journal of Competitiveness, Asia Pacific Journal of Marketing and Logistics, Total Quality Management & Business Excellence, Marketing Intelligence & Planning, Economic and Industrial Democracy, International Journal of Emerging Markets, Chinese Management Studies, Autex Research Journal, SAGE Open, Quality & Quantity, Industria Textila, Journal of Islamic Marketing. He can be contacted at: abrarphd@gmail.com, abrarphd@gcuf.edu.pk

Maha K. Al Balushi is the Head of the Marketing Department and the former director of the MBA program in the College of Economics and Political Science at Sultan Qaboos University. Dr Maha is the faculty fellow at the Centre of Excellence in Teaching and Learning (CETL) in SQU. She teaches both undergraduate and graduate courses. She has published papers in reputed journals. Her research interests include consumer behavior and branding in sports, food, fashion and tourism together with AI- enabled customers service and branding. Dr. Maha has successfully supervised and examined Master and PhD theses. She also served as program reviewer and verifier for various local programs. Specifically, she is the External Reviewer for Oman Authority for Academic Accreditation and Quality Assurance of Education.

Mohammed Al Hosni is a part-time MBA student at Sultan Qaboos University with a PhD in Geophysics and more than eight years of experience in the Oil and Gas industry with roles involving new technologies adoption, including AI models such as big data and machine learning. Mohammed's current research interest is in AI adaptation in the local market and organizational change management.

Amal Al Mamari is a part-time MBA student at Sultan Qaboos University while working as a researcher in the Foreign Trade and International Cooperation Office at the Ministry of Commerce, Industry and Investment Promotion. With a research interest in governmental policies aimed at enhancing international trade, Amal's research explores strategies that promote economic growth and global competitiveness. Her work contributes to the formulation of trade policies and fosters stronger international partnerships.

Aliya Anwar is a PhD scholar and has a strong background of research in the area of economics and management.

Nabeela Arshad is an active PhD Scholar with expertise in management sciences. She has published many articles in HRM, Finance, and Tourism.

Sajjad Ahmad Baig is an Associate Professor and Director at Faisalabad Business School, National Textile University Faisalabad, Pakistan. He holds a Doctorate in Total Quality Management from the University of the Punjab, Lahore. Dr Baig's research focuses on circularity, textile sustainability, TQM, and lean practices, aiming to minimize environmental impact and enhance efficiency through innovative strategies. With over 85 journal articles and five funded research projects, he has made significant contributions to sustainable and quality-driven textile production. Dr. Baig is dedicated to mentoring students and advancing sustainable practices in the textile industry.

Francesco Maria Barbini is an Associate Professor of Organizational behaviour at the Department of Management of the University of Bologna, where he teaches Organizational behaviour, Human resource management and Organization of tourism enterprises. He is the Director of the Center for Advanced Studies in Tourism at the University of Bologna. His research interests focus on organizational change and occupational health and well-being. He is the Director of the Advanced Center of Tourism Studies at the Campus of Rimini

Marisol B. Correia is a Coordinating Professor in the scientific area of Information Technologies and Systems at the School of Management, Hospitality and Tourism (ESGHT) of the University of Algarve (UAlg). She is a research member-investigator of CiTUR Algarve (Centre for Tourism Research, Development and Innovation), and she is a research member-collaborator of the CEG-IST (Centro de Estudos de Gestão, Instituto Superior Técnico, Universidade de Lisboa). She holds a PhD in Electronics and Computer Engineering, a master's degree in Electronics and Computer Engineering and a five-year undergraduate degree in Informatics Engineering. My research interests are computer science, business intelligence, website evaluation, and ICT applied to management, hospitality, and tourism.

Hafizullah Dar, Assistant Professor, Tourism and Airlines. LPU Punjab India

Nelson Matos is a marketing professional with more than two decades of experience in tourism, hospitality and sales. He is also an assistant professor of marketing since 2010 at the University of Algarve. He holds a PhD in Marketing and Strategy (2022) from the University of Minho, Portugal and another PhD in Tourism (2015) from the University of Algarve, Portugal.

Hamid Derviş is an Associate Professor in the Department of Information Management and Records at Kastamonu University. He holds a PhD in Information Management and Records from Hacettepe University, Ankara, Türkiye, where his research focused on the diffusion of nanotechnology in Turkey using social network analysis. Dr. Derviş has published numerous scientific articles in national and international journals, including the Journal of Informetrics and Scientometrics. He is selected as one of the world's top 2% of scientists in research done by Stanford University and Elsevier in the information & Library Sciences field for 2024.

Olukemi Adedokun Fagbolu has a PhD in Hospitality and Tourism Management from Assumption University, Thailand. She worked with Kwara State University, Malete and is now a Lecturer in the Department of Tourism Studies at the National Open University of Nigeria. Her research interests cover hospitality and tourism management, strategic tourism planning and development, sustainable tourism organization development, destination planning and management and hospitality and tourism management education.

Serkan Gün is an Assistant Professor at Siirt University, specializing in Tourism Management and Gastronomy. He holds a Doctorate from Hasan Kalyoncu University, where his thesis focused on the impact of destination image on visitor satisfaction. With a robust academic background, he has published numerous articles in international journals and authored several books on tourism and gastronomy. His administrative roles include Head of the Gastronomy and Culinary Arts Department and Vice Director of the Vocational School at Siirt University. Additionally, he has presented research at various international conferences, contributing significantly to tourism marketing and consumer behaviour. His work emphasizes the intersection of gastronomy and sustainable tourism practices.

Gulen Hashmi has more than twenty-six years of experience in the hospitality industry. Her doctoral specialization lies in tourism and hotel sustainability strategies and change management for sustainability and sustainable tourism. Her publications are on systemic, collaborative challenges of our time, such as collaboration for tourism and sustainability, the linkage between corporate well-being and societal well-being, and the alignment between organizational strategies and UN SDGs. Dr Gulen Hashmi has taught various hospitality and tourism courses at the National University of Sciences and Technology in Islamabad and the Emirates Academy of Hospitality Management in Dubai. She is a Lecturer in Responsible Business Management at Glasgow Caledonian University, Scotland, UK. Dr Hashmi may be contacted at Gulen.Hashmi@gcu.ac.uk. ORCID ID: 0000-0001-6949-6647

Khalid Jamil is working as a research associate at Beijing University of Technology. He has completed his doctoral degree with distinguished and published high-impact factor publications.

Ahmad Sohail Khan is a doctoral student at Lyallpur Business School, Government College University Faisalabad, Pakistan. He has long-standing teaching experience both at the undergraduate and graduate levels. His prime teaching and research interests are marketing, consumer behaviour, and branding. He has presented his work at multiple local and international conferences. He has a decent corporate experience. He has worked in one of the leading Islamic Banks in Pakistan.

Valeria Lo Presti is a Tourism Economics and Management graduate student at the University of Bologna, Rimini Campus. He is currently the Resident Manager of Palazzo Montegridolfo, a luxury hotel in Emilia Romagna. She is collaborating with the Cast on various research projects and has written a book with Prof. Presutti on the phenomenon of niche tourism in Italian villages.

Muhammad Hamid Murtza is an Assistant Professor at the Department of Tourism and Hospitality Management, The Islamia University of Bahawalpur, Pakistan. He holds a PhD from the Islamia University of Bahawalpur, Pakistan, and a Research Fellowship at The School of Hospitality Business, Broad College of Business, Michigan State University, USA. His academic and research interests lie in Organizational Behavior, Human Resource Management, and Hospitality

Operations, focusing on workplace envy, competitive psychological climate, and team collaboration in the hospitality industry. His scholarly contributions have been presented at leading conferences such as the Academy of Management Annual Meeting and the CentralCHRIE Conference at Purdue University. He has published in esteemed journals, including the Knowledge Management Research & Practice, the Journal of Hospitality and Tourism Technology and the Journal of Hospitality and Tourism Insights.

Aditi Nag is an Architect and Urban Planner currently serving as an Assistant Professor in the Faculty of Design at Manipal University Jaipur. She is pursuing a PhD in the Department of Architecture and Planning at Birla Institute of Technology, Mesra, Ranchi, India. Her research focuses on urban and rural planning, and she has several publications to her credit. She is the first recipient of the DST Inspire Fellowship in Architecture and Planning, awarded by the Ministry of Science and Technology, Government of India.

Uma Pandey is an Assistant Professor in the School of Hospitality and Tourism at Jagran Lakecity University, India. She holds a Ph.D. in Tourism Management. She has a deep belief in the transformative power of tourism. She believes that tourism can be a force for good in the world, and she is committed to using her research and teaching to promote sustainable tourism development. Her research interests include tourism, ecotourism, consumer behaviour, gender equality, and tourism education.

Panoraia Poulaki (BSc, MSc, PhD) is an academic laboratory teaching staff member in the Department of Economics and Management of Tourism at the University of the Aegean. She also teaches in the MSc Program in Strategic Management of Tourism Destinations and Hospitality Enterprises at the University of the Aegean. She holds a first degree in History and Archaeology from the National and Kapodistrian University of Athens, a Master of Science (MSc) in Planning, Management and Policy of Tourism from the University of the Aegean and a Doctor of Philosophy (PhD) in Tourism from the same University. She has written a book about the contribution of the Ottoman Monuments of Chios to the development of cultural tourism; she has published research papers in scientific journals and has presented her research work at international conferences. Her research interests focus on developing, planning and managing tourism, emphasising unique and alternative forms of tourism.

Manuela Presutti is an Associate Professor of Management at the Department of Management of Bologna. In 2003, she took a Ph.D in General Management at the University of Bologna - Rimini branch, where she teaches Management of Tourism and Tourism Management From 2005 to 2010 she was an Assistant Professor at the

Department of Management of Bologna. She participates in the research activities of the Advanced School of Tourism Sciences - Rimini Campus of the University of Bologna. Manuela Presutti's main research activity was originally focused on small firms and internationalisation process. During the last years, her research interest have included the analysis of social networks, entrepreneurship, and tourism management.

Theodoros Rachiotis (BSc, MSc, PhD Candidate) is an educator in the private sector and a PhD Candidate at the School of Physical Education and Sports of the Kapodistrian University of Athens, with a subject related to sports psychology and sports research methodology. He holds a first degree in History- Archaeology from the Aristotle University of Thessaloniki and a Master of Science (MSc) in Planning, Management and Policy of Tourism from the University of the Aegean. He has published research papers in scientific journals and has presented his research work at national and international conferences. His research interests focus on developing, planning and managing tourism and sports psychology.

Muhammad Imran Rasheed is an Associate Professor at the International Institute Dongbei University of Finance and Economics, China & University of Surrey, UK. He received his Bachelor of Hons, M.Phill, and Ph.D. in Business Administration. His current research focuses on Organizational Behavior and Industrial and Organizational Psychology, specifically in leadership, Career, personality, tourism/hospitality management and technology & people.

Anurag Singh Rathore is a tourism studies student pursuing a degree course in the Department of Tourism at IGNOU, New Delhi. He has a fascination with the field of modern tourism trends and traditional branding techniques.

Saqib Rehman (PhD) is an HR professional, trainer, and researcher with vast experience handling HR issues in Pakistan's private and public sector organizations. He serves as an assistant professor at Lahore College for Women University, Lahore, Pakistan, and supervises master & doctoral students. His research interests include Human Psychology & Behaviours, Organizational Development, Human Resource Management & IT, Leadership, Knowledge Management, Tourism Management and Sustainable Businesses.

Julie Roberts is the Programme Leader of the Doctorate of Business Administration at Glasgow Caledonian University with an interdisciplinary background, crossing disciplines of science/business. She is a Senior Lecturer, teaching in areas including Innovation, Operations Management, Entrepreneurship, Research Methodology and Academic skills & Reflective practice. Julie is a Senior

Fellow of the Higher Education Academy, actively engaging in pedagogical research, including using critical incident techniques to understand student learning. Her research interests also include creative responses by businesses to disruption in the hospitality sector and utilising essential incident techniques to understand learning behaviour you're. She participates in funded research with industry and recently participated in an EU-funded Interreg project with the Cultural and Creative sector, utilising the Quintuple Helix (5H) innovation model to support post-pandemic recovery. ORCID Id: 0000-0001-6652-6994

Rizwan Shabbir has been working as an Assistant Professor at the Lyallpur Business School, Government College University, Faisalabad, since 2015. He got his Ph.D. in Marketing Management from Huazhong University of Science and Technology, China. He also did his MS from Lund University, Sweden, in 2011. Dr Rizwan Shabbir has published research in many highly reputed international journals, including the Asia Pacific Journal of Marketing and Logistics, Psychology Research and Behavior Management, and Frontiers in Psychology. He has supervised many MS and Ph.D. students. His teaching interests include digital marketing, marketing research, and sustainable supply chain management. He wants to research value creation, industrial marketing, branding, and cross-cultural decision-making differences. He also provides industrial consultancy to many reputed international and national organizations, like Walmart, KPMG, and Tencent Technologies (WeChat).

Mario Sierra Martin, Professor at the University of Malaga since 2018. Marketing and Market Research Area.

Mohammad Soliman currently works in the Marketing Department at Sultan Qaboos University, Oman. He previously served as Head of the Research and Consultation Department at UTAS, Salalah, Oman. He is also a Full Professor at the Faculty of Tourism and Hotels at Fayoum University, Egypt. He has published multiple papers in high-rank journals indexed in ABDC, WoS, and Scopus (e.g., International Journal of Hospitality Management, Tourism Management Perspectives, Journal of Destination Management & Marketing, Current Issues in Tourism, Technology in Society, Tourism Review, Journal of Service Theory & Practice, International Journal of Human-Computer Interaction, Journal of Consumer Behaviour, Journal of Tourism and Services, etc.). Additionally, he sits on the editorial board of different academic journals and is an associate editor and reviewer for several top-tier journals. He has successfully supervised and examined several master's and PhD theses. His research interests include destination marketing, tourism marketing, branding, consumer behaviour, AI in education & marketing, PLS-SEM, and review studies.

Nil Sonuç, currently Assist. Prof. Dr. at İzmir Katip Çelebi University, Faculty of Tourism. Her bachelor(Education in English & French) and PhD are from Dokuz Eylül University, Tourism Management. PhD thesis on Social Tourism in İzmir. 4th year of bachelor and MSc at Université de Savoie, in Chambéry/France "Masters of European Hospitality Management". Internship in Guadeloupe. Master thesis in French on Sustainable Tourism Development in Guadeloupe. Pedagogical Formation at Dokuz Eylul University, for Teaching English. Licensed tour guide in French and English. Since 2007 teaches at universities in İzmir & by Erasmus Teaching Exchange at European Universities; Belgium, Germany, Italy, Portugal & Denmark. Publications on sustainability and tourism, sustainable tourism marketing, environmental and social sustainability of tourism, sustainable tourism product and planning, accessible tourism, digitalisation and tourism, wellness tourism, gender in tourism guidance, yoga tourism, destinations in Turkey and Europe, slow tourism, western European cuisine, bar management, mythology, tourism and hospitality management, tourism education, cultural heritage and tourism..

Aman Ullah holds PhD in Management from Deakin Business School, Deakin University, demonstrating my academic foundation in the field. He supplemented his academic qualifications with a Graduate Diploma in Pedagogy (professional teaching qualification) from the Melbourne Graduate School of Education, the University of Melbourne, reflecting my dedication to pedagogy and teaching excellence. Also, Aman completed the Tutoring in Business and Economics (TBE) program at WCLA, Faculty of Business and Economics, University of Melbourne. Currently, he is a peer mentor in the WCLA team and contributes positively to teaching excellently at FBE. Aman has published in the leading peer-reviewed impact factor journals.

Vasilakis Nikolaos, BSc, has studied history at the Ionian University in Corfu Island. He teaches Greek and International History and Culture. He also teaches Greek and Latin languages. He is a history, culture, and tourism researcher and has published research papers in scientific journals and collective volumes. He has also presented his research work at international conferences, and his interests focus on the development, planning, and management of tourism, emphasising cultural tourism.

Index

D

T

U

V

W

ingramcontent.com/pod-product-compliance
Content Group UK Ltd.
Milton Keynes, MK11 3LW, UK
12332151224
K00006B/59